Gandhi and Civil Disobedience

T0204674

Gandhi in 1931, aged 62 (by permission of the Government of India)

Gandhi and Civil Disobedience

THE MAHATMA IN INDIAN POLITICS

1928–34

JUDITH M. BROWN

Lecturer in History
University of Manchester

CAMBRIDGE UNIVERSITY PRESS

CAMBRIDGE

LONDON · NEW YORK · MELBOURNE

CAMBRIDGE UNIVERSITY PRESS
Cambridge, New York, Melbourne, Madrid, Cape Town, Singapore, São Paulo

Cambridge University Press
The Edinburgh Building, Cambridge CB2 8RU, UK

Published in the United States of America by Cambridge University Press, New York

www.cambridge.org
Information on this title: www.cambridge.org/9780521212793

First published 1977
This digitally printed version 2008

A catalogue record for this publication is available from the British Library

Library of Congress Cataloguing in Publication data
Brown, Judith M.
Gandhi and civil disobedience.
Bibliography: p.
Includes index.
1. Gandhi, Mohandas Karamchand, 1869–1948.
2. India – Politics and government – 1919–1947.
3. Passive resistance – India. I. Title.
DS481 .G3B73   954.03′5′0924 [B]   76–10407

ISBN 978-0-521-21279-3 hardback
ISBN 978-0-521-06695-2 paperback

To my Mother

Contents

Tables

Preface

Few twentieth-century public figures have attracted as much attention as M. K. Gandhi. Description and analysis of his career from many angles and diverse disciplines has given rise to a voluminous literature. This book is intended as a contribution to understanding his political career; because his significance for his contemporaries and to some extent for later generations lay in his role as a political leader and innovator, and because he realized that he could only publicize and implement his ideals through political involvement. It is based on evidence recently made available, which permits more detailed enquiry than has hitherto been possible. My analysis of the first phase of Gandhi's career in India, which was published in 1972, concluded with his imprisonment in 1922 and the collapse of his first continental campaign of non-cooperation against the British raj: this volume, fruit of recent research in India and Britain, continues the analysis. It is in a sense a parallel to the earlier work, in that its subject is Gandhi's re-emergence at the end of the 1920s in a position of singular importance in Indian politics and the reversion of many of his compatriots to his technique of non-violent civil resistance to the raj, followed by the disintegration of his position and the collapse of the civil disobedience movement. The book stands by itself as an investigation of Gandhi's politics and their relevance to his country-men during a particular period of time, but the comparisons which can be drawn with the analysis of the earlier phase of his political dominance make it also a means of focussing on the changing nature of Indian politics.

I gratefully acknowledge the help of several institutions in this enterprise. My own university of Manchester made a grant from Hayter funds which enabled me to work in India in 1973, and gave me a term's leave of absence in 1975 to write. From the universities of Canterbury, Otago and Wellington in New Zealand, and the Australian universities of New South Wales and Flinders I received the opportunity as visiting lecturer in 1974 to try out some of the ideas which have finally taken shape here: while to the Australian National University at Canberra I owe gratitude for the particularly generous grant of a Visiting Research Fellowship in the Research School of Pacific Studies which permitted me to attend a conference on 'Congress and the Raj' in 1974, at which I presented a paper on Gandhi's role as an all-India leader and benefited from the comments and discussion of the participants. To the libraries which house the sources referred to in the bibliography I owe thanks for permission to consult the material in their care: the National Archives of India, the Nehru Memorial Museum and Library, and the Gandhi Memorial Museum in Delhi; the British Library and the India Office Library in London; the John Rylands University Library and the Central Reference Library in Manchester. Dr Richard Bingle, Smt Dhan Keswani and Shri V. C. Joshi have been particularly generous with their time and archival knowledge.

I would also like to express my gratitude to several scholars who have extended both salutary criticism and encouragement during the making of this book, though the arguments and emphases in it are my own, as are the errors that remain. Professors John Gallagher and Eric Stokes read the manuscript: Professor Anthony Low gave unstintingly of his time and his own research material in illuminating discussions during my visit to Canberra.

In the preparation of this volume I have benefited from the courtesy and expertise of Robert Seal and the staff of the Cambridge University Press. Dr Angus McDougall and his calculator helped with the tables. To my brother, Peter, I am particularly indebted. He read the manuscript, cast out many inconsistencies and stylistic errors, and helped to prepare it for publication. To the many friends in India and Britain who have supported me in my work and entertained me on my travels I offer my thanks; and particularly to my family for their tolerance and encouragement.

All Hallows Eve 1975   JUDITH M. BROWN
Manchester

Abbreviations

AICC	All-India Congress Committee
AISA	All India Spinners' Association
AITUC	All-India Trade Union Congress
B.M.	British Museum (now British Library)
C.P.	Central Provinces
CWMG	*The Collected Works of Mahatma Gandhi*
DCC	District Congress Committee
D.I.B.	Director of Bureau of Intelligence
D.S.P.	District Superintendent of Police
FICCI	Federation of Indian Chambers of Commerce and Industry
FR1	Provincial fortnightly report for first half of month
FR2	Provincial fortnightly report for second half of month
HFM	*Source Material for a History of the Freedom Movement in India*
Home Poll.	Home Political File
I.C.S.	Indian Civil Service
I.N.C.	Indian National Congress
IOL	India Office Library
K.-W.	Keep With to file
MLA	Member of Legislative Assembly
MLC	Member of Legislative Council
M.P.	Member of Parliament
NAI	National Archives of India
NMML	Nehru Memorial Museum and Library
N.-W.F.P.	North-West Frontier Province
PCC	Provincial Congress Committee
P.S.V.	Private Secretary to the Viceroy
R.S.S.	Rashtriya Swayamsevak Sangh
S of S	Secretary of State for India
SWJN	*Selected Works of Jawaharlal Nehru*
U.P.	United Provinces of Agra and Oudh
V	Viceroy

Introduction

Gandhi's leadership of the civil disobedience movement which began in India in 1930 probably marked the peak of his political influence over his countrymen and the British raj. This, his second continental campaign of non-cooperation with the imperial structure, was the most serious country-wide agitational challenge in the name of nationalism which the British faced in their Indian empire. It attracted considerable popular participation and even wider public sympathy in India, and brought the Mahatma and his claims to the attention of a world-wide audience. His personal prestige and authority were displayed when with the Sovereign's representative he concluded a 'pact' which temporarily ended civil disobedience in 1931; and when later in the year as sole spokesman for the Indian National Congress he attended the Round Table Conference in London on India's new federal constitution. He was the leader whose decision reactivated the campaign on his return to India, and whose agreement both Congressmen and government sought in attempts to procure the end of civil disobedience in 1933–4. Many of India's sober and sophisticated politicians, professional and business men regarded him with respect and affection despite his denunciation of many of their priorities and practices. He had a large circle of devotees to whom he was a spiritual guide; and beyond the ranks of those who knew him personally he attracted popular adulation throughout the subcontinent which at times bordered on veneration of a messianic figure.

However, Gandhi's Indian career was not a smooth progression to a peak of political power. There was always a groundswell of hostility to his methods and aims which became more articulate and strident as he lost the support of the bulk of Muslims in the 1920s and incurred the suspicion of overtly communalist Hindus. Moreover at certain times his political programme was ignored by the Indian National Congress. Gandhi had gained control of Congress in 1920 with dramatic swiftness after his return from two decades of campaigning in South Africa for Indian rights, because his political interests and methods served the purposes of men who had until that time exerted little permanent influence in the politics of Congress. His Non-cooperation movement of 1920–2 attracted wider and deeper support than any previous political movement because to a greater extent than the older style of Congress politics it served a diversity of local needs and provided a channel for a host of particularist drives. However, in 1922 he abandoned the movement which had carried him to continental fame and influence because violence erupted among its participants, striking at the heart of his philosophy of non-violent action as the only moral means of changing men and their world. Thereafter for nearly a decade men thought him a spent political force, as his former Congress colleagues haltingly trod the paths of constitutional cooperation with their rulers while he was in jail for sedition and then in semi-retirement from politics after his release. Gandhi's reassertion of authority in Congress in 1928–9 and subsequent leadership of a powerful civil disobedience movement, thereafter, require as much explanation as his initial rise to power in Indian politics.[1]

Understanding of Gandhi's whole political career must rest on analysis of its separate phases because of the length of time that career spanned. Gandhi was a major figure in Indian politics for over thirty years, years of change in himself and his environment. In 1930 he was sixty-one; but late middle age did not mean for him mental rigidity. Returning from Africa in 1915 he had responded to the stimulus of Indian public life by refining his beliefs and adapting his methods to new situations. His sojourn in jail from 1922 to 1924 and his elected 'year of silence' in 1926 allowed time for reflection not usually given to established leaders. Moreover his religious commitment to what he perceived as truth made him receptive and flexible in applying his principles. He was not afraid to be called inconsistent, although he maintained that there was an underlying consistency in his apparent inconsistencies.[2]

As Gandhi remained responsive to new experiences the Indians and British he encountered in politics changed, as did the formative influences on them and the context in which they operated. In 1920 India's main continental political leaders were men slightly older than himself – a Surendranath Bannerjee, model of Victorian constitutionalism, a Tilak, herald of Maharashtrain revivalism. In 1930 the older men were dead and dying or were being challenged by a new generation, some of whom like Jawaharlal Nehru were fired by the examples of European socialism and the Russian revolution. In 1930 Gandhi was also dealing with a new breed of imperial politicians whose Indian policies were formulated in the setting of post-war disillusion and economic stringency. The ultimate authority of the raj, moreover, lay in a Parliament where the balance of power had been

---

[1] No detailed analysis of this phase of Gandhi's career exists, largely because the evidence for such a study has only recently become available, for example in the expanding collection of private papers and AICC material at the Nehru Memorial Museum and Library, and in the official and private papers in the National Archives of India and India Office Library opened to research under the operation of the 30-year rule. The most satisfactory accounts of these years of Gandhi's career are S. Gopal, *The Viceroyalty of Lord Irwin 1926–1931* (Oxford, 1957); P. Moon, *Gandhi and Modern India* (London, 1968); R. J. Moore, *The Crisis of Indian Unity 1917–1940* (Oxford, 1974); B. R. Nanda, *Mahatma Gandhi. A Biography* (Boston, 1958); D. G. Tendulkar, *Mahatma*, vols. 2 & 3 (revised edn, Dehli, 1961).

[2] *Young India*, 13 February 1930, *The Collected Works of Mahatma Gandhi* (in process of publication, New Delhi), XLII, 469 (hereafter *CWMG*).

transformed by the emergence of the Labour Party. In India itself the framework of political life had changed. The 1919 reforms had modified the structures by which imperialists sought to control their subjects, and power over a wide area of life was available to Indians who could attract the votes of the enlarged electorate and organize themselves for conciliar activity in collaboration with their rulers. Consequently, during the 1920s the provinces became an increasingly significant unit of political aspiration and action. Not only the arenas of politics open to Indians and their relative values to different social groups had changed: so had other economic and ideological forces which impelled men into political life. India's economy was increasingly welded into a world-wide network of trade and production; and as a primary producer and exporter India was dangerously vulnerable to economic trends and pressures originating outside the subcontinent. Within India growing communal tension produced further incentives to new styles of political action, while from Europe came the tidings of socialism and communism which also provided the impetus and ideological content for novel forms of political commitment. Changes in Gandhi and his environment therefore meant that the reasons for his emergence as a dominant figure between 1915 and 1922 can only partially explain his influence and role in the early 1930s.

It might be argued that study of an all-India figure such as Gandhi produces a distorted picture of Indian politics. It credits the continental figure with powers of initiative and influence which belonged to local men whose hands were on the pulse of provincial and district life near the heart of Indian politics. By stressing nation-wide action and nationalist rhetoric it obscures the divisions in Indian society and the calculated alliances of diverse groups out of which were constructed political movements which flew the banner of the nationalist struggle against the imperial ruler. There is no doubt about the importance of the geographically restricted political arena, whether of town, district or province, and of the men whose political aspirations and styles were geared to these arenas.[3] With their networks of allies and clients they determined to a great extent the success or failure of continental moves, agitational and constitutional alike; and constrained the actions of those who aspired to all-India leadership. Yet all-India leaders existed. Their presence, and the authority and glamour attached to their positions indicate that they were a necessary element in Indian politics. But necessary to whom? What functions did they perform and what forces impelled them into such positions and determined their influence? To grapple with the dynamics of an all-India's leader's career is as important in the understanding of Indian politics as to locate the local origins of political ambition and organization. It is indeed the necessary corollary,

[3] The trend in recent analysis of Indian politics has been towards detailed local studies as a necessary foundation for a deeper understanding or Indian politics. See for example, C. A. Bayly, *The Local Roots of Indian Politics. Allahabad 1880–1920* (Oxford, 1975); C. J. Baker, *The Politics of South India 1920–1937* (Cambridge, 1976).

indicating some of the ways in which local and particularist movements were welded into larger unities, their differences adjusted, overcome or masked as a prelude to attaining power in the constitutional structures of the state at provincial and continental level.

The phenomenon of the continental leader demands a two-pronged analysis – of the potential leader, his personal drives, career aspirations and qualifications for particular styles of political activity, and the needs he could satisfy of people in politics, including those outside the range of his potential followers. All-India politics occurred at the juncture of diverse worlds, those of India's localities and of Britain itself, a political interaction increasingly observed by people outside either country as communications improved and whose reactions affected the major participants. At this meeting-point, observed by international opinion, both Indians and British needed all-India 'leaders' who could play various roles – figureheads, ideologues, spokesmen, negotiators, compromisers, organizers and mobilizers. The origins of all-India leadership lay in the creation of sets of relationships between the individual with the internal drive towards such status and people for whom he could perform a useful function in a specific context. The context was crucial: it was compounded of many variables, such as the issues and interests at stake at that particular time, the institutions and personalities involved, the strategies available and the ideologies current. As the context changed in any of these respects so might a particular leader cease to be able to perform the function on which his acceptance as a leader had been based. Such sets of relationships in specific contexts were the foundations of continental leadership positions, providing the explanation of who 'led' whom in all-India politics and revealing the constraints inherent in their positions of leadership. My study of Gandhi's role as civil disobedience leader in the 1930s investigates a particular example of the phenomenon of continental political leadership. It seeks to show how far Gandhi's politics became those of other Indians during the civil disobedience movement. In fulfilling its primary aim of charting Gandhi's personal political career in one of its most remarkable phases it raises questions of initiative, influence and perceived unity essential to an understanding of the complexity of Indian politics.

The phase 1928–34 in Gandhi's life is not as sharply demarcated as the period 1915–22 when he first emerged as a powerful figure in India between his return from Africa and his first experience of an Indian jail. 1928 marked his reassertion of authority in Congress affairs, and 1934 saw his apparent retirement from Congress. Yet neither was a clear-cut change. He was not politically inactive before 1928 or after 1934. But the phase is a whole in the sense that within it occurred the creation of his new continental leadership position, the exercise of that leadership role, and its disintegration as the context changed and Gandhi could no longer perform the functions which had been his passport to prominence. It shows that Gandhi's leadership position was no static phenomenon but one which altered over time as the context changed and his peculiar ambitions and aptitudes meshed with and served the interests of other people and groups. Now his position depended far more on his ability to serve the diverse needs of both British and Indian groups engaged in tortuous political interplay at a time when the rules and relationships of politics were plunged into turmoil by the prospect of reform, when economic pressures strained the structures of social and political control to the point of collapse and when the emergence of new ideologies and the growth to political awareness of younger men generated demands for new political attitudes and alignments. In the process of interaction his technique of *satyagraha* was crucial, as was the repute he brought with him from the days of the Non-cooperation confrontation with the raj; because his position depended largely on the degree to which his politics channelled local and sectional drives and became an integrative force in political life. People turned to Gandhi as leader and then recoiled from him according to their judgement of how he could assist them in their political relationships.

The sources for an investigation of Gandhi's role pose distinct problems apart from those of focus and balance inherent in studying any continental leadership position. As in the records which survive any heated confrontation, there is considerable bias. Accounts of events and judgement of people's intentions from British sources are coloured by the anger and frustration of rulers combating what they perceived as senseless subversion. On the Indian side letters and reports were equally part of the process of political encounter, often designed more to rouse support, cover tracks or prepare the ground for a new move or alignment than to impart factual information. Purveyors of intelligence, whether police or Congress informants, were often inefficient and inaccurate, and the records they have left behind are not always reliable. Moreover, statistics for involvement in political activities were inadequate and in some cases prepared for propaganda purposes.

Evidence about Gandhi is particularly difficult to handle because reactions to him were and are so strong. Men have loved and hated this enigmatic figure. British and Indian alike wrestled with his quirks, his obstinacy and apparent inconsistency. This was exemplified in the comments of one Viceroy on the attitude towards the Mahatma of Sir George Lloyd, who had been Governor of Bombay during Non-cooperation.

> Lloyd always had a notion that Gandhi under his plea of non-violence was at heart a violent revolutionary who would one day come out in his true colours, and that might be at any moment...I cannot myself think that Gandhi is as astute a politician as Lloyd would have you believe, but I do accept the view that he is a party politician desirous of leading the multitude, quick to use his advantages as a man of religion and spirituality and very susceptible to the adulation of the crowds. He is an extraordinary person, full of contradictions, at heart an idealist, truthful, courageous and on a high ethical plane. But nevertheless, the idol's feet are of clay as was shown during 1921–22. Towards

the last...shortly before his arrest, according to all accounts to me, he displayed unmistakable symptoms of megalomania.[4]

Faced with such a controversial and dynamic figure the historian often lacks evidence of those elements in Gandhi's relationships with individuals and groups which were unquantifiable but of undoubted significance in the creation of his leadership position. His almost messianic appeal to vast crowds, the devotion he elicited from individuals, his material concern for the intimate lives of his followers, his sense of humour and iron will are qualities which historical records assume or merely hint at. In Gandhi's case his use of English, often twisting words and phrases to pour into them the meaning his convictions demanded, and the inadequacy of English translations of his Gujarati, are further barriers to those who cannot hear him speak or feel his presence.

Gandhi's self image even more than his public image presents difficulties. Here was a man who claimed to be governed by religious commitment, who was hailed as a Mahatma, but who traded in the doubtful currency of politics. Any assessment of him comes up against this apparent dilemma. Moreover there are few 'private' papers on political matters in the usual sense of the word, from which one might discern the roots of his public actions. Gandhi's commitment to satyagraha, truth force, demanded that all his activities and the agonizings of conscience which lay behind them should be open to the public gaze. Therefore there is often little difference between 'public' pronouncements and 'private' interchanges. Ostensibly private letters tend to read like public speeches of similar date. He quoted his correspondence extensively in his didactic journalism; and reported private meetings to the public as he unravelled for them his trains of thought. Consequently the observations of close friends and associates like his secretary, Mahadev Desai, are often more revealing than those of Gandhi himself about his intentions and calculations.

Precisely because public and private life were one and the same for Gandhi, because religion and politics were intertwined, it is essential to trace the development of his interior life. His autobiography does not cover this period; but his growing repute as a *Mahatma* or 'Great Soul' and the expanding numbers in the religious community or *ashram* he had founded at Sabarmati outside Ahmedabad in 1915 meant that people increasingly looked to him for guidance on spiritual matters and questioned him on the relationship between his roles as religious leader and politician. His replies came in a voluminous correspondence and the columns of his papers, *Young India, Navajivan* and eventually *Harijan*. Self-analysis had more scope while he was in jail when letters on overtly political subjects were banned. During this phase of his career he referred increasingly to the 'Inner Voice' as the guiding fact in his life, though he acknowledged that others could not be expected to accept the existence or the validity

---

[4] Reading to Oliver, 24 July 1924, IOL, Reading Papers, Mss. EUR.E.238 (7).

of that voice.[5] This study of Gandhi's politics sets his arguments and explanations beside assessments of him by his contemporaries and evidence of the external factors which certainly or probably impinged on his decisions: for though material constraints had a significant effect on Gandhi's actions his personal convictions and drives were crucial in determining what he made of the political opportunities offered to him by the needs of Indians and the British in the particular circumstances of 1928–34.

[5] Gandhi to C. F. Andrews, 20 December 1932, *CWMG*, LII, 244–5.

CHAPTER 1

The recreation of a political leader
1922–8

Gandhi was active in Indian public life when politics on the subcontinent were undergoing swift and significant change. From the latter part of the nineteenth century India's society, economy and administrative structures were increasingly modified by the pressures which stemmed from the British presence. The nature and balance of power in society began to alter: old forms of control were eroded, and new paths to influence laid down, by a variety of means – the revenue and legal apparatus which determined the extent and stability of land-holding, the decline of old trading patterns and the expansion of new commercial and industrial enterprises, the growth of an anglicized educational system and the opportunities it provided for employment in the administration and the new western-style professions. Moreover India's different regions, with their varied social structures and material resources, experienced these social and economic changes in different ways and at different paces, as they were thrust into new relationships with each other and the world beyond the subcontinent under the aegis of the raj.

Politics as the concern for power and its use in the community began to change in response. As new sorts of power became available and old ones declined so new arenas of political enterprise became important to some Indians, and new activities and organizations necessary and profitable. Consequently by the early twentieth century a multiplicity of political arenas existed – the village community, the municipality, the caste council, the religious association, the Bar, the university senate, and ultimately the new legislatures. In each arena particular types of power and influence were sought; each had its appropriate styles of action, and each threw up the particular form of leader whose skills and style could forward the aims of the participating interest groups and alliances. Often old and new overlapping or ran in parallel. Some people needed only to concern themselves with one political arena, while others operated in several simultaneously, using the resources of one arena to forward their enterprises in another. India had not one political system but many, a set of interlocking, interacting systems in which Indians jockeyed for position and influence over each other and in relation to their rulers.

The British responded to the complex political changes their presence helped to create by consciously retraining themselves as politicians in so far as their preconceptions, their imperial experience outside India, and

British public opinion permitted. In so doing they accelerated political change and helped to determine its course. They refined the instruments with which they hoped to elicit Indian alliances in their imperial enterprise, by opening more doors into the administration, expanding the range of recipients of honours, modifying the apprenticeship of I.C.S. recruits, and supremely by inaugurating new constitutions. British administrators were thin on the ground and their administrative apparatus was light in relation to the size of the subcontinent. Cheap and effective imperial domination thus demanded Indian collaborators. In the previous century the British had relied heavily on the alliance of local notables in town and countryside both as administrative agents and as nodules of loyalty; and had solicited their cooperation through informal consultation and the dispensation of patronage. As social and economic change gradually weakened the authority of such men the alien rulers began to supplement their durbari style of politics and informal alliances with provincial and central legislatures designed to attract not only these older collaborators but also men who had begun to exercise more influence in society as a result of their expertise and success in the new professions and business. Many of these were increasingly critical of the imperial regime which had largely excluded them from administrative authority and influence in the decision-making processes of government. They couched their demands and protests in the arguments of nationalism familiar to, and to a considerable extent imported from, the history of Europe.

The 1909 experiment in constitution-making offered little power to Indians. In marked contrast were the Montagu–Chelmsford Reforms of 1919, conceived when the British had their backs to the wall during the Great War and were anxious to secure the loyalty of key groups of their Indian subjects. In 1917 Edwin Montagu, Secretary of State for India, had announced that the British wished increasingly to associate Indians in the administration of their country, and develop self-governing institutions, with the ultimate goal of responsible government in India as part of the empire. In 1919 the reform act implementing the immediate intention provided for expanded legislatures in Delhi and the provincial capitals, and created the system of dyarchy or dual government whereby certain areas of administration were handed over to provincial control; though some of these were reserved under the governor's authority specified topics such as education, public works, municipal government and agriculture were transferred to the control of ministers responsible to the elected legislatures. However, despite the principle of ultimate responsible government enunciated in Montagu's declaration, few British officials or M.P.s envisaged any form of self-government in the foreseeable future. The reforms were an exercise in conciliation to protect the empire in a time of crisis not to demolish it: and the new constitutional edifices were erected as buttresses for the raj in changing economic and social conditions.

In the twentieth century constitutional reform was a major factor in the development of Indian politics, as the extension of local self-government had been at the end of the nineteenth. It created a new range of institutions in which greater power was offered to Indians. In so doing it altered the balance of importance of different political arenas; for once power over a wide spectrum of public life was available through the politics of the legislatures, few Indians concerned with the exercise of power in public life could afford to ignore them for long. Landlords and tenants, business-men and shopkeepers, lawyers and ratepayers all realized that decisions made in them would affect their lives significantly. Moreover, by extending the franchise the British forced aspirant legislators and their backers into new relations with potential voters. Thus, both by the range of power it made available and the pathways to such power it constituted, the raj altered the relationship between different arenas of Indian politics, pro-pelling its subjects into new forms of political activity, alliance and leadership.[1]

Indians were quick to perceive that under Britain's imperial dispensation all-India pressure on the raj was more effective than isolated pockets of demand; and that a general, inclusive appeal was essential as a link between the multiplicity of regional and interest groups who were manoeuvering for power among themselves and in relation to the British. The Indian National Congress was proof of this awareness. From its foundation in 1885 all-India politics, and their concomitant, all-India leadership, became estab-lished political phenomena. The continental leader was a curious figure, influential yet vulnerable. He was often deemed necessary by his compat-riots and the British in this key area of political life, were India's regional political systems meshed with each other and with the world of British politics. Yet his was a hazardous position. Annual Congress sessions were little more than agglomerations of local leaders valiantly trying to preserve a credible degree of unity. Not only was Congress's continental cohesion precarious. Its organization was thinly spread through the subcontinent, and had but shallow roots in the local politics of many regions. Local men used or abused the Congress name, captured, ignored or walked out of its structures as it suited them. Though more like a political party than any other political group, it was essentially a constellation of changing alliances rather than a corporate body with shared and defined goals and ideas. Without the backing of an efficient organization and a following with clear aims which he was equipped to promote, the all-India leader seldom had access to material resources or wielded sanctions as powerful as those which local leaders could deploy. Although some combined the roles of local and

[1] The relationship between different arenas of politics is analysed from all-India and local angles in J. Gallagher, G. Johnson & A. Seal (ed.), *Locality, Province and Nation. Essays on Indian Politics 1870–1940* (Cambridge, 1973): it is also the theme of H. A. Gould's study of a particular U.P. district, 'The Emergence of Modern Indian Politics: Political Development in Faizabad', *The Journal of Commonwealth & Com-parative Politics*, XII, 1 (March 1974), 20–41.

continental leader, building the latter on the former, the tensions between local priority and all-India necessity, the clash between the needs of followers at the different levels, often became acute. Tilak had experienced this at the turn of the century: Vallabhbhai Patel and Jawaharlal Nehru were to discover it during civil disobedience. The all-India leader's influence rested largely on the perceptions of local leaders of his significance in their particular situations and on their judgement of the service functions he could perform for them in their relations with their peers, their followers and their rulers. Sometimes it stemmed too from the needs of the raj itself for Indians through whom it could deal with groups of its subjects as social and economic change broke down the old imperial patterns of political control. The corollary was that when these perceptions and needs changed, the all-India leader could find himself rapidly deprived of his functions and therefore of his position.

Gandhi rose dramatically to prominence in Indian politics in the aftermath of the 1914–18 War because his idiosyncratic ideology and techniques enabled him to perform a crucial all-India function for his compatriots. He had only returned in 1915 from South Africa, where for two decades he had championed the immigrant Indian community in the face of racial discrimination: in the process he had become a religious thinker and self-taught political leader, expert in varieties of civil resistance. In India he was little known and viewed with suspicion by many of the western educated who participated in all-Indian politics and were the backbone of Congress. It was precisely because of his difference from established Congress leaders in attitude and style that he presented a formidable challenge to them.

Since the foundation of Congress its adherents had advanced beyond their early tentative pleas for more influence in government, and by the second decade of the twentieth century most of them backed the demand for home rule couched in the strident language of nationalism. Yet their politics of petition, protest and debate failed to produce a radical change in British policy or to shift the foundations of the raj. In 1920 Gandhi inaugurated a movement of Non-cooperation designed to erode the acquiescence and collaboration by Indians on which the raj rested. It also provided scope for the expression of diverse political aspirations and conflicts which had rarely found a place in Congress politics. Moreover Gandhi took his stand on wide and emotive issues on which existing leaders had proved unconcerned and impotent; the Khalifah's status after Turkey's defeat by the allies which disturbed Indian Muslims, and the British firing on an unarmed crowd which had gathered for a political protest in the Jallianwalla Bagh in the Punjabi town of Amritsar early in 1919. In so doing Gandhi attracted the support of men from areas, groups and communities which had previously exercised little influence in all-India politics partly because those politics offered little means of forwarding their sectional and local interests which could be more effectively pursued in other political arenas. Consequently he also gained the reluctant and temporary alliance of many leading Congressmen who feared his power and gambled on the pay-offs of unity and the new technique the Mahatma offered for dealing with the British. For a brief period his leadership and tactics appeared to integrate many of the activities and interests which had previously been isolated in distinct political arenas. But the diversity of allies he gathered under the Non-cooperation banner and the variety of local and sectional political drives which were channelled through his campaign distorted the non-violent blueprint he had laid down. When violence erupted, most devastatingly in the massacre of twenty-two policemen at Chauri Chaura in 1922, he called off the campaign's most potent aspect, civil resistance.[2] Shortly afterwards the British imprisoned him, saving him from the fiercest recrimination of his compatriots and the undermining of his all-India leadership position at their hands as they realized he could not perform a useful function for them in their relations with each other and their rulers.

In 1924 Gandhi emerged from his forced seclusion in jail, convalescent after an emergency appendicectomy: he faced a political world markedly different from the one he had left in 1922 as architect of Non-cooperation. In the five years which followed, Lord Reading and his viceregal successor, Lord Irwin, judged him to be a spent force politically. After meeting Gandhi in 1927, Irwin described him as 'rather remote, and moving in a rarefied atmosphere divorced from the political facts of the situation . . . his main interest now lies in social matters, and he is reluctant to re-enter the arena of politics.'[3] Despite this apparent detachment from political life, the years 1922–8 were of considerable significance for Gandhi. They witnessed his recreation as a political leader. Confronted with the collapse of Non-cooperation, a blasted hope of *swaraj* or home rule in one year and the disintegration of the bases on which his power had rested in 1920, Gandhi re-examined his priorities and methods. Unlike most middle-aged politicians, he had the chance to take stock, personally and politically. Jail, illness and deliberate choice provided opportunities for physical rest, study and reflection. When he returned to public activity he had considered afresh his goals and the following he wished to attract. Meanwhile his distance from the manoeuvres of political life helped him retain the public image of an idealist and national spokesman, unsullied by party loyalty and intrigue. By 1928 he was refashioned as a potential all-India leader, able to use the moment when the political context changed and people's needs

---

[2] Judith M. Brown, *Gandhi's Rise to Power. Indian Politics 1915–1922* (Cambridge, 1972).

[3] Irwin to Birkenhead, 3 November 1927, IOL, Halifax Papers, Mss. EUR.C.152 (3). See also Irwin to Birkenhead, 16 June 1926, Mss. EUR.C.152 (2); V to S of S, telegram, 17 October 1925, Mss. EUR.E.238 (19). Moon calls the years 1922–8 'partial eclipse', *Gandhi and Modern India*, pp. 116–32.

produced an opportunity for a new phase of leadership on terms acceptable to him.[4]

I   THE POLITICAL CONTEXT

When Non-cooperation collapsed in 1922 the agitational links across regions, between local arenas of politics, and between them and an all-India campaign, snapped. Within the context of the Montagu–Chelmsford constitution, the relationship between India's different types of politics settled into a new pattern. Because the 1919 reforms offered considerable power and prestige to Indians who would collaborate with the British in the new constitutional structures, the drives of much local political awareness and ambition were soon channelled through the new structures in anticipation that they would be satisfied by the fruits of legislation and influence in the administration. Small landowners' concern for the relative burden of rural and urban taxation, local pressures for water supplies, roads, bridges, medical relief and educational facilities, politicians' needs to gain access to patronage – such was the stuff of local politics, and increasingly men pursued these goals through constitutional mechanisms.

Despite this movement, however, there was still marked discontinuity between the politics of the legislators and those of the electorate, even at election time. Few legislators felt the necessity for a permanent party-type organization of supporters: few interest groups set up candidates and kept watch on their activities in council. As Bihar's governor noted, 'Of course no one tries to organise the electorate as such. All efforts are directed towards getting hold of the men with local influence who can tell the others how to vote.'[5] Beyond the narrow circles of the enfranchised and their representatives, economic change produced rural tension and urban disruption which began to alter the context and content of political interchange, so that even imperialists had to abandon their complacent assumption that politics concerned only a microscopic minority of their subjects. However, they took comfort from the fact that there appeared

---

[4] Gandhi's Bengali critic, Subhas Chandra Bose, writing in the context of Gandhi's retirement from Congress in 1934 commented, 'The Mahatma will not play second fiddle to anyone. As long as it will be possible for him to guide the political movement, he will be there – but if the composition or the mentality of the Congress changes, he may possibly retire from active politics. . . A temporary retirement is like a strategic retreat. . . We have had experience of the Mahatma's retirement from active politics once before – from 1924 to 1928.' S. C. Bose, *The Indian Struggle 1920–1942* (2nd edn, New York, 1964), p. 296.

An introductory study of the significance of Gandhi's years of retirement is M. Ryburn, 'Mahatma Gandhi 1922–1928' (M.A. thesis, Canterbury University, N.Z., 1974).

[5] Sir Henry Wheeler, Governor of Bihar & Orissa, to Irwin, 22 April 1926, Mss, EUR.C.152 (20). On the local goals which were increasingly pursued through the legislatures see Sir Malcolm Hailey, Governor of U.P., to Irwin, 9 September 1928, Mss. EUR.C.152 (22); comments by Goschen, Governor of Madras, reported by Lytton to Birkenhead, 25 February 1926, enclosed in Birkenhead to Irwin, 20 May 1926, Mss. EUR.C.152 (2); Goschen to Irwin, 24 April 1926, Mss. EUR.C.152 (20).

to be little connection between the disturbing activities of rural tenants and urban labourers and the manoeuvres of the English educated who came to Delhi and the provincial capitals as assembly and council politicians; though as good democrats they regretted that no political group had created a permanent organization of voters and supporters at national or local level.[6]

The opportunities the reforms offered in provinces where the electoral rules did not weight conciliar influence too heavily in favour of landlords or Europeans presented Congressmen with acute dilemmas. Should they stick to Non-cooperation with the conciliar structure, forgo these gains and risk the support of their local adherents and the voters who might run after those prophets of constitutionalism who could prove their point with material benefits? Or should they forget their brave protestations of self-reliance and national unity, and plunge into the collaboration and manoeuvring inherent in constitutional activity? Few of them had participated in Non-cooperation in the expectation that their movement would undermine the raj, despite Gandhi's assertions and expressed hope of swaraj within a year. The vast majority of them were not revolutionaries by temperament, belief or interest. Unconstitutional opposition to the raj was only one end of a wide spectrum of interaction with their rulers which shaded from overt and illegal conflict to varieties of local and continental cooperation in the structures of administration and consultation. Individuals and groups moved through the spectrum as at particular times different stances suited their interests, judged in relation to their rulers and their compatriots. Through political activity they undoubtedly sought strategies to pressurize the raj into conceding more power through the constitution, but this was only one element in the rationale of their political decisions. Interwoven with their desire to influence the British was their need to cement alliances and attract followings among fellow Indians which would enable them to wield influence in a broad range of institutions, organizations, and relationships which composed public life. In the complicated calculations which ensued, continental pressures and possibilities had to be weighed against local opportunities and constraints, as did the fruits of extra-constitutional agitation against the benefits of legal political action. At times collaboration in the institutions of government seemed the most productive mode of relating to their rulers, their peers, potential leaders, clients and followers: at other times the pressures which could be exerted on the British and the linkages with their countrymen which could be forged through agitational politics seemed more profitable.

In the 1920s most Congressmen were to judge that the processes of

[6] For the disorganization of the Bombay labour force, for example, and government belief that there was little danger of a Congress–Labour alliance, see Sir Frederick Sykes, Governor of Bombay, to Irwin, 26 January 1929, IOL, Sykes Papers, Mss. EUR.F.150 (1); Govt. of India, Home Sec., to Govt. of Bengal, Chief Sec., 23 October 1929, NAI, Home Poll., 1930, File No. 257/1 & K.-W.

constitutional politics were the more valuable to them in their relations with other Indians and the British, though their reversion to these processes was no more permanent than their conversion to Non-cooperation had been in 1920. Motilal might take to Assembly politics, his son and Vallabhbhai Patel to urban administration, but like many erstwhile non-cooperators turned constitutionalists they recognized that the tactics of conflict might again prove valuable as political circumstances changed. In the early 1920s the trend in Congress towards constitutional action was swift and strong. Yet the process of changing tactics was painful for individuals and the organization as a whole. It was embarrassing to justify without appearing defeatist; moreover, it provided occasion for factional and personal rivalries to rear their heads, and for regional differences to become marked. Congress split on the tactical questions posed by the collapse of Non-cooperation. Its continental unity, fashioned in joint opposition to a common foe, broke up on the rocks of local opportunity and expediency and genuine ideological differences, the divisions hardening as a result of personal antipathies.

In the debris of Non-cooperation 'No-changers' who adhered to Gandhi's tactics faced 'Pro-changers' who wished to steer Congress once more into constitutional paths. The latter won the day, forming Swaraj parties which became the main instruments of Congressmen's political activities. Motilal Nehru and C. R. Das tried to create an all-India party with a single policy and effective organization. The Swarajists never had sufficient men in the central Assembly to pursue a wholesale policy of obstruction; and in the provinces local Swarajist groups never submitted to continental discipline when it threatened their local positions and prospects. Fissures widened on the issues of obstructing council work, accepting ministerial office, and the role of Muslims in the party, and by the end of 1925 Swarajist disunity had spawned Responsive Cooperation groups in several provinces under such prominent leaders as M. R. Jayakar, N. C. Kelkar, and Dr B. S. Moonje. Significantly in the Central Provinces and Berar, one of the only two provinces where Swarajists had been numerous enough to wreck dyarchy and force the governor to take over the transferred subjects, they had by 1926 decided temporarily that constitutional tactics and ministerships made greater sense for them locally.[7] When Motilal organized a 'walk-out' in the Assembly, local Swarajist groups chafed at the directive, and the protest was short lived. Assam was not the only province where the governor could report, 'Swarajists have always objected strongly to the walk-out policy and have greatly resented having to obtain the permis-

[7] Sir Montagu Butler, Governor of C.P., to Irwin, 4 August 1926, Mss. EUR.C.152 (20).

D. E. U. Baker, 'The Break-Down of Nationalist Unity and the Formation of the Swaraj Parties, India, 1922 to 1924', *University Studies in History*, v, 4 (1970), 85–113; R. A. Gordon, 'Aspects in the history of the Indian National Congress, with special reference to the Swarajya Party, 1919 to 1937' (D. Phil. thesis, Oxford, 1970).

sion of the All-India Congress Committee to attend sessions of the local Council. Several of them, too, I have good reason to believe, would accept a Ministership if it was offered to them.' In neighbouring Bihar, moreover, it was plain that Swarajists were no stable, coherent group united by all-India loyalty and discipline. Local politicians adopted any label which they thought would facilitate their election, and tied temporary tags on themselves to gain access to electioneering organization and funds.[8] The rationale of provincial situations and the opportunities the councils offered had triumphed over the all-India unity and leadership Gandhi and Congress had provided during Non-cooperation, and which Motilal had tried to replace. The Swarjist rout in the 1926 elections confirmed this triumph.

The erosion of national unity and leadership in the context of the reformed constitution was equally marked among India's Muslims and in their relation to Congress politics. The 1920s saw the disintegration of the Muslim League–Congress alliance, the hardening of political divisions among Muslims from different provinces, and the loss of control by Muslim political 'leaders' over the actions of Muslims in town and countryside. The communal alliance in Non-cooperation had been fortuitous. Gandhi had seized on anxiety about the Khalifah's status after Turkey's defeat in the 1914–18 war to bring Muslims into a movement with Hindus which he hoped would forward his ideal of swaraj, an essential ingredient of which was Hindu-Muslim unity. The resulting strains within Non-cooperation were blatantly clear even before Gandhi called it to a halt. The Turks' abolition of the Khilafat in 1924 effectively removed the issue from Indian politics, thereby snapping the brittle links between Congress and League which had survived the collapse of joint agitation.

In 1924 the League met separately from Congress for the first time since 1918. It called for the solution of the problem of India's Muslim minority through a federation of autonomous provinces and the provision of separate electorates. These resolutions and the separation from Congress indicated that Muslims were rethinking their position in the light of their experience of the new constitution. In Bengal and Punjab Muslims in a majority had learnt swiftly that the enlarged franchise on a communal basis and the devolution of power through dyarchy paid dividends. If set in a federation where Hindu preponderance in India as a whole could be offset by provincial autonomy, this promised to be a sound recipe for future Muslim power and hence security.[9] The pursuit of this claim not only widened the gulf between League and Congress, which was committed to joint electorates. It also split the Muslims along provincial lines. In March 1927, at an informal Muslim conference in Delhi of members of the provincial and central legislatures, M. A. Jinnah floated a scheme whereby

[8] Sir Henry Wheeler to Irwin, 12 December 1926, Sir John Kerr, Governor of Assam, to Irwin, 30 September 1926, Mss. Eur.C.152 (20).

[9] R. Coupland, *The Indian Problem 1833–1935* (London, 1942), pp. 74–5: Moore, *Crisis of Indian Unity 1917–1940*, pp. 21–4.

Muslims would give up the demand for a separate electorate provided that
their security was protected by the creation of three more Muslim majority
provinces, the North-West Frontier, Sind and Baluchistan, within a federal
constitution. Jinnah, a Bombay Muslim lawyer, had been an isolated political figure since his withdrawal from Congress activities when Gandhi led
it into unconstitutional paths in 1920. He was moved to his new stand partly
by his own political need to establish a new appeal and alignment as a base
for his own claims to political leadership. Immediately, however, his step
towards a rapprochement with Hindu politicians was disowned by some
who had attended the Delhi meeting, and condemned by the Assembly
representative of the North-West Frontier, Sir Abdul Qaiyum, by the
Punjab Muslim League and the Bengal Provincial Muslim Conference.[10]
The Muslim majority areas spoke with one voice: separate electorates best
safeguarded their position, whatever the attraction of joint electorates in
return for concessions for their co-religionists who could never hope for
local dominance. Controversy erupted within the League in the summer
of 1927 on the venue of the next morning, M. M. Shafi and the Punjabis
endeavouring to steer the League away from Madras where it would
coincide with Congress and they might be swamped by Jinnah and his
supporters who favoured joint electorates. The League split into two parts,
Jinnah's group going their way in Calcutta, and Shafi's adherents affirming
their policy in Lahore.

Not only the logic of provincial politics under the dispensation of dyarchy
divided League from Congress. These constitutional essays occurred amid
deteriorating communal relations in towns and villages. Communal rioting,
rivalry for office, attempts to unify each community and reconvert the fallen
were its sinister hall-marks. In 1924 all the Hindus fled the Frontier town
of Kohat in fear of their lives in one of a series of outbursts which scarred
many north Indian cities. In the twelve months following a serious communal riot in Calcutta in April 1926, there were forty riots resulting in 197
deaths and injuries to nearly 1,600 people. In the United Provinces alone
between 1923 and 1927 eighty-one were killed and 2,301 injured in eighty-
eight communal riots. This was a far cry from the communal fraternization
and joint political endeavour of Non-cooperation days. Over these manifestations of communal strife neither aspiring all-India leaders nor local
politicians exercised control.[11]

The fears thus generated, moreover, provided material for politicians
in search of potent rallying cries, and disposed people to look to explicitly

[10] V to S of S, telegram, 26 March 1927, Mss. EUR.C.152 (8); Irwin to Birkenhead,
11 May 1927, Mss. EUR.C.152 (3).

[11] For the politicians' inability to control communal tensions see V to S of S,
telegram, 18 April 1923, Mss. EUR.E.238 (17); Sir Hugh Stephenson, Governor of
Bihar & Orissa, to Irwin, 19 June 1927, Mss. EUR.C.152 (21). For the manifestations
of communal antagonism and their origins see *Report of the Indian Statutory Commission Volume I – Survey*, P.P., 1929–30, XI, Cmd. 3568, 252–3; P. Hardy, *The Muslims
of British India* (Cambridge, 1972), pp. 201–9.

communal bodies for protection. It was in the 1920s that the specifically Hindu organization, the All-India Hindu Mahasabha, began to gain support in north and central India, though its origins ante-dated the First World War, deeply rooted in the concerns and alignments which made up the provincial politics of Punjab and U.P. in particular. Like Congress itself the Mahasabha's local and continental unity was extremely fragile, and even though it became more overtly political during the decade, many of its adherents and major figures such as M. M. Malaviya, N. C. Kelkar, M. S. Aney and B. S. Moonje remained within or on the fringes of Congress. But the changing communal context gave a new edge to old divisions and armed these 'Communalists' (as they have somewhat inaccurately become known in too stark a contrast with Congressmen) with new means of attracting local and cross-regional support.[12] This compounded the splits in the Swarajist front, underlining the loose nature of political groupings during the decade and boding ill for common action by Congress as a united body when the redistribution of power in the state structures became imminent and demanded new political stances.

In the 1920s Gandhi was confronted by the collapse of continental political unity and discontinuity between actions in different political arenas. His countrymen evidently saw little value in the role he had performed for them in 1920–2. For this Gandhi was partly responsible by calling off the civil disobedience element in Non-cooperation, thereby throwing into question the viability of this all-India strategy. But as important a cause of his redundancy in the mid-1920s as his 'failure' of 1922 was the fact that once a new constitution was operative Indians did not have the same need to make a continental response to the raj of the type Gandhi's campaign had facilitated. They did not need the linkages with each other across regions and within regions which Non-cooperation had forged. Politicians in the provinces could pursue their goals in local interchanges with their rulers through the councils; and in this enterprise they had no need of popular support. The only functions an all-India leader could now attempt to perform were to arrange alliances between provincial groups of politicians and to organize a central party in the Assembly. These were roles Gandhi was neither equipped nor prepared to play. Moreover, the two politicians who preeminently aspired to these roles, Jinnah and Motilal Nehru, were by 1927 leaders without an all-India following, their endeavours shattered by the logic of provincial diversity and the differing needs of local groups of politicians.

In 1927 Motilal thought the Assembly 'not at all a place for decent men' and painted for his absent son a vivid picture of the confusions of the political scene, as he hankered after the unity of Non-cooperation.

> In short conditions in India have never been worse. The reaction of the N.C.O. movement which set in in 1922–23 has since been slowly but surely

[12] R. Gordon, 'The Hindu Mahasabha and the Indian National Congress, 1915 to 1926', *Modern Asian Studies*, 9, 2 (April 1975), 145–203.

undermining all public activity. There is not much of it left now but the rot is still proceeding – at a quicker pace now than before. The only education the masses are getting is in communal hatred. It is not true today as it certainly was a couple of years ago that communal strife was confined to cities and was not known in the villages. The latter now are more frequently the scenes of communal riots than the former. The older people among the nationalists have given way to despair. The younger men are taking greater interest in their own advancement by whatever means & however reprehensible in their own opinion of 2 years ago. Imagine Congressmen in the Assembly & the Councils tumbling over each other to shake hands with officials, stealthily attending official functions after taking care that their names are not reported to the press, actually applying for invitations to such functions, complaining of the *zulum* of their leader at preventing them from coming into close contact with officials while he himself was in high favour with them.

A fortnight later he lamented, 'I don't think there is one man among the old or the new sort of Congressmen who will not go into a fainting fit on hearing the words complete independence for India.'[13]

The British, too, had no need of a continental figure to help them construct collaborative alliances with key groups of their subjects. They were content with the cooperation forthcoming in and outside the legislatures which so disgusted Motilal. When the acting Governor of Bombay invited Gandhi to see him in 1926 in a move to avert a possible boycott of the Royal Commission on Agriculture, he was firmly rebuked by the Viceroy, for the double reason that this might suggest to the public that government was afraid of Gandhi's influence in politics, and that since Gandhi was an uncertain quantity such a private confabulation could bring little benefit. This brief interchange was highly significant. Gandhi's all-India role was in part made possible by the British. At times they were willing to risk high stakes for his cooperation because of their reading of his public image and his influence over his compatriots. At other times they closed the doors to him, opening them to other Indians whose support they believed could provide a surer buttress to their raj. Their willingness or refusal to deal with Gandhi affected his value to Indians: when they treated him as an all-India leader they confirmed him in that position, and when they refused to do so they tended to erode his standing. Calculating the benefits and disadvantages of contact with Gandhi in 1926 the Viceroy would have preferred no contact; but he did not insist on the cancellation of the meeting lest this should in its turn be used as a stick to beat the raj.[14]

[13] M. to J. Nehru, 30 March & 14 April 1927, NMML, J. Nehru Papers, part I, vol. LXIX. *Zulum* means oppression, and weight of the taunt lies in the fact that the word was often used to describe police harassment. For Jinnah's discomfiture at being an aspirant leader without a following or a role see Irwin to Birkenhead, 8 & 15 March 1928, Mss. EUR.C.152 (4).

[14] Sir Henry Lawrence, Acting Governor of Bombay, to V, 22 April 1926, V to Lawrence, 28 April 1926, Mss. EUR.C.152 (20); V to S of S, telegram, 27 April 1926, Mss. EUR.C.152 (7).

Gandhi's singular personal repute gave him a potentially unique position of leverage over the British and their subjects, because of the role each calculated Gandhi could play in their relationship with each other. In the mid-1920s, however, neither needed him to facilitate that relationship. All-India leadership only came to Gandhi when they did.

Late in 1927 there were signs of change in the political context which had in the three years since Gandhi's release prevented his assumption of a continental leadership role. The act creating the 1919 constitution had provided for a Statutory Commission to enquire into the working of the constitution at the end of ten years. Britain's Tory government appointed the Commission under Sir John Simon earlier than the scheduled date in order to retain control over the choice of its members, fearing that this might slip from its grasp at the next general election. Now the British needed public support from Indians whom they hoped could lead their compatriots in constructive cooperation with the Commission. Significantly Gandhi was among those whom Irwin interviewed to urge them not to throw away the opportunity of the Commission.[15] Its announcement, in fact, aroused intense opposition from a wide spectrum of political opinion because it included no Indian. Indians who favoured boycotting it turned to Gandhi as they realized their need on an all-India issue to present a united front to the government. Punjabi Hindus, for example, suspended judgement, awaiting news of the attitude not only of their Punjabi leader, Lajpat Rai, but of Gandhi – 'to which they attach a good deal of importance'. Gandhi played no part in the Madras Congress of 1927, but in Jawaharlal Nehru's words, 'he was frequently consulted, and little of importance was done without his knowledge'.[16] In the new situation Motilal, recognizing the potential of Gandhi's name and political techniques, kept him minutely informed on developments within Congress and negotiations for a joint Hindu–Muslim reply to the Commission in the form of an all-parties' constitutional scheme. In December 1928 when the fate of that scheme, the Nehru Report, hung in the balance, Motilal insisted that Gandhi should go to Calcutta where the issues would be decided.

The prospect of reform threw political relationships into the melting pot – the relationships of Indians to their rulers, the relationship of India's regions and different political arenas to each other in the framework of a new constitution. On their part many Indians saw that they needed to put an end at least temporarily to their political divisions and discontinuities. They needed cross-regional alliances and evidence of support for their claims from within their own areas if they were to extract favourable terms for the future from the raj. The raj in its turn could not afford to embark on possible consideration of another new constitution without some guarantee that enough Indians would cooperate within it to ensure its success

[15] Irwin to Birkenhead, 3 November 1927, Mss. EUR.C.152 (3).
[16] J. Nehru, *An Autobiography* (London, 1936), p. 167; Sir Malcolm Hailey, Governor of Punjab, to Irwin, 7 November 1927, Mss. EUR.C.152 (21).

as a means of safeguarding British interests and the imperial link. What Gandhi made of the changing political context and the new needs of Indians and the raj depended on the way his perceptions and activities had developed since he had last played a continental leadership role.

II   THE MAHATMA TAKES STOCK

The years 1922-8 were for Gandhi a time of stock-taking, during which he was forced by government and his countrymen to rethink his personal priorities and his role in public affairs. The first stage in this process was his two-year spell in jail. He throve on the regular, disciplined life prison demanded. His daily routine was similar to that which he laid down for his ashram, though in Yeravda jail near Poona, undisturbed by the demands of public life, he was able to give six hours a day to reading and four to spinning and carding. He read over 150 books; reading for the first time the whole of the *Mahabharata* and the six systems of Hindu philosophy in Gujarati, he steeped himself afresh in his Hindu heritage. Reading and the solitary reflection promoted by rhythmic handwork merely confirmed his views on religion and politics, as he admitted on his release.[17] He re-emerged from Yeravda with clearer priorities and a stronger conviction that he must pursue his own path even if he could find no companions to share it. He had become a man with a much surer sense of himself and his potential public role than the fumbling pragmatist of his first years back in India.

The foundation of Gandhi's attitude to public affairs was his conviction that religion could not be relegated to the realm of private opinion but must influence and permeate all men's activities. For himself he maintained that if he was to be true to his spiritual vision he could not stand apart even from political action. He told an English audience in 1931,

> although to all appearances my mission is political, I would ask you to accept my assurance that its roots are...spiritual. It is commonly known though perhaps not believed, that I claim that at least my politics are not divorced from morality, from spirituality, from religion. I have claimed...that a man who is trying to discover and follow the will of God cannot possibly leave a single field of life untouched. I came also... to the conclusion that if there was any field of service where morality,

[17] Answers to questions on his release, February 1924, *CWMG*, XXIII, 196. Gandhi's jail reading list is in *CWMG*, XXV, 83-5. He described his jail life to H. A. Khan, 14 April 1922, *CWMG*, XXIII, 129-36. It was clear from this letter that spinning was increasingly important to him as an aid to meditation and a means of coming 'nearer to the poorest of the poor, and in them, to God'. He professed to be 'as happy as a bird' and not to feel that he was 'accomplishing less here than outside the prison. My stay here is a good school for me and my separation from my fellow workers should prove whether our movement is an independently evolving organism, or merely the work of one individual and, therefore, something very transient.'
For the ashram routine see Draft Constitution, 1915, *CWMG*, XIII, 97, and *Young India*, 14 June 1928, *CWMG*, XXXVI, 410.

where truth, where fear of God, were not essential, that field should be given up entirely.

But I found also that the politics of the day are no longer a concern of kings, but that they affect the lowest strata of society. And I found, through bitter experience that, if I wanted to do social service, I could not possibly leave politics alone.[18]

Religion for Gandhi was not the doctrinal formulation of any one religious system but a basic truth underlying all formal religions. He described this as the struggle for truth, the striving of the permanent element in human nature to find and express itself, to know its maker. His own desire, he wrote in 1925, 'what I have been striving and pining to achieve these thirty years – is self-realization, to see God face to face, to attain *moksha*. I live and move and have my being in pursuit of this goal. All that I do by way of speaking and writing, and all my ventures in the political field, are directed to this end.' He agreed that in turning to service of humanity without the shackles of attachment, in seeking truth and salvation, self-realization, through social action he was following one path within Hinduism, that of the *karma yogi*; though he had not appreciated this until other people used this title of him.[19]

Central to Gandhi's interpretation of religion and perception of his own *dharma*, or religious duty, as self-realization through service, was the affirmation that there could be no double standards, no public and private morality. 'Unfortunately a belief has today sprung up that one's private character has nothing to do with one's public activity. This superstition must go.' Those who believed with him that public life must be purified must first reform themselves. 'This spiritual weapon of self-purification, intangible as it seems, is the most potent means for revolutionizing one's environment and for loosening external shackles.' This lay behind his agonizings over his own drives and motives, and the moral standards observed in the Sabarmati ashram where he hoped to train a hard core of workers committed to following him in the purification of public life.[20]

The commitment to a single moral standard presented Gandhi, as an idealist pursuing his ideals in public affairs, with the problem not only of right intentions but of right means. On this question he was adamant. Means could not be separated from ends, since wrong means would only distort the end. As he told the Madras politician, S. Satyamurti, in 1931, he sought political power for Congress for the sake of the improvements in people's lives which this would enable: but if that power could only be obtained in

[18] Speech in London, 23 September 1931, *The Guildhouse*, 23 September 1931, *CWMG*, XLVIII, 50.
A valuable study of Gandhi's main ideas is Raghavan N. Iyer, *The Moral and Political Thought of Mahatma Gandhi*, (New York, 1972).
[19] Gandhi to Ramdas Gandhi, 7 November 1932, *CWMG*, LI, 373–4. See also the introduction to Gandhi's autobiography, subtitled, 'The Story of my Experiments with Truth', 26 November 1925, *Navajivan*, 29 November 1925, *CWMG*, XXXIX, 3.
[20] Interview reported in *Young India*, 28 March 1929, *CWMG*, XL, 63–4.

ways which would jeopardize the goal, then he would rather do without it.[21] His solution to the problem of ends and means, as of the indivisibility of public and private morality, was satyagraha, truth-force. This was the Gujarati word he concocted to describe striving non-violently to the point of sacrifice rather than fighting to attain one's vision of truth. It was to him the only means which was pure because it did not violate the integrity of the opponent, forcing him to deny his own perception of truth. Its very action in refining the character of its exponent and converting the opponent made it both means and ends. In practice satyagraha could take a wide variety of forms – fasting, non-violent picketing, various types of non-cooperation and ultimately in politics civil disobedience in willing anticipation of the legal penalty.

Gandhi's commitment to satyagraha went back to his South African days when he incorporated an initially pragmatic tactic of passive resistance into his perception of life as an 'experiment with truth'. After his release in 1924 he was even more deeply committed to it, despite the apparent failure of Non-cooperation and India's blindness to what he saw as the spiritual importance of non-violence. Admitting he was out on a limb from his contemporaries he nonetheless asserted in 1927.

> For me there is no hope save through truth and non-violence. I know that they will triumph when everything else has failed. Whether therefore I am in the minority of one or I have a majority, I must go along the course God seems to have shown me. Today non-violence as a mere policy is a broken reed...[This] is the time for the out-and-out believer in non-violence to test his creed. Both my creed and I are therefore on our trial.

A year later he reiterated his affirmation that satyagraha presupposed divine guidance, and that it alone would prove to be the most practical politics. 'All this may sound foolish and visionary...But I would be untrue to the nation and myself if I failed to say what I feel to be the deepest truth.'[22]

Here manifestly was one fired with internal conviction, eager to prove himself and his creed, steeled by years of discipline to drive himself in the face of ridicule and opposition. It promised to be an explosive mixture if applied to politics. But it was unclear how far Gandhi would be prepared to involve himself in politics, precisely because his attitudes and self-image were so different from the majority of Indian politicians. Where they manoeuvred for political power and place and interpreted their goal of swaraj as Dominion Status or independence, Gandhi spoke of personal transformation as the only solid foundation for the reformation of public

---

[21] For the correspondence with Satyamurti see articles in *Young India*, 2 July, 6 August 1931, *CWMG*, XLVII, 90–2, 251–3. Gandhi's insistence on the inseparability of means and ends is clear in an article on *dharma* as truth and non-violence in *Navajivan*, 21 July 1929, *CWMG*, XLI, 209–11.

[22] *Young India*, 2 August 1928, *CWMG*, XXXVII, 113; *Young India*, 1 December 1927, *CWMG*, XXXV, 353.

For the African origins of Gandhi's commitment to satyagraha see Brown, *Gandhi's Rise to Power*, pp. 6–8.

life and the attainment of swaraj, true self-rule. The differences between Gandhi and his compatriots on the aims as well as the standards of political life were even more marked on his release from Yeravda than they had been during Non-cooperation. Gandhi's ideal of swaraj was an India composed of truthful, fearless individuals who were capable of regulating their own affairs, who treated each other with equality and tolerance, and resolved their differences through satyagraha. It meant returning to a religious outlook on life and throwing off the shackles of modern civilization with its false standards of wealth and success, and the opportunities industrial society created for man to exploit man.

Gandhi opposed the British government because he believed that the raj, as the herald of modern ways, was the instrument of India's growing degradation; and that under its emasculating influence Indians would never attain full equality with their rulers and have the power to refashion their country according to its true *dharma*. This had been clear in his trial statement in 1922: in 1928 he was equally firm in his stand.

> To promote...disaffection is the bounden duty of every nationalist... We have no quarrel with men, but if we are worthy of swaraj, we must destroy the existing system of Government by all legitimate and peaceful means...The whole of my being is worked in order to achieve the destruction of this Government and to that end to spread disaffection as wide as possible.[23]

Gandhi's condemnation of the raj did not sound quite so drastic when he came down to the practicalities of political aims and possible constitutions. On his release from jail he defined swaraj as full partnership for India with other parts of the empire on an equal footing with Dominions like Canada; and a year later he said swaraj meant government of India by the consent of the people as ascertained by the vote of adults who contributed to the state by manual labour and had registered as voters. He believed that such government should be possible within a British connection, but if that connection impeded India's growth and full equality it should be severed.[23]

Just as Gandhi quarrelled with the British for the form of government they imposed on India, so he differed from those Indians who believed that swaraj was a constitution which could be given to them by the British. He argued that it would only come as the result of their own efforts, for they were as much responsible for their own degradation as were the British, because of their moral weaknesses, their acceptance of modern ways, and their acquiescence if not active collaboration in official institutions. Reform of evils in Indian society such as the treatment of women, Untouchability, and Hindu–Muslim hatred, was an essential element in the creation of

---

[23] *Young India*, 23 February 1928, *CWMG*, XXXVI, 43–4. Gandhi's trial statement, *Young India*, 23 March 1922, *CWMG*, XXIII, 115–19. The content of Gandhi's true swaraj is described in a booklet he wrote in 1909, *Hind Swaraj*, *CWMG*, X, 6–68.

[24] Gandhi's answers to questions on his release, February 1924, *CWMG*, XXIII, 196; *Young India*, 29 January 1925, *CWMG*, XXVI, 50.

swaraj, for swaraj was a state to be created not a status to be snatched or accepted from their rulers. 'An Act of Parliament might give you constitutional swaraj. But it will be a mere chimera that will profit us but little if we are unable to solve these internal problems. In fact, ability to solve these problems is the alpha and omega of real swaraj, the swaraj of the masses that we all want.'[25]

The Gandhi who left Yeravda was a man more resolutely committed to the creation of new people and a new social order from which would grow new forms of government and new political relationships between Indians, and between India and Britain. His aim was to create a new identity for Indians and a new unity among them; to build up their strength so that they could create their own swaraj, and so to shatter the psychological roots of British power which were Indian acquiescence and disunity. Only if this aim was fulfilled could his over-arching ambition be satisfied – that of spreading the swaraj message throughout the world.[26] Speaking in Gujarat nearly a year after his release he explained how he saw the significance of his time in jail.

> I see a great purpose in God saving me from a serious illness in Yeravda Prison and releasing me for your service. The purpose is that I should come to you and give you self-confidence, put before you the fruit of profound meditation in prison, namely the key to swaraj lies in fulfilling three conditions alone – in the spinning-wheel, in Hindu-Muslim unity and in the removal of untouchability.

He had already made clear on his release that he proposed to resume his 'activities for the attainment of swaraj' as soon as he was well again.[27]

The second phase in Gandhi's personal and political stock-taking was forced on him by his Congress colleagues. Re-entering public life in the circumstances of 1924, he had to decide how to pursue his 'activities for the attainment of swaraj'. Naturally enough Motilal and C. R. Das wanted the prestige his support for them would bring in the controversy between the No-changers and the Pro-changers. But Gandhi refused to compromise with them during discussions at Juhu in March 1924. He immersed himself in editing *Young India* and *Navajivan*, considering that job 'quite enough'; and he wrote in his first *Young India* article after his release that he had no new message or programme. 'My faith in the old is just as bright as ever, if not brighter.'[28]

[25] Speech at Bardoli, 12 August 1928, *Young India*, 13 September 1928, *CWMG*, XXXVII, 168. See also *Navajivan*, 9 & 16 September 1928, *ibid*, pp. 250, 266.

[26] *Young India*, 12 January 1928, *CWMG*, XXXV, 457.
For Gandhi's denunciation of the hypnotic and corrupting effect of involvement in the British system see *Young India*, 13 December 1928, 10 January 1929, *CWMG*, XXXVIII, 210, 257.

[27] Answers to questions on his release, February 1924, *CWMG*, XXIII, 195; speech at Godhra, 2 January 1925, *Navajivan*, 11 January 1925, *CWMG*, XXV, 536.

[28] *Young India*, 3 April 1924, *CWMG*, XXIII, 340; *Navajivan*, 15 June 1924, *CWMG*, XXIV, 255.

Late in June at an All-India Congress Committee (AICC) meeting in Ahmedabad he forced a confrontation to test support for the Non-cooperation programme, particularly *khadi* (hand-spun cloth) and non-violence, and to gauge how far Congressmen would submit to all-India discipline. Despite objections from Nehru and Das he moved four resolutions, enjoining daily spinning on Congress office-bearers, exclusion from office in Congress of those who did not obey Congress directives and did not observe the Non-cooperation boycotts (of mill cloth, courts, schools, titles and legislative bodies), and condemning a recent terrorist murder as inconsistent with the Congress creed. These were the terms on which he would accept all-India leadership again, he told the AICC. If the means and instruments he needed were available, he would take up the role: they must accept his conditions or choose another leader.[29] The showdown was dramatic. Nehru and Das left the hall with about fifty-five supporters during the discussion of the spinning resolution, and would have decamped from Ahmedabad had they not heard of the subsequent removal of the penalty clause ousting from office those who defaulted on their spinning. But it was the narrow majority of under ten on the violence issue which really shattered Gandhi, making him weep publicly. He described himself as 'defeated and humbled', and considered retirement from Congress to devote himself to communal unity, *khadi* and the removal of Untouchability.[30]

At the urging of his Swarajist opponents he stayed within Congress, and began to work either for a Congress unanimously behind his programme or for a separate organization through which he could pursue his programme in parallel with Congress's constitutional work. 'I know that there is room for both the *policies*,' he wrote. 'Fields of action must be different. They will not then clash but help. I am seeking means of exit from the Congress without a fireworks display. In Mr. Tilak's own time, I had no difficulties in working along my own lines.'[31] By September 1925 the problem was resolved by demarcating zones of work. Gandhi 'surrendered' to the Swarajists, blessing their constitutional work as an integral part of Congress activity, and advocating the suspension of Non-cooperation apart from the refusal to wear foreign cloth. But he secured the creation of a

[29] Speech at AICC, 28 June 1924, *ibid.* pp. 306–11.
For the resolutions he proposed to move see article, 'The Acid Test', *Young India*, 19 June 1924, *ibid.* pp. 267–70.
[30] Article on AICC meeting, 'Defeated And Humbled', *Young India*, 3 July 1924, *ibid.* pp. 334–40. Viceroy's report on AICC meeting in telegram to S of S, 21 July 1924, Mss. EUR.E.238 (13).
[31] Gandhi to Bhagwandas, 27 July 1924, *CWMG*, XXIV, 462. He told J. Nehru in a letter, 15 September 1924, 'I do so feel like retiring from the Congress and doing the three things quietly. They are enough to occupy more than all the true men and women we can get. But even that ruffles people...They do not realise that I shall cease to be useful as soon as I cease to be myself. It is a wretched situation but I do not despair. My faith is in God.' J. Nehru, *A Bunch of Old Letters* (2nd edn, Bombay, 1960), p. 41.

new body, the All-India Spinners' Association at an AICC meeting in Patna. The AISA was to be integral with, yet independent of Congress, and its members were to spin 1,000 yards of yarn a month, wear *khadi* and popularize the spinning wheel.

In Ahmedabad Gandhi had tested the political context in which he would now have to operate. By late 1925 he had not only taken stock of the situation but carved out a role for himself in public affairs outside the main stream of Congress politics. He had made clear that he stuck to the beliefs and programme which Yeravda had reinforced; and refused to compromise them for leadership on terms which would make him false to himself and place only feeble instruments at his disposal. He had his own organization and sphere of work, enabling him to reach beyond the ranks of India's educated to the people whose lives he wished to reform, among whom he wished to generate the strength for true swaraj.

Gandhi now set his sights on mass contact through *khadi*, maintaining that he would have been 'thoroughly useless to the masses as an Anglicized, denationalized being knowing little of, caring less for and perhaps even despising their ways, habits, thoughts and aspirations'.[32] But after the Ahmedabad debacle his attitude towards India's educated seems to have mellowed, as his perception of the value of Congress to India showed. The lessons of Non-cooperation were not lost on him. Until India's masses had been roused and organized for political action, Gandhi needed his educated compatriots just as they had needed him in 1920–2. Moreover they were essential to the purpose of mass education, and as such had to be converted and integrated into the new Indian nation. Writing of his 'surrender' in 1925 he commented,

> I must carry the educated with me in my attempt to convert the Congress into a mass organization. We cannot be true representatives of the masses so long as we do not do physical work to qualify ourselves for membership of the Congress. But I have not been able to convince the educated class of this...I must have patience and make it as easy as possible for [them] to join the Congress.[33]

Moreover, in reply to those who criticized Congress for its weaknesses, divisions and wordy protestations, he defended it as a venerable institution maintaining the ideal of a united, free India. He advised that they, like him, should remain silent where they could not participate in or serve it, and observe non-violence even towards erring Congressmen.[34]

From 1925 Gandhi remained sympathetically aloof from Congress deliberations. His deliberate year of silence on political matters in 1926 and

---

[32] *Young India*, 5 July 1928, *CWMG*, XXXVII, 21.

[33] *Navajivan*, 26 July 1925, *CWMG*, XXVII, 422. On 1 April 1928 Gandhi wrote significantly to J. Nehru, 'some day we shall have to start an intensive movement without the rich people and without the vocal educated class. But that time is not yet.' *CWMG*, XXXVI, 174.

[34] Gandhi to P.C. Ghosh, 22 February 1928, *ibid.* p. 42; Gandhi to C. F. Andrews, 1 October 1927, *CWMG*, XXXV, 68.

his collapse from overwork in March 1927 confirmed this position. Early in 1928 he declared that he had no political moves to suggest and 'no desire even now to interfere with the present evolution of the national movement except through occasional writings'.[35] A clear indication of how he saw his political role was a comment to Dr B. C. Roy, the Calcutta politician, in May 1928:

> I am biding my time and you will find me leading the country in the field of politics when the country is ready. I have no false modesty about me. I am undoubtedly a politician in my own way, and I have a scheme for the country's freedom. But my time is not yet and may never come to me in this life. If it does not, I shall not shed a single tear. We are all in the hands of God. I shall therefore await His guidance.[36]

However, Gandhi still attended the annual sessions of Congress, was consulted, and made his views known through correspondence and the press. In 1926 at the Gauhati Congress, for example, he spoke out on the resolution to redefine swaraj as complete independence, warning members not to bite off more than they could chew. They should aim for what was currently possible and make it clear that they wished to remain as imperial partners if this permitted equality and the evolution of true swaraj.[37] During 1927 he was in close confabulation with Motilal Nehru, at the latter's instigation, on the election of the Congress president for that year. The close cooperation between Gandhi and the two Nehrus, despite the confrontation of 1924 and continuing disagreement on many issues, was a vital element in Gandhi's influence in all-India politics, now in the Mahatma's partial retirement, and later when the crucial decisions on civil disobedience were made. The three men, and then Jawaharlal and Gandhi after Motilal's death in 1931, recognized that alliance was a mutual source of strength although their goals were markedly different. Motilal had suggested Jawaharlal as a gesture of the older generation that they were prepared to give place to younger men in Congress. Gandhi believed that this would be a waste of Jawaharlal's time, enmeshing him in intrigue and communal rancour when he should be making contact with the masses. He therefore began exerting private and public pressure in favour of the Congress Muslim and his colleague of the Khilafat movement, Dr M. A. Ansari, on the grounds that he could best promote the scheduled communal unity resolution and prove that Congress was not a Hindu body.[38]

Ansari did preside at Madras in 1927, but it was this very session which

---

[35] *Young India*, 9 February 1928, *CWMG*, XXXVI, 15; *Young India*, 9 January 1928, *CWMG*, XXXV, 447.

[36] Gandhi to B. C. Roy, 1 May 1928, *CWMG*, XXXVI, 287.

[37] Speech at Subjects Committee, 28 December 1926, *CWMG*, XXXII, 468.

[38] See for example Gandhi to M. Nehru, 14 & 25 May 1927, Gandhi to J. Nehru, 25 May 1927, *CWMG*, XXXIII, 320–1, 366, 364–5: M. to J. Nehru, 19 May 1927, J. Nehru Papers, part I, vol. LXIX.

For Gandhi's pressure for Ansari as President see Gandhi to Sarojini Naidu, 25 June 1927; *Young India*, 21 July 1927; Gandhi to M. A. Ansari, 10 August 1927; *CWMG*, XXXIV, 57–8, 213–14, 305.

elicited some of Gandhi's most scathing comments on Congress politics. He attended the open sessions but took no part in the formulation of policy, and did not attend the Subjects Committee meetings although he was a member. Somewhat surprisingly a resolution put by Jawaharlal that Congress's goal should be complete independence was passed, whereas similar proposals had been defeated in 1926 and earlier sessions. It owed its passage to the disgust of Jawaharlal and some of his younger supporters at the torpor of Congress as guided by entrenched politicians, and to Srinivasa Iyengar's exploitation of this feeling as a weapon to fight his rival, Motilal, the man who, as leader of the Swarajists, advocated policies of non-participation in the councils which offered nothing to Tamil Nad Congressmen who desperately needed in their local situation to exploit the opportunities of legislative politics. Motilal was in Europe at the time but he opposed the idea because it would split Congress and also detach from Congress peripheral political groups such as the Liberals, Nationalists like Lajpat Rai and Malaviya, and Jinnah with the Independents, whose sympathy was essential if there was to be effective boycott of the Simon Commission. Although the resolution was manoeuvred through the open session, this signified little change in the attitude of most Congressmen whose sights remained set on Dominion Status.[39] In *Young India* Gandhi castigated Congress for its irresponsible talk and indiscipline. He singled out the resolutions on independence and boycott of British goods as ill-conceived, unlikely to be given effect and therefore sure to make an exhibition of Congress weakness: 'we have almost sunk to the level of the schoolboy's debating society.' He held fast to swaraj as the goal, opposing the cry for independence on the grounds that the Hindustani word described for ordinary people what they were striving for, a state they alone could create but which might be fashioned within an imperial link. Privately he rebuked Jawaharlal for encouraging 'mischief-makers and hooligans' and for not thinking out the whole situation and the resolutions which might be appropriate.[40]

Gandhi's reaction to Congress after his 'surrender' to the Swarajists was respect muted by sadness at what passed for political work among its adherents. Although he was only a peripheral figure in Congress he did not count himself as politically retired. Rather his vision of the scope of politics and the actions demanded for their purification thrust him into activities he considered more important because they were the building

[39] J. Nehru, *An Autobiography*, pp. 167–8; Goschen to Irwin, 5 January 1928, Mss. EUR.C.152 (22); Note by Govt. of India Publicity Officer on Congress demand for independence as opposed to Dominion Status, enclosed in Irwin to Peel, 15 November 1928, Mss. EUR.C.152 (4).

For the logic which led Tamil Nad Congressmen towards the councils, see D. Washbrook, 'Country Politics: Madras 1880 to 1930', in Gallagher, Johnson & Seal, *Locality, Province and Nation*, pp. 206–7.

[40] *Young India*, 5 & 12 January 1928, *CWMG*, XXXV, 437–9, 454–7; Gandhi to J. Nehru, 4 January 1928, J. Nehru, *A Bunch of Old Letters*, p. 58; Gandhi to J. Nehru, 11 January 1928, J. Nehru Papers, part I, vol. XXII.

blocks of swaraj. At the end of his year's reflection in 1926 he reiterated his conviction that 'swaraj is impossible to be attained if there is no Hindu–Muslim unity, if we still suffer from the curse of untouchability and if our middle classes refuse to understand the gospel of swadeshi.'[41] He threw himself into this triple programme with exhausting country-wide tours, a battery of press articles and his massive personal correspondence. In so doing he not only fulfilled his conception of his proper public role. He also kept himself in the public eye, yet unsullied by the divisions and antagonisms which rent the Congress, as he talked on matters which affected the lives of people who would never come within range of a Congress session.

Subhas Chandra Bose noted the function of Gandhi's apparently apolitical *khadi* campaign in the recreation of his leadership role. As AISA branches spread throughout India, 'the Mahatma was once again building up his own party which was to be of invaluable service to him when he desired to recapture the Congress machinery once again'.[42] To Gandhi the organizational potential of *khadi* was certainly one of its most important aspects. 'If cooking had to be revived and required the same organization, I should claim for it the same merit that I claim for khaddar.' He could see no other way of making contact with India's villagers; nor another issue which would appeal to them and yet could be used to retrain India's educated to value their poorer countrymen and so unite all social groups, thereby laying the foundations of a new national identity. Its economic importance was a further strand in his argument. In a country of poverty and under-employment spinning in every home would provide extra income and help the poor to cast off the shackles the rich imposed on them. Moreover on a national scale, if India produced all her own cloth there need be no imports from Lancashire and this would weaken Britain's will to hold India at any cost. By the power of the spinning-wheel he hoped to create a new India whose unity and self-reliance would achieve swaraj more swiftly than airy Congress resolutions. But it was a hard slog. As Motilal reported to his son in August 1927, 'He is pushing up Khadi & Charkha with all the energy he can command but though he did not say so in so many words his despondency in making it the success he had hoped was apparent from the manner in which he talked. For the rest he had only three words: wait, watch and pray.'[43]

---

[41] Speech at Wardha, 20 December 1926, *Young India*, 30 December 1926, *CWMG*, XXXII, 441.

[42] Bose, *The Indian Struggle 1920–1942*, p. 124.

By 1926–7 the AISA had 748 workers under its control, 204 centres and 177 *kahdi* production centres. Hand-spinning under AISA agency was done in 2,381 villages, 83,339 spinners serving 5,193 weavers. Sales were worth Rs. 33,48,794. *Young India*, 5 April 1928, *CWMG*, XXXVI, 186–7.

[43] M. to J. Nehru, 11 August 1927, J. Nehru Papers, part I, vol. LXIX. Important statements by Gandhi on the significance he attached to *khadi* are in *Young India*, 29 January 1925 & 17 March 1927, *CWMG*, XXVI, 48–9, XXXIII, 165–6.

Gandhi's despondency was particularly marked over his efforts to cement Hindu–Muslim unity. The collapse of the communal alliance he had so carefully constructed during Non-cooperation hurt him personally. He claimed it was the only question for immediate solution because disunity barred the way to swaraj, for as long as Indians were disunited there was room for imperial manoeuvre and the reliance of one group on British support. Confronted with communal riots and communal constitutional claims Gandhi pleaded for voluntary effort on both sides to restore friendliness and exhorted Hindus on political matters not to bargain but to trust Muslims and concede their demands.[44] He then tried the tactics of the fast and the conference to bring Hindus and Muslims together, but without permanent success. By January 1927 he was admitting, 'I dare not touch the problem of Hindu–Muslim unity. It has passed out of human hands and has been transferred to God's hands alone.' At the end of the year he stated,

> My interest and faith in Hindu–Muslim unity and unity among all the communities remains as strong as ever. My method of approach has changed. Whereas formerly I tried to achieve it by addressing meetings, joining in promoting and passing resolutions, now I have no faith in these devices...I therefore rely upon prayer and such individual acts of friendship as are possible...
>
> I am out of tune with the present temper of both the communities. From their own standpoint they are perhaps entitled to say that my method has failed.[45]

The rift between Gandhi and the Ali brothers, his closest Muslim colleagues of Khilafat days, after the Kohat riots was symbolic of the fact that few Muslims now felt that acceptance of the Mahatma's leadership could promise any safeguards for Muslim interests. Gandhi could no longer be of service to the majority of Muslims in the new political context once the agitational alliance between Congress and Khilafat supporters, founded on mutual need, had collapsed. In his new position of isolation and weakness as a Muslim leader, Gandhi naturally relied more heavily on Ansari and the handful of Muslims within Congress to be a link between him and their community, and to give the lie to assertions that Congress was a Hindu body. This was to give them particular leverage over him in the course of civil disobedience. Gandhi's loss of the Khilafat issue also made him particularly anxious to support causes which could be used in a similar way as bases for renewed cooperation in joint action where negotiation had failed to foster unity.[46]

---

[44] 'Hindu–Muslim Tension: Its Cause And Cure', *Young India*, 29 May 1924, *CWMG*, XXIV, 136–54; also *Young India*, 29 January 1925, *CWMG*, XXVI, 52.

[45] *Young India*, 1 December 1927, *CWMG*, XXXV, 353; *Young India*, 13 January 1927 in M. K. Gandhi, *The Hindu–Muslim Unity* (Bombay, 1965), p. 83.

[46] The Salt and the North–West Frontier movement led by Abdul Ghaffar Khan were two such cases. For evidence of the rift between Gandhi and the Alis see *Young India*, 1 December 1927, *CWMG*, XXV, 353–4; S. Ali to Gandhi, 23 October 1928,

The other fissure in Indian society which Gandhi condemned categorically was that of Untouchability. He campaigned against it relentlessly in speeches and in the press, maintaining as he had done during Non-cooperation that without this reform swaraj would be an illusion. He urged Untouchables to clean up their own habits, while to caste Hindus he asserted that 'this blot poisons the whole [caste] system, even as a drop of arsenic would poison a tankful of milk'.[47] Meanwhile a significant change was occurring in Gandhi's attitude to caste itself as he did battle with this grossest form of social inequality. In contrast to his earlier more orthodox position he was by 1926 distinguishing between caste as seen in India and *varnashramadharma*, the four ideal divisions of Hindu society defining a man's calling but imputing no distinctions of inferiority and superiority. It was on the basis of this redefinition of his idea of caste that he proceeded to attack the realities of caste in practice and to argue for radical reform of which the removal of Untouchability was the essential preliminary. Here, as in his work for communal unity and *khadi*, he sought to create a new Indian society bonded by mutual trust and obligation.[48]

In Gandhi's endeavour to create a new community capable of swaraj, his ashram had a prominent role. On the banks of the Sabarmati at Ahmedabad, Gujarat's main city, it had been his headquarters since his return from Africa. It was designed as a laboratory for experiments with truth and a power house which would produce public workers for the service of their country. To it Gandhi devoted much of his attention in the 1920s, particularly during 1926. Late in 1928 he again felt like burying himself at Sabarmati: the importance of ashram inmates in the Bardoli satyagraha convinced him that if he could make of the ashram what he wanted then he would 'be ready to give battle on an extensive scale'. In 1929 he called it his 'best creation'.[49]

Gandhi's attempts to remodel men and through them society spread far beyond the circle of inmates and visitors at Sabarmati, however. Through his speeches, tours, the press, and his vast correspondence he dealt with a wide range of topics concerning the lives of ordinary people but which most politicians did not consider to be the stuff of politics. To Gandhi health,

Gandhi to S. Ali, 30 November 1928, *CWMG*, XXXVIII, 436–8, 129–32; Hardy, *The Muslims of British India*, pp. 210–11.

[47] *Young India*, 19 April 1928, *CWMG*, XXXVI, 233; speech at sweepers' meeting, Ahmedabad, 27 March 1928, *ibid*, pp. 146–7. A collection of Gandhi's writings on this issue is available as M. K. Gandhi, *The Removal of Untouchability* (reprint of 1954 edn, Ahmedabad, 1959).

[48] A study of this critical change in Gandhi's attitude to caste is D. Dalton, 'The Gandhian View of Caste, and Caste after Gandhi', in P. Mason (ed.), *India and Ceylon: Unity and Diversity* (London, 1967), pp. 167–76. A collection of Gandhi's writings on this topic is available as M. K. Gandhi, *Varnashramadharma* (Ahmedabad, 1962).

[49] *Young India*, 31 January 1929, *CWMG*, XXXVIII, 417; Gandhi to M. Nehru, 21 August 1928, *CWMG*, XXXVII, 194.
 The new draft constitution of the ashram including details of activities, daily timetable, finances etc. is in *Young India*, 14 June 1928, *CWMG*, XXXVI, 398–410.

morals, social and personal habits were more important than constitutions because they were symptomatic of individual's attitudes to life: all would have to be permeated by religion and transformed before the advent of swaraj. He wrote to an English friend,

> You seem to think lightly of my having invited suggestions with reference to sanitary matters. In my own humble opinion we needlessly divide life into water-tight compartments, religious and other. Whereas if a man has true religion in him, it must show itself in the smallest detail of life. To me sanitation in a community such as ours is based upon common spiritual effort. The slightest irregularity in sanitary, social and political life is a sign of spiritual poverty. It is a sign of inattention, neglect of duty.

Consequently latrine cleaning was a prominent feature of ashram discipline, and Gandhi shot virulent articles into the press on lack of public hygiene. He advised scores of people on their personal and family problems, and the state of their souls and their digestive systems, as well as giving advice on more obviously public matters such as the payment of debts by hard work or the framing of public appeals.[50]

Gandhi's range of concerns and care for individuals bound men to him, educated and uneducated alike. They helped to establish the country-wide reputation whose manifestations caused him embarrassment and distress. Included in the instructions sent before a *khadi* tour in 1929 was the warning.

> I have a horror of touching-the-feet devotion. It is wholly unnecessary as a mark of affection, it may easily be degrading. It interferes with free and easy movement, and I have been hurt by the nails of the devotees cutting into the flesh. The performance has often taken more than fifteen minutes to pass through a crowd to a platform only a few yards from the farthest end.[51]

Gandhi's commitment to his perception of swaraj and the paths he believed led to it was even clearer towards the end of the decade when the Simon Commission convinced many Indians in and out of Congress that an all-India stand against the raj was necessary. Despite the opportunities this development offered for a new continental leadership role, Gandhi steered his own particular course: he stuck to his own forte and declined involvement on terms other than his own.

The Simon Commission appeared to Gandhi an 'organized insult to a whole people', and he urged the organizers of the protest against it to go

---

[50] Gandhi to Rajagopalachariar on how a public appeal should be framed, 21 October 1928, *CWMG*, XXXVII, 386; Gandhi to S. Biswas on the payment of his debts, 17 June 1928, *CWMG*, XXXVI, 424.

Gandhi's letter on the significance of sanitation to H. Alexander, 22 June 1928, *ibid*, p. 449; two examples of articles on this are 'A National Defect', *Young India*, 25 April 1929, *CWMG*, XL, 283–4; 'Does a Village mean a Dunghill?', *Shikshan ang Sahitya*, 22 September 1929, *CWMG*, XLI, 445–8.

[51] *Young India*, 5 September 1929, *ibid*. p. 351.

on with demonstrations and hartals. However he refrained from interference, largely because the terms would not have been of his own choosing,
as he explained to a missionary in Calcutta.

> If I could see my way clear leading to boycott movement, do not
> imagine that I should sit still for a single moment. But the way is not
> clear... I want a living faith on the part of known workers in the boycott
> as I have prescribed from time to time in... *Young India.* I am positive
> that no other boycott can possibly succeed, and I am equally positive
> that this boycott must succeed if there is enough work behind it. Huge
> demonstrations that have been taking place in Calcutta are good in their
> way, but not good enough for me. There is no reality behind them. They
> have their use too, but they cannot enthuse me as an active soldier.[52]

He also professed total lack of interest in the Commission's work, believing
that it was entirely ignorant of the true state of things in India. His
disregard for it lay partly in his conviction that constitutions handed out
by imperial rulers could not bring swaraj. Whatever the source of constitutions they were not his way to swaraj; and his lack of interest applied to
other constitution-making endeavours.[53]

Gandhi took no formal part in the All-Parties Conference and its committee meetings which during 1928 attempted to frame a constitution based
on communal agreement, which would be the boycotters' answer to the jibe
by Birkenhead, the Secretary of State for India, that Indians were incapable
of producing their own constitution. Nevertheless he was kept fully
informed of the proceedings, not least by the two Nehrus, and he did all
he could behind the scenes to end the communal wrangling which so
grieved him. It was at his suggestion that a small committee, chaired by
Motilal in May, set about framing a report when the Conference itself
seemed stuck on communal safeguards.[54] Uppermost in Gandhi's mind,
however, was the need for some sanction to back the national demand,
without which it would mean little more than the windy rhetoric of the
Madras Congress. He explained his order of priorities to Motilal in March
1928.

> Personally I am of opinion that we are not ready for drawing up a
> constitution till we have developed sanction for ourselves... Unless we

[52] Gandhi to B. W. Tucker, 24 February 1928, *CWMG*, XXXVI, 49; *Young India*,
9 February 1928, *ibid.* pp. 14–15; Gandhi to M. Nehru, 29 February 1928, *ibid*, p. 67.

[53] Gandhi to C. F. Andrews, 21 September 1928, *CWMG*, XXXVII, 291. When
invited by Arthur Moore, editor of *The Statesman*, to consider informal discussions
on a future constitution Gandhi replied, 'I confess to you that neither the Statutory
Commission nor constitution-making interests me much. I am concentrating my
attention upon the means of attainment of swaraj. Neither the Statutory Commission
nor constitution-making appeals to me as part of the means.' 10 June 1928, *CWMG*,
XXXVI, 391.

[54] Gandhi's interest in the All-Parties Conference and the flow of information on
it to him is clear, for example, in J. Nehru to Gandhi, 23 February 1928, *ibid*, p. 58,
fn. 1; Gandhi to J. Nehru, 26 February 1928, *ibid*, p. 58; M. Nehru to Gandhi, 24
February 1928, *ibid.* p. 67, fn. 1; Gandhi to M. Nehru, 29 February 1928, *ibid.* pp.
67–8; S. Ali to Gandhi, 23 October 1928, *CWMG*, XXXVIII, 436–7.

have created some force ourselves, we shall not advance beyond the
position of beggars, and I have given all my time to thinking over this
one question, and I can think of nothing else but the boycott of foreign
cloth...I would have exclusive concentration upon this thing if I had
my way.

In *Young India* the theme of foreign-cloth boycott was given much greater
emphasis from this point within Gandhi's overall argument for *khadi*.
Foreign-cloth boycott alone would enable ordinary people to participate
in the movement without making any great sacrifice: it alone, therefore,
could unite the masses and the educated, thereby generating a sanction
which was powerful because created by joint activity.[55]

In spite of Gandhi's greater concern for the sanction than the possible
constitution, he threw his whole weight behind the Nehru Report which
emerged from the All-Parties Conference committee. Before the Conference met at Lucknow to consider the report, he published an appeal
for a united, national approach. 'There is room enough under the constitution devised by the committee for all to rise to their full height. Every
legitimate interest has its protection guaranteed if it has enough vitality in
itself for expansion. The franchise is the broadest possible.' Subsequently
he expressed delight at the measure of unity achieved at Lucknow. His
stress on unity rather than the provisions of the constitution, however,
reflected his order of priorities in the quest for swaraj which his time of
stock-taking had reinforced.[56]

III   THE TERMS OF LEADERSHIP

After his release from jail Gandhi had increasingly devoted himself to
constructing the social foundations of swaraj, holding aloof from the
politics of councils and Congress because his priorities and expertise did
not fit or forward the felt needs of Indians concerned with their constitutional relationships with each other and the British, or of the British in their
search for Indian allies. However in 1928 two episodes thrust Gandhi into

[55] Gandhi to M. Nehru, 3 March 1928, *CWMG*, XXXVI, 76–7; *Young India*, 15 March
& 5 April 1928, *ibid*, pp. 105–6, 188.

[56] *Young India*, 23 August 1928, *CWMG*, XXXVII, 196–7; *Young India*, 6 September
1928, *ibid*. pp. 233–4; Gandhi to M. Zafarulmulk, 8 September 1928, *ibid*. p. 243.
   For the terms of the Nehru Report see R. Coupland, *The Indian Problem 1833–1935*,
pp. 87–94.
   The report envisaged a single state for the whole of India including the princely
states, possibly on federal lines. It was to have full responsible government as in the
self-governing Dominions. Devolution of power to the provinces was to go no
further than in the 1919 reforms, and residual powers were to remain at the centre.
There were to be joint electorates everywhere, and reservation of seats for Muslims
only at the centre and in the provinces where they were a minority: the only
concessions to communal demands and fears were a declaration of right in the
constitution assuring full liberty of conscience and religion, and agreement that the
North–West Frontier Province and Sind should become full provinces. (Baluchistan
was added at the Lucknow meeting.)

the political limelight. The Bardoli satyagraha and the 1928 Congress session heralded his return to all-India leadership, though they came to him unsought. Both were occasions when others in public life calculated that they needed the Mahatma: he responded because he felt he could satisfy those needs with his particular expertise, on terms which were acceptable to him, promising to promote his wider vision of swaraj.

The campaign against enhancement of the land revenue demand was led by Vallabhbhai Patel in Bardoli, a Gujarat *taluka* where the locally dominant Patidar community was well organized and experienced in disciplined protest under the Congress banner. Had it not been for the Chauri Chaura violence in 1922, Bardoli would have been one of Gandhi's chosen areas for civil disobedience. The campaign of civil resistance to the tax demand lasted from February to August 1928 and succeeded in its attempt to extract from the Bombay government an enquiry into the level of enhancement.[57] This success depended on the efficient organization of the district for resistance by Vallabhbhai and a group of prominent Bardoli Patidars, and on the publicity which produced a wave of popular support in Bombay and throughout India for the Bardoli defaulters. This caught the Bombay government at a time when it was vulnerable to local unrest: it also exposed it to pressure from the Government of India with its continental perspective.

Sir Leslie Wilson, Governor of Bombay, was justifiably anxious that if there was no settlement with the Bardoli resisters the vote in his legislative council scheduled for the end of July would go against the setting-up of a committee to cooperate with the Simon Commission. The Indian Merchants' Chamber, influenced by the Gujarati loyalties of many of its members, was threatening to withdraw its representatives from the council if the government did not convene a conference including Patel and Gandhi; eleven MLCs had already resigned, eight representing Gujarat and three Bombay. By mid-July Wilson believed that if he had to act against Vallabhbhai and even Gandhi the whole of Gujarat would erupt and he would lose his Hindu ministers and probably his Hindu MLCs too. Bombay was in the throes of a general strike in the cotton mills, and the impending arrival of a new governor, Sir Frederick Sykes, made a quick settlement even more necessary to prevent his term of office getting off to a bad start. To make matters worse, the local government was hampered by the early inaction of the Surat Collector, and the circumstances of the assessment itself. The initial reassessment of 30% by an inexperienced Indian revenue officer had been rejected by the Settlement Commissioner, whose proposal of 29% had

---

[57] Accounts of the Bardoli satyagraha are M. Desai, *The Story of Bardoli* (reprint of 1929 edn., Ahmedabad, 1957); A. Bhatt, 'Caste and Political Mobilisation in a Gujarat District', in R. Kothari (ed.), *Caste in Indian Politics* (New Delhi, 1970), pp. 299–339; B. G. Gokhale, 'Sardar Vallabhbhai Patel: the Party Organizer as Political Leader', in R. L. Park & I. Tinker (ed.), *Leadership and Political Institutions in India* (Princeton, 1959), pp. 87–99.

in turn been reduced by the Bombay government to 20%. The Government of India for its part was convinced that the whole settlement issue had been grossly mismanaged; and Irwin, the Viceroy, was not convinced that the satyagraha was politically motivated from the start. He told the Governor of Madras, 'I have been cudgelling my brains to suggest ways to Leslie Wilson by which...he might extricate us all from a very threatening position.'[58] He sent his Home Secretary, Harry Haig, to Bombay and then met Wilson himself. The evidence of Bombay's vulnerability to local pressure and Government of India promptings complements the evidence of Bardoli's cohesion and organization in suggesting that satyagraha even on a limited scale achieved its most striking effects over a governmental opponent when that government was weak, severely embarrassed in some other respect, or susceptible to influence from higher authority. The pattern had been similar in Gandhi's earlier local and continental satyagrahas: it was to be repeated in civil disobedience.

Bardoli was indeed one of Gandhi's satyagrahas although Vallabhbhai did the main organizational and directive work in the district. Vallabhbhai sent the Bardoli spokesmen to secure Gandhi's consent before he himself would lead the campaign, and thereafter Gandhi was constantly behind Vallabhbhai. He stated in *Navajivan,*

> Let it be known to the readers that I have associated myself with the Bardoli Satyagraha from its very beginning. Its leader is Shri Vallabh-bhai and he can take me to Bardoli whenever he needs me. He does all the work whether small or big on his own responsibility. I do not go to attend the meetings, etc., but this is an understanding reached between him and me before the struggle began. My health does not permit me to carry on all kinds of activities.[59]

Gandhi's surviving letters to Vallabhbhai confirm the importance of Gandhi's advisory role; so does the shuttle service between Bardoli and Sabarmati maintained by Mahadev Desai as Gandhi's private secretary. Early in June Gandhi drafted a letter to the Governor to be sent from Vallabhbhai. In July he sent a statement Vallabhbhai was to issue as a reply to a speech by Wilson, and when negotiations reached a crucial stage he told Vallabhbhai the minimum they could accept. His back-stage direction

[58] Irwin to Goschen, 11 July 1928, Mss. EUR.C.152 (22). Evidence of the local government's predicament and Delhi's interpretation of the situation comes from: Wilson to Irwin, 28 June 1928, *ibid.*; Wilson to Irwin, 2 July 1928 & enclosing Bombay Revenue Sec. to Govt of India, Home Sec., 1 July 1928, *ibid.*; Wilson to S of S, 19 July 1928, enclosed in Wilson to Irwin, 19 July 1928, *ibid.*; Wilson to Irwin, telegram, 6 August 1928, *ibid.*; Irwin to Birkenhead, 19 July 1928, Mss. EUR.C.152 (4); Sethna to Saleh, 18 July 1928, NMML, Sir Phiroze Sethna Papers.

The Bardoli Enquiry Report by a revenue and judicial officer in April 1929 and the discussion of provincial Revenue Members in May 1929 showed that Irwin's suspicions were correct and that Bombay's revenue system was in need of drastic overhaul.

[59] *Navajivan*, 22 July 1928, *CWMG*, xxxvii, 85. For Vallabhbhai's insistence on Gandhi's consent for the campaign see Desai, *The Story of Bardoli*, pp. 28–9.

was even clearer when he sent a draft letter for Wilson to be despatched by Vithalbhai Patel, Vallabhbhai's brother and President of the Legislative Assembly, who had entered the fray in support of Vallabhbhai by corresponding with Wilson and interviewing Irwin. On 20 June Gandhi had received the prominent Bombay businessman, Sir Purshotamdas Thakurdas, at Sabarmati. In response to attempts by the Indian Merchants' Chamber to mediate between them and government, Gandhi backed Vallabhbhai in taking a tough stand, despite Thakurdas's warnings that they might not be in such a good bargaining position if they held out longer. In July Gandhi also explained the terms he was prepared to accept to the Gujarat MLCs with whom the government had elected to deal. Finally at the beginning of August he went to Bardoli at Vallabhbhai's request in preparation for the latter's expected arrest.[60] Apart from these personal interventions Gandhi's main assistance in the Bardoli campaign took the shape of continuous publicity, encouragement and instructions in the columns of *Young India* and *Navajivan*; while some of his hand-picked workers from Sabarmati such as Desai went to help Vallabhbhai on the spot.

Gandhi's press articles on Bardoli indicate why he was prepared to accept the burden of leadership on this particular issue. For him it was not just a local satyagraha for the redress of a specific grievance, such as he had conducted in Champaran in 1917. It was a crucial demonstration of the road to swaraj, just as the Lucknow meeting of the All-Parties Conference had, he believed, opened the way to purely constitutional swaraj. Right at the beginning of the struggle he had asserted that although the object of the satyagraha was specific and local, not the attainment of swaraj, yet it had 'an indirect bearing on swaraj. Whatever awakens people to a sense of their wrongs and whatever gives them strength for disciplined and peaceful resistance and habituates them for corporate suffering brings us nearer swaraj.'[61] He argued that the very method purified its exponents and created the swaraj character in them. It generated a new courage and liberty of mind guaranteed to shatter the foundations of a government which relied on the collaboration of weak, cowardly subjects. It provided occasions for demonstrating communal unity, and united people in activity for common rather than individual benefit. These were the very stuff of swaraj which Gandhi had preached but failed to find in what passed as political activity among his contemporaries. It was therefore not surprising

[60] Evidence of Gandhi's personal participation is in: Gandhi to Vallabhbhai Patel, 3 June, 24 & 31 July 1928, M. K. Gandhi, *Letters to Sardar Vallabhbhai Patel* (Ahmedabad, 1957), pp. 9–10; Gandhi to V. J. Patel, 7 June 1928, and enclosed draft to Governor, *CWMG*, xxxvi, 373–5; Sir P. Thakurdas to G. D. Birla, 28 July 1928, NMML, Sir Purshotamdas Thakurdas Papers, File No. 74 (I)/1928; Wilson to Irwin, 28 July 1928, Mss. EUR.C152 (22); Wilson to S of S, 7 August 1928, enclosed in Wilson to Irwin, *ibid.*; *Young India*, 9 August 1928, *CWMG*, xxxvii, 118–19.

Vithalbhai's role in the campaign is evident from letters between Irwin and Wilson, Mss. EUR.C.152 (22).

[61] *Navajivan*, 9 September 1928, *CWMG*, xxxvii, 249; *Young India*, 8 March 1928, *CWMG*, xxxvi, 90.

that he should associate himself with a movement promising such opportunities for creating new men and a new society on which a new framework
of state authority could be built.[62]

The repercussions of Bardoli on Gandhi's career were far-reaching. It
publicized Gandhi and his methods throughout India: the satyagraha's
success in gaining an enquiry helped to offset the memory of Non-
cooperation's sputtering end. As the great business magnate and supporter
of the Mahatma, G. D. Birla, remarked, 'I am glad the Bardoli affairs are
all settled and the triumph has been for the people. I think this one
instance will be an eye opener to...all concerned and will put new life into
the dwindling forces of nationalism.' Moreover the publication of the report
of enquiry vindicating the resisters' stand extended the publicity value of
Bardoli well into 1929, underlining the efficacy of satyagraha as opposed
to consitutional action in extracting concessions from the raj.[63]

More important still, Bardoli lifted Gandhi out of the depression into
which he had sunk in 1927 because of continuing communal tension and
the slow progress of *khadi*. Once more he began to see a role for himself
as the leader of a movement which was non-violent yet rooted in popular
support, even if he had failed to convert the majority to non-violence as
a creed. While the outcome was still in doubt he said that the Bardoli
struggle 'has revived our drooping spirits, it has brought us new hope, it
has shown the immense possibilities of mass non-violence practised not
from conviction, but like most virtues with most of us as a policy.' After
its successful conclusion he spoke of Bardoli as reviving faith in non-violent
methods and in the power of the masses, and proving that the people
were stronger than the government if they shook off fear and remained
non-violent.[64] The long-term importance of satyagraha's local success in
Gandhi's perception of his potential as an all-India leader became apparent
early in 1930 when the Bardoli experience was running in his mind as he
prepared for civil disobedience. More immediately, Bardoli offered to
Gandhi the solution to the problem of a sanction to back the national
demand which so disturbed him, contributing to his reluctance to become
involved in constitution-making. Without teeth Indian demands were
wordy futilities. In April he had asked Jawaharlal 'if you have noticed what
I sense everywhere, utter absence of seriousness and disinclination to do

[62] Examples of Gandhi's explication of the importance of Bardoli are *Young India*,
17 May & 14 June 1928, *Navajivan*, 3, 10 & 17 June 1928, *CWMG*, xxxvi, 321–2, 411,
360, 384, 419–20.

[63] G. D. Birla to Sir P. Thakurdas, 7 August 1928, Thakurdas Papers, File No. 74
(I)/1928; Notes On The Press. U.P., No. 20 of 1929. For week ending 18 May 1929,
No. 21 of 1929. For Week ending 25 May 1929. (I owe this reference to D. A. Low.)
Irwin commented on the report, 'It will of course be hailed by the opponents of
Government as no mean victory, and I fancy they will be fully entitled to make
the most of it.' Irwin to Peel, 18 May 1929, Mss. EUR.C.152 (5).

[64] *Young India*, 12 July 1928, *CWMG*, xxxvii, 46; Gandhi to R. B. Gregg, 14 August
1928, *ibid.* p. 176; *Young India*, 16 August 1928, *ibid.* pp. 179–80; *Navajivan*, 19 August
1928, *ibid.* pp. 190–1; Gandhi to C. F. Andrews, 24 August 1928, *ibid.* p. 200.

any concrete work demanding sustained energy'. In Bardoli he thought he had found the answer, whereas previously he had stressed foreign-cloth boycott as the best sanction. He therefore returned to Congress with renewed hope.[65]

The Calcutta Congress session in December 1928 confirmed Gandhi's re-emergence as an all-India leader in the Congress arena as well as in the sphere of constructive work. As in Bardoli, the pressure to take up a new role came from other people. By mid-year manoeuvrings were under way in preparation for a Congress which was obviously going to be of more than ordinary importance for communal relations, and the relations of Congressmen with each other, their local followers and the government. As the pattern of political alignments was thrown into the melting-pot men turned to Gandhi.

The first sign of this was in mid-June when Bengali Congressmen, anxious for Motilal's election as president, tried to enlist Gandhi's support. J. M. Sen Gupta asked him to persuade the Gujarat PCC to vote for Motilal. Gandhi asked Motilal what he thought, adding the rider that the time was perhaps not yet ripe for Jawaharlal to take the office. Motilal, however, favoured Vallabhbhai as a mark of appreciation for his Bardoli work, and failing him Jawaharlal. His reply indicated that he felt himself a spent force in politics, unable to rally much significant support except that of Gandhi, while he saw Jawaharlal as representing the rising generation:

> He has no doubt frightened many of our goody goodies by his plain talk. But the time has come when the more energetic and determined workers should have their way of guiding the political activities of the country. There are I admit points of difference between this class and the one to which you and I belong but there is no reason why we should continue to force our views on the former. Our race is fast dying out and the struggle will sooner or later have to be continued by men of Jawahar's type. The sooner they begin the better.

Gandhi responded by talking to Vallabhbhai, who preferred to devote his attention to Bardoli. In these circumstances Gandhi therefore agreed with Motilal 'that we should give place to younger men. And amongst them, there is no one even to equal Jawahar': he would accordingly recommend Jawaharlal's name to the PCCs unless Motilal dissented.[66]

When Gandhi wired Motilal's attitude to Sen Gupta, the latter and Subhas Chandra Bose wrote separately to Motilal urging him to accept the presidency at this critical juncture when they needed as much unity as possible and an agreed constitution. Motilal's reply to them, refusing the offer

[65] Gandhi to J. Nehru, 17 April 1928, *CWMG*, XXXVI, 237; Gandhi's declaration that Bardoli had shown the way to a non-violent sanction for the national demand, *Young India*, 6 September 1928, *CWMG*, XXXVII, 234.

[66] Sources for this paragraph are Gandhi to M. Nehru, 19 June 1928, *CWMG*, XXXVI, 432–3; M. Nehru to Gandhi, 11 July 1928, NMML, M. Nehru Papers, File G-1; Gandhi to M. Nehru, 15 July 1928, *CWMG*, XXXVII, 64.

reiterated the argument he had used to Gandhi. He clearly had in mind the report he was largely instrumental in preparing for the All-Parties Conference and believed that Jawaharlal's presidency could help to pilot it through Congress in the face of 'the considered opinion of the younger set'. Having received copies of the two Bengali letters Gandhi intervened once more, urging Motilal by wire to accept the office 'especially for Bengal's sake'. In a *Young India* article hard on the heels of this wire, he argued strongly for Motilal as president on the grounds that Bengal wanted him, that he was widely respected, acceptable to many Muslims, and imbued with 'a spirit of conciliation and compromise which makes him an eminently worthy ambassador of a nation that is in need of and is in the mood to take an honourable compromise...Let the impatient youth of the country wait a while.' In Gandhi's mind unity in the forthcoming Congress was evidently of fundamental importance. Moreover, Congressmen in Bengal, the host province, were divided into two factions and if Sen Gupta and Bose, representing both factions, backed the same candidate this would lessen the chance of local disunity affecting the whole session.[67]

By September 1928 Motilal, as president-elect, was pressing Gandhi to take a fuller part in Congress affairs. Gandhi replied that he did not want to attend the AICC and was even contemplating absence from the Calcutta session. He still felt that what he termed constructive work, not constitution-building, was his particular forte, and that India must generate her own strength of mind and power of resistance. Moreover, he said, recent outbreaks of Hindu–Muslim violence unfitted him for planning constitutions. Yet a further reason for his reluctance to go to Calcutta was the type of *swadeshi* exhibition that Calcutta was laying on: he regretted the admission into it of mill-made cloth, and the AISA had decided not to exhibit there. Consequently, he did not want to place himself or his hosts in an embarrassing position by his presence in Calcutta in such circumstances. In mid-October he agreed to 'obey' Motilal's wish that he should go to Calcutta; and subsequent correspondence with B. C. Roy led to the Bengalis modifying the type of exhibition so that Gandhi was able to advise *khadi* organizations to exhibit if they could at such short notice. Motilal's importunity and the Bengalis' pliancy over the exhibition indicated the value they placed on Gandhi's presence at Calcutta. But though Gandhi for his part felt bound to accede to Motilal's request after pressing him to become president, he could see no immediate prospect of assuming leadership. That, he maintained, could only happen when there was a 'national call' for him, and he felt sure of widespread support for a non-violent following whom he could control.[68]

[67] J. M. Sen Gupta to M. Nehru, 17 July 1928, J. Nehru, *A Bunch of Old Letters*, pp. 61–2; S. C. Bose to M. Nehru, 18 July 1928, *ibid.* pp. 62–3: M. Nehru to J. M. Sen Gupta & S. C. Bose, 19 July 1928, *ibid.* pp. 63–4; M. Nehru to Gandhi, 19 July 1928, *ibid*, p. 65; Gandhi to M. Nehru, telegram, 23 July 1928, *CWMG*, XXXVII, 90; *Young India*, 26 July 1928, *ibid.* pp. 91–2.
[68] Interview on 1 November 1928, *The Hindustan Times*, 3 November 1928, *CWMG*,

When Gandhi arrived in Calcutta it was abundantly clear why Motilal had wanted him there. In the months after his election as President, the report which bore his name and recommended a constitution envisaging Dominion Status for India, had been published and discussed at length. Divisions on the subject now gaped within Congress, while pressure from outside the Congress establishment against the report was increasing. Before Congress began, over 50,000 mill labourers occupied the *pandal* for nearly two hours and passed a resolution in favour of complete independence for India. Moreover a powerful pro-independence faction within Congress had built up led by Srinivasa Iyengar (who as in 1927 was manoeuvering against Motilal), and two spokesmen of the younger men, Jawaharlal and Bose. These two had made their position plain at the Lucknow Conference: but there, rather than divide a meeting which augured well for Hindu–Muslim unity, they had preferred to state their position and then to organize an Independence for India League to rally support for the goal of complete independence. Both were aware of swelling discontent among younger men at the paltry role their elders expected them to play in Congress and at the goals to which Congress aspired under their guidance. In September 1928 Jawaharlal had presided over an All-Bengal Students' Conference which advocated complete independence, and Bose had declared at a Youth Congress in Calcutta in December, 'The youths of India are no longer content with handing over all responsibility to their older leaders and sitting with folded hands, or following like dumb driven cattle. They have realised that it is for them to create a new India – an India free, great and powerful.' How far these two could control their following was debatable. Assured of votes and vocal backing from the Bengal student body and from the large bloc of ex-terrorists and terrorist sympathisers who had entrenched themselves in the Bengal Congress organization in the 1920s, they came to Congress just as the Dominion Status supporters were weakened by the death of one of their foremost spokesmen, the Punjabi, Lala Lajpat Rai.[69] There seemed no chance that the facile accord of the two groups

[69] *India in 1928–29* (Calcutta, 1930), pp. 49–52; S. C. Bose, *The Indian Struggle 1920–1942*, pp. 152–5; J. Nehru, *An Autobiography*, pp. 172–3; J. Nehru to N. S. Hardikar, 8 October 1928, NMML, N. S. Hardikar Papers, File No. II; note on the Youth Association in Bengal, June 1929, by F. J. Lowman, D.I.G., Police, enclosed in Govt of India, Home Dept., to Under-Sec. of State, 26 September 1929, IOL, L/PJ/6/1976; Brief Note on the Alliance of Congress with Terrorism in Bengal, 25 January 1932, by R. E. A. Ray, Special C.I.D. Superintendent, Home Poll., 1932, File No. 4/21. J. Nehru's appeal to youth, 18 March 1928, and response to it, NMML, AICC Papers, 1928, File No. 12. The mill-labourers' demonstration was reported in *Report of the Forty-Third Session of the Indian National Congress held in Calcutta in December 1928* (IOL, microfilm, Neg. 996).

which had occurred at Madras in 1927 could be repeated at Calcutta in 1928.

When Motilal realized the danger that Congress would reject his report he made it known that he would resign as President if this was the case; and he looked to Gandhi to concoct some formula of reconciliation. The Mahatma was peculiarly fitted to perform this function. His immense public repute outside the ranks of the politicians marked him out as a national figure whose conciliation might be acceptable to all parties. Since he had devoted his main efforts to constructive work in the preceding years he was not aligned with either Congress group. However he had reaffirmed his support for the Nehru Report in *Young India* early in December. The basis of that support was his belief that the report could provide a focus for unanimity, and that unanimity behind the call for Dominion Status, rather than independence, therefore made Dominion Status a practical possibility. Such concern for the unifying potential of the report, rather than its actual substance, meant that Gandhi might still be flexible on the issue if he felt that unity would be jeopardized rather than cemented by sticking to it at all costs. The value he placed on Congress as India's premier political organization made him anxious to avoid any major split in its ranks. The assassination of an official in Lahore on 17 December by Bhagat Singh highlighted the depth of feeling among some younger political activists: Gandhi deplored this action and in his press articles there appeared a sense of impending crisis for the creed of non-violence. He must have wondered whether the time was imminent for renewed satyagraha in order to 'sterilize' the violence visible in public life – a conclusion he had drawn before when violence in politics seemed dangerously near the surface. Moreover by the time Congress met he was aware that the Nehru Report was being rejected by a wide range of Muslim opinion. The Muslim reaction had begun within days of the Lucknow meeting he had so welcomed. It was underlined while Congress was actually in session by Jinnah and his section of the Muslim League in Calcutta and by an All-Parties Muslim Conference in Delhi under the presidency of the Aga Khan, both of which repudiated the report. In such circumstances the report was a feebler instrument for affecting unity than Gandhi had earlier thought.[70]

At Congress Gandhi's first essay was in the Subjects Committee on 26 December. He moved the resolution adopting the Nehru Report while

[70] V (Home Dept.) to S of S, telegram, 19 January 1929, L/PJ/6/1976; J. Nehru, *An Autobiography*, pp. 184–5; *Young India*, 6 December 1928, *CWMG*, XXXVIII, 137–8. For Muslim opposition to the Nehru Report see Irwin to Birkenhead, 6 & 13 September, 3 October 1928, Irwin to Peel, 7 November, 12 December 1928, Mss. EUR.C.152 (4); K. K. Aziz (ed.), *The All India Muslim Conference 1928–1935 A Documentary Record* (Karachi, 1972), pp. 17–56: Moore, *Crisis of Indian Unity 1917–1940*, pp. 36–8. Gandhi's comments on the Lahore assassination are in *Young India*, 27 December 1928, *CWMG*, XXXVIII, 274–6. His sense of impending crisis is evident in *Young India*, 6 & 27 December 1928, *ibid.* pp. 162–3, 245. For a survey of terrorism in the Punjab, see H. W. Hale, *Political Trouble in India 1917–1937* (reprint, Allahabad, 1974), pp. 53–80.

abiding by the Madras declaration on complete independence, with the proviso that if the British did not accept it by 31 December 1930 Congress would revive non-violent Non-cooperation by advising the country to refuse taxation and every aid to the government. As he admitted, this was in itself an attempt to find a *via media* between the two schools of thought in Congress, but he recommended it as the beginning of their desired end which was independence according to the Madras resolution. Speaking 'as a man of business wanting to serve the nation, wanting to educate the masses and influence the masses and desiring to enlist active co-operation of the masses,' he also warned delegates of the confusion they would cause in the country at large if they began to propagate and distinguish between the two concepts of Dominion Status and independence. Amendments put by Jawaharlal and Bose indicated that even this compromise was not acceptable to them; they wanted no time of grace for British acceptance of Dominion Status and advocated complete independence as India's goal.[71]

Two days later in the Subjects Committee Gandhi moved a new resolution of his own drafting which cut the time limit to 31 December 1929. This step was the result of intense private negotiations. Gandhi explained that he preferred the first resolution he had moved, but this one was essential to the national interest because it would hold all parties in Congress together in an acceptable compromise. 'If we want unity, then adjustment and readjustment, a series of compromises honourable to both parties and to variety of opinions, is to be effected.' Here again his emphasis was on the necessity for unity in Congress. He also reiterated the themes which had recurred in all his observations on current political activity – the need to reorganize Congress and establish discipline within its ranks, and to cement communal unity if they were to be prepared to give battle to the government in deeds as a sanction to their words. His resolution was passed by 118 votes to 45. In answer to those who asked whether he would return to leadership of a national movement as in 1920 if they voted for his resolution, Gandhi had said that he would only return if they subjected themselves to his discipline. 'Today I have come to perform a sacred duty to my country,' he said of his compromise proposal, 'and after that my back is turned upon Calcutta and I retire to Sabarmati. I say to you that beyond putting this resolution before you, you may not expect anything unless these inexorable terms are granted to me by you.' There could have been no starker

[71] Gandhi's speech in Subjects Committee, 26 December 1928, *CWMG*, XXXVIII, 267–73. The text of J. Nehru's amendment is in B. P. Sitaramayya, *History of The Indian National Congress Volume I (1885–1935)* (reprint of 1935 edn., New Delhi, 1969), p. 330. Gandhi's proposed compromise overturned an earlier attempt at compromise between the two groups in Congress effected at a Delhi AICC meeting on 3 November, by which Congress would accept the Nehru Report's recommendations for settlement of the communal question but would reiterate the demand for complete independence. Neither Motilal nor Gandhi was satisfied with this, as Gandhi indicated in his speech and Bose reported in *The Indian Struggle 1920–1942*, p. 157.

declaration of his intention only to lead when the terms were right. He made the terms clearer by moving in the Subjects Committee on 29 December the resolution demanding constructive action, designed not only to revive the Congress organization but also to remove Untouchability, boycott foreign cloth, spread *khadi* and temperance, reconstruct villages, remove women's disabilities and encourage them to take part in nation-building, and to remedy specific grievances by the Bardoli method – just those activities which he had fostered in his 'retirement' as the road to true swaraj.[72]

The critical day in the open Congress was 31 December. When Gandhi arrived there was a great uproar and the whole audience stood to greet him with shouts of '*Bande Mataram*'. He moved and Ansari seconded the compromise proposal on the Nehru Report envisaging Non-cooperation if the British did not accept it by the end of 1929. Addressing his speech principally to younger Bengalis, Gandhi affirmed that there was no opposition between independence and Dominion Status. He did not want Dominion Status which would interfere with their growth, but independence which would permit their growth to their fullest height: and as he had in 1920, so now he promised that swaraj would come in the year if they helped him and followed the programme laid down. Bose then moved an amendment which Satyamurti seconded, that Congress should stick to the goal of independence. Gandhi was aggrieved at this because Bose was resiling on the compromise to which he had been a party with Jawaharlal and Srinivasa Iyengar. But Bose was clearly pushed by the wishes of his Bengali followers, and admitted that he moved the amendment at the wish of the majority of Bengali delegates. Jawaharlal's position at this point was highly ambivalent. He had absented himself from the Subjects Committee when Gandhi proposed the compromise resolution, such was his dislike of the agreement to which he had been party. Now, in open Congress at the end of the long discussion on it, he supported Bose, though 'half-heartedly' according to his own account.

Bose's amendment was ultimately lost, 973 for, 1,350 against, with forty-eight remaining neutral. Gandhi's resolution was then adopted with deafening shouts of '*Bande Mataram*' and '*Mahatma Gandhi-ki-jai*'. Bose said later that the vote was not a free one; Gandhi's supporters gave out that he would retire from Congress if the resolution was defeated, and consequently many supported it rather than force Gandhi out of Congress. Gandhi's stance in the Subjects Committee gave substance to this complaint.

[72] Gandhi's speeches in Subjects Committee, 28 & 29 December 1928, *CWMG*, XXXVIII, 283–96, 299–300; J. Coatman, *Years of Destiny. India 1926–1932* (London, 1932), pp. 224–7; Tendulkar, *Mahatma*, vol. 2, pp. 334–5. M. Brecher records that Bose told a friend that he did not press his case in the AICC because he did not wish to embarrass Jawaharlal, who he thought would come round to his side in the open session, and because he wished to keep his hands free to make an appeal in the open session; M. Brecher, *Nehru A Political Biography* (London, 1959), p. 133, fn. 1.

The following day the resolution on Congress's programme of organization and constructive work was passed with only two opposing votes. Gandhi had moved the resolution, supported by Srinivasa Iyengar as a symbol of the compromise which had been effected.[73]

As with most political compromises, however, the differences of opinion remained: Gandhi's conciliation had engineered a very uneasy peace. Moreover it evoked opposition from those more moderate politicians loosely described as Liberals, who were as staunch as Congressmen in their desire for a reformed relationship between India and Britain, but who opposed violence and unconstitutional agitation and were prepared to wait longer for the status of a Dominion if it could be achieved by persuasion and constitutional pressure. Led by such prominent figures as Sapru and Srinivasa Sastri they were significant elements in any Congress confrontation with the raj because of the weight they carried in imperial counsels as reliable though critical collaborators. The gap between Congressmen and Liberals had narrowed during joint opposition to the Simon Commission and preparation of the Nehru Report. But now the All-India Liberal Federation, meeting in Allahabad while Congressmen gathered in Calcutta, supported the Nehru Report and demanded immediate Dominion Status, making clear that it would not stray from the path of constitutional agitation whatever 'the displeasures of a section of our own countrymen'.[74]

The occasion for Gandhi's re-emergence in a leadership role in Congress had not been of his own seeking. He commented to Motilal,

> No apology whatsoever is necessary for taking me to Calcutta. Of course I had never expected to have to take such an active part in the deliberations as circumstances forced me to take. But it was as well. I was quite happy over it and it gave me an insight into the present working of the Congress organisation which I certainly did not possess. And after all we have to battle both within and without.[75]

The session's opportunity for Gandhi and the response he made set the seal on his recreation as an all-India political leader which had been in process since the collapse of Non-cooperation.

[73] *Report of 43rd I.N.C.;* Gandhi's speeches in open Congress, 31 December 1928 & 1 January 1929, *CWMG*, XXXVIII, 307-10, 311-14; R. Prasad, *Autobiography* (Bombay, 1957), pp. 289-90; Bose, *The Indian Struggle 1920-1942*, p. 157; J. Nehru, *An Autobiography*, p. 186.

[74] Part of speech by the Federation's President, Sir Chimanlal Setalvad, quoted in account of the Allahabad meeting on 30 December 1928, *India in 1928-29*, pp. 52-4.

Irwin described the divisions which remained in Congress to Peel, 2 & 17 January 1929, Mss. EUR.C.152 (5). He believed that the younger men accepted the compromise in order 'to place themselves in a position where they can come to the Congress in a year's time and say that, in deference to Gandhi's appeal, they had agreed to a year's delay, that they had always known the British Government would do nothing within that time and that now therefore they demand the full support of Congress for a policy of which they should be the accredited leaders instead of men who have been shown powerless to produce any results.' Irwin to Peel, 9 January, *ibid.*

[75] Gandhi to M. Nehru, 17 January 1929, M. Nehru Papers, File G-1.

Gandhi emerged from Calcutta in good health, knowing that he could stand up to the irregular life political involvement demanded.[76] His political position had changed markedly by contrast with early November when he had been reluctant to attend Congress and unsure of his political role. Congress divisions and the absence of another acceptable conciliator played into his hands and he re-established a temporary leadership position within Congress on this ticket. Moreover he had stated the terms for sustained leadership of a country-wide Congress campaign, and by the resolution on constructive work had in theory gained much that he had demanded.[77]

In a time of political uncertainty when political relationships between Indians, and between Indians and the raj, were in a state of flux, Congressmen turned to Gandhi. The uncertainty was caused partly by the imminence of constitutional change and partly by economic and ideological pressures which caused a new generation to stake their claims for a new role in and new goals for political life. Congressmen needed a stance towards the raj which would neither threaten their prestige by backing down from the Madras declaration nor wreck their unity by making a sharp distinction between the independence and Dominion Status demands. In the complexity of their interlocking relationships with each other and the British, Gandhi's ability and willingness to act as compromiser provided him with a crucial functional role. His programme, moreover, offered a new way of relating to the government and of extending their connections with other sections of society. The constructive programme was to be the preparation for a showdown with the British in which unity and mass contact were essential. However Calcutta also showed that Gandhi's new leadership role was unlikely to be that of a dictator. In asserting the authority Calcutta had offered him, he would be constricted by the very divisions which had opened the door to him and by the degree of success he gained in the coming year in organizing Congress and in attracting support in the country.

[76] Gandhi told Rajagoplachariar, 13 January 1929, that he was none the worse for the Calcutta strain. In spite of less food, bad hours and want of sleep he lost only 1 lb in weight which he regained in a week back at Sabarmati; *CWMG*, XXXVIII, 347.

[77] The constructive resolution and Gandhi's article on it in *Young India*, 17 January 1929, *ibid.* pp. 313–14, 354–5.

The constructive campaign was similar to that of 1920–1 except that it included the raising of women's status, village reconstruction and organization of city labour, and excluded boycott of legislatures, law courts, educational institutions and titles. The inclusions and exclusions were signs of changes which had taken place in public life since 1920 and Gandhi's response to the new environment. He had included the organization of city labour at Satyamurti's suggestion. He would have liked boycott of legislatures etc., but he realized that most Congressmen would not accept this.

CHAPTER 2

The assertion of authority

Fifteen months elapsed after Calcutta before it was clear what Gandhi's compromise resolution in Congress would mean in practice for India's relationship with the raj. During this time, if Gandhi was to accept the opportunity for all-India leadership which Calcutta had offered, he had to assert his authority and convince people that he was worth following. Moreover, he had to be sure in himself that the opportunity was worth taking up in view of his personal priorities.

An effective all-India leadership position needed foundations in the Congress organization and policy-making gatherings, and in the country at large. Success or failure to assert authority in these two areas interacted on each other. Without widespread support Gandhi was unlikely to prove of permanent value to Congressmen in conclave and therefore unlikely to retain the position of dominance Calcutta had proffered. But without control of the Congress organization and the loyalty of local Congress leaderships he would probably be unable to direct and control a country-wide movement, judging by the fate of Non-cooperation. In both Congress and in the country Gandhi's main problems were cohesion and control. Only a united and disciplined movement stood a chance of success, whether in the political sense of putting pressure on the raj or in Gandhian terms of achieving true swaraj. The Mahatma had before him the lamentable example of Non-cooperation as evidence of what could happen when a continental agitation against the government disintegrated into a series of local and sectional protest movements often with conflicting aims, generating discord and even violence among their participants and weakening satyagraha as an all-India weapon. Yet he had an apocalyptic view of satyagraha as the ultimate moral weapon in politics which could purify political life, affecting both parties in a conflict by its very operation. The political realist within him therefore jostled uneasily with the visionary as he tackled the problems of cohesion and control in three main phases: between January and October 1929 while Congress awaited a British response to its ultimatum, in the final weeks of 1929 when Congress had to decide the next move after Britain's response in Irwin's Declaration, and finally between January and March 1930 when Gandhi cast around for a tactic which would give effect to the Congress decision and precipitate a confrontation with the raj yet would ensure a cohesive movement over which he had maximum control.

41

1 JANUARY–NOVEMBER 1929: WAITING FOR THE RAJ

Immediately after Calcutta Gandhi had no clear idea of what his role might be as Congress waited for the raj's response to its Calcutta ultimatum. He abandoned a proposed European tour, feeling responsible for the constructive programme laid down by Congress at his insistence, although he admitted, 'It may be that I shall have to do nothing during the year in respect of the programme.' He announced that he would turn his attention to his ashram and to Gujarat.[1]

Throughout the period of waiting and preparation for possible civil disobedience Gandhi made it plain that he hoped for a peaceful settlement which would enable India to remain in the Empire. Word came to Irwin within days of Congress, via Vithalbhai Patel, that Gandhi was 'quite categorically...in favour of the British connection and that he would not make difficulty about an accommodation of the Dominion Status idea by which Foreign Affairs, Political and possibly Defence should be reserved in some manner to be defined.'[2] At the end of February when Gandhi and Irwin met at a tea-party given by Vithalbhai they talked of missions, diet and communal tension. On the Calcutta Congress Gandhi had, according to Irwin, 'nothing very exciting' to say.

> The principal thread running through his thought was that the constitution of India was a thing in the settlement of which she herself ought to have the predominant voice, Parliament subsequently ratifying what India decided to ask for. There is of course nothing new in that, but what was interesting was his statement that if such freedom of choice were left to Indians, we should be astonished by how much they would desire to leave in our hands through lack of self-confidence.

Gandhi's report on the occasion in *Young India*, referring to it as one of 'Patel's many creditable freaks', stated that India was not ready for any advance just as the British were still reluctant to budge.[3]

Soon after fraternizing with Irwin Gandhi was in court in Calcutta for burning foreign cloth in a public park. But even at the illegal bonfire he warned his audience that the time for civil disobedience had not come. He called himself a man 'mad...[and] hungry after freedom', yet he recognized the risks attendant on civil disobedience, was determined to take every precaution against them, and hoped that 'we shall settle our business

[1] *Young India*, 31 January 1929 and *Navajivan*, 3 February 1929, *CWMG*, XXXVIII, 416–17; Gandhi to M. Nehru, 24 January 1929, *ibid*. p. 394.

[2] Note by Irwin, 11 January 1929, on interview with Vithalbhai Patel that day, enclosed in Irwin to Peel, 17 January 1929, Mss. EUR.C.152 (5). Irwin also heard from Sir C. Setalvad that he was sure Sapru, Motilal and Gandhi did not expect full Dominion Status in the near future; Irwin to Peel, 24 January 1929, *ibid*.

[3] *Young India*, 28 February 1929, *CWMG*, XL, 46; Irwin to Peel, 21 February 1929, Mss. EUR.C.152 (5).

It is significant that though Irwin was prepared to meet Gandhi at a party he refused to invite Gandhi to meet him, thus indicating his awareness that government actions influenced the credibility of Indian leaders; Irwin to Peel, 13 & 21 February 1929, Mss. EUR.C.152 (5).

with Government without having to resort to civil disobedience...Believe me I shall strain every nerve to avoid that issue.' Simultaneously he was thinking of attending discussions with the British on reform if the invitation was genuine; and envisaged Dominion Status as the final form of government for India provided it meant 'a partnership at will on a basis of equality with full freedom for either party to secede'.[4]

Meanwhile Gandhi constantly reminded those who flocked to hear him or read his papers that swaraj would not come to them as a gift; it could only be created by working out the triple constructive programme of foreign-cloth boycott through *khadi*, temperance and the abolition of Untouchability. His concern during the months of waiting for the raj was not so much what might happen at the deadline of 31 December but rather to forge a sanction for any declaration that Congress might then make. As in 1928, so now, he proclaimed the need for Indians to operate within a totally new cognitive structure. Defining swaraj in terms which promised equality for Hindu and Muslim, rich and poor, worker and landlord, advising quiet work which would not alienate the timorous and moderate, he preached a new unity among Indians. Hammering home the message that the empire rested on Indians' fear and acquiescence he urged them to have courage in their own ability to win freedom.[5]

Gandhi's principal activities after Calcutta were designed to create this new cohesion in Indian society and to make the country at large capable of disciplined activities under Congress control should the need arise. *Khadi* took up most of his time. As Working Committee adviser on foreign-cloth boycott, he prepared a scheme which appeared in *Young India* on 24 January. It recommended recruitment of volunteers to collect foreign cloth and take *khadi* orders, *khadi* progaganda, public incineration of foreign cloth, peaceful picketing of foreign-cloth shops, and enlisting help from 'all political and other organizations' and 'patriotic ladies'. The AISA should stamp and price all *khadi* and help in its distribution, and Congress should form a special committee to oversee the boycott campaign. But he pointed out that the scheme depended on the existence of a working Congress organization throughout India. On 17 February the Working Committee accepted this scheme and appointed a Foreign Cloth Boycott Committee under Gandhi's chairmanship.[6]

[4] Answers to questions put in Rangoon, 10 March 1929, *CWMG*, XL, 122; speech in Calcutta, 4 March 1929, *ibid.* p. 80.

[5] *Young India*, 7 March 1929, *ibid.* 92; speech in Agra, 11 September 1929, *Young India*, 19 September 1929, *CWMG*, XLI, 377–8. Gandhi spoke in Benares on 26 September 1929 on the equality for all he envisaged in swaraj; *Aaj*, 28 September 1929, *ibid.* p. 477. The D.S.P., Ahmedabad, commented on the function of constructive work in soothing and incorporating the more moderate in Congress activity; Bombay Secret Abstract, 1929, par. 1790–A, *Source Material for a History of the Freedom of Movement in India Vol. III Mahatma Gandhi Part II: 1922–1929* (Bombay, 1968), p. 452 (hereafter *HFM, III, II*).

[6] Account of Working Committee in Delhi, *Navajivan*, 24 February 1929, *CWMG*, XL, 26; Gandhi's scheme, *Young India*, 24 January 1929, *CWMG*, XXXVIII, 388–9; Gandhi to P. C. Ghosh, 20 January 1929, *ibid.* p. 374.

The brunt of the committee's work was borne by the Sindhi Congressman, Jairamdas Daulatram, based in Congress House, Bombay. He wrote to local administrative bodies requesting their cooperation, supplied MLAs and MLCs with *khadi* and boycott literature, issued boycott bulletins, and circularized Congress committees about progress in their provinces and possible programmes.[7] However his work was unrewarding. One of the main obstacles was the sluggish response of local Congress committees. By September 1929 only 27 out of 172 DCCs had sent reports of work done towards the boycott. Repeated reminders went unacknowledged, and even some PCCs ignored Jairamdas's appeals. Nothing had been heard from Delhi, Hindi C.P., Burma, Assam, Andhra, Ajmer and the North-West Frontier. While Gandhi was scathing about this evidence of indifference and indiscipline, government reports also noted the failure of the cloth-burning campaign on any large scale. Irwin reported that Congressmen in Bombay 'after collecting foreign cloth for a week...were only able to make a small bonfire of rags and cast-off clothes. The same story is told everywhere of similar efforts. Muhammadans have stood aloof entirely, and at meetings speakers have to take their audience to task for wearing foreign cloth!'[8]

Although the committee's work produced paltry results, Gandhi's other *khadi* tactic, the personal tour, was much more spectacular. In April–May, for example, he toured in Andhra, covering immense distances and setting himself and his attendants a shattering pace. He would tour between 6.0 a.m. and 9.0 a.m., then camp till the cool of the evening, when at 5.0 p.m. he would start off again, settling at a new camp at about 8.0 p.m. He sent rigorous instructions ahead, forbidding expensive shows or demonstrations, requiring the provision of simple food and at least six hours a day for his correspondence and secretarial work. His dictatorial demands were necessary for survival: 'I insist on my requirements being met. I have to if I am to finish the tour without collapsing...I am in first class health.'[9]

It is impossible to quantify most of the effects of these tours. Certainly Gandhi's visits did not permanently change the clothing habits of the majority. But he collected thousands of rupees which swelled the Congress coffers. By 31 May in Andhra alone he had collected over Rs. 264,000, mostly in cash but part in jewels which were then sold. More important were the

[7] Evidence of the activities of J. Daulatram and the committee in organizing the boycott are in *CWMG*, XL 261, 279–81, 430–1; XLI, 19–21, 172–3, 289–90. An account of a committee meeting on 23/24 May in Gandhi's Bombay home (attended by Gandhi, M. & J. Nehru, Ansari, J. Bajaj, Vallabhbhai Patel, S. C. Das Gupta & J. Doulatram), Bombay Secret Abstract, 1929, par. 1015, *HFM*, III, II, p. 437.

[8] Irwin to Peel, 17 April 1929, Mss. EUR.C.152 (5); report on boycott movement, Home Dept., Govt. of India, to Under-Sec. of State, 9 May 1929, L/PJ/6/1976; *Young India*, 29 August & 5 September 1929, *CWMG*, XLI, 336–7, 350–1.

[9] Gandhi to Mirabehn, 5 May 1929 (written at 5.30 a.m.), *Bapu's Letters to Mira* [*1924–1948*] (reprint of 1949 edn, Ahmedabad, 1959), p. 94. Tour time-tables, instructions etc., *Young India*, 7 March, 2, 5, 9, 30 May 1929, *CWMG*, XL, 88–90, 317–22, 342–3, 359–63, 432.

less tangible results. Gandhi gained immense knowledge of rural India from the experience. Moreover thousands of ordinary people across regional and provincial boundaries saw him and heard of his activities, a degree of publicity enjoyed by no other politician. He also used the tours to educate local Congressmen in organization, discipline and handling public funds.[10] Younger Congressmen like Jawaharlal disliked Gandhi's concentration on an apparently apolitical issue, and his seeming glorification of poverty in appealing for money for *Daridranarayan*, 'the Lord of the Poor'. Yet they cannot have failed to observe the reception he was given throughout India compared with the 'suspended animation' of their Independence for India League.[11]

On one occasion Gandhi fell foul of the law during the boycott campaign. Without the knowledge of the Governor of Bengal Gandhi was arrested in Calcutta making a bonfire in a public place. He bailed himself out and in the intervening period before the trial Irwin made sure that there was no question of Gandhi going to jail for the offence. The Bengal government took the Viceregal hint: the issue was treated as a test case on a minor point of law and Gandhi was fined one rupee. When the Secretary of State twitted the Viceroy on Gandhi's release on bail Irwin replied that they in India saw things rather differently from Peel in London: the situation was potentially very serious and much depended on how it was handled in the next few months.

> The really important feature...of the whole affair seems to me to be that Gandhi's position is at present hanging in the balance. It might not take much to restore him to something approximating to his old position as a national leader. Nothing could be a greater mistake than to embark on a policy of pin-pricks with regard to Gandhi, and to give him the opportunity of undergoing a short period of imprisonment. Nothing would give him and the cloth boycott movement a better advertisement. We should have done the work of our opponents for them.[12]

The episode indicated the government's sensitivity to Gandhi's public image and awareness of his potential political role, as also its own contribution to that role by its policy towards him.

---

[10] Statement of collections and expenses in Andhra tour, *Young India*, 6 June 1929, *CWMG*, XLI, 14–16. J. Nehru commented on the significance of Gandhi's *khadi* tours in *An Autobiography*, pp. 191–2.

[11] J. Nehru, *ibid.* p. 192; for the fate of the Independence for India League see J. Nehru to League Council members and provincial officers, 10 April 1929, AICC Papers, 1929, File No. 17; J. Nehru to Gandhi, 13 July 1929, *Selected Works of Jawaharlal Nehru* (in process of publication, New Delhi), vol. 4, p. 156 (hereafter *SWJN*).

[12] Irwin to Peel, 4 April 1929, in reply to Peel to Irwin, 7 March 1929, Mss. EUR.C. 152 (5). See also Sir Stanley Jackson, Governor of Bengal, to Irwin, 6 & 14 March 1929, Irwin to Jackson, 11 March 1929, Mss. EUR.C.152 (23); Officiating Chief Sec., Govt. of Bengal, to Home Sec., Govt. of India, 10 April 1929, forwarding 26 March judgement of Chief Presidency Magistrate on Gandhi's case, P & J 1556, 1929; Gandhi's statement in court, *Forward*, 27 March 1929, *CWMG*, XL, 180–2.

Apart from his *khadi* campaign, Gandhi devoted time to other aspects of constructive work which he hoped would unify and discipline his compatriots. As he stated after Calcutta, he turned his attention to the Sabarmati ashram because its inmates would be the spearhead of any campaign he decided to lead. While he was away from Sabarmati he was in constant touch with Chhaganlal Joshi who directed the community for him. He urged Joshi to write about anything concerning the ashram, however paltry it might seem, and deluged him with advice, even on such minor matters as how to cure cracks in the soles of his feet. The ashram caused Gandhi considerable anxiety. There were tensions between the residents – for example, among the women on whether they should have separate rooms. More seriously, a cousin of Gandhi's was found to have been stealing for several years and had to leave. Mrs Gandhi was discovered keeping money for personal use; and the seduction of a widow by an ashram inmate came to light. These major lapses Gandhi condemned publicly in the press, taking a share of the blame. His satyagrahi's commitment to openness and the indivisibility of public and private morals drove him to this public confession. It also had the effect of scotching possible unsavoury rumours about the ashram, and of publicizing himself as a man dedicated to the service of the nation.[13]

Gandhi's experiment with uncooked food in June–August 1929 had similar publicity value, though it was a somewhat unusual concern for the organizer of a potentially seditious campaign. Press accounts of it demonstrated the depth of his commitment to non-violence and celibacy, and he underlined its possible public consequences. 'If it succeeds it enables serious men and women to make revolutionary changes in their mode of living. It frees women from a drudgery which brings no happiness but which brings disease in its train.'[14] The treatment of women in India had long been one of Gandhi's concerns. In 1929 he continued to speak and write on such problems as widow marriage, divorce, dowries, child brides and wife beaters; but this was now within the context of the Congress constructive programme which included the amelioration of women's position in society. Moreover he began a deliberate appeal to women to participate in establishing swaraj. He played on the Hindu theme of Sita. Women should model themselves on Sita, he urged, becoming pure in mind and body, liberating their sex from social abuses, refusing to observe Untouchability, giving away their jewels for *khadi* work and wearing *khadi*.[15]

[13] 'My Shame and Sorrow', *The Bombay Chronicle*, 8 April 1929, *ibid.* pp. 209–12; Gandhi to Chhaganlal Joshi, 11 February 1929, *CWMG*, XXXIX, 453–4, 17 April 1929, *CWMG*, XL, 254–5; Gandhi to Gangabehn Vaidya, 14 April 1929, *ibid.* pp. 250–1.

[14] *Young India*, 13 June 1929, *CWMG*, XLI, 34–6; *Navajivan*, 16 June 1929, *ibid.* pp. 52–4. Gandhi eventually gave up the experiment; further comments are in *CWMG*, XLI.

[15] Examples of Gandhi's use of Sita in appealing to women are speech at women's meeting, 10 February 1929, *Young India*, 21 February 1929, *CWMG*, XXXIX, 447; speech to women, 13 April 1929, *The Hindu*, 15 April 1929, *CWMG*, XL, 237. For

The particular call to women, stressing their role in *khadi* was part of Gandhi's attempt to integrate all sections of society into a newly perceived community and to discipline them for united action. His educational efforts to this end continued to include general exhortations against such habits as spitting in public and lack of public sanitation. To those who complained that such issues diverted attention from swaraj he replied that they were swaraj work, and underlined their uniting and disciplinary potential.

> Indeed if swaraj is to be had by peaceful means it will only be attained by attending to every little detail of national life. Such work will promote cohesion among workers and create an indissoluble bond between them and the people – a bond necessary for the final overthrow of the existing system of government.

Jawaharlal marvelled at the way Gandhi 'disciplined our lazy and demoralised people and made them work', a quality which had earlier earned him the nickname of 'beloved slave-driver'.[16]

Although this wide span of constructive rather than overtly political activity was aimed at uniting and disciplining Indians and publicized Gandhi's credentials as a national leader, there was a significant element in Indian society which held out against his blandishments – the Muslims. Hindu–Muslim unity was not part of the Congress constructive plan laid down at Calcutta. It was nevertheless one of Gandhi's constant concerns and was becoming more urgent in view of the possible struggle with the British in 1930, and the evidence of a widening schism between Muslim leaders and those who called themselves Indian nationalists. In March 1929 Muslims in the Legislative Assembly made it clear that they did not accept the Nehru Report, while Jinnah drafted a fourteen-point resolution to unite the various blocs of Muslim politicians. Although it failed in its attempt, its similarity to the resolutions of the All Parties Muslim Conference in Delhi in January showed the trend of Muslim political opinion away from agreement with Congress, and its focus on a common communal demand to safeguard Muslim interests in the face of constitutional change and threatened Congress agitation. The All Parties Muslim Conference was itself symbolic of this. An ad hoc body which had emerged in reaction to the Nehru Report and under the presidency of the Aga Khan had attempted to challenge that report and both mask and heal the divisions among Muslim politicians and in the Muslim League itself, its continued existence and authority as Muslim mouthpiece in subsequent months demonstrated the split with Congress and a new unity among Muslim politicians which was in marked contrast to their disunity during the 1920s. On 8 September the Conference's Executive Board urged Muslims not to participate in the next Congress session as this would be 'in the highest degree of detrimental

Gandhi's attitude to women's rights see *Young India*, 17 October 1929, *CWMG*, XLII, 4–6.

[16] J. Nehru, *An Autobiography*, p. 255; article on public sanitation, *Young India*, 25 April 1929, *CWMG*, XL, 283–4.

to the best interests of the country in general and the Muslim community in particular'.[17] Moreover Gandhi himself was criticized in the Muslim press. A U.P. paper for example urged Muslims to keep aloof from events during Gandhi's local *khadi* tour, and to tell him that the Nehru Report had laid an axe at the political life of the community.[18]

Gandhi lamented evidence of Muslim politicians' alienation from Congress, and during his work throughout the country he attempted to soothe Muslim suspicions with assurances that swaraj, even his vision of a godly society, *Ramarajya*, did not mean Hindu raj. At Motilal's arrangement he had discussions with Jinnah at Delhi in February, on Muslim complaints about the Nehru Report, but with no tangible results. In August Sarojini Naidu engineered two encounters between Gandhi and Jinnah, and Gandhi and the Ali brothers. Gandhi however told the public that these were merely friendly explorations of possible avenues to peace and not significant meetings in which he was acting in a representative capacity. Despite this assurance M. R. Jayakar voiced the fears of some Hindus, urging Gandhi that there should be no attempt at a communal solution outside the terms of the Nehru Report.[19] The Mahatma was caught in cross currents of hostility between those he wished to unite behind him. If he advised concessions to Muslims he risked Hindu support, particularly those for whom the Mahasabha spoke. If he made no gestures to Muslims he confirmed their suspicion that swaraj in Congress terms meant Hindu domination. In such circumstances he was impotent, unable to lead because of the conflicting pressures on him. Or, as he preferred to put it, the issue was in God's hands, and all he could do was to wait and pray. However, his support for the Nationalist Muslims who broke away from the Muslim League in July showed where he would look for Muslim support in the future to give credence to his claims to national leadership and those of Congress to represent all Indians.[20]

During the months of waiting for the raj Gandhi spent considerable time and energy on trying to reinforce the fragile unity of Congress and to refurbish it as an organization capable of embarking on effective resistance.

[17] Aziz, *The All India Muslim Conference*, pp. 57–8. Jinnah's 14 points are in C. H. Phillips (ed.). *The Evolution of India and Pakistan 1858 to 1947 Select Documents* (London, 1962), pp. 235–7. Irwin's description of Legislative Assembly debate to Peel, 21 March 1929, Mss. EUR.C. 152 (5).

[18] Note on the Press, U.P. No. 39 of 1929. Week ending September 28, 1929. (I owe this reference to D. A. Low).

[19] M. R. Jayakar to Gandhi, 23 August 1929, *CWMG*, XLI, 574–5; Gandhi's reply to Jayakar, 24 August 1929, assured him that he had merely listened to Jinnah and the Alis; he had no representative capacity and wished to bind nobody, *ibid.* p. 319. Gandhi's public comments on the meetings, *Young India*, 15 August 1929, *ibid.* p. 289, *Navajivan*, 24 February 1929, *CWMG*, XL, 27–8.

[20] Message to first meeting of Bombay Congress Muslim Party, 28 July 1929, *The Bombay Chronicle*, 29 July 1929, *CWMG*, XLI, 234. The All-India party came into being at Allahabad: it included A. K. Azad, M. A. Ansari and T. A. K. Sherwani.
Gandhi's awareness of his impotence on the communal question is clear in *Young India*, 29 August 1929, *CWMG*, XLI, 321; *Young India*, 30 May 1929, *CWMG*, XL, 426.

Although country-wide contact and sympathy were essential to him, he realized that his plans were unworkable unless Congress itself was united and organized. Three committees had been set up after Calcutta, the Foreign Cloth Boycott under himself and Jairamdas, one for Prohibition under Rajagopalachariar and one for anti-Untouchability work under Jamnalal Bajaj; but their work was impossible without an effective country-wide Congress organization as Gandhi had pointed out in his cloth boycott scheme. He set himself to publicize the inadequacies of the Congress organization and to prod it into reform.

When he heard of irregularities and manipulation behind the delegations from Andhra, Punjab and Bengal to the Calcutta Congress he told Jawaharlal as Congress General Secretary that he must put the Congress committees in order. 'Unless by some unforeseen circumstances there is an honourable settlement with Great Britain, there will be practically no other party save the party of independence in the country. But the cry will be ineffective if we cannot put up a proper fight. If that fight is to be put up through the Congress, then the Congress must be a living thing.' Through the press he castigated Congress squabbles and somnulence in the provinces, using Sind as a notorious example.[21] He also underlined Congress's need of a sound financial base. But he refused to use the proceeds of his *khadi* tours to subsidize local Congress committees, insisting that they must finance themselves by commanding 'the confidence of the public independently of the services of all-India men'.[22]

Gandhi's criticisms of the congress organization were well founded. The AICC General Secretaries reported large debts owed to the AICC by individual Congressmen and some PCCs, the largest being Rs. 139,003 due from Bengal. Both the AICC and other provinces had relied on Bombay's generosity, and the AICC had been living off its capital which by the end of 1929 was severely depleted. By the end of February 1929, the closing date for provincial contributions, Andhra, Assam, Bengal, Burma, Marathi C.P. and Delhi had produced nothing. The other provinces had given ridiculously small amounts, Bombay's being the largest contribution (Rs. 1,000) followed by Gujarat (Rs. 500), U.P. (Rs. 300) and Bihar (Rs. 200).[23] These figures were symptomatic of an almost total paralysis in the Congress organization at provincial level and below. In accordance with a Working

[21] *Young India*, 21 February 1929, *ibid*, pp. 10–12; Gandhi to J. Nehru, 1 February 1929, J. Nehru Papers, part 1, vol. XXII; Gandhi to M. Nehru, 1 February 1929, M. Nehru Papers, File G. 1.

[22] Gandhi to K. S. Rao, 14 February 1929, *CWMG*, XXXIX, 467.

[23] Handwritten report by J. Nehru, 22 May 1929, submitted to AICC on 24 May 1929, AICC Papers, 1929, File No. 20. Of the other provinces Utkal sent Rs. 105, Punjab, Hindi, C.P., Karnatak and Tamil Nad Rs. 100 each, N.-W.F.P., Maharashtra, Sind and Berar Rs. 50 each, and Kerala Rs. 25.

For further evidence of Congress's financial disarray see report by S. C. Bose and J. Nehru, AICC Gen. Secs., 10 December 1928, *43rd I.N.C. Report*; statistics on AICC finance prepared for Working Committee in November 1929, AICC Papers, 1929, File No. 17.

Committee resolution of 17 February Jawaharlal, aided by Gandhi, arranged for the audit and inspection of PCCs. These investigations proved the depths to which the Congress organization had sunk since its reconstruction during Non-cooperation. Moreover the reluctance of provinces like Bengal and Andhra to submit to this investigation was for Gandhi 'an evidence of the chaos that reigns supreme in our house. For what I see throughout Andhra is true almost of every province.'[24]

By the end of May proof had accumulated that only the PCCs of Bombay, Bengal, Bihar, Burma, Punjab, U.P., Gujarat and Tamil Nad were functioning as proper offices. But even in these provinces lower level organization was often weak or non-existent. Bombay was only a shadow of its former self with very few members; and Jawaharlal who inspected it himself urged the PCC 'to shake up the city of Bombay' and to make the Congress organization representative of all sections of the city's life including labourers and younger people. In Bengal the rural areas were scarcely organized at all: in Punjab only ten out of thirty districts had DCCs and these had very few members. Gujarat by contrast reported that its five districts all had properly elected DCCs, and beneath them thirty-five *taluka* committees. U.P. began to take itself in hand under Sri Prakasa, helped by Jawaharlal. It organized its own local inspection, but this only indicated the level from which it would have to raise itself, as Prakasa reported.

> During the last four years the Congress organization in our province, as perhaps, in other provinces also, had become dormant. Soon after the upheaval caused by the Non-co-operation movement had subsided, propaganda and work in the villages was more or less given up; and as the natural result of this the Congress machinery could not function at all effectively. Work came to be totally confined to the head-quarters of districts and larger cities. Once in a while when the elections of the PCC or for the official Councils approached, interested persons enrolled some members and set up some sort of Congress committees. During the last year or two in many districts even this was not done: in more than half of the districts, the district committees, have either disappeared or have existed only nominally on paper. Even the provincial office suffered from the prevailing reaction and remained only in name.[25]

Prasaka stressed the need for finance if provincial work was to flourish. Sind which had already come in for the Mahatma's public lashing underlined the point: without funds to give full time workers an assured maintenance allowance they could not begin political work. In the provinces where PCCs had no proper office, conditions were lamentable. Assam had no proper organization. Hindi C.P.'s PCC had no office or fixed abode, and Marathi C.P., torn by factions, had only just started from scratch, though

[24] Gandhi to J. Nehru, 10 May 1929, *CWMG*, XL, 368.
[25] Prakasa's report, 5 May 1929, to J. Nehru, AICC Papers, 1929, File No. P 24. See also provincial reports in same AICC file; handwritten report by J. Nehru, 22 May 1929, submitted to AICC on 24 May 1929, AICC Papers, 1929, File No. 20; J. Nehru to Sec., Punjab PCC, 13 March 1929, *SWJN*, 4, pp. 141–3; J. Nehru to Sec., Bombay PCC, 6 May 1929, *ibid*. pp. 149–50.

nine of its eleven DCCs were reportedly in tolerably good order. What went on at a lower level in C.P. remained a mystery as the auditors failed to get access to the books of the Jubbulpore and Nagpur town committees. Neither could the Delhi PCC account book be found. It had apparently disappeared at the beginning of the year when new officials took up their charge; and both old and new officials blamed the other for its loss.

Understandably the statistics for membership which such an organization could produce were extremely sketchy. Jawaharlal, reporting to the AICC in May, had to use the previous year's figures for Bengal (25,500), Delhi, (789), Maharashtra (2,000), Karnatak (4,796) and Tamil Nad (2,000). The current figures showed the following totals, though some were qualified by special comments: Ajmer – 14,594 (high figure probably due to the fact that Congress elections were in progress and each group was recruiting members); Bihar – 30,000 (highest provincial total: best district was Champaran); Bombay – 1,210 (only 3 districts reported to date); Burma – 800; Karnatak – 800 (not clear from the report why this was so different from the previous year's figure or why both were included); Punjab – 731; U.P. – 6,000 (probably too low a figure); Gujarat – 500; Kerala – 90; Sind – 1,336; total 56,061.

Gandhi noted with wry humour to Jawaharlal, 'Copies of the reports make sad reading. I suggest your sending 10 pies to the respective committees with your observations & suggestions.'[26] At the AICC in Bombay which received these gloomy tidings, Gandhi moved a resolution calling on provinces to reorganize themselves from PCC to village level in accordance with minimum quotas laid down in relation to population and the number of districts, *tahsils* and villages. He suggested, for example, that DCCs should have at least 1 % of their population as members, and should have representatives from at least 50 % of the *tahsils* within them. Provinces which had not fulfilled their quota of enrolment by 31 August were to be disqualified. He called his resolution a radical measure to meet an emergency situation; and it was passed, albeit in a watered-down version – the 7½ lakhs of members called for was only one-eighth of what he wanted. Even so Dr B. S. Moonje, Maharashtrian Mahasabhite and critic of Gandhi from Noncooperation days grumbled into his diary, 'What a utopian idea and all cheered Mahatmaji but there was not one who affected to feel that such a proposal is thoroughly unpractical. I was glad to note that Dr Khare raised his hand in opposition; he was practically the only man who opposed the Resolution. Others laughed at him in ridicule. I remained neutral.' The previous day he had noted that there was no personality who could give a practical and constructive lead to the country, and to all 'practically minded people' Congress appeared 'a sham show of tall talk'.[27]

[26] Gandhi to J. Nehru, 5 June 1929, J. Nehru Papers. (Pice were the small coins which made up a rupee).
[27] 24, 25 May 1929, NMML, Microfilm, Diary of B. S. Moonje. Accounts of AICC meeting, the relevant resolution & Gandhi's speech, 25 May 1929, *CWMG*, XL, 420–1;

TABLE I. *Congress membership during the second half of 1929*

Province	Quota	Members enrolled	
		I	II
Ajmer	1,120	14,594 (disputed)	14,591
Andhra	36,763	29,000	29,685
Assam	8,337	?	—
Bihar	72,558 (72,588)*	17,107	90,525
Bengal	1,24,413	93,385	93,385
Berar	7,688	7,688?	7,688?
C.P. (Hindustani)	20,505	23,827	28,827
C.P. (Marathi)	6,586	11,651	11,651
Bombay	17,000	11,889	12,689
Delhi	6,954	6,071	6,071
Gujarat	7,396	15,990	17,807
Karnatak	13,244 (13,654)	10,038	13,092
Kerala	7,747	3,265	3,380
Maharashtra	21,720 (21,542)	24,608	26,499
N.-W.F.P.	2,000	2,000?	2,000
Punjab	51,718	27,490	29,122
Sind	8,200	2,615	2,613
Tamil Nad	51,784	4,500?	36,087
U.P.	1,07,724 (1,06,529)	67,849	75,710
Utkal	12,421	6,945	6,945
Burma	2,000	1,904	1,904
Total	5,87,908 (5,86,105)	4,48,418	5,10,276

* Figures in parentheses are those given in the Annual Report.
SOURCE: Column I – *Young India*, 10 October 1929, quoting a Congress
            Bulletin, *CWMG*, XLI, 537–8.
            Column II – Annual Report for 1929 presented by Congress General
            Secretaries to AICC, Appendix I of *Report of the 44th Annual Session*.

The results of the intensive recruiting drive which followed this meeting
were significant (see Table 1). Gujarat had doubled its quota by October;
Bihar, the two C.P.s and Maharashtra had more than their quotas; Berar
and N.-W.F.P. had just fulfilled their requirement. But the other provincial
figures were below their quota. Consequently at its Lucknow meeting late
in September the AICC waived the penalty laid down in May rather than
disqualify most provinces, including U.P. and Bombay. Gandhi's warning
against nominal enrolment indicates that these figures like their predeces-
sors are only rough indications, not accurate statistics, and prove little about
the real depth of support Congress had tapped, let alone the discipline it
could impose by the end of 1929. The annual Congress report for 1929
suggested that Congress barely functioned in Assam, and work done in
Kerala, Sind, Berar and Marathi C.P. was unsatisfactory. Again a group

Bombay Secret Abstract, 1929, par. 1014, *HFM, III, II*, pp. 435–6. Gandhi's comments
on resolution, *Young India*, 30 May 1929, *CWMG*, XL, 428–9.

of provinces failed to send in annual reports (Ajmer, Assam, Berar, Burma, the two C.P.s, Delhi, Sind, and Utkal). Moreover, the provincial contributions were little better than they had been in February.[28]

Recruitment of volunteers recommended by the Calcutta constructive resolution had similarly been patchy in its results. The volunteer movement was strongest in Bengal under S. C. Bose, though the numbers fell short of the 1,000 per district he wanted. Otherwise volunteering only made headway in Punjab where a corps was established for work during the forthcoming Lahore session.[29] More worrying to the government and ultimately to Gandhi than the failure to create a strong volunteer organization, was the attitude of many who should have been potential recruits. In Bengal, for example, a section of the All-Bengal Youth Conference in March 1929 approved of their president's attack on Gandhi's *khadi* programme and his attempt 'to show the Bengalis how to fight for freedom'. The Punjab government noted with concern the activities of the Nau Jawan Bharat Sabha, a youth movement founded in March 1926 which had grown markedly since 1928 among students, and aimed at independence for India. Its relationship with Congress was ambivalent. One of its meetings had criticized Motilal's refusal to allow a motion of sympathy for two of its members, Bhagat Singh and B. Dutt, in the July AICC meeting, because this would be in contravention of Congress's non-violent creed. Yet local officials believed that Congress had definitely encouraged the Sabha's violent policy. This link made the provincial situation particularly difficult, although 'The Congress organization is weaker in the Punjab than in any other province and if the local Government had to deal only with plans initiated and organized by the Provincial Congress Committee, it would view the situation with equanimity.'[30]

The problems of cohesion and control stemming from the failure to integrate such burgeoning youth movements into a Congress organization confronted Gandhi most forcibly at the Lahore Congress in December 1929. But episodes had occurred earlier in the year which taxed his skill in keeping a semblance of unity within Congress. The divisions which had permitted his re-emergence at Calcutta limited the extent to which he could exert authority, as did the weakness of the Congress organization.

[28] Annual Report for 1929 presented by General Secs. to AICC, Appendix 1 of *Report of the 44th Annual Session*, IOL, Microfilm Pos. 2274; *Young India*, 10 October 1929, *CWMG*, XLI, 537–9.

[29] Sir Stanley Jackson to Irwin, 10 May 1929, Mss. EUR.C.152 (23); Weekly Report of D.I., 26 September 1929, appended to Govt. of India, Home Dept. to S of S, telegram, 11 October 1929, L/PJ/6/1976.

[30] Chief sec., Punjab Govt., to Home Sec., Govt. of India, 25 February 1930, Home Poll., 1930, File No. 130 & K.-W. (this file is on the Nau Jawan Bharat Sabha); Weekly Report of D.I., 26 September 1929, appended to Govt. of India, Home Dept. to S of S, telegram, 11 October 1929, Govt. of India, Home Dept., to Under Sec. of State, 18 July 1929 with enclosures, L/PJ/6/1976. Bhagat Singh and B. Dutt had been sentenced to transportation for life for throwing the bombs in the Assembly in April. For the Bengal Youth Movement see Home Poll., 1930, File No. 212/30.

The rift between Motilal and Srinivasa Iyengar which had influenced the independence–Dominion Status controversy at Madras and Calcutta gaped even wider in May 1929 when the Tamil Nad PCC, apparently packed by Iyengar, resolved in favour of accepting office. Motilal poured scorn on the apparent incongruity of this action by a leader of the independence group.[31] Yet it proved that the rift between the two leaders was not so much an ideological one as the surface symptom of local Congress divisions and the tension felt by Iyengar between all-India policy and local necessity. Like Iyengar most Congressmen maintained an uneasy balance of priorities as they oscillated between consideration of their local situation and the all-India problem of relations with the raj. The tension thus generated which had wrecked Swarajist unity, threatened Congress again on a wide front in 1929 on the issue of attending the new session of the legislatures. It fell to Gandhi to try to succeed where Motilal had failed to enforce a continental policy.

In May 1929 Irwin decided to postpone the elections scheduled for the autumn so that they could be held after Simon's report was published. He was anxious to prevent electioneering condemnation of the report before it appeared, to curtail the propaganda opportunities open to Congress politicians at the end of their 'year of grace' for the raj, and to see what would happen on 1 January.[32] Motilal's response was that Congressmen should not attend the legislatures during their extended life, and the topic was tabled for discussion at the 24/25 May AICC in Bombay. It was expected to be an exceedingly lively meeting because of Tamil Nad's proposal on office acceptance. But on 25 May Satyamurti defused the tension by withdrawing the proposal, in view of opposition from other provinces and the Viceregal extension of the legislatures. The meeting delegated responsibility to the Working Committee for deciding the action of Congress legislators in the forthcoming session.[33]

Motilal sent a presidential circular on 1 June to all Congress legislators announcing that, because of the extension of the legislatures, the AICC and Working Committee called on them to abstain from attendance until further notice, and to devote their time to furthering Congress work in the country where the real strength of the nation must be built up before the end of 1929. Gandhi published this appeal in *Young India*, giving it his full support. It did, of course, coincide with his long-held views that council work had benefited India little.[34]

However, Motilal was immediately deluged with letters of protest from Congress legislators who were perturbed when they realized what absten-

[31] M. Nehru to M. R. Jayakar, 17 May 1929, NAI, Papers of M. R. Jayakar, Correspondence File No. 407, part i; Irwin to Peel, 23 May 1929, Mss. EUR.C.152 (5).

[32] V to S of S, telegrams, 23 April, 6 May 1929, Mss. EUR.C.152 (10).

[33] Bombay Secret Abstract, 1929, par. 1014, *HFM, III, II*, pp. 433–5.

[34] 1 June circular from M. Nehru, M. Nehru Papers, Subject File, I.N.C.: *Young India*, 13 June 1929, *CWMG*, xli, 42–3; *Hindi Navajivan*, 6 June 1929, *ibid.* p. 27.

tion might mean in their local situations. An Assam legislator told Motilal that important measures on land revenue and opium were pending on which Swarajists were pledged to their voters to put up a big fight: they did not want to alienate the electorate or miss the chance of electing an assembly president from their ranks. From Madras came word that Congressmen wished to have a say on the Malabar Tenancy Bill; while Bombay men wanted to oppose a measure to control trade unions lest they should lay themselves open to the charge of betraying the cause of labour. A Punjab MLC wanted to be present for discussion on the extension of the Punjab Alienation of Land Act on which Hindus felt strongly. From U.P. G. B. Pant wrote to tell Motilal that his colleagues were very agitated over the Working Committee resolution. They needed to be present in the next session for bills on which they had already expended time and effort, and they feared that their absence would not only weaken the progressive element in the legislature but would alienate electors already sceptical about Congress non-cooperation in the councils. Faced with such local arguments, Motilal arranged a Working Committee for 5 July – significantly when he knew Gandhi could attend.[35] The Committee met in Ansari's Delhi home: although it supported the resignation tactic, it referred the matter for approval by the AICC.[36]

The AICC met at Allahabad on 26/27 July, representing all provinces except Assam. The largest group was the local one from U.P., 80 strong; Bengal sent 30, Bihar and Orissa, 15, while the other provinces produced 10 or less. Gandhi did not attend the open meeting on 26th, but devoted himself to private discussions on the Council entry question at the Nehru home with a subjects committee composed of Working Committee members and selected provincial delegates. There was complete deadlock, Bombay, Andhra, the Karnatak and Delhi favoured boycott, while U.P., Maharashtra, Bengal and Madras opposed it. Eventually Gandhi promised to produce a proposal the following day. On 27th the inner group met again at the Nehru house, and Gandhi produced an acceptable compromise, though some of the boycott diehards said they would oppose it in the AICC. Gandhi moved his own proposal in the formal meeting – that the question of Congress resignations be held over until the Lahore Congress because of the feeling in Congress on the issue. This was seconded by Bose who argued that they could not afford to divide Congress when it needed all

[35] Letters of protest are in M. Nehru Papers, Subject File, I.N.C., e.g. G. B. Pant to M. Nehru, 5 June 1929. Motilal explained his attitude at length to J. Mehta, 20 June 1929, also in this file. He was determined that Congress should take its Calcutta resolution seriously and believed that the extension of the legislatures meant that the Nehru Report would not be considered, let alone accepted by 31 December. In this situation Congress must do something effective at the end of 1929, or it would stultify itself; it would be difficult to prepare for such action while collaborating with the administration in the legislatures.

[36] Bombay Secret Abstract, 1929, par. 1327, quoting from Delhi Secret Abstract, 6 July 1929, par. 173, *HFM, III, II*, p. 443.

its resources to fight the foreign bureaucracy. Despite some opposition the compromise was accepted by an overwhelming majority, only four members voting against it. Gandhi said he moved the resolution simply because he was not prepared to face a split in Congress. Maintaining the same attitude towards Congress he had shown at Calcutta, he was willing to perform a similar conciliatory role, assuming prominence within a Congress conclave because of the divisions among its members.[37]

Congress disunity boded ill for united action at the end of the year. It was also clear that some Hindus on the periphery of Congress were increasingly hostile to Gandhi's assumption of leadership. B. S. Moonje disliked M. S. Aney's anxiety to attend the July AICC.

> I wonder why he should be so anxious to set right the Swarajists who have been maintaining their position by misleading the people on the strength of Mahatma Gandhi's support about the Council work. If the Congress decides upon Council Boycott which I doubt if it will ever do once having tasted the advantages of Council entry, others and particularly the Hindu Mahasabha will be free to organize the work in the Legislatures on sound logical and practical basis.[38]

Gandhi's concern for Congress unity was also an element in his refusal to preside over the 1929 session. He evidently discussed the question with Jawaharlal during his *khadi* tour of U.P. in June, and thought he had persuaded him to preside. Early in July he pressed him to make a firm decision. Jawaharlal was reluctant to take on the office. He wished to renew contacts with rural areas rather than burden himself with organizational work in which he was unskilled, and felt that those who backed him only did so in order to keep someone else out. He urged Gandhi to preside. At Jawaharlal's request Gandhi did not renew his pressure until after the crucial July AICC, but then he weighed in with a public appeal in *Young India.* He argued for Jawaharlal as president on the grounds that the young must have their place in Congress, and that responsibility would mellow and train them. He professed himself unfitted to attend to detailed office work, and to be out of accord with younger men, asserting that he could best use his 'special qualities...by remaining detached from and untrammelled by...office. So long as I retain the affection and the confidence of our people, there is not the slightest danger of my not being able without holding office to make the fullest use of such powers as I may possess.'[39]

---

[37] Printed agenda and hand-written agenda by J. Nehru for AICC, AICC Papers, 1929, File No. 7; typed account of AICC meeting, AICC Papers, 1931, File No. G-11; Bombay Secret Abstract, 1929, par. 1450, quoting U.P. Secret Abstract, 3 August 1929, par. 441, *HFM, III, II*, pp. 444–9; Gandhi's speech in AICC, 27 July 1929, *CWMG*, XLI, 228–9.

[38] 24 July 1929, Diary of B. S. Moonje.

[39] Gandhi to J. Nehru, *c.* 1 July 1929, *CWMG*, XLI, 153; J. Nehru to Gandhi, 9 & 13 July 1929, *SWJN*, 4, pp. 155, 156–7; *Young India*, 1 August 1929, *CWMG*, XLI, 239–41. Gandhi wrote to M. Nehru on 6 July 1929, 'I am sure Jawahar should preside. Let young men have their innings. We must stand behind them.' M. Nehru Papers, File G. 1.

Nineteen out of twenty-one provinces made ther views known. Ten backed Gandhi and five voted for Vallabhbhai, and the Reception Committee endorsed this, electing Gandhi. Gandhi heard of his election on 19 August and immediately refused the office, insisting that he lacked the energy and was 'out of tune' with many things done by Congressmen, and urging the Reception Committee to elect Jawaharlal. In accordance with the Congress constitution the matter was referred to an AICC meeting on 28 September. Gandhi maintained his stand despite pressure from Motilal and continuing reluctance on Jawaharlal's part.[40] In *Young India* he professed regret for forcing this on the AICC; but after listing his political credos he asked if it was any wonder that as president he would feel like a square peg in a round hole since only 'a microscopic minority' of Congressmen agreed with him and to most of them at least some of his ideals were a positive stumbling block. Once more he was stating his own terms. Jawaharlal saw this after a long talk with him, and reported to Motilal, 'Briefly put he feels that few people are prepared to follow him although they demand loudly for his presidentship. If he was convinced that he was seriously wanted to lead and not merely to be exploited he would I think agree to preside.'[41] At the AICC in Lucknow Gandhi was asked to reconsider his decision, but he spoke briefly, referring his audience to *Young India* for his reasons. He assured them that he did not intend to keep aloof from the Congress programme and would help Jawaharlal as best he could. 'I shall be prepared for the worst if the chance comes. I am not to run away from the coming battle on the 1st January, 1930. I shall willingly extend every help in formulating the programme and scheme for Congress work. The AICC thereupon elected Jawaharlal – much to the younger man's annoyance and humiliation. 'I did not come...by the main entrance or even a side entrance; I appeared suddenly by a trap-door and bewildered the audience into acceptance. They put a brave face on it, and, like a necessary pill, swallowed me.'[42]

The reasoning behind Gandhi's pressure for Jawaharlal's presidency was partly his concern for Congress unity. By putting Jawaharlal, one of the major spokesmen for independence at Calcutta, in the Lahore chair he hoped both to use him to heal the cleavages of generation and ideology

[40] Longhand draft by J. Nehru of Congress Bulletin No. 13, 13 September 1929, giving voting figures and explaining the reference of the matter to the AICC; AICC Papers, 1929, File No. 43.
Gandhi's wire refusing presidency, to I.N.C. Lahore, *c.* 19 August 1929, *CWMG*, XLI, 303, in reply to wire of 19 August, *ibid.* p. 303, fn. 2.
M. Nehru to Gandhi, telegram, 21 August 1929, *ibid.* p. 305, fn. 4; J. Nehru to Gandhi, telegram, 21 August 1929, *ibid.* p. 305, fn. 3; Gandhi to J. Nehru, 22 August 1929, J. Nehru Papers.
[41] J. to M. Nehru, 30 August 1929, M. Nehru Papers; *Young India*, 12 September 1929, *CWMG*, XLI, 378–9.
[42] J. Nehru, *An Autobiography*, pp. 194–5; longhand draft by J. Nehru of Congress Bulletin No. 14, 5 October 1929, AICC Papers, 1929, File No. 43; speech by Gandhi at AICC, 28 September 1929, *CWMG*, XLI, 482–3.

in Congress and also to prevent him becoming a focus and mouthpiece of opposition to a less extreme demand – if that should appear necessary in the circumstances of December. As he commented to Abbas Tyabji, 'I have no misgivings about Jawaharlal's conduct in the chair.'[43] At the same time there was evidently a growing pessimism in the Mahatma's mind about his own wish or capacity to lead a movement of protest, in view of the feeble enactment of the terms of leadership he had laid down at Calcutta.

The Congress organization was not the living reality he wanted, and politics still seemed to him frivolous and disorderly compared with the hard labour for swaraj he recommended. There were increasing signs of violence and the resurgence of terrorism, particularly among students: the bombs thrown by Punjabi students in the Assembly in April were but one example. Congress was split by faction in several regions, and Gandhi was powerless to intervene in local disputes. He could only appeal to the divided Punjabis, for example, to put nation before party and to rally round the Congress; and express the hope that local pressure would resolve the faction splits in Bengal. Such a Congress would be an incubus if he presided over it, inhibiting his pursuit of his *dharma* as a servant of the people. Most serious of all, he could not count on country-wide support. In September, just when he was refusing the presidency he told *Young India* readers.

> It is a gross misrepresentation of the true situation to say that the masses are impatient to be led to civil disobedience, but that I am hanging back. I know well enough how to lead to civil disobedience a people who are prepared to embark upon it on my terms. I see no such sign on the horizon. But I live in faith. I am still hoping that a way out of the 'encircling gloom' will be found on 1st January next.[44]

Gandhi was more than a little irritated at the circumstances in which he was caught. Seeing neither the cohesion nor means of control vital for a national campaign his thoughts turned to the ashram where his control over a united group of workers was more sure. To Chhanganlal Joshi he admitted that he had no plan, but that his responsibility for doing something in January had increased as he had refused the presidency. In this the ashram was to be vital. 'If the country is able to do nothing and if I see the fitness of the Ashram inmates, something can certainly be done through them.'[45]

[43] Gandhi to A. Tyabji, 19 October 1929, *CWMG*, XLII, 18.

[44] *Young India*, 5 September 1929, *CWMG*, XLI, 276. Further evidence of Gandhi's pessimisim about the political context in which he was being expected to lead is in: *Navajivan*, 11 August 1929, *ibid.* pp. 249–50; *Young India*, 22 August 1929, *ibid.* p. 318; *Young India*, 18 April 1929 (on the bomb thrown in the Assembly), *CWMG*, XL, 259–61; Gandhi to J. M. Sarkar on Bengali disputes, 3 November 1929, *CWMG*, XLII, 91–2; *Young India*, 7 November 1929, appeal for Punjabi unity, *ibid.* p. 111.

[45] Gandhi to C. Joshi, 6 October 1929, *CWMG*, XLI, 519. Gandhi professed to be fighting against anger to C., Joshi, 16 September 1929, *ibid.* pp. 412–13.

II NOVEMBER – DECEMBER 1929: RESPONSE TO THE RAJ

Congress entered the final weeks of 1929 in a state which augured ill for decisive and effective action if the raj failed to meet its deadline for acceptance of the Nehru Report. Its disunity was manifest in the clashing policy priorities of different regions and generations, and in the feuds which divided Congressmen within provinces. It was still scrambling to refurbish its organization and recruit members. Its President-elect was angry and humiliated at the role he was being forced to play. While the Mahatma, on whom it had relied to cover its rifts if he could not heal them, had not only refused to preside at Lahore but was openly pessimistic about the viability of a mass campaign.[46]

The main Congress leaders outside the Jawaharlal–Bose group were very close to the Liberals in desiring cooperation with the British. They needed some formula for advance which would permit this, saving them from the uncertain benefits of a repetition of 1920–2 and certain isolation from the Liberals who opposed civil disobedience yet were important for a united anti-British front. Srinivasa Sastri and Sapru both indicated that they would retire from politics rather than become non-cooperators.[47] In March Motilal had made known to Irwin through an intermediary that he was anxious to find some way out, and that Congress would present its case in London if it was assured of Dominion Status as India's future form of government. In July he appealed to the Labour Government which had come to power in Britain in June to 'invite the representatives of India to a round table conference to discuss the constitution of India with a committee of the Cabinet on the basis of Dominion Status before it is too late'. Moreover it was clear that the term 'Dominion Status' was amenable to various interpretations in the interests of an accommodation. Gandhi's views on this were reported to Irwin in January. B. S. Moonje told the Governor of C.P. that even Congress people, although they could not be expected to eat their words, would be satisfied with a constitution which was capable of automatic expansion into full Dominion Status. When asked how Congress would adjust to this position he replied, 'there need be no anxiety on this score. Mahatma Gandhi will do the rest.'[48]

[46] Weekly report of D.I., 26 September 1929, appended to Home Dept., Govt. of India, to S of S, telegram, 11 October 1929, L/PJ/6/1976; M. Nehru to B. C. Roy, 10 October 1929, M. Nehru Papers, Correspondence File R 10.

[47] Sir Grimwood Mears, Chief Justice Allahabad High Court, to Irwin, on Sapru's position, 29 April 1929, Mss. EUR.C.152 (23); V. S. S. Sastri explained his position to Sir P. S. Sivaswami Aiyar, 19 September 1929, T. N. Jagadisan (ed.), *Letters of The Right Honourable V. S. Srinivasa Sastri* (2nd edn, Bombay, 1963), p. 182: 'In no conceivable circumstances shall I join N.C.O., become a law-breaker, wear *khaddar* or assume membership of the Congress. Should the revised Constitution be no real advance with Assembly powers curtailed, Dominion Status disavowed, or the British hold tightened, I may denounce it and seek the retirement which you once before recommended to me. Leading an agitation of waving red flags and shouting war-cries – is not in my line. Martyrdom must come to me, if at all, in other forms.'

[48] 25 October 1929, Diary of B. S. Moonje. For Motilal's attitude see Sir Grimwood Mears to Irwin, 26 March 1929, Mss. EUR.C.152 (23); M. Nehru to editor of The

The British made a dual response to the post-Calcutta situation. Realizing as clearly as Gandhi that their rule depended on the acquiescence of the majority of their subjects and the active cooperation of a strategic minority in the structures of the raj, they took steps both to conciliate and to control in order to shore up the foundations of their empire. Their experience a decade earlier of war-time pressures for constitutional advance and the challenge of Non-cooperation underlined the need for a delicate balance between the two prongs of policy; and to the records of Non-cooperation they returned in January 1929.[49]

The general guidelines for control were laid down in a Government of India policy letter in February 1929. This asserted that the political situation was potentially dangerous despite divisions in Congress. Independence was no longer an academic ideal, and direct action, probably after publication of Simon's report, might create a situation worse than the one which hampered the introduction of the 1919 reforms. Moreover Congressmen like Jawaharlal who did not object to using force might enter into temporary alliance with the Communists who had been active among the industrial workers of Calcutta and Bombay. Judging from past experience it seemed unlikely that a non-cooperation movement would die of its own weakness or split, or that moderate Indians would range themselves effectively against it. Therefore, the government must take the initiative and deal with it at an early stage, denying Congress the opportunity to develop its organization and strategy, and strike when it thought best. The Government of India wished to be kept informed of any local government action which would affect the general situation, promising in return general appreciations of the situation. Meanwhile it advised local governments to deal swiftly with incitements to violence and boycotts involving picketing and intimidation; to adjust measures to local situations but not to act against important leaders without considering the wider implications of their speeches. Existing laws vigilantly and firmly used should be adequate and were, Delhi argued, far more effective than supplementing the law. During the next two months it buttressed this letter with detailed history notes on previous manifestations of no-tax, boycott and volunteer movements, drawing out the lessons to be learnt from them.[50]

Simultaneously the central government decided to crack down on lead-

Leader, 1 July 1929, M. Nehru Papers, Correspondence File L 2. For Gandhi's views see above, p. 42.

[49] Irwin to Peel, 9 January 1929, Mss. EUR.C.152 (6). Peel asked Irwin to work out detailed plans for dealing with civil disobedience much as the British government had done in preparation for the General Strike. 'I attach great importance to this, because it is the claim of Swarajists that they can reduce us to submission by making government impossible. It will be our business to show conclusively that they cannot.' Peel to Irwin, 17 January 1929, *ibid.*

[50] Secretary, Govt. of India, Home Dept., to all local govts., 21 February 1929, enclosed in letter from Govt. of India, Home Dept., to Under-Sec. of State, 21 February 1929; letters to all local govts. from Home Dept., enclosing notes on no-tax, boycott, and volunteer movements, 25 March, 7 May 1929; L/PJ/6/1976.

ing Communists in order to break their organization and hopefully to provide a basis for proclaiming Communist associations illegal in the future. It launched the Meerut Conspiracy case against thirty-one leading Communists in March; and the following month promulgated the Public Safety Ordinance after Vithalbhai Patel had refused as President of the Assembly to allow the introduction of a Public Safety Bill.[51] By June the Home Department judged that its tactics of control were working well against Congress and Communists. It suggested no modification of policy to local governments although it asked them to watch out for marked developments in youth and volunteer movements and for the emergence of specific grievances which would affect large groups or become occasions for widespread misrepresentation. Like Gandhi it clearly had taken Bardoli to heart; but like him, too, it saw no mass response yet to the Congress appeal.[52]

Meanwhile Irwin bent his mind to the problem of conciliation. His aim was not merely to prevent a possibly violent confrontation with Congress, but to attract the active cooperation of educated India's main political association in plans for constitutional reform set in train by the appointment of the Simon Commission. Within days of the Calcutta Congress, the Liberal, Sir Chimanlal Setalvad, urged on him the need for some generous British gesture, possibly a declaration that Britain's goal was Dominion Status for India. Although Irwin dismissed the suggestion at the time he reported it to the Secretary of State.

> ...for what it is worth, not so much because I feel that we are necessarily here touching anything that might offer substantial foothold, but because it is indicative of what I more and more come to believe is true, namely, that in nearly all quarters except the most extreme there would be very genuine relief if some face-saving device which afforded an excuse for the introduction of saner counsels could be found.[53]

Irwin was under pressure not only from Indians. He was reminded by one of his governors, Goschen of Madras, that there could be no standing still whatever the attitude of British diehards, and that government had only been possible in the previous months because people were waiting to see what the Simon Commission would suggest. If they resorted to a backtracking policy, they would probably have to use troops to suppress an upheaval.

> Would the country at home stand this? Would other countries remain onlookers? Especially if we had not given the Indian people the chance

---

[51] Irwin to Governors of Madras, Bombay, Bengal, Punjab, Burma, Bihar & Orissa, 25 February 1929, announcing likelihood of comprehensive conspiracy case, Mss. EUR.C.152 (23). Irwin's statement on the Public Safety Ordinance, 13 April 1929, Philips (ed.), *The Evolution of India and Pakistan*, pp. 256–8. For the Meerut Case and the Ordinance see Gopal, *The Viceroyalty of Lord Irwin*, pp. 38–45.

[52] General survey, 24 June 1929, Home Dept. to all local govts., enclosed in Govt. of India, Home Dept., to Under-Sec. of State, 27 June 1929, L/PJ/6/1976.

[53] Irwin to Peel, 24 January 1929, Mss. EUR.C.152 (5).

of showing what they could do under advances in Self-Government. I may be wrong in all this, but I do feel there would be a grave risk just as I feel there would be a risk in going forward, but that would be a lesser one, and the one I feel we ought to incur in view of what has been said to India.

Set in this wider context the need for accommodation with Congress seemed critical.[54]

Even before the Calcutta Congress Irwin had been considering a conference between representatives of Parliament, British India and the Princely states, as a means of attracting wide support for whatever reforms emerged, and of neutralizing Indian hostility to the Simon Commission. By April 1929, after listening to reports of the similar trend of opinion among Liberals and moderate Congressmen, he had connected the conference plan with the idea of a declaration that the goal of British India was Dominion Status. Here possibly was the appropriate 'face-saving device'. It would satisfy what he gathered to be the main Indian political demand, yet meant no drastic British concession for it was declared in his Governor-General's Instructions that the end envisaged for British India was a place among the sovereign's dominions. He discussed this with Simon, Sir Malcolm Hailey, Governor of U.P., and referred questions relating to the implications of Dominion Status for India to his Home Department. In July he reached England for mid-term leave, bringing these twin ideas for a conciliatory move.

He found support in the new Labour Government. The plan came to fruition in his declaration of 31 October that he was authorized by His Majesty's Government 'to state clearly that in their judgement it is implicit in the declaration of 1917 that the natural issue of India's constitutional progress, as there contemplated, is the attainment of Dominion status'. It also presaged an invitation to representatives of British and Princely India to meet the government after Simon's Commission had reported 'for the purpose of conference and discussion in regard both to the British-Indian and All-Indian problems'. But Irwin's initiative was lucky to have survived. Eminent jurists, Birkenhead and Reading, former Conservative Secretary of State for India and Liberal Viceroy respectively, opposed it in alliance, as eventually did Simon. They took their stand on the policy issue involved and the repercussions of the declaration on the standing of the Parliamentary Commission which had yet to report: but it became in Lloyd George's hands a stick to beat the government with and also a weapon in a Tory intrigue to remove Baldwin from the Conservative leadership. The announcement's survival in the cross currents of British party politics owed much to the determined cooperation of the Tory Viceroy and the Labour Cabinet, but also to a web of misunderstanding which kept Baldwin and Simon neutral till a late stage in the planning. At the last moment when the issues were clear and the virulence of the Tory opposition exposed,

---

[54] Goschen to Irwin, 26 February 1929, Mss. EUR.C.152 (23).

Baldwin tried to get the declaration postponed. He failed because Irwin refused point blank, and was backed by the Cabinet. The Viceroy argued that Indian political leaders and Princes had already been told privately of the announcement, and any postponement would jeopardize what augured well to be a successful venture.[55]

Irwin and his governors had seen prominent Indians in the week before the announcement was due, to pave the way for a cooperative response. From Jinnah and Sapru he gathered that Gandhi and Motilal would respond favourably and agree to go to London. He reported to his ally at the India Office, Wedgwood Benn, 'I accordingly hope for the best... But in any case I have little doubt that we shall rally enough support to introduce into ranks and policy of opponents a good deal of difficulty.'[56] On 26 October he wrote personally to a selection of leaders including Sapru, M. M. Malaviya, Motilal, Vithalbhai Patel, Shafi, Jayakar and Purshotamdas Thakurdas – but not Gandhi – announcing the purport of the declaration. His U.P. intermediary, Sir Grimwood Mears, described Sapru as 'pleased beyond measure' when he received the letter, though Motilal was less pleased and of course constricted by party commitments in the response he could make. Sapru still believed that Gandhi would take it favourably, and promised that he would do all he could to win over the older

[55] S of S to V, telegrams, 29 & 30 October 1929; V to S of S, telegram, 29 October 1929, Mss. EUR.C.152 (10). On 14 November Benn wrote to Irwin explaining the crisis which hit the plan for a declaration after Irwin had returned to India: he enclosed a Secret Cabinet Paper (C.P. 307 (29)) giving details of the episode: Mss. EUR.C.152 (5).

A very detailed analysis of the genesis of the Irwin Declaration, the campaign against it in England and the Parliamentary debates on it is in Moore, *Crisis of Indian Unity*, pp. 51–94. The government maintained that the Declaration meant no real policy change; and it was the presence of this goal stated in his Governor-General's Instructions which gave Irwin the confidence to go ahead with the initiative. The opponents of the idea were worried that it would be interpreted as a sign of radical policy change, and argued that Dominion Status was a considerable advance on the goal of responsible government declared by Montagu in 1917, in view of Balfour's 1926 definition of Dominionhood. They also based their attack on the grounds that by issuing before the Simon Commission's report it would compromise the liberty of the Commission.

G. Peele argues that Irwin deliberately attempted 'to delude and pacify Indian opinion' by using a phrase which to Indians would mean equality with the white Dominions, knowing that English politicians would consider it meaningless in India's case. However she bases this argument solely on two accounts by Lord Salisbury of discussions with Irwin in 1929, during which Irwin apparently maintained that the fulfilment of this goal was not in sight. It should however be remembered that this was precisely what moderate Indians were arguing privately, and in no way detracted from their desire for a declaration such as Irwin was proposing. See G. Peele, 'A Note on the Irwin Declaration', *The Journal of Imperial and Commonwealth History*, I, 3 (May 1973), pp. 331–7.

See also Templewood, *Nine Troubled Years* (London, 1954), pp. 45–6; Halifax, *Fulness of Days* (London, 1957), pp. 117–19. The text of Irwin's Declaration is in *India in 1929–30* (Calcutta, 1931), pp. 466–8.

[56] V to S of S, telegram, 26 October 1929, Mss. EUR.C.152 (10); Sir Grimwood Mears to Irwin, 25 October 1929, Mss. EUR.C.152 (23).

Congressmen.[57] M. A. Ansari considered Irwin's statement 'a godsend', and went with Vallabhbhai to Meerut to discuss it with Gandhi, whom they found 'less enthusiastic, more cautious, but on the whole, taking a very favourable view of the announcement'.[58]

Moonje had predicted that Gandhi would smoothe the Congress path to acceptance of such an offer. Congress's response to the imperial overture was decided in two types of gathering – the inner group of the Working Committee meeting with prominent Liberals, and then the annual session. Here was a new test of Gandhi's all-India leadership. He had to 'lead' in intensive discussion and negotiation once a concrete government proposal was on the table; and sell the decision of the inner group to the open Congress.

The first round of discussion, between the Working Committee and interested Liberals, occurred in November. In this setting the interaction of Gandhi, the two Nehrus and Sapru was of prime importance. However, each of them had to look beyond their immediate circle of negotiators to those whom their decision would affect, and on whose reaction depended the viability of any course they chose. Shades of the Liberals, Mahasabha Hindus, Muslims, and of the independence-wallahs who would flock to Lahore, hovered over the main decision-makers, reminding them of the parameters within which they could act.

Their informal meeting in Delhi on 1/2 November produced a joint statement appreciating Irwin's declaration and the government's 'desire ...to placate Indian opinion'; and hoping that they would be able to cooperate in their effort to evolve a scheme of 'Dominion Constitution suitable for India's needs'. The signatories noted that they interpreted the declaration as meaning 'that the Conference is to meet not to discuss when Dominion Status is to be established but to frame a scheme of Dominion Constitution'; and that they felt that before such a conference could succeed it was vital that certain steps should be taken to inspire trust and ensure the cooperation of Indian political organizations. The points they listed were (i) a policy of general conciliation, (ii) a general amnesty for political prisoners, and (iii) the effective representation of progressive political organizations at the conference, the largest contingent being that of Congress. They also hoped that India would be administered in a more liberal spirit before the new constitution came into existence.[59]

[57] Mears to Irwin, 30 October 1929, *ibid.* Irwin's letter to prominent Indians, 26 October 1929, *ibid.* (This was apparently sent to the Chancellor and Standing Committee of the Chamber of Princes, Sapru, Malaviya, Maulvi Muhammad Yakub, Motilal Nehru, Vithalbhai Patel, Sir Abdul Qayum, Mian Shah Nawaz, Shafi, Jayakar, Thakurdas, Sir Ibrahim Rahimtullah, V. S. S. Sastri, A. H. Ghaznavi, Sir Ali Imam, the Nawab of Chhitari, Mahmudabad and Bikaner. However this list appended to the letter is evidently incomplete because in the J. Nehru Papers (part I, vol. XXVIII) there is a similar letter dated 26 October from Irwin to J. Nehru.)

[58] M. A. Ansari to Gandhi, 13 February 1930, NMML, Microfilm, M. A. Ansari Papers.

[59] Joint Statement, 2 November 1929, *The Hindustan Times*, 4 November 1929, *CWMG*, XLII, 80–1.

It looked as though unanimity had been reached: but behind the joint statement there was serious discord. Gandhi had told Sastri that he knew that the new constitution could not embody full Dominion Status, but he wanted limitations on such topics as the army and the Princely states to be removable automatically on a specified date, and to be laid down with Indians' full consent. He was obviously very concerned about an amnesty for political prisoners. Not only did he identify emotionally with them as one committed to sedition: he must also have realized that on their fate would hinge the reaction of many younger men in and outside Congress to the decision the Working Committee made. To Sastri he appeared almost casual about risking the proposed conference on this issue. 'On the whole, he seemed rather carried away by the idea that the Congress ultimatum fixing the 31st December had won its object, and that the promise of further result lay along similar lines and not along a different procedure which might give us unripe fruit.'[60] The Mahatma, anxious about the younger generation and buoyed up by the success of his Calcutta compromise, faced a divided gathering. Liberal leaders with the backing of Ansari and most of the prominent Congress Muslims pressed for an unconditional acceptance of Irwin's offer. Bose opposed acceptance, in company with Jawaharlal who believed that it gave no assurance of Dominion Status in the near future. Jawaharlal's attitude stiffened his father's. Ultimately the rifts were covered – to the extent of a joint statement. But Gandhi had had to put extreme pressure on Jawaharlal to sign, arguing that he could not go against the wishes of the Working Committee when he was a member, and that it was wisest to accept whatever was given and fight on from there. For the sake of unity with the Liberals Gandhi waived his original stipulation that the three points noted in their statement should be called conditions, and adopted Sapru's formula which appeared in the published version. The Liberals led by Sapru agreed on these terms to strengthen Gandhi's hand 'in keeping Congress on the right side of the line'.[61]

[60] V. S. S. Sastri to Vaman Rao, 7 November 1929, NAI, V. S. Srinivasa Sastri Papers, S No. 525.

[61] V. S. S. Sastri to Vaman Rao, 7 & 13 November 1929, Sastri Papers, S Nos. 525 & 528; Sapru to V. S. S. Sastri, 10 November 1929, Sastri Papers, S No. 526; V to S of S, telegram, 2 November 1929, MSS. EUR.C.152 (10); M.A. Ansari to Gandhi, 13 February 1930, Ansari Papers. For Gandhi's pressure on Jawaharlal see G. Birla to Thakurdas, 3 November 1929, Thakurdas Papers, File No. 91/1929; 2 November 1929, Diary of B. S. Moonje; M. to J. Nehru, 7 November 1929, J. Nehru Papers, part I, vol. LXIX; S. C. Bose to his Mother, 5 November 1929, S. K. Bose (ed.) *Subhas Chandra Bose Correspondence 1924–1932* (Calcutta, 1967), p. 403.

For J. Nehru's attitude see draft for a response to the Declaration, *SWJN*, 4, pp. 175–8; this is misplaced in the published collection, as is pointed out in D. A. Low, 'The Purna Swaraj Decision 1929: new potentialities for Indian Nationalist Biography', Wang Gungwu (ed.), *Self and Biography: Essays on the Individual and Society in Asia* (Australian Academy of the Humanities, 1975). This is an important, detailed article on the November–December discussions, with particular emphasis on the interplay between the two Nehrus, Gandhi and Sapru.

Some Liberals who were not at the meeting criticized Sapru and Sastri for signing the statement. But they argued back that their support for Irwin's move was unconditional and that it would be disastrous for the country and themselves if they allowed Congress to be isolated and Gandhi to be swayed by Jawaharlal and his sympathizers. Sapru was prepared for compromise with Congress if it heralded.

> peace and goodwill. Can we honestly deny that the Congress represents the majority political party and has got a hold on popular mind which we Liberals have not got and are not likely to get[?] If the Liberal Party is going to play the part of respectable conservatives I can foresee a much more gloomy future for it than its past. This is just one of those occasions when the Liberal Party can rescue itself from its present position if it will function as a centre party in the country and be the connecting link between the Government and the people.

In Sapru's endeavour to relate the Liberals both to the raj and to their compatriots, he turned to Gandhi as their link with Congress, believing him to be the one who could exert the necessary pressure on Jawaharlal. It looked as if Jawaharlal, too, had calculated that he needed Gandhi, though for him the object was unity behind the one man who had proved able to lead a mass movement.[62] As at Calcutta the different needs of Indians impelled Gandhi into a position of particular leverage. Gandhi, though ambivalent about the declaration and the political methods it presupposed, was willing to play this lubricant role rather than break decisively with Liberals whose support would be influential in negotiation with the government, with the Nationalist Muslims whose adherence to Congress 'proved' its representative character, or with Jawaharlal whose supporters could make or mar any plans for a non-violent united campaign against the raj. In so doing he kept his options open, a course in keeping with his attitude to Congress and his future role in the months since Calcutta.

However, the unity of the Delhi statement was short-lived. On the same day Bose resigned from the Working Committee to free himself for public criticism of the statement; and Jawaharlal followed suit on 4 November, resigning from the Working Committee and as General Secretary of the AICC.[63] He wrote in anguish to Gandhi defending his resignation in view of his opposition to the statement. In retrospect his allegiance to the Trade Union Congress, the Independence for India League and the youth movement weakened the appeal Gandhi had made to disciplined cohesion within the Working Committee. Gandhi realized that if Jawaharlal broke with him openly and refused to preside at Lahore his own refusal of the Congress presidency in favour of Jawaharlal would be rendered useless and

---

[62] Sapru to D. G. Dalvi, 12 November 1929 (D 8), A.N.U., Sapru Papers, Series II; for J. Nehru's desire to keep Congress ranks close knit on the eve of a struggle with the British see his *An Autobiography*, pp. 196–7.

[63] S. C. Bose to AICC President, 2 November 1929, J. Nehru to AICC President, 4 November 1929, AICC Papers, 1929, File No. G 117; Bose, *The Indian Struggle 1920–1942*, p. 172.

his plan to incorporate younger men into the Congress establishment and draw the fire of their opposition shattered. He wrote and wired at once to soothe Jawaharlal, urging him not to resign because it would affect the national cause and there was in any case no principle at stake. Motilal, too, weighed in. He had been exhorting people to sign the Delhi statement. But on receiving his son's letter of resignation he encouraged him with the argument that the government was unlikely to accept the statement's 'conditions' and the Working Committee, strengthened with the agreement of those who had signed at Delhi, would be able to recommend to Congress civil disobedience and complete independence as its goal. He urged him not to rush into resignation, and when he heard news of the House of Lords debate on Irwin's Declaration he wrote, 'Congrats... There is no question of resignations now. The dustbin is the only safe place for the Delhi statement. The matter for immediate consideration is the mobilization of our own forces.'[64]

An open rift between Jawaharlal and Gandhi was averted; but on 9 November Sapru saw Motilal and scented danger that the working Committee might backtrack when it met in Allahabad in mid-November. However, he still hoped he might in alliance with Malaviya prevail over this trend towards the Jawaharlal line.[65] Vallabhbhai and Vithalbhai Patel were also disturbed at the prospect of the Working Committee throwing over the Delhi statement. Vallabhbhai wrote in this vein to Gandhi, telling him, too, of Jinnah's belief in the Labour Government's good faith and offer to act as intermediary with Irwin in an attempt to make the most of an opportunity which should not be missed.[66]

As pressure on Gandhi built up, for and against the Delhi statement, during the first fortnight of November his views hardened and he evinced a growing mistrust of British intentions, in reaction to news of the Parliamentary debates on Irwin's Declaration and presumably also to Jawaharlal's outburst. After the Delhi meeting Gandhi had professed himself 'dying to give and secure true heart cooperation'. In *Young India* on 7 November, an article which must have been written during his interchange with Jawaharlal, he spoke of the Delhi statement as based on trust which might turn out to be illusory, and argued that if this happened Congress would be more justified in taking strong action than if it had not made the gesture. Moreover he made it plain that the points noted in the statement

[64] J. Nehru to Gandhi, 4 November 1929, Gandhi to J. Nehru, 4 November 1929 (telegram), 6 November 1929, and 8 November 1929, J. Nehru Papers, part 1, vol. XXII; M. to J. Nehru, 6 & 7 November 1929, *ibid.* vol. LXIX. Irwin reported these attempts 'to keep Jawaharlal in play' to Wedgwood Benn, 13 November 1929, Mss. EUR.C.152 (5).

[65] Sapru to V. S. S. Sastri, 10 November 1929, Sastri Papers, S No. 526; Sapru to V. J. Patel, 11 November 1929 (P 12), Sapru Papers, Series I.

[66] Vallabhbhai Patel to Gandhi, 11 November 1929, *CWMG*, XLII, 517–18; 12 November 1929, Diary of B. S. Moonje; V. J. Patel to Sapru, 13 November 1929 (P 13), Sapru Papers, Series I,

were in reality conditions. 'Stripped of the courtesy becoming a document of that nature, the co-operation promised there is conditional upon certain events happening.' In the next three days he announced that there could be no peace without a 'full response to what must be frankly considered to be the conditions enumerated in the leaders' manifesto'; and advised people not to take too much interest in leaders' parleys but to concentrate on developing their own strength which alone could bring swaraj.[67]

Two days before the Working Committee met he stated that he still wished to cooperate. 'I can wait for the Dominion Status constitution, if I can get the real Dominion Status in action, if, that is to say, there is a real change of heart, a real desire on the part of the British people to see India a free and self-respecting nation and on the part of the officials in India a true spirit of service.' He included in his conception of Dominion Status the ability to end the British connection and noted that it was 'highly likely that the Labour Government has never meant all the implications mentioned by me'. He also told the M.P., Fenner Brockway, that the Parliamentary debates did not reassure him that the conference might not prove a dangerous trap, and he proposed to do what he had done with Smuts in South Africa, require an assurance before cooperating.[68]

The Working Committee on 16/19 November was attended by the two Nehrus, Gandhi, Malaviya, A. K. Azad, M. A. Ansari, J. Bajaj, J. M. Sen Gupta, P. Sitaramayya and Subhas Bose – despite his resignation. They were joined on 18th by a group of signatories to the Delhi statement. Among these was Sapru who gathered from meetings with Gandhi, Motilal, and Malaviya on the previous two days that they did not want to mar the proposed conference. He had persuaded Gandhi that they should give the government a chance to show itself in earnest over Irwin's Declaration. However Gandhi had indicated to him that his leadership position was delicate: he needed something from the government to enable him to put the younger men into 'a reasonable and hopeful frame of mind'. This meant, for example, the release of political prisoners not charged with violence. At the joint meeting Gandhi stuck by his agreement with Sapru, while Jawaharlal renewed his attack on Irwin's Declaration and the Delhi statement, supported by Jamnadas Mehta, Bose and Sen Gupta. Significantly his only Muslim backer was Dr Alam of the Punjab. Jawaharlal's hand was strengthened, as Motilal had predicted, by the Parliamentary debates on the Declaration during which opposition from many Conservatives and Liberals was plain and the government underlined that the Declaration meant no new policy. After the clash among Congressmen discussion was

[67] Telegram to ed., *Daily Express*, c. 3 November 1929, *CWMG*, XLII, 87; *Young India*, 7 November 1929, *ibid.* pp. 112–13; Gandhi to ed., *Kaiser-i-Hind*, 8 November 1929, *ibid.* p. 123; *Navajivan*, 10 November 1929, *ibid.* pp. 132–3.
[68] *Young India*, 14 November 1929, *ibid.* pp. 150–1; Gandhi to Fenner Brockway, 14 November 1929, *ibid.* p. 161.

postponed for several hours; but ultimately a resolution was passed endorsing the Delhi statement with the proviso that it was 'clearly understood that this confirmation is constitutionally limited to the date of the holding of the forthcoming session of the Congress'.[69]

It looked as if Jawaharlal had bowed to the Mahatma once again, in agreeing to the confirmation and withdrawing his resignation at the Working Committee's request. But Gandhi had moved significantly since Delhi and indicated this to Jawaharlal. He had, presumably during the adjournment on the 18th, given Jawaharlal a draft resolution to peruse, with a covering note urging him to take his full part in the evening discussion and not suppress himself except where he felt he should, since everyone had to serve according to his own lights and not to borrowed ones.[70] Gandhi's draft was subsequently modified to set the Lahore Congress as the deadline of the phase during which the confirmation of the Delhi statement would be valid whereas the original had approved the act of the Congress signatories at Delhi and deferred consideration of the matter to Lahore. Moreover it was understood between Gandhi and Jawaharlal after Gandhi's note that he would not subject Jawaharlal to such pressure as he had in Delhi, or the previous year at Calcutta.

Jawaharlal was convinced that the struggle was on. When Srinivasa Iyengar resigned from the Working Committee, alleging that its resolution was unjustified and departed from Congress's goal of independence and its stand at Calcutta, Jawaharlal replied:

> The proceedings of the so-called leaders' Conferences are strange enough but they must appear stranger at a distance. The great redeeming feature however is the approach of the Congress which will automatically put an end to all such conferences and their activities. It is clear enough that there is not an outside chance of the British Government acceding to the four conditions laid down. So that even moderate Congressmen will have no alternative left except to stick to independence.[71]

Moreover, speaking at Nagpur as President of the All-India Trade Union Congress on 30 November, he told his audience that he stood by independence still, that excitement over Irwin's Declaration was 'rapidly cooling

[69] Longhand draft by J. Nehru for Congress Bulletin No. 15, giving account of Working Committee meeting, AICC Papers, 1929, File No. 43; Sir Malcolm Hailey to Irwin, 20 November 1929, Sapru to Irwin, 25 November 1929, Mss. EUR.C.152 (23); Coatman, *Years of Destiny*, pp. 263–9, on the parliamentary debates and their repercussions in India souring Indian opinion and prejudicing Irwin's efforts. The Lords debate on 5 November is reported in *The Parliamentary Debates (Official Report). Fifth Series – Volume LXXV. Lords. 1929–30. Vol. 75*, cols. 372–426; the Commons debate on 7 November is reported in *ibid. Vol. 231, Commons, 1929–30*, cols. 1303–39.

[70] Gandhi's draft resolution for Working Committee, 18 November 1929, *CWMG*, XLII, 181; Gandhi to J. Nehru, 18 November 1929, J. Nehru Papers, part I, vol. XXII.

[71] J. Nehru to S. Iyengar, 20 November 1929, AICC Papers, 1929, File No. G 117. See also J. Nehru's letters to B. V. Burli, 20 November 1929, and Satyapal, 21 November 1929, *SWJN*, 4, pp. 172, 173–4.

as subsequent events have revealed the true inwardness of the situation'
and they should prepare for the struggle ahead. Irwin, however, took this
speech overall to mean that Nehru was 'still trying to keep one foot in each
camp. His heart is no doubt with the Independence men and ultra-extremists
generally, but his reason tells him that his material interests and his
political future depend, for the present at any rate, on his alliance with Mr
Gandhi.'[72] Sapru was uneasy about Gandhi's position despite the apparent
success of the moderate line at Allahabad; and he urged Irwin to see Gandhi
to strengthen his hand as a man of peace in relation to his fiercer followers.
Sastri, too, was worried. From the tone of Nehru's Nagpur address he
feared that Jawaharlal was going to 'swallow Gandhi'. More pessimistic than
Sapru, he also believed Gandhi would accept that position and was perhaps
eagerly awaiting a chance to use his 'mighty weapon' of satyagraha.[73]

Gandhi told C. F. Andrews, an intimate friend and British sympathizer
of long standing, that he was doing his 'utmost best to smooth the way
of Lord Irwin'. But an American who visited him at Sabarmati with a
conciliatory message from Irwin reported back that the situation was very
serious. Gandhi appeared quiet and gentle, but he was not looking for a
compromise and reiterated the four points of the Delhi statement as his
last word. He thought that although Irwin and the Labour Prime Minister
and Secretary of State were eager to grant Dominion Status in a reasonable
time the Labour Cabinet was divided and lacked power in Parliament to
carry through a programme which would satisfy India. He would advocate
independence as India's goal and would be ready to initiate civil disobedience if the four points were not met; but he was willing to see Irwin with
Motilal if there was discussion on the four points, though he had little hope
of agreement.[74] Gandhi's reluctance to slam the door to negotiation even
at this late stage, combined with a tough stance on the Delhi 'conditions'
reflected his wish to keep Congress united. Outright rejection of Irwin's
offer or outright acceptance would split the Congress, and the Mahatma
maintained a fine middle course. The government recognized his political
dilemma:[75] but it was too sanguine in its calculations of the forces making
Gandhi a man of peace. During the year, as Congress had waited for the
raj's response to its ultimatum, a militant determination to resort to direct
action and abandon the caution of the established Congress leaders had

[72] J. Nehru's presidential address to AITUC, Nagpur, 30 November 1929, *ibid.*
pp. 49–55; V to S of S, telegram, 12 December 1929, Mss. EUR.C.152 (10).

[73] Sapru to Irwin, 25 November 1929, Mss. EUR.C.152 (23); Sastri to Sir P. S.
Sivaswami Aiyar, 2 & 10 December 1929, Jagadisan, *Letters of Srinivasa Sastri*, pp.
183–4, 186.

[74] Gandhi to C. F. Andrews, 19 November 1929, *CWMG*, XLII, 187; Sherwood Eddy
to Irwin, 3 December 1929, Mss. EUR.C.152 (23). Gandhi's public pronouncements
in early December confirmed Eddy's report: see *Navajivan*, 24 November, 8 December 1929, *CWMG*, XLII, 208–9, 250–1.

[75] H. G. Haig to P.S.V., 24 November 1929, Home Poll., 1930, File No. 98; Irwin
repeated this almost exactly to the Secretary of State, telegram, 26 November 1929,
Mss. EUR.C.152 (10).

hardened among many younger Congressmen and radical groups on the fringes of Congress. Simultaneously many experienced Congressmen in the middle and older generations were increasingly convinced that the British intended to make an inadequate response to their demands, and aware that unless they toughened their stand they risked losing the support of their more militant countrymen. J. M. Sen Gupta put these arguments firmly to Motilal in mid-December, impressing on him the importance of changing the Congress creed to incorporate the goal of independence at the forthcoming session and avert accusations of 'vacillation or half-heartedness'. The need to attract support from younger men and fringe groups was particularly important in his own Bengal where the local Congress was split into two main factions, goading both to seek local support, and where the challenge of terrorism to constitutional politics was formidable.[76] The logic of confrontation with the raj was clearer in late December when Irwin and Gandhi met.

Irwin knew that he could do nothing to assure Congress on the major points raised at Delhi. The proposed conference could not frame a Dominion constitution; Indian representatives would have to come from all groups and shades of opinion, and therefore Congress could not expect the lion's share; and there could be no amnesty. However, he tried to handle the situation delicately, not wanting to 'hit people over the shins while they are trying not too ungracefully to climb down off a high pedestal which they have found uncomfortable'.[77] In late November conversation with Jinnah convinced him that the amnesty question would be crucial in determining the Congress decision, and he referred the matter to his Home Member in case there was any area of compromise. But on Crerar's advice he decided that an amnesty would not conciliate the men Gandhi had in mind as he pressed this demand. He did, however, urge his governors to go slow with new prosecutions for sedition while Congress was still vacillating.[78] Moreover he agreed through Jinnah's mediation to see

[76] J. M. Sen Gupta to M. Nehru, 18 December 1929, AICC Papers, 1929, File No. G-99.

[77] Irwin to Wedgwood Benn, 6 November 1929, Mss. EUR.C.152 (5); Irwin's reaction to the Delhi statement is in V to S of S, telegram, 3 November 1929, Mss. EUR.C.152 (10).

[78] Irwin to Governors of Madras, Bombay, Bengal, U.P., Punjab, Burma, Bihar & Orissa, C.P., Assam, 12 December 1929, Mss. EUR.C.152 (23).
  Irwin told Wedgwood Benn how he thought about an amnesty on 12 December 1929, Mss. EUR.C.152 (5): he referred the matter to Sir James Crerar, his Home Member, on 21 November and Crerar replied on 2 December, Mss. EUR.C.152 (23). Crerar argued, 'We must consider who are really interested in the amnesty question. The Moderates are not very really or directly interested. The wild young men will not be placated by anything we can give. The less extreme Congress men want to have something to show in the way of concession by Government to keep these young men from extreme courses. I am afraid, therefore, that our original position that all we can do is likely to bring us little gratitude or profit still in the main stands, and the great body of moderate opinion in India, including such elements as the Muhammadans and all the men of substance who are not politicians – not merely

Gandhi, Motilal, Sapru, Vithalbhai Patel and Jinnah, more in the hope of strengthening the moderate politicians than of influencing Congress policy.[79]

Gandhi approached the meeting with Irwin without any hopes of a compromise. Meanwhile Motilal had moved further away from Sapru and Ansari. The latter, asked his opinion by Motilal on 22 December, advised against breaking with Irwin in view of their internal dissensions, weakness and lack of preparation for conflict: Motilal merely said his observations were based on weakness.[80] On 23rd, the day they were to meet Irwin, Motilal, Jinnah, Patel and Sapru had preliminary talks and agreed on the subjects of political prisoners, the conference date and personnel. Sapru had no idea that he, Patel and Jinnah were going 'to be let down so badly' by Gandhi and Motilal; although Sarojini Naidu warned him to be careful as he was getting into the car bound for the Viceregal interview.[81]

Gandhi opened the discussion courteously by expressing horror at the bomb attack on the Viceroy's train that morning; but then plunged straight into the controversy by saying that it was pointless to have discussions until it was clear that the function of the proposed conference was to frame a Dominion constitution. Irwin stood by his Declaration: the conference was free to discuss any proposals put before it but they could not lay down beforehand that it was to draft a particular constitution. Gandhi maintained that he could not participate in it unless Irwin assured him that the Cabinet would back his demand for immediate Dominion Status at the conference and in Parliament. Motilal lined up with Gandhi, while Jinnah and Sapru reasoned with them at length. As the discussion appeared to get bogged down, Irwin said that the real test was whether Gandhi and his colleagues believed in the British purpose. Gandhi replied that he recognized the sincerity of individuals but doubted broadly the sincerity of British intentions. There followed further discussion between Irwin's visitors whether the new position was any advance on the position established by the 1919 Act. (This had of course been fiercely debated in Parliament.) The conversation then moved to the communal question, and Gandhi made it clear that he did not wish to go to London, weakened as Indians were by these divisions. As Motilal remembered, 'Your idea so far as I could gather was

the Ditchers and last-ditchers – would be, as it always is, distressed and depressed by anything that could be represented as a climb-down by Government.'
[79] Irwin to Crerar, 21 November 1929, Jinnah to Irwin, 3 December 1929, Mss. EUR.C.152 (23); Irwin to Wedgwood Benn, 19 December 1929, Mss. EUR.C.152 (5). Jinnah had been to Ahmedabad to achieve this meeting, and had talked for several hours with Gandhi and the Patel brothers: he still judged from talking to Gandhi that the situation was hopeful, but he thought Sapru's presence essential at the meeting with Irwin; Jinnah to Sapru, 3 December 1929, Sapru Papers, Series II.
[80] M. A. Ansari to Gandhi, 13 February 1930, Ansari Papers; Sir Malcolm Hailey, Governor of U.P., to Irwin, 19 December 1929, Mss. EUR.C.152 (23); Gandhi to M. Trikumji, 21 December 1929, *CWMG*, XLII, 301.
[81] Sapru to Sir Ali Imam, 5 January 1930, Sapru Papers, Series II; Sir Grimwood Mears to Irwin, 6 January 1930, Mss. EUR.C.152 (24).

that it was owing to this very weakness that you considered it necessary to have the assurance of support from the British Cabinet and that if we were united the Government could not refuse the demand for Dominion Status.'[82] After two and a half hours the discussion closed, without touching on the other points of the Delhi statement such as the amnesty and the personnel of the conference.

During this encounter Gandhi was the main Congress spokesman. For him and Motilal the crux of the matter was the degree to which power would be transferred from Britain to India as a result of the conference. For Gandhi this was tied to the question of Indian weakness which stemmed largely from Indian disunity. Throughout the 1920s he had preached self-strengthening and unity as the only road to swaraj. Now when offered a conference he knew that his negotiating hand would be weak as Indians had not responded to his exhortations. The only remedy was guaranteed backing from the Cabinet. Irwin, like Sapru, was deeply disappointed at the failure of the meeting. At the time Irwin urged that they should not let slip an opportunity for 'doing something big'; but his pessimism before the meeting soon hardened into belief that the conference spokesmen had never wanted to attend the Round Table Conference. In his judgement they preferred a detached position from which Congress could grudgingly accept or violently criticize. If government had prejudged the conference and given the assurance Gandhi demanded Congress would have been from the start successful champion of a popular cause, and protected from the wreck of its national claim on the rock of communal differences.[83]

In the two months between Irwin's Declaration and the Lahore Congress Gandhi was the central figure in Congress deliberations. Contemporaries among Liberals and in government thought that the way Gandhi threw his weight would be crucial: they angled for his support and attempted to strengthen his hand. Moreover it was to Gandhi alone that Jawaharlal would bend. Gandhi gained a unique position of leverage in the face-to-face negotiations of November and December because the different groups involved needed him to ease their relations with each other. However

[82] M. Nehru to Gandhi, 18 February 1930, M. Nehru Papers, Subject File – Viceroy's Conference. In this letter Motilal noted his own corrections of the minutes of the meeting with Irwin, which he enclosed. The minutes, by G. Cunningham, Irwin's P.S.V., are also in the Sapru Papers and in L/PO/14, with corrections made by Sapru. Motilal and Sapru both inserted further evidence of Gandhi's reluctance to go to the Conference because of communal disunity. The first report of the meeting was in V to S of S, telegram, 24 December 1929, Mss. EUR.C.152 (10). See also *India in 1929–30*, pp. 92–3. Cunningham's minutes are quoted fairly fully in B. R. Nanda, *The Nehrus. Motilal and Jawaharlal* (London, 1962), pp. 322–3.

Gandhi in retrospect played down the influence of younger opinion on him in the break with Irwin, insisting that he had never been sanguine about the proposed Conference '...the central thing I insisted on was that the Conference should apply itself to a scheme of Dominion Status suited to the needs of India'. *Young India*, 20 March 1930, *CWMG*, XLIII, 44.

[83] Irwin to Wedgwood Benn, 26 December 1929, L/PO/14; Irwin to Wedgwood Benn, 3 October 1930, Mss. EUR.C.152 (6).

Gandhi 'led' not just in the November compromises but in the December break with Irwin. This demonstrated the constraints within which he had to operate if he was to lead. Gandhi realized that he must not risk a split in Congress on the lines which he had averted at Calcutta. Faced with the choice of forgoing Liberal support or abandoning Jawaharlal, he chose the former, adhering to the tactic of integrating and taming Jawaharlal for the sake of his admirers and adherents which he had pursued first in the engineering behind Jawaharlal's election as Congress President. Jawaharlal was symbolic of a large build-up of frustration directed at Congress's established leaders: if Gandhi broke with him now and back-peddled on the Calcutta ultimatum Congress would probably split apart, creating still further cleavages in the unity Gandhi was attempting to forge among Indians. Communal divisions also restricted the Mahatma's manoeuvring space. As the meeting with Irwin indicated, the logic and opportunities of confrontation made more sense than negotiation from a divided base. Within Gandhi himself there was a further force making for conflict rather than compromise. In the distressing political scene of communal demands, provincial differences and erupting violence, satyagraha was the only weapon he could conceive of as purifying public life and neutralizing violence. In the darkest hour satyagraha and its devotees must prove themselves. As Sastri had realized, this was Gandhi's mighty weapon and as a satyagrahi he resorted to it when the conditions for a conference did not appear to ensure success.[84]

Late in December the focus of the political scene shifted to Lahore, where Gandhi's leadership was tried in a different kind of gathering. The question now was whether he had correctly judged the trend of opinion outside the Working Committee and would be able to sell the result of the negotiations to the Congress session in such a way as to ensure a measure of cohesion and control in the forthcoming confrontation with the raj.

Before delegates met in Lahore the problems of cohesion and control promised to be grave. Evidence from the provinces suggested that there was little unanimity among Congressmen or willingness to submit to continental discipline. Only after heated discussion and by a majority of 139 to 103 did the Bihar PCC pass a resolution that the Lahore Congress should decide for complete independence. The Assam PCC was clearly anxious to avoid an extreme policy and rejected a resolution recommending the start of an independence movement from 1 January if the government did not give India Dominion Status by 31 December. In Bengal the split between the factions led by Sen Gupta and Bose competed in virulence with an eye to the support of younger Bengalis, but despite 'the general expectation...that the Independence resolution will be carried...grave doubts are expressed whether any boycott will be successful.'[85] Any chance of a com-

---

[84] V. S. S. Sastri to Sir P. S. Sivaswami Aiyar, 2 December 1929, Jagadisan, *Letters of Srinivasa Sastri*, pp. 183–4; *Navajivan*, 8 December 1929, *CWMG*, XLII, 251.

[85] Bihar & Orissa FR1, December 1929, Assam FR1, December 1929, Bengal FR2, December 1929, Home Poll., 1929, File No. 17.

munal alliance such as Gandhi had engineered in the aftermath of Turkey's defeat in 1918 was out, too; and there was likelihood of considerable Muslim and Sikh opposition in Lahore itself during the Congress session.[86] Turbulence and anti-Congress feeling was rife among students and others who converged on Lahore. A large Kirti-Kisan conference expressed distrust of the Congress leadership, supported by large numbers from the simultaneous Nau Jawan Bharat Sabha conference which condemned Motilal and Gandhi and shouted revolutionary slogans.[87] Equally disquieting for Gandhi were signs that many experienced and influential Congress stalwarts and some of his valued colleagues were perturbed at the new stance he had taken partly in the hope of controlling those who clamoured for conflict. These were men at the other end of the Congress spectrum who had rejoiced in Congress's critical cooperation in the institutions of government in the previous decade and were loth to forgo its benefits, as they had made clear when Motilal had tried to impose a boycott of the legislatures earlier in 1929. For some the ramifications of the communal problem reinforced their opposition to conflict with the raj. Syed Mahmud had a long talk with Gandhi on 24th and emphasized the Hindu–Muslim problem, and Ansari repeated the views he had voiced in Delhi on 1 November and to Motilal on 22 December. Pandit Malaviya, N. C. Kelkar and Sarojini Naidu also made known their opposition. Moreover Kelkar presided at a parallel Hindu conference where the opposition of many Punjabi Hindus to the move towards independence demonstrated not only the tensions within Congress produced by regional diversity, but the power behind the Mahasabha's opposition to the efforts of Gandhi and the All-Parties Committee to reach a communal agreement.[88]

[86] Punjab FR1, December 1929, *ibid.* Sir Geoffrey de Montmorency, Governor of Punjab, told Irwin in letter of 29 December that Gandhi and Motilal had been angling for Sikh and Muslim support. 'Of the latter I think Gandhi has now despaired. Old lieutenants like the Ali Brothers have completely gone against his blandishments; but he still has hopes of the Akali Sikhs... Their price is at present too high as to win them he would certainly have to promise publicly special concessions to claims and his colleagues are not likely to stomach this; on the other hand, Gandhi knows that up in this part of India at any rate the campaign must fail unless he can get Muslims and Sikhs to join it.' Mss. EUR.C.152 (23). One result of the discussion between Motilal, Gandhi and some Sikhs was a resolution which had not been among Gandhi's original proposals, assuring Sikhs in particular and Muslims with other minorities in general that Congress would not accept any communal solution in a future constitution which did not satisfy the parties concerned: *CWMG*, XLII, 359, fn. 1.

[87] Punjab FR1, December 1929, Home Poll., 1929, File No. 17; Punjab Govt. to Govt. of India, telegram, 27 December 1929, Home Poll., 1930, File No. 98.

[88] *idem*; S. Mahmud to M. A. Ansari, n.d., Ansari Papers; M. A. Ansari to Gandhi, 13 February 1930, Ansari Papers; Coatman, *Years of Destiny*, pp. 272–3. For the dilemma of Punjabi Hindus see Chief Sec., Punjab Govt., to Home Sec., Govt. of India, 3 January 1930, Home Poll., 1930, File No. 98: 'The Punjab Hindus are between the devil and the deep sea. They distrust the Congress because they fear that it would not hesitate to sacrifice their interests if by so doing it could reach a settlement with Muhammadans. They loathe the idea of Muhammadan domination,

Gandhi therefore came to Lahore with several urgent priorities. He had to soothe those who pressed for peace and prevent a revolt on their part which would shatter the unity he considered so vital. Yet it was essential to integrate the generations within Congress and conciliate the radical, setting the seal on Jawaharlal's presidency and the break with Irwin. He needed to stem the rising tide of violence and provide another outlet for the feeling of which it was symptomatic; and he also had to appeal for communal cooperation in any confrontation with the raj. In this unenviable situation it fell to him 'to conceive and frame practically every resolution'.[89]

On 27 December in the Subjects Committee Gandhi supported the resolution which endorsed the Working Committee's action on the Delhi statement, but now rejected the conference proposal and declared that swaraj in the Congress creed should mean complete independence, *purna swaraj*. The resolution appealed for communal cooperation now that the communal solution proposed in the Nehru Report was no longer at issue since the report had lapsed; and Gandhi underlined this in his speech. He also urged boycott of the legislatures as envisaged in the resolution, as a preparation for civil disobedience which the AICC would be authorized to start when it deemed fit.

> If you like to take part in the legislatures and local bodies, I must frankly tell you that civil disobedience is an impossibility. Civil disobedience undoubtedly requires much discipline, much vigour, and, most of all, absorbing concentration. If you go to the councils, you cannot work up all these absolutely requisite conditions for civil disobedience. If you want to do what has been done in Bardoli, you should now cease to think about such things as the legislative councils, the Assembly, etc. It must be admitted that the country is not at present prepared for civil disobedience, and the country must be prepared for it. If you want me to conduct the civil disobedience movement, I would conduct it. But you must be soldiers of the battle and you must acquire all that is required for civil disobedience.[90]

Gandhi's stand evoked stout opposition largely from those who valued the resources to which constitutional collaboration gave access. He had to fight in committee for the resolution on 29 and 30 December before his opponents gave way and allowed it to be carried forward to the open

and although they could probably rely on the support of the Sikhs in communal matters, they could not obtain their support in questions where the issue was rural *versus* urban. An influential section of the Punjab Hindus, therefore, favours the attitude of the Mahasabha, which is non-commital.'
On the dilemma an all-India Congress presented to Punjabi Hindus see G. A. Heeger, 'The Growth of the Congress Movement in Punjab, 1920–1940', *The Journal of Asian Studies*, XXXII, 1 (November 1972), 39–51.
[89] *Young India*, 20 March 1930, *CWMG*, XLIII, 43. Gandhi's draft resolutions circulated to the Working Committee, *The Hindustan Times*, 28 December 1929, *CWMG*, XLII, 320–2.
[90] Speech in Subjects Committee, 27 December 1929, *ibid*. pp. 324–6.

session. He chided the committee for such unbusinesslike obstruction when the Working Committee was entrusted with drawing up resolutions on its behalf. He fended off the plea by Kelkar and Malaviya to postpone a decision, a request to abandon council boycott because of the feelings it aroused, objections to the preamble endorsing the Delhi statement and expressing appreciation of Irwin's attempts at a settlement, and doubts about the effectiveness of a non-violent campaign for independence. The restrictions on Gandhi's ability to lead the sort of campaign he wanted were clear not just from the opposition but also from his omission from the main resolution of tactics which he favoured but realized Congressmen would not accept – boycott of schools and courts, and non-participation in local boards and municipalities.[91] Moreover, two of his suggested resolutions designed to increase Congress efficiency were thrown out by the Subjects Committee. One which would have made into autonomous organizations the three boycott committees created after Calcutta was defeated by an overwhelming majority: the other which would have cut the size of the AICC to 100 was lost by 111 to 101 votes. By the time he spoke on this question he was thoroughly annoyed at the Subjects Committee's obstruction and uttered a criticism which showed how his mind was working for the coming campaign. 'You want civil disobedience. But you can never expect civil disobedience to be a practical thing with such an unwieldy national body which is to set to the work. I am living for civil disobedience and if need be I will carry on civil disobedience separately.[92]

While Gandhi did battle in committee, the Congress opened on 29 December. The welcome speech from S. Kitchlew as Chairman of the Reception Committee indicated that in this arena Gandhi would face pressure from those who still felt him to be too moderate. Kitchlew demanded a good fighting programme against alien domination which would mobilize peasants and workers and take the form of well organized mass and individual civil disobedience in selected areas. He hoped that Congress

[91] Speeches in Subjects Committee, 29 & 30 December 1929 on the main resolution, and on 30 December 1929 on boycott committee resolution, *ibid.* pp. 329–34, 335–6, 339. Boycott of schools and colleges had been part of Non-cooperation, but Congressmen had worked in local government organs, often to promote Non-cooperation. By March 1930 Gandhi was wishing he had pushed for the boycott of local boards, too, criticizing the energy rival Congressmen dissipated in attacking each other during municipality elections just when the country was preparing for civil disobedience: *Young India*, 12 March 1930, *CWMG*, XLIII, 55 and note by J. Nehru on Bengali Congress disputes, 29 March 1930, *SWJN*, 4, pp. 263–4.
It was understandable that many Congressmen wished to work through local boards because this meant access to resources which were important in local affairs. In Bombay Presidency in 1930–1, for example, local boards had a total income of Rs. 239.81 lakhs, from local levies, taxes and government grants. The major proportions of this were spent on education, public works and medical relief. *Bombay – 1930–31. A Review of the Administration of the Presidency* (Bombay, 1932), pp. 143–4.
[92] Speech in Subjects Committee on size of AICC, 30 December 1929, *CWMG*, XLII, 340–1; speech in Subjects Committee on proposed autonomy of boycott committees, 30 December 1929, *ibid.* pp. 336–9.

4

would make independence it goal, and appealed to Gandhi to lead and the young to follow him and bear the brunt of the battle. 'My appeal is...to Mahatmaji. He is the one leader in whom the masses have faith. He is the one leader who commands nation-wide respect and affection. I appeal to Mahatmaji to lead us in our struggle for...National Independence.' Significantly he added that there should be no suspension of civil disobedience like that which Gandhi imposed after the Chauri Chaura violence in 1922 'which severely disappointed the workers and the country and played havoc with morale'. Jawaharlal followed this up with a presidential call for the goal of complete independence and a struggle through economic and political boycotts.[93]

On 31 December the temper of the open session showed itself. Gandhi moved the resolution deploring the bomb attack on the Viceroy's train, realizing that he was flying in the face of most youthful opinion in Congress. He was opposed by Swami Govindanand from Sind and Dr Alam; and when the vote was taken 942 were for the resolution and 794 against. The vote was disputed and had to be retaken, indicating both the strength of feeling on the violence issue and the narrowness of Gandhi's majority. Most provinces were fairly evenly divided in the vote, but Bengal and Punjab were heavily against Gandhi's resolution, while a large majority within the Gujarat, Andhra, Bihar and Hindi C.P. delegations supported him.

Gandhi then moved the main resolution on independence and civil disobedience: Motilal seconded it. There followed two and a half hours of opposition from various angles, during which a cross section of Congressmen moved amendments. Malaviya, for example, repeated his appeal to postpone any decision until the All-Parties Conference had reconvened and considered the prospect of a Round Table Conference. M. S. Aney wanted Congress to accept the conference invitation and postpone any change of its creed. Kelkar argued that they should try to capture all the power offered in the legislatures: Satyamurti favoured council entry as part of a wide anti-government campaign. At the other end of the spectrum Bose called for a far more adequate campaign than the one Gandhi proposed, involving peasants, workers and young people, and backing civil disobedience and general strikes with an attempt to form a parallel government. He also opposed endorsement of the Working Committee's support for the Delhi statement. Alam argued against expressing appreciation of Irwin's efforts for a settlement. After listening to the outpouring against Gandhi's resolution two men got up to support it, Viswanathan from Andhra and J. M. Sen Gupta, Bose's local Bengali rival. Their main point was that only by supporting this resolution could they win Gandhi to the side of independence and secure his leadership. Sen Gupta's question, 'Do you have in India today any other leader who can lead the country to victory than Mahatma Gandhi?' was greeted with cries of 'No, No'.

[93] *44th I.N.C. Report*; J. Nehru's Presidential address, *SWJN*, 4, pp. 184–98.

Gandhi was not present during the debate, but when he returned he spoke at length rebutting the amendments and asking Congress to accept the resolution *in toto*. Jawaharlal declared that twelve amendments were admissible and should be voted on. All were lost, but the vote on Alam's (802 for and 987 against) again showed that Gandhi's margin of victory was narrow. Of the provinces whose vote was not evenly split, Bengal voted heavily for Alam's amendment, while Gujarat, Andhra, Bihar, Hindi C.P. and Punjab opposed it strongly The resolution congratulating Irwin on his escape from the bomb attack was also narrowly passed, by 904 to 823: but Gandhi's resolution went through with only a handful of opponents amid cries of '*Mahatma Gandhi-ki-jai*'.[94] Gandhi crowned this victory with an eye to the future campaign by insisting on a Working Committee of his choice, arguing that it must be of one mind. Srinivasa Iyengar and Bose were not on the Mahatma's list, and they argued that the committee should be properly elected. When their plea was rejected they formed the Congress Democratic Party, but its basis was personal pique.[95]

Bose described Gandhi as dominating proceedings at Lahore, and the session as a great victory for him, while pressmen noted the adulation given to him. In a sense it was a triumph for him as an all-India leader. He pushed his most important resolutions through a hesitant Subjects Committee and a more militant open session. He secured a Working Committee of picked men – without a major split in Congress. His reading of the political situation in November–December had been correct: by being sensitive and pliant to pressures in Congress he avoided the revolt which threatened in the wake of Irwin's Declaration and also secured his own position. But at Lahore he knew that there was no chance of a Congress–Muslim alliance, and he had frighteningly tangible evidence of the turbulence of many of those on whom he would have to rely for the enactment of his campaign. Moreover, his stand disturbed and alienated not merely Liberals outside Congress but many moderate men within the Congress camp. As a senior CID officer commented, 'Within the Hindu community the Congress has satisfied nobody. Gandhi's bargaining aptitude saved the session itself from dissolution from within, but every point in his programme is bitterly distasteful to one important section or another.'[96]

Opposition to Gandhi at Lahore, voiced and muted, indicated that his leadership position did not rest on the support of a solid bloc of adherents.

[94] *44th I.N.C. Report*; voting figures on bomb outrage resolution and Dr Alam's amendment, AICC Papers, 1929, File No. 33.
For Bose's scorn at Gandhi's lack of plans for an effective campaign see his *The Indian Struggle 1920–1942*, p. 174.
[95] *ibid.* pp. 174–5; J. Nehru to A. Rahim, 7 January 1930, *SWJN*, 4, pp. 205–6: Sitaramayya, *History of the Indian National Congress Volume I*, p. 360.
[96] Appreciation of Lahore Congress by Deputy Inspector-General, C.I.D., in Punjab FR2, December 1929, Home Poll., 1929, File No. 17. This was quoted verbatim in Bombay Secret Abstract, 1930, par. 197, *Source Material for a History of the Freedom Movement in India Vol. III Mahatma Gandhi Part III: 1929–1931* (Bombay, 1969), pp. 3–5 (hereafter *HFM, III, III*).

He was accepted because of the degree of unity his resolution permitted, and because a mass campaign without him appeared impossible. In such circumstances opposition to him looked not only fatal to individuals' political careers but positively unpatriotic.[97] On his part, though he gave way on resolutions he would have liked, he stuck out for his main resolution which he felt would secure the unity he required and the type of campaign he was willing to lead, banking on the fact that he was indispensable to many of those present, and appealing to Congress discipline. But the cracks were barely covered. Gandhi found himself leading Congressmen who presented the appearance of an ill-assorted rabble rather than a group of disciplined followers.

III THE DILEMMAS OF CONFRONTATION

The opening weeks of 1930 were crucial for Gandhi's assertion of authority as an all-India leader. He and Congress were committed to civil disobedience and he faced the dilemmas of actual confrontation with the raj, as the unifying formulae of procrastination until the close of 1929 had run their course. But he had increasingly realized in later 1929 that the continental instruments at his disposal for such action were lamentably weak and undisciplined: and his mind had turned to some form of demonstration which involved himself and his ashram 'storm-troops' alone. Nevertheless such action had to be effective, and this posed for Gandhi the problem of what civil disobedience was meant to effect.

There was little thought and even less unanimity in Congress about the goal of civil disobedience. A few had firm ideas. Bose envisaged it as a step towards establishing a parallel government, while Motilal assumed that they were working for the collapse of the administration.[98] But for most Congressmen it was merely a dramatic means of protest, a catch-all remedy reminiscent of the great days of Non-cooperation. Moreover it could be tailored to suit their particular needs without threatening their local positions or cutting all their links with the administration and its fruits. Gandhi's reluctant concession on boycott of schools, courts and local bodies proved that. Divided among themselves Congressmen resorted to civil disobedience as a cover for a variety of options, and delegated responsibility for precise plans to the AICC, which meant effectively to Gandhi.[99]

Gandhi's perception of the object of civil disobedience, therefore, assumed particular significance. He spoke of civil disobedience for establishing

[97] S. Mahmud told M. A. Ansari (undated letter) that he wanted to press Gandhi further on the communal point, 'but Maulana Azad & yourself were quiet & therefore I thought nobody would hear me & even you two may not like it. The Lahore Resolution was passed & I thought it my duty as true Congress man to support it whether I liked it or not.' Ansari Papers.

[98] Bose, *The Indian Struggle 1920–1942*, p. 174; M. Nehru to Vithalbhai Patel, 12 June 1930, M. Nehru Papers, File P-6.

[99] *Young India*, 9 January 1930, CWMG, XLII, 376; J. Nehru, *An Autobiography*, p. 202.

purna swaraj, complete independence. His more careful exposition of his thoughts showed that he did not intend or envisage a total collapse of the raj. His aim was through the corporate action of satyagraha to generate among Indians the interdependent qualities of strength and unity, fundamental to his ultimate goal of swaraj but vital also in the short term to enable some of them to go to the conference table to negotiate as national representatives, accepted as such by their rulers and their compatriots. The connection in Gandhi's mind between civil disobedience and attendance at a constitutional conference on the right terms, was evident at the Calcutta Congress and immediately after Lahore.[100] In March–April, as he perfected his plan, he described civil disobedience as 'a process of developing internal strength', 'not designed to establish independence but to arm the people with the power to do so'. Moreover in July 1930 when negotiation with the raj was on the cards, he told Jayakar that he was not fighting for victory but to create an intensity of feeling as a demonstration – presumably directed at both British and Indians, combatant and non-combatant.[101]

For Gandhi, therefore, civil disobedience was designed to affect Indians equally or more than the British. This was consistent with two constant themes in his teaching; that satyagraha was both means and ends because of the moral revolution it worked in its exponents, and that real swaraj must grow from within Indian society and could not be wrested from or distributed by an alien power. The precise form of satyagraha had to be adapted to those it was intended to influence. Since Gandhi's primary subjects were his countrymen, he had to plan a campaign which would weld them together in a disciplined unity, gather the maximum support and ensure at least the benevolent neutrality of non-participants.

Gandhi's main consideration was Congressmen. As he knew to his cost they were split by local and vested interest, temperament, ideology and age. Against those who clamoured for decisive action Gandhi had to weigh the hesitant and moderate, those who opposed the idea of council boycott and civil disobedience yet refrained from overt opposition at Lahore and after out of loyalty to Congress. M. M. Malavy resigned from the Working Committee on New Year's Day as a protest at the policy and programme adopted the previous day; and information swiftly reached Gandhi of opposition from many other quarters, particularly on the council boycott issue which had proved intractable in July 1929. Jawaharlal reported on 7 January, 'Rajagopalachari's idea that we may get some of the non-

---

[100] Speech in Subjects Committee, 28 December 1928, *CWMG*, xxxviii, 289; *Young India*, 9 January 1930, *CWMG*, xLii, 377–8. On 23 January 1930 B. Shiva Rao reported to Sapru that Gandhi had apparently not dropped the idea of participating in the Round Table Conference; Sapru Papers, Series ii. An example of Gandhi's shorthand description of civil disobedience for *purna swaraj* is in letter, 30 April 1930, published in the Bombay Congress Bulletin, 2 May 1930, AICC Papers, 1930, File No. G-118.

[101] M. R. Jayakar to T. B. Sapru, 4 August 1930, Jayakar Papers, Correspondence File No. 770; *Young India*, 12 March & 24 April 1930, *CWMG*, xLii, 56, 306.

Congress members out of the legislatures seems to me to be amazingly optimistic. There is no chance of this happening. Indeed it is clear that many Congress members even will stick on or resign and then seek election.'[102] Most of Motilal's intimate friends, among them Rangaswami Aiyengar, M. A. Ansari, A. K. Azad and Sarojini Naidu, felt that he had let them down by throwing in his lot with Jawaharlal and Gandhi in such a policy. Aiyengar, who reported this disarray to B. Shiva Rao, thought that though many Congressmen would resign from the legislatures because of the Congress mandate they would soon revert to council entry even if Congress stuck to the boycott.[103]

Gandhi's new Working Committee, meeting on 2 January, had taken immediate steps to implement the boycott decision, and on 6 January Jawaharlal sent a presidential directive to all PCCs that they should ask MLAs and MLCs in their province to resign from the legislatures, and should report the response to the AICC office immediately. When the Working Committee met on 14–16 February it decided to call for the resignation from Congress elective bodies of all those who had disobeyed the boycott mandate or resigned from councils only to seek re-election. This decision, backed by the threat of disciplinary action, was circulated to PCC secretaries and to offenders.[104] It provoked even more hostility. Nilakantha Das, for example, refused to resign on the grounds that the AICC was a deliberative and not an executive body. M. S. Aney also argued that the AICC and PCCs were not executive bodies, but nevertheless resigned from the AICC since Congress had embarked on a tough struggle and he professed the wish not to embarrass it further 'by raising constitutional questions and opening new grounds of factions or widening old split'. Among others who resigned from the AICC were N. C. Kelkar, N. C. Bardaloi and C. Khaliquzzaman. Kelkar had made his stand at Lahore, and subsequently in *Mahratta* he denounced the Lahore resolutions as an unconvincing bundle of inconsistencies and indicated that if the Working Committee threatened disciplinary action he would not hesitate to break from Congress temporarily. 'That the Congress should so surrender its

[102] J. Nehru to Gandhi, 7 January 1930, *SWJN*, 4, p. 207; see also J. Nehru's press statement, 9 January 1930, in which he noted that 'Leading Congressmen have described the main resolution as outrageous and others have stated that this resolution does not represent the view of the country.' *The Hindu*, 10 January 1930, *ibid.* p. 208.

M. M. Malaviya's letter of resignation, 1 January 1930, AICC Papers, 1929, File No. 117.

[103] B. Shiva Rao to T. B. Sapru, 9 January 1930, Sapru Papers, Series II.

[104] J. Nehru to PCC Secretaries, 6 January and 25 February 1930, *SWJN*, 4, pp. 203, 253–4; a reflection on the Congress organization was Jawaharlal's protest in 25 February letter that most PCCs had not sent him the information requested on 6 January.

Sri Prakasa, AICC General Secretary, to all members of elective Congress committees who had not resigned seats in legislatures or had resigned and sought re-election, 5 March 1930, with covering letter from J. Nehru to selected AICC members, 4 March 1930, AICC Papers, 1930, File No. G-1 (ii).

conscience to Mr Gandhi speaks volumes to the credit of his personality. But it also speaks volumes to the discredit and ignominy of the Indian Political world.'[105]

As a result of Working Committee pressure 33 members of the Central Legislatures had resigned by the end of January. In Bombay by mid-February only 7 provincial legislators had resigned. Responsivists such as Kelkar and Jayakar stuck to their guns, and Jamnadas Mehta resigned as President of the Bombay PCC and then from the provincial assembly, to seek re-election as an Independent Nationalist. The Bombay PCC had on 11 January called on all Congressmen to carry out the boycott, but on 12 January the Maharashtra PCC resolved in favour of participation in the Round Table Conference on the terms of the Delhi statement and asked Congress not to emphasize Council boycott as this would only create bitterness within Congress. Madras Congressmen were divided, Andhra men favoured boycott while Srinivasa Iyengar and Satyamurti opposed it. Eventually 17 MLCs resigned in Madras, including Satyamurti, though several were re-elected as independents. In Bengal 40 out of 47 Swarajist MLCs resigned – all of them Hindu. In U.P. 17 out of 23 Swarajist MLCs resigned, though in some cases with considerable reluctance: and there was no shortage of replacements. In Bihar and Orissa, 30 resigned being almost the whole Swarajist contingent. Again there was no lack of new candidates, and two of the five Orissa Congressmen stood for re-election. In C.P. 15 Congress MLCs resigned, though apparently with little conviction that their gesture was useful. In Assam 12 out of 16 Swarajists resigned, but Punjab produced only a single resignation.[106] These rifts among Congressmen meant that certain types of civil disobedience were almost certainly not viable on a large scale, and that Gandhi in turning away from any attempt forcibly to bring down the raj was only facing reality. They meant, too, that he would have to select issues and styles of action which would heal as far as possible the breaches in Congress caused by council boycott.

More serious than the resentments of anti-boycotters within Congress were the signs of opposition among Congress Muslims to the Lahore resolutions and the Mahatma's drift from cooperation with the British. Gandhi needed to keep these men above all if Congress was to gain credence as a nationally representative body. M. A. Ansari resigned as President of the

[105] Extract from *Mahratta* quoted in Bombay FR1, January 1930, Home Poll., 1930, File No. 18–11.
Resignations from AICC and protests are in AICC Papers, 1930, File No. G-1 (ii).
It is noteworthy that J. Nehru told M. S. Aney that the AICC would be the poorer for his absence; his advice and cooperation would always be welcome, and he was invited to attend the AICC at Ahmedabad; 16 March 1930, *SWJN*, 4, p. 282.

[106] These figures relate to January and February 1930. They are gathered from Home Poll., 1930, File No. 18-11; *Bihar And Orissa in 1929–30* (Patna, 1931), p.4; Report on Satyagraha Movement in Utkal, January 1930–March 1931, AICC Papers, 1930, File No. Misc. 24; *The Central Provinces and Berar 1931–32. A Review of the Administration of the Province. Volume II* (Nagpur, 1933), p. 11; *Report on the Administration of the United Provinces of Agra and Oudh. 1929–30.* (Lucknow, 1931), p. iv.

Delhi PCC because of his opposition to the Lahore policy, but refused
to leave Congress or weaken it by overt hostility. Exhorting T. A. K.
Sherwani not to do anything more drastic, he admitted that there was no
other political option for men like them. They could not join the Liberals
who would work whatever constitution the British gave, nor could they join
communalist Muslim leaders with whom they differed on principle and
from whom they had just extricated themselves to form the Nationalist
Muslim Party. 'To leave the Congress, would be to commit political suicide,
to oppose the Congress would be a crime. Therefore, we must remain in
the Congress and let those who believe in the present policy and programme
carry on.'[107]

Ansari had hoped to attend the Working Committee at Sabarmati on 14–16
February when the plans for civil disobedience were to be laid: but his
medical services were required in Jaora State by a sick Begum. He wrote
a quick note to Gandhi on 10 February urging him to remember the advice
he had given Motilal in Delhi and Gandhi himself in Lahore, and not to
think that the response to Independence Day on 26 January was a true guide
to the support they could expect for real action. He followed this up with
a long, impassioned appeal from Jaora on 13 February, in which he
reminded Gandhi of his opposition to rejecting the British offer from the
time of the Delhi meeting on 1 November until Lahore, where out of
loyalty to Congress and friendship with Gandhi and the Nehrus he kept
quiet, indicating his feelings by refusing to be General Secretary or a
Working Committee member, and by resigning as President of the Delhi
PCC and member of the provincial executive. In his view the country was
not ready for civil disobedience. Compared with 1920 when there was much
anti-government feeling, many people now believed in the goodwill of the
Labour Government and Irwin's sincerity; Hindu–Muslim unity had reached its 'lowest water-mark' by contrast with the communal alliance of 1920,
and Sikhs were almost entirely against Congress whereas then they had
been firm supporters. Moreover there was within Congress disunity, even
overt revolt, 'diversity of purpose, complete lack of enthusiasm among the
workers', and the virtual certainty of violent outbreaks. He argued that to
embark on civil disobedience in such a situation would 'do an incalculable
damage', and they should concentrate on enrolling members and volunteers, collecting funds, and – the cardinal need – achieving communal
unity. Such an appeal must have hurt Gandhi to the quick: it reiterated
the precise doubts and criticisms of Congress and Indian disunity he had
voiced throughout 1929. But he merely replied on 16 February after the
civil disobedience plan was laid that he could not turn back now. Although
he agreed that the Hindu–Muslim problem was fundamental, he believed
that it must be dealt with in a new way. Political adjustment was only
possible if there was some trust between the communities and Congress
could only command such trust 'by becoming fearless and strictly just. But

[107] M. A. Ansari to T. A. K. Sherwani, 6 January 1930, Ansari Papers.

meanwhile the third party – the evil British power – has got to be sterilized. There will be no charter of independence before the Hindus and the Muslims have met but there can be virtual independence before the charter is received.'[108]

Not surprisingly, Ansari was perturbed by the Working Committee's decision to launch civil disobedience. His Nationalist Muslim colleagues expressed acute anxiety when they learnt of Gandhi's reply. Khaliquzzaman wrote on behalf of Sherwani and others to ask Ansari's advice, as it seemed that Gandhi did not think that communal unity was an essential preliminary for a struggle for independence. If they accepted Gandhi's apparent order of priorities and time scale, they would in effect be abandoning all claims to Muslim leadership: 'we indirectly proclaim to the Muslim community to find its champions in people who believe that communalism in India is a fact'. Syed Mahmud had been to the Sabarmati Working Committee and spoken of the danger of civil disobedience erupting into communal riots. Having read Ansari's letter to Gandhi (presumably at Sabarmati), he wrote to tell Ansari that he wished he had shared his doubts earlier because his silence had helped to convince him, Mahmud, that he should not publicly oppose the Lahore resolutions. He, too, asked for advice, torn between loyalty to Jawaharlal and dislike of the policy, reinforced by his need to earn a living at the Bar.[109] All Ansari could advise was that his friends should try to get men of their views elected to the council of the Muslim League so that at least a Nationalist Muslim voice would be heard at the Round Table Conference although Congress had cast Irwin's offer aside.[110] There was little else they could do. U.P. men predominantly, they shared their Urdu cultural traditions with Hindus like Jawaharlal, they had cooperated with Gandhi and Congress in 1920–2 on the Khilafat issue, they were a minority community in their own province and the arguments of Bengali or Punjabi communalist leaders made little local sense to them. To abandon Congress where they had leverage and repute would be to commit political suicide. Yet their resistance to civil disobedience was a factor influencing Gandhi because he needed their overt

---

[108] M. A. Ansari to Gandhi, 10 & 13 February 1930, Gandhi to Ansari, 16 February 1930, Ansari Papers.
For the Working Committee's decision and Gandhi's train of thought on the communal problem see below, pp. 93–6.

[109] C. Khaliquzzaman to Ansari, 1 March 1930, S. Mahmud to Ansari (undated, marked 'Please destroy'), Ansari Papers. Khaliquzzaman's resignation from AICC was accepted by the Working Committee on 20/21 March. He had earlier told Jawaharlal that his withdrawal from Congress was caused by ill health and family debts rather than by his disapproval of the Lahore policy and his belief that the country was not ready for a battle for independence: Khaliquzzaman to J. Nehru, 1 February 1930, Ansari Papers.

[110] Ansari, Sherwani, Khaliquzzaman and R. A. Kidwai cooperated to bring Nationalist Muslims to the council meeting of the Muslim League on 28 February: Ansari gave Rs. 500 for this. Ansari to Khaliquzzaman & Sherwani, 18 February 1930; Ansari to Khaliquzzaman, 24 February 1930; R. A, Kidwai to Ansari, 4 March 1930; Ansari Papers.

support in his campaign to generate unity and burnish Congress's 'national' image.

Gandhi had also to tailor his tactics to Indians outside the divided Congress, whose support or at least neutrality were essential. Muslims and Sikhs had somehow to be welded into civil disobedience and weaned from cooperation with the British in the Round Table Conference. Gandhi did not need Ansari's pessimistic assessment of communal relations to tell him that he could count on little Sikh support.[111] Moreover, at Lahore when Congress was in session the Muslim Conference Executive Board resolved to attend the Round Table Conference, and in March announced that Muslims could not participate in civil disobedience because it was merely a tactic 'to frighten the Government into accepting Dominion Status with the communal settlement embodied in the Nehru Report'. Even Muslims like Sir Ali Imam and Jinnah appeared to be taking an overtly communal line in the choice between conference-going or civil disobedience, and in March the Shafi–Jinnah split in the League was healed in the shadow of the Congress campaign. Symbolic of the collapse of the old alliance on which Gandhi had built Non-cooperation was Shaukat Ali's appeal to Muslims not to join civil disobedience because its goal was Hindu raj.[112]

Liberals and non-Congress Hindus were a further factor in Gandhi's planning. He knew that their presence at a constitutional conference would undermine Congress standing in British and Indian eyes, and that some of them exercised considerable influence in New Delhi. If a programme could be contrived which would attract their sympathy, there was more hope that Congress would eventually find itself at the negotiating table with a strengthened hand. Reading's offer of a conference was made in 1921 when Liberal sympathy for government disintegrated in the face of repression. But Liberals had declared their opposition to civil disobedience at their Federation in Madras while Congress met in Lahore.[113] As Gandhi brooded on tactics after Lahore, Sapru and another prominent Liberal, Sir Phiroze Sethna, tried to organize an All-Parties Conference of those who supported the goal of Dominion Status rather than complete indepen-

[111] The only Sikhs who supported Gandhi and Congress were those in the Akali Dal led by Sardar Kharak Singh: even they claimed 30% representation in the Punjab legislatures should there be communal representation in a future constitution. Sikhs in general opposed constitutional changes which would permanently subordinate them as a minority community in the Punjab. Congress was of course limited in the offers it could hold out to Sikhs because of its difficulties with Punjabi Hindu fears and its wish not to antagonize Muslims.
Chief Sec., Govt., of Punjab, to Home Sec., Govt. of India, 3 January 1930, Home Poll., 1930, File No. 98; Punjab FR1, January 1930, Home Poll., 1930, File No. 18-11.
[112] Muslim Conference Executive Board Resolutions, Lahore, 30/31 December 1929, New Delhi, 18 March 1930, Aziz, *The All India Muslim Conference*, pp. 58–60; Irwin to Wedgwood Benn, 6 March 1930, Mss. EUR.C.152 (6); *Young India*, 12 March 1930, *CWMG*, XLIII, 55–7.
[113] *India in 1929–30*, pp. 96–8; Madras FR1, January 1930, Home Poll., 1930, File No. 18-11.

dence, including the Madras Justice Party, the Hindu Mahasabha and Muslim leaders. The Mahasabha men were the most intransigent, opposing any conference if it discussed communal questions before Dominion Status. Ultimately an informal airing of views in Delhi at the beginning of March achieved nothing, leaving the crucial issue of communal representation in the hands of a large committee.[114] This failure at least relieved Gandhi of the challenge of a united opposition platform and made his definite stand more attractive to Hindus who did not relish the accusation of collaboration with the raj.

Finally Gandhi had to consider how best to integrate into his campaign those whose support could make or mar a mass movement. Business support for foreign-cloth boycott was an urgent necessity. Moreover without commercial assistance a large-scale campaign would have inadequate financial foundations since Congressmen's reluctance to tax themselves in aid of a national campaign had become plain in 1929. But businessmen were apprehensive about the repercussions of the Lahore resolutions, and before they would donate they would have to be assured of the protection of their long-term interests.[115] The Mahatma had also to satisfy the demands for a strong offensive by younger men on the Congress peripheries, yet channel their proclivities to violence. If he failed to do this he would alienate businessmen and Liberals, and bring down on civil disobedience a policy of official repression. Symptomatic of the dangers from the Youth Leagues was the Bombay case in January of the local league breaking up a Liberal meeting organized to explain the Liberal programme; and the All-India Naujawan Bharat Sabha's declaration that its first objective was to establish a free republic of workers and peasants.[116] But most important of all, Gandhi had to delineate some issue and define a tactic which would appeal to a wide spectrum of the population and give them opportunities for participating in the movement. He needed a rallying cry and an educative strategy which would do what he had hoped *khadi* might do.[117]

---

[114] Evidence of this attempt is in Sapru Papers, Series II, January–June 1930; Sapru to Irwin, 4 January & 3 February 1930, Mss. EUR.C.152 (24); Sethna to T. Drummond Shiels, 21 January 1930, & to McBain, 29 January 1930, Sethna Papers; 30 January, 26 February & 1 March 1930, Diary of B. S. Moonje; Irwin to Wedgwood Benn, 6 March 1930, Mss. EUR.C.152 (6).

[115] The apprehensions of the Bombay business community are reported in Bombay FR1, January 1930, Home Poll., 1930, File No. 18-II; Sapru had apparently raised or been promised over Rs. 60,000 from Bombay businessmen in his attempt to form a non-Congress alliance; Sir Grimwood Mears to Irwin, 6 January 1930, Mss. EUR.C.152 (24).

[116] Sethna to McBain, 29 January 1930, Sethna Papers; pamphlet containing constitution of All-India Naujawan Bharat Sabha as passed by its Working Committee in Delhi, 2 February 1930, AICC Papers, 1930, File No. Misc. 10.

[117] Gandhi's belief that Congress must cease to be 'a pantomime, a holiday show' steered by lawyers, and become deeply rooted in popular support, 'responsive to the needs of the dumb millions', if it was to be the instrument for achieving independence was clear in *Young India*, 16 January & 13 February 1930, *CWMG*, XLII, 400–3, 468.

Although Indians were the primary target of civil disobedience the British were the other group Gandhi wished to influence; consequently they too were a constraining influence on his strategic planning. He had been through Non-cooperation with them before, and knew that on utilitarian grounds a non-violent campaign was desirable. Non-violent resistance embarrassed; whereas violence by Indians not only united official ranks and gained the raj the support of British and world public opinion, but also attracted policies sufficiently severe to depress public enthusiasm. At this juncture his reading of the situation was that although Irwin and the Cabinet were genuine in their liberal plans for India, the chief stumbling blocks to advance were the I.C.S. and British parliamentary opinion. Therefore he had to evolve a strategy which would undermine the administration and also convert public opinion in Britain and abroad into sympathy for Congress demands.

These external dilemmas of confrontation were not the only ones facing the Mahatma. Internal constraints also affected his choice of tactics – more significantly than in the case of most political leaders because his sights were set not so much on acquiring power but on a moral and social revolution which could be jeopardized by the wrong means. He maintained, moreover, that it was a satyagrahi's *dharma* never to miss an opportunity for compromise provided that no fundamental principle was at stake.[118] Therefore any campaign must leave room for manoeuvre and adjustment and could not aim at mere destruction of the system or people opposed. As a satyagrahi he was also concerned to spread non-violence in public life, quite apart from the practical consideration that violent resistance attracted repression. Not only were terrorist outbreaks evidence of willingness by some to use violence. It was common knowledge that many of his adherents only adopted non-violent resistance as an expedient tactic.[119] After Lahore Gandhi's public pronouncements displayed a conviction that non-violence faced a crisis of credibility and viability. He generated within himself a missionary zeal for proving his technique, and as he put it of 'sterilizing' the violence in public life emanating from his countrymen and their rulers.

However Gandhi faced a crucial question. In the event of an outbreak of violence equivalent to Chauri Chaura in 1922 during a non-violent campaign should he call off civil disobedience? His refusal to continue in 1922 had disturbed many supporters and cast doubts on the satyagraha technique; for as Jawaharlal reasoned, 'if Gandhiji's argument for the suspension of civil resistance was correct, our opponents would always have the power to create circumstances which would necessarily result in our abandoning the struggle'. In the last weeks of 1929 Gandhi wrestled with the possibility of repetitions of Chauri Chaura, and his personal dilemma

[118] *Navajivan*, 8 December 1929, *ibid.* p. 251; Gandhi to B. W. Tucker, 12 March 1928, *CWMG*, XXXVI, 102.

[119] 18 November 1929, Diary of V. S. S. Sastri, NMML, J. Nehru's presidential address at Lahore, 29 December 1929, *SWJN*, 4, p. 195.

of reconciling such with his commitment to non-violence. He sought a
formula which would permit the movement to continue in such an event,
though even after Lahore he had no concrete plan in mind.[120] Significantly,
by mid-January he proclaimed, 'Votary as I am of non-violence, if I was
given a choice between being a helpless witness to chaos and perpetual
slavery, I should unhesitatingly say that I would far rather be witness to
chaos in India...to Hindus and Mussalmans doing one another to death
than I should daily witness our gilded slavery.'[121]

   While Gandhi did battle with his conscience over violence he also brooded
on past campaigns. South Africa was on his mind, evoking memories of
personal negotiation with Smuts, and civil disobedience inaugurated first
by himself and a few picked companions as a prelude to a mass movement.
The success of the Bardoli satyagraha also permeated his planning, convincing him that disciplined action by a non-violent group and effective
publicity for hard facts could bring the civil service off its pedestal to the
negotiating table.[122] He was drawing inspiration from experiences other
than his earlier all-India satyagraha, having realized that a repetition of
1920–2 would be ineffective, in relation both to Indians and the British, and
that he must evolve some new form of satyagraha appropriate to the new
circumstances. Moreover he was anxious to try the experiment while
Jawaharlal was Congress President, while he had a critical ally in office who
could place the Congress machinery at his disposal and whose presence
might help to draw behind the Gandhian programme many to whom the
Mahatma had little direct appeal.[123]

[120] Sherwood Eddy reported to Irwin, 3 December 1929, his three-day visit to
Sabarmati during which Gandhi said he would not join an independence party which
sanctioned violence, but 'he would not regard himself as responsible for individual
acts of violence in a vast country which no man could fully control and that his mind
was seeking a formula whereby, after a campaign of non-violent non-co-operation
and civil disobedience is launched, he would not feel called upon to stop the
campaign even if individual acts of violence should occur'. Mss. EUR.C.152 (23).
Similar pronouncements by Gandhi are in *Navajivan*, 10 November 1929, *CWMG*,
XLII, 129; press interview, *c.* 1 January 1930, *Young India*, 30 January 1930, *ibid.* pp.
360–1.
   J. Nehru's doubts as a result of the 1922 suspension of civil disobedience are
expressed in his *An Autobiography*, pp. 84–5.
[121] Speech at Gujarat Vidyapith, 11 January 1930, *CWMG*, XLII, 388.
[122] For the influence of Gandhi's South African experiences on his thinking see
Gandhi to Fenner Brockway, 14 November 1929, *ibid.* p. 161; Gandhi to J. Nehru,
10 January 1930, AICC Papers, 1930, File No. Misc. 26. Accounts of Gandhi's
African campaigns are available in M. K. Gandhi, *Satyagraha in South Africa* (revised
2nd edn., Ahmedabad, 1961); R. A. Huttenback, *Gandhi in South Africa British
Imperialism and the Indian Question, 1860–1914* (Ithaca & London, 1971). In his 10
January letter Gandhi told Jawaharlal to study the former volume.
   For evidence of the influence of the Bardoli example on Gandhi as he planned
civil disobedience see *Young India*, 6 February 1930, *CWMG*, XLII, 454; L. K.
Elmhirst to Irwin, 1 March 1930, on interview with Gandhi on 28 February, Mss.
EUR.C.152 (24).
[123] Gandhi to J. Nehru, 10 January 1930, AICC Papers, 1930, File No. Misc. 26;
speech to Gujarat Vidyapith, 11 January 1930, *CWMG*, XLII, 388.

The first development after Lahore apart from the council boycott call to Congressmen was the decision of the Working Committee on 2 January to celebrate 26 January as Independence Day. This was primarily a holding and publicity tactic, not the first step in a confrontation with the raj, the strategy for which Gandhi had not yet conceived. It was not intended as a day to start civil disobedience or proclaim independence, 'but to declare that we will be satisfied with nothing less than complete independence as opposed to Dominion Status so-called'. Moreover Gandhi tried to avoid processions as part of the celebrations: they could not ask for licences but he did not wish to advocate unlicensed processions. He even deprecated speeches, because he was 'anxious to avoid anticipation of a crisis' and 'would value perfect calm for ushering in civil disobedience'.[124] The programme recommended to PCCs was, therefore, very restricted. Its essentials were hoisting the national flag and holding a solemn evening meeting at which a declaration should be read in the provincial language and approved by a show of hands: the decision whether to have processions was left to PCCs. Between 10 and 17 January Gandhi and Jawaharlal worked out the text of the declaration, Gandhi composing the draft and having the final say in alterations. It proclaimed 'the inalienable right of the Indian people . . .to have freedom and to enjoy the fruits of their toil and have the necessities of life, so that they may have full opportunities of growth'; and since the raj had deprived India of that freedom it declared that India must sever the British connection and attain complete independence. The major portion consisted of an inventory of the ways in which Britain had ruined India – economically, politically, culturally and spiritually, with heavy stress on the economic pressure of foreign rule. Couched in these terms it reflected Gandhi's personal assessment of the evils of British rule. It was also appealing to a wide spectrum in Indian society, including those who paid land revenue, businessmen concerned with customs and currency control, and those who aspired to administrative employment.[125]

The Government of India decided against interference with the celebrations and did not subsequently regret its stance. Taken on a continental scale the national flag processions and meetings to read the declaration appeared to evoke little enthusiasm. Muslims were noticeably uninvolved, and in Dacca demonstrations led to a serious communal riot. The only local governments uneasy at the manifestations were Punjab, U.P., Delhi and Bombay. In Punjab the cause for official disquiet was student participation. Celebrations occurred in all large towns and many small ones, but they were small-scale except in district headquarters, and Muslims kept aloof though

[124] Gandhi to J. Nehru, 10 January 1930, AICC Papers, 1930, File No. Misc. 26; J. Nehru to G. V. Ketkar, 25 January 1930, *SWJN*, 4, p. 227. *Young India*, 23 January 1930, *CWMG*, XLII, 426.

[125] Text of pledge and J. Nehru's circular to PCCs enclosing it and suggesting plans for the day, 17 January 1930, *SWJN*, 4, pp. 215–18. The exchanges between Gandhi and J. Nehru in drafting the declaration are in *CWMG*, XLII & *SWJN*, 4.

Sikhs were fairly active. In Delhi the Congress had a very good day; a very large crowd attended the evening meeting despite the absence of Muslims and Sikhs and of any great numbers of students and millhands. A significant feature was the number of Hindu women volunteers. In U.P. student participation gave demonstrations their main strength, and in Allahabad university students flew national flags on hostels and processed, in defiance of the Vice-Chancellor's wishes. Towns were the centres of observance, about 3,000 attending a Lucknow meeting and 7,000 at Agra and Cawnpore: as yet rural areas did not seem affected. In Bombay celebrations were small outside Bombay City, even in Gujarat. In Ahmedabad a 2,000 strong procession had to have police protection against Muslim attacks. In Bombay City, however, national flags were raised in nearly all wards in the morning before audiences ranging from 50 to 2,000. An evening procession of about 10,000 ended in a massive meeting on Chowpatty beach; of the 25–30,000 present many were merely sightseers. Disturbing to officials and Congress-men was the invasion of the platform by 1,000 millhands of the Girni Kamgar Union, led by Mrs Suhasini Nambiar, G. L. Khandalkar and S. V. Deshpande, whose forcible substitution of the red flag for the national flag ended the meeting. Although the all-India picture was pre-dominently of urban and Hindu celebration, while the numbers involved were no indicator of those who could be relied on in lengthy conflict, the formidable array of local reports to the AICC, many in Hindi and from district level, indicated that despite Gandhi's pessimism about the Congress organization there was a basic network for distributing informa-tion if not a structure of command, through which a country-wide campaign could be initiated.[126]

Meanwhile Gandhi had retired to Sabarmati to brood on the strategy of a broad-fronted confrontation with the raj. The support on which he could count and the dangers of violence were uppermost in his mind. On 10 January he told Jawaharlal, 'Ever since we have separated at Lahore, I have been evolving schemes of civil disobedience. I have not seen my way clear as yet. But I have come so far that in the present state of the Congress no civil disobedience can be or should be offered in its name & that it should be offered by me alone or jointly with a few companions.' By the beginning of February he had still not seen his way clear. He told a *Daily Express* correspondent that he was hoping in seclusion 'to evolve a plan of civil disobedience which will not cause destruction or involve bloodshed, but which will be large enough to make the impression I desire'. To C. F. Andrews he disclosed his conviction that it would be 'stupid if not cowardly'

---

[126] Congress reports on 26 January are in AICC Papers, 1930, File No. G-136 (Kw) (i), Parts I & II; official reports are in Home Poll., 1930, File No. 88. For Bombay Presidency see Govt. of Bombay to Govt. of India, telegram, 30 January 1930, Mss. EUR.F.150 (2). Ansari warned Gandhi not to be misled into an incorrect estimate of rank and file support. 'It is one thing to join a procession, but it is quite another to face hardship and to withstand repression when time comes for real action.' 10 February 1930, Ansari Papers.

to sit still in the face of the violence among his compatriots Lahore had revealed to him, and the violence present in government 'exploitation'. He had decided to take 'the boldest of risks' and combat violence with civil disobedience, though how and with whom he did not know.[127]

While precise plans for civil disobedience were still in embryo, Gandhi embarked on the first part of a broad strategy of confrontation. In *Young India* on 30 January he made an offer to Irwin. If the British would satisfy eleven 'simple but vital needs of India' there would be no civil disobedience and Congress would 'heartily participate in any conference where there is perfect freedom of expression and demand'. The eleven points were, (1) total prohibition, (2) reduction of the sterling: rupee ratio to $1/4d$, (3) reduction of the land revenue to at least 50% and its subjection to legislative control, (4) abolition of the salt tax, (5) reduction of military expenditure, (6) reduction of I.C.S. salaries, (7) a protective tariff on foreign cloth, (8) passage of the Coastal Traffic Reservation Bill, (9) discharge of political prisoners not convicted of murder or attempted murder, (10) abolition of the C.I.D. or its popular control, and (11) issue of firearms licences under popular control. [128]

At first glance it was a fantastic proposal, politically impossible for Irwin and apparently unconnected with the demand for Dominion Status Gandhi had pressed on Irwin on 23 December. It provoked bewilderment and hostility among Indians who looked to Gandhi for tough leadership. *Vanguard*, the organ of the Bombay Youth League, commented that it 'read more like tit-bits than a self-respecting revolutionary counter offer. One is simply amazed at the Mahatma's complete somersault.' To Motilal it appeared a virtual surrender and reversion to the position of the Delhi manifesto, and he deprecated 'purposeless talk like this' which only lowered morale. Jawaharlal, too, failed to grasp the significance of the eleven points for Gandhi.[129]

In Gandhi's plan of confrontation with the raj they served an important function. They were to fill out the word 'independence', giving it meaning to ordinary people. Like the Independence Day resolution they were a publicity enterprise and a means of appealing to and uniting as wide a spectrum of Indian opinion as possible – from financiers and businessmen, discontented taxpayers and cultivators to those who had fallen foul of the C.I.D. They showed Gandhi's sensitivity to the aspirations and needs of the

[127] Gandhi to J. Nehru, 10 January 1930, AICC Papers, 1930, File No. Misc. 26; interview to *The Daily Express*, 22 January 1930, *The Searchlight*, 12 February 1930, *CWMG*, XLII, 419; Gandhi to C. F. Andrews, 2 February 1930, *ibid.* p. 444. *The Daily Express* correspondent told Irwin that after three hours with Gandhi he had the impression that Gandhi wanted to avoid doing anything definite; Irwin to Wedgwood Benn, 6 February 1930, Mss. EUR.C.152 (6).

[128] *Young India*, 30 January 1930, *CWMG*, XLII, 434–5.

[129] Bombay FR1, February 1930, Home Poll., 1930, File No. 18/III; M. to J. Nehru, 4 February 1930, J. Nehru Papers, part I, vol. LXX; Gandhi to J. Nehru, postcard, 6 February 1930, *ibid.* vol. XXII.

diverse groups he hoped to weld into a unity by leading civil disobedience. Among Bombay and Ahmedabad businessmen who were in touch with Gandhi there were mixed feelings of apprehension at threats of boycott and disorder, and hope that here was a political leader who could obtain for Indians real power over economic policies. Gandhi's points on currency ratios, tariffs and public expenditure soothed their fears and confirmed their belief that only by supporting Congress would they exert leverage over the raj.[130] Expounded in terms of these eleven points the demand for independence might also accommodate Muslims, Liberals and other non-Congress Hindus. Moreover the proposal opened a chink through which compromise feelers might be extended. Mahadev Desai said that only salt, cloth boycott, temperance and land revenue were really important to Gandhi, and on the basis of these four points he would be willing to negotiate. Gandhi himself admitted that if the British 'were to concede a few main points and couple the concession with a promise that the rest would be conceded as soon as possible, I would be prepared to consider a proposition for a Conference.'[131]

Having marked out a very broad area of confrontation Gandhi tackled the problem of a precise mode of civil disobedience. The Working Committee met in the Sabarmati ashram from 14 to 16 February behind closed and guarded doors. The formal outcome was a resolution endorsing Gandhi's proposal that since different attitudes to non-violence co-existed in Congress, only those who believed in non-violence as an article of faith rather than an expedient policy should initiate and control civil disobedience. Under its terms Gandhi and his associates were authorized 'to start civil disobedience as and when they desire and in the manner and to the extent they decide'. The Mahatma's ability to determine both the timing and the plan of civil disobedience was not just the result of his success in the Congress session but the consequence of the procedural device of reserving decisions on precise details to the Working Committee, which consisted of his chosen men. This pattern of removing decisions on the details of strategy to a small body free from the pressures which could be generated in a larger gathering gave him peculiar influence at critical junctures now and in the following months – early in 1931, for example, when he was chosen as sole Congress delegate to the second Round Table Conference, or at Poona, in 1933 when the decision to adopt 'individual civil disobedience' was taken after the departure of most Congressmen who had attended an informal conference to discuss strategy, and

[130] Gandhi's justification of his 'eleven points', *Young India*, 13 February 1930, *CWMG*, XLII, 469–70; *Young India*, 12 March 1930, *CWMG*, XLIII, 57–9. See also Sethna to Sapru, 17 & 18 January 1930, Sapru Papers, Series II: A. Sarabhai to P. Thakurdas, 28 March 1930, Lalji Naranji to Thakurdas, 28 March 1930, Thakurdas Papers, File No. 91/1929.
[131] The possibility of compromise was clear in answers to questions, *c.* 11 March 1930, *Young India*, 20 March 1930, *CWMG*, XLIII, 45; Collector of Ahmedabad to Home Dept., Govt. of Bombay, 2 April 1930, Home Poll., 1930, File No. 247/II.

in defiance of the expressed wish of the majority who had attended. The Working Committee's February decision was Gandhi's solution to the dilemma of possible violence, the formula for which he had groped since November. He had demarcated the civil disobedience experiment as an activity solely for those whom he could control, and on whose non-violence he could depend; if violence erupted among other Congressmen it would not be his direct responsibility. On this ticket he felt free to embark on the campaign which he intended should both combat violence and prove the supreme value of satyagraha; and on the evening of 15th at the ashram prayer meeting he warned residents to prepare for the fight, asserting that the ashram had been started to prepare them for the struggle for *purna swaraj*.[132]

Informal discussions at Sabarmati produced a decision on the issue on which civil disobedience should be offered. This, like the timing and the personnel, was crucial if Gandhi was to avoid violence and attract wide support and sympathetic neutrality. One of his eleven points had been the abolition of the salt tax, and even before the Working Committee met, rumours circulated in the press that the government's salt monopoly and tax were to be the initial point of conflict. On 27 February he confirmed the rumours in *Young India* with a stringent attack on taxing 'the starving millions, the sick, the maimed and the utterly helpless'.[133]

Salt, apparently such a side issue beside the great claim for independence, was a superbly ingenious choice, solving many of the dilemmas which faced Gandhi after Lahore. In the first place it was not a major threat either to government finances or to Indian vested interests. Consequently it would not alienate non-Congressmen who feared attacks on their pockets or a tough fight with the raj. Since it would not evoke strong repressive measures it would serve as an educative tactic, initiating large numbers into the movement without fear of great inconvenience or harsh reprisals. But it could be made into a highly emotional issue. Condemnation of a tax on a necessity of life for all by an exploitive foreign government could serve as a mass rallying cry and would probably rouse sympathy in England and America, elevating the whole campaign to a moral plane which would embarrass the raj. There was a long tradition of opposition to the salt tax, but most particularly Gandhi's stand would evoke for many politically minded Indians of all shades memories of a confrontation with the govern-

---

[132] Accounts of Sabarmati meeting of Working Committee, undated note by Bhagwan Das, *ibid.;* Bombay Secret Abstract, 1930, par. 405-A, *HFM, III, III,* pp. 8–10 (this account also gives Gandhi's address at the prayer meeting). Those present at the Working Committee were Gandhi, the two Nehrus, J. Daulatram, P. Sitaramayya, Rajagopalachariar, Vallabhbhai Patel, Satyapal, Sardar Sardulsingh, Sri Prakasa, S. Ahmed, and J. Bajaj. Text of resolution and Gandhi's comments on its significance, *Young India,* 20 February 1930, *CWMG,* XLII, 480–3. The reasons for his determination to launch civil disobedience are clear in answers to questions, *c.* 11 March, *Young India,* 20 March 1930, *CWMG,* XLIII, 42.
[133] *Young India,* 27 February 1930, *CWMG,* XLII, 499–501.

ment over the tax in 1923. Reading's government had felt it essential to double the tax to balance the budget, and when the Legislative Assembly had refused to sanction this Reading used his powers of certification, admitting that there was 'no step I have taken as Viceroy that I have disliked more'.[134] The purely economic issue dropped out of sight behind the anger of Indian legislators at the use of executive powers which confirmed their suspicions of the reality of the power offered to them in the 1919 constitution.

Although salt had such value for a broad appeal and emotive publicity, and such a low violence potential, one aspect of it weighed particularly heavily with Gandhi and apparently clinched the matter in his mind. He was convinced that a joint struggle on a basic common issue was the only way to unite India's different communities since negotiation and political accommodation had failed. Consequently he brushed aside Ansari's appeal to put communal unity before civil disobedience, having decided by mid-February that civil disobedience over salt was the only way to communal unity. Motilal took up the argument with Ansari having read his letter to Gandhi. Negotiations had failed them and they could only create Hindu–Muslim unity without either community realizing that they were working for unity: this could only be done on an economic issue in a joint struggle against the foreign oppressor. 'The master mind has amidst much ridicule and misrepresentation discovered one such economic basis in the breaking of the salt laws. The thing, to use his own favourite phrase, is "incredibly simple". The only wonder is that no one else ever thought of it.'[135] Gandhi himself replied to another message from Ansari that only a fight in a common cause could bring unity, reminding him of the communal unity which had flowered in Gujarat during floods four years previously. He was convinced that 'a few more such lessons will certainly set them right. I want you to realise the new orientation I have given to the struggle. I seek independence through a redress of the age-long grievances which touch the masses more than us.'[136] The phrase 'the new orientation' was Gandhi's description of the eleven points he had put to Irwin. These, including salt,

[134] Reading to Peel, 22 March 1923, Mss. EUR.E.238 (6); his letters to Peel on 2 & 17 May 1923 (*ibid.*) showed the political significance with which the tax became invested in the course of the 1923 confrontation.

For other evidence about Gandhi's reasons for choosing salt see J. Nehru's circular to PCCs, 22 February 1930, *SWJN*, 4, p. 272; note by Sir Malcolm Hailey, Governor of U.P., 17 April 1930, Home Poll., 1930, File No. 247/11; R. Prasad, *Mahatma Gandhi and Bihar. Some Reminiscences* (Bombay, 1949), pp. 80–1. Prasad commented 'that even the poorest man did not feel the pinch' of the tax, and that salt was cheap despite the duty on it. In Ahmedabad district for example, in 1929–30 salt cost Rs. 2.4.7. per maund, of which Rs. 1.4.0 was duty. The total revenue from salt for the central government in 1929–30 was Rs. 67,646,354 out of a total of Rs. 800,443,369. It compared with Rs. 512,566,229 from customs and Rs. 167,060,821 from income tax. *Statistical Abstract for British India from 1924–25 to 1933–34* (Delhi, 1936), p. 147.

[135] M. Nehru to M. A. Ansari, 17 February 1930, M. Nehru Papers, File No. A 15.   [136] Gandhi to M. A. Ansari, 3 March 1930, Ansari Papers.

were in his mind as possible replacements for the Khilafat issue which brought Muslims into a joint struggle beside Congressmen in 1920-2.

The issue for civil disobedience was settled at Sabarmati, but there was still no precise plan of campaign. Jawaharlal sketched a vague outline to PCCs on 22 February. The first stage would probably be 'some form of civil disobedience' by Gandhi and his assistants, the second stage action similar to Gandhi's organized by the Working Committee, AICC and PCCs after Gandhi's arrest, gradually developing into forms suitable for different localities. The third stage would be mass civil disobedience when most Congress leaders would probably be in jail, and little local planning was therefore possible. He merely requested PCCs to look at locally viable forms of civil disobedience and particularly to consider ways of attacking the salt monopoly. Two days later Motilal acknowledged privately that they had 'not yet arrived at definite and final conclusions about the precise method of the actual start'; and Gandhi's article in *Young India* on 27th merely stated that he intended to start the movement with his ashram co-workers.[137]

The mode of disobedience was still vague in Gandhi's ultimatum to the Viceroy on 2 March, though 11 March was named as the date. This letter, when published the day the salt satyagraha began, performed the same function as the eleven points. It filled out those points, laying particular stress on the financial burdens of British rule and emphasizing that the freedom Gandhi sought would benefit not only a small group of Hindu politicians. It also contained an offer to talk on the substance of the letter with Irwin, thereby satisfying Gandhi's personal needs as a satyagrahi for readiness to compromise and openness with the opponent. However the only reply was a brief note from Irwin's Private Secretary, regretting that Gandhi should contemplate action which would lead to violation of law and danger to the public peace.[138]

Irwin was in no mood for compromise and admitted that he was finding it 'very hard to preserve any mental patience with Gandhi'.[139] But he like the Mahatma was speaking for a variety of groups with different priorities, and was therefore subject to conflicting pressures as his government laid its plans for dealing with the confrontation Gandhi had engineered. Wedgwood Benn reminded him that political conflict threatened serious repercussions on India's credit in the world's money markets; and that the Labour Cabinet with an eye to its supporters in Britain would, though backing him in necessary action, nevertheless be 'profoundly grateful when you can produce an atmosphere which makes action unnecessary'. The Governor of Bombay saw the situation from the position of his Presidency

[137] J. Nehru to PCCs, 22 February 1930, *SWJN*, 4, pp. 271-3; M. Nehru to B. C. Roy, 25 February 1930, M. Nehru Papers, File No. R. 10: *Young India*, 27 February 1930, *CWMG*, XLII, 496-8.

[138] Gandhi to Irwin, 2 March 1930, G. Cunningham (P.S.V.) to Gandhi, 5 March 1930, Mss. EUR.C.152 (4).

[139] Irwin to J. H. Whitley, 14 March 1930, Mss. EUR.C.152 (4).

which would probably bear the brunt of Gandhi's campaign. When Irwin visited Bombay in January, Sykes argued against the policy of treating civil disobedience uniformly throughout India as far as possible under ordinary laws. His government also told the Government of India officially that it considered the ordinary law insufficient to check such acts as non-payment of taxes and picketing of liquor shops. It argued that government must act swiftly to check such movements, to protect its prestige and hearten the loyal: and to this end it pressed for executive powers against illegal organizations and full support and assistance from Delhi. Irwin agreed that they could not allow Congress to perfect seditious plans unchecked. However he had also to consider those Indians who had shown willingness to participate in the Round Table Conference on India's future, announced in his October declaration: he was determined not to alienate them by unnecessary severity.[140] From these conflicting pressures emerged a decision to adhere to the policy already laid down, of conciliating those who were amenable to conciliation, and of adjusting response to opposition according to local conditions, relying as far as possible on the ordinary law. If Gandhi broke the law, as seemed inevitable, he would be arrested at once on the grounds that although his arrest would cause an outcry even among moderate politicians, failure to arrest him would frighten government's friends and encourage Gandhi's supporters.[141]

Awaiting the Viceroy's reply to his 2 March ultimatum Gandhi made the final decision in his strategy of confrontation. Repeating a tactic he had used in South Africa he would march from the ashram with a column of satyagrahis to break the law. It would be a live drama, generating interest and support in the region he knew best and attracting press publicity throughout India. By restricting his companions to men from the ashram, carrying copies of the *Gita*, he would make it a lesson in discipline and non-violence. He made his announcement at ashram prayers on 5 March, setting the date for 12 March. Only three days before he was due to leave he said that Vallabhbhai had selected Jalalpur *taluka* on the Surat coast where there were good opportunities for salt making.[142]

By March Gandhi had attempted an ingenious solution to the dilemmas of actual confrontation with the raj, by expounding the reasons for confrontation in broad terms and using an emotive symbol as the immediate point of attack, by playing a dramatic personal role through correspon-

[140] S of S to V, telegram, 24 January 1930, Mss. EUR.C.152 (11); Wedgwood Benn to Irwin, 27 February 1930, Mss. EUR.C.152 (6); Irwin to Wedgwood Benn, 9 January 1930, *ibid.*; F. Sykes, *From Many Angles. An Autobiography* (London, 1942), p. 382; Govt. of Bombay to Govt. of India, Home Dept., telegram, 17 January 1930, Mss. EUR.F.150 (2).

[141] Govt. of India to S of S, telegram, 9 January 1930, Govt. of India to all local govts., 30 January 1930. Home Poll., 1930, File No. 98; V to S of S, telegram, 9 March 1930, Mss. EUR.C.152 (11).

[142] Gandhi's announcements, 5 March 1930 & *Navajivan*, 9 March 1930, *CWMG*, XLIII, 12–13, 31; J. Nehru's announcement to press, 6 March 1930, *The Searchlight*, 9 March 1930, *SWJN*, 4, pp. 274–5.

dence with Irwin and a public march, and by limiting active resisters to close, disciplined adherents. Thus he removed the independence goal from the realm of political definition where it had destroyed Congress unity and alienated non-Congressmen, and used trustworthy instruments in place of those he had failed to create in 1929. Although he thereby convinced many people that he was the only all-India leader worth following at this juncture his leadership position depended on his ability to resolve the dilemmas of confrontation more permanently and produce perceptible gains as the political context changed. He recognized that the solutions he had propounded were temporary, describing them as 'the last throw of a gambler', but insisting that the risk even of violence was worth it.[143] Realizing that he would almost certainly be arrested and that Congress would take over direction of the campaign, on the eve of the march he suggested that breaking salt laws should be followed by picketing liquor and foreign-cloth shops, non-payment of taxes, boycott of courts and resignation of government servants.[144] To date his newly achieved leadership role had been that of conciliator, educator and tactician, but his tactics of conflict relied heavily on his presence. A country-wide campaign when he was removed from active participation would be a more searching test of his leadership.

[143] *Young India*, 20 February & 27 March 1930, *CWMG*, XLII, 483, XLIII, 133–4.
Gandhi clearly envisaged wide outbreaks of violence after his arrest; L. K. Elmhirst to Irwin, 1 March 1930, Mss. EUR.C.152 (24).
[144] Speech at ashram prayers, 11 March 1930, *Young India*, 20 March 1930, *CWMG*, XLIII, 46–8.

CHAPTER 3

Civil disobedience: the test of leadership

During civil disobedience Gandhi was in his own eyes on trial as an all-India leader. He embarked on the campaign with a sense of spiritual exaltation, guided, he claimed, not by reason but by inner inspiration. He spoke of the struggle as a holy war, a fight to the finish from which there could be no retreat, and possibly his own 'last chance'.[1] Yet only civil disobedience in practice would prove to him whether public response and the conscience-saving formula he had secured from the Working Committee would satisfy him and permit him to continue his personal pursuit of *dharma* as a continental political leader. For his countrymen, too, civil disobedience was the test of his leadership. On its repercussions in terms of personal fulfilment and political gain, the threats it posed and the pressure it generated, depended their future relationship with Gandhi. A wider world also watched the satyagraha experiment, wondering whether in the teeth of a struggle the Mahatma would prove a charlatan and political twister rather than the non-violent zealot for truth he claimed to be. Moreover the judgement by British officials of the response Gandhi elicited in India and abroad influenced their future dealings with him. Consequently, although civil disobedience could be assessed in Gandhian terms of the moral regeneration of society as the foundation of a new political order, or measured against the diverse intentions of participants, in the context of Gandhi's political career and position it must be analysed primarily in terms of its depth of support and degree of cohesion, and on the product of these, Congress's negotiating position at the end of the campaign.

The type of evidence available also poses problems in measuring the success or failure of civil disobedience. Statistics for acts performed and people convicted, even if reasonably accurate, can only hint at the depth and nature of the response to Gandhi's call. Attitudes and perceptions are beyond the realm of quantification, while the intensity of the conflict bred bias and propaganda in contemporary assessments which are the only

---

[1] Interview to *The Manchester Guardian*, c. 11 March 1930, *The Hindu*, 11 June 1930, *CWMG*, XLIII, p. 39.

Gandhi's horoscope allegedly predicted that he would die in 1930; Irwin to Wedgwood Benn, 7 April 1930, Mss. EUR.C.152 (6). I have found no evidence that this influenced Gandhi; rather he seems to have felt that if he did not seize this moment violence might overwhelm Indian public life and prevent a further opportunity for him to guide India as he wished. See also Gandhi to M. Desai, 9 & 25 April 1930, *CWMG*, XLIII, pp. 217, 321.

supplement to the bare figures. Regional variations were much greater than in 1920–2, because Gandhi and the Working Committee learnt from that experience and gave PCCs much greater tactical liberty than during Non-cooperation. Furthermore once an appeal for action was made to the whole population a host of factors came into play which were not primarily political but determined popular response to a great extent. Most significant of these were the effects of the world economic depression which coincided quite fortuitously with the civil disobedience campaign. The depression's main manifestation in India was a catastrophic fall in prices in 1930–1 which continued for several years subsequently but at a slower rate (see Table 2). Unlike war-time inflation which had generated distress on which Non-cooperation fed a decade before, depression hit producers more than consumers, but its ramifications in the economy and in social relations were wide. Farming tenants found their crops fetched too little cash to pay their rents, landlords and cultivating owners experienced difficulty in paying land revenue, and sources of vital rural credit dried up. Businessmen received lower prices for their goods at home and abroad, and their stocks piled up for lack of purchasers. Some were forced to make their clerks and other employees redundant, while factories either shut down or laid off some of their labour force. Even government, the greatest single employer in the economy, its revenues from excise, customs, land and income tax drastically reduced, cut down its staff and reduced their salaries. But the impact of this economic crisis was not uniform throughout the sub-continent: different regions were affected according to the nature of the local economy, and consequently the attractions of agitational politics varied from area to area.

TABLE 2. *Index of prices, 1924–34*

1924	221	1930	171
1925	227	1931	127
1926	216	1932	126
1927	202	1933	121
1928	201	1934	119
1929	203		

100 = base in 1873

SOURCE: *Statistical Abstract for British India, 1924–25 to 1933–34*, p. 816.

I   SALT SATYAGRAHA

The salt satyagraha began with the carefully staged drama of Gandhi's month-long march on a 240-mile route from Sabarmati to Dandi, on the Gujarat coast. The satyagraha lasted about two months after his inaugural gesture on the Dandi shore, petering out when the monsoon arrived. This phase of civil disobedience was peculiarly Gandhi's own. It was a point of conflict he had carefully chosen to create the maximum unity central to his plans; and for most of the time he led the satyagraha in person.

The march was not strictly part of civil disobedience, but a dramatic prelude. On 9 March *Navajivan* printed the first week's tentative itinerary and Gandhi's instructions for the march. The column would travel in the early morning and the cool of the evening, stopping at one village in the morning and another at night. They would sleep in the open and eat the simplest food, sparing host villages the expense of accommodation, bedding, betel nuts or sweets. All he asked of villagers was the raw food, a clean resting and washing place, and information on their human and animal population, the extent of *khadi* and spinning, their drinking habits, land revenue demand and salt consumption. The march was designed not just to publicize his appeal for civil disobedience but to educate villagers and those who read of it in the press. Like his *khadi* tours it was to be a walking lesson in the qualities necessary for true swaraj, and a demonstration of his claim and credentials for leadership. It was also a dramatic contrast to the imperial exploitation which he had condemned in his 'eleven points' and his letter to Irwin of 2 March: he pointed this out when he criticized his walking companions for ordering fresh milk and vegetables by lorry from Surat, for taking to motor cars at the slightest pretext, and for forcing a labourer to carry a heavy kerosene lamp to light the night march. Volunteers from the Gujarat Vidyapith in Ahmedabad, went ahead to prepare for Gandhi's reception, and seventy-eight male companions marched with him. They were selected as people obedient to ashram discipline and representative of most provinces, a wide generation span, Muslims, Christians and Untouchables; and Gandhi tried to generate among them a religious zeal for their march as a pilgrimage rather than a party or a political gesture. Many of them felt the physical strain, some fell sick and some complained of the harshness of Gandhi's regulations; but the Mahatma continued 'regrettably hale and hearty'.[2]

At each village where the party stopped Gandhi spoke briefly. He attacked the salt tax in terms reminiscent of his argument to Ansari and the reasoning behind his 'eleven points'. 'Who can help liking this poor man's battle? The cruel tax is no respecter of persons. It is therefore as much the interest of the Mussalman as of the Hindu to secure its abolition. This is a fight undertaken in the name of God and for the sake of the millions of the paupers of this country.'[3] He filled out his political appeal with exhortations relevant to village life, on *khadi*, cow-protection, cleanliness and Untouchability. His appeal was not for money but for a change of attitudes; and symbolic in a village context of the courage and cohesion

[2] *Navajivan*, 9 March, 13 April 1930, *Young India*, 3 April 1930, *ibid.* pp. 33–5, 144, 146–9.
  Gandhi's companions were listed in *Young India*, 12 March 1930, *ibid.* pp. 454–5; for complaints, drop-outs etc. see *Navajivan*, 13 April 1930, *ibid.* pp. 97–8, Bombay Secret Abstract, 1930, par. 575, *HFM, III, III*, p. 13, Irwin to Wedgwood Benn, 26 March 1930, Mss. EUR.C.152 (6).

[3] Speech at Broach, 26 March 1930, *Young India*, 3 April 1930, *CWMG*, XLIII, 127; his speeches during the march are in *ibid.*

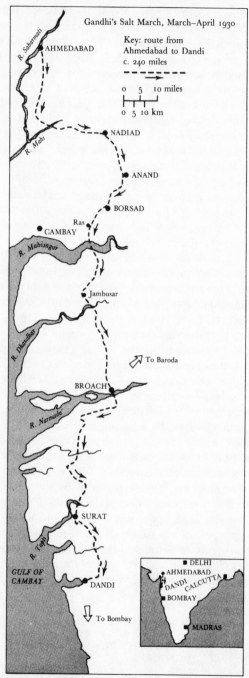

The route of Gandhi's salt march, March–April 1930

he was trying to generate, he called on village officials to resign their posts which buttressed the exploitive regime.

As he journeyed Gandhi continued to give press interviews and to write for *Navajivan* and *Young India*, spreading his message of swaraj and the duty of disobedience to a corrupt state, and giving advice for the future conduct of the campaign. He missed an AICC meeting at Sabarmati on 21 March, but a resolution he had drafted for it was passed with few alterations, endorsing the Working Committee's resolution of 16 February and authorizing PCCs to organize civil disobedience subject to Working Committee directions. The initial thrust was to be salt satyagraha, when Gandhi finished his march and gave the word, or on his arrest if he did not reach the coast. After the salt phase provinces were to be free to adopt whatever form of satyagraha suited them.[4] When the AICC put the ultimate timing decision on Gandhi he announced that civil disobedience should probably start on 6 April; that date was the start of the planned National Week and the anniversary of the hartal inaugurating the Rowlatt satyagraha in 1919 which had culminated in the well-remembered Jallianwalla Bagh massacre at Amritsar. But still he urged great care and preparation to avoid violence, and advised only contravention of salt laws for the time being. His instructions on types of social boycott of officials and collaborators emphasized the need for non-violence, as did his final instructions on 6 April.[5]

Gandhi and Vallabhbhai could not have chosen a more suitable area for the salt march than south Gujarat. Not only was it a large salt-producing area. It was also their own home ground. Their joint concern and campaigns for local issues dated back to the Kaira satyagraha of 1918 and had won them the support, shading in Gandhi's case into real veneration, of the Patidars, the prosperous cultivating caste who dominated the region. Since the Bardoli satyagraha Vallabhbhai had concentrated on organizing the locality and building swaraj ashrams as permanent centres. A temperance campaign was under way in Surat district, involving picketing, social ostracism and cutting of toddy trees. Further north in the Matar taluka of Kaira he had organized an 'economic survey' by students of the Gujarat Vidyapith, which officials feared might lead to a no-tax campaign.[6]

[4] Article by J. Nehru on AICC meeting and future plans, *Young India*, 27 March 1930, *SWJN*, 4, pp. 287–8; handwritten draft by J. Nehru for Congress Bulletin No. 6, 26 March 1930, AICC Papers, File No. 43/1929. This draft gives 21 March AICC resolutions; a draft of the civil disobedience resolution in Gandhi's hand is in J. Nehru Papers, part I, vol. XXII. One clause of Gandhi's omitted in the resolution as passed called on all educational institutions to suspend work and concentrate on the campaign for liberty.
[5] *Young India*, 27 March, 3 April 1930, *Navajivan*, 30 March 1930, *CWMG*, XLIII, 135–7, 170–1, 150–3; J. Nehru to PCCs, 4 April 1930, *SWJN*, 4, pp. 297–8.
[6] For evidence of organization in Gujarat see Report by D.S.P., Surat, in Bombay Police Abstract, No. 5, 2 February 1929, Home Poll., 1931, File No. 5/17; Bombay FR2, December 1929, Home Poll., 1929, File No. 17; Bombay FR1, January 1930, Home Poll., 1930, File No. 18/II. The Bombay government's anxiety about Gujarat was indicated to the Government of India, Home Dept., in telegram, 17 January

With such organization and deep support Gandhi could expect a march to generate wide local enthusiasm which would duly be reported in the continental press. His appeal for support was made easier by a local magistrate who arrested Vallabhbhai at Ras on 7 March – without the prior approval of the Bombay government. When news of this arrest reached Ahmedabad all the mills closed, as did schools, theatres, Hindu shops and the Municipality's administrative offices. A protest meeting gathered two and a half thousand, and the Millowners' Association passed a resolution condemning the government's action.[7]

The march itself was peaceful but impressive. This stark figure, staff in hand, outstriding his companions, fearless with a messianic zeal for his cause, quietly confident in combat with the raj, compelled respect and awe as he made his symbolic journey to the sea. Jawaharlal, who joined him briefly on his journey, remembered it as the most significant picture of the Mahatma he could call to mind.[8]

Excitement built up when Gandhi reached Kaira and Surat districts. At Nadiad, Kaira's largest town, his meeting drew a crowd of 20,000, many of whom attended from Bombay with 3,000–4,000 from Ahmedabad. At Anand he drew over 10,000, at Broach 15,000 and at Surat 30,000. In other places he attracted between three and six thousand, while his village meetings were attended by several hundred. Muslims were conspicuous by their absence, the largest number being about 200 at Broach. Moreover, there was some overt hostility to Gandhi's insistence on introducing Untouchables to his meetings, as there had been during Non-cooperation: and at Gajera on 21 March many women left rather than attend in Untouchable company.[9] Gandhi's call for the resignation of village headmen was good strategy as the attitude of these local collaborators of the raj did much to influence the reception their villages gave to him. As the march proceeded, so pressure of publicity and social boycott built up, and resignations began to occur in larger numbers. By 22 March approximate numbers of resignations were 4 from Ahmedabad district, 27 from Kaira (of whom 16 were from Borsad taluka), 17 from Broach and 2 from Surat. But Surat soon became the most affected district: by 5 April 140 out of 760

1930, Mss. EUR.F.150 (2). It warned, 'The bulk of the population...is not politically inclined, but cannot stand out against Congress organisation so long as the latter holds the field unchecked. With adequate protection from illegal pressure they would probably remain loyal and thus cause the breakdown of a movement depending on mass disobedience...experience has shown that such a movement is much more difficult to deal with if allowed to develop at the outset and to absorb a large section of the population who, after committing themselves, rely on the Congress to see them through and protect them from consequences.'

[7] V to S of S, telegram, 10 March 1930, Home Poll., 1930, File No. 247/11; Bombay Secret Abstract, 1930, par. 579–B (2), *HFM*, *III*, *III*, pp. 13–14.

[8] J. Nehru's Foreword, 30 June 1951, to Tendulkar, *Mahatma*, vol. 1, p. xii.

[9] File containing daily reports on the salt march, Home Poll., 1930, File No. 247/11; Bombay Secret Abstract, 1930, paras. 384, 633, *HFM*, *III*, *III*, pp. 14–27.

village headmen had resigned, and ten days later the figure had risen to 227.[10]

Statistics for meetings and resignations give at best a sketchy indication of the response to Gandhi's march in Gujarat. The Collector of Ahmedabad noted the religious aura which surrounded Gandhi's journey as he and his followers kept quoting the Gospels, presumably likening Gandhi to Christ setting his face to go to Jerusalem and certain capture. The sale of Bibles to Ahmedabad Hindus shot up. As a result Gandhi's position was, the Collector judged, of a different order from that of any other leader, and his arrest would probably stir even the politically apathetic. In the rural areas of Surat and Kaira local officials were becoming seriously disturbed at the growth of ashrams as bases for propaganda and the organization of village officers' resignations and boycott of the reluctant. In Nadiad taluka alone three such volunteer centres had opened, and three more were about to open in mid-April. As Irwin reported to London, the situation in the Gujarat countryside was grave. 'Here the personal influence of Gandhi threatens to create a position of real embarrassment to the administration. He is using with effect the weapons of boycott and intimidation, and in some areas he has already achieved a considerable measure of success in undermining the authority of Government.'[11] From the other side of the confrontation Mahadev Desai wrote to Jawaharlal of the reserves of energy, new courage and self-confidence for public speaking he had drawn from the immense public response during the month of Gandhi's march, as he held the fort at Sabarmati and nominally edited Gandhi's two papers.[12]

Outside Gujarat the repercussions of the march were understandably less dramatic, but even in provinces where the Gujarati Bania had previously attracted less support than in the Bombay Presidency he received much attention and publicity. In Madras his march completely overshadowed the wrangling of local Congressmen on council entry; and though it was generally considered theatrical and his programme impracticable he was held 'in such personal reverence by the Hindu public generally' that the local government viewed the political repercussions of his probable arrest 'with considerable misgiving'. In Bengal, too, Gandhi's activities received lengthy press publicity, but there was little actual enthusiasm for civil disobedience of the salt acts. Moreover Muslims were notably hostile to the

[10] Governor of Bombay to S of S, telegram, received 15 March 1930, L/PJ/6/1998; draft note by Govt. of Bombay for discussion in Delhi, 27 March 1930, Mss. EUR.F.150(2); Bombay Special Dept. to Govt. of India, Home Dept., telegram, 5 April 1930, Home Poll., 1930, File No. 247/11; Sykes to Irwin, 15 April 1930, Mss. EUR.C. 152 (24).

[11] Irwin to Wedgwood Benn, 24 April 1930, Mss. EUR.C.152 (6); Collector of Ahmedabad to Govt. of Bombay, Home Dept., 2 April 1930, Home Poll., 1930, File No. 247/11; note on policy proposals by Gujarat district officers, 7 May 1930, Home Poll., 1930, File No. 247/IV.

[12] M. Desai to J. Nehru, 7 April 1930, J. Nehru Papers, part I, vol. XVII.

idea. A factor interfering with Gandhi's publicity throughout India was the enforcement of the Child Marriage Act from 1 April, and there occurred a rush of Muslim marriages before that date which deflected public attention and encouraged liquor sales, to the Mahatma's chagrin.[13]

Gandhi reached Dandi on 5 April, a considerable feat for an elderly man who had collapsed in 1927 and tended to have high blood pressure. The following morning he bathed in the sea and then picked up a lump of mud and salt as a sign that he had broken the salt laws. Batches of volunteers then filled pots and pans with sea water and boiled it to extract the salt. An orderly crowd of about 2,000 gathered to watch in holiday mood, many of them having arrived in motor lorries.[14] Gandhi had been expecting arrest since he left Sabarmati, and in this unsought period of liberty he had hastily to mark out a role for himself. Concentrating on salt for the first week he decided thereafter 'to utilise this golden opportunity' for a temperance and anti-foreign-cloth campaign which would incorporate women into the movement and appeal as righteous issues to international opinion. He still wished to keep resistance to land revenue as a last resort. Refusing invitations to go to other parts of the country he confined his activities to Gujarat, and to Surat district in particular, and threw himself into this triple campaign in press articles and personal actions. He addressed general meetings, women's gatherings and groups of police patels, issued advice on picketing foreign cloth and liquor shops, and urged people to cut down their toddy trees.[15]

When Jawaharlal was arrested on 14 April Gandhi refused to become Congress President, and on his advice Motilal took up the office. His own liberty appears to have embarrassed him, and having exhorted his compatriots 'to force the jail doors open' after Jawaharlal's imprisonment he forced a personal conflict with the government. He announced on 24 April that he would lead a raid on the Dharasna and Chharvada salt works, and on 4 May drafted a letter to Irwin announcing his intention.[16]

These two months after Gandhi's March ultimatum to Irwin demon-

[13] Irwin to Wedgwood Benn, 3 April 1930, Mss. EUR.C.152 (6); Madras FR1 & Bengal FR2, March 1930, Home Poll., 1930, File No. 18/IV.
[14] Bombay Secret Abstract, 1930, par. 633, *HFM, III, III*, p. 28; press interview after breaking the law, *The Amrita Bazar Patrika*, 7 April 1930, *CWMG*, XLIII, 199–200.
[15] Gandhi to M. Desai, 9 April 1930, *ibid.* pp. 216–17; statement to press, 11 April 1930, *The Hindu*, 12 April 1930, *ibid.* p. 243. For examples of Gandhi's press advice on picketing, hartals, social boycott, see *Young India*, 24 April 1930, *Navajivan*, 27 April & 4 May 1930, *ibid.* pp. 312–13, 341–2, 379–82. Gandhi's activities between 6 April and his arrest are reported in Bombay Secret Abstract, 1930, paras. 659,-A,-B, 681, 706, 749-B, *HFM, III, III*, pp. 29–43.
[16] Draft letter to Irwin, 4 May 1930, *Young India*, 8 May 1930, *CWMG*, XLIII, 389–93. Gandhi's appeal after Jawaharlal's imprisonment, *Hindi Navajivan*, 17 April 1930, *ibid.* pp. 275–6. Jawaharlal had nominated Gandhi as his successor and failing him Motilal, in letter to Working Committee, 10 April 1930, *SWJN*, 4, p. 304; Gandhi's refusal to Motilal, telegram, 15 April 1930, *CWMG*, XLIII, 260; Motilal's acceptance of office in wire to Gandhi, 17 April 1930, *ibid.* p. 260, fn. 2.

strated that the Government of India worked within as severe constraints in planning its response to civil disobedience as the Mahatma did in shaping his strategy. The government's general policy towards the impending satyagraha was laid down on 26 March. It aimed to avoid opportunities for confrontation and misrepresentation, but where confrontation proved inevitable prompt and disorganizing action against leaders was deemed preferable to wholesale arrests. In cases of salt satyagraha arrests might be avoided by confiscating illicit salt and the equipment for its preparation. Gandhi was considered a special case. In Irwin's words, the British would be 'clumsy-footed' if they 'thought that the law could successfully treat him as it treats any other mundane and immoral law-breaker'.[17]

How to treat Gandhi, having acknowledged his extraordinary position, proved an extremely tricky problem for Irwin. Although the Government of India had decided before the march began on swift arrest, once Gandhi was en route it stayed its hand, and Irwin admitted, 'Most of my thought at the moment is concentrated upon Gandhi. I wish I felt sure what the right way to deal with him is.'[18] Like Gandhi Irwin had to consider the effects of his actions on the diverse groups interacting in the political sphere – Congressmen of various hues, Liberals, Mahasabhites, different Muslim groups, the normally apolitical who nonetheless revered Gandhi, the services, foreign and British public opinion and the extent to which this constrained the home government. The Viceroy faced not just the question of Gandhi's arrest but the spectre of his hunger-striking in jail. Gandhi's scrupulous avoidance of violence was a factor inhibiting his arrest. So was the unease of the Labour Secretary of State at the prospect of repression. 'If the whole escapade fizzles out in some ridiculous way, I shall be only too pleased,' he wrote, 'and I devoutly hope that no strong measures will be required. The halo of martyrdom is obviously what he is after, and I hope it will be possible to avoid adorning him with it.' A cogent appeal for firm action, however, came from Sykes, concerned at the effect of the Mahatma's action on public opinion in his Presidency, particularly among loyalists and government servants, and the possibility that satyagraha might develop into refusal to pay land revenue. He discussed policy with Irwin and with Crerar and Haig, the Government of India's Home Member and Secretary, in Delhi on 27 March, and argued firmly for Gandhi's arrest and a long sentence, and for the provision of extra-legal powers under Ordinance to inspire confidence among the loyal public and government servants.[19]

---

[17] Irwin to Wedgwood Benn, 7 April 1930, Mss. EUR.C.152 (6); Govt. of India to Govt. of Bombay, Special Dept., telegram, 5 April 1930, Home Poll., 1930, File No. 247/11; Govt. of India to all local govts., 26 March 1930, *The Civil Disobedience Movement 1930–34* (New Delhi, 1936), pp. 40–3. [IOL, Mss. EUR.E.251 (34)]

[18] Irwin to Wedgwood Benn, 13 March 1930, Mss. EUR.C.152 (6).

[19] Irwin to Wedgwood Benn, 26/27 March 1930, *ibid*; draft note by Govt. of Bombay for discussion at Delhi, memorandum of Delhi discussion, 27 March 1930, Mss. EUR.F.150 (2); S of S to Sykes, 20 March 1930, *ibid*.

Sykes was not alone in thinking that the Government of India displayed woeful weakness in letting Gandhi go free. The Bombay correspondent of *The Times* and *The Daily Telegraph* spread the same criticism in Britain. But as Irwin's Director of Public Information later pointed out, the Viceroy faced 'a desperate dilemma'. He was playing for the stake of a successful Round Table Conference to solve India's constitutional problems, and in mid-1930 many Hindu politicians 'between the Centre and the Left were nicely poised on the razor edge of indecision. The immediate arrest of Mr Gandhi, before he had committed any offence, would, it is known, have precipitated these leaders down on the side of Congress and non-co-operation again.' Gandhi himself put Irwin's dilemma in a nutshell. 'The Government's plight is that of the serpent which has swallowed a rat. It would find it hard to resort to either course of action – allowing me to remain out or putting me behind the bars.'[20] What the Government of India had feared in 1926 when it criticized the acting Governor of Bombay for interviewing Gandhi, and in 1929 when it refused to make an issue of Gandhi's cloth-burning in Calcutta, had now happened. Because of Gandhi's public repute outside the ranks of the politicians and his peculiar leadership position in Congress he now held a strategic position in the relationship of the raj with its subjects. He had become a special all-India case, and whatever policy it adopted towards him only underlined that position. If it arrested him it risked massive public outcry; if it let him remain free it appeared to be frightened of his power and unwilling to back its own supporters.

However, for the first fortnight of April Irwin was satisfied with his 'very illogical' policy of not arresting Gandhi.[21] Thereafter pressure built up from numerous quarters, convincing Irwin of the increasing gravity of the political situation. Sykes argued by letter and wire that Gandhi's liberty was putting police and other local officials in a very difficult situation in Surat district, and that his arrest was urgently needed, coupled with Ordinance powers against such manifestations as intimidation and boycott. From Sapru and Mohammed Ali, politicians of very different hues, yet neither aligned with Gandhi over civil disobedience, came warnings of the danger of the situation: while E. Villiers, President of Calcutta's European Association, saw Irwin on 21 April and told him that the government's apparent fear of arresting Gandhi was generating a dangerous atmosphere in Calcutta. Other news from Bengal was even more disquieting. On the night of 18 April the Chittagong group of the Jugantar terrorist party successfully raided the police and auxiliary force armouries in what was clearly a well planned and well financed operation. Other provinces reported

[20] *Navajivan*, 6 April 1930, *CWMG*, XLIII, 188; Coatman, *Years of Destiny*, p. 279; Moore, *Crisis of Indian Unity 1917–1940*, pp. 107–8; S of S to V, telegram, 11 April 1930, Mss. EUR.C.152 (11).
[21] Irwin to Sir George Stanley, Governor of Madras, 14 April 1930, Mss. EUR.C.152 (24).

serious clashes between police and public as a result of arrests of salt satyagraha leaders. One of the worst occurred in Karachi on 16 April when a crowd of 7–8,000 broke into the compound of the City Magistrate's Court where six Sind leaders were being tried: the police fired, killing two people.[22]

By 21 April Irwin and most of his Council were coming down in favour of Gandhi's arrest. The following day the Home Department asked local governments whether the balance had now swung in favour of arresting Gandhi in the light of disquiet in England and among Indian supporters of government, and of Bombay's increasingly difficult situation. The consensus of the replies was that Gandhi's arrest would not bring new elements into his campaign although serious disturbances were likely as a result. Most governments favoured arrest if the campaign took a more active turn. Bombay urged that there should be no more delay: Gandhi's guiding brain must be removed although that would not break the movement without concurrent steps under Ordinances 'to maintain Government prestige and restore public confidence, and to afford a rallying point for moderate and minority opinion'. What worried Bombay was not just the insidious attack on its local agents but the tendency of many sane and reasonable men to join Gandhi's movement, 'not because they expect any definite results from anti-salt laws campaign but because belief that British connection is morally indefensible and economically intolerable is gaining strength among educated Hindus, Gujaratis mostly but others also'.[23] Gandhi's attempt through satyagraha to shatter the psychological roots of collaboration on which the raj stood had evidently succeeded to a very significant extent, as had his redefinition of independence in his 'eleven points' and his anti-salt tax campaign.

A sign of the hard line emerging against Gandhi was Irwin's flat refusal to negotiate with the Mahatma when Vithalbhai Patel made the suggestion.[24] What tipped the balance in favour of Bombay's argument was Gandhi's announcement that he intended to lead the raid on the salt works, and the catastrophic events which engulfed Peshawar from 23 April, adding to the humiliation the government had suffered in the Chittagong raids.

[22] For the accumulation of pressure on Irwin see Governor of Bombay to Irwin, 9 April (telegram) & 15 April 1930, M. Ali to Irwin, 15 April 1930, Sapru to Irwin, 20 April 1930, Mss. EUR.C. 152 (24); Irwin to Sir Malcolm Hailey on Villiers' visit, 21 April 1930, *ibid.*; description of Chittagong Raids, Hale, *Political Trouble in India 1917–1937*, pp. 17–21; on Karachi riot, Bombay FR2, April 1930, Home Poll., 1930, File No. 18/v.

[23] Govt. of India, Home Dept., to Govt. of Bombay, Special Dept., telegram, 22 April 1930, Bombay's reply, telegram, 26 April 1930, Home Poll., 1930, File No. 257-VIII & K.-W; also in Mss. EUR.F.150 (2). Govt. of India telegram to all local govts. except Bombay, 22 April 1930, & replies, 23–26 April 1930, Home Poll., 1930, File No. 257-VIII & K.-W. Irwin to Sir Malcolm Hailey on his Council's views, 21 April 1930, Mss. EUR.C.152 (24).

[24] Irwin to Wedgwood Benn, 24 April 1930, enclosing his exchange of letters with Vithalbhai Patel on 23 April 1930, Mss. EUR.C.152 (6).

The North-West Frontier was always a sensitive area in official strategy, and Peshawar itself was a potentially turbulent city as the focus for a wide variety of immigrants from the border tribes, Afghanistan and central Asia. As late as December 1929 there seemed little danger of a link between Frontier problems and the Congress challenge. The Frontier Congress group was weak, drawn mainly from the tiny urban Hindu minority in this Muslim area; and when outsiders came to recruit volunteers for the Lahore Congress with promises of half the cost of uniform and travelling expenses they only attracted about fifty. However, among those who went to Lahore was Abdul Ghaffar Khan, a prominent Pathan who though western-educated had been influenced by the Haji of Turangzai, a dourly puritan Muslim opposed to the infidel government of the British. Abdul Ghaffar Khan professed himself a devotee of Gandhi's non-violent methods, and after Lahore linked a Pathan nationalist movement to the Congress name and organization, in a relationship which was always ambiguous and often strained. On his return from Lahore he began touring, particularly in Peshawar district, preaching the Congress creed, laying the foundations of an Afghan Youth League and a Central Afghan Jirga, and recruiting a body of volunteers, the 'Servants of God', *Khudai Khitmatgars*, whose distinctive mark was their red shirts. Outside Peshawar district sympathy for Congress appeared only in the few towns where Hindu traders clustered, and such political activity as this generated was channelled through Congress bodies and Nau Jawan Bharat Sabhas. On 23 April a Congress Enquiry Committee on the Frontier Crimes Regulation was excluded from Peshawar city. This led to violent speeches, the dissemination of anti-government pamphlets and posters, and the eruption of mob violence in the city; while mass Red Shirt meetings occurred in outlying parts of the district. Abdul Ghaffar Khan was among those arrested. From 24 April civil authority collapsed in the city until 4 May, and Congress sympathizers seized the initiative though certainly not control of the situation. As significant in government calculations as this local breakdown was the proof that the services might not always be a buttress against civil disorder and sedition provided when two platoons of the Garhawal Rifles refused to help in the reassertion of authority.[25]

Confronted with a rapidly deteriorating situation of which Peshawar was the *coup de grace*, Irwin promulgated the Press Ordinance on 27 April to curb the spread of anti-government exhortations; and his Council decided on 29 April both to regain control of Peshawar and to arrest Gandhi in the near future at a time convenient to government. Irwin realized that the arrest would bring matters to a head, but he felt it unavoidable 'unless

---

[25] *1929–30. Administration Report of The North West Frontier Province* (Peshawar, 1931), p. 2; *1930–31. Administration Report of The North West Frontier Province* (Peshawar, 1933), pp. 1–6; Coatman, *Years of Destiny*, pp. 283–4, 366–9.

For the ambivalent relations between local Congressmen, the Working Committee and Abdul Ghaffar Khan's supporters see evidence from 1931 below, pp. 219–20, 265–6.

Government is to abdicate in favour of Gandhi and the Congress, by admitting to ourselves and the public our inability to arrest him at all'. It was crucial for the administration to demonstrate its intention to govern – throughout India, but particularly in Gujarat 'where in certain parts authority of Government has almost disappeared'.[26] Somewhat fraught interchanges followed between Bombay and Delhi on the date of Gandhi's arrest, as Bombay argued for liberty to arrest him at once if he started for the salt works, while Delhi wished to fix a date, 4 May, in order to warn other governments. Delhi ultimately bowed to Bombay's wish but since Gandhi merely drafted a letter of intent and took no action he was arrested and interned on the date decided, under Regulation xxv of 1827, to avoid the necessity of a trial or fixed sentence, and to assuage Hindu sensitivity by not using the penal law on the Mahatma. Before Gandhi could send his minatory letter he was arrested during the night of 4/5 May and taken by train and car to Yeravda jail in Poona once again, where his captors thought he looked remarkably fit, years younger than in 1922 and thoroughly happy to be under arrest.[27]

The trouble ensued which Irwin and his governors had anticipated. Every province reported hartals and demonstrations in towns: only in the North-West Frontier, embroiled in its own turbulence, did people take little notice. Muslims however were generally not involved. In Delhi they closed their shops for fear of being looted when Congress organized hartals and processions, but in Bombay's E. Khandesh district a communal riot erupted when Muslims refused to participate in the hartal. In Bombay City and Ahmedabad troops were stationed in advance to prevent disturbances, but none occurred. The worst confrontations happened in Delhi where police fired on the Sisganj Gurdwara when they were heavily stoned from it; and in Sholapur where mob violence led to military occupation of the city and the declaration of martial law. As it turned out government's handling of Gandhi could hardly have discredited it more. First it raised doubts of its own strength and will by delaying Gandhi's arrest. Now it evoked India-wide hostility and the corollary of sympathy for Gandhi, not just among those it considered 'irreconcilables' but among many of those whose support it had hoped to retain by tactical handling of the Mahatma: ten Bombay MLCs for example resigned after the arrest.[28]

The continental repercussions of Gandhi's arrest were a remarkable demonstration of the political position of the man whom contemporaries

[26] V to S of S, telegram, 29 April 1930, Mss. EUR.C.152 (11).

[27] For the use of the Bombay Regulation see V to S of S, telegram, 28 April 1930, *ibid.*; telegraphic interchange between Govts. of India & Bombay on the date of Gandhi's arrest, 28 April – 1 May 1930, Mss. EUR.F.150 (2). Report to Bombay Home Member, 5 May 1930, *HFM, III, III*, p. 124.

[28] Provincial FRis, May 1930, Home Poll., 1930, File no. 18/vi; Governor of Bombay to S of S, telegram, 5 May 1930, L/PJ/6/1998. Irwin told Wedgwood Benn, 8 May 1930, that reaction to Gandhi's arrest was less than they had anticipated; Mss. EUR.C.152 (6).

had believed to be a spent force politically in the mid-1920s. Yet protest
at the arrest of one who had deliberately worked to represent in his own
person the struggle with the raj was not a true index of his leadership
strength. Willingness to follow his plans was more significant. After he had
broken the salt law there was no province which did not witness some form
of salt satyagraha, except for the Frontier, though the demonstrations
varied in type and intensity. Facilities for making salt or raiding salt works
were partly responsible for the regional diversities, although the law could
be broken by such variants as illicit sales. In 1933–4 the major production
areas were:[29]

Northern India	...	12,771,725 maunds
(most from Punjab mines and Sambhar Lake sources)		
Madras	...	12,980,838 maunds
Bombay	...	11,766,894 maunds
Sind	...	1,352,334 maunds
Bengal	...	751 maunds
Burma	...	1,042,810 maunds

Bombay was the most seriously affected area. Its major source of supply
was sea salt made in works owned or leased out by the government, the
main works being at Dharasna and Chharvada on the south Gujarat coast,
with others like Wadala within thirty miles of Bombay City. At the beginning
of the satyagraha the salt administration department destroyed natural salt
formations; and initially a popular method of contravening the law was
boiling sea water or water containing brine. The salt produced thus was
expensive and unpalatable, but the method had peculiar advantages as an
observer noted in Bombay City, where prominent Congressmen did it
ceremoniously on the Esplanade Maidan.

> The operation consisted of boiling sea water in a receptable over a fire,
> – the performer with a few attendants being surrounded by concentric
> rings of Congress volunteers with tightly linked arms, the rings number-
> ing not infrequently from six to twelve. On one occasion no less than
> thirty rings were used, three of which consisted of Sikhs and three of
> women. For the police to break through these rings of volunteers
> without inflicting injuries was an extremely prolonged and exasperating
> task, and when, – as was usually the case, – they had succeeded in doing
> so the crowd more often than not became violent and pelted them with
> stones.[30]

There was some salt smuggling from Goa and States territory and sales
of contraband salt, for example, in Ahmedabad. But the really serious phase
of the salt satyagraha occurred in May and early June when Congress
started raids on salt works. After Gandhi's arrest a war council was established to carry out his projected campaign at Dharasna; it consisted of Abbas
Tyabji and other prominent Gujarati Congressmen. Their main attack was
on 21 May, the effort of about 3,000 volunteers from Gujarat and Bombay,

[29] *Statistical Abstract for British India from 1924–25 to 1933–34,* p. 285.
[30] *India in 1930–31* (Calcutta, 1932), p. 660.

encouraged by several thousand sightseers. The police held them off with *lathi* charges, and there were about 300 casualties as a result. Minor subsequent attacks were fended off more easily, new columns of volunteers were stopped en route, and a volunteer camp was demolished. From 25 May a series of attacks was directed against the Wadala works, within easy train, tram and lorry distance of Bombay City. Thousands of Congress supporters and actively encouraging spectators streamed out to the three-mile front of the salt pans, and considerable amounts of salt were stolen. The police had to have military aid and they made numerous *lathi* charges. Prisoners from Worli Temporary Prison attempted to break out to join the Wadala raids, encouraged by large crowds, while women from the neighbourhood obstructed repair work on the prison fencing. Although the greatest turbulence occurred to the north of the city, in the southern suburban district at Ville Parle Maharashtrian Congressmen opened a salt satyagraha camp, which was followed by others on the coast down to Ratnagiri and Shiroda. Inland where salt could not be made, as at Poona and Nasik, contraband salt was sold. The salt satyagraha was effectively ended by the arrival of the monsoon at the beginning of June.[31]

TABLE 3. *Average consumption of salt per head per year in Bombay Presidency*

Area	Year	Average (in lbs)
Gujarat	1928–9	14.64
	1929–30	13.68
	1930–1	13.52
Konkan, Deccan and	1928–9	14.46
southern Maratha	1929–30	14.02
country	1930–1	13.89

SOURCE: See below n. 32.

The effects of the salt raids showed up in the Salt Department's books. Practically no salt was made at Dharasna and Chharvada in May 1930, and sales for the financial year 1929–30 were down by 18,230 maunds on the previous year: in 1930–1 they had dropped by a further 121,897 maunds. Moreover the average annual consumption of salt per head in the Presidency dropped noticeably (see Table 3).[32] But more important from the satyagrahis' point of view was the publicity value of the raids and the police

---

[31] *idem; Report on the Administration of the Salt Department of the Bombay Presidency (excluding Sind and Aden). For the year 1929–30* (Calcutta, 1930), pp. 17–20; Bombay FR, 21 June 1930, L/PJ/6/1998; Maharashtra Satyagraha File, AICC Papers, 1930, File No. G-148.

[32] Statistics on salt sales & consumption are in *Salt Administration Report, 1929–30, & Report on the Administration of the Salt Department of the Bombay Presidency (excluding Sind and Aden). For the year 1930–31* (Calcutta, 1931).

methods their suppression elicited. The raids were not intended to get salt but to force the government into violent retaliation, even to the extent of firing on unarmed crowds, to show not just to local sightseers but to a world-wide public 'the fangs and claws of the Government in all its ugliness'.[33] Congress proved to have an excellent publicity machine. Accounts of the raids and blood-curdling accounts of police brutality and injuries caused were reported in *Young India*. A Congress Free Hospital Medical Report for 22 May–21 July gave details and photographs of injuries to Congressmen treated. The Gujarat PCC also published a pamphlet, subsequently banned, *The Black Regime at Dharasana* [*A brief Survey of the 'Dharasana Raid'*], 'solely meant to show what depth of depravity, an alien Government, bent upon keeping its sway over a deliberately disarmed and emasculated nation, can go'. On 11 June the Bombay Government felt it necessary to issue a communique rebutting stories of savage police beatings at Dharasna. News of these accusations spread beyond India, and C. F. Andrews wrote to Wedgwood Benn asking that European officers present should be tried publicly, basing his demand on reports from Gandhi's English devotee, Mirabehn, in *Young India*, and a personal letter to him.[34]

Outside Bombay the only provinces where the salt satyagraha proved more than a token gesture were Bengal, Madras and U.P. In Bengal Bipin Chandra Pal's description of it as 'a great nation's tragic puerility' probably echoed the feelings of many political activists. In the districts of 24-Parganas and Midnapore, however, salt manufacture was brisk in April. In the former, satyagrahis' energy was diverted into boycott and picketing liquor shops at the end of the month, but in Contai sub-division of Midnapore, traditionally an area where salt was illegally made for home consumption, forty villages were involved, and the movement of *bhadralok* volunteers and sympathetic villagers was only crushed by the end of May with a vigorous programme of arrests.[35] In Madras salt making did not last long on any large scale, though E. and W. Godavari, Kistna, Guntur and Vizagapatam were all affected early in April. On the Tamil Nad PCC Srinivasa Iyengar, Satyamurti and their associates were eclipsed by their old rival, Rajagopa-lachariar, who had remained loyal to Gandhi and his techniques through the 1920s and now reaped the reward by becoming PCC President. He led

[33] J. C. Kumarappa in *Young India*, 29 May 1930, Microfilm, John Rylands University Library of Manchester: Gandhi had argued similarly in his draft letter to Irwin, 4 May 1930, *Young India*, 8 May 1930, CWMG, XLIII, 389–93.

[34] C. F. Andrews to Wedgwood Benn, 25 June 1930; *Young India*, 12 June 1930 (account of injuries after Dharasna raid by Mirabehn): Bombay Govt. communiqué, 11 June 1930; Congress Free Hospital. Medical Report. 22 May – 21 July 1930; L/PJ/6/1998. *The Black Regime at Dharasana* [*A brief Survey of the 'Dharasana Raid'*] (Ahmedabad, 1930), British Museum, PIB 29/3.

[35] *Report of the Administration of Bengal, 1929–30* (Calcutta, 1931), p. viii; Bengal PCC to AICC, 11 April 1930, AICC Papers, 1930, File No. G-86 (Kw) (i) Part 1; Bengal FR1, April 1930, Home Poll., 1930, File No. 18/v.

the salt satyagraha in the Tamil districts. The laws were broken daily in Madras City for two weeks under T. Prakasam's direction until the police dispersed crowds on 27 April. Rajagopalachariar then embarked on his own march from Trichinopoly to Vedaranniyan with 100 volunteers; but the Tamil campaign was effectively squashed by his arrest and that of the whole camp at Vedaranniyan.[36] In U.P. salt laws were broken by manufacturing and selling illicit salt in Agra, Cawnpore, Benares, Allahabad, Lucknow, Meerut, Rae Bareli, Farukhabad, Etawah, Balliah and Mainpuri early in April. The two Nehrus sold salt in Allahabad daily; but Jawaharlal was dubious that even a packet of salt collected by Gandhi would fetch a decent price at public auction there – Rs. 4–500 at the highest. There were not many arrests, and there was little rural interest, the peasants being too busy harvesting.[37]

In Punjab the salt satyagraha aroused no enthusiasm and swiftly degenerated into a farce; and little interest was shown in Delhi. The Assam PCC bluntly remarked that it was not deemed feasible locally, and on 19 April decided to postpone civil disobedience until its finances and organization were in better shape. In C.P. and Berar the absence of such easy targets as salt works or the sea shore discouraged local activity, and salt laws were defied briefly only in the Hindi districts. Just as C.P.'s natural target was forest regulations, so in Bihar Rajendra Prasad and the PCC leaned towards civil disboedience on a local issue, the chaukidari tax. As Gandhi was openly discouraging the PCC agreed to follow the Gandhian line. However, the campaign collapsed very swiftly except in Balasore on the Orissa coast where salt making was practicable and there was local dislike of the prohibition of Orissa's old salt industry.[38]

Neither in India as a whole nor in any province was the government's salt monopoly ever threatened by the salt satyagraha: but Gandhi and the Working Committee had not expected or intended this. Neither did it succeed, however, in Gandhi's aim of uniting the Hindus and Muslims in a common struggle. But it performed an important preparatory function in the civil disobedience campaign by generating widespread demonstra-

---

[36] Madras FR1, April 1930, *ibid.*; *Report on the Administration of the Madras Presidency for the year 1929–30* (Madras, 1931), pp. xiii-xvii; report on satyagraha in Tamil Nadu to 1 October 1930, Tamil Nad PCC to AICC, 4 October 1930, AICC Papers, 1930, File No. G-189.

[37] J. Nehru to M. Desai, 12 April 1930, *SWJN*, 4, pp. 308–11; UP FR1, April 1930, Home Poll., 1930, File No. 18/v.

[38] *Punjab Administration Report, 1930–31* (Lahore, 1932), pp. 3–5; Sir Geoffrey de Montmorency, Governor of Punjab, to Irwin, 14 April 1930, Mss. EUR.C.152 (24); Delhi FR2, April 1930, Home Poll., 1930, File No. 18/v; report from Assam PCC, 10 June 1930, AICC Papers, 1930, File No. G-145; *The Central Provinces and Berar 1929–30. A Review of the Administration of the Province* (Nagpur, 1931), pp. 1–2; annual report of Marathi C.P. PCC, AICC Papers, 1930, File No. Misc. 24; letter of Berar Provincial War Council Secretary, 9 November 1930, AICC Papers, 1930, File No. G-84; Bihar & Orissa FR2, February 1930, Home Poll., 1930, File No. 18/III; *Bihar and Orissa in 1929–30*, pp. xvii, 3.

tions of contempt for laws considered oppressive and for British authority.[39] It had also given local Congress committees occasion to try out their publicity mechanisms and organizational links.

II MASS CIVIL DISOBEDIENCE

Internment at Yeravda removed Gandhi from active leadership of civil disobedience, but there remained the dilemmas of confrontation he had hoped to solve through the salt satyagraha. These stemmed from the nature of Congress and the political context. It was an alignment of diverse groups confronting a raj it wished to change radically, but which most of its adherents had no wish to see go down amid a collapse of the political and social order. Moreover Congress had to choose its tactics in an environment where many other groups actually or potentially impinged on its relationship with the raj. The diversity of opinion and interest in Congress was a major obstacle to successful civil disobedience. There was no solid commitment to this style of action, and the majority adopting it at Lahore represented many shades of opinion. They accepted it partly as a tactical compromise rather than split the only national political organization which evoked considerable loyalty and appeared vital in the conflict with the British: and partly because Gandhi's exhortations to non-violence and his moralistic definitions of the goal lifted it from the plane of common or garden sedition. Moreover no other leader offered himself with an acceptable alternative in terms of a rallying cry or a tactic. But the problem once Gandhi was removed from active leadership was whether the programme he had initiated would elicit support and remain controlled, thereby uniting different political groups and integrating different levels of political awareness and expertise in a mutually beneficial stance in relation to the raj. Would civil disobedience become a political bandwaggon and buttress Gandhi's leadership position despite his incarceration, or would it disintegrate, shattering the fragile unities he had fostered and wrecking his own political credibility?

There was no all-India blueprint for civil disobedience in 1930–1 as there had been in 1920–2, and the movement in practice became a series of loosely coordinated local conflicts. The Working Committee's tactical decisions permitted extensive provincial flexibility, and its communications with PCCs were more often suggestions than directives. At its 15 May meeting, for example, it resolved in favour of complete boycott of foreign cloth and continuing salt satyagraha, but though suggesting that the time had come for new forms of civil disobedience, such as non-payment of land revenue and the chaukidari tax, and contravention of forest laws, it left the initiative in the hands of PCCs. Through 1930 it stuck to the basic guidelines laid down by Gandhi, adding disobedience to the Ordinances with which the

[39] Irwin to Wedgwood Benn, 24 April 1930, Mss. EUR.C.152 (6).

government combatted the campaign, withdrawal of post office savings and publication of its June resolution exhorting soldiers and police to treat satyagrahis as brothers. On controversial tactics, however, it merely made suggestions: non-payment of taxes was always left as a PCC decision, while students were not instructed to withdraw from college but merely encouraged to participate fully in civil disobedience, even to the extent of suspending their studies. The rationale of this approach by the Working Committee lay partly in the virtual certainty of Congress disorganization at government hands, as Jairamdas Daulatram warned in *Young India.*

> Each town, each village may have...to become its own battle field. The strategy of the battle must then come to be determined by local circumstances and change with them from day to day. The sooner the workers prepare for this state of things, the earlier shall we reach our goal. They should need little guidance from outside. They know that there must be no deviation from the principles of civil disobedience as laid down by Mahatma Gandhi or from the main programme of action as fixed by the Congress.[40]

For various reasons tight central control of civil disobedience on a rigid continental pattern was impossible. Each province provided opportunities for satyagraha particularly attractive to Congess's local adherents and potential recruits. This was demonstrated by the hankering of inland areas such as C.P. and Bihar for opposition to forest laws and the chaukidari tax while Gandhi planned the salt satyagraha. As the economic crisis deepened through 1930 affecting different regions in varying ways and degrees, so local strains became more sharply differentiated, increasing local Congress leaders' need for freedom from central control if they were to exploit local discontents and channel them into civil disobedience. Provincial governments also had different points of vulnerability, and effective campaigns had to be tailored to probe such weaknesses.[41]

Moreover as Gandhi's organizational efforts in 1929 indicated, Congress was not a modern political party with an efficient organization, sound

---

[40] *Young India*, 17 July 1930, G. Sharp, *Gandhi Wields the Weapon of Moral Power* (Ahmedabad, 1960), p. 172. For Working Committee meetings, resolutions and instructions see Home Poll., 1930, File No. 257/III; Bombay FR2, July 1930, Home Poll., 1930, File No. 18/VIII; J. Nehru's circular to PCCs, 14 October 1930, 'making certain suggestions...to guide your committee in its future work', *SWJN*, 4, pp. 397–400.

[41] The Government of Bihar was particularly vulnerable to a temperance agitation. It was a poor province, and in 1929–30 its largest head of revenue was excise, forming 32% of the total. Its capacity to levy land revenue was limited by the permanent settlement, and in 1929–30 this produced only 29.9% of the total. Neighbouring U.P. was heavily dependent on its land revenue.

The need of Congress leaders in the provinces to keep the momentum of a local campaign going was well indicated by J. Daulatram in Hyderabad, Sind, to J. Nehru, 17 June 1930, J. Nehru Papers, part I, vol. XXXV. 'We are getting on fairly well here. On the whole Government is avoiding arrests. We are going to force the issue now & compel arrests. Without arrest or something sensational the public enthusiasm may wane.'

finances and effective channels of information and command. Since it was an alliance of local groups, needing each other's support under an all-India banner and wishing to exploit the limited funds and organization which were nonetheless superior to those of any other political body, there was always within it an uneasy balance between local and central aims and initiative. Provincial politicians wanted access to the prestige and resources of the all-India body but they did not hesitate to modify or even ignore central advice if this clashed with provincial interests. Even within provinces there were different levels of leadership operating in specific areas, and when the aspirations of district men were out of line with those of provincial leaders the latter had little control within their provinces, and Congress became an even less effective mechanism through which all-India plans could be disseminated and implemented.[42]

The raj realised that the Working Committee had limited control over civil disobedience, and the experienced governor Sir Malcolm Hailey, cautioned Irwin,

> ...I know of course the military argument...that the most effective way to cripple the enemy is to strike a crushing blow at his most vital point. I am always a little mistrustful of General Staff advice on civil affairs, and I would think more of the argument if the blow was really likely to be crushing, and if the Working Committee were to-day the real motive and directive force behind the movement. It issues resolutions, but does very little actually in the way of organization or direction.[43]

Nonetheless officials were surprised at the strength and depth of Congress organization displayed in civil disobedience: and when early in 1931 local governments were asked whether Congress could reorganize civil disobedience if it had been effectively called off, they were unanimous that it could, and very swiftly.[44]

The Working Committee issued advice through the press as long as editors, with an eye to government controls, would accept its material. It issued its own leaflets and bulletins until regular presses refused the work. When letters and telegrams were increasingly stopped by censors it used special messengers. But governmental controls strangled the all-India

[42] The clearest case of a province in conflict with the all-India body was Bengal. See J. Gallagher, 'Congress in Decline: Bengal 1930 to 1939', Gallagher, Johnson & Seal (ed.), *Locality, Province and Nation*, pp. 269–325. For conflict and cooperation within a province between different levels of leadership affecting all-India plans, see B. Stoddart, 'The Anatomy of a Discontent. Politics in the Telugu Country 1925–1937', D. A. Low (ed.) *Congress and the Raj* (forthcoming).

[43] Governor of U.P. to Viceroy, 25 June 1930, Home Poll., 1930, File No. 257/111. Irwin told Wedgwood Benn, 10 July 1930, that 'a lot of people...have been hanging on the fringe of the civil disobedience movement, such as Youth Leagues and so on, whose purposes are quite different and who are not really under the control of Gandhi or Motilal'. Mss. EUR.C.152 (6).

[44] Wedgwood Benn to Irwin, 5 June 1930, *ibid.*; local government replies to Home Dept. enquiry of 28 January 1931 on the possibilities of reorganized civil disobedience, Home Poll., 1931, File No. 5/45.

organization;[45] and the brunt of the work fell to provincial Congresses whose mechanisms for publicity and control varied in efficiency. Many of them published bulletins and news sheets, some typed, some crudely written by hand and cyclostyled, which served the dual purpose of disobedience by evading press control and breaking the Ordinance against unauthorized news sheets, and of spreading propaganda and information about civil disobedience in their own and other regions. U.P. and Bihar are known to have organized local messenger services, and in U.P. towns drummers were used to spread Congress notifications. Regional reports on satyagraha came to the AICC erratically, but they indicated that provincial organization and all-India communication were never at a complete standstill.[46] Probably the best organized and best equipped of the local Congresses was that in Bombay City, where the hub was Congress House at 414 Girgaum Back Road. A May raid on this and the Jinnah Hall uncovered two cyclostyle machines and other material for issuing cyclostyled bulletins. But the Bombay Congress bulletin continued to appear to the ire and discomfiture of the local government, the publicity department of the Bombay Youth League being primarily responsible for it.[47]

Organization even on this scale required considerable funds. Bombay, for example, had to finance its bulletin, equipment and uniform for volunteers, and lorries for ferrying volunteers through the city. It was estimated that the satyagraha camps in Surat and district alone were costing Rs. 8–10,000 a month.[48] All provinces faced the problem of paying some of the volunteers and helping the families of those in jail. The availability of funds determined to some extent the number of activists local Congresses could attract into the campaign, and also the leverage which the all-India body could exert over the provincial organizations as pay-master.

[45] J. Nehru lamented that the AICC office did not seem to be functioning, and urged Syed Mahmud to 'make the place hum. If there is not enough work make the staff stand on their heads. Anything to keep them working.' n.d., November/December 1930, V. N. Datta & B. E. Cleghorn (ed.), *A Nationalist Muslim and Indian Politics* (Delhi, 1974), p. 102. For evidence of central organization see J. Nehru, *An Autobiography*, pp. 236, 256–7; C.I.D. Special Branch Memorandum, 20 January 1931, on printed instructions for Independence Day, 26 January 1931, sent by special messenger to PCCs asking them to distribute these in the vernacular to district and *taluka* committees, Home Poll., 1931, File No. 5/45.

[46] Provincial reports on satyagraha are in AICC Papers; for example (1930, G-94) contains the publicity organs of the Delhi Congress in Urdu, Hindi and English, the English Congress Bulletin costing 2 pies. See also J. Nehru to M. Desai, 12 April 1930, *SWJN*, 4, p. 308; J. Nehru, *An Autobiography*, pp. 236–7; Braj Kishore Prasad to Vallabhbhai Patel, 21 July 1930, enclosing note on satyagraha in Bihar, AICC Papers, 1930, File No. G-80, part II.

[47] Bombay FR1, June 1930, Home Poll., 1930, File No. 18/VII; Bombay FR1, July 1931, Home Poll., 1931, File No. 18/VII.

[48] Note by Govt. of India Home Member, H. G. Haig, 13 June 1930, on visit to Bombay, Home Poll., 1930, File No. 257/V & K.-W.; report by Surat District Magistrate to Bombay Home Dept., 1 August 1930, Home Poll., 1931, K.-W. to File No. 5/36.

No accurate assessment is possible of the funds Congress had at its disposal. Some AICC accounts survive, but there is little evidence about local Congress finances. The Governor of Bombay admitted that his government had only occasional clues and little accurate information about the location of Congress funds, and the AICC took precautions to remove funds to 'safe custody' in mid-1930 when it believed government would try to freeze or seize Congress money deposited in ordinary banks.[49] No provincial administration, however, found a satisfactory way of seizing Congress funds.[50] The hints of the financial backing for civil disobedience suggest that at certain times local Congresses had considerable resources, that AICC finances were in a far healthier condition than in 1929, and that the Mahatma was a superb fund-raiser with whom it was profitable to keep company.

The AICC's income came from provincial contributions, delegates' fees and subscriptions. It also had access to sizeable reserves in the All-India Tilak Memorial Swaraj Fund which Gandhi had collected during Non-Cooperation, and which stood in September 1929 at around Rs. 90,000. Some of these reserves were earmarked for specific purposes such as *khadi* and publicity, but in February 1930 the AICC had over Rs. 32,000 available for general expenditure, and in July over Rs. 28,000. AICC expenditure in February and March 1930 ran at about Rs. 4,300, though in July it shot up to Rs. 30,000. As some of its outgoings were into bank accounts it is difficult to trace their ultimate destination, but the AICC was evidently spending considerable sums on volunteering and publicity. In addition there were the funds for *khadi* which Gandhi had collected in 1929, which totalled Rs. 760,000; and hefty donations to Congress made early in 1930 – Rs. 50,000 for Gandhi's expenses in connection with civil disobedience from his Muslim friend, Dr Rajab Ali, Rs. 5 lahks from B. Desai and nearly Rs. 2 lakhs from Motilal. In February 1930 moreover G. D. Birla gave Gandhi a gift the exact amount of which was unknown, but which rumour put at between one and five lakhs of rupees.[51]

In the provinces there was also considerable financial buoyancy in the early months of the campaign. The governments of Bombay, U.P., Punjab, Bengal and Assam all reported businessmen supporting Congress with donations. Some of these contributions were reluctant, the result of social pressure; while others were designed to embarrass commercial rivals, as in the case of Allahabad men out to attract business from a Bombay disrupted by civil disobedience. In June some leading Hindu zamindars

[49] Sykes to Irwin, 18 September 1930, Mss. EUR.C.152 (25); AICC to Bombay PCC, 15 June & 16 July 1930, AICC Papers, 1931, File No. Misc. 63.
[50] Report of Conference of Police Officers held at New Delhi, 19–24 January 1931, part II, Home Poll., 1931, File No. 152.
[51] AICC Treasurer's Account, February & July 1930, AICC Papers, 1930, File Nos. Misc. 15 & 21; note by Sir David Petrie, D.I.B., on Congress funds, 26 May 1930, Home Poll., 1931, File No. 5/40.

in Bihar replenished Congress coffers and enabled a revival of picketing.[52] Congress funds were raised in Calcutta by street and house collections; but the local gold mine was the Calcutta Corporation which, under the control of Subhas Bose's brother, levied tolls from shop and stall keepers and from contractors with whom it did business.[53]

However from September onwards there were signs in the localities that Congress funds were drying up; and that this spelt the end of active local disobedience. The Secretary of the PCC in Malabar reported that his committee and the local satyagraha committee had only Rs. 400, but they were having to spend Rs. 200 a month on such things as butter, oil, milk and soap for prisoners in Cannanore jail. Correspondence intercepted from Tamil Nad indicated that lack of money was proving an insurmountable obstacle there. From Bihar news came to the AICC of an immediate need for Rs. 25,000 if civil disobedience was to carry on for six months more: volunteers could be fed in villages with ease, but little cash was forthcoming locally and volunteers could not be moved about.[54] The AICC could not foot these local bills.

If the character of Congress and the relationship between the central body and the provinces was an effective obstacle to any centralized civil disobedience campaign the policies of the government confirmed this tendency. A vigorous campaign of arrests followed the promulgation of Ordinances, designed to knock out the movement's leadership, cripple its organization and stifle its publicity mechanisms. The Prevention of Intimidation Ordinance and Unlawful Instigation Ordinance, both promulgated on 30 May, were aimed at the main manifestations of civil disobedience – picketing to procure the boycott of foreign cloth and liquor, and to intimidate government servants, and the instigation of no-tax campaigns. These lapsed at the end of November, but the latter was renewed on 23 December. The Press Ordinance of April was reinforced on 2 July by the Unauthorised News-sheets and Newspapers Ordinance intended to stop the flow of Congress propaganda. These, too, were renewed on 23 December after lapsing in October. Moreover the correspondence of all Working Committee members and PCC Presidents was censored to give governments advance

[52] Notes for speech by Sykes at Governors' Conference, Simla, 21–25 July 1930, Mss. EUR.F.150 (2); report by Governor of Punjab in Minutes of Governors' Conference, Simla, 23 July 1930, Mss. EUR.C.152 (25); U.P. FR2, April 1930, Home Poll., 1930, File No. 18/v; Assam FR2, August 1930, Home Poll., 1930, File No. 18/IX; Govt. of Bengal to Govt. of India, 12 January 1931, Home Poll., 1931, File No. 13/3; Bihar & Orissa FR2, June 1930, Home Poll., 1930, File No. 18/VII.

[53] Note by Sir B. L. Mitter, Govt. of India Law Member, 15 May 1930, Home Poll., 1930, File No. 248/11; Sir Stanley Jackson, Governor of Bengal, to Irwin, 30 June 1930, Mss EUR.C. 152 (24).

[54] Report in Kerala satyagraha file, 30 September 1930, AICC Papers, 1930, File No. G-107; Bombay FR2, November 1930, Home Poll., 1930, File No. 18/XII; handwritten report from Bihar, probably mid-October, AICC Papers, 1930, File No. Misc. 11, part I.

warning of Congress plans. Local governments were at first expected to deal with the different bodies within and aligned with the Congress organization under the Criminal Law Amendment Act of 1908. When it became clear that they could not seize property and buildings of associations declared illegal under the Act, they were armed with the Unlawful Association Ordinance of 10 October 1930.[55]

Irwin's government adopted these repressive measures with marked hesitation; and when the Ordinances lapsed towards the end of the year the Viceroy tried to avoid rearming the administration with extra-legal powers lest he embarrass the Secretary of State during the Round Table Conference at which many Liberals and other Hindu sympathizers of Congress were present. But against this consideration he had to weigh the increasing strain on local administrative services particularly the police, the recrudescence of terrorism in Bengal and the barrage of requests from Sykes in Bombay for tough action. Sykes, in the teeth of the storm, argued that the Government of India's policy of 'steady pressure' would fail in Bombay and would exhaust his services: they must choose between political conciliation or a knockout blow at civil disobedience.[56] The degree of repression permitted by Delhi and London did not break civil disobedience. Its effect was to emphasize the movement's regional diversities as it incarcerated the main all-India leaders. Moreover the imprisonment of recognized provincial leaders delivered the movement into the hands of men prompted by purely local visions and drives, who ignored such advice as issued from central Congress sources. In the U.P. this had happened as early as August 1930, and the release of some prominent provincial leaders in October and November only led to a more coherent campaign tailored to local conditions. By December disintegration of a recognized leadership was clear even in Bombay.[57]

An assessment of civil disobedience in relation to Gandhi's political

[55] *The Civil Disobedience Movement 1930–34*, pp. 4–9; text of 1930 Ordinances, *ibid.* pp. 96–129. For action taken against the press see also N. Gerald Barrier, *Banned. Controversial Literature and Political Control in British India 1907–1947* (Missouri, 1974), p. 115.

[56] For Irwin's reluctance to take powers by Ordinance see e.g. V to Governor of Bombay, (telegram) 7 May 1930, (letter) 10 May 1930, Mss. EUR.C.152 (24); V to S of S, telegrams, 18 & 20 December 1930, Mss. EUR.C.152 (11); D.A. Low, '"Civil Martial Law": The Government of India and the Civil Disobedience Movements 1930–34', Low (ed.), *Congress and the Raj.*
Examples of pressure from Sykes are Governor of Bombay to Viceroy, telegram, 8 May 1930, Mss. EUR.C.152 (24); Sykes to Irwin, 21 May 1930, Mss. EUR.F.150 (2); Sykes to Irwin, 4 July 1930, Mss. EUR.C.152 (25). Sykes made his views plain at the Governors' Conference, 21–25 July 1930: see notes for his speech, Mss. EUR.F.150 (2), and Sykes, *From Many Angles*, p. 402–3. Sykes wanted a comprehensive Defence of the Realm measure and had made a study of Britain's war-time DORA at the Home Office before reaching India: *ibid.* pp. 363–4.

[57] U.P. FR2, August 1930, Home Poll., 1930, File No. 18/IX; Sykes to Irwin, 23 December 1930, Mss. EUR.C.152 (25).

standing must however take into consideration both the local manifestations of the movement and their cumulative effect. The former indicate the degree to which Gandhi's tactics could be tailored to serve local needs, thus rooting his campaign deeply in popular support. The cumulative impact was equally important because it affected the British and non-combatants in the struggle, helping to determine their subsequent attitude to Gandhi, and the corollary, the position of leverage he attained in the relationship between them and those who had participated in the movement which was peculiarly his own. The survey which follows of the continental and local effects of civil disobedience is intended to demonstrate the nature of Gandhi's political position and the repercussions of the movement on it, not to provide a comprehensive account of the campaign.

As early as May 1930 it was clear that civil disobedience was a very severe challenge to the British on a continental scale. Purshotamdas Thakurdas, sober businessman and established though not uncritical ally of the imperial regime, warned Irwin that Gandhi had attracted immense public support, partly because the start of civil disobedience coincided with the effects of the depression, and that the degree of mass sympathy was markedly greater than in 1921. Irwin recognized that the raj faced 'a formidable menace to constituted Government' and would need all its resources to combat it; while his Home Member confessed that he had gained 'the impression during the last week or two from various parts of India that in spite of all that has been done Government may not be retaining that essential moral superiority, which is perhaps the most important factor in this struggle'.[58] By the beginning of July all provinces had been affected, Bombay City and Gujarat being the storm centres, and only C.P. and Assam had escaped serious difficulty in coping with its manifestations. Thereafter regional variations became sharper; and from August onwards the all-India situation improved from the government's viewpoint, the exceptions being areas like U.P. and C.P., where the movement moved into rural areas, and Gujarat where it had been so from the start. By the end of the year no fresh areas or modes of conflict were developing. In the first two months of 1931 the movement's manifestations ceased to be serious and in Madras and Punjab at least no longer affected ordinary life or inconvenienced the administration.[59]

[58] Thakurdas to Irwin, 28 April & 12 May 1930, Thakurdas Papers, File No. 99 (Pt. 1)/1930; V to S of S, telegram, 24 May 1930, Mss. EUR.C. 152 (11); H. G. Haig to J. E. B. Hotson, 25 May 1930, Home Poll., 1930, File No. 257/v & K.-W.

[59] *India in 1930–31*, pp. 66–137. J. Nehru, *An Autobiography*, p. 238, noted the weariness of the urban movement by autumn 1930; provincial FRs for September showed that civil disobedience was waning swiftly, Home Poll., 1930, File No. 18/x. Irwin was seriously concerned at the prospects of rural agitation when the autumn harvest came on the market after the catastrophic slump in the price of all the staple agricultural products; Irwin to Wedgwood Benn, 2 August 1930, Mss. EUR.C.152 (6).

TABLE 4. *Civil disobedience – prisoners in jail on 15 November 1930*

Province	Hindus	Muslims	Others	Total	Males	Females	Total	Juveniles under 17
Madras	2,930	31	5	2,966	2,923	43	2,966	23
Bombay	3,986	110	18	4,114	4,014	100	4,114	99
Bengal	4,684	106	—	4,790	4,716	74	4,790	669
U.P.	4,740	108	—	4,848	4,803	45	4,848	256
Punjab	1,094	226	523	1,843	1,792	51	1,843	230
Bihar and Orissa	6,285	37	1	6,323	6,316	7	6,323	615
C.P.	2,536	27	—	2,563	2,559	4	2,563	88
Assam	411	4	—	415	413	2	415	44
N.-W.F.P.	42	434	—	476	476	—	476	4
Delhi	646	69	1	716	683	33	716	22
Total	27,354	1,152	548	29,054	28,695	359	29,054	2,050

NOTES: The Bengal figures for the period up to 29 November; Punjab figures are to 31 December.

In the Punjab total 'others' are almost certainly Sikhs. On 14 March 1931 (Home Poll., 1931, File No. 23/26) the Govt. of Punjab informed the Govt. of India that 472 males, 2 females and 49 juveniles under 17 from the Sikh community were political prisoners.

SOURCE: Home Poll., 1931, File No. 23/26.

The official estimate of civil disobedience prisoners actually in jail in February 1931 was 23–24,000; and 60,000 the number who had been through jail in the course of the movement.[60] The most comprehensive set of figures relates to prisoners in mid-November when the total was just over 29,000. Broken down by province, community, sex and age they demonstrate that throughout India juveniles and women (except understandably on the Muslim frontier) were deeply involved in civil disobedience – a departure from previous patterns of involvement in political agitation. In marked contrast to Non-cooperation Muslims participated in very small numbers except on the Frontier where the campaign was *sui generis*. The statistics suggest that Bihar and Orissa, U.P., Bengal and Bombay were the most active provinces. But provincial governments had different arrest strategies and different opportunities for catching offenders: little could be done, for example, in Bombay when tax defaulters fled across the border into Baroda. This explains the contrast between the Bihar and Bombay figures, indicating that statistics alone are not accurate measurements of the intensity of civil disobedience (see Table 4).

[60] V to S of S, telegram, 3 February 1931, Mss. EUR.C.152 (11). An AICC estimate of the total number of convictions during the 1930–1 civil disobedience was just over 92,000, the highest provincial totals being those of Bihar & Orissa, Bengal, U.P. and Punjab; AICC General Secretary to Nagpur enquirer, 15 October 1930, AICC Papers, 1931, File No. G-1.

The imprisonment of such numbers put an immense strain on provincial jail services, stretching accommodation and demanding extra expenditure just at a time when depressed prices hit government revenue, as agriculturalists had to be relieved of some land revenue demands, legal liquor consumption and excise plummited, and customs collections declined. Bengal, for example, spent Rs. 7½ lakhs more on jails in 1930 than in 1929, half of which went on providing space for 7,000 extra prisoners. Bihar's increased expenditure on jails was Rs. 10½ Lakhs, and Bombay spent Rs. 2,747,000 on jails in 1930–1 compared with Rs. 2,437,000 in 1929–30 and Rs. 2,369,000 in 1928–9. C.P.'s overcrowding problems in jails were relieved by using go-downs, work sheds, and old cook-houses, and by building temporary huts – expedients paralleled elsewhere.[61]

Extra cash had to be found, too, for the police. Even in Assam expenditure went up from Rs. 2,492,545 in 1929 to Rs. 2,676,960 in 1930; while the cost of Bihar's civil police rose from Rs. 81½ lakhs in 1929–30 to Rs. 87½ lakhs in 1930–1. Bombay Presidency police costs rose from Rs. 39 lakhs to Rs. 41½ lakhs in the same period. Some of this went on extra police to combat civil disobedience – 200 temporary armed police in Bombay City, for example, and 500 additional armed police in Bengal. Where additional police were stationed in particularly troublesome areas the costs were borne by the local inhabitants, as in Midnapore and parts of Bihar.[62] More disturbing than the effects of civil disobedience on the cost of the police were its repercussions on their efficiency and morale. The control of ordinary crime gave place to the struggle against mobs, processions, forest burners and recalcitrant tax-payers, in an atmosphere of recrimination and boycott directed at policemen and their families. Bombay was the province where this was most marked, and the Inspector-General of Police penned a stiff note to Bombay's Home Secretary on the possible unreliability of his men because of the government's policy of attrition, particularly in Gujarat; he added in his annual report for 1930 that Kaira district was 'virtually in a state of war for a substantial part of the year'.[63] Despite the unpleasant conditions of service and the dangers of physical assault as well as social

---

[61] *Report on the Administration of Bengal 1930–31* (Calcutta, 1932), pp. 36–7; *Bihar and Orissa in 1930–31* (Patna, 1932), p. 20; *Bombay – 1928–29. A Review of the Administration of the Presidency* (Bombay, 1930), p. 222; *Bombay – 1929–30. A Review of the Administration of the Presidency* (Bombay, 1931), p. 219; *1930–31 Bombay Administration Report*, p. 154; *The Central Provinces and Berar 1930–31. A Review of the Administration of the Province* (Nagpur, 1932), p. 45.

[62] *Report on the Administration of Assam for the year 1929–30* (Shillong, 1931), pp. 10–11; *Report on the Administration of Assam for the year 1930–31* (Shillong, 1932), pp. 10–11; *1929–30 Bihar & Orissa Administration Report*, p. 69; *1930–31 Bihar & Orissa Administration Report*, p. 62; *1929–30 Bombay Administration Report*, pp. xiii–xiv; *1930–31 Bombay Administration Report*, pp. xiv–xv; *1930–31 Bengal Administration Report*, pp. 19–22.

[63] Bombay Inspector-General of Police to Bombay Home Secretary, 29 May 1930, Home Poll., 1930, File No. 257/v & K.-W.; his annual report was quoted in *1930–31 Bombay Administration Report*, pp. 35–44. For a general review of the strain on the police see *India in 1930–31*, pp. 532–76.

ostracism, recruits for the police forces continued to come forward in adequate numbers.

The ill-fated elections to local Legislative Councils and the Assembly, postponed in 1929, took place in September, just when the peak of civil disobedience was past in most provinces. It provided a firm continental demonstration, however, of the spread and depth of the Congress campaign, to the government and to non-combatants who stood for election or were preparing to attend the Round Table Conference. In 1920 the effects of Non-cooperation on the elections had been difficult to gauge because they were the first to be held under the reformed constitution. By 1930 there had been two 'normal' elections since 1920 and the percentage poll had risen each time. In 1930 the poll dropped sharply in every province, the fall being most marked in the Hindu seats, particularly in towns. The Muslim poll dropped but generally only slightly, the exception being Bombay where the Muslim urban vote fell from 36.5% in 1926 to 12.0% in 1930, though the Muslim rural vote actually rose. Bombay was the province most affected overall, the Hindu urban vote plummeting from 35.59% in 1926 to 8.0% in 1930 (see Appendices I and II). The elections passed off peacefully in most areas, although there was a riot in Moradabad (U.P.), and disturbances in Bombay City and suburbs, Surat and Ahmedabad. The fall in the poll was partly due to Congress picketing of booths, but more to the abstention from the elections of Congress candidates who in previous years had been the only ones with a real programme and some form of organization. In some places Congressmen put up dummy low caste candidates; in C.P. apparently with the idea of discrediting the Legislative Council, but in U.P. as a fund-raising mechanism to force genuine candidates to buy off the opposition. However, in the Punjab Hindus showed their disapproval of this tactic when they realized it would mean less Hindu representation in a Council where Muslims already had a majority.[64]

Similar reluctance to jeopardize their longer term local positions was evident in Congressmen's apathy towards a boycott of the Census early in 1931. Although the idea was publicized in an illegal edition of *Young India* as a continental form of satyagraha, few places posed problems to the enumerators, since all communities feared that boycott would lead to their under-enumeration and subsequent disadvantage when official decisions were based on the 1931 figures in the following decade. Only in Bombay was there serious interference with Census. Officials faced petty harassment, small boys in the Congress 'Monkey Army', Vanar Sena Corps, obliterated numbers on houses; but ultimately only the returns for some Gujarat towns were incomplete or defective.[65]

[64] Provincial FRs for September & October 1930, Home Poll., 1930, File Nos. 18/X & 18/XI; Govt. of Bombay to S of S, telegrams, received 3 & 12 September 1930, L/PJ/6/1998.

[65] *Census of India, 1931. Vol. 1. – India. Part I – Report* (Delhi, 1933), pp. ix-x; Irwin to Sykes, 4 January 1931, Mss. EUR.C.152 (26); Kaira District Magistrate to Bombay

The main all-India index of the spread and strength of civil disobedience was the boycott movement against foreign goods, particularly cloth. By contrast with Non-cooperation when picketing was haphazard and boycott depended on mass willingness to forego foreign goods, in 1930 Congress had refined and strengthened its techniques for enforcing boycotts. These were directed at customers and vendors. 'Volunteers', often paid, picketed foreign-cloth shops to prevent sales, pursued those who did buy until they gave up or handed back the purchase. Irwin heard of one case where picketers followed to their home women who had paid Rs. 750 for foreign silk for a wedding, and then frightened their mother with tales of an unlucky marriage if the silk was used. 'The old woman burst into tears and insisted on her daughters taking the stuff back, and the shopkeeper, partly from public opinion and partly from his kind heart, gave them back their Rs. 750 and put back the cut lengths of silk into stock. What are you to do about that?'[66] More effective was the extraction of pledges from merchants not to order or sell foreign cloth, sealing of foreign-cloth stocks and their periodic inspection by Congressmen, posting of watchers to detect sales, fining of dealers who broke their pledges, physical obstruction of lorries carrying cloth by volunteers prostrate in the streets, and in places severe social boycott with the help of caste panchayats of merchants who refused to comply. One of the most unpleasant styles of social pressure was *Siapa*, or mock mourning, when effigies of recalcitrant merchants were cremated and mourning ceremonies performed in front of their homes. Women were prominent in boycott activities, and the pressure they put on other women and on men was intense. Moreover overt physical violence was never far below the surface, despite Gandhi's detailed instructions on picketing and social boycott before his arrest and instructions from the Working Committee designed to eliminate physical compulsion. In some cases threats even turned into shooting. The dilemmas of the businessman were clear in the case of C. L. Nayar, head of one of Amritsar's biggest piece-goods firms, whose business was completely smashed by March 1931. To protect himself he first tried to deal with local Congressmen, and 'did some business under a blackmail system. Finding the latter too high a percentage off profits, he then tried the police. He did good business with the help of the latter for a time; & then he & his partners under the influence of their women who were terrified by social boycott, gave in & shut down business.'[67]

Home Dept., 18 December 1930, Home Poll., 1931, K.-W. to File No. 5/36; Govt. of Bombay to S of S, telegram, received 9 January 1931, L/PJ/6/1998.

J. C. Kumarappa argued for census boycott in *Young India*, 18 December 1930, Sharp, *op. cit.* pp. 187–8.

[66] Irwin to Wedgwood Benn, 5 September 1930, Mss. EUR.C.152 (6).

[67] Sir Geoffrey de Montmorency, Governor of Punjab, to H. W. Emerson, Govt. of India, Home Sec., 2 March 1931, Home Poll., 1931, File No. 33/6. Note on Congress boycott programme by D.I.B., 16 February 1931, *ibid.*, File No. 35/XI.

Details of boycott techniques are in provincial reports to AICC. Bihar told of the

While local groups adopted tactics which promised success in their area those members of the Working Committee who remained at liberty made efforts to impose some uniformity in the boycott because it was the main all-India plank of the Congress campaign. Following its tough resolution of 15 May the Committee put pressure on Congressmen who tried to come to local settlements with businessmen by which the latter would be allowed to dispose of existing stocks or relieved of picketing pressure in return for pledges not to sell foreign cloth.[68] It also issued a list of Indian mills to be boycotted because they used foreign cloth or were owned and managed by Europeans.[69] Motilal Nehru and S. Banker, Secretary of the AISA, pursued negotiations with Bombay and Ahmedabad millowners on lines suggested by Gandhi in an attempt to secure their cooperation in the boycott, to protect the *khadi* movement and to ensure that the price of Indian mill goods was not raised to exploit the boycott situation at the expense of the consumer. Considerable friction ensued, particularly between Banker and the millowners, and ultimately only the Ahmedabad men joined the *Swadeshi Sabha*, the organization set up to achieve these ends in June.[70]

The results of local boycott campaigns and Working Committee pressure were felt throughout India. Major centres of the foreign-cloth trade such as Calcutta, Bhagalpur, Delhi, Amritsar and Bombay came to a virtual standstill for part or most of 1930 as a result of hartals, picketing and self-imposed closures by businessmen. In Amritsar, for example, Rs. 6 crores worth of cloth was locked up and sales of piece-goods in June fetched Rs. 2 lakhs whereas the comparable figure over the previous two years was an average of Rs. 25 lakhs. This boycott was maintained without the need for picketing. The Bombay Native Piece Goods Merchants' Association closed its Mulji Jetha market from the end of July, and in October when its attempt to reopen attracted severe picketing it caved in and merchants who wished to trade were forced to go to other markets.[71] Only

use of caste panchayats, picketing & sealing stocks; reports in AICC Papers, 1930, File No. Misc. 11, part I. Working Committee rules for picketing are in AICC Papers, 1930, File No. G-151.

[68] Correspondence on local 'agreements', M. Nehru to G. Birla, 30 May 1930, Mrs G. M. S. Captain to M. Nehru, 14 May 1930, M. Nehru to Mrs Captain, 16 May 1930, AICC Papers, 1930, File No. G-150, part II; AICC to Jullundur DCC & Punjab PCC, 28 June 1930, AICC Papers, 1930, File No. G-151; Utkal PCC to AICC, 29 September 1930, AICC Papers, 1930, File No. Misc. 24.

[69] Undated list of 56 Indian mills to be boycotted, Thakurdas Papers, File No. 100/1930; correspondence on what constituted swadeshi mills, AICC Papers, 1930, File No. G-177.

[70] For negotiations leading to the foundation of the *Swadeshi Sabha* see AICC Papers, 1930, File Nos. G-150, part II, G-157 & G-177; Thakurdas Papers, File No. 100/1930; Bombay FR2, June 1930, Home Poll., 1930, No. 18/VII. Gandhi's suggestions to millowners appeared in *Navajivan*, 13 April 1930, *CWMG*, XLIII, 247-8.

[71] Summary by Governor of Punjab in Minutes of Governors' Conference, Simla, 23 July 1930, Mss. EUR.C.152 (25); Punjab FR1, June 1930, Home Poll., 1930, File No. 18/VII; Bombay FR2, July 1930, FR1, October 1930, Home Poll., 1930, File Nos.

in Tamil Nad was the boycott movement a complete failure. After the arrest of T. Prakasam and N. Rao, the main leaders in Madras City, and stern police action against picketers, recruits dried up and foreign cloth was freely sold. In Madura, the only Tamil district where civil disobedience was strong, foreign cloth could not be boycotted because the main financiers of the movement were members of the Sourashtra community who were the local traders in foreign cloth.[72] Overall India's imports of cotton manufactures dropped from Rs. 59 crores in 1929–30 to Rs. 25 crores in 1930–1: imports of cotton piece-goods contracted from 1,919 million yards valued at Rs. 50 crores to 890 million yards valued at Rs. 20 crores. The slump in world prices, the contraction of good markets for Indian goods and raw material and the consequent decrease in Indian purchasing power, were partly responsible for a general decline in India's foreign trade. But in the piece-goods trade boycott clearly had a marked effect since the decline in imports was greater than that of other commodities and affected British goods more than those from any other country.[73]

The economic situation was a factor predisposing some Indian dealers to cooperate with a boycott movement which in normal times would have hurt their interests. Sykes met representatives of various professions and communities in Bombay in September, and learnt that many businessmen were glad of a patriotic excuse to put off fulfilling obligations they could not meet in a period of falling prices. Two prominent businessmen, Sir Cowasji Jehangir and H. P. Mody, even urged that the Bombay Chamber of Commerce should organize a temporary suspension of imports partly to induce merchants to break the boycott in defiance of Congress, but partly on the economic grounds that there were such large stocks piled up in Bombay. Purshotamdas Thakurdas confirmed Sykes's impression when he told Irwin that the bulk of mercantile support for boycott came 'from people who, seeing themselves for other reasons on the verge of bankruptcy, had been anxious to cover their tracks in a cloud of patriotism'.[74] Other economic arguments came into play – the deep feeling that the government's policies were largely responsible for India's economic ills, and that it was worth a traumatic upheaval to get Indian hands on the country's purse strings, the wish of industrialists outside Bombay to gain trade as Bombay lost it – over and above the effects of picketing and pressure. However, even

---

18/VIII, 18/XI; Governor of Bombay to S of S, telegram received 25 November 1930, L/PJ/6/1998.

[72] *1929–30 Madras Administration Report*, pp. xiii-xvii; reports on Tamil Nad satyagraha, AICC Papers, 1930, File Nos. G-116, G-189.

[73] *India in 1931–32* (Calcutta, 1933), pp. 136–8; *Statistical Abstract for British India from 1924–25 to 1933–34*, pp. 702–3.

For the difficulties of particular companies see report of Manchester deputation to India Office, 20 August 1930, enclosed in Wedgwood Benn to Irwin, 22 August 1930, Mss. EUR.C.152 (6); file on picketing experienced by Dunlop Rubber Co. (India) Ltd, Home Poll., 1930, File No. 201/42.

[74] Sykes to Irwin, 25 September 1930, Mss. EUR.C.152 (25); Irwin to Wedgwood Benn, 10 October 1930, Mss. EUR.C.152 (6).

in July some Bombay merchants were looking for a compromise between Congress and government, and by September/October there were signs of revolt among cloth dealers in Bombay, Delhi, Amritsar and Cawnpore. In Amritsar, for example, in early September dealers were unloading their stocks on to the retail market at considerable profit, and thereafter foreign cloth was sold more freely than for months. By the last quarter of the year the boycott held only in Bombay, and Congress leaders were in no doubt as to commercial feeling when a deputation of cloth merchants urged Motilal to come to some accommodation with the government as they could not hold out much longer.[75]

The real strength of civil disobedience cannot be gauged from these all-India manifestations although they indicate a continental response to the Congress appeal on a significant scale. The movement varied in strength and kind between localities as it dovetailed with local political patterns: it was particularly strong where it suited the purposes of local leaderships or provided a vent for local strains. Its variations indeed went right down to district and village level.[76] A survey of the regional incidence of civil disobedience cannot disclose the multifarious drives behind it in the localities but it suggests the extent to which it did mesh with local political drives, thereby integrating various levels of politics, in contrast to the disintegration so manifest in the 1920s, when all-India Swarajist tactics found little response among many provincial politicians and bore even less relevance to the aspirations and activities of men in districts and villages. The degree to which the localities became involved in the all-India campaign was crucial for Gandhi's political position, both reflecting and partly determining the way Indians saw him and his ability to satisfy their diverse needs with his style of politics. It also affected the raj's perception of him and the depth of his support. Moreover the drives behind local support for the campaign affected the degree to which his 'followers' proved amenable to central control on Gandhian lines and constricted his room to manoeuvre in ending the movement when he deemed that the time was right. Whether involvement in civil disobedience stemmed from considered political commitment to Gandhi, semi-religious adulation of him, exploitation of a convenient tactic he provided, or sheer lack of any alternative, determined the extent to which his all-India role was that of a leader or a mere figurehead and focus.

[75] Sapru & Jayakar to Irwin, 28 July 1930, enclosed in Irwin to Wedgwood Benn, 2 August 1930, Irwin to Wedgwood Benn, 5 September & 3 October 1930, Mss. EUR.C.152 (6); Sir George Schuster to Irwin, 20 September 1930, Mss. EUR.C.152 (25); Delhi FR1, September 1930, Home Poll., 1930, File No. 18/x; Punjab FR1 & 2, September 1930, FR1, October 1930, *ibid.* & File No. 18/xi; Thakurdas to D. Khaitan, 8 October 1930, Thakurdas Papers, File No. 99 (Pt. i)/1930.

[76] For variations between villages in Gujarat see D. Hardiman, 'The Crisis of the Middle Patidars. Kheda District Gujarat. 1900–1935', Low (ed.), *Congress and the Raj.*

A note by the Deputy Commissioner, Almora, stressed the peculiarities which made the Pali sub-division of U.P. a particularly fertile area for Congress in 1932, Home Poll., 1932, File No. 14/28.

Bombay Presidency was undoubtedly the area where civil disobedience elicited the deepest support and affected the administration most seriously. In May Sykes admitted, 'it is now necessary frankly to recognise the fact that we are faced with a more or less overt rebellion, for which the term "non-violence" is merely camouflage, and that it is supported either actively or passively by a very large section of the population. We have, for one reason or another, practically no openly active friends.' The gravity of the situation necessitated daily situation reports to the Government of India and the Secretary of State.[77] The movement reached its peak in July, and later in the year as the government used Ordinance powers its intensity lessened. Volunteers began to dry up in Bombay City, and the seizure of ashrams and *chhavnis* in Gujarat surprised Congressmen and disrupted the rural movement. But even in January 1931 Gujarat was still causing Sykes 'grave concern', and there was considerable picketing in Bombay City.[78]

Of the four main areas of the Presidency, Sind was the quietest during 1930. In November Sykes toured Sind and found that even in comparatively small, isolated villages Congress could organize hostile demonstrations, particularly among the young. The bulk of the population, a Muslim peasantry under Muslim zamindars, was outside the movement, however, in striking contrast to Non-cooperation; and in Sukkur town and district Muslims looted Hindus in a wave of communal violence in August.[79] In the central and southern divisions of the Presidency the movement attracted wide support when its organizers chose an issue of immediate local concern. Picketing of liquor shops, cutting of toddy trees, and foreign-cloth boycott had limited appeal: only three talukas considered non-payment of taxes a viable enterprise, one of these being Bassein *taluka* where land revenue was a grievance of two years' standing. But forest satyagraha caught on. It took such forms as cutting trees and grass, grazing cattle in closed forests, refusal to pay grazing fees, burning forests and obstructing forest officials. It was organized in the central division by the Maharashtrian

[77] Sykes to Irwin, 21 May 1930, Mss. EUR.F.150 (2). On 14 December Sykes told Willingdon, Irwin's successor, that Bombay faced a more difficult problem than other local governments because civil disobedience was a mass movement there, and the local government was dealing with 'a population which has a very special understanding of the meaning of non-violent civil disobedience, and which has completely mastered the art of exercising every conceivable means of rendering Government impossible'. Mss. EUR.F.150 (3).
For the daily reports see L/PJ/6/1998; Home Poll., 1931, File Nos. 116/I–IV.
[78] Sykes to Irwin, 2 January 1931, Mss. EUR.C.152 (26); Govt. of Bombay to S of S, telegrams, received 3, 8, & 13 February 1931, L/PJ/6/1998. For the tailing-off of civil disobedience see Sykes to Irwin, 25 August & 5 November 1930, Mss. EUR.C.152 (25); Bombay FR2, September 1930, Home Poll., 1930, File No. 18/X, FR2, October 1930, *ibid.* File No. 18/XI.
[79] Sykes to Irwin, 3 December 1930, Mss. EUR.C.152 (25); H. T. Lambrick, 'Prospects for a United India after the Cessation of British Rule, as these appeared in Sind 1930–46', C. H. Philips & M. D. Wainwright (ed.), *The Partition of India. Policies and Perspectives 1935–1947* (London, 1970), pp. 506–8; President, Sind Satyagraha Council, to A. K. Azad, 18 August 1930, AICC Papers, 1930, File No. G-106.

War Council from Poona and Ville Parle, and in the southern division by the Karnatak Congress Committee and the volunteer organization, the Seva Dal, radiating out from local camps such as the one at Sangamner from which about 100,000 villagers broke forest laws in mid-July. Partly as a result of this, and partly because the general trade depression reduced the market for forest produce, the Forest Department suffered a severe loss of revenue – Rs. 27.50 lakhs down compared with 1929–30, and Rs. 23.40 lakhs less than the average of the preceding five years.[80]

The inconvenience caused to the administration in the south of Bombay was minimal compared with its almost total collapse of control in parts of Gujarat. Here Congress had been building up its organization for over a decade, often in alliance with the Patidar community. By 1930 its ashrams were the most imposing buildings in the villages and served as campaign centres as well as standing challenges to government prestige by their contrast with the inferior local offices of the raj. For this reason Sykes pressed hard for powers to forfeit Congress buildings, and was disappointed to receive only powers of temporary seizure from a Government of India which was hoping to ease the way to a necessary future peace, and could press the Labour Government for no firmer action. In Gujarat, too, Gandhi's prestige and influence were at their highest, reinforced by the Bardoli satyagraha and the salt march. As Haig reported after his visit to Bombay in June, a very large part of the Gujarati population was genuinely and strongly anti-government, and confident of success, convinced by Gandhi's Bardoli satyagraha that they had only to maintain their opposition long enough and the government was bound to give in.[81]

Local support for Congress varied within Gujarat, and was not uniform even within the dominant castes. For some the land revenue burden was a real and long-standing issue, and in 1929–30 economic conditions not only heightened existing rural pressures but generated new ones. The season of 1929–30 was only moderate for the Presidency, and Gujarat suffered particularly from little rain from mid-July until the end of September. The resulting decline in crop outturns that year was temporary, however, as 1930–1 was one of the best seasons since the war (see Table 5). But this brought little relief as the good crop coincided with the slump in prices which set in in May 1930 and became crushing by the winter when the *kharif* crop came on to the market (see Appendix III). Peasant proprietors with high economic expectations, an unusual degree of social solidarity and political experience, caught in an unprecedented price depression, were fertile ground for civil disobedience.

[80] Undated report on civil disobedience in Maharashtra, AICC Papers, 1930, File No. G-148; Bombay FR2, June 1930, Home Poll., 1930, File No. 18/VII; *1930–31 Bombay Administration Report*, pp. xx, 82–3.

[81] Note by H. G. Haig, Govt. of India Home Member, 13 June 1930, Home Poll., 1930, File No. 257/v & K.-W.

On the question of forfeiture see Sykes to Irwin, (telegram) 13 August, 25 August & 18 September 1930, Irwin to Sykes, 12 & 26 September 1930, Mss. EUR.C.152 (25).

TABLE 5. *Outturn of crops in thousands of tons in Bombay Presidency*

	1927–8	1928–9	1929–30	1930–1
Gujarat	674	734	542	641
Deccan	2,366	2,103	1,743	2,173
Karnatak	889	993	941	914
Konkan	710	686	665	682
Total	4,639	4,516	3,891	4,410

SOURCE: *1929–30 Bombay Administration Report*, p. 60; *1930–31 Bombay Administration Report*, p. 58.

One of the movement's major manifestations was social boycott of government servants and pressure, often from caste panchayats, for their resignation, on the lines Gandhi had initiated while marching to Dandi. In June the Kaira District Magistrate reported resignations of Patidar *talatis* and clerks following a resolution of the panchayat of twenty-two Patidar villages of Borsad and surrounding Baroda territory; and a Nadiad Patidar *talati* from a Borsad village alleged that he would be fined Rs. 1,100 if he did not resign. Resignations snowballed in mid-1930. Towards the end of the year some of these were withdrawn, more particularly in Ahmedabad and Broach districts compared with Kaira and Surat[82] (see Table 6).

The other main prong of Gujarat's civil disobedience was refusal to pay land revenue. On 10 May at Congress's Bardoli ashram a meeting of over 1,000 Bardoli farmers resolved not to pay their revenue without orders from Gandhi or Vallabhbhai Patel.[83] The movement spread throughout Gujarat in May, and of the areas where government considered that there was no excuse of economic hardship the *talukas* where the percentage of arrears was greatest were Borsad (12.5%) and Nadiad (11.0%) in Kaira; Jambusar (47.0%) in Broach district; Bardoli (57.0%), Valod (31.0%) and Chorasi (20.0%) in Surat. The winter collection of revenue was brought forward to October to enable officials to remove the standing crops in lieu of revenue before farmers could sell them, and there was an exodus of over 16,000, mostly from the Patidar community, into neighbouring Baroda territory where many Patidars had relatives who encouraged their migration. District Magistrates reported Surat and Kaira villages desolate in November, with only a few labourers left behind.[84]

[82] Kaira District Magistrate to Bombay Home Dept., 25 June 1930, Home Poll., 1931, K.-W. to File No. 5/36.
For resignations in June & July 1930 see Chief Sec., Bombay Revenue Dept., to Govt. of India, 17 June 1930, Home Poll., 1930, File No. 214; Bombay FR2, July 1930, Home Poll., 1930, File No. 18/VIII.

[83] Bombay FR1, May 1930, Home Poll., 1930, File No. 18/IV.

[84] Chief Sec., Bombay Revenue Dept., to Govt. of India, 17 June 1930, Home Poll., 1930, File No. 214; Bombay FR2, October 1930, Home Poll., 1930, File No. 18/XI; Bombay FR1, November 1930, *ibid.* File No. 18/XII; Bombay FR1 & Baroda FR2,

TABLE 6. *Resignations of village officials in Gujarat, November 1930*

District	Total no officials	No. resigned	No. resignations withdrawn	Net resignations
	Patels			
Ahmedabad	823	203	105	98
Kaira	655	310	164	146
Broach	545	183	71	112
Surat	760	369	134	235
	Talatis			
Ahmedabad	166	1	—	1
Kaira	260	24	12	12
Broach	151	—	—	—
Surat	246	38	23	15
	Inferior village servants			
Ahmedabad	1,197	260	114	146
Kaira	1,286	523	322	201
Broach	1,880	360	129	231
Surat	1,824	101	62	39

SOURCE: Bombay FRI, November 1930, Home Poll., 1930, File No. 18/XII.

The Bombay government's problems in Gujarat were complicated by the weakness of the police, particularly in Kaira where recruiting and discipline had been substandard for some years. It was also embarrassed by police brutality during the suppression of civil disobedience, which received publicity even in England. Moreover, the municipalities and local boards openly supported the movement, the Broach and Ahmedabad municipalities requiring primary school staff and pupils to participate in political demonstrations so often that the government withdrew their educational grants. In Surat, Broach and Ahmedabad children's corps were founded, and older students picketed schools and colleges in Ahmedabad, Surat and Kaira districts when they reopened in June after the vacation.[85] The cumulative effect of civil disobedience was so great that in June Sykes

December 1930, *ibid.* File No. 18/XIII; Kaira District Magistrate to Bombay Home Dept., 7 November 1930, Bardoli District Magistrate to Bombay Home Dept., 16 December 1930, Home Poll., 1931, K.-W. to File No. 5/36; Hardiman, *loc. cit.*

[85] For police problems see Bombay Inspector-General of Police to Bombay Home Sec., 29 May 1930, Home Poll., 1930, File No. 257/V & K.-W.; H. N. Brailsford to Wedgwood Benn, 2 November 1930, enclosed in Wedgwood Benn to Irwin, 17 November 1930, Irwin to Wedgwood Benn, 6 December 1930, Mss. EUR.C.152 (6); Brailsford to Irwin, 9 November 1930, Mss. EUR.C.152 (25). Brailsford published some of his accusations of police brutality after touring in Gujarat in *The Manchester Guardian*, 12 January 1931.

For local boards' and student involvement see Notes on Gujarat officials' conference, 16 April 1930, enclosed in Sykes to Irwin, 22 April 1930, Mss. EUR.C.152 (24); *Bombay – 1931–32. A Review of the Administration of the Presidency* (Bombay, 1933), pp. 135–6; Bombay FR2, June 1930, Home Poll., 1930, File No. 18/VII.

reported that in 'most of Gujarat we have practically a mass movement, and we cannot effectively apply coercion unless we are prepared for a clash on a very large scale, inevitably involving military action and very far-reaching political consequences'.[86]

Sykes's diagnosis of Gujarat's condition applied to Bombay City. Here, too, contemporary accounts suggested a virtual collapse of government control and an immense accession of prestige and support to Congress. Large processions organized from Congress House, bands of picketers, morning song-processions waking people with nationalist propaganda in the early hours, the continuing appearance of the Congress Bulletin, all demonstrated the ascendancy of Congress. As one British General put it, 'the Congress really runs Bombay – when things are quiet the police are *en evidence*, but when the Congress wants – its people take over the show!' Haig, visiting Bombay in June, had no illusions about the strength of civil disobedience in the city.

> The Congress House openly directs the movement of revolt against Government, Gandhi caps fill the streets, volunteers in uniform are posted for picketing with the same regularity and orderliness as police constables. One sees an occasional body of earnest young men in khaddar marching along. It is not surprising that all this intense feeling with its open and apparently successful defiance of Government has produced a profound impression on Bombay as a whole. Nothing, perhaps, had done more to deepen the impression than the series of processions that have been organized by the Congress. The numbers, the discipline, the organization and the brushing aside of the ordinary functions of police control of traffic have combined to produce a vivid impression of the power and the success of the Congress movement.[87]

The group most deeply involved in civil disobedience was the city's large Gujarati population who were mostly businessmen, traders and employees in commercial firms. The world-wide depression hit them in a rather different way from their rural compatriots. Falling prices were welcome to them as consumers (see Appendix III), but the decline in trade caused bankruptcies and unemployment. One cotton merchant and share broker calculated that the majority of merchants were insolvent and as many as 50,000 clerks and assistants jobless by mid-July. In 1929–30 imports of private merchandise fell by Rs. 1½ crores compared with the previous year, while exports of Indian produce fell by Rs. 9 crores; and Bombay's entrepot trade fell by over Rs. 50 lakhs. In 1930–1 the figures were even worse. Bombay's total trade was 22% down in value and 12% down in tonnage compared with 1929–30, imports falling by Rs. 25.71 crores (31%), exports

---

[86] Sykes to Irwin, 20 June 1930, Mss. EUR.F.150 (2).
[87] Note by H. G. Haig, Govt. of India Home Member, 13 June 1930, Home Poll., 1930, File No. 257/v & K.-W.; Field Marshall Sir William Birdwood to Irwin, 6 August 1930, reporting impressions of a *Times of India* correspondent and of General Weir, Mss. EUR.C.152 (25); Note by an observer on the Civil Disobedience Movement in Bombay City, *India in 1930–31*, pp. 660–1.

by Rs. 17 crores (24%) and the entrepot trade by Rs. 1.29 crores. The desperation engendered by such conditions predisposed many Gujaratis to civil disobedience, but their actions only produced a vicious circle, the frequent hartals and closure of the cloth market increasing the economic dislocation caused by external factors.[88] Gandhi's name and teaching exerted an extraordinary appeal to this group. 'Preaching of Gandhi and his followers has worked them up to a state of fanatical excitement in which they are prepared to suffer extreme violence while remaining for the most part non-violent.'[89] Women took a particularly prominent part in the picketing and processions: and such an atmosphere was engendered that other educated and middle class groups were swept into a potent anti-government movement. In Sykes's words,

> ...the public will not allow themselves to be kept out of it. Those who know Bombay well tell me that they have never known anti-Government feeling so high and so widespread. The population as a whole seems to have been carried away on a wave of semi-hysterical enthusiasm, and even Parsis and Christians, women and children, are possessed with the mania for martyrdom, and even the most responsible people are either infected by it or do not dare to stand up against it.

Even Europeans who had earlier called for tough measures were by mid-summer advocating negotiation with Congress or a laissez-faire approach to save themselves from business boycott.[90]

Nevertheless there were sections of the city's population which kept out of civil disobedience, even if they provided no active support for the government. Millworkers in general were unresponsive to Congress overtures, despite the closure of many of the cotton mills as a result of the depression. By late August over 44,000 were out of work, and Congress tried to exploit this situation by holding meetings, organizing a Labour Week from 18 August and establishing a Labour Camp in the mill area of Parel. Most of the labour force were migrants from the Konkan and Deccan and thus shared no regional solidarity with the Gujaratis. Moreover their union, the Girni Kamgar Union, was divided; and although its president, G. L. Khandalkar, favoured cooperation with Congress, S. V. Deshpande, its secretary, and a staunch Communist minority of the managing committee regarded Congress as a capitalist body and had no wish to see labour become a Congress pawn. The failure of the 1929 mill strike was a further disincentive to millhands to participate in civil disobedience, and the prospect of a labour–Congress alliance faded when mills began to reopen in October and the number of unemployed fell to about 22,000.[91]

[88] 1929–30 Bombay Administration Report, pp. vi-vii; 1930–31 Bombay Administration Report, pp. vi-viii; J. Ujamshi to M. R. Jayakar, 25 July 1930, Jayakar Papers, Correspondence File No. 771; Sykes to Irwin, 20 June 1930, Mss. EUR.F.150 (2).

[89] Govt. of Bombay to Govt. of India, telegram, 5 June 1930, ibid.

[90] Sykes to Irwin, 4 July 1930, Mss. EUR.C.152 (25); Sykes, From Many Angles, p. 392.

[91] Bombay FRs, August 1930, Home Poll., 1930, File No. 18/IX; Bombay FRs, October 1930, ibid. File No. 18/x; for details of Labour Week (Unemployment Day,

Muslims, too, did not join in any numbers. Public meetings were held to urge them both ways. Mohammed Ali presided over one of about 5,000 on 23 April and argued that civil disobedience was different from Non-cooperation and was aimed at establishing Hindu raj: the meeting resolved that Muslims should not participate. The Congress Muslim party worked to integrate Muslims into the movement, importing maulanas from other provinces to argue the Congress case. On 3 June S. A. Brelvi, leader of Bombay's Nationalist Muslims and editor of *The Bombay Chronicle*, presided over a meeting of about 10,000 including a large number of Hindus, which called on all Muslims to cooperate in the campaign. Despite exploitation of events in Peshawar and the death of five Muslims after police firing in a riot in Bombay's Bhendy Bazaar, no large-scale Muslim support was forthcoming.[92]

Outside Bombay Presidency support for civil disobedience was much more varied, depending on the extent to which Gandhian tactics suited local needs. Only in Bengal was there an area which witnessed as severe a breakdown in governmental control as in Gujarat and Bombay City. That was Midnapore on the Bengal–Orissa boundary, where salt satyagraha was followed by the boycott of government servants, intimidation of chaukidars and a series of assaults on the police. The district was honeycombed with Congress volunteers and village Congress committees, and when the police appeared conch shells were blown as the sign of attack on them. The Governor of Bengal, Sir Hugh Stephenson, called it practically a rising; and a Midnapore magistrate described in June how one area of about ten miles round Chechna *hat* was completely out of control and under the sway of volunteers who had made themselves comfortable in a fenced building, were receiving food and money from villages and were holding paramilitary training sessions. In July the thrust turned against the chaukidari tax which had to be collected by force. In Sabang *thana* in August the magistrate was attacked by three large crowds when he reconnoitred over the border with a view to collecting the tax, and had to return with three columns of police converging on Sabang from different directions. Not surprisingly Midnapore provided more convicts than any other Bengal district with the exception of Calcutta. The Bengal Council of Civil Disobedience reported 1,079 jailed by 10 October compared with Calcutta's 1,702 out of a provincial total of about 10,200. The worst affected part was the Tamluk sub-division where the bulk of the population were Mahisya cultivators. The success of civil disobedience among them lay not in any sudden conversion to Gandhian tactics but to the avail-ability of an all-India campaign through which long-standing agricultural

Bread, Day, Independence Day, Congress Day, etc.) see telegrams from Bombay Govt. to S of S, L/PJ/6/1998.
[92] Bombay FR2, April 1930, Home Poll., 1930, File No. 18/v; Bombay Govt. to Govt. of India, 14 June 1930, Home Poll., 1930, File No. 257/v & K.-W.; communications between Govt. of India and India Office, L/PJ/6/1998.

strains found a vent, as they had done in the same area during Non-cooperation.[93]

In Bengal's rural districts apart from Midnapore there was some participation in civil disobedience, but only where local grievances provided the incentive. Moreover eastern districts were markedly free of civil disobedience because the predominant Muslim and Namasudra communities were hostile to tactics matured on the banks of the Sabarmati. In Faridpur, for example, in one week of June fifty-four meetings were held opposing civil disobedience, of which eight were organized by Muslims and two by Namasudras. In Calcutta, too, Muslim gatherings expressed hostility to the Congress campaign and Muslim legislators supported demands for extra finance for jails and police.[94]

Among Calcutta's Hindu middle class population there was considerable support for civil disobedience. Boycott and picketing were widespread in the early part of the campaign, and Congress organization pressurized those who were not already anti-government. Particularly noticeable were the thousands of students and teachers who became Congress volunteers. In July Calcutta University law examinations had to be abandoned because of picketing, and attendance at colleges in the city was small, though most remained open. Towards the end of 1930 there was a decline in civil disobedience in the Presidency as a whole; and consultations between local Congress bodies and the AICC about the use of schoolboys in demonstrations indicated that the campaign was impossible in many places outside Calcutta if schoolboys were not recruited.[95] More disturbing to the government were signs that old terrorist names were cropping up among the movement's leaders, and that terrorist attacks were on the upsurge under cover of civil disobedience. Terrorist 'outrages' jumped to thirty-six compared with four in 1929, causing nineteen deaths compared with one the previous year. Among the victims were Lowman, Inspector-General of Police; while Hodson, Superintendent of Police, and Sir Charles Tegart, Calcutta's Police Commissioner, narrowly escaped.[96]

[93] 6 November report to AICC on civil disobedience in Bengal, AICC Papers, 1930, File No. G-86; Bengal FRs, May 1930, Home Poll., 1930, File No. 18/VI, FR1, June 1930, *ibid.* File No. 18/VII, FR2, August 1930, *ibid.* File No. 18/IX; file of details on Midnapore attacks on police, Home Poll., 1930, File No. 248; Stephenson to Irwin, 25 June 1930, Mss. EUR.C.152 (24); *1929–30 Bengal Administration Report*, pp. vi–xvi. See also *Law and Order in Midnapur. 1930. As Contained in the Reports of the Non-Official Enquiry Committee* (Calcutta), British Museum PIB 9/32.

[94] Bengal FRs, May 1930, Home Poll., 1930, File No. 18/VI; FR2, June 1930, *ibid.* File No. 18/VII; FR1, August 1930, *ibid.* File No. 18/IX; J. Gallagher, 'Congress in Decline: Bengal 1930 to 1939', Gallagher, Johnson & Seal (ed.), *Locality, Province and Nation*, pp. 269–325.

[95] Note by Govt. of India Law Member, Sir B. L. Mitter, 15 May 1930, on situation in Calcutta, Home Poll., 1930, File No. 248/II; Bengal FRs, July 1930, Home Poll., 1930, File No. 18/VIII; letters to AICC from Bengali Congress bodies, 12 & 24 July 1930, AICC Papers, 1930, File Nos. G-86, (Kw) (i) part 1, & G-151.

[96] Note by R. E. A. Ray on alliance of terrorism & Congress in Bengal, 25 January 1932, Home Poll., 1932, File No. 4/21; note on recruitment of terrorists in schools

The exception to Muslim hostility towards Congress's campaign so apparent in Bengal was the North-West Frontier, where the situation was without parallel in the rest of India. Troops restored order in Peshawar, and in Kohat after the Peshawar breakdown was duplicated in mid-May. In Bannu there was extensive rural agitation and troops were used to seal off the city from rural incursions; while in Dera Ismail Khan though the district was quiet Congress was active in the city and troops were necessary for arrests after an upsurge of picketing. Thereafter the situation was complicated by a series of tribal incursions which had nothing to do with Congress or civil disobedience: extensive military operations were launched to control the situation, and in August the province passed under martial law.[97]

Bombay, Gujarat, Midnapore and Peshawar were the only places where civil disobedience or its offshoots seriously threatened the government. Elsewhere Congressmen saw the tactics of satyagraha as locally profitable or viable only to a limited extent. In Madras, for example, only Andhra delta districts were deeply affected because district leaders found in civil disobedience a means of integrating a local campaign against an increased revenue assessment into an all-India movement. Volunteers were recruited in large numbers, meetings held at which proscribed literature was read, liquor shops were picketed; and there was much talk of non-payment of taxes and some social boycott of the police. But by mid-1930 overt manifestation of the campaign were declining.[98] In Tamil districts by contrast civil disobedience barely left the ground and there was little of the public sympathy apparent in the Telugu districts. According to a Congress report in early October there was virtually no civil disobedience in Tamil Nad, even in Madras City. The arrest of leaders and swift police action had stopped the movement at its inception, and by later 1930 temperance was the only form of agitation visible. In Madura the Sourashtra Oolya Sangam was holding daily temperance meetings, and as a result of picketing of toddy and liquor shops sales dropped markedly. Reports from Malabar were equally dispiriting. Memories of the Moplah rebellion during Non-cooperation proved a deterrent to popular support, police action had removed the leadership and the bulk of volunteers, and though the PCC still functioned there was practically no village or district organization. Picketing drink shops was the only possible form of civil disobedience; non-payment of land revenue proved out of the question as the landholders who paid revenue had no sympathy for the movement. The PCC secretary claimed in September that he sent weekly reports for the AICC to Madras

& colleges in Bengal, May 1932, Home Poll., 1932, File No. 4/40; Hale, *Political Trouble in India 1917–1937*, pp. 17–30.

[97] *1930–31 N.-W. F.P. Administration Report*, pp. 1–6.

[98] Govt. of Madras to Govt. of India, 27 May 1930, Home Poll., 1930, File No. 257/III; Madras FRs, May 1930, Home Poll., 1930, File No. 18/VI, June 1930, *ibid.* File No. 18/VII; Stoddart, *loc. cit.*; C. J. Baker, *The Politics of South India 1920–1937* (Cambridge, 1976).

but that for months there had been nobody to receive them.[99] A measure of Madras's tranquillity during 1930 was the fact that Stanley never had to apply the Ordinances in his Presidency. Almost the only tangible effect of civil disobedience was the drop of nearly 20% in the excise revenue, but even this was partly due to people's reduced purchasing power during the economic depression.[100]

U.P. was a province where Non-cooperation had struck deep roots in local politics as a result of Muslim involvement in the Khilafat campaign and the peasant agitation in the Kisan Sabha movement aligned to urban Hindu support for Congress. In early 1930 U.P.'s rural population had little interest in civil disobedience, unlike the Telugu delta men. Moreover Muslims showed no inclination to join the movement. At first it was a purely urban phenomenon consisting of meetings, hartals, processions and press propaganda, supported by students, the Hindu intelligentsia and some businessmen. In April the general attitude towards the government in towns was officially recognized as 'one either of criticism or of hostility'.[101]

The interest in the movement taken by women of all social backgrounds was particularly noticeable, and extended beyond the numbers who actually joined processions or made speeches. In July–August there was an effective attack on educational institutions, and Allahabad, Lucknow and Benares Universities ceased to function although they remained nominally open. The authorities of Benares Hindu University complained to Vallabhbhai Patel as Congress President that under the auspices of the Benares Congress Committee, picketing amounted to physical obstruction – lying down in passages and forming cordons to prevent staff and students going to classes and peons and clerks from reaching offices. Vallabhbhai wired to the committee that this must stop. Control of local workers was a persistent problem, and Motilal had insisted that 'undesirable volunteers' should be expelled: 'there need be no delicacy in the matter'. Volunteers from Youth Leagues at first played an active part in Congress meetings and propaganda, but they soon removed themselves from the Congress ranks in favour of more riotous pursuits and frankly revolutionary aims.[102] A further source of support for civil disobedience was local bodies who controlled large educational establishments; and the government struggled to prevent their resources and personnel from being used in the Congress cause. In some cases local bodies required all their schools to exhibit 'independence' flags,

[99] Reports on satyagraha in Malabar & Tamil Nad, AICC Papers, 1930, File Nos. G-107, G-116, G-189.
[100] Stanley to Irwin, 15 December 1930, Mss. EUR.C.152 (25); *Report on the Administration of the Madras Presidency for the year 1930–31* (Madras, 1932), pp. ix, 144–5.
[101] U.P. FR2, April 1930, Home Poll., 1930, File No. 18/v; Hailey to Irwin, 25 June 1930, Mss. EUR.C.152 (24).
[102] U.P. FRs, August 1930, Home Poll., 1930, File No. 18/ix; *1929–30 U.P. Administration Report*, p. viii; correspondence on picketing at Benares Hindu University, July 1930, AICC Papers, 1930, File G-151; M. Nehru to P. Tandon, 18 May 1930, M. Nehru Papers, File T-1.

compelled teachers and pupils to wear *khadi*, used teachers as propaganda agents and allowed Congress parties daily into schools for indoctrination sessions.[103]

From the autumn civil disobedience acquired more rural adherents. In September villagers were recruited for the first time in considerable numbers as Congress volunteers, and in October the PCC sanctioned a no-tax campaign, though it did not itself declare it. Several districts took up the new tactic formally or informally, including Agra, Allahabad and Rai Bareli.[104] In part this switch to rural agitation was a deliberate design by U.P. leaders, particularly during Jawaharlal's brief period of liberty in October. He was perturbed at the extreme caution of the PCC and the staleness of a movement which to date had depended on urban support. 'There is no verve – no dash – no jumping into the fire – no gambling for big stakes – no reliance on the masses & specifically the peasantry. There is a very middle class cautious approach to problems and no striking decisions.'[105] Moreover economic conditions had prepared the peasantry for a degree of involvement which had not been forthcoming at the start of the campaign. The spring harvest of 1930 had been good, but thereafter agricultural prices collapsed in the province (see Table 7), hitting the cash position of cultivators already weakened by a series of bad harvests preceding the 1930 *rabi*, who needed the money to pay their land revenue or their rents if they were tenants. The rise in the number of landlords' suits for enhancement of rent from 4,650 to 8,246 in 1929–30 compared with 1928–9 was evidence of acute cash problems in the countryside; as was the decline in the consumption of liquor and the growth of illicit distillation which stemmed only partially from Congress's boycott campaign.[106] However U.P. Congressmen were by no means unanimous in wishing to use peasant distress. Many of them were small zamindars, substantial tenants or money lenders, and the realization that rural radicalism unleashed threatened their interests prevented them from meshing the national campaign with the local drives which would have given it real vigour and destructive potential.[107]

Economic strains on U.P. peasants benefited Delhi organizers of civil disobedience, however. A letter from a U.P. Congress official, intercepted by the C.I.D., showed that volunteers were being drained to the capital with the lure of warm clothing and better pay – at the rate of two annas a day.

[103] U.P. FR2, June 1930, Home Poll., 1930, File No. 18/VII; Hailey to Irwin, 30 October 1930, Mss. EUR.C.152 (25).

[104] U.P. FRs, September 1930, Home Poll., 1930, File No. 18/IX; J. Nehru, *An Autobiography*, pp. 232–8; G. Pandey, 'A Rural Base for Congress: U.P. 1920–39', Low (ed.), *Congress and the Raj*. See also G. Pandey, 'The Indian National Congress and Political Mobilisation in the United Provinces 1926–1934' (D.Phil. thesis, Oxford, 1974).

[105] Undated note written by J. Nehru, apparently in late 1930 in jail, on the strategy for civil disobedience, NMML, S. Mahmud Papers, File No. 121 (viii).

[106] *1929–30 U.P. Administration Report*, pp. 20, xliv–xlv, 96, 98.

[107] Note by J. Nehru, late 1930, S. Mahmud Papers, File No. 121 (viii).

BGC

TABLE 7. *U.P. food grain prices in seers to the rupee*

	Wheat	Barley	Gram	Rice
July 1928	6.91	10.95	8.82	5.40
December 1928	5.63	6.99	6.47	5.02
July 1929	7.25	9.50	7.75	4.75
December 1929	7.25	10.25	7.25	5.25
July 1930	11.50	16.73	11.16	6.45
December 1930	15.14	25.04	15.34	10.23

SOURCE: *1929–30 U.P. Administration Report*, p. xix.

Students were also the object of Congress propaganda in Delhi through speeches in schools and colleges and street meetings, often with school-masters' collaboration. Collections were also taken in examination centres and classrooms. The main effects of the movement locally, however, were the dislocation of the piece-goods trade and the temperance agitation: five country liquor shops were closed for part of the year and when they reopened licences for them had to be granted at a reduced rate.[108]

In C.P. there was little civil disobedience during the early months of the continental movement; but just when other provincial administrations gained a respite a mass wave of forest satyagraha hit the whole province. The Governor, Sir Montagu Butler, expressed his fears at the spreading movement which was attracting women, children and villagers, and inculcating a semi-religious enthusiasm when he left for the Governors' Conference in Simla at the end of July. On his return he reported,

> Things had deteriorated in my absence, and Nagpur and Jubbulpore are both out of hand, whilst large bands of maenads are ranging the forests, emotionally cutting grass and wood, in several different places. I shall have to hit hard and may have to shoot a bit, but that is kinder, and more efficacious, than indiscriminate beating, while the new buck-shot is most humane, so much so that I hope the mobs won't find it out.[109]

The situation in fact deteriorated so much that the police fired six times and punitive police were imposed in twelve areas. Forest satyagraha started in the Hindi districts, organized by the PCC at Jubbulpore, and reached a peak in June–September. Marathi leaders joined in in July in the province and in Berar, including local Responsivists with an eye to publicity for the forthcoming elections. Even M. S. Aney and B. S. Moonje started forest satyagraha in Yeotmal district in a flourish of publicity on 10 July; while

[108] Delhi FR2, December 1930, Home Poll., 1930, File No. 18/XIII; note by T. Hussain, 21 March 1930, Home Poll., 1930, File No. 256; *Report on the Administration of the Delhi Province for 1930–31* (Calcutta, 1932), p. 77.

[109] Butler to Irwin, 30 July 1930, Mss. EUR.C.152 (25); minutes of Governors' Conference, Simla, 23 July 1930, *ibid.*

the militant Hindu R.S.S. permitted its members to join civil disobedience as individuals. The Berar War Council estimated that at its peak it had 106 centres for the forest movement, with 1,460 volunteers and 225 workers. Its main tactics were grass cutting, theft of firewood, arson, and picketing fuel and timber auctions. The movement spread deep into the countryside, involved the tribal population and led to clashes with the police. By mid-October, however, police action had quelled it, though not until forests had been damaged to the extent of Rs. 70,000. The distribution of damage was extremely uneven, the cost to Amraoti, for example, being Rs. 11,916 compared with 10 annas in Yeotmal![110] The success of this peculiar brand of civil disobedience proved the point made by U.P.'s experience, that widespread and deep support developed where local leaders adapted the campaign to suit felt local needs. C.P. leaders were aware of this, and deliberately avoided non-payment of land revenue as potentially disruptive of the social order; but unlike their U.P. counterparts they discovered another local issue which gave meaning to a national campaign among villagers and tribal people.[111]

Liquor boycott also had some success in C.P. Caste panchayats exerted pressure for prohibition by levying fines. In Jubbulpore at least picketing took the aggressive form of volunteers lying down in front of liquor warehouses; and Vallabhbhai Patel when consulted tried to stop this style of picketing as he did several days later in the case of Benares Hindu University. The government believed that the economic situation was partially responsible for the decline in liquor consumption (by 33 % in 1930); and the increase in illicit distillation indicated that true temperance was not the cause. In November the sales of licence fees for country liquor shops were down 25–60%, and the gross excise revenue declined from Rs. 12,544,054 in 1929–30 to Rs. 8,627,268 in 1930–1 – a serious matter for an administration whose second largest head of revenue was excise.[112] The other main provincial manifestation of civil disobedience was the August–October boycott of schools and colleges to an extent unparalleled elsewhere in India. All government colleges closed for part of the period, as did

---

[110] *1929–30 C.P. Administration Report*, pp. 1–2, 10, 15; C.P. FR1, July 1930, Home Poll., 1930, File No. 18/VIII; reports on civil disobedience from C.P. & Berar, AICC Papers, 1930, File Nos. G-84, Misc. 24.

[111] A report from C.P. (Hindi) late in 1930 explained why a no-tax campaign was deemed locally impossible in view of the prevalence of landlords, known as Malguzars: 'But the Malguzari system is so obnoxious that even if the tenants do not pay the Malguzars will be compelled to make full payments or lose their property for which they are not at all prepared. Hence a sort of class war will be introduced if the compaign [sic] is undertaken in this province which is undesirable under the present conditions. The possibilities of this compaign [sic] are being enquired into in the Raitwari tracts of this province which are very few.' AICC Papers, 1930, File No. Misc. 24.

[112] Annual report from C.P. (Marathi) PCC, *ibid.*; Hindi C.P. PCC to AICC, 13 July 1930, & reply, 17 July 1930, AICC Papers, 1930, File No. G-176; C.P. FR2, November 1930, Home Poll., 1930, File No. 18/XII; *1929–30 C.P. Administration Report*, pp. 21–3; *1930–31 C.P. Administration Report*, pp. 23–5, 67.

eighteen government high schools and four Anglo-Vernacular middle schools.[113]

Sir Hugh Stephenson, Governor of Bihar, comparing his province with C.P. and Bombay, told his fellow Governors in July that his government faced no semi-religious hysteria. In June he had compared his local situation with 1921–2 when Bihar's experience as one of the most disturbed areas had induced despair in the services; whereas now his men were 'pretty cheerful'.[114] However there was evidence of considerable potential for Congress organization of a wide campaign in his province, and early in June the police occupied a satyagraha camp of some months standing at Bihpur, an important railway junction. It had been the centre of Congress activity since civil disobedience began and had become a semi-military training camp for volunteers who proceeded to prominent roles in the salt satyagraha and picketing of cloth and liquor shops. This ashram had also been the hub of pressure on village officials, and at one time 130 out of 250 chaukidars had resigned as a result of its efforts.[115]

Refusals to pay the chaukidari tax were one of the major prongs of civil disobedience in Bihar after the swift waning of the salt satyagraha. It spread to Champaran, Saran, Muzaffapur, Monghyr and to a few places in Patna and Shahabad, precipitating rural riots, widespread arrests and the imposition of additional police. Bihar was saved from worse rural disruption in the form of a no-revenue or rent campaign by two main factors. One was the lower incidence of land revenue and rent than in neighbouring U.P. This cushioned rural people from the degree of cash shortage felt by their U.P. counterparts, although they experienced a collapse in agricultural prices in the last quarter of 1930. The price of rice averaged twelve to fourteen seers to the rupee compared with eight to twelve seers the previous year, and the harvest price of winter rice in 1930 was 68% below the average for 1922–7. The other force preventing rural upheaval was the social origin of Congress's local leaders, who were often small landholders and lawyers, and like many of their U.P. counterparts wished to keep at bay any developments which might threaten their interests.[116]

One line of attack against the Bihar government proved particularly popular – excise. This hurt no Congressman's pocket, and the Bihar administration, poor at the best of times, depended on excise as its major source of revenue, bringing in 32% of its total revenue in 1929–30. Moreover

[113] *ibid.* pp. 1–2; C.P. FRs, August–November 1930, Home Poll., 1930, File Nos. 18/IX–18/XII.

[114] Minutes of Governors' Conference, Simla, 23 July 1930, Mss. EUR.C.152 (25); Stephenson to Irwin, 2 June 1930, Mss. EUR.C.152 (24).

[115] M. G. Hallett, Officiating Chief Sec., Govt. of Bihar, to Home Sec., Govt. of India, 28 June 1930, Home Poll., 1930, File No. 252/1; *1929–30 Bihar & Orissa Administration Report*, pp. xviii–xxviii. A further organ of Congress teaching was the *Bihar Satyagraha Samachar*, a handwritten cyclostyled news sheet; copies of May–June 1930, AICC Papers, 1930, File No. G-81.

[116] Report on civil disobedience in Bihar, 1930, AICC Papers, 1930, File No. Misc. 11, Part I; *1930–31 Bihar & Orissa Administration Report*, pp. xvi, xix–xxi, 11, 92.

it was particularly easy to break the excise regulations locally because palm and mahua trees (whose flowers made country spirit) were in everybody's reach. Tree cutting and picketing liquor shops were rife: caste panchayats joined in exerting social pressure. As in the case of cloth boycott the methods employed were humiliating, frightening and effective. Offenders' faces were smeared with tar, they were paraded on donkeys, and one Patna liquor-seller's women folk were hemmed within their house and prevented from leaving, even to answer the calls of nature. The drop in Bihar's excise revenue was catastrophic. In 1930 it fell by Rs. 43 lakhs, in one month alone by Rs. 3 lakhs. Volunteers did not scruple about encouraging illicit distillation; and cases of this actually discovered were up nearly 120% in 1930.[117]

The two provinces least affected by the all-India campaign apart from Tamil Nad were Assam and Punjab. Like Bihar Assam was markedly quieter that in 1920-2 when the tea plantations had become centres of mass unrest. Early in the year Assam Congressmen were clearly reluctant to become involved in Gandhi's campaign, and in April the PCC postponed any form of disobedience on the grounds of inadequate organization, and decided to concentrate on foreign-cloth boycott, prohibition and meetings. From the start the participation of women and very young people was marked: the Governor noted on 1 May, 'Ludicrously enough we are confronted by an agitation supported chiefly by women and schoolboys'. Schoolboy involvement produced a circular of 19 May 1930 from J. R. Cunningham, Director of the Education Department, informing all guardians who wished to enrol children in government schools after the vacation that they must undertake to keep the Department's rules which included not participating in political propaganda. This caused considerable hostility in the Assam Valley and about 3,000 pupils did not enrol for the new term. By mid-September about 15% of schoolboys were still away from government schools, and they used their freedom to picket. School property also came under attack, and seven government-controlled or government-aided high schools were burnt down.[118]

In the Punjab the Muslim majority were not involved in civil disobedience and were often overtly hostile to it. The Sikhs were a more uncertain quantity, and despite the failure of Gandhi and Motilal to engineer a firm alliance with them at Lahore officials were worried lest the police firing on Delhi's Sisganj Gurdwara in the wake of Gandhi's arrest would effect what the Mahatma had failed to secure in person. However, throughout 1930

[117] *ibid.* pp. 71–6; reports from Bihar in AICC Papers, 1930, File Nos. G.-80, parts I & II, Misc. 11, part I; *1929–30 Bihar & Orissa Administration Report*, pp. 12, 79–87, xviii–xxviii.

[118] Assam FR2, February 1930, Home Poll., 1930, File No. 18/III, FR2, March 1930, *ibid.* File No. 18/IV; report from Assam PCC, 10 June 1930, AICC Papers, 1930, File No. G-145; Sir Laurie Hammond, Governor of Assam, to Irwin, 1 May & 17 September 1930, Mss. EUR.C.152 (24) (25); *1930–31 Assam Administration Report*, pp. i, 42–3.

the Sikhs remained divided in their attitude to civil disobedience, which eased the Punjab government's problems. These were never great at any time, and the disruption of the Amritsar piece-goods trade was the main thrust of the movement locally. Bands of Congress preachers began in mid-year to turn their sights from towns to the countryside but met with little support, even among Hindu cultivators; while many members of the Nau Jawan Bharat Sabha and Kirti Kisan party who participated in civil disobedience despite their hostility to Gandhi were soon in jail.[119]

The movement Gandhi initiated and left to develop with mainly local impetus and organization when he was jailed was certainly national in its geographical spread. No part of British India escaped it, though its manifestations and intensity varied widely in the proportion to which it serviced local needs. Moreover it gathered into the ranks of political activists a wide range of social groups, among them some who were rarely involved in the more sedentary politics of the Congress session or the Council chamber.

Women were prominent in active participation, a new political departure to which PCCs, governments and the statistics for imprisonment bore witness. Men realized their value in embarrassing police attempts to control demonstrations, despite Gandhi's insistence that it was cowardly to exploit British reluctance to harm women by using them as a shield against police violence. Moreover, as men were jailed, their wives, sisters and daughters took their places in the minimal organizational structures behind local campaigns, as 'Dictators' and members of War Councils. Tactics and leadership vacancies were partly responsible for the extraordinary enthusiasm of educated women of good families for civil disobedience. So too was Gandhi's propaganda for a new role for women in Indian society, and his calculated appeal to them before his arrest to come forward into politics and make *khadi* and prohibition their particular concerns, and picketing their special activity. By the end of the movement police chiefs gathered at New Delhi in January 1931 had decided as a result of dealing with civil disobedience that in future they could not be 'chivalrous' to women who participated in illegal demonstrations.[120]

Active sympathy for Congress was apparent among a large proportion of those Hindus whom contemporaries referred to loosely as the moderate middle class: government's counter-propaganda difficulties demonstrated this. But sympathy had also spread far beyond the ranks of the educated and influential. Observers spoke of a mass movement even outside Gujarat

[119] Minutes of Governors' Conference, Simla, 23 July 1930, Mss. EUR.C.152 (25); Sir Geoffrey de Montmorency, Governor of Punjab, to Irwin, 14 April & 10 May 1930, Mss. EUR.C.152 (24); Irwin to Wedgwood Benn, 14 May & 12 June 1930, Mss. EUR.C.152 (6); Punjab FRs, June & October 1930, Home Poll., 1930, File Nos, 18/VII, 18/XI; *1930–31 Punjab Administration Report*, pp. 3–5.
[120] Part II of report of police officers' conference, New Delhi, 19–24 January 1931, Home Poll., 1931, File No. 152. For Gandhi's appeal to women to make *khadi* and prohibition their particular role, and his assertion that they would contribute more than men to the struggle, see *Navajivan*, 6 April 1930, *CWMG*, XLIII, 154–5.

and Bombay City. Srinivasa Sastri impressed this on the Secretary of State, and Sapru reported in plain language to Irwin:

> I have been compelled by personal experience to revise some of my opinions. The Congress has undoubtedly acquired a great hold on popular imaginations. On roadside stations where until a few months ago I could hardly have suspected that people had any politics, I have seen with my own eyes demonstrations and heard with my own ears the usual Congress slogans. The popular feeling is one of intense excitement. It is fed from day to day by continuous and persistent propaganda on the part of the Congressmen – by lectures delivered by their volunteers in running trains and similar other activities. Very few people understand what they say or what they do, but there is no doubt whatever in my mind that there is the most intense distrust of the Government and its professions.[121]

Mass sympathy for Congress was one thing; mass involvement quite another. Of the unprecedented numbers who participated in demonstrations and ended in jail some were out of work and hungry. But many were men of some substance in rural areas who realized that the Gandhian political style could at this juncture serve their purposes, and who were genuinely attracted by the new interpretation Gandhi put on independence. Gujarati peasant proprietors were only one example of the blend of vested interest and ideological enthusiasm which linked men primarily interested in local power into an all-India movement.

Gandhian tactics not only integrated different levels of political awareness and activity. They also helped to unite different generations in a common campaign – an outcome he had intended in order to heal divisions in Congress and divert into constructive work the frustrations which bred violence. There was no official educational boycott in 1930 as there had been in 1920–2: Congress only called on students to cooperate in the struggle. Regional reports underlined the participation of the student age group and younger children in civil disobedience, as did statistics for prisoners. However the cooperation of students with established leaderships was not without strain, as demonstrated by the Bengali recrudescence of terrorism and the splitting away of the Nau Jawan Bharat Sabha members from the main Congress programme in U.P. and Punjab.[122]

If young people provided vital manpower for the campaign, businessmen were essential for its financial backing. In almost every province mercantile communities poured funds into Congress in the early part of the campaign and either cooperated in the foreign-cloth boycott or submitted to its

[121] Sapru to Irwin, 19 September 1930, Mss. EUR.C.152 (25); S of S to V, telegram, 30 May 1930, Mss. EUR.C.152 (11).
[122] For the effects of government retrenchment and parental hardship which were more influential in determining the numbers receiving education than civil disobedience, see *Progress of Education in India 1927–32. Tenth Quinquennial Review. Vol. I* (Delhi, n.d.). The quinquennium was a difficult one in which growth slowed markedly at the end.

pressure. Sethna commented that although 'the Civil Disobedience Movement is leading to the financial & economic ruin of the country...the merchant class, which community suffers most under the existing conditions, very strongly supports Gandhi's campaign. They urge that any country in a period of war must suffer, & they are prepared to suffer to any extent necessary. They regard the present troubles as a war between England & India.' Some were forced into this relationship with the political activists by economic circumstances or the pressure of their employees; while others hoped that Gandhi's presence and planning would be a safeguard against revolutionary violence.[123] The major reason for business support of Gandhi and his campaign, however, was the hope thereby to gain Indian control over financial policy. This was clear in the pressure of the Indian Merchants' Chamber in Bombay on the government for rapid constitutional progress and the end of repression, which Thakurdas put forcibly to Irwin during the summer of 1930.[124] Whatever businessmen's intentions, they cooperated with political activists in agitational politics to a far greater extent than in 1920–2.

The great failure of civil disobedience as an integrative force lay in the very area where Gandhi had hoped it would be most effective. Muslims failed to cooperate with Congress in any numbers, in marked contrast to Non-cooperation; and this seriously weakened the movement in the Muslim majority regions of Bengal, Punjab and Sind, and in provinces such as Assam or U.P. where Muslims were a sizeable or influential minority. It also undermined the Congress claim that its appeal and support were national in more than a geographical sense. The harassed government seized on the evidence of Muslim neutrality or hostility towards civil disobedience as the greatest saving feature of the situation from its point of view; while Gandhi made special appeals to Muslims to cooperate before he was jailed, and Congress appeared particularly sensitive to charges that civil disobedience was a purely Hindu campaign. The Working Committee passed a resolution in June reiterating its Lahore pledge that it would accept no constitutional solution to the communal problem which was not acceptable to Muslims, and appealing for Muslim support while rebutting accusations of Muslim apathy. It also made efforts to import pro-Congress Muslim speakers into strategic areas such as Delhi.[125] However, without a

[123] Sethna to H. Lewis, 18 July 1930, Sethna Papers. Ahmedabad millowners appear to have supported Gandhi in the belief that he was a force against violence and would protect their industry from disorder; Collector of Ahmedabad to Govt. of Bombay Home Dept., 2 April 1930, Home Poll., 1930, File No. 247/II.

[124] Thakurdas to Irwin, 12 & 31 May, 10 June 1930, Mss. EUR.C.152 (24); Sykes to Irwin, 15 April 1930, *ibid.* Lalji Naranji also told M. R. Jayakar, 25 July 1930, that merchants had supported civil disobedience because constitutional methods and the 1919 reforms in particular had failed to give them freedom from Whitehall over financial policy; Jayakar Papers, Correspondence File No. 771.

[125] Irwin to Wedgwood Benn, 24 April, 8 & 14 May, 12 June 1930, Mss. EUR.C.152 (6); speech by Gandhi, 1 May 1930, *Navajivan*, 11 May 1930, *CWMG*, XLIII, 373–4; resolutions passed at Working Committee in Allahabad, 4–7 June 1930, AICC

religious issue to attract the ulema and hence the Muslim majority as in the days of the Khilafat campaign there was little chance of widespread Muslim cooperation. Neither the Sardr Act prohibiting child marriages nor events on the Frontier aroused the call of Islam in danger, and salt proved useless as a ground for a common agitation. Moreover, many Muslim politicians believed that critical collaboration with the government in the Round Table Conference would bring more political benefits than sedition in Congress company. The Muslim delegation to London, led by the Aga Khan, included Shafi and Fazl-i-Husain from the Punjab, Fazlul Huq and A. H. Ghaznavi from Bengal, Jinnah and Mohammed Ali, Gandhi's old Khilafat comrade – a remarkable cross section of the community's opinion.[126] Gandhi had proved unable through civil disobedience to convince either Muslim politicians or the Muslim masses that he was a leader worth following.

However, the cumulative effects of civil disobedience did help to stiffen the courage of the waverers among the Nationalist Muslims. Despite their discomfort while the crucial decisions were being made in November–February, once Gandhi was arrested and the movement gained strength and attracted repression they joined in. If they wished to remain credible political spokesmen for their co-religionists they had no other choice as communalist leaders prepared for London. Sherwani, Kidwai and Syed Mahmud were among those jailed. Ansari maintained silence over his opposition to the Lahore policy and programme until Vallabhbhai Patel appealed for his return to the Working Committee in July after the arrest of the two Nehrus. Then he issued a press statement of guarded support for Congress, urging the government to negotiate: the statement indicated that he was prompted to this move by the unexpected success and non-violence of civil disobedience, the government's stern counter measures, and the 'shockingly retrograde' recommendations of Simon's Report.[127]

Similar pressures induced many Hindu politicians in the spectrum of opinion ranging from Responsivist to overtly communalist to participate in civil disobedience although they had made their hostility to the prospect plain in 1929. Vithalbhai Patel, Madan Mohan Malaviya and Jamnadas

Bulletin No. 10, 8 June 1930, AICC Papers, 1930, File No. Misc. 1 & Home Poll., 1930, File No. 257/111; file on Congress efforts to attract Muslims, AICC Papers, 1930, File No. G-44; Delhi FR2, April 1930, Home Poll., 1930, File No. 18/ v.

[126] For the hostility of Muslim political leaders to civil disobedience and their attendance in London see *India in 1930–31*, pp. 76–7; Moore, *Crisis of Indian Unity 1917–1940*, p. 121.

Even the Jamiat-ul-Ulema-i-Hind, a pro-Congress organization dating from Non-cooperation, split on the civil disobedience issue at Amroha in May, a large group following the Ali brothers in opposition to the Congress movement. Irwin tried, at Sir Malcolm Hailey's suggestion, to influence this meeting through the Nawab of Bhopal; Hailey to Irwin, 26 April 1930, Irwin to Bhopal, 30 April 1930, Bhopal to Irwin, 3 & 10 May 1930, Mss. EUR.C. 152 (24).

[127] M. A. Ansari to S. A. Brelvi, 2 April 1930, NMML, S. A. Brelvi Papers, file of correspondence with M. A. Ansari; Vallabhbhai Patel to Ansari, 13 July 1930, n.d. press statement by Ansari, probably July 1930, Ansari Papers.

Mehta went to jail. Bombay and C.P. Responsivists joined in the fray, as did members of the R.S.S. B. S. Moonje and M. S. Aney both did a spell in jail, although Butler of C.P. considered this an electioneering stunt. The many facets of the movement meant that such men had a variety of practical options of varying intensity which would attract public acclaim but from which they could draw back should the occasion demand it. Moonje as Working President of the Mahasabha implored Gandhi not to make concessions to Muslims in early May, but still pledged Responsivist support for foreign-cloth boycott. He also broke the salt law. Both were comfortably neutral activities which did not preclude cooperation with the government in the legislatures or at a conference. In June he poured scorn on the idea that the Hindu Mahasabha might boycott the Round Table Conference and regretted the Responsivists' decision to work under the Congress banner and resign from the Legislatures. Ultimately Moonje attended the Conference in company with M. R. Jayakar, S. B. Tambe and Raja Narendra Nath of the Punjab, who represented other shades of Hindu communal opinion. However, the decision of such men whether or not to throw in their lot with Gandhian satyagraha was not an easy one. The wave of enthusiasm for the movement, the government's response and the prestige of Gandhi's name were severe pressures to withstand, particularly as no other leader appeared capable of providing an effective challenge to Gandhi. It was understandable that many of them hedged their bets.[128]

Liberal Hindus did not take to satyagraha, but they too felt embarrassed and constrained by the response to Gandhi's call and the tactics the government used against the movement. Moreover the span of support for Congress suggested that any reform scheme concocted at a conference would have little chance of success in operation unless it received Congress support. Even in April there were signs that Liberals were feeling pressure to become more extreme if they wished to remain a credible political group. H. N. Kunzru advocated their support of the foreign-cloth boycott for this reason. He pressed Srinivasa Sastri

> ...hard to consider the desirability of our moving forward politically in view of the present political situation. I felt strongly that we would have no political future if we refused to revise our opinion and take account of changed circumstances. I think he was impressed somewhat by what I said but mainly by my insistence on being bolder if we wanted to remain in politics...I should frankly like to tell you that I am coming to feel strongly on the boycott question. Both in view of the political temper of the public and in the political and economic interests of the country I feel drawn to the boycott policy.[129]

[128] Butler to Irwin, 14 July 1930, Mss. EUR.C.152 (25); Moonje to Gandhi, 1 May 1930, *The Times of India*, 7 May 1930, Jayakar Papers, Correspondence File No. 354; 11 & 15 June, 31 July 1930, Diary of B. S. Moonje. For Jayakar's hostility to government's repressive measures see his speech in the Legislative Assembly, 12 July 1930, Jayakar Papers, Correspondence File No. 357, part III.

[129] H. N. Kunzru to Patwardhan, 7 April 1930, S. No. 542, Sastri Papers.

Through the summer of 1930 Liberals increasingly supported Gandhi's campaign, not by participation but by insisting to the government that the campaign had gained such wide support that the raj must change its stance and negotiate with Gandhi while also providing some concrete assurance that the pledge of Dominion Status was not hot air. Liberals in mid-1930 in fact sounded like Gandhi at his December meeting with Irwin.[130] Setalvad and Sapru both pressed Irwin in May for some statement that the Round Table Conference would discuss Dominion Status, and urged the priority of conciliation over repression. Thakurdas joined their pleas in July, arguing that the government's refusal to let Motilal see Gandhi in jail displayed an attitude guaranteed to alienate a public who were not going to be cowed into submission by repression. As he told a British M.P., government's policies really made him suspect that it did not want an amicable settlement, and this combined with what they knew of Simon's Report would soon leave very few who were not suspicious of British intentions.[131] Even when official contacts with Gandhi through Sapru and Jayakar had been permitted and proved abortive, Liberals continued to press Irwin and to emphasize the embarrassment of their position. Sir P. C. Mitter asked for the London conference to be delayed if Congress would not participate, and C. Y. Chintamini couched his acceptance of the conference invitation in the statement

> that Indians going there are on the horns of a dilemma. At home they will have to face on their return obloquy and even social boycott, in England itself the elements that conduce to the success of the Conference in the manner in which Your Excellency and Your Excellency's supporters wish are not quite strong. These [there?] will be, we fear, a tough fight both among the delegates from India and between them and the English politicians, not merely on details but on basic principles themselves.[132]

Chintamini's warning showed the complexity of the political environment. The world of British politics was interacting with that of all-India political figures, who were in turn constrained by the forces at work in the provincial and local arenas of Indian politics, as shown in civil disobedience. It was in this situation of tortuous interplay that Gandhi had gained a unique position of leverage as leader of civil disobedience. His movement

[130] P. C. Sethna to Sapru, 22 April 1930, Sapru Papers, Series II.

[131] Note of interview between Irwin & Setalvad, 10 May 1930, enclosed in Irwin to Hailey, 12 May 1930, Mss. EUR.C.152 (24); Irwin to Sapru, 27 May 1930, Sapru to Irwin, 31 May 1930, *ibid.*; Thakurdas to Irwin, 1 July 1930, Thakurdas to Major Graham Pole, M.P., 9 July 1930, Thakurdas Papers, File No. 99 (Pt. 1)/1930.

Irwin hoped that the Secretary of State could reaffirm government policy in Parliament after the publication of Simon's report, but he dropped the scheme when he realized that Tory opposition to it would exacerbate Indian suspicions. Instead he made a speech himself, boosting the power of the conference. Moore, *Crisis of Indian Unity* pp. 108–13.

[132] Chintamini to Irwin, 10 September 1930, Mss. EUR.C.152 (25); P. C. Mitter to Irwin, 2 September 1930, *ibid.*

had elicited a surprising degree of active support and an unprecedented spectrum of public sympathy in India. It thus confronted the raj not merely with the danger of local collapses of authority but a threat to the whole prospect of controlled constitutional change with Indian cooperation on which depended the future protection of British interests in India. Moreover Gandhi could properly be called the movement's leader. Although he was in jail for much of 1930 his name was constantly on people's lips, his advice was often repeated, and he exerted an unparalleled public appeal.[133] This appeal lay partly in his personal style of political activity, so redolent of Hindu tradition. It also stemmed from his broad definition of the movement's goal and the flexibility of the tactics he suggested, which could be adapted to suit most localities and so integrate their levels of political concern and capacity into a continental campaign.

The relationship of local drives and central intention and control was however the crucial point in Gandhi's leadership position. In 1920–2 local drives had shattered the all-India campaign, splitting it asunder and precipitating violence which alienated moderate sympathizers and forced Gandhi to call it off. In 1930 the impetus of the localities was equally important in determining the nature and intensity of civil disobedience. The campaign proved remarkably disciplined within the realistic limits set by Gandhi and Congress. There were problems with aggressive picketers; some peripheral groups were beyond Congress control; and violence erupted, ranging from terrorist attacks to mob confrontations with the police.[134] But this was not surprising considering the size of the country and the government's own inability effectively to control the activities of its law-enforcing agents. On a continental scale civil disobedience operated within the loose guidelines laid down by Gandhi and the Working Committee, controlled by the memory of Gandhi's exhortations and Congress publicity and organization.

However continental leadership consisted not just in calling up the genii of agitation. It also had to manoeuvre the time and terms of peace. Gandhi, therefore, if he was to sustain his all-India leadership position, had to play the role of negotiator. He had to translate the gains of agitation into a negotiating position and secure a peace which would satisfy the diverse aspirations of the groups who had participated in civil disobedience for reasons only partially connected with his own political intentions.

[133] Thakurdas told Irwin on 28 April 1930, 'So great is the support to Mahatma Gandhi in this movement here, that the masses here, and in fact, everywhere, will not stand anything said against him publicly. It is impossible in Bombay to think of having a public meeting to point out the dangers of this movement. However deplorable this may be, this is a fact, and what applies to Bombay in this connection, applies with equal force, as far as I am aware, to other places in India.' Thakurdas Papers, File No. 99 (Pt. 1)/1930.
[134] Note on instances when civil disobedience led to violence, Home Poll., 1931, File No. 14/15.

CHAPTER 4

A time for peace

The immediate object of civil disobedience in Gandhi's eyes was to create a situation in which Congressmen could go to the conference table as accredited national representatives with a strong negotiating hand. Soon after Gandhi was jailed, Irwin announced that the Round Table Conference would be held in London in October. The Mahatma was sharp in his response. He argued to Irwin that the current wave of arrests reflected a deep discontent at British exploitation of India, and only a response on the lines of his 'eleven points' would bring peace. 'No Round Table Conference can therefore be of any avail, unless you see things from our standpoint and leaving coercion rely simply on carrying conviction. Even those who you think are with you, are with the Congressmen so far as our wants are concerned.'[1] Before he judged that the time had come for peace and negotiation he would have to be convinced of some shift in the British stance, enabling him to parley without going back on his stated position. He would also need the conviction that he could 'lead' a peace move without jeopardizing his own political influence and following. In deciding on a time for peace, similar considerations would weigh in his mind as in choosing the time and issue for conflict, namely the effect of such a move on the whole spectrum of British and Indian groups interacting politically.

However, the initiative for peace was not in Gandhi's hands while he was a prisoner. It lay with the raj: and before approaches to discussion with Gandhi could develop, officials, too, needed convincing that it was necessary to deal with Congress and with the Mahatma as its effective leader. In 1929 Irwin had been willing to risk a break with Congress. The evidence of support for civil disobedience since then and its effects on commercial life and on non-Congress politicians at the precise time when the stake, the success of the Round Table Conference, became more important, began to modify his attitude. Moreover, he and his colleagues became convinced that Gandhi was the man with whom it would be productive to talk, as they witnessed his appeal and degree of control over the campaign; though they also knew that any negotiation with him would confirm his authority and increase his prestige. The development of civil disobedience, its strength and cohesion, were therefore crucial data on which potential negotiators

---

[1] Gandhi to Irwin, 18 May 1930, handwritten original in IOL, Sir George Cunningham Papers, Mss. EUR.D.670. (Cunningham was Irwin's Private Secretary at the time.) For Irwin's statement published on 13 May 1931 see *India in 1930–31*, pp. 77–8.

on both sides judged whether the time had come for peace between Congress and the raj.

As a State Prisoner Gandhi was not subject to ordinary jail rules, and the flow of information to him from outside was considerable. He received whatever newspapers and books he requested. His correspondence was not a source of political news as the permitted fifteen ingoing and outgoing letters a week were censored; and moreover he refused from mid-July to receive his quota of two interviews a week with members of his family because the government would not include in this category the many ashram inmates and other devotees who, Gandhi claimed, were as close to him as relations.[2] However Gandhi's internal resources and personal priorities were such that he accepted the opportunity for rest, study and reflection which Yeravda gave him, and cooperated with the prison authorities by not trying to send political messages or to retain active guidance of satyagraha.[3]

He lived in two roomy cells with back and front verandahs and a garden plot, and was allowed whatever food he wished. This consisted of fruit, soda bicarbonate, curds and milk, the goat actually being milked in his presence. He maintained good health and a fairly constant weight of around seven and a half stone throughout his incarceration: Jayakar commented early in August that he had never seen Gandhi in such good health, and that he was the only one of the Congress leaders who throve mentally and physically in jail. His day lasted from 4 a.m. to 9 p.m. with a one and a half hour nap. He spent two hours in washing etc., an hour in prayer, three in preparing and eating meals, six hours in spinning and allied work, an hour and a half walking in the yard and two hours reading and meeting jail officials. Compared with his time in Yeravda a decade before, spinning was now much more important to him, and he read less; though he started Marathi and began to learn the *Gita* by heart, using time in the lavatory for that purpose – a combination of activities he realized might shock people at the ashram! His correspondence from prison touched on a wide range of moral, dietetic and health problems, and ashram concerns; it included discourses for the ashram on its vows and on the *Gita*. These reflected his development as a thinker and spiritual guide in the years since his previous imprisonment, when he had immersed himself in religious literature rather than being the source of inspiration to others. Here was a man content with the peace prison gave, fulfilled by the role it permitted

[2] For the privileges allowed to Gandhi see Sec., Govt. of Bombay, to Bombay Inspector General of Prisons, 8 June 1930, *HFM, III, III*, pp. 260–2. Gandhi had asked for *The Bombay Chronicle, The Times of India, Indian Social Reformer, Modern Review, Young India & Navajivan*; Gandhi to E. E. Doyle, 10 May 1930, *CWMG*, XLIII, 401. For the correspondence over visitors see *ibid.* pp. 435–6, *CWMG*, XLIV, 10–13, 32.

[3] Gandhi to N. Gandhi, 25 September 1930, *ibid.* p. 186; Gandhi to R. V. Martin, 2 October 1930, *ibid.* p. 191; interview by D. B. Kalelkar who had been allowed as Gandhi's jail companion, *The Bombay Chronicle*, 1 January 1931, *ibid.* p. 347.

him, unlike a Jawaharlal to whom prison was a torment and grievous frustration as he heard news of outside events and longed to be out chivvying his countrymen into more radical tactics.[4]

Despite the philosophical welcome Gandhi gave to jail life, there were signs that negotiation on possible peace terms was at the back of his mind within days of his tough letter to Irwin on the futility of the forthcoming London conference. A *Daily Herald* journalist, George Slocombe, interviewing him on 20 May, received the impression that he would be prepared to recommend the suspension of hostilities and Congress participation in the conference, provided that its terms of reference included framing a constitution giving India 'the substance of independence', that there was satisfaction over the repeal of the salt tax, prohibition and a ban on foreign cloth, and that an amnesty for political prisoners coincided with the end of civil disobedience. As Gandhi remarked, his life had been 'nothing but a record of settlements'.[5]

On the British side there was no possibility of talks with Gandhi at this stage. In mid-May Mohammed Ali was refused permission to see Gandhi because the Government of India thought attempted mediation would be both fruitless and dangerous. Sykes argued cogently against bargaining with Gandhi while civil disobedience continued, on the grounds that it would prejudge the Round Table Conference and be a surrender to unconstitutional agitation which would endanger the position in India, possibly bring down the government in Britain, while it probably would not satisfy Gandhi and his friends. More picturesquely, Hailey from U.P. pressed a similar warning against negotiation:

> ... just at the moment even the terms offered as a basis of negotiation would be impossibly high and could not even be discussed without prejudging the Conference and its decisions. I myself jib nervously at the very notion of bargaining with these gentlemen; I would as soon sup with Old Nick, and indeed much rather, for our own particular Satan has often shown himself a bit of a sportsman, and notoriously sticks to his bargains. But it is no use discussing this at the moment, because the time is entirely unripe for any effort of the kind.[6]

However, as the weeks of conflict passed, the attitude of the Viceroy at least began to soften towards possible talks with Gandhi. The unexpected

---

[4] For evidence of Gandhi's jail life see Bombay Govt. to Govt. of India, telegram, 10 May 1930, *HFM, III, III,* pp. 140–1; periodic health reports, *ibid.* eg. pp. 151–2, 211; Gandhi to N. Gandhi, 12, 18/21 May, 22/23 June 1930, *CWMG,* XLIII, 403–4, 417–19, 439–42; Gandhi to N. Gandhi, 4 November 1930, *CWMG,* XLIV, 276–7; Jayakar's comment to Moonje, 2 August 1930, Diary of B. S. Moonje.

For the contrast with Jawaharlal see J. Nehru's prison diary and letters, *SWJN,* 4, pp. 317–88, 413–62.

[5] Interview with Slocombe, 20 May 1930, *The Bombay Chronicle,* 23 May 1930, *CWMG,* XLIII, 415–17.

[6] Hailey to Irwin, 23 May 1930, Irwin to Sykes, telegram about M. Ali's proposed visit, 17 May 1930, Mss. EUR.C.152 (24); 'Some Reflections. May 1930', printed note by Sykes sent by him to Irwin, 28 May 1930, Mss. EUR.F.150 (2).

strength and spread of civil disobedience was clear from official reports and anxious protestations by such prominent Indians as Thakurdas. Moreover Irwin was confronted with evidence of Gandhi's personal position of influence. Sapru reported, 'I accept him neither as a prophet nor as a politician nor as a leader, but I do feel that somehow or other he has captured the imagination of considerable sections of the population.' The Government of India's publicity secretary confirmed this when he noted that landowners gave no signs of forming loyalty movements because of a combination of apathy and fear of arousing 'the hostility of their tenants who regard Mr. Gandhi as a saint and over whom he exercises considerable influence'. Sykes, too, joined the chorus that they had underestimated Gandhi's influence.[7] Irwin consequently began to think that the Mahatma was the leader with whom they would have to deal; and in a long assessment of the political situation for Wedgwood Benn on 2 June 1930 he noted, 'If ...Gandhi had thrown his influence the other way, popular opinion which is always ready to follow individuals would have quite happily ranged itself for co-operation.' In his judgement repression would not solve the problem which had now developed: it was unlikely that Gandhi would call off civil disobedience unconditionally, and he could not forecast whether the movement would snowball or peter out. Therefore he believed that government should be in a receptive mood to secure peace with honour. It should consider responding to a suspension of civil disobedience by withdrawing most of the special powers, releasing non-violent political prisoners, while re-pledging the British goal of Dominion Status and stating that the conference's function would be to secure maximum agreement consistent with this purpose and that the British government would make proposals to Parliament based on a scheme agreed at the conference. He realized that the timing of this would be delicate, but he thought it would be right to assure 'third parties' on these lines and so mobilize them to get Gandhi to stop civil disobedience on the strength of an understanding that such official action was likely to follow.[8] Irwin moved in this direction not just because of evidence about Gandhi's influence and the strength of civil disobedience. He was also harried by the realization that moderate Indian opinion was increasingly gloomy about the prospects of the constitutional conference – a gloom which deepened with the publication of the Simon Report and its omission of any reference to Dominion Status.

Following his 2 June telegram to London, Irwin initiated a double-pronged policy of conciliation to counterbalance firm action against civil disobedience. One prong was to reassure Indian opinion of the sincerity of British intentions and the scope and power of the forthcoming conference. His original suggestion to this end envisaged a parliamentary statement by

[7] Sykes to Irwin, 21 May 1930, *ibid.*; note by R. S. Bajpai, Govt. of India Publicity Secretary, enclosed in Irwin to Wedgwood Benn, 14 May 1930, Mss. EUR.C.152 (6); Sapru to Irwin, 20 May 1930, Mss. EUR.C.152 (24).
[8] V to S of S, telegram, 2 June 1930, Mss. EUR.C.152 (11).

Wedgwood Benn and one by himself in the Assembly, but he withdrew it rather than face acrimonious debate in Parliament of the sort which had done so much to wreck his Dominion Status initiative. In his speech to the Assembly on 9 July he went as far as British politics would permit, stating that the terms of the forthcoming Round Table Conference were those implied in his 1 November statement, and that it would 'be free to approach its task, greatly assisted indeed, but with liberty unimpaired' by Simon's Report; while any agreement reached by it would become the basis of proposals the British government would submit to Parliament.[9]

While his suggestion was under discussion in London during June, Irwin made plain to his governors the second prong of his conciliatory approach. As he told Sykes on 17 June, they ought to hit the Congress hard and also encourage peace moves.

> I have never taken the view that we could expect Gandhi to call off his movement unconditionally, or that there was anything improper in keeping one's mind open as to the probability that at some stage or other we should be approached for some general indication of the line Government would take if and when the movement were abandoned. But all this...does not seem to me in any way incompatible with pursuing a vigorous policy as long as the movement is in full swing and as long as those supporting it are resorting to every means to encompass the downfall of Government.[10]

However he drew a sharp distinction between negotiating and giving an indication of what government might do if civil disobedience ceased. He was prepared to countenance only the latter in order to reconcile non-Congress Hindus and smooth the path of the Round Table Conference and the subsequent constitution: and he assured the men who bore the brunt of the battle that there would be no negotiation and no settlement without regard for those who had proved to be government's friends.[11] Meanwhile the Secretary of State put in blunt terms to Irwin that they might have come to a point where they needed to work through Gandhi in order to secure the support of the majority who would never understand the details of a constitutional settlement, and to control the spread of political violence.[12]

By mid-June 1930 both Viceroy and Secretary of State were disposed

[9] Irwin's 9 July speech, *India in 1930–31*, pp. 80–2. For Irwin's original suggestion and its fate see V to S of S, telegrams, 12 June & 2 July 1930, Mss. EUR.C.152 (11). For Tory opposition to Irwin's suggested reiteration of the Dominion Status declaration see Baldwin to Irwin, enclosed in S of S to V, telegram, 4 July 1930, *ibid.*; Moore, *Crisis of Indian Unity*, pp. 108–13. The Labour Cabinet decided on 25 June to make opposition leaders realize that the Round Table Conference would be a real conference with power unfettered by the Simon Report; S of S to V, telegram, 25 June 1930, Mss. EUR.C.152 (11).

[10] Irwin to Sykes, 17 June 1930, Mss. EUR.C.152 (24).

[11] Irwin to Sykes, 27 June 1930, Memorandum by Irwin sent to Governors other than Sykes, 22 June 1930, *ibid.*

[12] Wedgwood Benn to Irwin, 20 June 1930, Mss. EUR.C.152 (6).

to resume contact with Gandhi, provided this could be done without suggestions that negotiations were in the air. Irwin insisted on this when Thakurdas approached the Bombay government with a request that Motilal might visit Gandhi. Sykes and his Home Member viewed the proposal favourably, thinking it might have a good effect on Bombay opinion, but Irwin and his Council refused permission though they would have liked to ease Sykes's local predicament. 'Effect on public opinion both here and in England of our granting this concession would I fear have been bewildering and damaging. General impression of our allowing the two prime movers in Civil Disobedience to meet would have inevitably suggested that we were prepared to negotiate with Congress with result of encouraging our enemies and disheartening our friends.'[13] However, when an offer of contact with Gandhi was made by two leaders untainted by civil disobedience, Sapru and Jayakar, Irwin consented, hoping that if the Mahatma proved unreasonable the abortive enterprise would at least encourage non-Congress politicians to cooperate in the Round Table Conference.[14]

The Sapru–Jayakar initiative originated immediately after Gandhi's interview in jail with Slocombe of the *Daily Herald*. Sethna seized on Gandhi's eventual concession to Slocombe that he desired 'the substance of independence' rather than 'Immediate independence' from the conference, as a chance to get Gandhi to London; and with other Bombay politicians including Jayakar and Jinnah, the businessman Lalji Naranji, and the Maharaja of Bikaner, discussed how this could become the basis for mediation between Gandhi and the raj by men like Jayakar and Sapru.[15] Motilal, however, replying on 12 June to an enquiry from Vithalbhai Patel, said he attached little importance to Slocombe and would not go out of his way to meet him, though he was prepared to give him a few minutes if they coincided in Bombay. He made plain that his priority was conflict, and the collapse of the administration, whatever the cost.[16] A week later he was in Bombay having protracted and only partially fruitful negotiations with Bombay and Ahmedabad millowners over cloth boycott; and prominent businessmen, notably Thakurdas, took the chance to impress on him the gravity of Bombay's commercial position. Motilal also met Slocombe and indicated that a settlement was not out of the question. Together they prepared terms on which Congress would participate in the Round Table Conference; and at this stage Slocombe brought Jayakar into the discussions, pressing him to see Motilal even though they were politically opposed. The three men discussed and modified the proposed terms on 25 June,

[13] V to S of S, telegram, 24 June 1930, Mss. EUR.C.152 (11); Irwin to Thakurdas reiterating the argument, 5 July 1930, Thakurdas Papers, File No. 99 (Pt. 1)/1930.
[14] Minutes of Governors' Conference, Simla, 23 July 1930, Mss. EUR.C.152 (25).
[15] Sethna to Sapru, 21 May, 9 & 18 June 1930, Sethna Papers.
[16] M. Nehru to Vithalbhai Patel, 12 June 1930, M. Nehru Papers, File No. P-6; M. Nehru to Thakurdas, 12 June 1930, *ibid.* File No. P-14.

and Motilal approved them though he would not sign them. They were given to Jayakar who went to Simla, where he proposed to enlist Sapru who had been suggested by Motilal when Jayakar had expressed the wish for a companion mediator 'in this delicate task to provide against possibilities of a charge of misrepresentation of one party to the other'.[17] Under the terms, Motilal agreed to take to Gandhi and Jawaharlal 'a private assurance' from the British authorities in India and Britain 'that they would support a demand for full responsible government for India subject to such mutual adjustments and terms of transfer as are required by the special needs and conditions of India and by her long association with Great Britain, and as may be decided by the Round Table Conference'. If this assurance was forthcoming and was accepted, general reconciliation could follow whereby Congress would call off civil disobedience and participate in the conference, provided the government stopped its repressive measures and allowed a generous amnesty for political prisoners.[18]

However, the first thing Jayakar heard when he reached Simla was that Motilal had been arrested on 30 June. On 27 June the Working Committee at Allahabad had reaffirmed its 7 June resolution calling on soldiers and police to treat satyagrahis as brothers: three days later it was declared an illegal body in the U.P. and its members, including Motilal, were arrested. This jeopardized the prospect of successful mediation from the start. It alienated Motilal just at the point when he had come round to considering accommodation with the British, and predisposed him 'in his present state of embitterment' to 'adopt a somewhat truculent attitude'. Moreover it brought him into the same cell in Naini jail, Allahabad, as his son who, as his prison diary showed, hoped that the struggle would 'go on to the bitter end. Nothing more unfortunate than a premature compromise could take place.'[19] Jinnah told Irwin that Jawaharlal was quite intractable and that Motilal would be pulp in his son's hands: the only person with whom it would be possible to do a deal was Gandhi, though even with him the chance was not very high. Gandhi's own comments, restrained by prison conditions, confirmed Jinnah's assessment. He wrote on 11 July to a Birmingham M.P., 'From a prison cell it would not be proper for me to enter into any argument. But you may depend upon my not missing a single real opportunity for cooperation. But I confess that I see no sign as yet in the midst of fraud, falsehood and force that appear to surround so many of the acts of the powers that be.'[20]

[17] Jayakar to Sapru, 14 November 1934, Sapru Papers, Series II; Bombay FR2, June 1930, Home Poll., 1930, File No. 18/VII; statement made by Motilal to Slocombe, 20 June 1930, Jayakar Papers, Correspondence File No. 771.

[18] Statement approved by Motilal on 25 June as basis of informal approach to Irwin, *ibid.*

[19] 31 May 1930, J. Nehru's Diary, *SWJN*, 4, p. 357; Sapru to Jayakar on Motilal's attitude, 15 July 1930, Jayakar Papers, Correspondence File No. 770.

[20] Gandhi to W. Wellock, 11 July 1930, *CWMG*, XLIV, 15; Irwin to Wedgwood Benn giving Jinnah's assessment, 10 July 1930, Mss. EUR.C.152 (6).

Nevertheless Jayakar continued with his mission, contacting Irwin and Sapru the day he reached Simla. Irwin opposed any suggestion of general or private assurances as proposed in Motilal's terms, believing that this would expose the government to 'great risks of misunderstanding and suggestions of bad faith'; but he was prepared to discuss the general constitutional problem with Sapru and Jayakar and to let them convey their impressions to the civil disobedience leaders if they thought the British genuinely meant business. On 4 July Irwin's Council agreed that the two aspirant mediators should see Motilal and Gandhi in an attempt to get them to call off civil disobedience. The Viceroy tried to persuade Jinnah to join them, as a reassurance to Muslim opinion, but Jinnah drew back as he thought the enterprise would prove fruitless.[21]

During the following week Irwin, Jayakar and Sapru had further discussions which coincided with Irwin's conciliatory speech in the Assembly on the role of the Round Table Conference. Irwin showed them the reply he proposed to send to their letter asking to see Gandhi and Motilal to persuade them to cooperate in restoring 'normal conditions' so that the constitutional issue could be solved in a calm atmosphere; and the exchange of letters took place on 13 and 16 July. Irwin's reply gave the consent they sought, couched in a reference to his Assembly speech emphasizing the government's intention to fight civil disobedience and to solve the constitutional problem by agreement. Although Irwin tried to balance the two policy elements in his reply, Sapru at least was not entirely optimistic about its reception, since it condemned civil disobedience, gave no definite assurance on the constitutional issue, and referred to the valued cooperation of those who had supported the government against civil disobedience. One factor in the response Gandhi and the Nehrus made was bound to be fear of losing their supporters, but Sapru still thought the risk was worth taking since Irwin was obviously willing to go a long way with them with probable Cabinet backing. He was convinced that civil disobedience would only lead to disaster and never to Dominion Status, and that they should seize this chance of a peaceful solution. Significantly he commented that none of them, not even Gandhi or Motilal, thought they would get immediate Dominion Status, but they were all anxious to get the principle unequivocally recognized and a constitution as near as possible with safeguards on such topics as finance and the army.[22]

Irwin's decision to permit this peace move showed his government's need of all-India leaders who could ensure the support of the bulk of Hindu political opinion for the forthcoming constitution and secure 'normal conditions' in the country. It also set in motion negotiations which showed

[21] Irwin to Wedgwood Benn, 3 & 10 July 1930, *ibid.*, telegram, 5 July 1930, Mss. EUR.C.152 (11).

[22] Sapru to Jayakar, 12 July 1930, Jayakar Papers, Correspondence File No. 770; Sapru & Jayakar to Irwin, 13 July 1930, Irwin's reply to Jayakar, 16 July 1930, Mss. EUR.C.152 (25); V to S of S, telegrams, 13 & 16 July 1930, Mss. EUR.C.152 (11).

the limits within which Gandhi operated as he attempted to 'lead' a continental political movement.

Jayakar and Sapru were not alone in wanting peace. Ansari knew about their possible mediation early in July and thought Gandhi was more likely than the Nehrus to agree to a compromise on the basis of Irwin's speech and his probable reply to their letter: he encouraged an approach to Gandhi followed swiftly by a visit to Motilal lest the latter's personal embitterment should increase.[23] Jayakar was also armed with a letter from a group of Bombay merchants who saw him on 21 July and put their views in writing to be conveyed to Gandhi if Jayakar thought it advisable. They described a steady decline in India's trade since the fixture of a 1/6d exchange rate for the rupee in 1925, capped by the depression. With business now at a standstill and all credit and confidence gone, they hoped that Gandhi and Jayakar could procure an honourable settlement, though they were careful not to blame civil disobedience for their financial crisis and insisted that in any future financial settlement complete fiscal autonomy and the control of financial policy should be in Indian hands without interference from Whitehall.[24] Srinivasa Sastri in London also weighed in, with a wire to Gandhi supporting the Jayakar–Sapru move. To this Gandhi replied that he would do his best and was praying for light, though to G. A. Natesan he admitted that he saw no 'ray in this impenetrable darkness'.[25]

The two mediators saw Gandhi in Yeravda on 23/24 July, taking with them their letter to Irwin and his reply. Gandhi was clearly disturbed when he saw, too, the letter from the Bombay businessmen and learnt that Sarojini Naidu and other Congress colleagues disliked civil disobedience. He made it clear that he would only act in alliance with the Nehrus, and that Jawaharlal's must be the final voice. He gave them a note for the Nehrus in Naini jail, which indicated support for Congress attendance at the conference 'if the Round Table Conference is restricted to a discussion of the safeguards that may be necessary in connection with full self-government during the period of transition...it being understood that the question of Independence should not be ruled out if anybody raised it.' If Congress agreed to go to London, naturally civil disobedience would be called off, though peaceful picketing against foreign cloth and liquor would continue as would popular salt manufacture. Simultaneously there would have to be an amnesty for all non-violent political prisoners, the return of proper-

[23] Jayakar to Sapru, 12 July 1930, Sapru Papers, Series II.
[24] Bombay merchants (including K. R. P. Shroff, President of Stock Exchange, V. Thakordas, silver merchant & Director of Bullion Exchange, J. Ujamshi, cotton merchant & share broker) to Jayakar, 22 July 1930, Jayakar Papers, Correspondence File No. 771. Ujamshi & Lalji Naranji also wrote separately to Jayakar on 25 July, both telling him that a settlement was essential if Bombay merchants were not to be ruined; *ibid.*
[25] Exchange of wires between V. S. S. Sastri and Gandhi, 21/22 July 1930, *HFM*, III, III, pp. 660–3; Gandhi to G. A. Natesan, a Madras moderate, 22 July 1930, *CWMG*, XLIV, 38.

ties confiscated and refund of fines exacted during civil disobedience, the reinstatement of village officers who had resigned or been dismissed, and the repeal of the Ordinances. Even if these terms were accepted Gandhi felt that he personally could not go to London unless there was some unity among Indian delegates over their minimum demands. However in an accompanying letter to Motilal he stressed that as a prisoner he could not give a decisive opinion; and though he did not want to block an honourable settlement if the time was ripe, the ultimate decision must be Jawaharlal's. His draft was only an indication of what would satisfy him personally but he would not hesitate to support a stronger position 'up to the letter of the Lahore Resolution'.[26] Here certainly was a softer approach than Gandhi had taken either at Lahore or in the interview with Irwin on 23 December, but Gandhi's deference to Jawaharlal indicated that the constraints on his freedom to make decisions did not originate solely among those who wanted peace.

Jawaharlal was temperamentally geared for conflict. He also believed that the suspension of civil disobedience might prove disastrous: it might create a split in the country and it would certainly be impossible thereafter to revive the movement at short notice.[27] When Jayakar and Sapru reached Naini jail with Gandhi's missives and interviewed the Nehrus on 27 July, they got a tough reception, although they told them of the views of the Bombay merchants who had been in touch with Jayakar. Motilal was extremely bitter at being jailed, and said he had consequently changed his views since his discussions with Slocombe in Bombay. Even before Sapru and Jayakar returned for a further talk on the 28th, the father and son had decided that the Round Table Conference was unlikely to achieve anything from their point of view unless all vital matters could be tied up in advance; and they felt unable to suggest definite truce terms without consulting Gandhi and other colleagues of the original 1930 Working Committee. They put this down in a memorandum for the intermediaries to take to Gandhi, and Jawaharlal wrote an accompanying letter to Gandhi admitting that they both disliked Gandhi's stand on the constitutional question. 'I do not see how it fits in with our position or our pledges or with the realities of today ...I do not see any appreciable advance yet from the other side and I greatly fear a false or a weak move on our part. I am expressing myself moderately. For myself, I delight in warfare.' To his diary he confided

[26] Gandhi to M. Nehru, 23 July 1930, J. Nehru Papers, Subject File: Sapru–Jayakar Papers; note for Nehrus dictated to Jayakar & Sapru, 23 July 1930, Mss. EUR.C.152 (25). The important documents in the Jayakar–Sapru initiative are also available in *Statement Issued on 5th September by Sir Tej Bahadur Sapru and Mr M. R. Jayakar, of the Course of their Conversations with the Congress Leaders, July–September 1930*, P.P. 1930–1, XXIV, Cmd. 3728.

For accounts of the 23/24 July interviews see note by Jayakar, 2 October 1930, Jayakar Papers, Correspondence File No. 771; Sir Grimwood Mears to Irwin, describing Sapru's account of interviews, 31 July 1930, Mss. EUR.C.152 (25).

[27] Note by J. Nehru, 22 July 1930, J. Nehru Papers, Subject File: Sapru–Jayakar Papers.

that he found Gandhi's note disappointing, and though they had hinted at a stiff attitude he wished they had definitely stopped all talk of peace.[28]

Sapru felt depressed at this stage in the negotiations. He realized that the Nehrus and Gandhi all suspected that the Labour Government would not support a scheme of Dominion Status with safeguards and that they would not get Dominion Status within a reasonable time; while at the same time they were buoyed up by the feeling that civil disobedience had succeeded and was 'likely to succeed more in the near future'. But he was not without hope and pressed on, not least because he knew that if mediation failed, men like him would face a general demand that they, too, should boycott the conference.[29] Jayakar alone took the Nehrus' note and letter to Gandhi on 31 July, and found the Mahatma still open to a settlement. He professed not to be shaken by the Nehrus' attitude, and thought he could persuade them that the time had come for peace since they had not fought for victory but to create intense feeling as a demonstration. When Jayakar saw him on 1 August Gandhi clearly believed he would go to London because he mentioned points he would raise at the conference of which he wished to warn Irwin though they were not conditions of his attendance. These included the right of secession from the empire and an independent tribunal to examine British claims and privileges in relations to India. He also returned to the question of preliminary agreement among Indian conference delegates, saying that agreement was essential for the success of the conference, though neither was it a condition of his attendance. His anxious queries about the side the moderate politicians would take if this mediation failed also underlined his primary intention of generating a new Indian unity, the vision which had permeated his activities in the previous decade and his satyagraha planning. He was in no doubt that his leadership decisions had to be made in the context not only of the wishes of his Congress followers and colleagues but also of the attitudes of other political groups which were as crucial for the end he had in view.[30]

Meanwhile Irwin had been told of the first round of meetings in Yeravda and Naini jails, and gave permission for the Nehrus to confer with Gandhi and Syed Mahmud but not with other Congress leaders who were still actively campaigning against the government. Jayakar was anxious to keep this restriction on the permitted discussions a secret from the Nehrus lest

[28] 1 August 1930, J. Nehru's Diary, *SWJN*, 4, p. 373; note from Nehrus to Gandhi, 28 July 1930, letter from J. Nehru to Gandhi, 28 July 1930, Mss. EUR.C.152 (25); J. Nehru's notes on interviews with intermediaries, on back of typed copy of Gandhi's letter to M. Nehru of 23 July, J. Nehru Papers, Subject File: Sapru–Jayakar Papers; note by Jayakar, 2 October 1930, Jayakar Papers, Correspondence File No. 771.
[29] Sapru to G. Pole, 31 July 1930, Sapru Papers, Series II.
[30] Jayakar to Sapru, 4 August 1930, Jayakar Papers, Correspondence File No. 770; notes dictated to Jayakar on points Gandhi wished to raise at the conference, Cmd. 3728.

they should make it a grievance and it should jeopardize the whole enterprise. What he envisaged was an ongoing strategy of accepting Irwin's offer and gradually enlarging the circle of Congressmen included in the discussions, backing each demand for enlargement with proof that the small gatherings had been fruitful. He had reason to believe that a larger Congress gathering would adopt less belligerent attitudes than the Nehrus alone, because Vallabhbhai Patel had told him that he really wanted an honourable compromise and would go with Jayakar to see Gandhi if the government allowed it, though he would not slacken his civil disobedience activities or publicly support their peace mission.[31] It was Sapru who took Irwin's agreement to the Nehrus, but he clearly did not withhold the fact that they would not be able to see Vallabhbhai and other members of the Working Committee. Moreover the Nehrus' hostility had not been decreased by news that Vallabhbhai, Malaviya, Sherwani and Jairamdas Daulatram had been arrested on 2 August. They nonetheless agreed to go to Yeravda to see Gandhi although they could see no chance of the three of them alone coming to a decision. Sapru judged that Jawaharlal without his father would actually have refused to go.[32]

Within forty-eight hours of the Nehrus' grudging agreement to go to Yeravda, they were whisked into a special train for Bombay. They stayed at Yeravda from 12 to 19 August, their return being delayed for two days by Motilal's rapidly deteriorating health as he developed a high fever and began to spit blood. The conversations between the Nehrus, Gandhi and the intermediaries spanned 13–15 August, and Vallabhbhai, Syed Mahmud, Jairamdas Daulatram and Sarojini Naidu were included. Vallabhbhai and Jairamdas were now prisoners, and very bitter about it: but it at least cleared the obstacle of Irwin's refusal to let them as active campaigners participate in the talks. However the result of their being together was a joint stiffening of their attitude despite the pressure on them from commercial opinion to call off civil disobedience. During the talks, Jayakar read out two letters from Bombay businessmen, arguing that civil disobedience would ruin Bombay's commercial life; and Motilal had received a personal appeal from Purshotamdas Thakurdas which emphasized that the economic situation had deteriorated since they had talked in Bombay in June.[33]

The upshot of these talks was a letter from the seven Congress leaders

[31] Sapru & Jayakar to Irwin, 28 July 1930, Mss. EUR.C.152 (6); Irwin's replies to them separately, 2 August 1930, Mss. EUR.C.152 (25); Jayakar to Sapru, 6 August 1930, Sapru Papers, Series II; Jayakar told Moonje of his talk with Vallabhbhai, 2 August 1930, Diary of B. S. Moonje. For Vallabhbhai's public opposition to compromise see *The Times of India*, 21 July 1930, HFM, III, III, pp. 663–4.

[32] Sapru to Jayakar, 8 August 1930, Jayakar Papers, Correspondence File No. 770; 9 August 1930, J. Nehru's Diary, *SWJN*, 4, p. 374.

[33] Thakurdas to M. Nehru, 10 August 1930, J. Nehru Papers, Subject File: Sapru-Jayakar Papers: Jayakar & Sapru to Irwin, 16 August 1930, Jayakar Papers, Correspondence File No. 770. One of the letters presented to the Congress leaders was probably that of F. E. Dinshaw to Jayakar, 11 August 1930, *ibid.* Correspondence File No. 771.

to Sapru and Jayakar stating that the time was not ripe for a peace honourable to the country. This was contrary to Gandhi's view as stated to Jayakar a fortnight before. Moreover the other Congressmen took the points Gandhi had intended to raise at the conference, expanded them and made them into essential elements of a solution which they would consider satisfactory. These were (i) India's right to secede from the empire, (ii) a national government responsible to India's people with powers including control over economic policy and defence and the matters raised in Gandhi's 'eleven points', and (iii) India's right to refer British claims, including the public debt, to an independent tribunal if the national government considered them unjust. If the British government was willing to make a declaration accepting these stipulations, then they would recommend that the Working Committee should call off civil disobedience simultaneously with government action on the lines laid down by Gandhi in his note to the Nehrus on 23 July. Sapru and Jayakar merely replied with a formal acknowledgement.[34] Jayakar thought that the letter was a bluff and that the terms laid down were open to substantial modification. Sapru thought otherwise, because Gandhi had asked Jayakar to tell A. K. Azad, Ansari, Malaviya and Vithalbhai Patel about the joint letter. This would mean that the views in it would become public knowledge, and their own mediatory efforts would be prejudiced by uncompromising speeches and press articles: '...it will complicate the situation and if I am not doing wrong to our friends whom we have met in jail it seems to me that they are not keen on a compromise though until now I have shared your conclusion that they were not willing to break off negotiations.'[35]

Jayakar took the Congress terms to Irwin on 21 August, with his own gloss that there was still room for negotiation. While they waited for Sapru to join them on 25th, Irwin told Wedgwood Benn that he planned a stiff reply that discussion on the basis of the Congress letter was impossible. He was increasingly pessimistic that the parleys would produce any result, and realized that even if Congress did participate in the conference its representatives might 'be very unreasonable and walk out'. Moreover he began to sense from provincial reports that the government was getting on top of civil disobedience and that Bombay commercial opinion was being driven back from supporting the movement by economic hardship. Therefore he concluded, 'although I shall continue to make every effort to build the bridge, I shall not break my heart if the girders prove to be too short'.[36]

When Sapru arrived, the two mediators had long talks with Irwin and

[34] The seven jailed Congress leaders to Sapru & Jayakar, 15 August 1930, reply from Sapru & Jayakar, 16 August 1930, Mss. EUR.C.152 (25).

[35] Sapru to Jayakar, 19 August 1930, Jayakar Papers, Correspondence File No. 771; Gandhi's request to Jayakar, 16 August 1930, *ibid.* Correspondence File No. 770; Jayakar's assessment of the situation to Irwin was reported by Irwin to Wedgwood Benn, 23 August 1930, Mss. EUR.C.152 (6).

[36] Irwin to Wedgwood Been, 23 August 1930, *ibid.*; V to S of S, telegram, 23 August 1930, Mss. EUR.C.152 (11).

members of his Council. On discovering the contents of the proposed viceregal reply which they could convey to the jailed Congressmen, Sapru and Jayakar urged Irwin to equip them with another private letter defining the government's attitude to the points raised in the Congress letter. They badly needed some material for negotiation. This Irwin resolutely refused to give, knowing that any private letter would eventually become public. He was determined to avoid entanglement in what he saw as a tortuous manoeuvre to extract a private assurance which went beyond official declarations; by now he was convinced that Congress leaders had no real wish for peace, and that the only thing which would bring them to a settlement was the knowledge that civil disobedience was beaten. The most he would permit Sapru and Jayakar to do was to tell Congressmen their own impression of what the official line would be on such questions as an amnesty.[37]

Armed with Irwin's formal reply of 28 August and an informal note of their conversation with him, Jayakar and Sapru travelled to Allahabad, where on 30/31 August they saw the Nehrus and Syed Mahmud in Naini jail. By this time the Nehrus' attitude was even tougher, and they refused to make the evidence the mediators brought from Irwin the basis of further discussions. As Jayakar recalled, 'They practically said that they were the belligerent power which had very nearly succeeded in bending the Government, and as such, all talk of a compromise must be with them directly, and on all essential points, leaving the Round Table Conference to register their decision.' However, they left one small loophole: they wanted Gandhi to take the final responsibility for closing down the talks. They wrote him a note confirming Irwin's impression that there was no basis for further discussion, in view of Irwin's reply and the official belligerence displayed in the arrest of most of the Working Committee on 27 August.[38] With this unyielding document the mediators shuttled once more to Poona and spent 3–5 September in discussion with Gandhi and other Congress leaders in Yeravda jail. The Gandhi they encountered was very different from the amenable one Jayakar had interviewed alone in Yeravda at the end of July. Now he was unswerving in his support for Jawaharlal and said that the time had not come for peace. He maintained that Irwin was unwilling to settle and that India must endure greater suffering before the official mentality changed. With Mrs Naidu, Vallabhbhai and Jairamdas, he signed a letter to the mediators confirming the opinion of the Nehrus and Mahmud; and the same day,

[37] Irwin to Wedgwood Benn, 28 August 1930, Mss. EUR.C.152 (6); Irwin's note, 27 August 1930, of meeting that evening with Sapru & Jayakar, attended by Sir G. Rainy & Sir B. L. Mitter, Mss. EUR.C.152 (25); Irwin to Sapru & Jayakar, 28 August 1930, *ibid.*

[38] Note by Nehrus & Mahmud for Gandhi, 31 August 1930, *ibid.*; note by Jayakar, 2 October 1930, Jayakar Papers, Correspondence File No. 771; note of impressions of Sapru & Jayakar on discussions with Irwin shown to Nehrus & Mahmud, Cmd. 3728.

5 September, Sapru and Jayakar wired to Irwin the news that the negotiations had broken down.[39]

The two-month saga of the Sapru–Jayakar peace move demonstrated the key position of Gandhi in the relationship of Congress leaders, the raj, non-Congress Hindu politicians and the Bombay commercial community. Congress leaders put the final decision on him. Other Indians put pressure on him and urged the Viceroy to do a deal with him. Irwin, too, believed that only Gandhi and the Nehrus could produce the atmosphere the British wanted for constitutional negotiations. Although these different groups looked to Gandhi as a leader, the tortuous discussions and final breakdown demonstrated the limited room in which Gandhi could manoeuvre if he wished to lead. In this case Jawaharlal was crucial in his thinking, outweighing Sapru and Jayakar and the groups they represented, and the evidence of commercial unrest at the continued civil disobedience. It was also significant that he made the major shift in his position early in August when it was still not clear that government would gain the upper hand in the confrontation. Moreover the main discussions were held at Yeravda in Bombay Presidency, where civil disobedience was strongest and the pursuit of peace attracted least public support. Jayakar confided to S. C. Mitra in Calcutta,

> I know of the sentiments of Congress people in your part of the country, but they happen to be different from those of the irresponsible people who are at present in charge of the Congress affairs in my city. The clamour which they raised had, I am sure, its effect upon the minds of our Congress friends in jail, and ultimately they found it difficult to agree to these terms.[40]

In the light of the evidence available to him and weighing the pressures on him at that juncture, Gandhi decided that he could not go for a settlement without risking the break with Jawaharlal he had so far avoided, and endangering the momentum of the movement which he saw as his last chance fundamentally to alter the Indian political scene. At the heart of his leadership position was sensitive pliancy to people whose responses

[39] Sapru & Jayakar to Irwin, telegram, 5 September 1930, Mss. EUR.C.152 (25); Gandhi & colleagues to Sapru & Jayakar, 5 September 1930, *ibid.*; note by Jayakar, 2 October 1930, Jayakar Papers, Correspondence File No. 771.

[40] Jayakar to S. C. Mitra, 13 September 1930, *ibid.* Mitra had told Jayakar on 2 September that Congress people in Calcutta were not averse to peace, *ibid.* Jayakar had commented on the prevailing atmosphere in Bombay to A. Rangaswami Aiyengar, 8 August 1930, *ibid.*: 'I know you are one of the few Congressmen who will welcome an early and honourable settlement. I wish I could say this of many of our Congress friends here who think one thing and talk another.' Evidence of the hostility of the executive committee of the Bombay Youth League and the Bombay 'War Council' to a settlement is in *The Bombay Chronicle*, 12 August 1930, *The Times of India*, 15 August 1930, HFM, III, III, pp. 676, 680.

Rajendra Prasad recorded that among his fellow prisoners in Hazaribagh jail, Bihar, only a few were opposed to any compromise and the majority were disappointed when the peace talks failed; Prasad, *Autobiography*, p. 326.

determined the viability of his political position. But now this prevented him from taking advantage of a situation when the government was vulnerable to attacks from civil resisters and pressure from potential conference-goers, and when there was considerable flexibility in the official position compared with December 1929. By breaking up the talks he passed the initiative back to the British, who became increasingly secure in their control of agitation and were now assured of the collaboration at the conference table of the politicians whose goodwill they had hoped to reinforce by letting the peace move occur.

Having secured the government's position against charges of implacable repression by non-Congress Hindu politicians, Irwin and his Council were more willing to permit local governments to deal firmly with civil disobedience, even before the Sapru–Jayakar talks finally collapsed. On 9 August 1930 Irwin confirmed to Sykes that he should take all measures necessary to counter civil disobedience, regardless of the current peace move; and assured him that the Government of India had already made a provisional draft of the forfeiture Ordinance which Sykes considered vital for Bombay. After the Governors' Conference at the end of July the Home Department also took up the question of an omnibus emergency powers Ordinance to be used in particularly troubled areas or on an extensive scale if the general situation deteriorated seriously. It proved an unnecessary precaution against events in 1930, but it showed the stiffening trend in official thinking.[41] After the talks had finished Irwin agreed that Hailey in the U.P. should adopt a more vigorous local approach than the 'steady pressure' which had been the policy slogan to date: and it was at this juncture in September 1930 that Irwin's Council decided to go ahead with the Ordinance to deal with unlawful associations. Moreover when Purshotamdas Thakurdas asked to see Gandhi within a fortnight of the failure of the Jayakar–Sapru move Irwin dismissed the suggestion on the grounds that it would be misrepresented as a desperate attempt by the government to sue for peace.[42]

As Irwin loosened the rein on his governors one of his primary concerns was to prevent further strain on the I.C.S. and the police, which the governors kept reporting as a dangerous aspect of the situation. He justified his reluctant renewal of Ordinance powers in December on these grounds: 'it is important to remember that many officers and the police generally have been subject to continuous strain for nearly nine months and that we

---

[41] Irwin to Sykes, telegrams, 9 & 16 August 1930, Mss. EUR.C.152 (25); H. W. Emerson, Govt. of India Home Sec., to all local govts., 20 August 1930, on omnibus Ordinance, Home Poll., 1930, File No. 13/8.

[42] Irwin to Sykes on Thakurdas's request, 17 September 1930, Mss. EUR.C.152 (25); Thakurdas to Irwin, 20 September 1930, Irwin to Thakurdas, 29 September 1930, Thakurdas Papers, File No. 99 (Pt. 1)/1930. Hailey to Irwin, 9 September 1930, Irwin to Hailey, 20 September 1930, Mss. EUR.C.152 (25).

Irwin's Council decided to recommend an Ordinance dealing with unlawful associations on 11 September; Irwin to Sykes, 12 September 1930, *ibid.*

cannot afford either to allow the strain to get heavier, if we can prevent it, or to let Local Governments and officers feel that we are postponing measures which are clearly necessary.'[43] Nevertheless he manoeuvred to keep his options open; and while sanctioning stiff measures still attempted to prepare the ground for peace. Sykes did not get the powers of forfeiture he wanted because Irwin's government felt that this would make a final settlement more difficult.[44] Irwin also had his eye on the Round Table Conference which opened in London on 12 November. In the closing weeks of 1930 did his best not to embarrass Wedgwood Benn, assuring him that he was 'constantly thinking whether there is anything to be done to assist the Conference in the way of conciliation towards the civil disobedience movement at this end'. When Irwin consulted his governors on the possible renewal of the lapsed Ordinances in December, he reminded them of the need to prevent hostile public opinion in and out of India on the grounds that government had more emergency powers than the situation warranted, and argued that he had a special responsibility to the Secretary of State while the conference was in session, although his colleague in Whitehall had not asked them to hold back because of the conference.[45]

Meanwhile, on the Congress side repression took its toll in the wake of the failure of the summer peace move. Declining support, incarceration of recognized leaders and the disruption of Congress's communications network made the continuation of the campaign increasingly difficult. Deepening economic distress heightened businessmen's anxiety to press the more amenable Congress leaders into cooperation with Britain to retrieve the economic situation; while some Bombay businessmen were increasingly suspicious that Congress was out to help Ahmedabad at their expense.[46]

In this situation the acting Working Committee was split on future policy. When some of its members met in Mussoorie in October, Motilal, recently released from Naini on health grounds, pressed for a resolution confirming the rejection of the peace terms brought by Sapru and Jayakar; but he was firmly opposed by Khaliquzzaman, K. F. Nariman from Bombay, and Sen Gupta from Bengal. The issue was postponed because Motilal felt too ill to discuss it, and because Jawaharlal was still in jail. But news reached Irwin that

> ...a storm is brewing amongst the Congress adherents. The rank and
> file are growing impatient and tired; there is much difference of opinion
> amongst the various leaders, and some of them are very annoyed at the

[43] V to S of S, telegram, 20 December 1930, Mss. EUR.C.152 (11). Bombay & Bengal were provinces where the services were particularly strained; pressure on these grounds for renewal of Ordinances also came from Sir Hugh Stephenson, Governor of Bihar, to Irwin, 2 December 1930, Mss. EUR.C.152 (25).

[44] Irwin to Sykes, 12 & 26 September 1930, *ibid.*

[45] Irwin to Wedgwood Benn, 3 November 1930, Mss. EUR.C.152 (6); Irwin to Governors, 9 December 1930, Mss. EUR.C.152 (25).

[46] Sir George Schuster to Irwin, 20 September 1930, reporting interview with Thakurdas that day, *ibid.*; J. Nehru, *An Autobiography*, pp. 256–7.

attitude of Panditji. Sen Gupta, along with others, has openly said that it is becoming a family affair, and that they are not there merely to endorse the opinions of Pandits Motilal and Jawaharlal.[47]

The younger Nehru enjoyed eight days of freedom from 11 to 19 October, during which he attempted to inject new vigour into the U.P. movement through a no-tax campaign. As Congress President he circularized all PCCs with an exhortation to disregard peace rumours and to continue the struggle, authorizing them to start no-tax campaigns where they thought these were feasible and proper. Despite his bold front he was impressed by the obvious decline and staleness of the movement where it had not been invigorated by forces born of rural distress. Further evidence of increasing disarray among campaigners came, for example, from Bombay City where there was overt hostility between those who had remained free and those who had been jailed, the latter complaining that the former had mismanaged Congress funds.[48]

In the war of attrition which followed the collapse of the Sapru–Jayakar peace mission, neither Congress nor government ranks were united in their attitude towards peace. Disorganization and weariness among the rank and file campaigners pushed a divided Congress leadership, weakened by the absence of their jailed colleagues, towards a truce; while on the government side local administrations were more concerned than Delhi to crush than to conciliate. Only events in London broke the stalemate and caused Irwin to take the initiative in resuming contact with Gandhi and the Working Committee.

Although Congressmen had excluded themselves from participation in the Round Table Conference representatives of the Liberals, Hindu Responsivists, Muslims and smaller minorities agreed to attend when nominated by Irwin. Fifty-eight of them, joined by a sixteen-man delegation from the Princely States, began arriving late in October in London, where they met the sixteen representatives of the British Government, the Conservative and Liberal parties. During the run-up to the conference and its sittings, Indian delegates joined forces in support of a plan for a federation which would include the Princely States. This produced a radical change in British willingness to countenance substantial constitutional advance. The government now found it could contemplate conceding apparently considerable power to Indians because Tories and Liberals agreed to support a proposal which guaranteed the conservative weight of the Princes at the centre; whereas they had opposed any idea of Dominion Status in the near future for British India alone. The result of the deal was the Prime Minister's

---

[47] Nawab of Bhopal to Irwin, 8 October 1930, Mss. EUR.C.152 (25).
[48] Bombay FRs, December 1930, Home Poll., 1930, File No. 18/XIII: J. Nehru to PCCs, 14 October 1930, *SWJN*, 4, pp. 397–400; undated note by J. Nehru, probably late 1930, S. Mahmud Papers, File No. 121 (viii); J. Nehru, *An Autobiography*, pp. 232–3.

statement at the close of the conference on 19 January that 'With a Legislature constituted on a federal basis, His Majesty's Government will be prepared to recognise the principle of the responsibility of the Executive to the Legislature.' There would be a period of transition during which statutory safeguards would operate, giving the Viceroy reserve powers on such topics as defence, finance and the protection of minorities; while in the provinces governors would have the minimum special powers necessary to maintain peace and protect the rights of the services and minorities. He concluded with the grandiose prayer 'that by our labours together India will come to possess the only thing which she now lacks to give her the status of a Dominion...the responsibilities and the cares, the burdens and the difficulties, but the pride and the honour of responsible self-government'.[49]

Whereas Irwin had parleyed in mid-summer to secure a reasonable attendance at the conference, now he was to play for a far bigger stake – constitutional advance on a scale inconceivable a year earlier which promised to solve the political problem with which he had grappled since the beginning of his viceroyalty. Immediately he explored avenues to peace which he had tried to prepare after the breakdown of the earlier conversations.

Even before the conference closed formally, plans for a settlement were in the air. Irwin and Wedgwood Benn had discussed the question of an amnesty for political prisoners, but Irwin was clear that he could not countenance such a move unless they secured in return the cessation of civil disobedience: in any case he anticipated that provincial governments would 'jib badly at the idea of amnesty'. He was equally sure, however, that they must seize the chance offered by the plan of federation with responsibility at the centre. On 1 January he telegraphed to Benn his view that such an opportunity for a political solution with reasonable safeguards in an atmosphere of goodwill was unlikely to come again for the next five to ten years. This was reinforced by his anxiety to avoid further widespread agitation when the government's services and financial resources were severely strained, and when the present agrarian distress alongside a landowning system always vulnerable to attack provided fertile ground for political agitators. Benn's thinking coincided with Irwin's; and after dining with Sapru, Jayakar and V. S. S. Sastri he wrote to the Viceroy suggesting that leading Congressmen, including the prisoners, should be allowed to meet, in the hope that if they decided to abandon civil disobedience and look critically at the conference proposals 'A situation might arise in which,

[49] Prime Minister's closing speech, 19 January 1931, *Indian Round Table Conference, 12th November, 1930 – 19th January, 1931*, P.P., 1930–1, XII, Cmd. 3772.

Wedgwood Benn's letters to Irwin during the conference were in diary form and showed the change in the political prospect once the Princes offered to come into the Federation; Mss. EUR.C.152 (6). Irwin was told secretly of the scheme in a wire from S of S, 29 December 1930, Mss. EUR.C.152 (11).

For a detailed account of the conference and the negotiations which led to the prospect of responsibility at the centre, see Moore, *Crisis of Indian Unity*, pp. 103–64.

without any bargaining being made we should be justified in doing something'.[50]

Irwin had already contemplated permitting Working Committee members still at liberty to meet in Allahabad although the body had been declared illegal in the U.P. The Prime Minister's 19 January statement provided the occasion and justification for this leniency, as MacDonald had appealed for Congress cooperation in the new constitutional venture and promised in reply to Sapru's appeal for an amnesty that if 'civil quiet' was 'proclaimed and assured' in India the government would 'certainly not be backward in responding to his plea'. On 20 January Irwin decided in consultation with Hailey's government to let the Working Committee meet, and he hoped to use the services of returned conference delegates to influence Congress discussions.[51] Simultaneously his government examined the possibility of releasing the jailed members of the Committee to give them a chance to discuss MacDonald's statement. He argued to his governors that if they did not do this there was little hope that Congress would cooperate, and the government would find it difficult to justify its stand to public opinion in Britain and India. A further factor was that this procedure would not commit the government to a wider amnesty until it was assured that civil disobedience would be called off. The governors either agreed or made no comment; though from Bihar and Bombay came the warning that any wider leniency would have a serious effect on the services' morale. After a lengthy Council discussion on 24 January Irwin made a public statement that all who had belonged to the Working Committee since 1 January 1930 would be released unconditionally as an indication of the government's wish to create the conditions in which they could implement MacDonald's undertaking.[52]

Irwin was aware of dangers even in this limited gesture; in particular its possible repercussions on local administrative morale and ability to contain the situation, and the opening it would give Congress to haggle and press for a general amnesty. de Montmorency from the Punjab had reported to him an intercepted letter written by Asaf Ali, a Delhi Congress Muslim, indicating that he envisaged an amnesty followed by a temporary truce: the Governor added his own gloss that he was sure Congress would only use a peace to reorganize its forces for a second rebellion, in the event

[50] Irwin to Wedgwood Benn, 26 December 1930, Mss. EUR.C.152 (6); V to S of S, telegram, 1 January 1931, Mss. EUR.C.152 (11); Wedgwood Benn to Irwin, 15 January 1931, Home Poll., 1931, File No. 5/45.

[51] U.P. Govt. to Govt. of India & Govt. of India reply, telegrams, 20 January 1931, *ibid.*; V to S of S, telegram, 21 January 1931, Mss. EUR.C.152 (11).

[52] Irwin's statement, 25 January 1931, *HFM, III, III*, pp. 652–3; Irwin to Governor of Burma, on 24 January Council meeting, 25 January 1931, Mss. EUR.C.152 (26). For the consultations leading to the decision see Irwin to Governor of Madras, 20 January 1931, *ibid.*; V to S of S, telegram giving text of two wires to governors on proposed policy and statement, 22 January 1931, S of S to V, telegram agreeing to proposed action, 23 January 1931, Mss. EUR.C.152 (11); Governors' replies to Govt. of India proposals, 23/24 January 1931, Mss. EUR.C.152 (26).

of which non-Congress Hindus might well not support what looked like a dying government. Irwin replied that he, too, was 'not very sanguine about the future', and thought that they were 'in for a very difficult period of pressure and haggling. The Congress people will be as difficult and niggling as they can, and I shall be surprised if they come into the further discussions.' Since Irwin lacked any real optimism about Congress leaders' intentions and was more concerned about the gesture's effect on non-Congress groups in India and abroad and its potential for dividing Congress opinion, he was cautious about further leniency and underlined to Whitehall the importance of amnesty measures occurring simultaneously with the cessation of civil disobedience. 'I have no desire to ask Congress to assume the position of defeated suppliants, but neither do I think we can ask Local Governments, Police, Services, and all our non-official friends to make so dramatic a gesture as universal release without any outward sign that this is to be accompanied by a corresponding concession to peace on the other side.'[53]

Concern for the effects of policy on groups other than Congress permeated intra-governmental discussions on the next move. On 28 January the Home Department sent a long analysis of the political situation to local governments, asking their opinion on the various forms of simultaneous government action which might occur if Congress gave sufficient assurances about the end of the campaign to justify the risk. To prepare itself for a dynamic situation in which it might have to make quick decisions, it wanted advance information on provincial attitudes to such questions as amnesty, withdrawal of Ordinances, restoration of forfeited lands and reinstatement of ex-officials. All local governments were apprehensive at the prospect of such actions, particularly Bombay which stuck out against the restoration of lands sold to third parties, and 'simultaneity of action' on the grounds that leaders could not guarantee the actions of local campaigners. Governors were haunted by the prospect of a stampede among minorities and former government supporters and the deterioration of service morale, though they realized that if Congress did take to constitutional methods they had everything to gain from a liberal response. Consequently, as the Home Secretary noted, they must 'judge any proposed course of action not so much by its possible effects on the Congress, but by its probable effects on our supporters and our officers and men. Desirable as it might be in normal conditions to go to the utmost limit of forbearance and concession in order to placate our enemies, we simply cannot afford to carry this process at the present time beyond circumscribed limits.' He therefore suggested that they must keep absolute confidence and cohesion on policy between governments in the provinces, Delhi and London, and make it plain that though they desired cooperation they were not begging for it.[54]

[53] de Montmorency to Irwin, 24 January 1931, Irwin's reply, 27 January 1931, *ibid.*; Irwin to Wedgwood Benn, 26 January 1931, Mss. EUR.C.152 (6).
[54] File containing 28 January 1931 Govt. of India letter to all local govts. with their replies, and Emerson's note, 12 February 1931, Home Poll., 1931, File No. 4/45.

The government's freedom to manoeuvre was severely restricted. Conflicting pressures on Congress leaders, and on Gandhi in particular, were of similar intensity. When the free members of the Working Committee met in Allahabad they were divided on the desirability of peace. Madan Mohan Malaviya had a considerable following when he urged moderation, but Motilal opposed him vehemently. A resolution was passed refusing to recognize the proceedings of the Round Table Conference, and stating that MacDonald's statement was too vague and general to justify any change in Congress policy. However, this was not published because a cable arrived from Sapru and other conference delegates urging the Working Committee to postpone a decision until they could consult with its members on their return to India. All that emerged formally from the Allahabad meeting was a circular to PCCs urging them not to relax. 'The struggle has to be continued with vigour and firmness until the goal is reached, and we should not be deflected from our course by anything that is happening until the Congress asks us to take any course different from that already chalked out.'[55]

At this juncture Gandhi and the rest of the Working Committee were released, on 26 January 1931. Questioned by the press as he left for Bombay, Gandhi said that he had no plan or policy mapped out and that he was prepared to study the situation with an open mind. But within days he had laid out the grounds of a negotiating position as Emerson had done for the government. He maintained that since civil disobedience was a mass movement the leaders could not dictate a course of action, and the release of all satyagraha prisoners must occur – an ingenious argument for a general amnesty and possibly a way of covering his position if he proved unable to secure a single Congress line on acceptable terms of peace or to control the rank and file in a truce period. He called MacDonald's statement 'wholly inadequate' on the face of it, arguing that even if it turned out after discussion with the conference delegates to provide adequate ground for Congress cooperation, Congress could never give up Indians' right to manufacture salt or to pursue boycott of foreign cloth and liquor even by picketing. Withdrawal of Ordinances and restoration of confiscated property were also essential in his view.[56]

The preliminary terms Gandhi laid down reflected not only his personal priorities of salt, temperance and *khadi*: they were evidence of his need to consider the people who had followed his appeals to the extent of being jailed or losing their lands. Once he was out of Yeravda he was confronted even more forcibly by such considerations, as well as the arguments of those

[55] Circular from R. Prasad, Acting Congress President, to PCCs, 22 January 1931, *ibid.*; Governor of U.P. to Viceroy, telegram, 23 January 1931, Mss. EUR.C.152 (26); unpublished Working Committee resolution, 21 January 1931, Sitaramayya, *History of the INC. Volume I*, pp. 424–5.

[56] Press interviews, 26 January 1931, *The Hindu*, 28 January 1931, 27 January 1931, *The Times of India*, 28 January 1931; cable to *Daily Herald*, 30 January 1931; *CWMG*, XLV, 125–6, 127–30, 130–1.

who wanted peace. On 27 January he had long talks in Bombay with Vallabhbhai Patel, Lalji Naranji, F. E. Dinshaw and Sir Chunilal Mehta, President of the Indian Merchants' Chamber, among others. Lalji Naranji urged that the Working Committee should reach no decision until it had met representatives of important commercial interests who were the real sufferers from civil disobedience, and of Gujarati cultivators who had also made sacrifices. Vallabhbhai, however, hammered home the problem of the Gujaratis who had lost their lands for refusing to pay revenue. He felt that people in the villages would never allow purchasers to cultivate the lands they had bought as a result of confiscations and urged that lands must be restored to their original owners; though Naranji thought this a small matter which should not prevent peace. Gandhi appeared open-minded, and said that he would support what the country seemed to want, whatever his personal view. Naranji judged that the omens were favourable for peace provided the government could satisfy Gandhi and his colleagues of their intention to meet Indian wishes.[57]

From Bombay Gandhi went to Allahabad where businessmen continued to put pressure on him for peace. Birla was there to consult with Gandhi; and he, too, reported to Purshotamdas Thakurdas that there was some hope of peace. Gandhi had enquired what the Bombay business community would consider minimum terms for constitutional advance. He received no precise answer because the Indian Merchants' Chamber was divided on policy, and Thakurdas replied that he would rather negotiate without laying down an ultimatum. The Chamber merchants were very anxious about the nature of the financial safeguards proposed in the new constitution: however they asked Birla to impress on Gandhi that the future might be catastrophic if there was no settlement soon.[58] Against this weighed Jawaharlal's uncompromising stand. He had made it clear from jail to Motilal, while the Working Committee considered the position, that he believed any haggling or appearance of waiting for results from the Round Table Conference would be disastrous for rank and file morale and might rend the Congress leadership asunder. Motilal was by this time very ill: but he nonetheless urged Gandhi to be firm, and when the Mahatma floated the idea of visiting Irwin he insisted that the invitation should come from the Viceroy.[59] Gandhi stood between the Nehrus and those who pressed for peace from outside Congress and, like Malaviya and Sen Gupta, from

[57] L. Naranji to P. Thakurdas, 31 January 1931, Thakurdas Papers, File No. 107/1931.
[58] Note for Irwin by Sir Joseph Bhore, 31 January 1931, Mss. EUR.C.152 (26). For further evidence of Bombay mercantile pressure on Gandhi for peace see Maharaja of Bikaner to Irwin, 6 February 1931, Sykes to Irwin, telegram, 7 February 1931, *ibid.*
[59] Note written by Jawaharlal in jail before MacDonald's statement, letter written by Jawaharlal to his father after seeing the statement (n.d.), *SWJN*, 4, pp. 453–61; on Motilal's position see note for Irwin by Sir Joseph Bhore, 31 January 1931, Mss. EUR.C.152 (26).

within its ranks, having behind him those who held the middle ground between the two extremes. Those who were manoeuvring to contrive a settlement believed, according to Irwin, that Gandhi was the key to the situation, while even such a sceptic about Gandhi's tactics as M. S. Aney wired to assure him of support for any decision he might make in consultation with Congressmen and returning conference delegates.[60]

Gandhi's position was analogous to the one he had occupied in the intricate manoeuvres at Delhi and Allahabad late in 1929, though his influence over the groups involved was now greater because of the response his tactics had elicited in 1930. He kept his options open in his speech to the Working Committee at Allahabad on 31 January before the conference delegates returned. Although he did not rule out the possibility of a truce, he declared that MacDonald's statement could only be considered if the government granted the demands they had made during the Yeravda negotiations (demands which did not appear as radical now in the light of the Round Table Conference), and an enquiry into allegations of police atrocities – the latter being, he conceded, a new condition of cooperation. The Committee passed a holding resolution that the campaign was to continue until there were explicit instructions to the contrary; and in tune with Gandhi's statements since his release, reminded the public that peaceful picketing of foreign cloth and liquor shops was the right of every citizen. In subsequent public statements Gandhi remained non-committal on the eventual Congress decision, but reiterated that no peace was possible 'with repression fouling the atmosphere hour after hour' and without an enquiry into police brutality.[61] Simultaneously he renewed contact with Irwin, though in the somewhat belligerent context of a request for an independent enquiry into alleged 'excesses' by officials during civil disobedience. Nonetheless Jayakar suggested that it was distinctly hopeful that for the first time 'Congress leaders have descended into definite particulars. I am inclined to take the view that this is a tactful move on the part of Mr. Gandhi to get again into touch with Government on an issue which will keep up his prestige.'[62]

As Gandhi managed to maintain a flexible position, pressing the government yet opening communications with Irwin, the balance of personalities within the Congress leadership was altered drastically by Motilal's death on 6 February. As Gandhi said, 'Confusion is worse confounded. Motilalji's

[60] Irwin to Wedgwood Benn, 2 February 1931, Mss. EUR.C.152 (6); M. S. Aney to Gandhi, telegram before 31 January 1931, *CWMG*, XLV, 131, fn. 1.
[61] Speech to Working Committee, 31 January 1931, *ibid.* pp. 132–4; Working Committee resolution, Sitaramayya, *op. cit.* p. 430; press interview, 1 February 1931, *The Hindu*, 2 February 1931, *CWMG*, XLV, 138–9; cable to *Daily News*, 3 February 1931, *ibid.* p. 148.
[62] Jayakar to Irwin, 7 February 1931, Mss. EUR.C.152 (26); Gandhi to Irwin, 1 February 1931, *ibid.*
Irwin declined to grant Gandhi's request; P. S. V. to Gandhi, 4 February 1931, *ibid.* Nevertheless he pressed Sykes to enquire into one of the incidents Gandhi had cited, telegrams, 4 & 6 February 1931, *ibid.*

death has upset my apple cart.' Irwin speculated what realignments might ensue, thinking that Jawaharlal's militancy would no longer be cloaked by his father's apparent moderation and that this might strengthen the more moderate men.[63] The loss of his father certainly isolated Jawaharlal politically and threw greater weight on Gandhi's shoulders in the decision-making process. It also made Jawaharlal more amenable to Gandhi in a time of personal loss when Gandhi's relationship with him became more tender and fatherly. The results of this redistribution of influence in Congress counsels was not clear for several weeks, and immediately after Motilal's death Gandhi still appeared to be feeling his way and professed to see no signs of a possible settlement.[64]

However, on the day Motilal died, the Round Table Conference delegates landed at Bombay. Sapru, Jayakar and Srinivasa Sastri hurried to Allahabad and threw their weight into the discussions in an attempt to safeguard their recent labours and future positions. Sastri noted, 'If the work of the Conference is rejected, the future is dark.' The three had long talks with Gandhi and attended the Working Committee to answer questions about the conference and future possibilities. The Committee was still divided; and their efforts to sway its members and Gandhi in particular towards peace were supported by the Nawab of Bhopal who called on Gandhi on 13 February, and by Nationalist Muslims and Pandit Malaviya from within the Congress circle. Jawaharlal meanwhile pressed for tough minimum conditions for a settlement.[65] The upshot of these discussions was a letter from Gandhi to Irwin requesting an interview. Gandhi said his practice was to get into personal touch with officials when this could help, and now the advice of the conference delegates coinciding with the increased responsibility put on him by Motilal's death made him 'feel that without personal contact and heart to heart talk with you, the advice I may give my coworkers may not be right'. Irwin agreed immediately, gathering that the critical need was now to win Gandhi's sympathy and convince him of British sincerity, and that this rather than hard bargaining over precise terms would be the key to Congress cooperation.[66]

Again Gandhi acquired a unique position of political leverage for

[63] Gandhi to G. Deshpande, 10 February 1931, *CWMG*, XLV, 169; Irwin to Wedgwood Benn, 9 February 1931, Mss. EUR.C.152 (6).

[64] Gandhi to T. Rangachari, 8 February 1931, to N. Gandhi, 10 February 1931, *CWMG*, XLV, 163, 170; de Montmorency to Irwin, 13 February 1931, Mss. EUR.C.152 (26).

[65] For the forces working for peace in the Allahabad discussions see 11/12/13 February 1931, Diary of V. S. S. Sastri; V. S. S. Sastri to D. V. Gundappa, 10 & 15 February 1931, to V. S. R. Sastri, 16 February 1931, Jagadisan, *Letters of Srinivasa Sastri*, pp. 207–9; Wedgwood Benn to Irwin, 13 February 1931, Mss. EUR.C.152 (6).

For J. Nehru's attitude see undated draft communiqué of Working Committee and note for Working Committee by Jawaharlal, *SWJN*, 4, pp. 470–4.

[66] Gandhi to Irwin, 14 February 1931, original in Mss. EUR.D.670; Irwin to Wedgwood Benn, 16 February 1930, Mss. EUR.C.152 (6).

which he was prepared by his satyagrahi's commitment to persuasion and his African experience of negotiating with the head of the government. Congress and non-Congress Hindu politicians, divided on acceptable peace terms, needed a means of accommodation with each other and the British and offered him the role of negotiator. The British seized on the idea in the hope of following through the Round Table Conference initiative to a constitutional solution accepted by all important political groups among their subjects. It was highly significant that the Viceroy at this junction was Irwin. An aristocrat and Tory, he was nonetheless sympathetic towards the political aspirations of Indians and keenly aware that the empire would only survive if it was founded on a broad span of agreement and cooperation. A devout Anglican, he was intrigued by and sensitive to Gandhi as another man of religion; and despite his political realism about Congressmen in general he hoped that a gesture of faith would attract the cooperation of the Mahatma as a leader of wider vision than his colleagues.

The first phase in the negotiations between the Mahatma and the Viceroy lasted for a week, beginning with two long interviews on 17 and 18 February. Sastri, Jayakar and Sapru endeavoured to soften them up for the encounter so that it could appear to both as a meeting of spiritual men rather than a confrontation of political opponents. 'This afternoon "the two uncrucified Christs" meet,' wrote Sastri. 'Sapru, Jayakar and I have prepared each for the other!'[67]

The purpose of these meetings was a preliminary investigation of issues at stake to see if there was substantial ground for talks between the government and Congress. At this stage both spoke only for themselves, Irwin not committing his local governments or the Secretary of State, and Gandhi not binding his Congress colleagues or formally representing their views. They covered first the scope of future constitutional discussions; and Irwin told Gandhi that the main principles of the proposed plan were federation, Indian responsibility, and reservations and safeguards. Gandhi raised the questions of possible secession from the empire, an enquiry into debt obligations, and the position of people in the Princely States; he was assured that he could raise such topics although Irwin warned him that mention of independence would probably have a very damaging effect on British opinion. Irwin was concerned to extract a firm statement from Gandhi that if Congress agreed to participate in constitutional discussions it would not suddenly revert to civil disobedience. Without such a commitment he was not prepared to recommend any form of reciprocal government action, a line which his Home Department had pressed since the possibility of peace became a real one. Gandhi said Congress could not give a pledge never to resort to civil disobedience, but if it entered discussions it would try to make them a success and would definitely not resort to civil

---

[67] V. S. S. Sastri to T. R. V. Sastri, 17 February 1931, Jagadisan, *op. cit.* p. 209; Irwin to Wedgwood Benn, 16 February 1931, Mss. EUR.C.152 (6).

disobedience while they were in progress. The rest of their talks covered practical points on possible government action if civil disobedience ceased – amnesty, the problem of confiscated lands and property, remission of fines, reinstatement of officials who had resigned or been dismissed, withdrawal of Ordinances and punitive police, an enquiry into police excesses, salt manufacture and peaceful picketing. On these details they merely exchanged views and did not negotiate, because the questions were academic until Gandhi and Congress were convinced that the constitutional plans within the principles sketched by Irwin were worth discussing. Irwin, however, remarked to the Secretary of State that it was on the details of government action that he expected trouble. The atmosphere of the conversations was friendly and Gandhi was pleased with them. Moreover he was convinced that the Viceroy really wanted to make peace, though he summed up Irwin's stance on 18th as 'Stiff today but still pleasant'. On 19th the two met again for just half an hour and agreed on the gist of their discussions to date which Irwin had prepared. He then explained that he would have to consult his local governments on the practical points raised, and with the Secretary of State on the scope of the constitutional discussions before there could be more extended talks.[68]

Irwin reported these proceedings to Wedgwood Benn on 19 February and received confirmation that the scope of future constitutional discussions would be contained within the three principles Irwin had expounded to Gandhi – federation but with safeguards during the transitional period on such topics as defence and credit, and Indian responsibility.[69] Meanwhile consultations took place within government circles in Delhi on the terms and procedure for an agreement with Congress. Sykes was up from Bombay for three days while Irwin's talks with Gandhi were in progress; he urged on Irwin and his Home Secretary, Emerson, that they should not yield on three cardinal points – an enquiry into alleged police excesses, the return of lands forfeited for non-payment of revenue and the reinstatement of village officials. Emerson's note circulated in advance of the Council meeting of 20th showed that the Government of India recognized the pressures on men like Sykes who had to deal with the repercussions of an all-India settlement in their specific local contexts. It stated that the general principles guiding a settlement should be the avoidance of enquiries into actions on either side during civil disobedience, and of anything which would imply that government was in the dock or would by implication censure or humilitate government officials, and would permit Congress to parade as victor. Within these parameters government policy should be as liberal as possible provided that Congress called off civil disobedience at least while

---

[68] Accounts of the 17/18/19 February 1931 meetings by Irwin and by Gandhi, *CWMG*, XLV, 185–91, 193–201, 205–7; 18 February 1931, Diary of V. S. S. Sastri; V to S of S, telegram, 19 February 1931, Mss. EUR.C.152 (11).

[69] V to S of S, telegram, 19 February 1931, S of S to V, telegram, 20 February 1931, *ibid.*

constitutional discussions were in progress. Sensitive to local government's attitudes and declining revenue in the recession, Emerson suggested that the Government of India should accept liability for any concessions which would require local government expenditure.[70]

The upshot of the Council discussion was a telegraphic reference to provincial governments on the possible terms of a settlement, and a decision on future procedure. Irwin and Gandhi had contemplated as the next step discussions among a wider circle including some Congressmen, some officials and conference delegates. Now the government abandoned this idea for fear that in such a gathering conference delegates might not be able to stand out against Congressmen, and Gandhi might say things which he could not withdraw as easily as if the discussions were more private. Therefore Irwin was to see Gandhi alone and leave him to bring his fellow Congressmen round. This decision confirmed the unique leadership role thrust on Gandhi in part by the perceptions and needs of the government.[71] The Commander-in-Chief, General Sir Philip Chetwode, who believed Gandhi to be 'as cunning as a cartload of monkeys', was appalled at the evidence the Council discussions gave of government's apparent weakness and need of Gandhi's cooperation. In his view although they had been laying down essential conditions which Congress must observe before there could be further clemency, they had spent far more time discussing the terms of a man who was not in a position to offer terms.[72]

In the brief intermission before the resumption of talks between Gandhi and Irwin there seemed to some at the centre of the negotiations a good chance that Gandhi would not only opt for a settlement but would sway the more militant in the Working Committee. Irwin anticipated much argument over details but believed that Gandhi would ultimately be won over and would bring Jawaharlal with him. Sastri thought Gandhi seemed conciliatory and that the Mahatma's 'influence over the Congress Working Committee is supreme and will prevail over Jawaharlal and others. It looks so. Events make it necessary for him to seek peace.' Although the pressures on Gandhi for peace were undoubtedly strong he was also criticized for his willingness to negotiate. He justified his action on the grounds that satyagraha implied gentleness and waiting where these seemed appropriate, and again his thoughts turned to his South African experience. As 'a seasoned soldier in satyagraha' he maintained that no cause had suffered by such action since satyagraha was 'a method of carrying conviction and of converting by an appeal to reason and to the sympathetic chord in human

---

[70] Sykes, *From Many Angles*, pp. 409–10; note by H. W. Emerson, 20 February 1931, Home Poll., 1931, File No. 5/45.

[71] Govt. of India to local govts., telegrams, 21 & 22 February 1931, *ibid.*; V to S of S, telegram, 22 February 1931, Mss. EUR.C.152 (11).

[72] Chetwode to Irwin, 22 February 1931, Mss. EUR.C.152 (26). For Chetwode's opinion of Gandhi see Sir M. Hallett to Wavell, 29 June 1944, N. Mansergh & E. W. R. Lumby (ed.), *Constitutional Relations between Britain and India. The Transfer of Power 1942–7. Volume IV* (London, 1973), p. 1058.

beings'. But he asserted that there would be no surrender of principle.[73] External constraints thus dovetailed with the Mahatma's perception of his proper stance as a satyagrahi, committing him to a role which political circumstances offered to him.

The second and really tough phase of the Gandhi–Irwin talks began on 27 February when the two men met for three and a half hours. As Irwin had anticipated the problems arose over the practical aspects of a truce, not over the scope of constitutional discussions which had been cleared by the Secretary of State. Gandhi readily assented to the formula Irwin put to him.

> The object of future discussions is to consider further the scheme for the constitutional government of India discussed at the Round Table Conference. Of the scheme there outlined, Federation is an essential part; so also are Indian responsibility, and safeguards... as being needed to secure such matters as Crown control of defence and external affairs; the position of minorities; the financial credit of India, and the discharge of obligations. The character and form of the arrangements, by which effect should be given to these fundamental principles of Federation, responsibility and safeguards, are matter for discussion.

Gandhi was satisfied with the assurance that he could raise such questions as secession and finance, though the total constitutional package fell short of the demand made by the seven Congress signatories at Yeravda. However he said that the official line presented insurmountable difficulties on three matters – picketing, enquiries into police excesses, and salt. The government position was that picketing repeatedly led to violence and must cease, there could be no general enquiry into allegations against government servants nor any condoning breaches of the salt law. After the interview Gandhi made no statement and was non-committal about the continuation of talks. He had told Irwin that the initiative for further discussion lay with him, and the Viceroy concluded that the outlook was bleak. 'He was in a very obstinate mood throughout the conversation and left a pretty clear impression on my mind that, beneath the guise of reasonableness, he was either bluffing or had made up his mind that he did not mean to settle except on his full terms.'[74]

The following morning Irwin saw Sapru and Jayakar, who were very

---

[73] Gandhi to R. Reynolds, 23 February, 1931, *CWMG*, XLV, 221–2; Irwin to Wedgwood Benn, 23 February 1931, Mss. EUR.C.152 (6); V. S. S. Sastri to D. V. Gundappa, 23 February 1931, Jagadisan, *op. cit.* p. 210.

[74] Note by Irwin, 27 February 1931, of interview with Gandhi that day, & note sent to Gandhi by G. Cunningham (P.S.V.), 28 February 1931, setting out the official view on points made by Gandhi, all enclosed in Irwin to Wedgwood Benn, 2 March 1931, Mss. EUR.C.152 (6); press interview by Gandhi, 27 February 1931, *The Hindu*, 28 February 1931, *CWMG*, XLV, 235.

For the Home Department's stress on these three issues see note by H. W. Emerson, 20 February 1931, Home Poll., 1931, File No. 5/45: he described the demand for an enquiry into police behaviour as 'an issue of first rate importance on which it is absolutely essential that we should stand firm'.

disturbed over the police question and pressed strongly that local governments should be made to hold enquiries into specific cases. But Irwin and
his advisors, Crerar, Emerson and Mitter, would only agree to communicate
important allegations to local governments and ask them to act as seemed
fit, reporting the outcome to the Government of India. Sastri hoped that
this might satisfy Gandhi; and Malaviya thought the Mahatma could be
persuaded to agree. Sapru and Jayakar supported Irwin's position on salt,
though they suggested some accommodation with Gandhi on various types
of picketing. A note of the government's attitude to points raised by Gandhi
was sent that afternoon to him with an assurance that Irwin would be glad
to see him the following day. It crossed with a note from Gandhi which
he had promised Irwin, clarifying his distinction between 'aggressive'
picketing and peaceful picketing 'predominantly for social and moral ends'
which would occur mainly in villages, directed at buyers rather than
sellers. It was the latter kind of picketing which Gandhi insisted should be
permitted to continue if peace was established.[75]

During the talks Gandhi stayed at Dr Ansari's house on the borders of
old and new Delhi in Daryaganj. With him were the whole Working
Committee, whom he kept constantly informed of the course of the discussions even if this meant waking them in the middle of the night for
consultation. He was also at the centre of a stream of visitors and journalists
who sensed that vital decisions were imminent and clamoured for news or
pressed their views on the Mahatma. Jayakar, Sapru and Sastri were the
main protagonists of peace, in daily touch with both the Congress group
in Daryaganj and officials at the Secretariat. Pulling in the opposite direction was Jawaharlal who argued against the contemplated compromise even
though he realized that it would be extremely difficult to reorganize the
struggle at this stage. On 28 February he reported to his sister, 'The long
conversations are at last drawing to a close and we have to prepare again
for jail or worse! This is all to the good.'[76]

Irwin, too, thought a break was inevitable at this juncture. He believed
it would be on the police question and was determined that it should occur
on a wider front including salt and picketing. Sapru and Jayakar, among
others, saw the Viceroy on the morning of 1 March and argued forcibly
that without some concession on the police issue there would be no settlement. When they half hinted that if this happened they would be less
inclined to cooperate in constitution-making, Irwin leaned on them extremely heavily, losing his temper 'partly by design and partly by accident'
on his own admission. News of this reached Gandhi and the Working

[75] Addendum dated 28 February to Irwin's 27 February 1931 note on interview
with Gandhi that day, note on government position sent by Cunningham to Gandhi,
28 February 1931, Gandhi's 28 February 1931 note on picketing – all enclosed in Irwin
to Wedgwood Benn, 2 March 1931, Mss. EUR.C.152 (6); V. S. S. Sastri to T. R. V.
Sastri, 28 February 1931, Jagadisan, *op. cit.* p. 211.

[76] J. Nehru to 'Nan', 28 February 1931, NMML, V. Pandit Papers; Prasad, *Autobiography*, pp. 330–1; J. Nehru, *An Autobiography*, pp. 250–7.

Committee rapidly, and Sastri spoke to the Committee for an hour on the need for some accommodation on the police question. The result was that when Gandhi came to see Irwin in the afternoon he proved far more amenable than Irwin had dared to hope.[77]

They restated their positions on picketing and left the issue undecided. On the police question Gandhi objected to the formula contained in the notes Irwin had sent him the previous evening, but responded when Irwin agreed that the formula was a bad one and explained his predicament.

> I told him quite frankly that I...couldn't invent anything better without putting the Police in the cart, which I was not going to do. In these circumstances, was it not better that he should drop it altogether? I accompanied this with a very earnest appeal, emphasising that the big work on which we were engaged was restoration of peace, and that by no stretch of the imagination could anybody suppose that peace would be assisted by ragging the Police.

Together they drafted a formula on the lines that Gandhi, in a desire to establish peace, agreed not to press allegations he had made and on which government declined to institute specific enquiries. Gandhi took this away to consider, and Irwin was optimistic that it would prove a satisfactory means of getting over the greatest hurdle. The Mahatma attached far greater importance to salt than Irwin had expected; and the question was left for discussion with Sir George Schuster, the Finance Member of the Government of India, though Irwin indicated that there was some latitude in the official position on this, at least to the extent of allowing some alteration in the executive administration of the law. Summing up, he believed that as a result of this interview the outlook was very promising over the police, while there was considerable room for manoeuvre on picketing and salt if the government so desired.[78]

The same evening Gandhi saw Emerson, who had been present for part of the afternoon interview. The Home Secretary got Gandhi to agree to the abandonment of boycott as a political weapon and the freedom of cloth merchants to do as they wished; both of which Irwin considered 'pretty substantial gains'. He had joined them at this juncture, and although the three reached no formula on picketing they parted in expectation of being able to do so eventually. Irwin believed that it might be worth a slight concession here provided government secured the end of picketing as a political weapon, though he would have preferred to have got rid of it entirely. At the close of the day which had begun so ominously the Viceroy was fairly opimistic that a settlement would emerge. Even if it proved to be only temporary he believed it would have real advantages. It would justify his release of the Congress leaders while opening the way to real

[77] Irwin to Wedgwood Benn, 2 March 1931, Mss. EUR.C.152 (6); 1 March 1931, Diary of V. S. S. Sastri.
[78] Irwin to Wedgwood Benn, 2 March 1931, & enclosed note by Irwin, 2 March 1931, on first interview with Gandhi on 1 March, Mss. EUR.C.152 (6).

agreement at the conference table. It would also please British traders and would lower the stock of British diehards, while relieving the strain in India and allowing Willingdon a fairly clean slate for the start of his viceroyalty in April.[79]

Gandhi returned to Daryaganj to enter his silence day on 2 March. Like Irwin he was considering those whom the proposed settlement would affect; and uppermost in his mind was the problem of Jawaharlal, who seemed to be out on a limb as at Allahabad in November 1929. As he had done then, so now he sent him a note. He asked him to use the free day to examine the proposals carefully. 'You seem to be feeling lonely and almost uninterested. That must not be, my strength depends upon you. I want your active support in what I am doing. And that I cannot get unless you criticise, alter, amend, reject and do many other things.' Jawaharlal made his view plain in a note to the Working Committee which described the government's attitude to picketing, punitive police, the police enquiry demand and salt manufacture as 'insurmountable barriers'. The package Irwin proposed seemed to him 'an unmistakable indication that...India is not to expect through the conference the freedom she has bled for during the past 12 months.' At about this time he also told B. C. Roy that there was an outside chance of an agreement but he was 'sick and tired' of negotiations.[80]

However, Gandhi pushed on with negotiations when his silence day had ended. On 3 March he reached a working formula on salt with Schuster, and in interviews with Emerson and Irwin which lasted well into the night he concluded agreements on all the outstanding matters. Irwin felt least happy from the government's point of view about the concessions couched in the formulae on picketing and salt; while Gandhi was clearly worried about Irwin's insistence that government could not actively support efforts to get forfeited lands in Gujarat returned to their original owners where they had already been sold. It was not certain, however, that the Working Committee would agree to the terms Gandhi and Irwin had reached.[81]

Events on 4 March showed that Gandhi was under no illusions that to lead a political settlement he had, as much as in leading a struggle, to consider the reactions of his colleagues and the rank and file. The question of forfeited lands, anxiety over which he had expressed to Irwin on 3 March, was by the morning of the 4th a barrier to the working of the whole settlement; and he prepared a letter for Irwin explaining that Vallabhbhai insisted that it would be impossible to implement the Congress side of the

[79] Irwin to Wedgwood Benn, 2 March 1931, & enclosed note by Irwin, 2 March 1931, on second interview with Gandhi on 1 March, *ibid.*

[80] B. C. Roy to J. Nehru, 5 March 1931, J. Nehru Papers, part I, vol. LXXXIX; undated note by J. Nehru for Working Committee, *SWJN*, 4, pp. 479–81; note from Gandhi to J. Nehru, 2 March 1931, *CWMG*, XLV, 242.

[81] Irwin to Maharaja of Bikaner, 4 March 1931, Mss. EUR.C.152 (26); V to S of S, telegram, 4 March 1931, Mss. EUR.C.152 (11); note by Irwin, 4 March 1931, on interviews with Gandhi on 3 March, *CWMG*, XLV, 243–5.

settlement unless lands were restored to their original owners. He showed this to Irwin in the afternoon, but Irwin remained firm that he could not press the Bombay government further and that sales which had occurred must officially be considered final. The most he could agree to do was to draw Sykes's attention to the problem as Gandhi saw it and ask him to give it his personal attention. At this point he left for a garden party where he met Sapru, Jayakar, Sastri, Thakurdas and Rahimtullah, and told them of the hitch, urging them to put all possible pressure on Gandhi to avert the wreck of the settlement. The first three hurried to Ansari's, where they found Gandhi in obvious distress but firm. They returned to Irwin after long talks, bearing alternative proposals. Ultimately the solution they reached was the inclusion of a note in the settlement that Gandhi had represented to the government that he believed some of the sales to have been unlawful and unjust though the government had not accepted this contention. With this the Indian mediators shuttled back to Ansari's where in the early hours of 5 March they gained Gandhi's assent. Gandhi did not like the idea but agreed to accept it 'for want of the proper thing', as he told Irwin's Private Secretary in a letter of 5 March enclosing an amended version of the 4 March letter to Irwin he had shown but not formally sent to him. Cunningham replied that Irwin would let Sykes know of Gandhi's feelings as he had promised.[82]

With the Gujarat issue shelved though not solved Gandhi was able to secure the Working Committee's assent to the truce terms he had so painfully negotiated with Irwin; and the government published them within hours lest Gandhi developed any more scruples of the sort which had nearly shattered the delicately contrived structure the previous day.[83] Under the settlement Congress was to discontinue civil disobedience while the government announced that it would withdraw the Ordinances and notifications declaring organizations unlawful under the Criminal Law Amendment Act, would release civil disobedience prisoners, remove punitive police, restore forfeited property provided this had not been sold to third parties and would treat liberally applications for reinstatement by village officials who had resigned provided their posts had not been permanently filled. There was to be no enquiry into allegations about police

[82] Note by Irwin on interview with Gandhi on 4 March & subsequent negotiations, *ibid.* pp. 246–7; 4 March 1931, Diary of V. S. S. Sastri; Gandhi to G. Cunningham, 5 March 1931, Mss. EUR.D.670; Gandhi to Irwin, 4 March 1931, Cunningham to Gandhi, 5 March 1931, enclosed in Irwin to Sykes, 6 March 1931, in which Irwin kept his word to Gandhi and indeed went further, asking Sykes to do his best to help original owners regain their lands; Mss. EUR.C.152 (26). Sykes replied that his government could only be neutral on the issue, particularly because their going back on their undertaking to purchasers of forfeited lands after the Bardoli satyagraha had undermined local belief in the government's good faith, had increased Congress prestige in Gujarat and contributed to their troubles there in 1930; Sykes to Irwin, 11 March 1931, *ibid.*
[83] Working Committee Resolution, 5 March 1931, *CWMG*, XLV, 250; text of settlement, 5 March 1931, *India in 1930–31*, pp. 655–9.

conduct and Gandhi agreed not to press the matter rather than jeopardize the peace with inevitable charges and countercharges. Boycott of British goods as a political weapon was to end, but peaceful picketing could continue provided it was not coercive or in contravention of the ordinary law. The government refused to condone breaches of the salt laws or substantially to modify them, but it agreed to permit people to collect or make salt for domestic consumption if they lived in salt-producing areas. Congressmen would now participate in the discussions on the scheme of constitutional reform discussed at the Round Table Conference: 'Of the scheme there outlined, Federation is an essential part; so also are Indian responsibility and reservations or safeguards in the interests of India, for such matters as, for instance, defence; external affairs; the position of minorities; the financial credit of India, and the discharge of obligations.'

Gandhi and Irwin both found it necessary to justify the settlement to their colleagues and subordinates. The Viceroy was surprised that the enterprise had worked. He told the Secretary of State that although it might have been possible to extract a stiffer settlement he believed it was better to have carried Gandhi with a personal appeal and commitment so that he threw himself with goodwill into searching for a permanent settlement. To his governors he repeated the argument that Gandhi was an ally worth having, and he pressed them to proceed promptly with the stated terms to this end. He explained that the settlement sacrificed nothing essential from the government point of view, and its most satisfactory aspect was the absence of any police enquiry. The points on which he had conceded more than he wished were picketing and salt, but both had proved unavoidable. It would have been difficult to deny people their legal right to picket, and the formula had probably deprived the tactic of its political and provocative thrusts; while without the concession on salt Gandhi would have refused to settle. Irwin disliked having had to concede on the issue on which civil disobedience had formally started, but he commented, 'You will have observed that we did our best to make it look fairly respectable by saying what we could not do and by justifying our concession on the basis of existing practice in some districts.'[84]

Gandhi, too, had to argue the respectability of the settlement. In a long press statement on 5 March he said the settlement was provisional and that the Congress goal remained *purna swaraj*. The proposed constitution might prove the framework for the attainment of this goal, though this was not certain.

> Federation may be a mirage or it may mean a vital organic state in which the two limbs might work so as to strengthen the whole. Responsibility, which is the second girder, may be a mere shadow or it may be tall, majestic, unbending and unbendable oak. Safeguards in the interests of

[84] Irwin to Governors of Madras, Bengal, U.P., C.P., Assam, & Delhi Chief Commissioner, 6 March 1931, Mss. EUR.C.152 (26); Irwin to Wedgwood Benn, 9 March 1931, Mss. EUR.C.152 (6).

India may be purely illusory and so many ropes tying the country hand and foot and strangling her by the neck, or they may be like so many fences protecting a tender plant requiring delicate care and attention.

It was up to Congress to make its position plain at the conference. He admitted that Congress had not secured victor's terms, but neither had the government; and moreover, Congress had not been fighting for outright victory. Again he returned to the considerations which had guided his thinking as he planned the struggle. Unity and discipline were essential if Congressmen were to gain credence as national representatives and therefore the leverage to secure an acceptable constitution. These qualities could be engendered and displayed by the organization of a peace as much as by battle. 'If Congressmen honourably and fully implement the conditions applicable to them of the settlement, the Congress will obtain an irresistable prestige and would have inspired Government with confidence in its ability to ensure peace, as I think it has proved its ability to conduct disobedience.' Moreover in practical terms it would have been folly to prolong the sufferings of satyagrahis when the opponent made it easy to enter into discussion about their aims.[85]

Speaking to journalists the next day Gandhi asserted that the settlement was consistent with the Lahore resolution and that Congress could take up that stand at the conference if it wished – a point he had cleared with Irwin at the start of the discussions. But even at Lahore, he reminded them, he had maintained that independence did not necessarily mean dissociation from Britain, but might be association for mutal benefit at the will of both nations. To Irwin privately on 7 March he confirmed that he wanted a partnership between an equal India and Britain when he spoke of independence, though if he failed to secure that he would go for what he saw as the lower ideal of independence in isolation. He would argue on these lines to Congress, but there could be no alteration of the Lahore Resolution as this would arouse too much opposition. His press interviewers also asked whether he had not been offered precisely the same thing in December 1929 and the turmoil of civil disboedience had therefore been unnecessary. To this he replied that then Irwin could promise nothing, nor did they know the attitude of Indian delegates to the conference: now Dominion Status was certain. Moreover, as he repeated later, they had the power to make Dominion Status mean complete independence as in the intervening struggle they had displayed their strength, and no longer appeared as beggars at the negotiating table.[86]

[85] Gandhi's press statement, 5 March 1931, *Young India*, 12 March 1931, *CWMG*, XLV, 250–6.

[86] Interview to journalists, 6 March 1931, *Young India*, 19 March 1931, *ibid.* pp. 263–7; *Navajivan*, 15 March 1931, *ibid.* p. 296; Irwin to Wedgwood Benn on interview with Gandhi on 7 March 1931, Mss. EUR.C.152 (6). Gandhi also insisted that he stood by his 'eleven points' as the substance of independence, and said that if Congress succeeded at the Round Table Conference the points would be secured: speech on 16 March 1931, *Young India*, 26 March 1931, *CWMG*, XLV, 300.

Jawaharlal, however, did not share Gandhi's view. He believed that the clause setting out the parameters of the proposed constitution marked a real limitation on their independence ideal as proclaimed at Lahore. According to Gandhi he even wept on the Mahatma's shoulder at what he saw as the betrayal of India. But he realized there was nothing he could do once Gandhi had committed himself to the package and when civil disobedience was as good as dead. He contemplated dissociating himself from the settlement, much as he had wavered on the Delhi manifesto. But after several days of distress he agreed to accept Gandhi's interpretation rather than indulge in a personal demonstration which could not affect the larger issue.[87]

The parallel with Jawaharlal's position in November 1929 was close. But now he gave way to the Mahatma rather than Gandhi bending to accommodate him. There were several reasons for this, among them the practical impossibility of any other policy in a political situation where the moderates and a large proportion of the Congress leadership were anxious to pursue the conference possibilities, where the rank and file were weary and disorganized, and where the British authorities, including the Parliamentary opposition, backed the moves of conciliation and construction. Another factor in Jawaharlal's changed position was his father's death. He believed that if Motilal had lived events in Delhi would have turned out very differently, and hurt Gandhi by saying so within hours of the truce. Subhas Bose thought that Motilal was the only one who could have dissuaded Gandhi from the pact with Irwin, and Thakurdas commented several days after the settlement that he believed Motilal would have thrown his weight against it and 'would not have allowed Mahatma Gandhi to negotiate with the Viceroy'.[88] In the circle of the Working Committee and in the wider spectrum of provincial leaders there were none of Motilal's stature who were willing to challenge Gandhi once he had assumed the negotiator's role. The Bombay leader, K. F. Nariman, feared that Gandhi was going to break with Irwin on what he saw as the side issues of the police and salt, and felt that if the negotiations foundered they should do so on the major constitutional issue. In his opinion only the AICC could decide on such a matter, and 'Howsoever great an individual, this sort of autocracy in a matter of such supreme importance is undemocratic & undesirable; everyone feels it but is afraid to speak.'[89]

The fact that the truce had disadvantages for both Gandhi and Irwin and those for whom they spoke proved that its terms were not to the

[87] J. Nehru, *An Autobiography*, pp. 257–60; note by J. Nehru on settlement, n.d., *SWJN*, 4, pp. 481–2; B. R. Nanda, *Gokhale, Gandhi and the Nehrus. Studies in Indian Nationalism* (London, 1974), p. 190, n. 18.

[88] 4 March 1932, J. Nehru's Diary, *SWJN*, 5, p. 363; Bose, *The Indian Struggle 1920–42*, p. 209; P. Thakurdas to M. A. Jinnah, 17 March 1931, Thakurdas Papers, File No. 107/1931.

[89] K. F. Nariman to S. A. Brelvi, 1 March 1931, Brelvi Papers, File of correspondence with Nariman.

striking advantage of either side. The government secured the peace it required for its constitutional experiment and the prospect of Congress cooperation, and it gave away nothing it considered vital. However in spite of the efforts Irwin put into making the terms look 'respectable' the head of the government had parleyed with the leader of a movement which was self-confessedly seditious. The corollary was a great increase in the prestige and respectability of Congress. It had secured, by implication, official recognition that it could ensure peace in the country and that no Indian representation at the Round Table Conference was effectively national without Congressmen – a far cry from the old British taunts that Congressmen were a microscopic minority in no way representative of the majority of Indians. Furthermore, by giving up civil disobedience for the moment, Congress secured the option of attending the Round Table Conference with the opportunities for further influence that that proffered. The scope of the Conference discussions moreover approximated to the demand Gandhi had made to Irwin late in December 1929.

However, it was not civil disobedience which had produced this change in the power on offer to Indians in a new constitution. The emergence of a real possibility of responsible government depended on the movement of elements in the political environment other than Congress – the alliance of Princes and other Indian delegates on the basis of a Federation, and the agreement of the British political parties to responsible government in a constitution where the Princes' presence guaranteed a conservative weight at the centre. Yet civil disobedience was an important factor in the shifting political scene. As a demonstration of the range and depth of Congress support it convinced the British, moderate politicians, commercial men and even some Princes that it was essential to incorporate Congress into the next round of discussions now that the stake appeared so much higher. The juxtaposition of London bargaining and Indian agitation put Gandhi as assumed civil disobedience leader in a unique position of leverage among the various groups interacting in politics. Added to this was the need of many in the middle and upper echelons of Congress for a respectable settlement so that they could relate to their rulers and their moderate compatriots in the new political context when powers were promised which they wished to exploit: while most of the rank and file campaigners hankered for normal conditions, and an end to jail-going, fines and punitive police. As a satyagrahi Gandhi was superbly flexible and could switch from being a battle tactician to acting as an architect of peace. His role as sole negotiator was in a sense thrust on him by the absence of any other aspirant to the part, and by the divisions among Congressmen on the prospect of peace. But he accepted it willingly: and the fortnight of discussions with Irwin and his officials greatly increased his personal influence with both the government and his compatriots.[90] As Nariman and

[90] Winston Churchill criticized Irwin's treatment of Gandhi in a Commons speech, 12 March 1931, *Parliamentary Debates. Fifth Series – Volume 249. Commons, 1930–31,*

Nehru hinted, once negotiations were under way the bandwaggon began to roll. People concluded that Gandhi was the leader of the moment and hurried to make their obeisances; and none was willing to challenge him openly, risking public odium as well as ineffectiveness.

Nevertheless Gandhi's influence as a leader depended on his sensitivity to the messages coming from his colleagues and the rank and file of the campaigners. These he had to weigh against each other as he had done in moving towards conflict in 1929, knowing that whatever his personal prestige and influence he could not lead either in peace or war if he flouted the signs around him of what would be politically possible. The tortuous details of the negotiations at Yeravda and then in Delhi showed the diversity of people who looked to him for all-India leadership, and his own slow testing of the situation and the support he could elicit in any particular move. By 1931 the tide had turned sufficiently among most campaigners, non-Congressmen and the British for him to follow his inclination for negotiation; whereas in 1930 he had deferred to the Nehrus despite his personal conviction that the time had come for peace. His insistence in Delhi on the minutiae of the reciprocal government action rather than the constitutional proposals was evidence of his political sensitivity to the priorities and perceptions of those he would have to lead, as well as his personal commitment on the salt issue. He realized that further conflict could do nothing to influence the constitutional planning, and that Congress would probably improve its negotiating position now by participating in talks and proving an efficient peace-keeping force. To those involved locally in civil disobedience constitutional details were less important than to men like Jawaharlal. Salt and picketing were the hallmarks of the Congress campaign; and having salvaged these and secured the release of prisoners and the return of forfeited property he had gone a long way towards maintaining Congress prestige in the popular estimation. He would have done so even more spectacularly if he could have forced concessions from Irwin on a police enquiry and the return of forfeited lands which had already been sold.

Vol. 249, cols. 1453–4.
'I notice that Mr Gandhi speaks of Lord Irwin in terms of strong approbation. It is no more than just. In the course of this year the Viceroy has fostered the growth of Mr Gandhi's power to an extent almost inconceivable, first, by neglecting to arrest him until his breaches of the law had gradually attracted and rivetted the attention of India; secondly, by arresting him when they did for his breaches of the law; thirdly, by not trying him upon any known charge or proceeding against him by any recognised process of the law but confining him under some old Statute as a prisoner of State; fourthly, by attempting to negotiate with him when he was still in prison; fifthly, by releasing him unconditionally; sixthly, by negotiating with him as an equal and as if he were the victor in some warlike encounter; seventhly, by conceding to him as a permanent emblem of triumph the legality of the very practice which he had selected for the purpose of affronting the Government.

This series of steps ought to be preserved as a patent prescription for building up the reputation of a political opponent, or rather of a revolutionary leader.'

The conclusion of the Gandhi–Irwin pact, as it came to be known, probably marked the peak of Gandhi's political influence and prestige in India. Political leadership, however, is not a static phenomenon, but a developing relationship in a context where the issues and arenas may change. In Gandhi's case he had to proceed from Delhi to a Congress session at Karachi, and thence to the fulfilment of the settlement in the country and to the conference table in London. To continue to lead he had to prove himself valuable in these arenas, dealing with new issues, to the British and non-Congressmen as much as to his colleagues and followers in Congress and their local clienteles. He could not rest on the laurels acquired in the particular circumstances of the Delhi negotiations with a Viceroy who was both willing and able to adjust to the Gandhian negotiating style.

CHAPTER 5

The constraints of peace

Between March and December 1931 Gandhi's political activities were directed towards maintaining and exploiting the settlement he had engineered with Irwin. His aim, as in the preceding conflict, was to weld Indians into a new, self-consciously national unity and to substantiate Congress's claim to represent that unity: by so doing he hoped to gain a constitution which would endorse that claim and permit India's unfettered growth into the state he called *purna swaraj*. In peace as in battle with the raj, his intention was to build a strong negotiating position, and in pursuing this object he had to consider the variety of groups whose attitudes and responses impinged on his enterprise. Foremost among these were Congress supporters, whose coordination and discipline were essential, as failure among former campaigners to observe the Congress side of the pact would wreck its claim to be the nation's spokesman. Of almost equal significance were Indians outside Congress, public opinion beyond the subcontinent, and the British who formulated and executed the raj's policies both in India and Britain.

The Mahatma's weakness as well as his strength as an all-India leader lay in the fact that he had no permanent and solid power base. He spoke for no bloc of supporters with a clear aim, let alone for a self-consciously national group. Support for him was disparate and fluctuating; and correspondingly his powers of control were limited, varying in time and place. His core of devotees based on the ashram could be deployed politically as in the long march to Dandi, but few of them carried weight in Congress counsels or could guarantee him political support beyond their personal adherence. Among all-India and prominent provincial politicians he could depend permanently on some close colleagues like Rajendra Prasad, Vallabhbhai Patel or Rajagopalachariar, who were bound to him by ideological commitment and personal affection as well as political calculation. Beyond their inner ring were men who made temporary alliance with the Mahatma in a running calculation of the benefits of alignment with his political stance and tactics. Some of these could guarantee local support for Gandhi, while others hoped to buttress or attain local support by trading on his name. In the subcontinent at large he had only a few permanent groups of adherents. Foremost of these were Gujaratis in Bombay City and the towns of Gujarat and some Gujarati peasant proprietors who believed he could promote their particular material interests and also venerated him as a

prophet and spiritual guide. Otherwise in the localities Gandhi's ability to
rally activists for his campaigns fluctuated in proportion to their capacity
to serve local interests at that juncture. He did, however, evoke remarkable
sympathy from many educated Hindus, and attracted vast crowds of the
awestruck or the merely curious, who rarely participated actively in his
campaigns but whose existence contributed to his public image. The presence of a wide band of sedentary sympathizers with Gandhi at every level
of Hindu society was a factor in the political environment in which British
and Indian alike made political decisions, though it was not a support bank
on which Gandhi could draw for active assistance.

Gandhi's strength as a political leader at a particular junction of circumstances in 1930 had been demonstrated by his remarkable success in welding
many Indians into a conscious unity during civil disobedience. He had been
able to do this because he was a figure apart from other politicians, not
aligned with a particular faction, interest or region, or set on a political
career; because his tactics were exploitable by groups with a variety of aims
and expertise; and because his teachings brought a new dimension to
political life, attracting to political activity men and women who would
probably never have participated in the politics of conciliar collaboration,
local jobbery or terrorist resistance. His path to renewed prominence as a
leader of non-violent resistance to the raj and then of peace-making was
paved by the meshing of his political perceptions and aspirations and the
needs of diverse groups in politics. But the weakness which stemmed from
the very source of his political influence was increasingly manifest as he
tried to maintain and exploit the peace in 1931. The often conflicting needs
of those who had looked to him for leadership restricted his freedom
to manoeuvre, initiate and bargain as he moved into the new environment of the settlement and negotiation with the raj at a second Round
Table Congress session. Changes in the issues at stake, the personalities
and institutions involved, and the viable methods of political action
created a new context in which Gandhi faced formidable dilemmas in
maintaining a continental leadership position, though the months which
ended in his solitary appearance for Congress in London may have
seemed the zenith of his power.

I   THE KARACHI CONGRESSS

The March settlement was on the Congress side predominantly the
Mahatma's handiwork, though he was in consultation with the Working
Committee. The terms therefore hung on his reading of opinion in the
committee and the country. His judgement was swiftly put to the test, first
by the Congress session at Karachi, where the pact was presented for
ratification, then by its enactment throughout the subcontinent.

After the government had published the pact the AICC asked all PCCs
to tell local committees to observe it, and communicated the immediate

essentials – the end of civil disobedience and the limits within which salt manufacture could continue.[1] The general reaction to the news was relief, and most Congressmen appeared willing to observe the terms. There was division of opinion on how much Gandhi had actually gained for Congress; but Muslims and other opponents of civil disobedience showed considerable depression and apprehension at the outcome of the Gandhi–Irwin parleys. More disturbing for Gandhi was the threat to the settlement from groups within or on the periphery of Congress who concluded that he had let them down, particularly by his failure to secure the release of all political prisoners. The governments of Punjab, Delhi, Assam and Bombay all reported signs of hostility to Gandhi among youth organizations; while the small 'workers and peasants' groups with extreme left wing views in Punjab and Bombay swelled the chorus of complaints, accusing the Mahatma of betraying India's workers.[2] The Bengali terrorists under trial in the Chittagong armoury case wrote to belabour him for ignoring those who believed in violence and widespread, indiscriminate murder of Europeans as the most effective political tactic.[3]

Even among Gandhi's closest colleagues there were signs that difficulties would arise in working the settlement, and that the position of Vallabhbhai and Jawaharlal as local leaders in Gujarat and U.P. might hamper Gandhi's stance as all-India guardian of the pact. Speaking in Lucknow and Allahabad within a week of the settlement Jawaharlal made it plain that he disliked its terms and regarded the peace as a truce during which Congress could recoup its strength: moreover he pronounced that if peasants and zamindars could not pay their rents or land revenue because of economic hardship they should not try to pay, even though Congress had suspended the no-tax movement as part of civil disobedience. In a circular he urged PCCs to consolidate the position Congress had gained during 1930 and make particular efforts in rural areas. 'If we now establish firmly definite centres of work and activity in rural areas we shall strengthen our organisation and prepare the people for any contingency that might arise. I need

[1] Syed Mahmud, AICC Gen. Sec., to PCCs, telegram, 5 March 1931, Home Poll., 1931, File No. 5/45. The Assam PCC, however, had not received a full copy of the agreement by June: Assam PCC to AICC, postcard, 19 June 1931, AICC Papers, 1931, File No. G-1.

[2] Provincial FRIs, March 1931, Home Poll., 1931, File No. 18/III; Sir Laurie Hammond, Governor of Assam, to Irwin, 20 March 1931, Mss. EUR.C.152 (26); Sykes to Irwin, 25 March 1931, *ibid.* For Gandhi's parrying of Communist criticisms at a labour meeting in Parel district of Bombay City, 16 March 1931, see *Young India*, 26 March 1931, *CWMG*, XLV, 298–300. At this meeting his main critics were B. T. Ranadive & G. Khandalkar; there were scuffles between Congress volunteers and members of the Young Workers' League who carried red flags and tried to hoist one beside the Congress flag on the platform: Bombay Secret Abstract, 1931, par. 940 (3), *Source Material for a History of the Freedom Movement in India. Mahatma Gandhi Vol. III, Part IV 1931–32* (Bombay, 1973), pp. 15–16 (hereafter *HFM, III, IV*).

[3] 'Brief Note on the Alliance of Congress with Terrorism in Bengal', by S. E. A. Ray, Bengal C.I.D., 25 January 1932, Home Poll., 1932, File No. 4/21.

not tell you that the provisional settlement at Delhi means a truce only and no final peace.'[4]

Meanwhile, in Bombay, Vallabhbhai's pronouncements were Janus-like, depending on where he was speaking. In Bombay City he argued for the settlement and defended Gandhi against labour criticisms that he had abandoned the cause of workers and non-satyagrahi political prisoners. However, when touring Gujarat in mid-March with Gandhi to explain the settlement he assured cultivators that they would not lose the lands which had been forfeited and sold as a result of their civil disobedience, but, as in the aftermath of Bardoli, their land would be returned to them. Although he agreed that those who had money should now pay their land revenue, he proclaimed that those who would have to borrow to pay, need not and would be given time by the government.[5] Gandhi, too, took a tough line, though obviously in deference to the pressures on Vallabhbhai lest he undermine the latter's leadership position in Gujarat. In Borsad he asserted:

> Of course, there is one thing that the Sardar and I would regard as a slap in our faces. The land which belongs to you and which has been given away to someone else is surely something which you cannot afford to lose...Although the Sardar had agreed to have your land restored to you, I had not. But there is no doubt that that land will be restored to you; it cannot be said when and how this will be done, but you will certainly get it back. Just this one thing is sufficient to test the Sardar and me, viz., the land which had been lost must be restored. And until this is done, you must believe that swaraj had not been won, that we are not your true servants. In order to do so, we shall ruin ourselves and not spare you either.[6]

Some contemporaries, anxious that the settlement should hold, were worried that Gandhi would be unable to pilot it through the Karachi session against the pressures of youth groups who regarded it as a betrayal and those established leaders who disliked its constitutional implications and local repercussions. The governor of Punjab feared Gandhi would 'have a tough time at the Congress; and it remains to be seen if he will find himself to be the Kerensky of a movement which really wants something more drastic and dreadful.' Sapru, despite his fears, thought Gandhi would win through at Karachi, as did public opinion in Bombay. Gandhi himself anticipated opposition; but when he saw Emerson on 19 March he appeared confident on the outcome.[7] Although the fate of the pact at Karachi remained in some doubt, he made immediate efforts to secure its

[4] J. Nehru to PCCs, 10 March 1931, Home Poll., 1931, File No. 33/XI; J. Nehru's speeches at Lucknow, 9 March 1931, & Allahabad, 10 March 1931, *The Leader*, 11 & 12 March 1931, *SWJN*, 4, pp. 497–8, 490–2.

[5] Bombay FR1, March 1931, Home Poll., 1931, File No. 18/III.

[6] Speech at Borsad, 12 March 1931, *Navajivan*, 15 March 1931, *CWMG*, XLV, 286.

[7] de Montmorency to Irwin, 26 March 1931, Sapru to Irwin, 17 March 1931, Sykes to Irwin, 25 March 1931, Mss. EUR.C.152 (26); Sapru to Jayakar, 16 & 25 March 1931, Sapru Papers, Series II; note by H. W. Emerson, 19 March 1931, on interview with Gandhi that day, *CWMG*, XLV, 445.

acceptance and implementation by both sides, continuing as intermediary and interpretor between officialdom and the diverse groups within Congress, the role he had made peculiarly his own since February.

On 19 March he saw the Viceroy and Home Secretary to air matters which seemed to threaten the peace. To Irwin he emphasized the House of Commons debate on the settlement with its display of Tory opposition and the Secretary of State's insistence that there could be no diminution of the financial safeguards already proposed. Gandhi also fielded Irwin's criticisms of Congress methods of enforcing *swadeshi* and of Jawaharlal's apparent desire for renewed combat. As he was leaving he raised the case of the Punjabi terrorist, Bhagat Singh, whose execution was scheduled for 24 March, the day the new Congress President reached Karachi. Irwin knew that Gandhi had been sharply criticized for his failure to extract government clemency in such cases, and that the timing of this execution would further embarrass the Mahatma's efforts to carry the pact at Karachi. He argued, however, that it would be improper to postpone it on political grounds and inhuman because it would suggest that he was considering commutation.[8] That evening Gandhi had a three hour interview with Emerson. The Mahatma raised the issues which were causing problems on his side, from specific cases to the range of political prisoners to be released under the agreement. The Home Secretary then produced the matters which were causing difficulty from the government's viewpoint. Among these was the evidence of pressure on millowners and foreign-cloth importers which government regarded as unacceptable, particularly the planned Congress black list of non-*swadeshi* mills and the scheme for the re-export of foreign cloth concocted by representatives of Congress and the Bombay millowners. Emerson also told Gandhi of official disquiet about U.P. because of Jawaharlal's continued belligerence and the danger of serious rural conflict as Congress appeared to be advising people to withhold rents and revenue on economic grounds even though civil disobedience had ended. Vallabhbhai's statements that Gujarati proprietors need not pay their revenue for several years were equally disturbing because 'the inevitable result of unwarranted delay on the part of revenue payers would be the recommencement of coercive processes and the creation of an unfavourable atmosphere'. He stressed that in both areas government would take into consideration genuine economic distress. Gandhi gave Emerson the general impression that he was anxious to implement the settlement, though he expected that Bhagat Singh's execution would complicate matters and that he might not always be able to restrain Jawaharlal from taking his own line.[9]

[8] Note by Irwin, 19 March 1931, on interview with Gandhi that day, *ibid.* pp. 313–16; Coatman, *Years of Destiny*, p. 340. For the Commons debate on 12 March 1931 see *Parliamentary Debates. Fifth Series – Volume 249. Commons, 1930–31, Vol. 249,* cols. 1416–1541.

[9] Note by H. W. Emerson, 19 March 1931, on interview with Gandhi that evening, *CWMG*, XLV, 438–46.

Gandhi, Shankarlal Banker, Vallabhbhai and Jawaharlal had met Bombay mill-

Gandhi followed up the problems Emerson had raised in their discussion; their ensuing correspondence demonstrating the conflicting pressures on him as he continued his mediatory role between government and his 'followers'. On 23 March he agreed to two official replies to be made in the Legislative Assembly about the black list and the scheme for re-exporting foreign cloth to questions arranged by the government in order to publicize the position to which Gandhi had agreed on 19th. Both stressed that there would be no interference with individual liberty, while the boycott list would be replaced by a list of *swadeshi* mills for advertisement only.[10]

The U.P. question proved much less amenable to compromise. By mid-March government was convinced that the local Congress was bent on entrenching itself in rural areas, and that provincial leaders were organizing a movement against full rent payment on economic grounds. Gandhi had appeared surprised and disapproving at the latter action when Emerson had told him of it, and on 21 March Emerson followed up the allegation with precise details. Gandhi immediately consulted Jawaharlal who armed him with a note stating the local Congress position. This was that during the Gandhi–Irwin talks it had been specifically understood that although the political movement would cease, economic distress in U.P. was such that the Congress 'could not...leave the tenantry or the zamindars in the lurch'. Consequently since the settlement the U.P. PCC had stated that provisionally it believed that 50–60% of rent should be remitted and had put this to the local government; but its aim was a peaceful agreement between peasants, zamindars and government, not rural strife. Gandhi sent this to Emerson with the comment that it indicated an irreproachable position on the part of the U.P. Congress, and that the scope of the movement had changed from non-payment of rent to a search for economic relief. Emerson responded that he was in touch with the U.P. government on the question, but asserted that neither he nor Irwin had gathered from their pre-settlement discussions with Gandhi that the Congress organization would continue to involve itself in rent and revenue matters as Jawaharlal's note had stated.[11] Nobody disputed that the continuing slump in prices was

owners on 17 March and formed an agency for the re-export of foreign cloth under the chairmanship of Sir Ness Wadia; Governor of Bombay to Viceroy, telegram, 20 March 1931, Mss. EUR.C.152 (26). The Congress black list of mills to be boycotted would include those which did not make a declaration of sympathy with national aspirations, that their personnel, banking, insurance etc. would be as Indian as possible, and that they would use no foreign yarn and only indispensable foreign articles; press statement by Syed Mahmud, Congress Gen. Sec., reported in *Times of India*, 10 March 1931, Home Poll., 1931, File No. 33/6.

[10] H. W. Emerson to Gandhi, 22 March 1931, enclosing two drafts of Legislative Assembly questions and answers; Gandhi to Emerson, 23 March 1931, *ibid.*

[11] Emerson to Gandhi, 21 March 1931, Gandhi to Emerson, enclosing undated note by J. Nehru, 23 March 1931, Emerson to Gandhi, 31 March 1931, Home Poll., 1931, File No. 33/XI.

An example of local reports of Congress leaders advising tenants not to pay their rents in full is Collector of Allahabad to Commissioner, Allahabad, 17 March 1931, *ibid.*

squeezing those who had to pay rent or revenue in cash. However the economic situation and local Congressmen's need to maintain their political credibility with the tenantry were already threatening to inhibit Gandhi's ability to help different groups to relate to each other in the new political context of the settlement and so retain an accepted continental leadership position. Sapru described the U.P. situation as 'really very bad so far as the peasantry is concerned. The economic distress in grain is immense and they have been thoroughly infected with the "no rent" doctrines'[12] – not a situation easily amenable to a Gandhian compromise from which peasantry, zamindars, Congress leaders and officials felt they could benefit.

Similarly in Bhagat Singh's case, Gandhi was unable to produce results for the different interest groups who looked to him for leadership. He had not influenced Irwin on 19 March towards clemency as many of his younger critics wished. Government also hoped to use him, as Emerson indicated in a letter requesting his cooperation over a meeting Subhas Bose was to address in Delhi on 20 March.

> I fully realise your difficulties in the matter and I think that you realise the difficulties of Government and also their desire at the present time to avoid, if possible, preventive action, which may, however, be unavoidable if excitement grows. If a meeting is held tonight, it is almost certain to increase feeling, especially if speeches of an inflammatory character are made. Government will much appreciate any assistance you feel able to give to prevent this.

Gandhi replied that he had 'already taken every precaution possible' and suggested that there should be no display of police force or interference with the meeting. He was caught between incompatible demands. He indicated this is an eleventh-hour appeal to Irwin to commute the sentence. 'Since you seem to value my influence such as it is in favour of peace, do not please unnecessarily make my position, difficult as it is, almost too difficult for future work.' His predicament was even clearer in his statement after the execution, in which he paid tribute to the memory of the terrorists yet urged the country's youth not to follow them; and criticized the government for dealing a blow at the settlement while arguing that it had not actually breached the settlement.[13]

Despite these difficulties, Gandhi attended an informal meeting on 21 March at the Viceroy's house where a number of Princes and Round Table Conference delegates discussed future procedure for the conference. Although Gandhi's participation on this occasion was a good omen for his presence at the conference table, he warned that if the communal question was not settled in advance Congress representatives might not go to

[12] Sapru to Jayakar, 25 March 1931, Sapru Papers, Series II.
[13] Emerson to Gandhi & Gandhi's reply, 20 March 1931. AICC Papers, 1931, File No. Misc. 2 (Kw) (i); Gandhi to Irwin, 23 March 1931, *CWMG*, XLV, 333–4; statement on 23 March 1931, *Gujarati*, 29 March 1931, *ibid.* pp. 335–6.

London.[14] Since his release Gandhi had reiterated his commitment to Hindu–Muslim unity. At a Muslim League Council meeting in February he proclaimed his wish to speak for all Indians, and referred to Hindu–Muslim unity as his life's mission: spectacularly on 7 March at a public meeting in Delhi, he advised Hindus to concede whatever Muslims wanted. This provoked immediate hostility from many Hindus, particularly in areas where they were a minority. The Sind Hindu Sabha, for example, convened an emergency meeting to discuss the threat Gandhi's speech appeared to contain for them. They feared he might prevail on Congress to concede the Muslim demand that Sind should be separated from Bombay to become a Muslim majority province, and the president asked M. R. Jayakar to put their position to the Mahatma and implore him not to sacrifice them, 'for though whatever he does is law to the whole world, the Hindus of Sind will be sheep in the mouth of wolves, if he so ordains'. Gandhi was left in no doubt of the communalist Hindu position when Mahasabha leaders conferred with him in Delhi in mid-March: a statement by the Mahasabha Working Committee on 23 March, insisting that there should be no communal electorates or reservation of seats for religious communities, indicated that it at least had no intention of following Gandhi's suggestion of a unilateral gesture of generosity.[15]

Gandhi had maintained since November 1929 that communal agreement was a precondition of Congress participation in a constitutional conference. There were sound tactical reasons for this, apart from the Mahatma's long-held commitment to communal unity as an essential element of true swaraj. Failure to present an agreed demand would play into the hands of those Princely and British politicians who wished to prevent responsible government in a Federation, while Congress's claim to command attention as the spokesman of the Indian nation would be proved a nonsense. Communal agreement was therefore fundamental to a strong Congress negotiating position. Hindu reaction to Gandhi's proposed unilateral generosity indicated that civil disobedience had not generated communal harmony as Gandhi had hoped. This fact was confirmed by bloody communal rioting in Cawnpore which erupted on the eve of the Karachi Congress, when Congressmen tried to induce Muslims to close their shops in memory

[14] Excerpts of report of 21 March meeting, *ibid.* pp. 320–6; Sapru to Jayakar, 25 March 1931, Sapru Papers, Series II.

[15] Gandhi's speech at Muslim League Council, 22 February 1931, *CWMG*, XLV, 216–17; Gandhi's speech at Delhi public meeting, 7 March 1931, *ibid.* pp. 269–74; President of Sind Provincial Hindu Sabha to M. R. Jayakar, 14 March 1931, Jayakar Papers, Correspondence File No. 354; Mahasabha Working Committee statement, 23 March 1931, AICC Papers, 1931, File No. G-85.

Dr R. Mookerji, who had been one of the Mahasabha's representatives in consultation with Gandhi, reported to Jayakar on 26 March that Gandhi had agreed to a governmental settlement if the communities could not settle their claims among themselves; Jayakar Papers, Correspondence File No. 354. Gandhi had avoided making a direct answer to the question of a governmental settlement at the 21 March informal meeting; *CWMG*, XLV, 322.

of Bhagat Singh. For several days the city was out of control. Loss of life, injury and destruction of property reached appalling dimensions, and thousands fled to the countryside to escape the carnage, carrying the communal bitterness with them. Gandhi condemned the strife immediately, saying that it was India's shame and a barrier to the nation's freedom.[16] It was, as he saw, devastating proof of a force which threatened his own political aspirations and position and weakened any Congress negotiator who went to London.

The last week in March was the time set for the Congress session which was to ratify or reject the settlement endorsed provisionally by the Working Committee. The committee's members immediately went into action to secure a gathering which would support them; and, having suspended the normal, lengthy election procedure for a President, chose Vallabhbhai Patel, one of Gandhi's staunchest supporters. Funds were evidently forthcoming from business sources anxious to secure a permanent peace to finance delegates who would support the settlement, and in Bombay there were allegations that Gandhi had done his best to pack the session. The Karachi venue clearly helped Gandhi since his most dependable followers were in the Bombay Presidency; while the continued imprisonment of political offenders accused of incitement to or actual violence kept some of the settlement's potential oponents away from Karachi.[17]

Nevertheless hostility to Gandhi and the settlement were apparent the very day he arrived in Karachi. At the station a band of Nau Jawan Bharat Sabha members paraded with black flags and truncheons after displacing the official Congress welcome party on the platform. They shouted 'Down! Down! Gandhi–Patel', 'Up! Up! Lenin!' and 'Who got Bhagat Singh hanged? Gandhi'; and they greeted the Mahatma with cries of 'Gandhi go back'. The next day, seven of them, all but one Punjabis, forced their way into the Congress camp and to Gandhi's quarters, calling 'Where is bloody Gandhi[?]' Jawaharlal had to intervene to save Gandhi from physical attack, persuading them to leave with the promise that they could later have an interview with the Mahatma. When they did have their private interview they asserted that the settlement could never pave the path to a workers' and peasants' republic. Gandhi countered their criticisms with the ambiguous assertion that he was a founder member of such a republic, working for sufficiency for every worker and the trusteeship of their riches by the wealthy for the benefit of the poor.[18]

However, Gandhi and the settlement were insulated from the brunt of such opposition in the Congress session itself by the fact that only delegates

[16] Statements by Gandhi on Cawnpore riots, 26 & 27 March 1931, *ibid.* pp. 345, 353–4.

[17] Sykes to Irwin, 25 March 1931, Mss. EUR.C.152 (26); Bose, *The Indian Struggle 1920–1942*, p. 202.

[18] Bombay Secret Abstract, 1931, par. 940 (6), *HFM, III, IV*, p. 18; Gandhi's discussion with Nau Jawan Bharat Sabha members, 27 March 1931, *CWMG*, XLV, 354–5.

could vote, while the recognized leaders who might have channelled and exploited this hostility muted their opposition. Subhas Bose, for example, judged that opponents of the pact were unlikely to achieve better results than Gandhi had done, despite his trenchant criticisms of Gandhi's tactics and concessions at Delhi; and he saw that to split the Congress would only strengthen officialdom still further. He therefore stated in the Subjects Committee that he would not attempt to divide the Congress on the issue; and, presiding over a simultaneous meeting of the All-India Nau Jawan Bharat Sabha, he urged its members to try to capture the Congress machinery rather than boycott it. His reluctance to oppose the Mahatma outright probably also stemmed from his recognition of Gandhi's considerable popularity at that juncture, despite the hostility of distinct groups, and the calculation that opposition would jeopardize his own political standing. Jawaharlal, too, refused to lead an anti-Gandhi bloc in Congress.[19] Gandhi made a concession to his younger critics, however, in drafting a resolution which condemned Bhagat Singh's execution as 'an act of wanton vengeance' and extolled his bravery, though it maintained Congress's disapproval of political violence. This was moved by Jawaharlal and passed by Congress on 29 March, though Gandhi later bitterly regretted his part in a tactic designed to have a restraining effect which was in subsequent months distorted and used as a passport for extolling violence.[20]

On the essential question of the settlement, however, Gandhi had his way. In the Subjects Committee on 28 March, he supported a resolution which both endorsed his pact with Irwin and declared that Congress's goal remained *purna swaraj*. It agreed that Congress respresentatives, of whom one should be Gandhi, should go to the conference table 'the way being otherwise open' to work for this goal,

> ...in particular, so as to give the nation control over the army, external affairs, finance and fiscal and economic policy, and to have a scrutiny, by an impartial tribunal, of the financial transactions of the British Government in India and to examine and assess the obligations to be undertaken by India or England, and the right to either party to end the partnership at will; provided, however, that the Congress delegation will be free to accept such adjustments as may be demonstrably necessary in the interest of India.

[19] Bose, *op. cit.* pp. 205–8.

In 1933 a critic lambasted Jawaharlal for his failure to lead 'the radical element' at Karachi against 'the compromising, opportunist leadership'. He maintained that this, combined with the control of the Congress machinery by the Working Committee, accounted for the failure to repudiate the established leadership. Dr Mahmud to J. Nehru, 15 October 1933, J. Nehru Papers, part I, vol. xxxxiv.

[20] Resolution on Bhagat Singh and his associates, moved by J. Nehru, 29 March 1931, *Report of the 45th Annual Session*, IOL, Microfilm Pos. 2274; note by H. W. Emerson, 26 October 1933, on interview with C. F. Andrews that day, Home Poll., 1933, File No. 169. For Gandhi's regret at the use to which the resolution was put see *Young India*, 16 April & 11 June 1931, *CWMG*, xlvi, 1–3, 357–9; speech at AICC, 6 August 1931, *CWMG*, xlvii, 262.

It was an ingenious formula, sticking to the goal stated at Lahore yet endorsing the settlement; opening the door to conference discussions, yet providing Congress representatives with such a brief that they could play the outcome either way, agreeing to 'demonstrably necessary' adjustments or standing by the demand for control over defence and finance and an impartial tribunal on the obligations of both countries. Moreover, in his speech Gandhi insisted that he and whoever accompanied him should have full authority to bind Congress provided they adhered to the terms of the resolution, and that their decisions should not be subjected to Congress ratification thereafter. He was manoeuvring for a flexible hand yet freedom from having to answer for his decisions on his return. Jayakar commented the next day on the Mahatma's political skill.

> I feel that Gandhi will succeed in taking matters through without much difficulty and will end by obtaining practically complete freedom to make adjustments detracting from Purna Swaraj, provided he thinks that such adjustments are in the interests of India. His formula, as embodied in the resolution adopted by the Working Committee, is very clever, and I believe the Congress will swallow it.[21]

The resolution came up for decision in open Congress on 30 March. In an astute tactical manoeuvre Gandhi asked Jawaharlal to move it. At first he refused, but at the last moment agreed rather than leave his attitude to Gandhi's position publicly in doubt. He was supported by Sen Gupta from Bengal, Satyamurti from Madras, and Abdul Ghaffar Khan who had come down from the Fontier with an impressive band of Red Shirts to back the Mahatma. Jamnadas Mehta opposed the resolution as a dilution of the Lahore resolution; and the Sindhi, Swami Govindanand, denounced the truce as unacceptable, arguing that they could have carried on the struggle and that a conference would never bring them independence. Like Bose in the Subjects Committee, however, he declared that those he called the 'Forward Party' would not divide Congress or oppose Gandhi's wish to attend the conference. He argued that if the conference proved fruitless the Working Committee should be as generous to them and allow them to control the Congress organization and attempt to win freedom in their way. The outcome of the debate was thus virtually assured; and Meharally's fiery diatribe as a spokesman for the younger men against compromise with imperialism and the exploitation of the people's sacrifices by such men as Birla and Thakurdas was not a real threat to the settlement. Gandhi concluded the debate with an assertion that at satyagrahis it had been their duty to agree to talk. However, he neatly secured himself a flexible position by insisting that it was not certain whether he would attend the conference, particularly in the light of the communal deadlock, and by warning that

---

[21] Jayakar to Sapru, 29 March 1931, Sapru Papers, Series II; text of resolution on settlement, enclosed in V to S of S, telegram, 5 April 1931, Mss. EUR.C.152 (11); Gandhi's speech in subjects committee on settlement, 28 March 1931, *CWMG*, XLV, 355–9.

he might well return from London empty-handed, in which case they would resume the fight. The resolution was then put to the vote and carried by a large majority.[22] Sethna commented that although the outcome was from a Liberal's point of view 'not all that we could desire yet I have no doubt that when Gandhi and his colleagues go over to England for the Conference, the atmosphere there will convert them to our way of thinking'.[23]

Sapru also admired Gandhi's political expertise in preserving his leadership position in Congress; but he feared he had 'paid a very heavy price for the allegiance of Jawahar Lal'. He was referring to the resolution on fundamental rights drafted by Jawaharlal with modifications by Gandhi which the latter moved successfully in open Congress on 31 March. This declared the rights of association, speech, conscience and so forth which all would enjoy under a swaraj government and listed the economic and social provisions such a government would make to ensure an egalitarian society. The latter included a substantial reduction of land revenue and rent, the right to form labour unions, an inheritance tax, the slashing of military and civil expenditure, total prohibition, exclusion of foreign cloth and yarn, abolition of salt duty, control of usury, and state regulation of the exchange ratio and control of key industries and mineral resources. It would do injustice to the subtle relationship of affection and mutual need between Gandhi and Jawaharlal to suggest that this was a blunt *quid pro quo* for Jawaharlal's public support of the settlement. Many of its suggestions Gandhi had preached for years and included in his 'eleven points' a year earlier, as he hastened to point out in his speech on the resolution. However, he had encouraged Nehru to bring the matter up during their long morning walks together in Delhi while the pact was being hammered out. The timing indicates that he must have hoped both that this would convince the younger man that their goal was the same though their paths to it appeared to diverge at times, and that Nehru's consequent adherence to him combined with the socialist aspects of the resolution would have some effect on those who condemned the Congress leadership as bourgeois betrayers of the workers and peasants. The youthful fringe responsible for what Sapru called 'a good deal of blowing of hot air at Karachi' might not be significant in terms of votes, but their breakaway from Congress would imperil the settlement in operation and would, like communal antagonism, undermine Congress's claim to speak for all Indians and thus weaken the position of the Congress representatives at the conference.[24]

---

[22] *Report of 45th I.N.C.*; J. Nehru, *An Autobiography*, pp. 265–6.
[23] Sethna to McBain, 31 March 1931, Sethna Papers.
[24] Sapru to Jayakar, 3 April 1931, Sapru Papers, Series II; Sapru to Sastri, 3 April 1931, NMML, V.S.S. Sastri Papers (2nd instalment); *Report of 45th I.N.C.*; Gandhi's speech on fundamental rights resolution, 31 March 1931, *CWMG*, XLV, 372–4; J. Nehru, *An Autobiography*, pp. 266–8.
Vallabhbhai also used Jawaharlal's acceptance of the settlement as a technique for ensuring younger men's support for it, arguing in his closing speech that they should have no misgivings about it if Jawaharlal approved of it; *Report of 45th I.N.C.*

The resolution demonstrated the constraints within which Gandhi was operating. Its very provisions, however, decreased his capacity to conciliate and arrange compromises between diverse Indian interests – a function which was an important basis of his leadership position and an essential precondition of a strong negotiating hand in London. As Sapru noted, prosperous agriculturalists and landlords were worried at the suggestion contained in it of a progressive tax on higher agricultural incomes, inheritance taxation threatened Muslims who did not have the loophole of the Hindu joint family, while talk of a Rs. 500 maximum salary for civil servants would frighten Indian and British officials and place a powerful weapon in Tory hands. If such groups refused from fear to deal with Gandhi as a leader and Congress spokesman, he would cease to perform a valuable function for his adherents within Congress.[25]

Nonetheless the Congress session was a signal triumph for him, as many of his political opponents admitted. Bose travelled with him for some days at this time observing the unprecedented crowds which gathered everywhere to welcome him both as a Mahatma and a hero of a political struggle. To Bose Karachi was 'undoubtedly...the pinnacle of the Mahatma's popularity and prestige'. The Bombay government reported Gandhi's 'increasing ascendancy on each subsequent day' at Karachi, culminating in 'his final triumph' when the settlement was endorsed. It was, however, an immense strain for him, and throughout April he had to sleep for two or three hours each day to recover from the exhaustion.[26] His success in Congress lay partly in the numbers of his supporters who came to Karachi and partly in the dynamics of decision making. As in 1920 potential opposition leaders decided that an overt challenge to the Mahatma would be politically unproductive in national and personal terms and perferred to give him time to prove or disprove his value as a leader. However, Gandhi's influence in Congress also had institutional foundations which were particularly significant between open sessions: and these were strengthened at Karachi. Although Gandhi still held no office in Congress, his closest supporters occupied key positions in the Congress machine. Immediately after the Karachi session, the AICC elected the Working Committee for the coming year, the list of names being drawn up by Gandhi in consultation with Vallabhbhai and Jawaharlal.[27]

One of the new committee's first acts was to resolve that Gandhi alone

[25] Sapru to Jayakar, 3 April 1931, Sapru Papers, Series II. Before Karachi Bihari landlords had feared that Gandhi would dominate the Round Table Conference and wondered 'whether it would be sound to enter into agreements with Gandhi at once to save what they can'. Sir Hugh Stephenson to Irwin, 16 March 1931, Mss. EUR.C.152 (26). The Karachi resolution clearly constrained Gandhi's freedom to effect compromises in this situation and so potentially weakened his position.

[26] Bose, *The Indian Struggle 1920–1942*, p. 213; Bombay FR2, March 1931, Home Poll., 1931, File No. 18/III; Gandhi to C. F. Andrews, 29 April 1931, *CWMG*, XLVI, 50.

[27] Bombay Secret Abstract, 1931, par. 1104, *HFM, III, IV*, p. 28; speech proposing Working Committee members at AICC meeting, 1 April 1931, *CWMG*, XLV, 378–80.

should speak for Congress in London, thus rejecting the opportunity to add further names to the list offered by the Congress resolution on the settlement. Why this course was adopted was a matter of contemporary speculation. Irwin did not understand the reasoning behind it; while the local police believed it was Gandhi's personal decision and caused great consternation in the committee. Jayakar later asserted that the decision sprang from Congressmen's distrust of each other when it came to constitutional construction and their reliance on men like himself, Sapru and Sir Chimanlal Setalvad. Gandhi stated that it was a measure to save money, to retain important leaders in India were real swaraj work was to be done, and to ensure that Congress spoke with one voice at the conference.[28] Judging by his previous political experience and predilection for personal appeal and encounter, it was probably his own wish. He almost certainly calculated that his austere figure would have a greater impact in Britain than a group of Congressmen who might disagree among themselves and whose social habits might well give the lie to Congress's claim to speak for India's poor.

Gandhi was able to secure for himself a unique role at the Round Table Conference as Congress spokesman because the decision rested with a small body over which he had peculiar influence. However, the position he acquired as a result of the Working Committee decision held for him potential for increased prestige or recrimination and declining authority, depending on the outcome of the conference. It exposed him, too, to the very strong political pressures which conference procedures were bound to generate, since he would not only be bound by the Congress mandate enshrined in the Karachi resolution on the settlement and whatever instructions the Working Committee sent thereafter, but would have to cope alone with the demands of the other Indian and British delegates, and single-handed parry the tactics of those who sought to exploit him.[29] Consequently he tried in the intervening months to secure for himself an impregnable negotiating base, founded on prior Indian and British acceptance of the Congress claim to represent all Indians.

[28] V to S of S, telegram, 4 April 1931, enclosing wire from Gandhi to P.S.V., announcing that the Working Committee had appointed him sole delegate to the Round Table Conference, Mss. EUR.C.152 (11); text of Working Committee resolution, *Young India*, 9 April 1931; Bombay Secret Abstract, 1931, par. 1104, *HFM, III, IV*, p. 28; Jayakar to P. R. Lele, 25 April 1932, Jayakar Papers, Correspondence File No. 407, part II; Gandhi's article, 'Sole Delegate', *Young India*, 9 April 1931, *CWMG*, XLV, 403–4.

[29] B. S. Moonje thought Gandhi would be at sea in London and commented, 'However if he will allow himself to be exploited by us, we can still retrieve a great deal of the position lost. There is nobody in the R.T. Conference who has the skill and strength to exploit Mahatmaji to the full except Jayakar and myself. If he will allow us, we shall use him as a chess player uses the King.' Moonje referred here to his calculation that Gandhi had thrown away a unique bargaining position in his settlement with Irwin. Like Bose and Nehru he criticized the pact as dealing with side issues and ignoring the major constitutional questions which should have been made the stake in Gandhi's negotiations with Irwin. 7 April 1931, Diary of B. S. Moonje.

BGC

II THE POLITICS OF PEACE

Gandhi's need of a strong base from which to attend the conference accounted for the loophole left in the Karachi resolution permitting him to back out of the conference if events made it seem unprofitable to attend. He was determined not to go to London merely as one of a number of bargainers; and having secured at Karachi the position of sole Congress delegate he manoeuvred during mid-1931 for Indian and British acceptance of Congress as a nationally representative body. His main problems in securing such recognition for Congress were the attitude of many Muslim political spokesmen, and the implementation of the settlement so as to demonstrate Congress authority and unity and wrest from government acceptance of Congress as intermediary between the raj and its subjects. The search for a solution to these problems generated Gandhi's intricate manoeuvres and apparent vacillation in mid-1931.

Gandhi's role was unique: he saw himself as 'directly responsible' for the delicate structure of peace.[30] He coordinated complaints from Congressmen in the localities about official behaviour and presented them to the Government of India; meanwhile he fielded government complaints about Congress observance of the settlement, and endeavoured to achieve a continental uniformity of observance by local activists in order to secure his own credibility with government as guarantor of the settlement and that of Congress as a uniquely representative body. He willingly functioned as a central point of contact and channel of communication, but this role was viable because officials and Congressmen were willing to use him for their own ends. The government exploited Gandhi's central position in the hope of securing the settlement as officials interpreted its terms; while local Congress groups similarly used Gandhi to press for its implementation as it suited them, trading on his prestige and leverage with the government. This role as lynchpin of the settlement, as lubricant between its parts which worked so uneasily together, gave Gandhi significant personal influence. It also exposed him to conflicting demands which he could not always satisfy, and to criticism from all those interested in the pact whom he failed to please.

One method by which Gandhi performed this lubricant function was correspondence with Government of India Officials. The Home Department collected files of Gandhi's complaints about alleged official breaches of the settlement made to him by local Congress leaders. Each one was meticulously examined in consultation with the local administration implicated, indicating the value the government placed on securing Gandhi's cooperation in maintaining the peace. The interchanges also showed how difficult it was both for Gandhi and for his all-India official counterparts, and even for provincial governments, to know precisely what was going on

[30] Gandhi to Willingdon, telegram, *c.* 21 May 1931, *CWMG*, XLVI, 197.

in the localities, let alone control the actions of their colleagues and subordinates.[31]

Gandhi also corresponded directly with local governments. These exchanges, too, underlined official eagerness to exploit Gandhi's peculiar leverage over his compatriots. The Governor of Bombay through his secretary asked Gandhi to use his influence over picketers of liquor shops so that their activities conformed to the settlement terms, over various Hindustani Seva Dal camps in the presidency where weapon training flouted the spirit of the settlement, and over those who still engaged in the daily *prabhat feris* (dawn song processions) in Bombay City and its suburbs, creating public disturbances in the early hours when they began at 5.30 a.m., and singing objectionable political songs. In such cases he hoped Gandhi's personal intervention would prevent official resort to legal proceedings which would generate bitterness. On the question of *prabhat feris* Gandhi queried what objection there could be to 'this innocent and beautiful institution which reminds citizens of their duty towards their Creator in the early morn'. Nevertheless through *Young India* he urged that the singers should perform in tune and choose only songs 'of worship and those dealing purely with constructive activities such as khadi, liquor prohibition, communal unity, untouchability and other social reform'; he reiterated this advice in Bombay to a group who came to sing beneath his window. For this he received official thanks.[32] In other cases Gandhi made the initial complaint, acting for local leaders who wished to bring their particular grievances to the notice of officials with the added weight of Gandhi's support.

Gandhi's primary concern in performing the function demanded of him by both sides in the uneasy peace was to secure recognition of Congress as the people's representative. This was particularly clear in his correspondence with J. H. Garrett, Commissioner of Bombay's Northern Division, which he then forwarded to the Bombay government. Ultimately it reached the Viceroy from Gandhi and the local government. The exchange began on 20 April with Gandhi's complaint to Garrett about a notice issued by a minor revenue official in Borsad: the following day in a further letter Gandhi made his real interest clear.

> The chief point fo[r] the moment is with reference to the status of the Congress in the settlement. If you agree that the settlement is between the Congress and the Government, and if it is the Congress that has to

[31] See, for example, Home Poll., 1931, File Nos. 33/12/I & II, 33/V (*re* alleged breaches of settlement in Bihar & Orissa), 33/30 (*re* picketing and boycott in Madras). For Gandhi's correspondence in March & June 1931 with H. W. Emerson on the implementation of the concessions on local salt manufacture see AICC Papers, 1931, File No. Misc. 2 (Kw) (i).

[32] R. M. Maxwell to Gandhi, 19 & 25 May, 18 July 1931, Gandhi to Maxwell, 29 May 1931, AICC Papers, 1931, File No. Misc. 4, part II; *Young India*, 4 June 1931; report of Gandhi's speech on 10 June 1931, *The Hindu*, 10 June 1931, *CWMG*, XLVI, 356.

implement its terms so far as they are applicable to the people, it follows that the Congress must be recognised as the intermediary between the Government and the people whom the Congress represents. If such was not the case, I suppose that I should have no right to see you or to correspond with you or to receive your replies in the several matters arising out of the settlement.

To the Governor's secretary he complained that if Sykes took the same attitude as the Commissioner 'it nullifies the whole settlement... To repudiate the Congress as the intermediary between the people and the Government means repudiation of the settlement.' He was soothed with a tactful reply which stressed the value Sykes put on Gandhi's personal influence in maintaining the settlement while noting that he did not imagine Gandhi had ever claimed that Congress was the only channel of communication between government and people.[33]

Although Gandhi agreed that he had never made this claim his desire to establish Congress's intermediary position, combined with his political style of personal encounter and persuasion, led him to interviews with officials as another means of propping up the pact. In this way he could enact the Congress's representative claim. The government, though repudiating his contention in words, confirmed his personal mediatory role in practice by allowing him such interviews in the hope of exploiting his influence for its own ends.

On 6 April, for example, Gandhi had a five hour session with Emerson. Before the meeting the Viceroy's Council issued two orders indicating precisely what the Home Secretary was to get across to the Mahatma. The burden of the message was that if the settlement was to continue in operation Gandhi and Congress must exert a restraining hand. The *swadeshi* movement must be kept strictly within the limits agreed by Irwin and Gandhi and later by Gandhi and Emerson; and unless the all-India 'leaders' controlled local activists in Gujarat and U.P., government would resort to the ordinary law or to extra powers. Emerson put these points strongly to Gandhi, who in his turn had brought to the meeting various specific complaints such as the cases of civil disobedience prisoners still in jail. Gandhi's attitude, according to Emerson, was 'very friendly and reasonable', but as the Home Secretary gathered from their prolonged discussion on U.P. and Gujarat, his role as mediator between Congressmen and officialdom and guardian of the settlement was an unenviable one. Often

---

[33] Gandhi to J. H. Garrett, 20 April 1931, Garrett to Gandhi, 21 April 1931, Gandhi to Garrett, 21 April 1931, AICC Papers, 1931, File No. Misc. 3; Garrett to Gandhi, 24 April 1931, AICC Papers, 1931, File No. Misc. 4, part I; Gandhi to Garrett, 26 April 1931, *CWMG*, XLVI, 42.

Gandhi to R. M. Maxwell, Sykes' secretary, 22 & 26 April 1931, Maxwell to Gandhi, 24 April 1931, AICC Papers, 1931, File No. Misc. 4, part I.

Sykes to Willingdon, 24 April 1931, enclosing some of the above correspondence, Mss. EUR.F.150 (3).

he was ignorant of the activities of his 'followers' and allies and had no dictatorial control over them.[34]

In Gujarat the problem as the government saw it was the virtual cessation of revenue payment since the settlement in particular *talukas*, the worst being Bardoli, Borsad and Kapadvanj. This was accompanied by social harassment of loyal government servants and people who had bought up land forfeited as a result of civil disobedience. For his part Gandhi argued that some of the patels who had replaced those who had participated in satyagraha were men of bad character and were persecuting the villagers, and that the government was not remaining neutral on the recovery of lands forfeited to third parties. The root of the problem was that in agreeing to a continental settlement with Irwin, Gandhi had sacrificed some local interests in Gujarat, in particular the lands and posts lost by those who had joined in civil disobedience. Now both his erstwhile followers in Gujarat and his closest colleague, Vallabhbhai, whose local repute depended on his defence of local interests, fought against the local implications of the pact – a situation Gandhi had feared in the final negotiations with Irwin. There was considerable truth in Emerson's concluding impression that 'Patel and his friends are making it as difficult as possible for Gandhi to honour the settlement; that they are holding up the payment of land revenue on one pretext or another in the hope that all Patels will be reinstated and all lands restored; that they are communicating to Gandhi all sorts of complaints, few of which have any foundation, and that Gandhi himself would like to find a way out, but cannot.' He believed that Gandhi would do his best, despite local opposition, to secure revenue payments and so prevent official resort to coercive processes.[35]

Gandhi's relationship to Congress leaders in U.P. and the local rank and file was similar, though in that province he had less personal influence in the villages than in Gujarat. Continuing economic distress and the realization of men like Jawaharlal that they must use this to attract wide rural support despite the terms of the all-India peace had caused problems for Gandhi even before Karachi. In early April these local pressures intensified. Peasants were turning to Congressmen who camped in the villages, petitioning for redress of grievances as if they were pleading before regular courts: they were told to pay what rents they could and to ask the government for remissions. By the beginning of April about 60% of the *kharif* instalment of revenue was in and landlords had probably collected about 75% of their rents. However firmly Gandhi, briefed by Jawaharlal, asserted that the U.P. Congress was merely standing by the whole rural community

[34] Orders in Council relating to meeting of 6 April 1931, Home Poll., 1931, File No. 33/XI; V to S of S, telegram, 8 April 1931, Mss. EUR.C.152 (11); note by H. W. Emerson on interview with Gandhi the previous evening, 7 April 1931, Home Poll., 1931, File No. 33/XI.
[35] *idem.*; Bombay FR2, March 1931, Home Poll., 1931, File No. 18/III; Bombay FR1, April 1931, Home Poll., 1931, File No. 18/IV.

in an economic crisis, the local government insisted that the campaign against full payment of rent and revenue was a political movement under an economic guise, organized by the PCC to consolidate the Congress position and cause strife between landlords and tenants. Officials noted the position as dangerous in Allahabad and disquieting in Partabgarh, Rae Bareli, Muttra, Farrukhabad, Etawah and Mainpuri. Nevertheless the U.P. government realized that presistent low prices, for wheat in particular, would make it impossible for tenants to pay full rents at the *rabi* harvest and therefore for landlords to pay revenue in full; and at the end of March the Governor announced a scheme for readjusted demands. When Emerson confronted Gandhi with this information from U.P. the Mahatma agreed that Congressmen should neither advise withholding rent or revenue nor stir up tenants against landlords. He was particularly anxious lest such strife should precipitate communal outbreaks in a province which had just witnessed the Cawnpore riots and where many of the large landlords were Muslims. Gandhi still clung to his assertion that Congress must support and speak for tenants, but he agreed to do what he could to control the anti-rent and revenue movement. Again Emerson concluded that Gandhi was ignorant of much that was happening in U.P., and that he would probably have difficulty in dealing with Jawaharlal and other local leaders, though as in the case of Gujarat he was likely to try rather than risk the total settlement, should local Congressmen's actions provoke the renewal of Ordinance powers which government threatened.[36]

Despite the problems inherent in relying on Gandhi as mediator and restraining hand, the Government of India acted on the list of allegations he had presented to Emerson on 6 April, sending them to local governments for investigation.[37] Gandhi turned his attention to the problems Emerson had raised, particularly to Gujarat, where he arrived on 10 April. One of his techniques was again to seek personal interviews with officials. He not only met Garrett as Commissioner of the division which covered Gujarat, but offered to see the Governor of Bombay if Sykes thought that personal contact was the best way of clearing up the points of conflict which had come to light in his talk with Emerson. He saw Sykes in Bombay on 17 April, the Governor having agreed to the interview because Irwin wished it. But their three hour encounter produced little but occasion for Gandhi to assert that his pact with Irwin gave Congress the status of intermediary between government and people in such matters as police behaviour, restoration of forfeited lands and reinstatement of village officials. Sykes denied this, pointing out 'that the principle at stake was the question of sovereignty,

[36] Note by H. W. Emerson on interview with Gandhi the previous evening, 7 April 1931, Home Poll., 1931, File No. 33/XI; note by Emerson, 3 April 1931, on interview that day with Sir Frank Noyce & the Governor of U.P., *ibid.*; U.P. FRi, April 1931, Home Poll., 1931, File No. 18/IV.
[37] Emerson to Chief Secs. of Madras, Bombay, Bengal, U.P., Punjab, C.P., and Bihar & Orissa, 14 April 1931, and local replies; Home Poll., 1931, File No. 33/12/1.

and that to concede these points would be a virtual acknowledgement that Congress and not the Government really ruled the country'.[38]

Thereafter Gandhi returned to Gujarat, spending the next three weeks in Bardoli and Borsad. By word of mouth and through the press he tried to exert a restraining influence as Emerson had requested. He argued against harassment of those who had bought forfeited lands and urged cultivators to be patient about getting their lands back: after all they had entered the conflict prepared for loss, and the settlement was not designed to make good those losses but to be a step towards swaraj, when certainly injustices would be righted and lands restored. On payment of land revenues he was firm. Cultivators who had not participated in or suffered substantially as a result of civil disobedience were to pay up, even if they had to borrow to do so: only those who had suffered substantially could withhold payment if payment would bring them into debt, but even they should remember that Gandhi believed it was in their interest to keep the settlement. The government considered that Gandhi's presence had a calming effect, but his intentions were often thwarted by Vallabhbhai's more bellicose speeches and open assertion that he did not share Gandhi's views on land revenue payment though he advised people to follow the Mahatma's advice. Moreover as Gandhi travelled through the villages he found it extremely hard to gauge the extent of 'suffering' as a result of civil disobedience and therefore the extent to which withholding revenue was permissible according to his rules of guidance. People were naturally inclined to paint as black a picture for him as possible, and the police were convinced that local leaders such as M. K. Pandya and Vallabhbhai himself 'coached' village spokesmen in this vein before Gandhi's arrival.[39]

Preoccupied with Gujarat, Gandhi did little at this juncture about the situation in U.P. He did however revert by letter to the question at issue between him and Emerson in their earlier correspondence and their April meeting – whether Congress had the right to interest itself in rent and revenue matters. He asserted that Congress was a peasants' and workers' organization – a pleasant irony in view of the charges of his radical critics after the March pact. It could not implement the settlement, he argued, if the local authorities refused to work with it when it spoke for the peasantry; and he suggested that U.P.'s difficulties could have been solved if officials had cooperated with Congressmen at district level.[40] Here, too, he was pressing for official acknowledgement that Congress occupied a unique position in Indian public life, an acknowledgement which might

[38] Gandhi to R. M. Maxwell, 11 April 1931, requesting interview with Sykes, AICC Papers, 1931, File No. Misc. 4, part 1. Sykes's account of his interview with Gandhi is in Sykes, *From Many Angles*, pp. 412–13.

[39] Bombay FR2, April 1931, Home Poll., 1931, File No. 18/IV; Bombay Secret Abstract, 1931, par. 1324 (2), HFM, III, IV, pp. 33–5. Gandhi's advice to Gujarat farmers, *Navajivan*, 19 April & 3 May 1931, speeches in villages, 24 & 26 April 1931, CWMG, XLVI, 13–15, 49, 36, 47.

[40] Gandhi to Emerson, 9 April 1931, AICC Papers, 1931, File No. Misc. 2 (Kw) (i).

make the journey to London worth while. Later developments in U.P., however, indicated that Gandhi could not control local Congressmen, and that they in turn might claim to speak for the peasantry but could not control their actions.

Outside these two areas local observance of the settlement was from the government's point of view far more satisfactory, with the exception of the North-West Frontier. Bengal and Bihar were probably the slowest of the other provinces to revert to a more normal situation. Bengali Congressmen called for consolidation in preparation for a further struggle. Picketing and boycott continued, processions and bellicose speeches were common, but other manifestations of civil disobedience subsided. Midnapore continued to be a disturbing centre of Congress power. In some parts of the district Congress 'militias' drilled and regularly patrolled villages, loyalists were subjected to severe social boycott, and about forty arbitration courts were established. Most of these collapsed by July, but while they lasted they tried a significant number of petty cases and the fines imposed helped to swell Congress coffers.[41] In Bihar and Orissa a revival of Congress activity followed the Delhi settlement, but by June this had subsided, partly because Congress funds dried up and with them the flow of volunteers. Picketing of foreign cloth and liquor shops continued spasmodically; though an enormous rise in the number of illicit stills indicated that the drive behind the Congress temperance campaign was scarcely the moral one Gandhi emphasized. Agrarian agitation occurred only in those districts with particular problems such as Gaya, where rents were peculiarly high, or where there were special objects of attack such as the European landlords of Champaran. In general rents and revenue demands were not high; moreover since many Congressmen were small landlords they would suffer from a no-rent campaign, while failure to pay revenue would lead to swift loss of land under the province's particularly stringent regulations in this matter.[42]

Assam, Punjab and C.P. all reported a fairly swift return to normal conditions, though Congressmen continued there, as in all provinces, to call the settlement a truce during which they must strengthen themselves for a further fight. All aspects of civil disobedience stopped, nonetheless, and even picketing produced few problems.[43] Picketing of liquor shops continued in Madras, however, though it varied in time and place, Madras

[41] *1930–31 Bengal Administration Report*, pp. xii–xiii; Bengal government report on Congress observance of the settlement, 24 December 1931, Home Poll., 1931, File No. 33/50.

[42] Bihar & Orissa government report on Congress observance of the settlement, 16 December 1931, *ibid.*; *Bihar and Orissa in 1931–32* (Patna, 1933), pp. 3–6. In the first nine months of 1931 excise revenue was down Rs. 29 lakhs compared with the same period in 1930; *1930–31 Bihar & Orissa Administration Report*, pp. xxi–xxii.

[43] Reports on Congress observance of the settlement from governments of Assam (10 December 1931), Punjab (29 December 1931), and C.P. (20 January 1932), Home Poll., 1931, File No. 33/50.

City, Malabar, Kistna and West Godavari being the most affected areas. The influence of Rajagopalachariar, a genuine temperance campaigner of long standing, was partly responsible for this. But it was generally unaggressive, and official objections to it were grounded on the opportunities it gave for Congress propaganda and its effects on the excise revenue: the Excise Commissioner anticipated a fall of Rs. 50 lakhs largely as a result of picketing. However the Madras government stated that it made no general charge against Congress of deliberately disregarding the Delhi settlement.[44]

The observance of the settlement was largely in inverse proportion to the intensity of the local drives which had been harnessed to the continental civil disobedience campaign in 1930. Where this intermeshing had been weak, as in Madras, the pact was accepted with little trouble: where it had been particularly strong, as in Midnapore or Gujarat, local politicians and their followers were not content to follow the fiat of the Mahatma and the AICC. On an all-India scale, however, the months after the Delhi negotiations justified Gandhi's decision and his judgement of the mood of provincial campaigners and their capacity to continue the conflict. The comparatively uniform observance of the terms he had secured also depended partly on his constant interventions and advice when discrepancies were brought to his notice. Local Congressmen referred questions of interpretation of the terms to him. His answers and the guidelines he issued through the press on such matters as picketing and panchayats were designed to secure peaceful and courteous pressure which would not alienate either the government or other Indians and would substantiate the Congress claim to special status. 'We cannot', he argued, 'be too strict in the observance of our part of the Settlement...Let us realize that the stricter we are, the greater will be our prestige and strength.'[45] His personal efforts to secure uniformity of observance were supplemented by those of his closest allies in their home provinces. Rajagopalachariar, as President of the Tamil Nad PCC, issued a circular of guidance on observing the settlement which attracted compliments even from Emerson.[46]

[44] Madras Chief Sec. to Govt. of India, Home Sec., 8 December 1931, C. Williamson to H. W. Emerson, 29 July 1931, *ibid.*; *1930–31 Madras Administration Report*, pp. xi–xiv. Excise revenue actually fell from Rs. 592.26 lakhs (1929–30) to Rs. 524.27 lakhs (1930–1) to Rs. 425.80 lakhs (1931–2) because of picketing and the acute economic depression; *ibid.* pp. 144–5, *Report on the Administration of the Madras Presidency for the year 1931–32* (Madras, 1933), p. 144.

[45] Gandhi's advice on picketing, *Young India*, 21 May 1931; guidance for panchayats, *Young India*, 28 May 1931. For references to Gandhi on implementing the settlement see AICC Papers, 1929, File No. 41 (Misc.); e.g. J. Daulatram to Gandhi, telegram 19 May 1931, Gandhi's telegram in reply, 19 May 1931, on admissible picketing of foreign-cloth sellers in Mirpurkhas.

[46] Rajagopalachariar's circular to all Congress workers in Tamil Nad, 22 April 1931, from Madras Secret Abstract, No. 16, 2 May 1931, Home Poll., 1931, File No. 33/9; Gandhi to Rajagopalachariar, 17 May 1931, *CWMG*, XLVI, 163.
Rajendra Prasad was also urging people to observe the settlement; Bihar & Orissa FR2, May 1931, Home Poll., 1931, File No. 18/v.

Even Gandhi's staunchest lieutenants could experience tension between the all-India reasoning and claims of the Mahatma and the demands of their local followers. When this occurred Gandhi's power to control events in the localities was limited, even in his home region. Vallabhbhai's local problems were so great that by late April Gandhi was saying that 'the Settlement itself runs the risk to being broken to pieces in Gujarat. Of course I am making every endeavour to see that it is honoured by the officials here.'[47] Only by demonstrating publicly that officials would listen to Vallabhbhai's allegations and cooperate with him could Gandhi ensure Vallabhbhai's local credibility and adherence to his line, and simultaneously open his own way to London. He let Emerson know of his fears for the settlement in Gujarat, asking for help in preventing a breakdown; and Emerson replied with the offer of another personal discussion.[48]

Their meeting occurred in Simla, spanning 13–16 May. The Home Secretary was even more convinced that Gandhi was anxious that the settlement should hold and was prepared to do his utmost to this end. He judged that the Mahatma had 'definitely mellowed during the past few months. He has been up against concrete difficulties and has had to face constructive work. This has made him less confident in regard to preconceived ideas and more ready to see the other side of the case, although I have always found him very fair in this respect.' Emerson recognized that close cooperation between Congress leaders and government officials would boost the former's prestige, yet he argued in his report on this meeting that the government should continue to proffer opportunities for such cooperation, as in Gandhi's case it seemed to have increased his disposition to be helpful. Again the government as a result of its own needs was confirming Gandhi in a position of peculiar political leverage.[49]

During this round of conversations Emerson and Gandhi covered a wide range of topics, from the situation in Gujarat and on the North-West Frontier, *swadeshi* and procedure for the Round Table Conference, down to supplies of salt for the fish-curing industry and the return of bicycles and a car seized by the government during civil disobedience. Gujarat was one of their major concerns, and Gandhi appeared happier over this area than at his last meeting with Emerson. In Kaira the revenue payment situation had eased since he had established a system of cooperation between himself and the Collector; but two matters still disturbed him and boded ill for future peace in Gujarat. One was the payment not of the current revenue demand but arrears as a result of the previous year's refusals to pay; because many cultivators were paying their current demand and part of their arrears in the expectation that the balance of the latter

[47] Gandhi to C. F. Andrews, 29 April 1931, also 5 May 1931, *CWMG*, XLVI, 51, 89.
[48] Gandhi to H. W. Emerson, 22 & 27 April 1931, *ibid.* pp. 25, 48; Emerson to Gandhi, 2 May 1931, *ibid.* pp. 396–7.
[49] Emerson's note, 18 May 1931, of his conversations with Gandhi, 13–16 May, Home Poll., 1931, File No. 33/9.

would be suspended. Emerson squashed what amounted to a claim that government should accept tax-payers' own judgement of what they could pay; but the problem was shelved until it should arise in practice – when the administration resorted to coercive processes to recover arrears. The other Gujarat problem they left unsolved was the reinstatement of village officials. In this case, as in that of forfeited lands, pressures from local groups bent on defending their particular interests hampered Gandhi's all-India attempts to safeguard a settlement which had recognized the validity of third party rights created in the aftermath of civil disobedience. Emerson also left Gandhi in no doubt that another area causing government increasing concern was the Frontier. Here since his release from jail Abdul Ghaffar Khan had continued to recruit Red Shirts, to make belligerent speeches about preparing for battle during the 'truce' and had attempted to spread agitation in the tribal areas, while refusing to meet any officials to discuss the situation. The current estimate of Red Shirt numbers was 13,000, and they appeared to be outside Abdul Ghaffar's control. Moreover in Peshawar district the crime rate had risen startlingly, and, with Abdul Ghaffar's encouragement, people were refusing to pay land revenue: in one subdivision payment had almost stopped. It was stressed to Gandhi that such disruptive activities were a threat to life and property, particularly of Frontier Hindus who were already voicing their apprehensions. Faced with such evidence Gandhi agreed to contact Abdul Ghaffar speedily.[50]

The Mahatma left Simla knowing the danger areas where he would have to try to exercise restraint over Congressmen or their allies if the settlement was to hold. He had also become more keenly aware of two factors which were to impinge on his calculations through the rest of 1931. One was the determination of the government 'to hit hard and hit at once', as Emerson had put it, if civil disobedience was restarted. In fact in April the Government of India Home Department had begun to draft a new, comprehensive emergency powers Ordinance to this end. The contrast with Irwin's reluctance in 1930 to act beyond the minimum requirements of the actual situation was clear. Emerson himself had minuted, 'we must regard the present draft Ordinance, not merely as a measure which would be useful if a grave situation developed, but also as a measure which would very materially assist in preventing the development of such a situation'.[51] This shift in government policy occurred just as Willingdon replaced Irwin as

[50] *idem.*; *1931–32. Administration Report Of The North West Frontier Province* (Peshawar, 1934), pp. i–x; note on Red Shirt movement by N.-W.F.P. Deputy Inspector General of Police, June 1931, Home Poll., 1931, File No. 33/8 part 1.

[51] Note by H. W. Emerson, 24 April 1931, Home Poll., 1931, File No. 13/8. The Bombay government had continued to press for an emergency powers Ordinance, as had Sykes in conversation with Irwin and Willingdon on 17/18 April when they were all in Bombay for the viceregal change-over: G. F. S. Collins, Home Sec., Govt. of Bombay, to H. W. Emerson, 8 April 1931, Mss. EUR.F.150 (3); Sykes, *From Many Angles*, p. 412.

Viceroy in mid-April. An Indian administrator of long experience, Willingdon was less flexible in political style than Irwin; and he tended to see
the Mahatma more as a slippery political schemer than a man of faith and
integrity. But the change in policy had deeper roots than the arrival of a
new Viceroy. It originated in the determination of Government of India
officials to work the settlement only on condition that they should not again
subject the services and their allies to the strain of renewed civil disobedience countered only with the limited weapons used in 1930. Just after
Emerson had seen Gandhi, the Government of India, arguing the case for
a hard blow at renewed civil disobedience, underlined the facts that Congress was clearly preparing for another struggle and that the settlement
had increased Congress prestige to the detriment of morale among officials
and loyalists; while the prospect of responsible government at the centre
was bound to hamper government in fighting civil disobedience. A tough
line if conflict erupted again was therefore an essential *quid pro quo* for the
settlement: 'if the situation deteriorates, the maintenance of the Settlement,
as the deliberate policy of Government, can be justified only if it is accompanied by the determination to strike at once and strike hard, if and when
the settlement breaks down.'[52]

The knowledge that government would wear no kid gloves in a renewed
struggle confirmed Gandhi's wish to play a moderating role and guard the
settlement through the summer of 1931. A further influence on his tactics
was his growing awareness of the importance of public opinion in Britain.
Emerson had stressed this in connection with Congressmen's boycott tactics
and their constant advocacy of preparation during the 'truce' for further
conflict. He told Gandhi that these aspects of Congressmen's behaviour had
caused considerable reaction in Britain, which might jeopardize constitutional discussions; and had suggested that the Mahatma's 'own position
would be very unpleasant if, when he was in London, a state of affairs
existed in India which irritated and even outraged public opinion in
England'.[53] In deciding whether to go to London Gandhi had to weigh the
obvious importance of 'converting' British opinion if he was to gain
permanent, constitutional results, against the probable futility of trying to
attempt this if events in India were simultaneously working to nullify his
British campaign, either by Congress alienating British opinion or by
government action in his absence implicitly denying the Congress claim to
speak for Indians.

After leaving Emerson in Simla Gandhi turned his attention to the three
areas where the peace was most precarious. On 20 May he saw the Governor

[52] Govt. of India to Under Sec. of State for India, 19 May 1931, Home Poll., 1931,
File No. 13/8. See also in this file discussion between Delhi and the provincial
governments on the proposed draft Ordinance. D. A. Low, '"Civil Martial Law":
The Government of India and the Civil Disobedience Movements 1930–34', Low
(ed.), *Congress and the Raj.*

[53] Emerson's note, 18 May 1931, of his conversations with Gandhi, 13–16 May,
Home Poll., 1931, File No. 33/9.

of U.P., Sir Malcolm Hailey, in Naini Tal, the province's summer capital. Emerson was largely responsible for this encounter, but Hailey was willing to follow the line Emerson had been pursuing in granting Gandhi interviews, hoping thereby 'to utilise his influence to assist in solving the difficulty which has arisen in our rural areas'.[54] By this time Gandhi was armed with an extensive note on the U.P. rent and revenue situation written by Jawaharlal before he went on a much-needed rest to Ceylon. This stressed the economic plight of tenants as the slump in agricultural prices continued, and called for substantial rent remissions. It also justified the role of Congress workers in attempting to publicize the facts and to arrange agreements between tenants and their landlords. Far from stirring up rural strife, it argued with considerable justification, they were trying to control a peasantry embittered by economic misfortune and by harassment from their landlords and sometimes the police. 'In spite of this great provocation however the tenantry have been generally kept in control and the lapses on their part, regrettable and unfortunate as they were, have been few.' Reports coming into the government confirmed that local Congressmen could not control the tenants, and that some were even refusing to pay the reduced rents agreed to by Congress 'representatives' in private arrangements with landlords.[55]

The U.P. government, despite its suspicions of the political drive behind Congress support of the peasantry, realized the gravity of the economic situation for all whose living came from the land. Prices of agricultural products, particularly of cereals and cotton, continued to fall, reaching a nadir in the second quarter of 1931. Consequently, the provincial administration sanctioned remissions of about 18.2% or Rs. 68 lakhs in tne *rabi* revenue demand and corresponding rent remissions of well over Rs. 2 crores. Gandhi claimed that this relief was inadequate and asked Hailey to accept the Congress figures as the basis for relief or to institute an enquiry in which Congressmen could participate. The latter course was unacceptable to Hailey who argued that the delay in payment involved in an enquiry would endanger the finances of the landlords and the government. Gandhi stuck to his position that the problem would only be solved by enlisting Congress cooperation in persuading tenants to pay: but he could not promise such cooperation or his personal intervention in favour of payment by tenants unless Congress could offer them something better than the remissions announced so far. Consequently Hailey judged their interview to have been pretty fruitless from the point of view of using Gandhi as an instrument for local control.[56]

[54] Hailey to Emerson, 2 May 1931, Emerson to Hailey, 2 June 1931, Home Poll., 1931, File No. 33/XI.
[55] Note on U.P. rent & revenue situation by J. Nehru, 18 April 1931, AICC Papers, 1931, File No. 4, part I; U.P. FR2, April 1931, Home Poll., 1931, File No. 18/IV.
[56] U.P. FRs, May 1931, *ibid.* No. 18/V; note by Sir Malcolm Hailey, 20 May 1931, on interview with Gandhi that day, Home Poll., 1931, File No. 33/XI.

Agricultural commodity prices reached their lowest in June 1931; for the

However three days later Gandhi indicated that he was prepared to intervene. He told Hailey that unless the government responded to any of his suggestions he proposed to issue a manifesto to the *kisans* telling them his opinion of the minimum they should pay. Hailey replied welcoming Gandhi's advice to pay at once and his condemnation of violence, but he felt that the manifesto's total effect would be to encourage tenants to pay only the minimum. He argued that the correct course was to allow collections to proceed, otherwise much of the rent would be permanently lost, to the detriment of landlord–tenant relations and government finances. However Gandhi published his manifesto, and in the same edition of *Young India* emphasized the priority of rural harmony in a parallel appeal to U.P. zamindars. He urged them to consider their tenants' present plight and long-term relationship with them as landlords; to cease their 'questionable perquisites', care for their tenants and become their 'trustees and trusted friends'. They should, he urged, trust the Congress as 'a bridge between the people and the Government' and even join it, and Congressmen would see that tenants fulfilled their obligations to their landlords. Gandhi was well aware that his manifestoes for rural peace might be of little avail and he underlined to U.P. Congressman, Mohanlal Saxena, the need to 'hold the *kisans* in check'. Provincial leaders' attempts to follow his line and sustain a continental settlement, however, undermined their authority in the villages; and when they felt forced to disown local militants such as Rae Bareli's Kalka Prasad, they cut their lines of communication and control with the grass roots of rural support where genuine distress had provided much of the strength of civil disobedience in late 1930.[57]

The problem of the U.P. exemplified Gandhi's predicament as a leader

deteriorating economic situation see *Report on the Administration of the United Provinces of Agra and Oudh. 1930–31* (Lucknow, 1932), pp. xv–xvi, 37–8.

[57] Gandhi to Hailey, 23 May 1931, draft manifesto to U.P. *kisans* by Gandhi, 23 May 1931, Hailey to Gandhi, 23 May 1931, Home Poll., 1931, File No. 33/xi; Gandhi's manifestoes to U.P. *kisans* and zamindars, *Young India*, 28 May 1931, *CWMG*, XLVI, 200–3, 233–5; Gandhi to M. Saxena, 15 June 1931, *ibid.* p. 384.

For Congress leaders' ambivalence towards *kisan* agitation when it was at its height see Pandey, 'The Indian National Congress and Political Mobilisation in the United Provinces 1926–1934', ch. 4. U.P. Congress leaders' ambivalence towards rural agitation was clear in the letter Jawaharlal wrote to A. Rahman on 30 July 1931 in reply to a letter from Rahman to Gandhi, 20 July 1931, which Gandhi had passed on to Jawaharlal: it also demonstrated Gandhi's role as a channel of communication and conciliation.

Jawaharlal insisted that the U.P. Congress was not an anti-zamindar body but stood for justice for all and had deplored *kisan* violence in various recent cases of agrarian rioting. 'Allow me to assure you that the U.P. Provincial Congress Organisation has no desire to do any injury to zamindars. Nor does it tolerate any violence or injury done by tenants to zamindars. My own views regarding the zamindari system are well known and I have not tried to hide them. But those views have no application to present day politics, and in any event the Congress is not committed to those views. The president of the U.P. Provincial Congress Committee is Mr. Tassaduk Ahmad Khan Sherwani, who is a zamindar. The general secretary of the Provincial Congress Committee is Mr. Sri Prakasa, who is also a fairly big zamindar, and among leading

whose position depended not on championing the cause of one particular group with a clear aim but on enabling a variety of groups to relate to each other politically with some benefit to all concerned. In this case he satisfied neither the government nor the U.P. tenants, failed to soothe the landlords or to extricate the local Congress leadership from its own ambivalent position. Having done his best to satisfy these incompatible needs he left Naini Tal for Gujarat where similar dilemmas confronted him. Establishing himself in Bardoli he studied Vallabhbhai's position and was careful to protect his local lieutenant's prestige. However, temporarily the situation improved from the government's point of view. Overt breaches of the settlement stopped and land revenue came in steadily, although there were still instances of social harassment, as in Kaira where a Patidar panchayat fined people who had paid their revenue during civil disobedience and a patel who had not resigned.[58]

Gandhi also took steps to protect the settlement on the Frontier, inviting Abdul Ghaffar to visit him in Gujarat. Gandhi's personal problems of lack of knowledge and power to control local events in U.P. and to a lesser extent in Gujarat were mirrored and magnified in Congress's relationship with the Frontier. The truth was that Congress leaders in India knew little of the Frontier situation and had little chance of acquiring accurate information or exerting leverage locally as Frontier Congressmen were at odds with Abdul Ghaffar and his Red Shirts. Realizing their predicament in trying to integrate Frontier politics into a continental programme, all-India leaders had at Karachi privately asked Frontier Congressmen to secure Abdul Ghaffar's cooperation within a formal Congress framework. On 30 May the Pathan leader's party were accordingly given office in the Frontier PCC, and when Abdul Ghaffar declined to become President his nominee, Mian Ahmad Shah, General Secretary of the Afghan Jirga, was elected. His main loyalties were however to the Pathan Afghan Youth League, and the tactic intended to integrate the Pathan political drive only precipitated a bitter split between him and the Peshawar City Congressmen. An element in this hostility was Frontier Hindu fear that the Red Shirt movement was developing into a blatantly violent and communal agitation, whatever the original intentions of Abdul Ghaffar. Eventually on 26 June the Peshawar faction of the Frontier PCC threw Mian Ahmad Shah from his presidential position and referred the whole position to Jawaharlal and the AICC. The deposed President also appealed to the AICC and to Gandhi, threatening to devote himself to Afghan Jirga work if the decision went against him. The AICC tried to keep this conflict from the public gaze, and without informing the

Congressmen in the province there are many zamindars. Thus there can be no question of the Congress as such being an anti-zamindar body. It is true however that the backbone of the Congress consists of kisans, and as the kisans are helpless and downtrodden it is the duty of the Congress to help and protect them.' AICC Papers, 1931, File No. G-140 Kw (i).

[58] Bombay FR2, May 1931, Home Poll., 1931, File No. 18/v.

press it quietly authorized Syed Mahmud as a Congress Muslim to go to the Frontier to arbitrate between the disputing parties.[59] In this situation Gandhi could do little. He entertained Abdul Ghaffar in early June and thereafter wrote to Emerson saying that he was convinced of the Pathan's genuine conversion to non-violence. Abdul Ghaffar maintained that he and his followers had not broken the settlement, and that he had refused to see the Frontier's Chief Commissioner for fear of being misinterpreted. However he was prepared to see Emerson or Willingdon if Gandhi accompanied him, and he also hoped Gandhi would visit the Frontier. Gandhi offered to do both things and urged Emerson that officials should see Abdul Ghaffar because the settlement presupposed mutual trust. The Home Secretary replied that though the Government of India appreciated the value of personal contact the best course was for Abdul Ghaffar to see the Chief Commissioner. Gandhi's request for permission to visit the Frontier was later turned down on the grounds that it would cause excitement and increase the difficulties of the Frontier administration. Instead Gandhi sent his son, Devadas, to investigate a situation which he realized he neither understood nor controlled.[60]

In the weeks after Karachi Gandhi was so absorbed in the minutiae of the settlement that he gave little thought to arrangements for the Round Table Conference. Harassed by local threats to the peace and the government's denial of Congress's claim to represent all Indians though officials were willing to use him personally as an intermediary, he hesitated through April and May to commit himself to going to London. However, his statements on this question always linked the communal question to the working of the settlement as the reason for his hesitation. Late in April he told C. F. Andrews, 'You have taken it for granted that I am going to London. I am not at all sure and I am certainly not going if there is no Hindu–Muslim solution. There is no immediate prospect. And then the Settlement itself runs the risk of being broken to pieces in Gujarat.' In May he repeated publicly and privately that a communal solution and the satisfactory working of the settlement were preconditions of his attending the Round Table Conference. But Emerson gathered from their mid-May conversations that most of Gandhi's close colleagues felt he should go; he judged that Gandhi would even if there was no prior communal

[59] P. Khan to J. Nehru, 23 October 1931, summarizing the Congress–Jirga controversy, AICC Papers, 1931, File No. P-17: undated press statement by Mian Ahmad Shah; Gen. Sec., Frontier PCC, to AICC, 27 June 1931, & to J. Nehru, 13 July 1931; J. Nehru to S. Mahmud, 13 July 1931; AICC Papers, 1931, File No. G-148: note on Red Shirt movement by N.-W.F.P. Deputy Inspector General of Police, June 1931, Home Poll., 1931, File No. 33/8 part 1: H. Polak to Gandhi, 16 June 1933, describing visit to Peshawar, S.N. No. 21477, Gandhi Papers.

[60] Gandhi to Emerson, 13 June 1931, Emerson to Gandhi, telegram, 17 June 1931, Emerson to Gandhi, 6 July 1931, Home Poll., 1931, File No. 33/8 part 1 (all these are also in AICC Papers, 1931, File No. Misc. 2 (Kw) (i)); Gandhi to Viceroy, 21 July 1931, *CWMG*, XLVII, 178–9.

agreement.[61] That Gandhi was keen to publicize his cause in England was clear from his professed willingness to go informally for discussion even if the absence of a communal agreement and the consequent weakening of his position at the conference table made his presence as a conference delegate impolitic. The only precondition for such an informal visit was the successful working of the settlement.[62]

After the Karachi Congress Gandhi tried to clear his path to London as a full conference member by attempting to secure a constitutional demand acceptable to all communities. Speaking to the Jamiat-ul-Ulema in Karachi on 1 April he affirmed that he would like to concede all the Muslims' political demands, and reiterated that Congress was not a Hindu body. Immediately afterwards he went to Delhi, where the All-India Muslim Conference was about to meet, having been deputed by the Congress Working Committee to consult with the Conference's spokesmen. A Muslim deputation from the Conference presented Gandhi on 4 April with Jinnah's '14 Points', and when Congress Muslims including Ansari and Sherwani denounced the call for separate electorates Gandhi had to drop the idea of negotiating an agreement on that basis. Whatever his personal wishes and declarations of willingness to give Muslims a 'blank cheque' he could not abandon the small group of Nationalist Muslims whose allegiance to Congress gave some credence to its claim to represent Muslims and Hindus.[63]

The possibility of agreement receded even further on 5 April when the Conference, under the presidency of Shaukat Ali, reiterated its standing claim for separate electorates and special weightage in the provincial and federal legislatures which would protect Muslims where they were minorities and secure their dominance in areas where they had small majorities – the latter being an important concern of the Punjabis, Fazl-i-Husain and Feroze Khan Noon, who were prime movers of the gathering. The Conference's insistence on the separation of Sind from Bombay and the transformation of the five settled areas of the North-West Frontier into a full province, and its determination that provinces should retain residual powers in any Federation, indicated that the whole package was designed to protect Muslims from Hindu domination when responsibility was handed over to an all-India federal government. The Conference also

[61] Gandhi to C. F. Andrews, 29 April 1931, *CWMG*, XLVI, 50–1; report in *Young India*, 21 May 1931, *ibid.* p. 153; Gandhi to Willingdon, telegram, *c.* 21 May 1931, *ibid*, p. 197; Gandhi to V. S. S. Sastri, telegram, 25 May 1931, AICC Papers, 1929, File No. 41 (Misc.); note by Emerson, 18 May 1931, on conversations with Gandhi, 13–16 May, Home Poll., 1931, File No. 33/9.

[62] Gandhi to M. A. Ansari, 26 May 1931, *CWMG*, XLIV, 224–5; Gandhi to V. S. S. Sastri, telegram, 25 May 1931, AICC Papers, 1929, File No. 41 (Misc.).

[63] Gandhi's speech to Jamiat-ul-Ulema Conference, 1 April 1931, *CWMG*, XLV, 380–4; Working Committee resolution of 1 April deputing Gandhi, Vallabhbhai and J. Bajaj to confer with Muslim leaders in Delhi, *Young India*, 9 April 1931; Bose, *The Indian Struggle 1920–1942*, pp. 214–15; J. Nehru to Mustafa Ali, 14 April 1931, *SWJN*, 5, pp. 243–4.

roundly attacked Hindus for 'wanton aggressiveness' in the recent communal riots in the U.P. and denounced 'the so-called non-violence of the Congress Satyagrahis' as 'mere sham... little short of an unclean political stratagem adopted in the face of the superior organized force of the State and cast off in dealings between communities'. Gandhi replied in a press statement on 6 April that although he favoured 'full surrender to any unanimously expressed wish' of Muslims and Sikhs, he could not accept the claim put to him on 4 April because it was not unanimous, as was proved by the hostility of Nationalist Muslims to the idea of separate electorates.[64]

One of the repercussions of the Delhi debacle was increasing Muslim hostility to Gandhi personally; and even his former Khilafat colleague, Shaukat Ali, proclaimed that Muslims could expect no justice from the Mahatma.[65] Gandhi's realization of his position in communal matters was demonstrated by his reluctance to ask for active support for the Nationalist Muslim Party even from the Patna Muslim, Hasan Imam, who had been deeply involved in Congress politics and helped him as far back as 1917 during his championship of Bihari cultivators in Champaran district.[66] After his attempts at Delhi he left negotiations for a communal agreement in the hands of the Nationalist Muslims, led by Ansari, Sherwani and Khaliquzzaman. These started at Bhopal on 10/11 May after mediatory intervention by the Nawab of Bhopal, and eventually broke down at the end of June on the question of separate electorates.[67]

Gandhi's abortive and idiosyncratic endeavours to secure a communal agreement not only weakened his position among Muslims. They also alienated Hindus who were locally in a minority and feared Gandhi's apparent willingness to conciliate other communities at their expense. A meeting of Hindus from Punjab, Sind and the Frontier in Lahore in early May under the auspices of the Hindu Sabha made this plain. Moonje, who presided over the meeting, later put these fears to Gandhi personally, backed by Sardar Ujjal Singh who spoke for Punjabi Sikhs. Gandhi still maintained that without an agreement they could not make the British listen to the Congress demands and that it was therefore a *sine qua non* of

[64] Gandhi's press statement on communal problem, 6 April 1931, *CWMG*, XLV, 394–5.

Muslim Conference Resolutions, 5 April 1931, Aziz, *All India Muslim Conference 1928–1935*, pp. 72–5; for comment on Muslim attitudes see Irwin to Wedgwood Benn, 2 April 1931 (part of letter dated 6 April after talking to various conference leaders on 5 April), Mss. EUR.C.152 (6); Jayakar to Sapru, 11 April 1931, Sapru Papers, Series II.

[65] Jayakar to Sapru, 11 April 1931, Sapru Papers, Series II; Delhi & Bombay FRIs, April 1931, Home Poll., 1931, File No. 18/IV.

[66] 'Twice I took up the pen to write to Syed Hasan Imam and twice I lacked the courage to write. I felt and still feel that it is best for me not to write to any Muslim friend so as to influence him [in] favour of the nationalist Muslim view.' Gandhi to Syed Mahmud, 19 April 1931, Syed Mahmud Papers, File No. 50.

[67] Muslim Conference Secretary's Statement on negotiations with nationalist Muslims, 23 June 1931, Aziz, *op. cit.* pp. 75–8; S. Mahmud to J. Nehru, 27 June 1931, Datta & Cleghorn (ed.), *A Nationalist Muslim and Indian Politics*, pp. 115–17.

his attendance at the Round Table Conference. He was also attracted by Fazl-i-Husain's idea of separate provincial settlements of the problem, which Moonje insisted would be suicidal because it would merely confirm existing weightage arrangements and secure for Muslims their majorities in Punjab and Bengal. He commented to his diary, 'Mahatma is absolutely a booby in the matters of conversations of this nature with opponents. That's how he allowed himself to be pocketted by Lord Irwin.'[68]

Despite Gandhi's continued reluctance to commit himself publicly to the conference table, in private he agreed that he was hoping to attend. To C. F. Andrews he wrote, 'My desire is certainly to go there but the inner voice says "no" and the external atmosphere confirms the guidance of the inner voice.' Among his non-Congress associates there was considerable pressure to get him to attend in the hope and expectation that he would prove reasonable in the different environment; while those who disliked the Delhi peace terms pulled in the opposition direction. Jayakar gathered from Bose that 'the wildest circles of the Congress' judged apprehensively that Gandhi would turn out more moderate even than Sapru and Jayakar if he reached London, and Jayakar himself interpreted 'Gandhi's vacillation and inconsistent speeches' as evidence of 'a steady purpose...to win over his associates to his ultimate desire to visit England and do his best'.[69] In the second week of June however the Working Committee gathered in Bombay made the decision for him, in as much as it depended on the communal question: the Mahatma should represent Congress at the conference even if the attempts to secure a communal agreement 'should... unfortunately fail, in order to avoid any possibility of the Congress attitude being misunderstood', provided that 'other conditions' were favourable.[70]

Gandhi argued against this resolution in the committee meeting; for though he wished to go to England he was determined that the scene should be rightly set for the role he envisaged for himself. In a *Young India* article he explained that he accepted the majority decision though he had opposed it in committee, partly from a wish to adhere to his repeated public declarations that he would not attend the conference without a communal agreement, and partly from fear that without such an agreement he would merely become one of a number of bargainers, unable to make the Congress claim as the nation's representative. Instead he proposed that Congress should abandon the conference path to a swaraj constitution until all communities could agree on a demand. Congress should consolidate its position among ordinary people and direct its activities towards obtaining *purna swaraj* by direct action, particularly by exercising satyagraha in specific causes affecting the welfare of the masses.

[68] 17 May 1931, Diary of B. S. Moonje; Punjab FR1, May 1931, Home Poll., 1931, File No. 18/v.

[69] Sapru to Jayakar, 30 May 1931, Jayakar to Sapru, 7 June 1931, Sapru Papers, Series II; Gandhi to C. F. Andrews, 2 June 1931, *CWMG*, XLVI, 275–6.

[70] 9 June 1931, Working Committee resolution, *CWMG*, XLVII, 1, fn. 1.

It all depends upon what we mean by and want through *purna swaraj.*
If we mean an awakening among the masses, a knowledge among them
of their true interest and ability to serve that interest against the whole
world and if through *purna swaraj* we want harmony, freedom from
aggression from within or without and a progressive improvement in
the economic condition of the masses, we can gain our end without
political power and by directly acting upon the powers that be.[71]

This seemed a dramatic about-turn, a rejection by Congress's major
figure of the struggle for a reformed constitution which he had been
leading since 1929. In fact Gandhi had hinted at this in his Delhi statement
on the communal problem in April; and it sprang from his long-held belief
that true swaraj was a quality of life which Indians could only generate
themselves and which could never be handed to them as a constitutional
package by their rulers. It reflected his deep distrust of all state structures
and of political power as commonly perceived of and sought after by
politicians. In later articles replying to private queries from Satyamurti,
Gandhi made his priorities plain. For him political power was not an end,
but only a means of enabling people to reform their lives through regulation
of the nation's life by national representatives: his ideal was enlightened
anarchy, a situation where national life became self-regulating and representation was therefore unnecessary. But as such an ideal was never fully
realized, he recognized that political power was necessary and he sought
it 'for the sake of the reforms for which the Congress stands'. If it could
be had only by expending much of the energy which should go on the
reforms – as threatened to be the case if communal conflict erupted – he
would prefer to concentrate on the reforms in his own way.[72] However,
even so close a colleague as Rajagopalachariar was mystified by Gandhi's
stand. He reasoned with Gandhi that he had campaigned for swaraj in 1930
when there was no communal agreement, and therefore stood convicted
of inconsistency: only if agreement proved impossible should they resort
to the chronic and continuous civil disobedience and its attendant evils
which Gandhi seemed to be advocating. He himself believed an agreement
could be reached away from India, using the simile of bargains which could
not be clinched in the village but were often made in the distant market.
Moreover, he thought Congressmen had 'overrated the value of joint
electorates with reservation of seats, and undervalued the methods of
working in groups. We are sacrificing far too much for this – what I call
– superstition of Congress politics.' He urged Gandhi to go to the conference and try to get as much as possible rather than let the constitution
be discussed in his absence: 'We cannot be worse off than we are now.'[73]

[71] 'Substance Not Shadow', article by Gandhi explaining his position in the
Working Committee, *Young India*, 18 June 1931, *ibid.* pp. 1–3.
[72] For Gandhi's earlier hint in this direction see his press statement on communal
problem, 6 April 1931, *CWMG*, XLVI, 394–5. His articles in response to letters from
Satyamurti are in *Young India*, 2 July & 6 August 1931, *CWMG*, XLVII, 90–2, 251–3:
see also Gandhi to S. Satyamurti, 30 June 1931, NMML, S. Satyamurti Papers.
[73] Rajagopalachariar to Gandhi, 2 July 1931, Home Poll., 1931, File No. 33/30.

Gandhi's contrary judgement sprang from an awareness of his own weakening position and the fact that in London his political skill would be tested in a very different context from the 1930 conflict to which Rajagopalachariar referred. Sethna realized what was going on in the Mahatma's mind and feared it might even lead him to bow to the reluctance of some Congressmen to maintain the peace. 'I am afraid', he wrote, 'whilst the general public do not know it Mr Gandhi himself is conscious that his power is perhaps waning. However much one may disagree from Mr Gandhi in some matters he on the whole is a force for good and it will be a pity if the other so called leaders get the upper hand.'[74] The communal impasse was a major force curtailing Gandhi's ability to manoeuvre, and undermining his credibility as a national spokesman in London and therefore his strength in making the Congress demand. Surrounded by men from the northern part of the subcontinent Gandhi was more sensitive to the intractability of this problem than his Madras colleague. Congress's attempted compromise formula of early June did nothing to remove this obstacle because the Muslim Conference rejected it outright, as did the Mahasabha and the Punjabi Hindus.[75]

By contrast with 1930, Congress finances and organization were in sad disorder. This, too, would weaken Gandhi's position as its conference spokesman because he could not count on its efficiency if he returned empty-handed and advised satyagraha. The position was similar to 1928/9 when he had argued so vehemently that Congress should train itself to provide an effective sanction to back the demand it made in the name of the nation. He urged Gujarati Congressmen to economize and make local committees financially independent of their PCC, for 'should fighting have to be resumed, we shall need to have the capacity to carry on with the minimum of funds or even without funds'.[76] He was not alone in realizing the need to discipline and reorganize Congress forces. At its July meeting the Working Committee resolved that the Hindustani Seva Dal should be recognized as the Congress's official volunteer organization operating directly under the Working Committee: all PCCs were required to form recognized volunteer corps whose members should subscribe to the Con-

[74] Sethna to Mr & Mrs Barns, 6 June 1931, Sethna Papers.
[75] The Congress compromise formula was contained in a resolution of the Working Committee meeting in Bombay, 7–12 July 1931, given in Congress Bulletin No. 3, 20 July 1931, Jayakar Papers, Correspondence File No. 356. Congress proposed to protect minorities by an acknowledgement of Fundamental Rights, adult suffrage and reservation of seats for minorities less than one quarter the population of any province. It also agreed that Sind, N.-W.F.P. & Baluchistan should be separate provinces and that residual powers in a Federation should rest with the federating units. However it did not concede separate electorates, a failure which helped to damn the proposal in the eyes of Conference Muslims concerned to protect Muslim majorities in Bengal & Punjab. For their rejection of it see Muslim Conference Executive Board Resulutions, Allahabad, 9 July 1931, Aziz, *op. cit.* pp. 78–81.
[76] *Young India*, 21 May 1931, CWMG, XLVI, 160–2. On 29 May a meeting of the Gujarat Prantik Samiti in Bardoli resolved to establish *chhavnis* in all Gujarat villages and voted Rs. 2 lakhs for this, a sum reduced from Rs. 4 lakhs at Gandhi's insistence: Bombay FR2, May 1931, Home Poll., 1931, File No. 18/v.

gress creed, and to disown any other volunteers who attempted to work in Congress's name. Jawaharlal's circular to PCCs about this noted the indiscipline and lack of uniformity in training and organization among volunteers in the 1930 campaign which led to this decision, while indicating that renewed conflict was an imminent possibility and further reason for reorganization of their forces.[77] Further proof of Congress's probable disarray in the face of a new campaign were the numerous factional disputes which erupted as elections to local Congress bodies took place in May and June. Congress was affected in most provinces, the bitter disputes undermining Congress unity and effectiveness as a political organization – a situation analogous to the one Gandhi had sought to remedy in 1929. Jawaharlal deplored the loss of prestige to Congress caused by the Delhi DCC election disputes, and Vallabhbhai in a Bombay meeting in June roundly condemned the election conflicts which were occupying the attention of most of the Presidency's local Congress leaders as 'vain disputes', and the disputants as enemies of Congress and the country.[78]

A further aspect of Gandhi's weakness as an aspirant national representative in London was his inability to control local situations in the sense either of restraining the activities of Congressmen and their local clientele or of ensuring that officials dealt with Congressmen as intermediaries with the people. The North-West Frontier and U.P. (where in June peasant violence was rife and a zamindar was murdered) were clear examples of the former: while in Gujarat not only was revenue collection plummeting again in June, but the Surat Collector issued warnings and then formal notices on about ninety proprietors in Bardoli and Valod that failure to pay would be followed by attachment of property.[79]

Gandhi's suggestion to the Working Committee that Congress should redirect its activities away from the struggle for political power fell on polite but unconvinced ears. Consequently he made yet another attempt to secure his position should he go to London. On 14 June after complaining to Emerson about the observance of the settlement by the Bombay and Madras governments he suggested that the time had come for 'a permanent Board of Arbitration to decide questions of interpretation of the Settlement and as to the full carrying out of the terms by the one party or the other',

[77] Resolution on Hindustani Seva Dal by Bombay meeting of Working Committee, 7–12 July 1931, Congress Bulletin No. 3, 20 July 1931, Jayakar Papers, Correspondence File No. 356; J. Nehru to all members of All-India Board of Hindustani Seva Dal, 16 July 1931, J. Nehru's circular No. 17 from AICC to all PCCs, 16 July 1931, AICC Papers, 1931, File No. G-8.

[78] Bombay FR2, June 1931, Home Poll., 1931, File No. 18/VI; Delhi FRs, July 1931, *ibid.* File No. 18/VII. Elections followed J. Nehru's circular to PCCs, 9 April 1931, *SWJN*, 5, pp. 240–1.

[79] Information on the settlement collected by Govt. of India in reply to Gandhi's 'charge sheet' in August, Home Poll., 1931, File No. 33/50. For Gandhi's inability to control the actions of U.P. *kisans* and the failure of the local Congress leadership to do so in Rae Bareli district, see Raja Sir Rampal Singh to Sapru, 9 June 1931 (S 344), & Sapru's reply, 12 June 1931 (S. 345), Sapru Papers, Series II.

following this up with the idea that local governments should appoint Boards of Enquiry consisting of a government and a Congress nominee to investigate the observance of the settlement by both sides in relation to picketing. If these suggestions had been accepted he would indeed have done much to retrieve the Congress's claimed status as representative and intermediary, on equal footing with the government, and his own consequent position at a conference table. Not surprisingly Emerson turned down both suggestions, arguing that since Congress obligations under the settlement were a matter of conformity to the law, such arbitration procedures would effectively suspend the ordinary law in the case of Congress 'offenders'.[80]

By the beginning of July, therefore, Gandhi knew that his attempts to force the government to recognize Congress's special position had failed – a failure confirmed by evidence which reached him from Gujarat and U.P. He was himself in Borsad where he wrote to Jawaharlal that he feared a 'burst-up', so great was the difficulty in getting both sides to observe the settlement. Jawaharlal, having returned from his holiday, was convinced that the U.P. government was ganging up with the zamindars against Congress and the peasantry and told Gandhi so. At the Mahatma's suggestion, however, he requested an interview with the Governor in order to strengthen the Congress case that it was leaving no stone unturned in trying to secure fulfilment of the settlement.[81] Gandhi's enthusiasm for going to England waned further in this atmosphere of apparent official distrust, but he pursued on a continental scale a similar course to the one he had recommended to Jawaharlal. When the Acting Governor of Bombay sounded him informally for Willingdon on his willingness to serve on the Federal Structure Committee of the conference, he replied that he would gladly serve if he found he could sail on time, but the working of the settlement was causing him great anxiety and occupying most of his time. Willingdon then told Gandhi he thought it was essential that he should go and offered his help in any way Gandhi wished – an offer the Mahatma accepted immediately, proceeding to Simla to lay before the Government of India his allegations that various provincial governments were not observing the settlement.[82]

Gandhi's stay in Simla from 15 to 22 July marked the beginning of his

[80] Gandhi to Emerson, 14 & 20 June 1931, Home Poll., 1931, File No. 33/30; Emerson to Gandhi, 4 July 1931, *CWMG*, XLVII, 428–9.

[81] Gandhi to J. Nehru, 28 June & 1 July 1931, J. Nehru Papers, part I, vol. XXIII; J. Nehru to Gandhi, 27 June 1931, enclosing two letters of his to J. Prasad, Chief Sec., U.P. Govt., 27 June 1931, AICC Papers, 1931, File No. Misc. 4, part II; J. Nehru to G. B. Pant, 18 June 1931, *SWJN*, 5, pp. 80–1.

[82] Sir E. Hotson to Gandhi, 30 June 1931, Gandhi to Hotson, 3 July 1931, Viceroy to Gandhi, 6 July 1931, Gandhi to Viceroy, telegrams, 9 & 10 July 1931, Viceroy to Gandhi, telegram, 11 July 1931, Gandhi to Viceroy, telegram, 12 July 1931, *CWMG*, XLVII, 429, 98, 122 fn. 2, 121, 122, 126 fn. 2, 126.
For Gandhi's waning enthusiasm for an English visit see Gandhi to G. D. Birla, 20 June 1931, *ibid.* p. 24.

final round of manoeuvring to get to the conference table on terms which would permit the role he hoped to play. He had lengthy talks with Emerson and Crerar, and produced for the Home Secretary a sheet detailing allegations of official breaches of the settlement. His main complaints, however, concerned the U.P., and on this both sides stuck to the positions thay had adopted as early as March. Officialdom regarded Congress activities as a breach of the settlement while Gandhi maintained that Congress had the right and duty to champion the peasantry, and that officials had given inadequate remissions in the current economic crisis while supporting the landlords against the tenants and Congress. His remedy was that district officers should consult Congress workers and on their advice fix the rent and revenue demands. Emerson countered that this was as unreasonable as suggesting that government should accept the landlords' advice on the level of rents. Gandhi insisted that he could not go to London without an impartial enquiry into allegations of official breaches of the settlement and while the peace was so precarious if, as he told Emerson, 'he thought that while he was there he would be constantly receiving telegrams about lathi charges, prosecutions of members of Congress and generally repressive measures'. Basically he wanted some continuing mechanism to establish Congress and its members in a special relationship with government which he claimed the settlement presupposed, a suggestion officials recognized would tie local governments' hands in maintaining law and order.[83]

As the week of discussions drew to a close Gandhi became increasingly bemused at the impossibility of getting at the truth behind Congress allegations and the evidence the government produced in refutation. He told Birla of his forebodings. 'No news from this end. Even if a compromise is reached, it will not make me happy. They no longer trust the Congress. Everywhere Congress workers are being prosecuted. How long can they hold out [empty] promises to me here? I ought to go to England but I do not feel like going.'[84] He added significantly, 'It is well that I do not worry over this thing. I find the fulfilment of life in simply doing the tasks that arise naturally from moment to moment' – a mental relaxation which helps to account for his stamina, but also for his tendency to become involved in minutiae at the expense of a longer-term view of the interests at stake. A crises was, however, temporarily averted at Simla. Gandhi's list of allega-

[83] Note by H. W. Emerson on discussions with Gandhi on 15 & 16 July 1931, note by Sir J. Crerar on discussion with Gandhi on 17 July 1931, Home Poll., 1931, File No. 33/23.

Emerson also had long talks with Nehru on 19 & 20 July, and gathered that he appreciated the long-term significance and potential of constitutional issues more than Gandhi. He also appeared to think that Congress should be represented at the conference and that there was an outside chance of the conference's success. Note by Emerson, 20 July 1931, on talks with J. Nehru, *idem*.

[84] Gandhi to G. D. Birla, 20 July 1931, *CWMG*, XLVII, 164; Gandhi to Emerson, 20 July 1931, Home Poll., 1931, File No. 33/26.

tions was despatched to local governments for investigation on 21 July, and
Willingdon assured the Mahatma in an interview that day that his government would get at the facts in all cases Gandhi cared to name, and if
non-observance by officials was proved the matter would at once be righted.
Gandhi was also told that there was no question of Congressmen acquiring
a favoured position under the law; whereupon he dropped that line of
request and asked for an impartial tribunal to decide upon matters of
interpretation of the settlement which either side might raise. This the
government promised to consider, believing that this request, considerably
less than his original June proprosal for a Board of Arbitration, was a tactic
to save face by securing a minor Congress 'victory' as a passport to London,
or if the government refused, to prove officialdom unreasonable and so
justify a break.[85]

A Working Committee was scheduled for early August, partly to decide
whether Gandhi should attend the conference. Between then and the Simla
discussions events increased the constraints on Gandhi, particularly as they
affected two of his most important allies, Jawaharlal and Vallabhbhai. In
the U.P., Sir Malcolm Hailey announced further rent and revenue concessions and the establishment of a Legislative Council Committee to consider
the appropriate levels. This went some way to satisfying Jawaharlal and
Gandhi. The former remained convinced nonetheless that government was
hounding Congress workers and coercing landlords and tenants to pay rent
and revenue; and he told the U.P. Chief Secretary, 'I am going to Bombay
and I shall place all these facts before Mr Gandhi.'[86] His pressure on Gandhi
in Bombay would obviously be reinforced by Vallabhbhai who was also
torn between all-India allegiance and local considerations. Vallabhbhai
told Nehru in a letter from Ahmedabad of the embarrassment of trying
to support Gandhi's all-India policy of restraint in Gujarat. 'You must have
heard about my position here... The opponent is firing heavily and the
Congress here is completely out of action. Poor peasantry believing on
Bapoo's word paid all their current dues. Now they are being prosecuted
for past arrears. I have never found myself in such a humiliating position
[in] all my life.' His humiliation was caused by the decision of the local
government to take coercive measures before the end of the revenue year
on the last day of July against cultivators in arrears on their revenue in
those places where it was sure non-payment was a deliberate policy by
people who had been deeply involved in the 1930 civil disobedience and
not the result of economic hardship. Thirteen of the 137 villages in Bardoli
taluka and Valod *mahal* in Surat were involved, and on several occasions

[85] Government of India to all local governments, 22 July 1931, Home Poll., 1931,
File No. 14/12.
Gandhi put his request in writing to Emerson the same evening, 21 July 1931,
CWMG, XLVII, 179–80.
[86] J. Nehru to U.P. Chief Secretary, 30, 31 July, 1 August 1931, *SWJN*, 5, pp. 108–9,
109–11, 111–13; note by Emerson, 20 July 1931, on talks with J. Nehru, 19/20 July
1931, Home Poll., 1931, File No. 33/23.

in July police accompanied the revenue parties – officially to guard the
revenue officers and the property attached in lieu of revenue.[87]

Gandhi reacted sharply to the news, telling the Indian Collector of Surat
that the measures were 'a breach of faith, if not of the Settlement' since
he and other Congress workers had been telling cultivators to pay all they
could of their current dues without having to borrow, on the assumption
that government on its part would not resort to coercion. He sent copies
of this to Sapru, telling him that a breaking-point in the settlement had
almost been reached, to the Commissioner of the Northern Division and
to the Bombay government. His wire informing Emerson of the situation
indicated that he, like Vallabhbhai, felt his personal credibility was locally
at stake because of his earlier assurances to cultivators that if they followed
his advice no coercive action against them would ensue. Willingdon hastily
requested Gandhi not to take precipitate action, to which Gandhi willingly
agreed. On 4 August he put the whole problem to Hotson, the Acting
Governor of Bombay, who promised to investigate.[88]

To cap the pressures on Gandhi generated by these local situations came
the government's refusal to concede Gandhi's request for a tribunal to
consider questions of interpretation of the settlement. Again its intention
was to avoid putting Congressmen in a privileged relationship with govern-

---

[87] Vallabhbhai Patel to J. Nehru, 21 July 1931, AICC Papers, 1931, File No. G-60;
Bombay memorandum on Gandhi's allegation of government's breaches of the
settlement, July 1931, Home Poll., 1931, File No. 33/23.
The Bombay memorandum gave the following figures for the distribution of
arrears:

Presidency excluding Sind:
total arrears for revenue year ending 31 July 1931:

Northern Division	Rs. 1.88 lakhs
Southern Division	Rs. 0.94 lakhs
Central Division	Rs. 0.09 lakhs
Bombay Suburban District	Rs. 0.25 lakhs.

Northern Division:

Ahmedabad	Rs. 17,000
Broach	Rs. 15,000
Kaira	Rs. 77,000
Panch Mahals	Nil
Surat	Rs. 71,000
Thana	Rs. 8,000

In Kaira Rs. 48,000 (Matar and Mehmadabad) of arrears were deemed to be due
to genuine economic hardship: the remaining arrears came mainly from Anand,
Borsad and Nadiad.
In Surat Bardoli taluka accounted for Rs. 57,000 of Surat's arrears, and Valod *mahal*
for Rs. 11,000.
[88] Gandhi to Sapru, 25 July 1931, enclosing letter of 24 July 1931 to T. T.
Kothwala, Collector of Surat, Sapru Papers, Series II; Gandhi to H. W. Emerson,
telegram, 24 July 1931, Gandhi to R. M. Maxwell, 24 July 1931, Emerson to Gandhi,
telegram, 25 July 1931, Gandhi to Emerson, telegram, 25 July 1931, *CWMG*, XLVII,
200, 200–1, 202 fn. 1, 202; Bombay FR1, August 1931, Home Poll., 1931, File No.
18/VIII.

ment or restricting local governments' freedom to enforce the law. The blow to Gandhi was only softened by a personal letter from the Viceroy assuring him that all his allegations against the government were under investigation and that he and the Governors took a personal interest in matters relating to the settlement. However, he urged Gandhi to attend the constitutional conference as 'the best way to obtain a real and lasting solution of present difficulties'.[89] Gandhi had indicated to him in reply to a formal invitation to attend the conference that despite the Simla discussions he was still hesitating; and on 25 July he described the chances as 99% against his attending. He was clearly reluctant to go because events in India implied denial of the position for which he had been manoeuvring since Karachi and consequently made his attendance of doubtful utility. To Abbas Tyabji he wrote, 'With reference to Simla we can say the mountain was in labour and did not bring forth even a ridiculous mouse...What is the use of my going to London if the things arising out of the Settlement are not put right? A debtor who cannot pay interest is never going to pay the capital.'[90]

From 4 to 15 August Gandhi was in Bombay, for the meetings of the Working Committee and the AICC and in readiness to sail on 15 August on the ship prepared to take the Round Table Conference delegates. The time for a final decision had come. Government officials and prominent moderate politicians insisted that he should go: he also knew that within Congress such colleagues as Sarojini Naidu and Rajagopalachariar were anxious lest he throw away the opportunity of putting the Congress case. Against them argued Jawaharlal and Vallabhbhai, prompted by the repercussions on their local positions if Gandhi left for London without extracting concessions with which they could satisfy their local clienteles. The recent wave of political assassinations, which Gandhi condemned at the AICC, and the hostility of local youth organizations to any truck with conference procedures, must also have swayed Gandhi towards staying in India. On previous occasions when violence had seemed particularly near the surface of political life, he had seen his personal mission as diverting violence into constructive action and 'sterilizing' its destructive power by launching satyagraha. Nevertheless such widely differing observers as Sethna and Abdul Ghaffar Khan thought Gandhi would ultimately decide to go to London.[91]

[89] Emerson to Gandhi, 30 July 1931, *CWMG*, XLVII, 442–4; Willingdon to Gandhi, 31 July 1931, Home Poll., 1932, File No. 14/30 – K.-W.

[90] Gandhi to Willingdon, 21 July 1931, Gandhi to Chhanganlal Joshi, 25 July 1931, *CWMG*, XLVII, 178, 206; Gandhi to A. Tyabji, 28 July 1931, S.N. No. 9576, Gandhi Papers. To Mr Bolton, 7 August 1931, Gandhi argued that events in Bardoli & U.P. were symbolic of British opinion in Britain as well as among officials in India, hence their significance; S.N. No. 17442, Gandhi Papers.

[91] For contemporary comments on the pressures on Gandhi and the likely outcome see 14 August 1931, Diary of B. S. Moonje; note by Govt. of India Law Member, 12 August 1931, Home Poll., 1932, File No. 14/30 – K.-W.; 17 August 1931, Diary of

Gandhi's inclination and ability to sway the Working Committee in favour of his sailing on the 15th were considerably reduced by two communications which reached him in Bombay from the governments with which Jawaharlal and Vallabhbhai had been in conflict. Bombay replied on 10 August to the points Gandhi had raised with Hotson on 4 August. The letter defended the local government against Gandhi's accusation of a breach of the settlement by attempting to collect land revenue in Bardoli, and the Collector of Surat against the allegation of a breach of faith. The reply also refused to refund the money collected by coercive measures, which Gandhi had requested, though it indicated a slight concession in that no further coercion was to be applied until the next revenue instalment was due early in 1932. Meanwhile Hailey from the U.P. argued to Gandhi that despite his allegations the U.P. government was attempting to hold the scales between landlord and tenant and mitigate the effects of the slump on cultivators. When Gandhi received the Bombay letter on 11 August he protested vigorously to the Governor's Private Secretary and told the Viceroy that in view of the attitude of the Bombay and U.P. governments he felt he must stay in India. The Government of India Law Member, Sir C. P. Ramaswami Iyer, gathered from talking with Gandhi that the main barrier to his departure was Gujarat, not U.P. or the North-West Frontier; and he noted for his colleagues that a little concession to the Mahatma's *amour propre* might do the trick. What Gandhi wanted was an undertaking that no coercion would be applied to those who could not pay, and the judgement of who could pay to rest not with the revenue collector: he felt that his personal honour had been impugned because he had helped in revenue collection on the understanding that there would be no coercion.[92]

Willingdon and his Council judged, however, that no gain would come from further discussion with Gandhi since they believed his aim was still

V. S. S. Sastri; Sethna to Mr & Mrs Barns, 24 July & 15 August 1931, Sethna to McBain, 18 August 1931, Sethna Papers; Chief Commissioner, N.-W.F.P., to Govt. of India, telegram, 30 July 1931, reporting interview with Abdul Ghaffar Khan that day, Home Poll., 1931, File, No. 33/8, part II.

For opposition of the Bombay Youth League to negotiation and its pressure for civil disobedience see Bombay FR1, June 1931, FR1, July 1931, Home Poll., 1931, File Nos. 18/VI & 18/VII. The Nau Jawan Bharat Sabha demonstrated outside the AICC meeting-place on 6 August and then met to condemn Congress participation in the Round Table Conference, Bombay FR1, August 1931, *ibid.* File No. 18/VIII.

Gandhi condemned the assassination of a judge in Bengal and the attempted assassination of the Acting Governor of Bombay in a speech to the AICC on 6 August 1931, *CWMG*, XLVII, pp. 260–5.

[92] R. M. Maxwell, P. S. to Bombay Governor, to Gandhi, 10 August 1931, Hailey to Gandhi, telegram, 6 August 1931, Gandhi to Viceroy, 11 August 1931, Home Poll., 1932, File No. 14/30 – K.-W.; Gandhi to Maxwell, 11 August 1931, *CWMG*, XLVII, 281–2; Hailey's wire was a reply to wire from Gandhi, 5 August 1931, *ibid.* p. 250; note by Govt. of India Law Member, 12 August 1931, Home Poll., 1932, File No. 14/30 – K.-W.

to secure for Congress a status of virtual equality with the government. The Secretary of State agreed with their refusal to concede such a status, and the principle of arbitration in which this was implicit. After discussion with the Prime Minister he urged nonetheless that Willingdon's reply to Gandhi should try to persuade him to leave for London, an approach which would strengthen the government's position if a rupture became inevitable. Consequently Willingdon wired to Gandhi that he regretted a decision which he felt sure must arise from a misunderstanding of the government's policy and had hoped that his personal assurance of concern for the settlement would have convinced Gandhi that he should go to London despite current difficulties arising from it. However, this was not enough to prevent the Working Committee from deciding on 13 August that the Congress should not be represented at the Round Table Conference, though the next day it passed a further resolution making plain that the refusal to send Gandhi to London should not be construed as ending the settlement. Gandhi told Willingdon of both resolutions, regretting the final outcome.[93]

What looked like a final decision in fact left slight room for movement. The Working Committee's refusal to reject the Delhi settlement held the situation rather than precipitating immediate conflict; while Gandhi's letter to Willingdon asserted that he was not insisting on a Board of Arbitration but would be satisfied with 'the justice to which I was entitled'. Gandhi in fact told the press that Congress hoped not to resume civil disobedience and that the door was still 'open for all kinds of negotiations, so long as they are designed to lead the Congress to its destined goal'. Nonetheless he was determined not to go to London unless the government made some sign of trust in Congress which would give him a unique status at the conference table, as he made plain in a press article entitled 'The Real Issue'. The issue between government and Congress, he argued, was the status of Congress as the intermediary between the people it represented and officialdom: Bardoli was the test of the official attitude and if that attitude was one of distrust he believed that the journey to London would be fruitless. The decision was for Gandhi not just a matter of political calculation, a judgement of his London prospects if he went with an indeterminate status, and a balancing act between the conflicting pressures on him. Such was the complexity of his mind, his stress on symbol and gesture and his understanding of political issues as religious questions, that he also saw the decision as a spiritual necessity. Realizing the blow this would be to his English friends, to Lord Irwin, and to Indian moderates such as Sastri, he told C. F. Andrews, 'But the voice within was

---

[93] V to S of S, telegram, 11 August 1931, S of S to V, telegram, 12 August 1931, V to Gandhi, telegram, 13 August 1931, Gandhi to V, 13 August (telegram) & 14 August 1931, *idem*. Text of 13 & 14 August Working Committee resolutions in J. Nehru to PCCs, 14 August 1931, *SWJN*, 5, pp. 12–13.

peremptory, and so when the Viceroy's wire came a great weight was lifted off my back.'[94]

Irwin and Gandhi's British lobby, including Andrews and Henry Polak, a friend from South African days, were shocked at the decision, which Sastri called 'another Himalayan blunder', using Gandhi's own sad description of his misjudgement in launching the Rowlatt satyagraha in 1919. To Sastri it was 'clear proof of the utter incapacity of Congress...and of Gandhi for real constructive work'. He suspected, though Gandhi denied this, that Muslim repudiation of the Mahatma's leadership was at the root of it. Sethna echoed Sastri, condemning the decision as 'monstrous and nothing short of a disaster'. The chorus of complaints was swelled from very different political sources, anxious that the Hindu hand should not be weakened by Congress abstention. *Mahratta* delivered the judgement that boycotting the conference was a national blunder when the constitutional future of India was at stake: compared with Gandhi's acquiescence in Bhagat Singh's execution, sticking on 'minor breaches of the Pact in Gujarat' savoured of 'swallowing a camel and straining at a gnat'. Malaviya was also deeply disappointed though he would not step out of line with Gandhi; while the scornful Moonje refused to stay away from the conference unless Gandhi and Congress capitulated to the Mahasabha on the communal issue.[95]

Immediately after the Working Committee had made its decision, Jayakar and Sapru went into action as intermediaries between Gandhi and the government, hoping to exploit the slight room for movement still present. When they left for London they entrusted the task to the Bombay Liberals, Sir Cowasji Jehangir and Sir Chimanlal Setalvad. They exerted pressure on the Governments of Bombay and India, and through the good offices of the Bombay Congressman, K. F. Nariman, extracted from Gandhi a statement of his terms for going to London. The formula he gave them was, 'Any enquiry into Bardoli collection would satisfy me if it is really impartial and public. Whilst that would be enough to send me to London it should not mean that Working Committee will not press for relief on other matters or failing this satisfaction press for public impartial enquiry.'[96] The Government of Bombay was reluctantly willing to agree to

---

[94] Gandhi to C. F. Andrews, 15 August 1931, S.N. No. 17470, Gandhi Papers; interview to press, 14 August 1931, *The Times of India*, 15 August 1931, CWMG, XLVII, 292–3; 'The Real Issue', *Young India*, 20 August 1931, *ibid.* pp. 319–22. Jawaharlal stressed that the decision had been taken 'particularly on account of U.P.' though he admitted that Bardoli raised a principle of paramount importance; speech in Allahabad, 20 August 1931, *The Leader*, 22 August 1931, *SWJN*, 5, pp. 18–21.

[95] *Mahratta*, 16 August 1931, Bombay Secret Abstract, 1931, par. 4028-A, *HFM*, III, IV, pp. 56–7; Sethna to Mrs Barns, 21 August 1931, Sethna Papers; V. S. S. Sastri to T. R. V. Sastri, 20 August 1931, Jagadisan, *Letters of Srinivasa Sastri*, p. 216; 14 August 1931, Diary of B. S. Moonje.

In a press interview Gandhi had denied that the communal impasse affected the decision, 14 August 1931, *The Times of India*, 15 August 1931, *CWMG*, XLVII, 298.

[96] Gandhi to K. F. Nariman, 17 August 1931, S.N. No. 17492, Gandhi Papers, in

an enquiry if the Government of India thought it a price worth paying for Gandhi's attendance in London, but on 18 August the Viceroy's Council rejected the idea despite the wish of Sir Joseph Bhore and Sir C. P. Ramaswami Iyer to pursue this line of accommodation with Gandhi. The majority argued that to concede an enquiry into Bardoli revenue collections would be but a prelude to other enquiries which Congress would demand and would undermine district administrations: it meant a 'surrender of principle we regard as vital and consequences of which might easily be more grave than those of Congress non-participation in Conference'. The Vice-regal reply to Gandhi's letter of 14 August went off the following day, giving away nothing though expressing government's intentions of adhering to the settlement. At this point Gandhi published the list of complaints he had given to Emerson in mid-July, his famous 'charge-sheet', which appeared in a lengthy edition of *Young India* of 20 August devoted to explaining how the government had broken the Gandhi–Irwin pact. The Government of India responded by publishing Willingdon's 19 August letter to Gandhi, though it withheld its detailed reply to Gandhi's charges at the request of the Secretary of State who feared that it would wreck any possibility of accommodation arising out of the soundings between Gandhi, Nariman, Jehangir and the Bombay government. On 20 August the Vice-regal Council decided unanimously that it must close down the Bardoli discussions and publish the government case. The two previously hesitant members had been swayed by the publication of Gandhi's 'charge-sheet' which would now make any concession look like a surrender; by the terms Gandhi gave Nariman which indicated that Congress would press for further enquiries even if Gandhi went to London; and by the views of governors that fundamental principles were at stake. The Council now felt it could not remain silent before Gandhi's charges as this would be an apparent admission of guilt and a failure to defend local governments. Moreover it was anxious to assure Muslims that they would have a fair deal at the conference table, assuaging their apprehensions on this count which, as Fazl-i-Husain warned the government, sprang from the fact that officials seemed intent on getting Gandhi's approval for a new constitution. The refutation was published on 24 August, despite the wishes of the Secretary of State.[97]

reply to Nariman to Gandhi, 16 August 1931, S.N. No. 17490. For the intermediaries' roles see Jayakar & Sapru to Sir C. P. Ramaswami Iyer, Govt. of India Law Member, 13 August 1931, S.N. No. 17458; Nariman to Desai, 18 August 1931, S.N. No. 17509; V to S of S, telegram, 18 August 1931, Home Poll., 1932, File No. 14/30 – K.-W.

[97] For exchanges between London, Simla & Bombay during this period see Home Poll., 1932, File No. 14/30 – K.-W. Willingdon's letter to Gandhi, 19 August 1931, is included and is also in Gandhi Papers as S.N. No. 17525.

Gandhi's 'charge-sheet', *Young India*, 20 August 1931; statement by Govt. of India with replies of local government to Gandhi's charges, *Gazette of India*, 24 August 1931, Home Poll., 1932, File No. 14/30 – K.-W. The Govt. of India did not however publish the general indictment of Congress activities during the settlement which it had ready in August: this is in Home Poll., 1931, File No. 33/50.

On 20 August it looked as if a stalemate had been reached, Gandhi and the Government of India both insisting that they could not give way on fundamental issues, although the London authorities were anxiously pushing Simla to do all it could to get Gandhi to London without jeopardizing its authority or placing any of its subjects in a particularly privileged position.[98] Gandhi, however, broke the impasse, and also prevented a conflict between Whitehall and Simla. On hearing of his publication of the 'charge-sheet' Sapru and Jayakar wired to him from Aden of their 'painful surprise' in view of their efforts to get the Viceroy and the London government to agree to an enquiry by an independent officer. Gandhi had insisted to the press that he was 'wholly unrepentant' about its publication and could not see that it jeopardized the chances of the government agreeing to an impartial enquiry. However he replied to Sapru and Jayakar that he had no idea that the publication could affect the issue. Largely because of their intervention he simultaneously sent a guarded feeler to Willingdon stating his position.

> I contend that the appointment of an impartial tribunal is implicit in the Settlement in the event of differences arising between the Government and the Congress regarding the interpretation of the Settlement or its working in practice. I have been prepared as I am now to waive such an enquiry if by quiet personal discussion or some such informal means reasonable satisfaction is given to Congress.

He said he would come to Simla if Willingdon thought discussions were necessary, an offer Willingdon took up at once.[99]

Gandhi reached Simla on 25 August, flanked by M. A. Ansari, Vallabhbhai, Jawaharlal and Abdul Ghaffar Khan, men whose particular local or communal positions had impinged heavily on his freedom to make and implement all-India policies for Congress. He approached the renewed discussions without great hopes of a change in the position. The Government of India was also pessimistic, though it was prepared to explore some accommodating formula on Bardoli provided this surrendered no principles it considered fundamental. Its strategy would be to attack the Bardoli question only after clearing away other important issues: it would adhere to its stated position on the question of arbitration and the settlement, and if Gandhi made complaints outside the area covered by the settlement it would agree to no special enquiry, while in future ordinary administrative

[98] S of S to V, 20 August 1931, Home Poll., 1932, File No. 14/30 – K.-W.
[99] Sapru & Jayakar to Gandhi, telegram, 20 August 1931, Gandhi to Sapru, telegram, 21 August 1931, Gandhi to Viceroy, telegram, 21 August 1931, AICC Papers, 1931, File No. G-7; press interview by Gandhi on publication of 'charge-sheet', 20 August 1931, *The Bombay Chronicle*, 21 August 1931, *CWMG*, XLVII, 329; Viceroy to Gandhi, telegram, 22 August 1931, S.N. No. 17575, Gandhi Papers; Gandhi to Viceroy, telegram, 23 August 1931, accepting invitation to Simla, S.N. No. 17582.
    After Gandhi had approached Willingdon he received a further wire from Sapru & Jayakar, 22 August 1931, saying that most of the conference delegates on the ship strongly urged him to make contact with the Viceroy; S.N. No. 17561.

procedures would apply to such complaints, which meant that officials would be the judges of whether any enquiry was necessary.[100]

The negotiations spanned three days, during which Gandhi saw Emerson and Willingdon and consulted with the colleagues who had accompanied him, while Sir Cowasji Jehangir was present at Viceregal Lodge to interpret the Congressmen's thinking to Emerson. As early as 25 August Willingdon thought the prospects were good, since Gandhi had in his first meeting with Emerson agreed to what the government had called the essential preliminary issues, and only Bardoli was left as a stumbling-block. On 27 August agreement was reached in what became known as the 'Second Settlement'. Gandhi agreed to represent Congress at the conference and the March settlement remained operative. The Collector of Nasik was to hold an enquiry into the allegations that certain Bardoli revenue-payers were coerced by use of the police to pay more revenue than would have been demanded had the same standard been applied to them as to other Bardoli villages where revenue was collected after 5 March without police assistance. However there was to be no enquiry into other matters raised by Congress. If complaints connected with the settlement arose in future government would consider any representations carefully; while complaints on matters outside the settlement's provisions would be dealt with according to ordinary administrative procedure. Attached to this statement were two letters which had passed between Emerson and Gandhi, the outcome of consultation between them in which Gandhi after discussion with his colleagues tried to safeguard Congress's right of direct action, even though civil disobedience was in abeyance, if grievances continued or arose and the government refused an enquiry. No agreement was reached on this question and the contrary views were merely stated and appended to the settlement. There was clearly room for future conflict here: but Gandhi insisted, and the government accepted his assurance, that Congress was not intending to revert to civil disobedience but wished to state its reservation of the right to do so if peaceful accommodation proved impossible, in order to guard itself against future misunderstanding or charges of breach of faith.[101]

The Government of India was well satisfied with the outcome. It had conceded a very limited enquiry over Bardoli; but as there was to be no general enquiry into past allegations and no future enquiries except at the discretion of the government it had secured in return an end to Congress claims for arbitration and special treatment, and the virtual merging of the settlement into the ordinary administration. This was a signal relief to

[100] V to S of S, telegram, 24 August 1931, Home Poll., 1932, File No. 14/30 – K.-W.; for Gandhi's pessimism see his letter to S. C. Das Gupta, 21 August 1931, S.N. No. 17545, Gandhi Papers.
[101] V to S of S, telegrams, 25 & 28 August 1931; note by H. W. Emerson, 28 August 1931, on discussions starting on 25 August and culminating in 28 August communiqué; four letters exchanged between Emerson & Gandhi of which the last two, 27 August 1931, were appended to communiqué; Home Poll., 1932, File No. 14/30 – K.-W. Text of second settlement, published 28 August 1931, *CWMG*, XLVII, 449–50.

officials embarrassed by the implications of Irwin's pact with Gandhi for their authority and freedom of action. As Willingdon told Sir Sam Hoare, the Secretary of State who had replaced Wedgwood Benn during the Simla consultations, 'These gains are of great importance and will, we hope, more than counteract grant of enquiry in Bardoli.'[102] From Gandhi's point of view the outcome of the talks had never been a foregone conclusion: up until the final hours he had believed he would be going home to the ashram rather than to London. He also viewed the prospects with considerable apprehension. To Willingdon he wrote on the day of the second settlement,

> Though the colleagues that have been with me have given their heartiest cooperation I know that the ultimate responsibility rests upon my shoulders. I have not come to the decision to go to London without fear, trembling and serious misgivings. Things from the Congress standpoint do not appear to be at all happy but I am relying upon your repeated assurances that you will give personal attention to everything that is brought to your notice.

He urged the Viceroy to trust Vallabhbhai, the other Working Committee members, and Abdul Ghaffar Khan, a plea he repeated to Emerson. Moreover on the train to Bombay he wrote appealing to Hailey to make personal contact with Jawaharlal. 'Seeing that the Settlement continues I venture to suggest that Congress may be trusted and all necessary help requisitioned from it.' In the last hours before he left India he was trying to groom his closest colleagues for the role he had himself performed during the summer. He had not secured formal acceptance of Congress's intermediary status but at least he could try to ensure that the major Congress leaders were accepted personally by government as spokesmen for the people.[103]

Gandhi's departure to London on 29 August to be the sole representative of India's premier political organization at a constitutional conference on the country's future looked like the ratification of very great political authority. It was also manifest that he attracted popular adulation on a scale and of a quality quite different from the support given to his contemporaries in politics.[104] However the concessions the government had actually made to him at Simla were minimal and there were voices which were not slow to comment on this. Moonje considered that Gandhi had made a series of blunders in vacillating through July and August, thus inviting official rebuffs, and then by agreeing to go to London when his prestige

---

[102] V to S of S, telegram, 28 August 1931, Home Poll., 1932, File No. 14/30 – K.-W.

[103] Gandhi to Hailey, 28 August 1931, *CWMG*, XLVII, 370–1; Gandhi to Emerson, 28 August 1931, Gandhi to Willingdon, 27 August 1931, both S.N. No. 17601, Gandhi Papers; Gandhi to R. B. Gregg, 29 September 1931, *CWMG*, XLVIII, 90.

[104] See for example Gandhi's condemnation of pictures which virtually placed him in the Hindu pantheon as 'excessive hero-worship' which 'borders on questionable idolatory, and is calculated to wound susceptibilities of the orthodox'; *Young India*, 4 June 1931, *CWMG*, XLVI, 304.

had been lowered and his position weakened by Muslim opposition. *Mahratta* reiterated its view that Gandhi should have left in mid-August, and pointed out that the delay had gained him 'practically nil' beyond the fuss of a special train from Simla to connect with the train for Bombay! Others were puzzled at this sudden about-turn in favour of London; while in places youth groups proclaimed that Gandhi and his capitalist friends had finally and irretrievably betrayed India's workers and peasants, and that the only hope was violent revolution.[105]

Since Gandhi's return to India from Africa neither British nor Indians had known where they stood with him; and his actions had often seemed incomprehensible to men with more conventional goals and notions of political rationality. His shifts and vacillations in mid-1931 can, however, be explained to a considerable degree by his pivotal position in the operation of the settlement. This was a position he welcomed because of his satyagrahi's perception of right political behaviour and his African experience; while personal pride also prompted him to act as guardian of a settlement of which he had been chief Indian architect at a peak of political influence and prestige.

Although he deliberately moulded a mediatory role for himself he could only play it because it served the interests of others. Local Congress groups welcomed the opportunity for their particular complaints and demands to the provincial and all-India authorities to be put through a person to whom they knew the authorities would listen. Officials confirmed his all-India status by using him as an intermediary with local leaders, in the hope that he would prove a restraining influence, despite their abhorrence of the March pact for having established him in Indian minds as a plenipotentiary who could deal with the government. Willingdon unconsciously betrayed official ambivalence towards Gandhi when he told Hoare of the embarrassment the pact had caused him on these grounds yet hoped that the Secretary of State would be able to make an ally of the Mahatma in London.

> You will find him I think amenable and anxious to help, with a real desire to work out a satisfactory constitution. I do not think you will find him in any way a violent extremist, or that he will be likely to walk out in order to create a demonstration. I must confess to a sense of extreme relief at having got rid of the little man for a few short months, for while we are the best of friends he certainly is the most difficult man to pin down in the matter of negotiations. He may be a saint, he may be a holy man; he is I believe quite sincere in his principles; but of this I am perfectly certain, that he is one of the most astute politically-minded and bargaining little gentlemen I ever came across. Still, I feel that in his new surroundings...he will be a help and not a hindrance.[106]

[105] 28 September 1931, Diary to B. S. Moonje; Bombay FR2, August 1931, Home Poll., 1931, File No. 18/viii; Punjab FR1, September, 1931, *ibid.* File No. 18/ix.
[106] Willingdon to Hoare, 28 August 1931, IOL, Templewood Papers, Mss. EUR.E.240 (5).

Gandhi was also impelled into a peculiar position of political leverage during the peace by the need of non-Congress Hindu politicians, particularly Moderates such as Sapru, Sastri and Sethna, to prevent further conflict between Congress and the raj and secure Congress cooperation in the next round of constitution-making. Not only had they staked much of their political prestige on the first Round Table Conference and therefore wished to prevent the wreck of their endeavours on the rock of Congress intransigence. They genuinely believed that this was the only way for their country to achieve freedom from British control in peaceful and ordered fashion. They saw Gandhi as the key to their hopes and looked to him to lead Congress into cooperation. Their relationship with him, of respect and friendship as well as political calculation, and their consequent pressure on the British to conciliate him, reinforced his all-India position.

However these forces which sustained Gandhi's continental influence in the politics of peace were a passport to leadership within severe constraints. The government would only go so far in doing a deal with Gandhi: and as the August settlement showed weighed the benefits of his cooperation against the repercussions of compromise with him on the services and the Muslim minority. Non-Congress Hindu politicians were unwilling to boycott the conference and let their views go unrepresented, even if it meant breaking with the Mahatma. Moreover local Congress leaderships on whose cooperation Gandhi depended for the implementation of the policies he had steered through the Working Committee and the Karachi session would only accept discipline from an all-India source to a limited degree. The pattern of alliances and the balance of influence between leaders at continental, provincial and district level varied from province to province; but Gandhi could rarely mobilize and control district level activists directly, and more often relied on provincial leaders as intermediaries. They in turn often traded on the Mahatma's prestige if they thought this would strengthen them in relation to officials and potential followers, but they themselves sometimes proved unable to control those who were politically active at district and village level. Consequently Gandhi faced agonizing dilemmas in trying to fashion a policy which would suit his different 'clients', knowing that although these diverse groups wished him to play a pivotal role in the settlement his failure to satisfy their conflicting needs would destroy the basis of his political leverage. These dilemmas lay behind his hesitations and inconsistencies in the summer of 1931.

Gandhi's political failures even more than his successes demonstrated the sources of his strength. His political influence lay primarily in a specific arena of politics, the all-India one where the worlds of Indian politics intermeshed with those of Britain. In local politics Gandhi had much less to offer, and there he exercised proportionately less power, except in Bombay Presidency. This was clear when he attempted to prevent local issues shattering the all-India peace; and when he failed to compose the local disputes of Congress factions.[107] Even in all-India politics some refused to recognize his leadership because they felt that to support or deal with him would only threaten their positions. The bulk of Muslim politicians were the most obvious example.

Gandhi realized that without Muslim support he would be unlikely to gain the concessions he sought from the British at the conference table and consequently would cease to be of such value to Congressmen. However, as he tried to conciliate Muslim spokesmen so he alienated Hindus in the Muslim majority provinces, generating hostility which in turn undermined the status he claimed as the nation's representative.[108] As he failed to conciliate Muslim politicians so he leaned more heavily on those Muslim allies he had, the Nationalist Muslims and Abdul Ghaffar: but they became his jailers and compounded his problems. His deference to the wishes of the group for which Ansari spoke made accommodation with other Muslim politicians even less likely; while his support for Abdul Ghaffar entangled him in a local situation which he neither understood nor controlled, and which threatened to thrust him into conflict with the raj in support of his Frontier ally when other considerations pointed towards peace.

By August 1931 Gandhi had reached a political impasse in India, having failed to secure the observance of the settlement in the manner and to the end he had intended. When he left for London his status as a national representative was not guaranteed. Yet a reversion to civil disobedience appeared impolitic since he had little hope of wide-scale support in the country, would alienate many Congressmen who wished for their views to be presented in London and non-Congress Hindus whose sympathy increased his influence with the government. Moreover a new campaign would attract swift suppression from the authorities.[109] His decision at Simla therefore made considerable sense; for in London, despite his weakness, he could try his hand alone in negotiation with the minorities and the British without constant pressure from his Congress colleagues. Furthermore he could appeal to a broader spectrum of British and world opinion in an attempt to circumvent what he saw as the barrier of official opinion in India blocking the path to swaraj. To go or to stay: it was an unenviable choice which demonstrated the constraints the peace imposed on one who claimed to lead a national campaign for independence.

[107] For example, Gandhi's failure to compose the dispute between the two warring factions of Bengali Congressmen, Gandhi to Dr B. C. Roy, 16 August 1931, Gandhi to B. K. Bhattacharya, 19 August 1931, *CWMG*, XLVII, 302–3, 316.

[108] V to S of S, telegram, 6 September 1931, Home Poll., 1931, File No. 155/I.

[109] Gandhi had known since May that the government intended to hit hard at any renewed campaign of civil disobedience. The extent of its determination is clear from a telegram of 4 August 1931 from Govt. of India to S of S (Home Poll., 1931, File No. 13/8). This recommended that if the Working Committee in Bombay decided in favour of civil disobedience it and local Congress organizations should be declared illegal, Gandhi should be arrested within ten days and the government should take wide Ordinance powers including those of the Emergency Powers Ordinance prepared that summer.

III GANDHI IN ENGLAND

When Gandhi reached England in September he moved into a new political context, where the personalities, institutions and pressures with which he would have to deal differed significantly from those he had encountered in India, and in which a different style of political behaviour was consequently demanded of him. His main task was to place the Congress demand on the conference table and support it in conference and informally among the delegates in negotiation and bargaining. Although Gandhi was a trained lawyer, it seemed unlikely at the outset that he would have the time or the expertise to do this effectively single-handed, particularly as he had so far shown himself to be skilled in more intuitive, face-to-face discussion and compromise than negotiation on constitutional details. His own apprehensions on these counts were muted by a spiritual conviction of vocation and guidance which he expounded to Rajagopalachariar.

> But I must bear the Cross alone and to the fullest extent. When I think of myself with all my limitations and ignorance I sink in utter despair but I rise out of it immediately, as I think and feel that it is God within Who is moving me and using me as His instrument. He will give me the right word at the right moment. That does not mean that I shall make no mistakes. But I have come to believe that God as it were purposely makes us commit mistakes if only to humble us. I know that this is a dangerous belief which can be utilized to justify any error. But I have no doubt about its correctness in respect of all unconscious errors.[110]

At the conference this strange figure, with all the unpredictability and drive of a visionary, encountered a range of Indian spokesmen many of whom were well versed in detailed schemes by which they hoped to preserve their interests under the new constitution. They included India's Princes, who though they had supported the Federal idea at the first Round Table Conference were now deeply divided on the shape of an acceptable Federation and willing to exploit divisions among spokesmen from British India to preserve their own positions. Muslim attitudes had also hardened during 1931, and they stuck to the demand for separate electorates and a weak centre in the forthcoming Federation. Representatives of other communal minorities, Anglo-Indians, Indian Christians, Sikhs and the Depressed Classes, were equally anxious to defend themselves against majority domination; while the Hindu delegates were divided among themselves, the Moderates hoping to get the Federal scheme rapidly into operation, and Mahasabha spokesmen remaining vigilant for the interests of Hindus locally in a minority as in Bengal and Punjab. British politicians were more concerned with their country's acute financial crisis than with India's future, and they were embroiled in the political uncertainties which accompanied the formation of the National Government at the end of

[110] Gandhi to Rajagopalachariar, 28 August 1931, *CWMG*, XLVII, 372.

August. A general election seemed an imminent necessity to give the new government a larger parliamentary majority, a prospect which boded ill for India's chances of a generous constitutional deal; for, as Hoare explained to Willingdon, conservative opinion in and outside the Tory Party was 'very nervous' on the Indian question.

> There is a general feeling that defeatism has corroded the machine of government...My own friends have had their suspicions increased by such speeches as have been made by certain prominent officials in India. They are horrified at the suggestion that we are engaged in shuffling out of our difficulties and liquidating a bankrupt state. Perhaps we here exaggerate these fears. Unfortunately, however, such incidents like the Cawnpore massacres have greatly aggravated them. My own view...is that the great body of opinion in this country is dead against anything in the nature of a surrender on the lines of the Irish Treaty. We are much more likely to make concessions if we feel that we are discarding from strength and not throwing down our hand.[111]

The election he had forecast occurred at the end of October. The result was 470 Tory M.P.s and a dominant Conservative influence in a Cabinet headed by Ramsay MacDonald as leader of a National Government.

To exercise influence in this situation and return to India with a package which would confirm his claim to leadership in Congress Gandhi would have to convince some of his fellow delegates that he could offer them something they wanted, or alternatively threaten something they feared, against which they had no other defence. In this process of interaction and exchange two aspects of Gandhi's position were crucial. One was his image of Congress and himself; particularly his claim as Congress delegate to speak for all Indians[112] – an assertion intensely offensive and provocative to other Indians present. The other was the brief from India to which he had to speak.

Before Gandhi reached England he said he was bound by the Karachi Congress resolution: this was his mandate, though he agreed that it gave him certain manoeuvrability. 'The Karachi resolutions demand control by India of finance, the army and foreign relations subject to safeguards "demonstrably in the interests of India" but also gave the delegation rather loose power to make adjustments necessary in the interests of

---

[111] Hoare to Willingdon, 2 September 1931, Mss. EUR.E.240 (1). Hoare had mentioned his fears that political uncertainty in Britain might delay decisions on India's future in a telegram to Willingdon, 28 August 1931, Mss. EUR.E.240 (11). The Viceroy replied that any delay would have grave political repercussions in India (possibly renewal of civil disobedience and exacerbation of communal antagonism) and might well precipitate a massive financial crisis, including the draining of India's reserves and the collapse of her exchange; V to S of S, telegram, 31 August 1931, *ibid.*

[112] Speech at Federal Structure Committee, 15 September 1931, *CWMG*, XLVIII, 14–17; speech at 30 November 1931 plenary meeting of conference, *Indian Round Table Conference (Second Session) 7th September, 1931 – 1st December, 1931. Proceedings*, P.P., 1931–2, VIII, Cmd. 3997.

India.'[113] However, the Working Committee in session at Ahmedabad, 8–11 September, put its own gloss on the Karachi resolution, and afterwards Jawaharlal and Vallabhbhai both sent Gandhi a note of the points which the Committee thought should be the basis of any settlement with Britain. The essential point was that India's future relationship with Britain should be more than Dominion Status: both parties must have the right to sever the connection. Among the more important details of a settlement should be full Indian control of defence forces (involving among other things immediate withdrawal of British troops) and complete freedom to direct economic policy and finance, which implied no special rights or protection for the British commercial community in India, and an impartial tribunal to assess the relative obligations of Britain and India in relation to the public debt. It also stated that since the services must be manned by people committed to the new order, many of the old civil servants would have to go. Nothing more was added to the Congress position on the communal question: this remained as stated in its July compromise proposal. The note was rigorous on the issue of the Indian States. Although Congress hoped that the States would join an all-India Federation, the minimum conditions for entry were that they should guarantee the fundamental rights of their subjects, that a Supreme Court should protect those rights, and that States' subjects should be represented in the central legislature on an elective basis. The message was plain. Congress was determined not to be swamped by a reactionary bloc of Princes at the centre who ruled their subjects in the old manner and appointed amenable 'representatives' of those subjects to the federal legislature.[114]

When the Mahatma arrived in England he was treated with particular respect. Among the public at large there was considerable curiosity at his dress and habits, even while he was on board ship. Mahadev Desai commented wryly on the voyage: 'There have been no "talks" of a political character for the simple reason none but Bapu is in a condition to carry on a talk. Bapu is thoroughly enjoying himself – if I may use the word "enjoy" about anything that he does. He sleeps on the floor on the deck without scandalising any one and we have our morning and evening prayers without a break.' *The Manchester Guardian* reported on this extraordinary phenomenon of a spartan, praying politician, whose companion, Pandit

[113] Interview at Marseilles, 11 September 1931, *The Daily Herald*, 12 September 1931, *CWMG*, XLVII, 414. Gandhi read out the Karachi resolution on the provisional settlement in the Federal Structure Committee, 15 September 1931, *CWMG*, XLVIII, 17.

[114] J. Nehru to Gandhi, enclosing note, 11 September 1931, J. Nehru Papers, part I, vol. XXIII; Vallabhbhai Patel to Gandhi, enclosing note, 10 September 1931, S.N. No. 17681, Gandhi Papers.
The terms proposed for the States were the same as Gandhi had put at Karachi in speech to Congress, 30 March 1931, *CWMG*, XLV, 368. Ansari, however, at the September Working Committee had tried unsuccessfully to secure agreement on some assurance to the Princes of their future constitutional position. Aney had supported him, but Jawaharlal's vehement opposition had swayed the Committee to reject the idea. M. A. Ansari to Gandhi, 10 September 1931, S.N. No. 17688.

Malaviya, brought with him gallons of ritually pure milk since he had been refused permission to bring a cow in the entourage. The paper continued to report the Mahatma's eccentricities and later published photos of him viewing prize goats at a dairy show in Islington. Crowds flocked to Kingsley Hall, the East End settlement where he stayed; he received hundreds of welcome letters and his appointment book was soon full for weeks ahead.[115] Hindu Liberals and British people who wanted a large measure of consti-tutional advance viewed his arrival with relief and hope; and Indian delegates, including the Princes, hurried to confer with him. He also had personal interviews with Ramsay MacDonald, Hoare, Sankey, Lothian and Irwin, addressed M.P.s of all parties, and was put on the Federal Structure and Minorities Committees. Hoare's first impression of the Mahatma coin-cided with the assessment Willingdon had wired to him as Gandhi left India. The Viceroy now sent an appreciation of the situation for the Dominion Governments: he felt that the results of Gandhi's presence in London were completely unpredictable, but he hoped that Gandhi might assist in a communal agreement and sway Congress into accepting concessions short of their demands if he was convinced of British sincerity and thought that outright rejection of what was offered would alienate world opinion and undermine his personal standing. On his side Gandhi announced, 'My expectations of the Conference are zero if I am to base them on a survey of the horizon[.] But being an optimist I am hoping that something will turn up to make the Conference a success from the national Indian standpoint.'[116]

The first problem confronting Gandhi in the conference was the com-munal impasse. In Sastri's words, 'This time Moslems are more sullen and militant.' When the Federal Structure Committee met on 14 September their demands were put by Shafa'at Ahmad, who with Zafrullah Khan was the strongest and the most unyielding of the Muslim delegation, in close touch with Fazl-i-Husain and orthodox Muslim opinion in India. He called for complete provincial autonomy in a Federation where there would be Muslim majorities in the Bengal and Punjab legislatures secured by sep-arate electorates and reservation of seats on a population basis, while in Muslim minority provinces the reservation would be according to existing ratios. Moreover, the Muslims refused to discuss any federal constitution until the minorities' problem was solved and the nature of representation at the centre of the mainly Hindu States was settled.[117] This stance of

---

[115] M. Desai to J. Nehru, 31 August & 16 September 1931, J. Nehru Papers, part I, vol. XVII; *The Manchester Guardian*, September–December 1931, microfilm, Central Reference Library, Manchester.

[116] Interview at Suez, 5 September 1931, S.N. No. 17643, Gandhi Papers; V to S of S, telegram, 6 September 1931, Home Poll., 1931, File No. 155/1; Willingdon to Hoare, 12 October 1931, Mss. EUR.E.240 (5).

[117] V. S. S. Sastri to V. S. R. Sastri, 24 September 1931, Jagadisan, *op. cit.* p. 219; Muslim Conference Working Committee Resolutions, 13 September 1931, Aziz, *op. cit.* pp. 81–2; note by G. Laithwaite on communal negotiations, 6 November 1931, Mss. EUR.E.240 (65).

course clashed with Gandhi's assertion that he represented all Indians more truly than their supposed spokesmen at the conference. He complained to the Prime Minister

> that the Conference was futile because the other delegates were only the nominees of Government and he was the sole genuine representative of the people. He thought that he could represent the Muslims and the Depressed Classes better than those who purported to do so. He and the British Government could settle the whole question if he was treated as representing everybody.[118]

Gandhi sought to demonstrate his claim for Congress's representative position by insisting that Dr Ansari should be present in London. He maintained that without Ansari he could not accept the Muslim delegates' demands, though he would try to persuade his Nationalist Muslim colleague to agree to them if he came.[119] Naturally Muslims in London resisted Gandhi's determination to import a man who they believed had sold their community's pass, unless they received a substantial *quid pro quo* from Gandhi on the communal question. Ansari disliked being a pawn in this acrid controversy and in desperation began to feel that Gandhi should go ahead alone. Jawaharlal, however, urged Ansari

> not to be so rash as to cable him to do what he chooses. This would put him in a false position. I sometimes wish I was there to have a loving chat with the Muslim delegation. There seems to me to be too much sugariness in its proceedings, at least so far as our side is concerned. That of course is Gandhiji's way and we must not complain. But a little pepper would add to the taste.[120]

Nehru's concern betrayed not merely his personal detestation of anything which smacked of communalism but also his apprehensions at Gandhi's style of negotiation if left to himself. In fact the Mahatma was fast expending his political credit. Tied both by his commitment to Ansari as leader of the Muslim group whose support gave credence to his claims for Congress's special status and by his desire to achieve a communal compromise he generated hostility among Indian delegates instead of convincing them of his leadership value as one who could help secure their aims. His insistence on Ansari's presence further alienated the Muslim delegates: while his frequent assertions that Hindus should give Muslims a blank cheque, and his suggestion that he would bring Ansari round to separate electorates, frightened the Punjabi Sikhs and almost all the other Hindus,

---

[118] Official note on interview between Gandhi & MacDonald, 30 September 1931, *CWMG*, XLVIII, 96.

[119] M. Desai to J. Nehru, 25 September 1931, J. Nehru Papers, part I, vol. XVII; 27 September 1931, Diary of B. S. Moonje.
Gandhi had told Willingdon before he left India that without Ansari he would be 'perfectly helpless' in Hindu–Muslim negotiations in London; 29 August 1931, *CWMG*, XLVII, 382–3.

[120] M. A. Ansari to J. Nehru, 30 September 1931, J. Nehru to M. A. Ansari, 4 October 1931, AICC Papers, 1931, File No. G-30.

including Sastri, Moonje and the normally pliant Malaviya. Hoare told Willingdon that Gandhi had been 'playing a furtive and uncertain game' and that the communal deadlock had prevented any real progress in conference deliberations on other topics[121]

However at the end of September Gandhi agreed to drop his insistence on Ansari's presence, when he was asked by the Muslim delegates to call together the representatives of the different communal groups to discuss the whole communal question. The Minorities Committee was adjourned for a week on 1 October to permit these discussions. *The Manchester Guardian* considered this a hopeful sign, judging that Gandhi would not have agreed if he did not think he could achieve something thereby. Devadas Gandhi, however, reported that his father was deeply pessimistic about the outcome, and believed that the British were exploiting the communal differences in order to retain power; moreover, he felt that he had been asked to chair the informal discussions in a bid to discredit him if they failed. In the event of failure he intended to state publicly that it was the fault of the British. Sastri, too, gathered that this was Gandhi's plan, and it confirmed the belief he had held for some days that the Mahatma was only looking for a decent excuse to pull out of the conference.[122]

At the outset of the discussions Gandhi said that he personally would give the Muslims a blank cheque, but that Congress was intent on a national solution of the communal problem and would therefore accept whatever the group decided on as an agreed demand. However, when the Untouchable, Dr B. R. Ambedkar, pressed for separate representation for the Depressed Classes Gandhi declared that Congress only accepted Muslims and Sikhs as separate political entities. When the Europeans, Anglo-Indians and Indian Christians added their claims for separate representation to those of the Muslims and Sikhs, and Moonje asserted that Hindus in Punjab and Bengal also needed protection, Gandhi was at a loss: according to Moonje he kept sighing and offered to give up the chair. He reiterated that he was tied by the Congress mandate and could not agree to separate representation for any but the Muslims and Sikhs, though he would cable Congress if they came up with a reasonable suggestion. The measure of his confusion and inability to provide leadership in the adjustment of competing interests was his statement on 5 October that he felt

---

[121] 18 & 27 September 1931, Diary of B. S. Moonje; Devadas Gandhi to J. Nehru, 2 October 1931, J. Nehru Papers, part I, vol. XXI; Hoare to Willingdon, 25 September 1931, Mss. EUR.E.240 (1).

The confusions in which Gandhi landed himself were evident in his letter to Sardar Ujjal Singh, 1 October 1931, S.N. No. 17925, Gandhi Papers. 'It is quite correct that I have personally said that I would give a blank cheque to the Mussalmans regarding their demands, but such a statement has added to it a similar assurance to the Sikhs; and for that matter all other communities.'

[122] *The Manchester Guardian*, 30 September & 2 October 1931; D. Gandhi to J. Nehru, 2 October 1931, J. Nehru Papers, part I, vol. XXI; V. S. S. Sastri to V. S. R. Sastri, 24 September 1931, to T. R. V. Sastri, 2 October 1931, Jagadisan, *op. cit.* pp. 218–19, 219–20.

sure Congress would abandon the legislatures if he advised it. By this time he seems to have made an offer to the Muslims that he would agree to their demands for separate electorates, majorities in the Punjab and Bengal legislatures, their present weightage in provinces where they were minorities, 33% of seats in the Federal legislature and residual powers in the provinces in the Federation – provided that the Muslims accepted the Congress demand and agreed to a referendum on the possibility of Joint Electorates when the new constitution came into operation. Although this was a very significant departure from the Congress scheme the Muslims were unsympathetic; and eventually the discussions collapsed on 7 October on the issue of the Punjab. Hindus and Sikhs were at loggerheads with the Muslims over the special problems of this province and could not agree on the appropriate body to adjudicate between their respective claims. The following day Gandhi announced the breakdown in a formal meeting of the Minorities Committee and suggested that they should nonetheless continue to hammer out the future constitution. He hoped that they might yet reach a communal agreement before the end of the conference, but if not he proposed that the constitution should provide for a judicial tribunal to decide unsettled points. He concluded by reading out the Congress Working Committee's July scheme, adding that if this was unacceptable, he was 'not precluded from endorsing any other reasonable scheme which may be acceptable to the parties concerned'. He did not, as Sastri had feared, make this an excuse to opt out of the whole conference procedure, but he did lay much of the blame on the British for having nominated so-called representatives of the communities and for expecting the committee to come to a solution before its members knew precisely what powers they were going to receive under the new constitution.[123]

Hoare reported that Gandhi's handling of the minorities' problem had 'thoroughly mystified everybody' and alienated the Muslims and other minorities, too. He had in fact given scant regard to the problems of the latter, concentrating on effecting a deal with the Muslims; and during the rest of October he renewed informal talks with them in the hope of striking a bargain by which they would support the Congress programme and not line up with the small minorities. On 16 October he apparently put to them the terms of such an arrangement. If they would abandon the minor minorities and submit to the Working Committee any provisional agreement they reached with Gandhi he would agree to the concessions he had already stated in the first week in October, or to an arbitration committee of some members of the Minorities Committee, or to a scheme

---

[123] 2, 3, 5 October 1931, Diary of B. S. Moonje; note by G. Laithwaite on communal negotiations, 6 November 1931, Mss. EUR.E.240 (65); Gandhi's speech at Minorities Committee, 8 October 1931, *CWMG*, XLVIII, 115–19. Gandhi continued to put the blame for the breakdown largely on the British for these two reasons: press interview, 13 October 1931, *Amrita Bazar Patrika*, 15 October 1931, *ibid.* p. 144, speech in Birmingham, 18 October 1931, *Young India*, 5 November 1931.

floated by an I.C.S. man, Sir Geoffrey Corbett, whereby Ambala district of the Punjab would be transferred to U.P., thus increasing the Muslim percentage of the Punjab population. However, this attempt also foundered, on a mixture of Muslim intransigence and the problem of the Punjab. Corbett's scheme which alone appeared to give a glimmering of hope of compromise was torpedoed by the Sikhs. By these manoeuvres Gandhi succeeded in adding the Sikhs to those who mistrusted him; simultaneously he hardened Ambedkar's bitter opposition to him by asserting that Ambedkar did not speak for all Untouchables and that the separate electorates he claimed for them would do them untold harm.[124] The upshot of these informal interchanges was the presentation of a bloc of proposals by representatives of the Muslims, the Depressed Classes, a section of Indian Christians, the Anglo-Indians and the European commercial community, at the next formal meeting of the Minorities Committee on 13 November. The Muslims had realized the strength of their position if they not only refused to do a deal with Gandhi on a compromise formula but attached to themselves other allies. Agreement on joint proposals had been reached on the basis of separate electorates and assured membership of provincial and central cabinets by representatives of the major minorities. Hindus and Sikhs rejected this package, and the committee closed its business, recording its failure to reach any agreed solution. Its chairman, the Prime Minister, offered to make a communal award but only if all the committee members asked him to do so and pledged their support for his decision.[125]

Gandhi's failure to break the communal deadlock showed the inherent weakness of his political position, despite the hope which had greeted his arrival. He had proved incapable of leading Indian delegates into a compromise agreement partly because of his inept and often tactless manner of political bargaining but even more because of his own perception and public assertions of the status of Congress and himself as its spokesman, and the mandate to which he was committed. These prevented him from entering into real negotiations which alone might have solved a problem which had become well nigh intractable once Muslims had drawn together and produced a concerted, hardened demand during the summer of 1931. The minorities' pact confirmed his weakness, strengthening the Muslims who even less than before viewed Gandhi as a leader who could guarantee them what they wanted or threaten what they feared. He had found the

[124] Hoare to Willingdon, 9, 16, 23 October 1931, Mss. EUR.E.240 (1); note by G. Laithwaite on communal negotiations, 6 November 1931, Corbett's scheme, 12 October 1931, Mss. EUR.E.240 (65).

Gandhi's attitude to Ambedkar was clear, e.g. in *The Spectator*, 24 October 1931, *CWMG*, XLVIII, 179. See also E. Zelliot, 'Gandhi and Ambedkar – A Study in Leadership', J. Michael Mahar (ed.), *The Untouchables in Contemporary India* (Arizona, 1972), pp. 69–95.

[125] Second Report of Minorities Committee and Minorities' package of proposals, Cmd. 3997.

whole communal wrangle an excruciating ordeal – torture as he called it even in early October – underlining as it did the contrast between the realities of Indian political life and his ideal of swaraj in which compatriots would trust and care for each other.

Gandhi rejected the minorities' pact outright as an instrument of 'vivisection', a scheme not to achieve responsible government but to share power with the bureaucracy. The Congress would have none of it, he declared in committee, but would 'wander no matter how many years in the wilderness rather than lend itself to a proposal under which the hardy tree of freedom and responsible government can never grow'. He repeated the Congress claim to represent all Indians and concluded with a fierce attack on the Untouchable demand for separate representation. In his view it could never remove Untouchability which he abhorred, 'this bar-sinister, which is the shame...of orthodox Hinduism', but would only create a division within Hinduism; and he for one would resist it with his life. Talking with Hindu delegates later he reiterated his intention to fight against the recognition of the Depressed Classes as a separate political entity.[126] He told Ramsay MacDonald that Congress would never countenance the extension of separate electorates or reserved seats to any but Muslims and Sikhs; but if MacDonald made an award in relation to Hindus, Muslims and Sikhs at the request of those who claimed to represent those three communities, Congress would not object to it. He himself would not sign the letter from the delegates asking MacDonald to make an award, as Prime Minister rather than in his personal capacity, because he felt this would embarrass him in presenting the Congress claim on the constitutional issue. He did, however, persuade Moonje to sign the letter, though Moonje had argued for arbitration by the League of Nations in the belief that the government was not impartial but definitely pro-Muslim.[127]

The Mahatma's obligations as a conference member did not rest with his efforts on the minorities' question. He also belonged to the Federal Structure Committee and participated in its lengthy and tedious deliberations on the details for a Federal Constitution which had been agreed in barest outline at the end of the first Round Table Conference. He attended it for the first time on 15 September when he declared the Congress claim to

[126] 22 November 1931, Diary of B. S. Moonje; Gandhi's speech at Minorities Committee, 13 November 1931, *CWMG*, XLVIII, 293–8. Gandhi later said that this speech was not prepared and that the final declaration, which led to his Poona fast in 1932, 'came irresistibly'. Gandhi to H. Polak, 17 October 1932, *CWMG*, LI, 252.

[127] Gandhi to Ramsay MacDonald, 14 November 1931, *CWMG*, XLVIII, 301–2; 4 & 14 November 1931, Diary of B. S. Moonje.

For Gandhi's attitude in March towards the prospect of a governmental settlement of the communal problem if the communities failed to agree, see above, p. 199, fn. 15. On 17 September Gandhi told Lothian that if the communities could not agree the government should secure agreement through the binding decision of an independent arbitrator, but that it should not arbitrate itself; note by G. Laithwaite on communal negotiations, 6 November 1931, Mss. EUR.E.240 (65).

represent all Indian communities, classes and interests, and read out the Karachi resolution which empowered him to attend the conference and gave him his brief. The tone of his speech was courteous – apologizing for intruding on Britain's domestic crisis – and, in the words of *The Manchester Guardian*, sensational for its moderation, because it stressed that Congress wished for a partnership between India and Britain as equals. Within two days, however, the conference atmosphere was oppressing Gandhi; he complained in committee that the delegates were government nominees rather than 'the chosen ones of the nation', and that the discussions seemed to be interminable and unproductive. He called on the government to put its cards on the table and give delegates concrete proposals to consider, a procedure which would have crystallized opinion rapidly and speeded up the proceedings, but was contrary to the British wish to elicit a working consensus as the basis of a new constitution.[128]

Although the government did not follow Gandhi's proposed procedure the Mahatma stuck doggedly to the work of the committee. In meeting after meeting he made his position plain, on major issues as on small details, from defence to his plea that the salt tax should go. He took his stand on the Congress mandate given at Karachi and in the Working Committee's September gloss, arguing, for example, for adult suffrage in elections to the Federal Legislature, for a Federal Court, for control over defence (though he was ambivalent over the withdrawal of British troops, in contrast to the Working Committee's note), and for an impartial tribunal to review the financial obligations of the existing government before a responsible Indian government could shoulder them: he followed the Congress line on the rights of British firms in India and the special rights of Europeans in criminal trials. He refused to agree to the proposed financial safeguards until he knew whether India was to have the degree of responsibility the Congress demanded, and hinted that in that event safeguards would probably be unnecessary or at least very different from those envisaged at present: his theme was the Congress complaint that Indian financial policy must be in the interests of the Indian people and in no way subordinated to foreign interests, taking the rupee exchange ratio as an example. In virtually every case he found himself a dissenting voice, as he admitted at the close of the conference.[129] By mid-November Hoare was resigned to the impossibility of reaching any compromise with Gandhi, as he reported to Willingdon.

[128] Speech by Gandhi at Federal Structure Committee, 15 September 1931, *CWMG*, XLVIII, 13–20; *The Manchester Guardian*, 16 September 1931; speech by Gandhi at Federal Structure Committee, 17 September 1931, *CWMG*, XLVIII, 26–38.
[129] Gandhi's speech at 30 November plenary meeting of conference, Cmd. 3997. For Gandhi's participation in the proceedings of the Federal Structure Committee see extracts from proceedings of that committee quoted in *CWMG*, XLVIII, 13–20, 26–38, 48–9, 131–2, 151–4, 169–71, 191–3, 209–13, 215–20, 265–6, 303–10, 314–25, 336–42, 342–8, 349–50.

I have had constant talks with Gandhi and as a result I am confirmed
in my view that we cannot possibly make an agreement with him. He
cannot accept anything like our terms and we cannot possibly accept his.
Unless, therefore, something very unexpected turns up, I am afraid we
must accept the fact that he will not agree to our conditions and that
the most that we can hope for is that we will send him back personally
friendly to me and other people, even though he may be politically
opposed to us.

As the Mahatma left London Hoare summed up the position, on which
he had been quite frank with Gandhi: 'there was not a dog's earthly of
satisfying his demand and ... there was an unbridgeable gulf between us.'[130]
   The proceedings of the Federal Structure Committee were not only
intolerably dull, as Hoare admitted; they were also decreasingly productive.
By the second week in November the press was reporting the evaporation
of enthusiasm, the drift of the Princes back to India, and the open pessimism of Gandhi and his friends. *The Manchester Guardian*'s correspondent
reported on 13 November that the conference had failed irretrievably,
blaming MacDonald for not giving a strong lead. A week later Gandhi
admitted that he could see no tangible result coming from the conference.
The communal impasse was largely responsible for this position. After the
breakdown of communal discussions the Muslim delegates would only
agree to continue with conference work provided it did not touch on the
communal question, and even this limited participation evoked condemnation from the Muslim Conference Working Committee. Moreover, the
Princes, fearful of the implications of Federation, took comfort from the
inability of British Indian delegates to agree and became even less willing
to commit themselves to a scheme which might consequently prove unnecessary from their viewpoint.[131]
   As the prospects receded of an agreed federal constitution emerging
from the conference the government considered other ways for British
India to achieve greater responsibility even if the federal idea failed for
the time being to provide the solution to its political problems which the
raj had so eagerly seized on at the end of 1930. In these discussions Gandhi
became involved. As early as 2 October, in a letter to Willingdon, Hoare
floated the idea of provincial autonomy as a first step; and the more
heavily Conservative National Government formed after the 27 October
election took up the idea with alacrity.[132] Sankey, who continued as Lord
Chancellor, investigated Gandhi's opinion on this procedure. Gandhi told
him and MacDonald, whom he saw on 3 November, that he would be
satisfied with a six to nine month postponement of central responsibility

[130] Hoare to Willingdon, 19 November & 3 December 1931, Mss. EUR.E.240 (1).
[131] Hoare to Willingdon, 2, 9, 16 October & 6 November 1931, *ibid.*; *The Manchester
Guardian*, 9 & 14 November 1931; Gandhi to J. Bolton, 21 November 1931, *CWMG*,
XLVIII, 329–30; Muslim Conference Working Committee Resolutions, 20 November
1931, Aziz, *op. cit.* pp. 82–3; Moore, *Crisis of Indian Unity*, pp. 223–32.
[132] Hoare to Willingdon, 2 October & 19 November 1931, Mss. EUR.E.240 (1).

if the provinces were granted what he called real autonomy, which meant depriving the centre of considerable power. When he reported his conversation to the Hindu delegates the following day, he was severely criticized by Moonje, Sastri and Sapru, who thought it was playing into government's hands to agree to such a two-phased approach. Consequently on 6 November he signed in company with the Hindu contingent a letter to MacDonald, drafted mainly by Sastri, which rejected anything but a comprehensive scheme and insisted that the communal deadlock should not be allowed to block the way to simultaneous advance to responsibility at the centre and autonomy in the provinces. The determination of Sapru and his colleagues to torpedo any suggestion of provincial autonomy until the Muslims would deal simultaneously with the centre was met with Muslim refusal to budge until the communal question was settled and they were assured of provincial autonomy on lines which suited them in the Punjab. In general, though, Muslims and other minorities seemed to favour the idea of provincial autonomy as a first step provided it was coupled with an assurance that central responsibility would come as quickly as possible.[133]

Despite hostility from his Hindu colleagues Gandhi continued to discuss his idea of provincial autonomy. He spent the weekend of 7/9 November in Oxford where he met at Balliol the Master of the college, A. D. Lindsay, the Beit Professor of Colonial History, Sir Reginald Coupland, Lothian, who was now Under-Secretary of State for India, and Malcolm MacDonald, son of the Prime Minister and Under-Secretary for the Dominions. With Gandhi were S. K. Datta, an Indian Christian conference delegate, and Henry Polak, now actively lobbying for Gandhi through the India Conciliation Group. Lothian and Gandhi had detailed discussions on ways of creating a Federal constitution, and the former returned to London with the hope that the government could start negotiations with Gandhi on the basis of immediate and more radical provincial autonomy and subsequent election by provincial legislatures of a national convention which would implement a Federal constitution. In the following week the government discussed a two-phased plan of advance circulated by Hoare, but it differed considerably from the idea discussed by Gandhi and Lothian in that there would be no change in the powers of the centre. Gandhi realized this when Hoare told him of his ideas on 12 November. The Cabinet, however, accepted Hoare's plan the following day, its conservative leanings appealing to the Tory members. There followed a political outcry. Sapru and his colleagues fought the proposal in private communication with the govern-

---

[133] Hoare to Willingdon, 6 November 1931, *ibid.*; 4 & 6 November 1931, Diary of B. S. Moonje; 4 & 6 November 1931, Diary of V. S. S. Sastri; S. K. Datta to J. Nehru, 12 November 1931, AICC Papers, 1931, File No. G-60; Gandhi and others (including Malaviya, Sastri, Sapru, Sethna, Jayakar, Mrs Naidu, Thakurdas, Rangaswami Aiyengar, Ujjal Singh & Moonje) to Prime Minister, 6 November 1931, *CWMG*, XLVIII, 271–2.

ment, and in public with the help of Labour supporters and *The Daily Herald*, which denounced the government for embarking on a retreat to the course recommended by Simon's Commission. Shafi and Jinnah who had agreed in private to the plan now repudiated it publicly, and Ambedkar was too nervous to state his support for it in committee.[134]

For his part Gandhi made it clear that his idea of provincial autonomy was very different from the government's plan. He rejected the instalment idea outright and stated three fundamentals of his own proposal.

> Firstly, the statute which embodies provincial autonomy must also embody responsibility at the Centre. Secondly, it must also fix a time limit within which the Federal Constitution with responsibility at the Centre will come into operation. I suggested six months. Thirdly, the provinces must enjoy practically sovereign rights.

The Constituent Assembly he envisaged would decide such matters as the strength of the Federal legislature, but the crucial decisions about central responsibility for finance, defence and foreign affairs would have to be taken at once in London. He enlarged on his ideas, particularly his vision of the scope of provincial power, and their manifest incompatibility with what the government was suggesting, in a meeting of the Federal Structure Committee on 25 November.[135]

The government dropped its plan for advance in two stages at the end of November, and when MacDonald closed the conference on 1 December he announced that the government's policy remained as it had been at the end of the first conference – an all-India Federal government enjoying responsibility subject to certain safeguards, founded on self-governing provinces and princely states: in deference to the delegates' opposition, he said, government would not urge the partial advance of the provinces alone. He also announced that since the communal deadlock held up all progress in the provinces and at the centre the government would make a provisional settlement of the communal question, but he urged the delegates to try to come to an agreement among themselves. Meanwhile the work of the conference would continue through a consultative committee in India and specialist committees on such topics as finance and franchise.[136]

Gandhi made his last major speech at the conference the night before the Prime Minister's statement, knowing that he could not influence the

---

[134] S. K. Datta to J. Nehru, 12 November 1931, AICC Papers, 1931, File No. G-60; Hoare to Willingdon, 26 November & 3 December 1931, Mss. EUR.E.240 (1); Moore, *op. cit.* pp. 235–7.

Hoare insisted in his 26 November letter to Willingdon that the government had no intention of reverting to Simon's proposals, and considered provincial autonomy as an interim measure as there was clearly going to be delay in achieving a Federation.

[135] Press interview, 14 November 1931, *The Hindustan Times*, 16 & 18 November 1931, *CWMG*, XLVIII, 300–1; speech at Federal Structure Committee, 25 November 1931, *ibid.* pp. 336–42.

[136] Prime Minister's statement, 1 December 1931, *Indian Round Table Conference 7th September – 1st December 1931*, P.P., 1931–2, XVIII, Cmd. 3972.

Cabinet's decision. It was an impassioned statement of his vision of Congress as representative of all Indians and a plea that the British should trust the Congress. He claimed that he had come for compromise and a permanent settlement, but only if India could thereby gain real liberty: so far, he confessed, he had seen no signs that Congress and the British meant the same thing when they spoke of liberty, and if this continued to be so there could be no compromise. He repeated his assertion on his arrival in London that he sought partnership with Britain, but said he feared they might have come to the parting of the ways and that if no honourable settlement was forthcoming he would again have to lead India into civil disobedience. Two days later he repeated his tentative opinion that the official attitude meant a break and the possibility of renewed civil disobedience, and he underlined the fact that though he had agreed to come to London for discussions his real hope for Indian swaraj lay in the Indian people themselves.

> I never believed that we would get anything more than what our own internal strength entitled. The Round Table Conference negotiations have been a method of finding out the measure of our strength compared with those with whom power at present resides. We have evidently failed. The Congress, therefore, must refill the battery so that it will be powerful enough to do its work.[137]

He maintained that he had no wish to renew the conflict, and he knew from conversations with Hoare that the government would crack down on a new civil disobedience campaign. But his vision of satyagraha as the great self-strengthening technique for its exponents must have made him feel that another campaign would be morally and politically productive compared with the unedifying and fruitless wrangling he had experienced during the conference. Hoare, having seen Gandhi on 4 December, judged that he did not wish to revert to civil disobedience; though he realized that he was disturbed at the safeguards proposed, the possible restrictions on the scope of the proposed standing committee's deliberations, and by the Ordinance powers taken by the Bengal government against terrorism. Hoare had replied that though safeguards were fundamental to the federal scheme there could be discussion on their machinery, while the government would not have decided to appoint a standing committee if it was not prepared to listen to its views on federal problems. When Gandhi wrote en route for India asking Hoare to confirm this conversation he obviously aimed at keeping the question of safeguards wide open, and in Hoare's judgement hoped that this would strengthen his hand in arguing for continued cooperation on his return home.[138]

[137] Gandhi's speech at second plenary meeting of conference, 30 November 1931, Cmd. 3997; press interview, 3 December 1931, *The Hindustan Times*, 6 December 1931, *CWMG*, XLVIII, 380–1.

[138] Hoare to Willingdon, 3 & 10 December 1931, Mss. EUR.E.240 (1); Gandhi to Hoare, 7 December 1931, Hoare to Gandhi, 16 December 1931, Mss. EUR.E.240 (16).

Gandhi's performance in formal conference business and in discussion with delegates and British officials was judged a disaster by some of his Indian contemporaries. Throughout the conference Moonje had been critical of what he saw as Gandhi's weakness and inconsistency. At the close of the conference he judged that the Muslims had been 'placated' and weaned away from Gandhi by the grant of provincial status to the Frontier and Sind and by the promise of provincial autonomy; and that consequently Gandhi would find it more difficult to revive civil disobedience. He believed they would actually get little more than Simon's proposals, predicting that central responsibility would be long postponed, the Princes under the thumb of the Government of India would not participate, while the Muslim provinces might similarly refuse to enter a Federation. Subhas Bose, who was not in London, considered that Gandhi absent in 1930 was more influential than Gandhi present in 1931. He put this down partly to lack of planning behind Gandhi's visit and the diversity of his activities in England, and also to the timing of his visit which he thought predisposed it to failure. Bose calculated that Gandhi should have gone to the conference table in 1930 if he intended to cooperate, but placed himself at a grave disadvantage the following year by attending without a prior assurance of Dominion Status, alone at a conference which was already in being, whose delegates were chosen on communal lines, and when Labour was out of power.[139] Bose also criticized the Mahatma's political tactics at the conference, and there was some truth in this. He had proved a skilled negotiator within Congress ranks, and was in his element making grand moral assertions and appeals and passionate personal commitments, but his aptitudes and interests ill fitted him for balancing the niceties of constitutional provisions among people suspicious of his intentions and anxious to protect their future positions. He proved unable to rally Indian opinion behind him either in the committee work or in the backstage negotiations. Hostility towards him increased among Indian delegates during the conference, though even Srinivasa Sastri had commented within days of his arrival that although it was good that Gandhi had arrived he was 'a PROBLEM himself!' Polak, moreover, had to urge Gandhi to be open to easy contact with Indian delegates and so dispel suspicion and misunderstanding.[140]

For the Bengal Ordinances see below, p. 265.

Moonje reported in his diary, 27 November 1931, that when Gandhi told them of his conversations with Hoare and the certainty of a severe government offensive against renewed civil disobedience he 'appeared bourne [sic] down by the responsibility of having to start again the Campaign of Civil Disobedience and the certainty of heavy repression by Govt.'

[139] 1 December 1931, Diary of B. S. Moonje; Bose, *The Indian Struggle 1920–1942*, pp. 226–31.

[140] Polak urged Gandhi to keep in touch with Sastri, Sapru, Jayakar and Ramachandra Rao, and also Ali Imam and Sultan Ahmed, for a start: Polak to Gandhi, 13 October 1931, S.N. No. 18092, Gandhi Papers; V. S. S. Sastri to G. V. Gundappa, 22 September 1931, Jagadisan, *op. cit.* p. 218.

Gandhi failed politically as an all-India leader at the Round Table Conference. Unable to solve the communal problem he became enmeshed in fruitless constitutional discussions and returned without either an assurance of Indian advance to the relationship with Britain which Congress had demanded, or recognition that Congress was more than one of a number of Indian parties involved in the political discussion. His weakness lay partly in his political style, but predominantly in the constraints imposed on him by his perception of his own role and the status of Congress, and by the terms of the Congress mandate. As a result of these limits to his flexibility he had little to give in exchange for support at the conference, given the hardening of Indian attitudes during 1931. Because of his attitude to the minorities and their 'representatives' in relation to Congress, and the nature of the Congress plan for a communal settlement, he could offer nothing but a threat to the minorities, whatever his conciliatory words. Instead of backing the Mahatma's demands to the British in return for an acceptable Congress assurance of their position in the new dispensation they looked to the British for protection *via* an award and a statute. Moreover, Gandhi's attempts to solve the problem or at least to find a way forward bypassing the impasse alienated many of the Hindu delegates who were his natural allies. As a result of this Gandhi lost the leverage he might have had over the British and the Princes as the spokesman of a united British Indian delegation, and they consequently had no incentive to countenance the claims he advanced in the Congress name. This was in marked contrast to his peculiarly influential position earlier that year when as leader of a surprisingly strong and popular civil disobedience movement he had seemed a valuable ally and potentially dangerous opponent to the British, the Moderates and even some Princes, one with whom it was therefore necessary to do a deal.

The Mahatma was well aware of his weak position. He had realized in 1929 that the communal problem would be crucial to the influence the Congress representatives could wield at any conference, and for this reason had insisted on a guarantee that Congress's claim of Dominion Status would be granted as a condition of Congress representation at the first Round Table Conference when prior communal agreement had proved impossible. It was for the same reason that in 1931 he fought for government recognition of Congress as a body representing all Indians and intermediary between the raj and its subjects. When he came to London in the autumn it was not because that recognition had been granted and his strength in conference assured, but partly because the political prospects for himself and the Congress were worse if he stayed at home when his colleagues and the rank and file were divided and at times uncontrollable, and when the government was ready to stamp on any renewal of direct action.

There was a further reason for Gandhi's journey to Britain. He was determined to circumvent the raj's bureaucracy and appeal to public opinion in Britain and the western world. He was under no illusion that his pact with Irwin was the result of any radical change in British policy towards India: he therefore wished to appeal to those who could put pressure on the raj, particularly British taxpayers and their representatives in Parliament, who finally called the British tune in India. In terms of his experience of satyagraha this made sense. His previous campaigns in India and Africa had succeeded in an immediate, political rather than personal and moral sense only when the authority against which they were directed was in turn pressurized by a higher authority which, for its own reasons, desired an end to the campaign. Champaran in 1917 and Bardoli in 1928 were the prime examples, when local governments had been forced to make concessions by the Government of India. Now Gandhi hoped to activate British public opinion and Parliament into forcing the Government of India to make concessions; and he insisted that his most important task in Britain lay outside the formal parameters of conference work.[141].

Gandhi's political activities in Britain outside the conference milieu were therefore directed to moulding British opinion, and he seized on every chance to inform the public of his personal priorities and the claims of Congress. In this he was assisted by a number of English friends, including C. F. Andrews, who helped to organize his timetable.[142] Press statements on particular issues and interviews discussing his general position were important means of contacting the public, and editors welcomed the Mahatma's eagerness to expound his views. Evelyn Wrench, editor of *The Spectator*, for example, published an account of an evening's conversation with Gandhi which covered his political hopes for India, communal differences, his religious beliefs and his daily diet.[143] Gandhi also spoke to individuals and groups outside the media who were significant spokesmen for sections of British opinion or influential in moulding public attitudes. Early in his visit he addressed M.P.s of all parties at a meeting at the Commons under the auspices of the Commonwealth of India League. Labour members were the most sympathetic and he spoke to them separately the day after his first speech at the conference, attracting considerable public comment by conducting his evening prayers in the Commons' precincts after the meeting. Hoare gathered that he did not make a good impression on most M.P.s who encountered him.[144] He also spoke to formal

[141] Speech at National Labour Club reception, 12 October 1931, *CWMG*, XLVIII, 139; speech in Birmingham, 18 October 1931, *Young India*, 5 November 1931.

[142] Andrews organized Gandhi's Lancashire visit at the end of September, for example; *The Manchester Guardian*, 19 September 1931: he also corresponded with people on the continent about arrangements for a possible European tour by Gandhi; Andrews to various people in Germany, 4 November 1931, S.N. No. 18242, Gandhi Papers.

Gandhi's activities in Britain were recorded in detail in articles and M. Desai's 'London Letter' which appeared in *Young India*, 24 September – 31 December 1931. A brief engagement diary, 14 October – 31 December 1931, is in *CWMG*, XLVIII, 459–68.

[143] *The Spectator*, 24 October 1931, *ibid.* pp. 175–81.

[144] *The Manchester Guardian*, 17 September 1931; Hoare to Willingdon, 25 September 1931, Mss. EUR.E.240 (1).

gatherings and small groups primarily concerned with imperial policy. His Oxford conversations in November were among the most important of such occasions: so was his speech on 20 October at Chatham House, where Lothian presided at a meeting arranged by the Royal Institute of International Affairs. On this occasion Gandhi presented a moderate and largely factual picture of India and depicted the Congress aim as a state whose primary concern would be the care of the masses. Only when questioned on the political situation did he agree that 'Congress wanted nothing short of complete political independence, and therefore complete control over the army, foreign relations and finance'. G. P. Gooch said that this meeting was one of the best he had known there, and Mahadev Desai unabashedly called it a great success. Even the critical Moonje conceded that Gandhi had been good on the present political situation though he abhorred Gandhi's condemnation of Untouchability as washing Hindu dirty linen in public.[145]

Concentrating on explaining his views to what he considered key segments of the British public, Gandhi visited a number of universities including Oxford, Cambridge and Manchester, when he spent whole weekends. He even accepted invitations to some major public schools. His tactics were clear when he told about fifty Etonians, 'You occupy a big place in England. Some of you will become prime ministers and generals in future and I am anxious to enter your hearts whilst your character is still being moulded': Mahadev Desai's account was headed 'Among Future Empire-Builders'. [146] Desai reported to Jawaharlal that Gandhi was also giving a lot of time to bishops and archbishops, and that an idea was abroad that the archbishops might appeal to the government to come to an agreement with India honourable to both sides. Even if no immediate political results ensued from such contacts, Gandhi evidently judged that a Christian lobby might be important for him. He had easy access to Christian groups through C. F. Andrews and his Quaker friends, including Horace Alexander; and it was in such circles that he could most easily put across the spiritual content of his message and what he saw as the morality of his political stand. Among the prominent Anglicans he met were the Archbishop of Canterbury and the 'Red Dean' of Canterbury, Bishop Bell of Chichester, and the Bishop of Birmingham. He also addressed a meeting at Church House, Westminster, which was presided over by the Archbishop of York and attended by thirty-two bishops and other church leaders.[147] He met Quakers in Birmingham, and spoke several times at the Friends' House in London. Other important encounters with Christian groups were a missionary conference on 8 October and a meeting in London on 22 September when he spoke on voluntary poverty to a group dedicated to

[145] Speech at Chatham House, 20 October 1931, *International Affairs*, November 1931, *CWMG*, XLVIII, 193–206; 20 October 1931, Diary of B. S. Moonje; M. Desai to J. Nehru, 23 October 1931, J. Nehru Papers, part I, vol. XVII.

[146] *Young India*, 12 November 1931.

[147]M. Desai to J. Nehru, 23 October 1931, J. Nehru Papers, part I, vol. XVII; *Young India*, 22 & 29 October, 5 November 1931; *The Manchester Guardian*, 22 October 1931.

Franciscan ideals which then published his talk. In this he emphasized his claim that the roots of his politics were a spiritual commitment to the service of humanity.[148]

Although Church leaders were a significant force in moulding vocal opinion towards India, Gandhi was determined to get to the grass roots of British society in his attempt to generate sympathy for his cause which would sway officialdom in India and the social class from which officials were drawn. H. N. Brailsford, who had reported on police activity in Gujarat in 1930 to the discomfort of the Governor and Viceroy, recorded that Gandhi intended to get at the middle class through the workers. It was partly for this reason that he chose to stay in an East End Settlement while he was in London rather than enjoy the comforts of a suite at the Ritz in the style of the Aga Khan or a West End flat like Malaviya. It was also of course a public demonstration of his identification with the poor of India. He was received in Bow with extraordinary curiosity and friendliness, thousands gathering to catch a glimpse of him and cheering when he appeared; a reception which astonished him and Desai.[149]

Friendliness from working people also greeted him in Lancashire, where he went for a weekend on 26 September. Realizing the political importance of the Lancashire lobby and knowing that the boycott of foreign cloth had hurt the Lancashire cotton industry at a time of depression and unemployment, he deliberately made contact with employers and operatives in the cotton trade in order to explain his position. He had a meeting with the Joint Committee of Cotton Trade Organizations in a private house near Bolton at the invitation of the Chairman, and received deputations from the unemployed. Although he expressed distress at local poverty and unemployment to which his campaign had contributed he insisted that Lancashire could never hope to revive its India trade, and that Indian poverty and unemployment were infinitely worse. Despite his firm stand on *swadeshi* both sides of the cotton industry were impressed by his honesty and humanity.[150] Gandhi's attempt to secure the sympathy of working people and their understanding of the issues involved for India was equally plain when he addressed a meeting of the Postal Workers' Union. Having described the state of Indian postmen and India's struggle for independence as he saw it he concluded, 'You can certainly mould public opinion. We may have to go through fiery ordeals of suffering and, when you hear of them, you will recall tonight's meeting and give your share. It is bound to count.'[151] Gandhi was evidently preparing British opinion

[148] Speech at Guildhouse Church, 23 September 1931, *CWMG*, XLVIII, 50–8; speech at missionary conference, 8 October 1931, *ibid.* pp. 120–8.

[149] *The Manchester Guardian*, 14 September & 13 October 1931 (Brailsford's article is in 13 October edition); M. Desai to J. Nehru, 15 September 1931, J. Nehru Papers, part I, vol. XVII.

[150] *The Manchester Guardian*, 28 September 1931; press statements, 26 & 27 September 1931, interviews with unemployed, 26 & 27 September 1931, *CWMG*, XLVIII, 65–6, 75–7, 68–9, 73–4.

[151] Speech at Postal Workers' Union meeting, 5 November 1931, *ibid.* pp. 268–70.

to assist him in any renewal of conflict with the raj. He returned to this idea the night before he left London, telling a small group of English friends that he foresaw a time of great strain ahead, during which he would need people in England who could interpret the Indian situation to the British public, 'who could pass between various circles here and who would keep closely in touch with India'[152]

Although the moulding of British opinion was perhaps Gandhi's major concern while he was at the conference, he also tried to appeal to a wider world audience; partly because he felt he had a universal mission to spread the doctrine of satyagraha, but more immediately because foreign pressure might well be a weapon in the Congress cause in any renewed conflict. Just as the Viceroy and Secretary of State had tried to guard themselves against foreign accusations of stubborn refusal to come to terms with Congress at the end of 1930, so Gandhi also played to a world audience. The day after he reached London he broadcast to America, calling for world-wide cooperation for India 'in her mighty struggle' for liberty. He stressed that India could only continue the glory of her ancient civilization as a free nation, and that Indians were breaking new ground in their non-violent attempt to achieve 'a successful, bloodless revolution'. As a result of this broadcast he received many letters from Americans, and followed up his publicity by accepting an invitation from American journalists to a luncheon at the Savoy.[153] He also contemplated a visit to America, and an extensive continental tour en route for home, telling Vallabhbhai that he thought acceptance of the many continental invitations he had received was 'likely to be serviceable to our cause'. However, news from India and Bengal in particular disturbed him, and at the end of October he asked Vallabhbhai whether it was advisable for him to be away from India until mid-January, the date he expected to return if he did travel on the continent. Vallabhbhai wired back that he personally hoped Gandhi would return as soon as possible because tension was increasing in India and failure at the conference seemed certain. However, he consulted the Working Committee at an emergency meeting on 7 November which only he, Jawaharlal, Aney, J. Bajaj, K. F. Nariman and J. Daulatram attended. They agreed with his personal reply to Gandhi but left the final decision to Gandhi as he had indicated that he considered his presence necessary in London. However, even before the opinion of this meeting reached Gandhi he cancelled his continental engagements, counting the influence he might exert in India more important than an appeal to European opinion.[154]

[152] Agatha Harrison to Gandhi, 2 December 1943, sent by her to L. Amery, 2 December 1943, Mansergh & Lumby (ed.), *The Transfer of Power 1942–7. Volume IV*, p. 510. Agatha Harrison of the Fellowship of Reconciliation took up this work in 1932, as Gandhi had suggested.

[153] Broadcast to America, 13 September 1931, published in *The New York Times*, 14 September 1931, *CWMG*, XLVIII, 8–10; *Young India*, 29 October 1931.

[154] Gandhi to Vallabhbhai Patel, 26 October 1931, *Letters to Sardar Vallabhbhai Patel*, p. 11; Gandhi to Vallabhbhai Patel, telegram, 31 October 1931, S.N. No. 18211, Gandhi Papers; Vallabhbhai's telegram in reply, 3 November 1931, S.N. No. 18240.

Bose later criticized Gandhi for not spending time in America and Europe contacting important politicians and League of Nations figures in order to make India an international issue; and was scathing about the apparently unimportant people the Mahatma chose to meet in England. He attributed this choice of contacts to Gandhi's dual role as a world teacher and political leader, concluding that the duality inhibited Gandhi as a political bargainer and wasted time he should have spent on rousing political support.[155] Nevertheless the pay-offs of Gandhi's diverse public appeals were considerable in the next three years when the Government of India was harassed by the knowledge of the Secretary of State's need to consider and conciliate those sections of the British and American public who saw Gandhi as a spiritual as well as political leader who could not be treated as a common or garden rebel. It was precisely because he had demonstrated that he was more than a politician, because he conceived of and presented his political aims in such wide terms, that he became a crucial figure in determining foreign reaction to Congress claims and the Indian political situation. This increased his significance to Indians and officials of the raj, adding a further dimension to the leverage he already exercised between interacting groups in Indian politics.

By the end of 1931 the disintegration of the unique leadership role Gandhi had built up occurred temporarily in situations where he had to descend from generalities to the particular – when he was not leading civil disobedience as a cohesive and integrating tactic for a wide span of people with diverse interests and ideals, or when he was not making sweeping claims in the name of liberty and morality. When precise issues were at stake, whether lands in Gujarat, rents in U.P., or the number of seats for a community in the legislatures, he was the prisoner of his own perceptions and the conflicting needs and demands of those he claimed to represent. Then his political resources, among them the tactics he could or would adopt, proved an inadequate foundation for leadership. Gandhi's political position would have been simpler, and on such occasions stronger, had he been the spokesman of a united group with a clear aim and had recognized himself as such. The events of 1931 after his pact with Irwin, in India but particularly in London, showed that his leadership position was neither static nor assured. His political influence, as one who exerted leverage because he was pivotal in the interaction of the groups who were active in or impinged on the world of all-India politics, depended on the issues at stake, the institutions involved, the people and perceptions which made up the political environment. During 1931 that environment changed, reducing Gandhi's utility to erstwhile followers and others involved in the processes of political interchange, lessening his leverage and so undermining his political strength.

For the Working Committee meeting on 7/8 November 1931 see Bombay FR1, Home Poll., 1931, File No. 18/xi; *Young India*, 12 November 1931. Gandhi announced the cancellation of his continental tour on 9 November 1931, *CWMG*, xlviii, 276.
[155] Bose, *op. cit.* pp. 226–31.

CHAPTER 6

The frustrations of conflict

I THE RENEWAL OF CIVIL DISOBEDIENCE

Gandhi's departure for London after the August settlement had been the choice of a lesser evil politically, the gamble of trying his hand alone in Britain rather than remaining enmeshed in certain controversy with the government generated by the needs of particular groups of Congressmen. The Simla settlement had not ended either these conflicts or divisions within Congress and London proved but a temporary escape for the Mahatma. During his absence events in India worked to curtail his options on his return, empty-handed, in December.

The rifts among Congress leaders left behind were clear when at the September meeting of the Working Committee Jawaharlal, with the support of Rajendra Prasad and K. F. Nariman, urged that Congressmen in U.P., Madras and Berar should be allowed to adopt 'defensive direct action' in response to what they saw as official breaches of the settlement. Vallabhbhai, as President and also as a Gujarati who knew that the enquiry conceded at Simla was easing his local situation, argued against their suggestion as one which might plunge the whole subcontinent into conflict for the sake of particular localities while the Mahatma was absent. He won the day, and all that emerged from the discussion was a rejoinder to the reply which government had made to Gandhi's 'charge-sheet'.[1]

Nonetheless Congress leaders' attempts to refurbish and strengthen the Congress organization looked ominously like preparations for further conflict. Jawaharlal exhorted PCCs to start village and *mohulla* committees and to organize volunteer units in preparation for a possible crisis before Gandhi's return, and 'for all contingencies and eventualities' should he return without success. Hardikar and Jawaharlal both spent considerable time in chivvying the provinces into forming volunteer groups, and handed Mrs Kamaladevi Chattopadhyaya the task of organizing a women's volunteer wing. Only Karnatak and Bombay produced a significant response, and even they came nowhere near the quota suggested in October 1931 by the Central Board of the Hindustani Seva Dal; while the standards of fitness and instruction in the Seva Dal's training camps were low.[2] Nehru

---

[1] Bombay FR1, September 1931, Home Poll., 1931, File No. 18/IX; Congress rejoinder in supplement to *Young India*, 24 September 1931 & subsequent issues.
[2] J. Nehru to PCCs, 31 August 1931, *SWJN*, 5, pp. 27–8.
For evidence on volunteer organizations see Bombay report on Congress obser-

and Patel took pains to try to integrate the youthful periphery into the main streams of Congress activity, urging that separatist activities only lowered Congress prestige and deprived it of the unity essential for strength in conflict.[3] Vallabhbhai in appealing for unity to the Bombay Youth League at the end of September now specifically stated that he thought it would be best to call Gandhi home and re-start civil disobedience. Among the reasons for this he cited the shooting of two detenus in Hijli camp in Bengal on 16 September by the police guard, and two matters under discussion in the Assembly – a Press Bill designed to suppress incitements to murder and violence, and the Emergency Finance Bill to cope with the continued fall in government revenue and maintain India's credit, which heralded heavy taxation and a 10% cut in government servants' pay. As one of Sapru's Bombay correspondents recognized, there was fertile soil for the seed of a further struggle. The growing agrarian crisis, increased taxation, government retrenchment slashing people's jobs, and business worries over the linkage between the rupee and the pound at 1/6d boded ill for Gandhi's ability to avoid a new campaign if he returned empty-handed.[4]

The real drive towards renewed conflict came however from specific local confrontations between the raj and Congressmen or their allies. Gujarat, in contrast to the earlier months of 1931, provided little occasion for controversy. Vallabhbhai protested to officials about the patels of the village of Ras who had not been reinstated, but few such controversial cases now remained. In November Congressmen withdrew from the Enquiry Commission because government would not disclose all its records. However, when in December Vallabhbhai told the people of Bardoli and Valod to prepare for a new fight it was a case of Vallabhbhai trying to goad the Gujaratis rather than their demands pushing him into battle. He himself admitted that it would be more difficult to bring Bardoli to its pitch of

vance of the settlement, 28 December 1931, Home Poll., 1931, File No. 33/50; Bombay FR1, Delhi FR1, October 1931, Home Poll., 1931, File No. 18/x; Bombay FR1, Delhi FR1, C.P. & Berar FR2, November 1931, *ibid.* File No. 18/xi; Madras FR1, C.P. & Berar FR2, December 1931, *ibid.* File No. 18/xii; correspondence between J. Nehru & N. S. Hardikar, October 1931, Hardikar Papers, File No. iii; report by Hardikar, 3 November 1931, on Hindustani Seva Dal work, 10 August – end of October 1931, AICC Papers, 1930, File No. Misc. 9.

The minimum suggested in October for the country was 6,000: by late October 1,137 were trained or being trained, including women and children; of these Bombay produced 220 and Karnatak 345. The work had been financed from existing Seva Dal funds (Rs. 3,000), donations from Bombay merchants (Rs. 1,000) and a Working Committee grant (Rs. 2,500).

[3] Punjab FR2, September 1931, describes Jawaharlal's criticisms of Punjab frittering away energies which should have been channelled into disciplined volunteer work, Home Poll., 1931, File No. 18/ix; he reported to Gandhi, 27 September 1931, that he had given the Punjab 'Naujawans...a severe drubbing', *SWJN*, 5, p. 47; J. Nehru's speech at Punjab Political Conference, 26 September 1931, *ibid.* pp. 295–6.

Speech by Vallabhbhai at meeting organized by Bombay Youth League, 30 September 1931, extract from report by Commissioner of Police, 1 October 1931, cited in Bombay report on Congress observance of the settlement, 28 December 1931, Home Poll., 1931, File No. 33/50.

[4] D. G. Dalvi to Sapru, 21 October 1931 (D 13), Sapru Papers, Series ii.

1928–30; and in most places in the district villagers refused to pay for his entertainment.[5]

In Bengal the terrorist attacks which Gandhi had condemned before he left continued, evoking official response which in turn became a source of pressure on Gandhi. Dacca's Divisional Commissioner was shot and wounded on 21 August, and a Muslim Police Inspector was shot dead while watching football in Chittagong a week later: these attacks were followed in October by assassination attempts on the Dacca District Magistrate and E. W. Villiers, President of the European Association. Young Hindu men were the assailants in each case, but in December two Hindu girls shot the Tippera District Magistrate at point-blank range. This situation caused the government increasing concern partly because of its devastating effect on the morale of local officials. One senior I.C.S. man in Bengal even suggested that all European officers should be withdrawn to headquarters towns and the districts left in charge of Indian officials. Moreover Muslims were roused by the murder of their co-religionist police officer, and the dangers of a European backlash were very real after the European casualties. Ironically the day before Villiers was attacked he had told Emerson that his Association had had great difficulty in restraining some of its members from taking self-protective measures against picketers and law-breakers.[6] This deteriorating situation lay behind the Press Bill which became law on 9 October, and the government's decision to take emergency powers under two Ordinances on 29 October and 30 November, enabling the arrest and detention of terrorists without trial and the cooperation of the civil and military authorities in rounding up terrorists in Chittagong. News of this disturbed Gandhi in London. It was just the sort of situation he had hoped to avoid by his summer manoeuvres. On 24 November he had forwarded to Hoare a cable he had received from Vallabhbhai recounting police activities under Ordinance regulations and pressure from Bengal's Europeans for further government action: he reverted to the question of the Bengal Ordinances in his final interview with the Secretary of State who judged that this was one of the potentially dangerous factors influencing Gandhi's attitude towards civil disobedience on his return.[7]

A further threat to all-India peace when Gandhi left London was the escalating conflict on the Frontier, an area specially significant to Gandhi because it had provided him with a bloc of Muslim adherents and a spectacular convert to satyagraha. The friction still continued between

[5] Bombay FR2, October 1931, FR1, November 1931, FR2, December 1931, Home Poll., 1931, File Nos. 18/x–xii; file on Vallabhbhai's allegations of official breach of the settlement in the case of Ras patels, Home Poll., 1931, File No. 33/42.

By the end of June 1931 out of 1,842 patels who resigned during civil disobedience in Bombay Presidency 1,596 had been reinstated. 148 had not because their appointments had been filled: of these 65 came from Surat & 37 from Broach. Bombay memorandum on Gandhi's allegations, July 1931, Home Poll., 1931, File No. 33/23.

[6] *India in 1931–32*, p. 25; Willingdon to Hoare, 20 December 1931, Mss. EUR.E.240 (5); E. Villiers to H. W. Emerson, 28 October 1931, Home Poll., 1931, File No. 5/53.

[7] Gandhi to Hoare, 24 November 1931, S.N. No. 18339, Gandhi Papers: Hoare to Willingdon, 10 December 1931, Mss. EUR.E.140 (1).

Abdul Ghaffar's men and Frontier Hindu Congressmen who feared the
Islamic and potentially violent nature of the Red Shirt movement. Devadas
Gandhi reported this after visiting the Frontier in July, and urged that
all-India Congress leaders should try to effect a compromise between the
warring groups when they met in Bombay in August. This Jawaharlal and
others attempted, arranging that Abdul Ghaffar would lead the local
Congress but would bring his *Khudai Khitmatgars* under Congress control
and substitute the 'national' flag for their own. Conflict continued nonetheless, as Jawaharlal gathered from a Peshawar Congressman who poured
out his complaints to him in Lahore in September. Jawaharlal was unable
to get evidence out of Abdul Ghaffar himself: reporting to Gandhi he
lamented that the August compromise was 'a difficult enough one to give
effect to. It becomes doubly difficult when the people concerned have little
notion of constitutions and the like, and are not fond of letter writing.' Yet
he still hoped to get the two groups working in harmony and integrate the
Pathan movement into a continental Congress strategy, because 'Abdul
Ghaffar's position in the Jirga is very strong and he can certainly deliver
the goods'[8] – the 'goods' in this case being power to the Congress from a
Muslim source. His attempts bore little fruit, nor did his exhortation to
Abdul Ghaffar's nephew, now secretary of the Frontier PCC, to organize
the local Congress efficiently in order to channel the available human
resources for possible conflict with the authorities. 'I have written to you
repeatedly', he chided in November, 'about the necessity of applying the
Congress constitution in its entirety to the Frontier Province and thus to
bring your provincial organization in line with the rest of the nation. Only
in this way can we build up our strength. The greater the uniformity the
greater our strength.'[9]

By the time Nehru wrote this letter the Red Shirts were not only out on
a limb from the local Hindu Congressmen and the continental Congress:
they were heading for confrontation with the government. From late
September they stepped up their picketing of foreign-cloth shops in Peshawar City: this was one of the factors in their strife with Hindu Congressmen. As many as 300 picketers were on duty at a time, and groups of fifty
marched through the city intimidating the shopkeepers and the public.
They also began to encourage non-payment of land revenue in Peshawar
district; and when another of Abdul Ghaffar's nephews landed in prison
for non-payment Jawaharlal queried sharply why this movement had not
been referred to the Working Committee. Conflict with the government
reached a climax in December when Abdul Ghaffar and his brother, Dr

---

[8] J. Nehru to Gandhi, 1 October 1931, J. Nehru Papers, part 1, File No. XXIII. Abdul
Ghaffar did however communicate with Gandhi, telling him in a letter, 16 October
1931, of the continued friction between 'the Peshawar wallahs' and Mian Ahmad
Shah: S. N. No. 18122, Gandhi Papers.

For further evidence of the August arrangement and subsequent friction see P.
Khan to J. Nehru, 23 October 1931, and other material in AICC Papers, 1931, File
No. P-17. D. Gandhi's report on N.-W.F.P. is in AICC Papers, 1932, File No. P-16.
[9] J. Nehru to Saadullah Khan, 10 November 1931, *SWJN*, 5, pp. 267–70.

Khan Sahib, declined an invitation to the Chief Commissioner's durbar at which it was known that constitutional reforms for the province would be announced; and when two days before the durbar the Frontier PCC proclaimed that the Red Shirts' aim was complete independence. The meeting proposed that the AICC should be asked to terminate the Gandhi–Irwin settlement and that Abdul Ghaffar should go to Bombay to concoct plans with Gandhi for renewed civil disobedience; and preparations were made for a mass meeting on New Year's Day when the Congress flag would be unfurled. The government reacted swiftly. On 24 December it took emergency powers under three Ordinances applicable to the Frontier, the Khan brothers were arrested, and on Christmas Day troops occupied Peshawar City.[10]

Although Jawaharlal was ambivalent towards the Red Shirts who were, from the all-India Congress viewpoint as from that of the government, unpredictable and uncontrollable, he was himself deeply involved in his own province in a local escalation of conflict with the administration which curtailed Gandhi's options on his return as tightly as did developments on the Frontier. The situation in U.P. while Gandhi was away became crucial for the ultimate decision on civil disobedience because it affected Jawaharlal who was the source of much of Gandhi's information and occupied a singular position in the Mahatma's affections and strategic thinking.

In U.P. the slump in agricultural prices continued to have a catastrophic effect on cultivators and landlords. One indication of the depth of the rural crisis was the increase in the suits from tenants wishing to relinquish their holdings since the money their produce now fetched made existing rents impossible: for the year ending September 1931 the suits rocketed from the previous year's figure of 20,860 to 71,430 in Agra, and in Oudh from 5,204 to 17,609. The Legislative Council Committee appointed to advise on the adjustment of rent and revenue necessary to meet this situation met early in August and suggested a formula for reduction based on rent levels of 1901 since prices had fallen to the level of that year. Its recommendations were largely accepted by the U.P. government which announced the remission of Rs. 110.90 lakhs of revenue and Rs. 426 lakhs of rent for the agricultural year 1339 *Fasli* which ran from the summer of 1931.[11]

The government had invited G. B. Pant to sit on the committee as Congress representative; but contrary to Gandhi's advice U.P. Congressmen decided that he should not.[12] The Committee's conclusions did not

[10] *1931–32 N.-W.F.P. Administration Report*, pp. i–x; J. Nehru to Saadullah Khan, 10 November 1931, *SWJN*, 5, p. 270.
Text of Ordinances, *The Civil Disobedience Movement 1930–34*, pp. 135–50.

[11] Recommendations of the committee, U.P. Government communiqué, 26 August 1931, Home Poll., 1931, File No. 33/36; *1930–31 U.P. Administration Report*, pp. xiii–xiv; *Report on the Administration of the United Provinces of Agra and Oudh. 1931–32* (Lucknow, 1933), p. 19, W. Neale, *Economic Change in Rural India. Land Tenure and Reform in Uttar Pradesh, 1800–1955* (reissue of 1962 edn., London, 1973), p. 115.

[12] J. Nehru to Gandhi, telegram, 15 August 1931, & Gandhi's reply, *SWJN*, 5, p. 114.

satisfy them and news soon reached Gandhi in London that in Jawaharlal's view conditions were very bad; ejectment of tenants for non-payment of rent continued and thousands had been dispossessed. He reported that he was engaged in lengthy correspondence on the situation with the U.P.'s chief secretary, Jagdish Prasad.[13] By mid-October it seemed as if Jawaharlal was not content with Prasad's courteous replies, and he decided to bring matters to a head. On 15 October he wrote two long letters to Prasad disputing the basis of the remissions granted and condemning the continuing coercion of tenants, their ejectment and other forms of harassment: he laid particular stress on the situation in Allahabad district. This followed a meeting of the Allahabad DCC that day which resolved to request the PCC and AICC for permission to advise tenants to withhold rents and revenue-payers their dues till a satisfactory solution was found. The following day Nehru sent a similar letter to E. C. Miéville, Willingdon's private secretary, and both cabled and wrote to Gandhi telling him of the position. Significantly he commented, 'I have taken all these steps on my own account more or less privately.' Gandhi cabled back that he should 'unhesitatingly take necessary steps meet every situation'; though Vallabhbhai on hearing the news of the DCC request tried to restrain Jawaharlal's apparent descent into civil disobedience with a wire urging him to tell Willingdon of the whole situation before taking the drastic action proposed.[14]

Vallabhbhai expressed his doubts when the Working Committee discussed the Allahabad request at its meeting in Delhi on 27/29 October. He was sceptical whether U.P. Congressmen could conduct such a campaign successfully as they were less in touch with grass roots opinion and assured of village support than he had been in Bardoli, though he agreed that the PCC was the best judge of the matter. Rajendra Prasad was very doubtful if the people would stand up to repression, and there was general hesitation to embark on civil disobedience in Gandhi's absence. Eventually the meeting rejected Jawaharlal's suggested campaign, referred the matter to the PCC and authorized Vallabhbhai to give the final decision.[15] On 1/2 November the PCC met in Lucknow and resolved to make one final attempt to gain relief from the government but if that failed to 'take the necessary permission' from Vallabhbhai to authorize the Allahabad and other DCCs to take defensive direct action as envisaged at Simla in August when Gandhi had explicitly stated that Congress reserved that right despite the second settle-

[13] J. Nehru to Gandhi, 1 September & 1 October 1931, J. Nehru Papers, part I, vol. XXIII; 4 October 1931, S.N. No. 17973, Gandhi Papers.

[14] J. Nehru to J. Prasad (2 letters) 15 October 1931, *SWJN*, 5, pp. 143–6, 148–51; J. Nehru to Miéville, 16 October 1931, Home Poll., 1931, File No. 33/36; J. Nehru to Gandhi (telegram) 16 October 1931, *SWJN*, 5, p. 155, (letter) 16 October 1931, Nehru Papers, part I, vol. XXIII; Gandhi to J. Nehru, telegram, 19 October 1931, AICC Papers, 1931, File No. G-25; V. Patel to J. Nehru, telegram, 20 October 1931, *ibid.*

[15] Delhi FR2, October 1931, Home Poll., 1931, File No. 18/x; R. Prasad, *Autobiography*, p. 341; J. Nehru to T. Sherwani, President, U.P. PCC, 30 October 1931, enclosing copy of Working Committee resolution, AICC Papers, 1931, File No. G-25.

ment. Vallabhbhai was duly sent a copy of the resolution by Jawaharlal and on 10 November reluctantly gave his consent. He would have preferred to wait for Gandhi's return but agreed as the new round of collections was due to begin on the 15th. The Government of India and the local administration judged from intercepted correspondence that Nehru was the moving spirit behind this decision and wanted to break the Delhi settlement to which he had objected at its inception. Clearly he was pushing Vallabhbhai, and probably other U.P. Congressmen, as there was evidence that some of them opposed the whole idea of the new campaign.[16]

The U.P. government told Delhi that Jawaharlal's allegations in his mid-October letters were unfounded, and that Congress was taking advantage of the fact that Allahabad had a lower rent remission rate than neighbouring districts because of its large number of occupancy tenants who had not, like statutory tenants, recently had their rents raised. Nevertheless Allahabad officials met a deputation sent by the PCC on 3 November to discuss the Allahabad situation. The discussions proved fruitless because the Congressmen wished to discuss the whole basis of remissions rather than the precise Allahabad figures. They thought rent reduction throughout the province should have been double what the government had sanctioned, and demanded the cancellation of all arrears and ejectments. Hailey told Sir James Crerar that he thought they could not reopen the whole question with the vast administrative exercise and legislation that would involve; but he assured him that in Allahabad and Meerut, where ejectments were more numerous than in previous years, officials were trying to get landlords to reinstate their tenants. He felt that the renewed discussions which Congressmen seemed to want would prove equally fruitless, but he was proceeding cautiously because he did not wish to precipitate a crisis. However within days the U.P. government in consultation with the Government of India decided that there could be no more talks until the PCC suspended a resolution it passed on 15 November authorizing the Allahabad DCC to advise the withholding of rent and revenue while negotiations were in progress, and until the Allahabad DCC's instructions to villagers to this end were cancelled. Sherwani and Patel were both informed of this decision.[17] Jawaharlal told Vallabhbhai on 26 November, 'the die is cast', but Vallabhbhai still tried to restrain his U.P. colleagues. He strongly advised against publishing their correspondence with the U.P. government lest it 'might

[16] J. Nehru to V. Patel, 2 November 1931, enclosing PCC resolution, *SWJN*, 5, pp. 167–9; V. Patel to J. Nehru, 10 November 1931, Home Poll., 1931, File No. 33/36; J. Crerar to Hailey, 29 October 1931, & Hailey's reply, 9 November 1931, *ibid.*

For opposition to Nehru among U.P. Congressmen see Sapru to B. L. Mitter, 4 January 1932, Sapru Papers, Series II; Secret report on Congress activities, 17 July 1932, Home Poll., 1932, File No. 5/67.

[17] Hailey to Crerar, 24 October 1931, J. Prasad to Emerson, 26 October 1931, Hailey to Crerar, 9 November 1931, J. Prasad to T. Sherwani, 22 November 1931, Emerson to V. Patel, 25 November 1931, Home Poll., 1931, File No. 33/36. (A copy of the Allahabad DCC instructions to peasants is in this file.) J. Nehru to J. Prasad, 3 November 1931, *SWJN*, 5, pp. 169–70.

appear as if we are taking the initiative in giving the challenge'. He urged Jawaharlal to keep the door open for renewed discussions and asked Emerson if there could be some temporary compromise (such as the simultaneous postponement of rent collection and suspension of the PCC resolution) so that discussions could continue. However before Vallabh-bhai's advice reached Jawaharlal the correspondence had been published, and initiative swung even more into the hands of Jawaharlal and local Congressmen. On 5 December the PCC authorized four more districts to take up the campaign, leaflets were distributed containing vows for peasant participants, and volunteers spread out into the villages from Allahabad and Cawnpore to further the movement. Revenue collection stopped completely in Allahabad, and in some districts rent payments stopped entirely.[18]

As the campaign gained momentum the Government of India decided to back the U.P. administration in firm action. It sent no reply to Vallabh-bhai's peace feeler, and on 30 November told Jagdish Prasad that whatever the repercussions on the Round Table Conference the primary considera-tion was to combat renewed civil disobedience and control a dangerous local situation. It left to the provincial government discretion over timing, and on 11 December U.P. replied that the time had come to arm itself with Ordinance powers. Three days later the U.P. Emergency Powers Ordinance was promulgated which permitted, among other emergency measures, the collection of rent and revenue arrears as notified liabilities, and the control of suspects; and brought instigation of the no-rent and no-revenue cam-paign within the jurisdiction of the 1931 Press Act. When the PCC was informed that it could only hold its proposed conference on 22 December if it undertook not to further the campaign, it postponed the gathering in order to wait for the Working Committee's advice, and Jawaharlal planned to meet Gandhi in Bombay and attend the Working Committee. When he started out on the 26th in defiance of an order under the Ordinance restraining him in Allahabad, he was arrested and jailed.[19]

[18] J. Nehru to V. Patel, 26 November & 7 December 1931, *ibid.* pp. 180, 187; V. Patel to J. Nehru, 1 December 1931, AICC Papers, 1931, File No. G-60; Patel to Emerson, 28 November 1931, Home Poll., 1931, File No. 33/36; V to S of S, 19 December 1931, telegram, Home Poll., 1931, File No. 155/1; U.P. FR1, December 1931, Home Poll., 1931, File No. 18/XIII.

On leaflets circulating in U.P. in November & December see G. N. Pandey's study of the periodical press & pamphlets in civil disobedience, 'Mobilization in a Mass Movement: Congress "Propaganda" in the United Provinces (India), 1930–34', *Modern Asian Studies*, vol. 9, pt. 2 (April 1975), 205–26.

[19] For the policy decisions culminating in the Ordinance see Home Poll., 1931, File No. 33/36; text of U.P. Emergency Powers Ordinance, 1931, *The Civil Disobedience Movement 1930–34*, pp. 129–34. J. Nehru to V. Patel, letter & telegram, 23 December 1931, *SWJN*, 5, p. 191. When served with the restraining order under the Ordinance Nehru replied to the Allahabad District Magistrate, 'I should like to inform you that I am not in the habit of taking orders from anyone except the great organization of which I have the honour to be a member. It is for the Indian National Congress to order me and I recognise no other authority.' He also asked him to take the trouble to spell his name correctly! 23 December 1931, *ibid.* pp. 192–3.

Willingdon had no doubts that Nehru was the architect of the campaign to withhold rent and revenue, and that it was a deliberate tactical move to force Gandhi's hand. 'I honestly believe', he told Hoare, 'that Jawaharlal has chosen this moment to do this thing because he always objected to Gandhi going over to London. He is afraid, I think, that he (Gandhi) may be inclined after his London visit to co-operate with us and he hopes that this action which Government has been forced by his agitation to take will send Gandhi completely over to the extreme Congress wing.' At the end of December he repeated this charge and included Abdul Ghaffar in the manoeuvre to ensure that Gandhi renewed civil disobedience.[20] Nehru later stoutly denied this, insisting that Sherwani as PCC President took the lead, and that the PCC did all it could to avoid a struggle until Gandhi returned. Contemporary evidence however, points to Jawaharlal's dominant influence. The likelihood is that he realized the declining influence of Congress among U.P. peasants, because of the reluctance of most of its leaders to align clearly with the peasantry and the backpedalling on the rent question enforced on the local Congress by the continental settlement of 1931: consequently he saw in emphasizing the real problems of the peasants a means of building a rural base for Congress – a necessity he had underlined during his September tour of Punjab – and of convincing the Working Committee and the Mahatma that tampering with the imperial framework through conferences would never bring swaraj or the redistribution of power in Indian society.[21]

The speed and severity of the government's response to challenges to its authority in Bengal, the Frontier and U.P. were symptomatic of the abandonment of Irwin's approach to civil disobedience and the hardening of policy which had culminated in the Government of India's demand on 4 August that London should sanction a package of measures for use if Congress decided to revert to civil disobedience. This included a declaration that the Working Committee and local Congress organizations (though not Congress as a body) were illegal, the swift arrest of Gandhi and selected provincial leaders, and the provision of a battery of Ordinances including the comprehensive Emergency Powers Ordinance which had been on the drawing board during the summer. It had not been necessary to put these plans into operation in August, but in October Delhi reverted to its proposals in case civil disobedience erupted again as the result of one of a variety of circumstances – Abdul Ghaffar Khan's activities, government measures to counteract 'defensive' satyagraha in any province, the breakdown of the Round Table Conference or Gandhi's departure from it as a protest. It received the Secretary of State's sanction in principle, though he stressed his assumption

[20] Willingdon to Hoare, 13 & 26 December 1931, Mss. EUR.E.240 (5).
[21] J. Nehru to K. M. Munshi, 29 April 1940, *SWJN*, 5, pp. 579–80; J. Nehru's speech at Punjab political conference, 26 September 1931, *ibid.* pp. 295–6.

that Gandhi would not be arrested unless he definitely associated himself with civil disobedience.[22]

Gandhi's reception was now also in preparation on the government's side. The Government of India felt itself under increasing pressure from a variety of quarters to aim a knock-out blow at any new continental civil disobedience campaign. Willingdon knew that the depression, the emergency budget and the government's retrenchment programme would provide Gandhi with a receptive audience for his propaganda should he return empty-handed, and he impressed on Hoare that this was why they wished to be able to hit hard and swiftly if civil disobedience was resumed.[23] He was also aware of the anxiety of some non-official members of the European community. Villiers, writing for the European Association in Calcutta, pressed for swift action in the event of a new confrontation, suggesting the seizure of all prominent leaders within twenty-four hours, compulsory production of bank accounts to uncover Congress financiers, a ban on the use of railways by Congress-approved mills to transport their goods, and the confiscation followed by destruction or sale of all property owned or used by Congress. He argued for an overwhelming display of government force: there should be no truce or pact, government must win 'quickly, decisively and completely', whereas half-measures would lead them into a desperate situation like that reached in Bombay in 1930.[24] Pressure against any repetition of 1930 likewise came up from provincial administrations. Understandably Sykes was one of the most vocal exponents of this view. Returning from sick leave, necessitated by an old ulcer which his anxieties in 1930 had reactivated, he complained to Willingdon that as no plans appeared to have been laid for combatting civil disobedience since his departure they were running a grave risk of being caught napping. He urged that they should be ready with a clear policy and the weapons to effect it, stressing particularly the need for an omnibus Ordinance. He quoted the views of Bombay's Commissioner of Police on any repetition of 1930.

> We cannot possibly embark on another campaign of this kind of warfare. It prolongs the agony and is undignified. Instead of fear, which is the root of all decent government, it begets contempt…It is…essential that the fact that the Government intends to treat a renewal of the civil disobedience movement with the severity which a rebellion demands should be clearly demonstrated.

[22] Govt. of India to S of S, telegram 4 August 1931, Home Poll., 1931, File No. 13–8; S of S's reply, telegram, 14 August 1931, Home Poll., 1931, File No. 14/12. Details of this policy were sent to local governments on 12 August 1931 with the request that they should be kept secret and not even communicated to district officers; *The Civil Disobedience Movement, 1930–34*, pp. 60–2. For the October return to the package see Govt. of India to S of S, 13 October 1931, S of S's reply, telegram, 27 October 1931, Home Poll., 1931, File No. 14/12.
[23] Willingdon to Hoare, 6 October, 2 & 9 November 1931, Mss. EUR.E.240 (5).
[24] E. Villiers to H. W. Emerson, 28 October 1931, Home Poll., 1931, File No. 5/53.

When Willingdon replied that they did have their August plans in readiness, Sykes countered that the issue lay deeper than specific emergency plans: they must make a policy decision whether the movement was a revolutionary drive to oust them from India, and if so must crush Congress as swiftly as possible. In 1930 they had remained on the defensive in view of the Round Table Conference rather than taking the offensive, and it had led them 'within measurable distance of disaster'.[25]

By the time Sykes wrote this Delhi had begun to activate the August policy – to prevent civil disobedience gaining initial momentum by swift action at the outset against leaders, organization, property and funds, and thereafter to quell unlawful activities by prompt action against individuals under the ordinary law and Ordinances. It was not however designed to shatter Congress itself, as Sykes seemed to be urging. Local governments were sent the proposed Ordinances in draft on 7 December, and on the 17th Willingdon's Council set out its strategy. It would make a final decision whether the Gandhi–Irwin settlement was still operative after the Working Committee had met in Bombay, but it would consider as a *casus belli* warranting the implementation of the August package decisions by the Committee in favour of civil disobedience, or support of the U.P. campaign, or boycott of British goods. Gandhi as the express or implied representative of Congress would not be allowed an interview with Willingdon or discussions with the Government of India on any matter while the U.P. campaign continued.[26]

Sanction to enact this plan was sought from London, though Willingdon explained privately to Hoare that he viewed such drastic action with distaste and felt like a budding Mussolini. He was sure that Gandhi's colleagues would force him into civil disobedience, but he felt he could not see Gandhi unless Congress called off its current activities. Such an interview would indicate to moderate people that this was the old story of Gandhi coming to do a deal with the Viceroy. Hoare agreed to Delhi's plan with the proviso that Gandhi might be permitted an interview if he had not definitely associated himself with the U.P. campaign or a Working Committee resolution in favour of illegal action. Delhi replied in effect that this was splitting hairs. Gandhi was in the public's eyes head of Congress and it was inconceivable that he would dissociate himself from Congress, and neither he nor Congress could have the advantages of consultation and cooperation with and subversive action against the government: both must choose either to cooperate or to fight. Willingdon assured Hoare that he would do all he could to give Gandhi a fair chance to cooperate if he was at all reasonable, but he judged that the Mahatma would be hard pressed

[25] Sykes to Willingdon, 12 November & 14 December 1931, Willingdon to Sykes, 26 November 1931, Mss. EUR.F.150 (3).

[26] Govt. of India to all local govts., 7 December 1931, Order In Council, 17 December 1931, Home Poll., 1931, File No. 14/12. Local govts. were told of the decisions in relation to Congress in letter, 19 December 1931, *ibid.*

to renew civil disobedience as a result of Jawaharlal's and Abdul Ghaffar's actions, and that 'his desire to remain the head of the great Congress Party will militate terribly against his coming in and working with us'.[27] While this exchange took place his government had conferred with Bombay on Gandhi's place of detention. A provisional booking had been made for him in Yeravda despite Bombay's reluctance to have him on its hands again. It would have preferred his removal outside Bombay, and argued that the moral effect of shipping him to Aden or the Andamans would be very great.[28]

Despite the draconian plan Willingdon's government had laid he not only disliked the prospect of unadulterated repression but realized its grave political implications. In late November he floated to Hoare the idea that the Viceroy should have complete freedom in selecting his Executive Council, so doing away with the existing ruling that three of its members must be I.C.S. men with ten years' service in India; and he wondered whether the India Council in Whitehall could not become a smaller body with more recent knowledge of India. An element in this proposal was certainly the Government of India's wish to free itself from restrictions from London, but at the same time the entry of more Indians into the Viceregal Council would be a counterpoise to repression. Willingdon argued that he could not use the big stick unless 'I can show the people at the same time, in some practical manner, what I sincerely feel and desire, namely some evidence of my desire to push them on towards responsibility for the management of their own affairs.[29] Backed by his three British Council members Willingdon, through December, January and February, pressed the idea of full discretion in making Council appointments, using the counterpoise argument. Hoare opposed it as likely to provoke a bitter reaction from the European community, and from Tories in Britain whose opposition might lead to a reversal of the long-term policy the government was manoeuvring through Parliament in the wake of the Round Table Conference. When Hoare eventually said he felt he must place their disagreement before the Cabinet, Willingdon reluctantly withdrew his proposal. There was to be no soothing concession to counteract the abrasive measures the Government had decided to apply to the Indian political situation on Gandhi's return.

So were the ingredients of Gandhi's welcome home prepared by officials

[27] Govt. of India to S of S, telegrams, 19 & 27 December 1931, S of S to Govt. of India, telegram, 21 December 1931, *ibid.*: Willingdon to Hoare, 20 & 26 December 1931, Mss. EUR.E.240 (5).

[28] Govt. of Bombay, Home Dept., to Govt. of India, Home Dept., 21 December 1931, reply, 24 December 1931, Home Poll., 1932, File No. 31/73.

Delhi agreed to look into the question of transferring Gandhi later to another Indian place of detention, but considered detention outside India impractical.

[29] Willingdon to Hoare, 30 November 1931, Mss. EUR.E.240 (5).

The continuation of this discussion, which lasted until Willingdon dropped the idea on 15 February 1932, is in Mss. EUR.E.240 (1) (5) (13).

and his fellow Congressmen. The latter were aware in considerable detail what the government had in store should civil disobedience be revived. Despite Delhi's attempts at secrecy Ansari knew virtually the text of the impending Ordinances. and Vallabhbhai, knowing of plans to seize Congress funds, arranged for the Gujarat PCC's money to pass into the custody of private individuals.[30] Despite the certain prospect of repression, pressure for renewed conflict built up in the Congress circles within which Gandhi would have to decide his course. Vallabhbhai's attempts to restrain Jawaharlal and Bombay men who were spoiling for a fight stemmed more from reluctance to precipitate a continental conflict without Gandhi's presence than from opposition to the prospect of conflict itself. At the end of November he was reported as urging those who gathered for the Congress flag-raising ceremony in Ahmedabad to prepare for a fight when Gandhi returned; and after Jawaharlal's arrest he and other Bombay Congressmen like Nariman spoke in similar vein at protest meetings. There was a consensus of opinion among officials, shared by some Indians, that Gandhi would find it very hard to resist his colleagues, particularly Jawaharlal and Vallabhbhai.[31] The timing of the Ordinances in U.P. and the Frontier and Nehru's arrest only served to intensify the influence of their arguments on him. However, there were some pulls in the opposite direction. In Bombay Presidency Congress had found difficulty in collecting funds except in Ahmedabad, which Sykes thought might affect Gandhi's decision; and D. G. Dalvi reported from Bombay to Sapru 'I... understand that the local commercial community will dissuade Mr Gandhi from starting trouble & if he insists he will get little financial help from them. I feel that the honours of the battle will, this time, be in your province, not mine.' Furthermore within Congress there were some like Rajendra Prasad and Ansari who were reluctant to revert to satyagraha.[32]

Before Gandhi left England he had been worried that developments in India would curtail his options, and several days before he reached Bombay he wrote an article for *Young India* on his English experiences in which he said that not until he knew at first hand how far the Indian situation 'permits of peaceful negotiations' could he decide on the renewal of satyagraha. The burden of his argument was that although he considered British ministers in London honest they could not grant Congress demands because they were fed with biassed, anti-national information by officials in India: therefore Congressmen must concentrate on changing the outlook

[30] R. Prasad, *Autobiography*, p. 343; daily report of Bombay Commissioner of Police, 24 December 1931, Home Poll., 1932, File No. 5/82.

[31] Bombay FR2, November & December 1931, Home Poll., 1931, File No. 18/XI, XII; daily report of Bombay Commissioner of Police, 24 December 1931, Home Poll., 1932, File No. 5/82; Sykes to Hoare, 30 December 1931, Mss. EUR.F.150 (3); D. G. Dalvi to Sapru, 26 December 1931 (D14), Sapru Papers, Series II.

[32] *ibid.*; Sykes to Hoare, 30 December 1931, Mss. EUR.F.150 (3); R. Prasad, *Autobiography*, p. 343. For Ansari's opposition to Gandhi's eventual stand see Sethna to an unnamed correspondent, 11 January 1932, Sethna Papers.

of the I.C.S. He would try the way of negotiation first, but if that failed he would not hesitate to advise direct action. Significantly he also stated that his journey abroad and contact with 'kindred spirits' had increased his faith in truth and non-violence. When Gandhi reached Bombay on 28 December he learnt of recent government actions in U.P. and the Frontier, and apparently on the ship received a letter from Jawaharlal which influenced him deeply.[33]

The day after he arrived the Bombay PCC arranged a very large welcome meeting on the Esplanade Maidan which almost all PCC and Working Committee members attended. Then and later at an evening meeting in the Majestic Hotel Gandhi expressed profound disquiet at the news of Willingdon's 'Christmas presents' to him – the U.P. and Frontier Ordinances and the arrests of Nehru, Sherwani and Abdul Ghaffar. He said he had come hoping for cooperation with the government and would still try his best, though what he had learnt since landing gave him little hope of being able to cooperate without losing his self-respect. He stressed again his increased faith in non-violence. This inner encouragement, combined with the news of the schoolgirl terrorists in Bengal, and the accusations he had heard in England that Indians were neither non-violent nor fit for swaraj (of which he also spoke at the two meetings), were almost certainly working to confirm his conviction that ultimately confabulations with officials were limited in value and only Indian self-transformation through satyagraha could be the foundation of swaraj.[34]

The following afternoon the Working Committee assembled at Gandhi's Bombay home, Mani Bhavan; they remained in conclave until 9.30 the next morning. The members present besides Gandhi were Vallabhbhai, Ansari, A. K. Azad, Rajendra Prasad, M. S. Aney, Mohamed Alam, Syed Mahmud, Nariman, J. Bajaj and J. Daulatram. No outsiders were admitted except those specially invited who represented provinces particularly involved in the gathering crisis – Subhas Bose, G. B. Chaudhuri, G. B. Pant, and also Rajagopalachariar, P. Sitaramayya and Konda Venkatappayya – the last two of whom could be expected to report on the movement in the Andhra delta districts against increased revenue assessment, news of which had also reached Gandhi in London. Bose argued that the Working Committee was indifferent to Bengal's particular problems, and pressed for the boycott of British goods as part of an aggressive satyagraha campaign to challenge the bureaucracy and incorporate into Congress work those who in despair now took to terrorism. Some members of the Committee argued in favour of a defensive satyagraha campaign, but Gandhi would not agree without

[33] *ibid.* I have found no copy of the letter which Sethna reported, on Ansari's authority, that Gandhi received from Jawaharlal as he reached Bombay. 'Retrospect', written by Gandhi on 23 December 1931, *Young India*, 31 December 1931, *CWMG*, XLVIII, 432–6.

[34] Speech at welcome meeting, 28 December 1931, *ibid.* pp. 446–50; speech at evening meeting, 28 December 1931, *ibid.* pp. 450–8; daily report of Bombay Commissioner of Police, 29 December 1931, Home Poll., 1932, File No. 5/82.

first discovering the government's intentions. Ultimately his view prevailed. The meeting did not declare the collapse of the settlement, and a wire was despatched from Gandhi to Willingdon, expressing surprise at the Ordinances and arrests which greeted the returning Mahatma. It stated, 'I do not know whether I am to regard these as indication that friendly relations between us are closed or whether you expect me still to see you and receive guidance from you as to course I am to pursue in advising Congress.' The Committee reconvened the same day, the 30th, while it awaited the Viceregal reply, and continued to discuss Bengal, U.P. and the Frontier. For his part Gandhi gathered what information he could about each province for his own guidance and counselled patience on the other members. He also advised Maharashtrians who were about to hold a provincial conference to take no hasty step until the Working Committee had made a decision.[35]

Meanwhile Delhi and London were in telegraphic communication on the substance of Willingdon's reply. The Viceroy proposed to recall events in U.P., Bengal and the Frontier and note that though government wished for cooperation with everyone this must be mutual, and Congress did not appear to be acting in a cooperative spirit. Hoare replied that he would like to modify the text slightly because he thought Gandhi was in a reasonable mood, and he did not wish the government to lose what might be the last chance of depriving the more belligerent in Congress of the great asset of Gandhi's support and prestige. He suggested that Willingdon should offer to see Gandhi on the grounds that he was not personally responsible for Congress activities in U.P. and the Frontier, and explain how he felt the Mahatma could help maintain cooperation. It was on the question of an interview that Delhi and London had failed to agree in their prior planning, and now Hoare again pressed the matter. In a private letter to Willingdon he explained that the intention behind his suggestion was not only to keep Gandhi out of the hands of Congress 'extremists' but to soothe the Prime Minister who was keenly interested in Indian affairs and whose support was essential from every point of view. But Hoare was as adamant as Willingdon that there could be no parallel to the protracted negotiations between Gandhi and Irwin, and he was content to leave the ultimate decision to the man on the spot.

> On no account would we dream of asking you to make anything in the nature of a pact with Gandhi. There can be no question of withdrawing Ordinances or altering our line of action against terrorism, revolution and anarchy for the purpose of buying off Congress opposition. All that we can do is to make it quite clear to Gandhi that the Round Table Conference policy is in no way changed and that we should like to have

[35] Daily reports of Bombay Commissioner of Police, 30 & 31 December 1931, *ibid.*; Gandhi to Willingdon, telegram, 29 December 1931, enclosed in V to S of S, telegram, 30 December 1931, Mss. EUR. E.240 (11).
Bose also made his views known in an interview to *The Bombay Chronicle*, published in that paper, 31 December 1931, Home Poll., 1932, File No. 5/82.

his co-operation for its next stages. As to our administrative action, it cannot be altered as a part of any bargain. We regard it as necessary for the good government of India and as absolutely essential if there is to be any constitutional advance . . . An interview on these lines, it seems to me might do good and it might be wiser to give it rather than by a refusal to drive Gandhi into the hands of Nehru and Patel. Naturally, however, we shall give the greatest possible weight to what you say and I do not at all wish to dogmatise from here with far less knowledge it [sic] my disposal than you have in India.[36]

Willingdon accepted Hoare's suggestion with slight alterations. The reply to Gandhi as sent began with Willingdon's initial suggestions but offered Gandhi an interview. The offer was on the understanding that he was neither personally responsible for Congress activities on the Frontier and in U.P. nor approved of them, and that in an interview they could not discuss government measures in those provinces and Bengal.[37] Willingdon's provisos and stated proposal to publish the correspondence made it virtually impossible for Gandhi to accept without publicly disowning colleagues who were among his closest political allies and personal friends, and in the special case of Abdul Ghaffar was a spectacular convert to satyagraha and symbol of Muslim support.

The Working Committee gathered on the 31st to consider the official cable and declared it unsatisfactory. They continued discussions into the early hours of the new year when Gandhi drafted a strongly worded resolution that the Committee considered official policy culminating in Willingdon's reply as a betrayal of faith and calculated to demoralize the nation, making it impossible for Congress to cooperate unless there was a radical change in the government's stance. Furthermore long-term British intentions as shown in the recent conference and in Parliament fell far short of the Congress demand for complete independence. It called for a public and impartial enquiry into events leading up to the Ordinances and asserted that it could only cooperate if Willingdon reconsidered his telegram, if relief was given over the Ordinances, if Congress had free scope in future negotiations to press its independence claim, and the administration was 'carried on in consultation with popular representatives pending the attainment of such independence'. The Committee declared that if government made no satisfactory response, it would assume that government had nullified the Gandhi–Irwin pact and would call on the nation to resume civil disobedience, Gandhi sent this resolution to Willingdon with his personal reply on 1 January 1932. He accused the government, on the evidence of the Ordinances and Willingdon's wire, of not wishing to cooperate on its side, and asserted that it would be dishonourable to disown either his colleagues or moral liability for their actions as Willingdon seemed

[36] Hoare to Willingdon, 31 December 1931, Mss. EUR.E.240 (1); V to S of S, telegram, 30 December 1931, S of S to V, 2 telegrams, 30 December 1931, Mss. EUR.E.240 (11).

[37] V to S of S, telegram, 31 December 1931, *ibid.*; P.S.V. to Gandhi, telegram, 31 December 1931, *India in 1931–32*, pp. 231–2.

to demand. Nonetheless he asked the Viceroy to see him 'as a friend without imposing any conditions whatsoever as to the scope or subject of discussion' and promised in that event to study with an open mind any facts he might present to him. Gandhi said that if he was then convinced that he and the Working Committee were misled in making their present stand he would not hesitate to advise a change of policy; but he warned that non-violence remained his creed, and he believed civil disobedience to be a people's natural right and an effective substitute for violence and armed rebellion. If Willingdon agreed to see him, civil disobedience would be suspended during their discussion in the hope that it could ultimately be given up. Ansari at least among Gandhi's colleagues was deeply disturbed at this turn of events and thought Gandhi's reaction intemperate and unjustified. Similarly Sapru, on being told by Gandhi in a telegram, urged him to see the Viceroy and do all he could to maintain peace. Gandhi only replied, 'My conscience is quite clear. The Government here simply do not want to see me unless I approach them with the straw in the mouth.'[38]

There was much truth in Gandhi's assessment that whatever the courtesy he had received in Whitehall, Willingdon had no time for his overtures of cooperation. Unlike Irwin the current Viceroy had scant regard for the Mahatma's sincerity or his utility to government. As he reflected to Hoare on his response to Gandhi,

> Gandhi could not control his extreme Congress people...[He] may say what he likes about his anxiety for co-operation, but...I am perfectly clear as I have always been that Gandhi is a sort of Jekyll and Hyde, and while he may possibly have his saint-like side, on the other he is the most Machiavellian bargaining little political humbug I have ever come across.

Consequently all Gandhi received in reply was a stiff wire of regret on 2 January closing the door to face-to-face contact. This was decided in Delhi without reference to London – a procedure Hoare accepted as necessary in the emergency conditions.[39]

Although the Working Committee had broken up in the evening on 1 January and the members had dispersed to their own provinces Gandhi remained in Bombay, receiving deputations, giving interviews, and spinning as usual. Deputations of cloth and bullion merchants and other commercial associations waited on him, and considerable support for his

[38] Gandhi to Sapru, 2 January 1932, Gandhi Papers; Gandhi to Willingdon, telegram, 1 January 1932, repeating Working Committee resolution, repeated by wire from V to S of S, 1 January 1932, Mss. EUR.E.240 (11); Sethna to unnamed correspondent, 1 January 1932, Sethna Papers; Sapru to Jayakar, 2 January 1932, Sapru Papers, Series II; 31 December 1932, Gandhi's diary, *CWMG*, XLVIII, 468; daily report of Bombay Commissioner of Police, 2 January 1932, Home Poll., 1932, File No. 5/82. The Working Committee resolution was issued in AICC Bulletin No. 9, 3 January 1932, AICC Papers, 1932, File No. 12 Misc.
[39] P.S.V. to Gandhi, 2 January 1932, *India in 1931–32*, pp. 237–8; S. of S to V, telegram, 4 January 1932, Mss. EUR.E.240 (11); Willingdon to Hoare, 10 January 1932, Mss. EUR.E.240 (5).

boycott programme was proffered. Among the non-Congress Hindu politicians who talked to him were Sethna and Jayakar, the latter swinging into a mediatory attempt after receiving a wire from Gandhi, about his efforts to see Willingdon which he took as a hint that the Mahatma would welcome his reversion to his former go-between role. Jayakar asked Willingdon by wire not to break with Gandhi on the interview question, and on 3 January he had a long talk with Gandhi, telling him bluntly that Congress had bungled in its correspondence with the Viceroy. When pressed by Jayakar Gandhi agreed to issue a statement condemning Bengali terrorism and to appeal for peace in Bengal and on the Frontier (neither of which would have required any deviation from his current position); but he was not prepared to let Jawaharlal down over the U.P. and would only advise calling off the provincial campaign if government agreed not to enforce payment of dues in disputed cases pending negotiations. That day he had replied to Willingdon's wire that whatever interpretation government put on his 1 January wire he was still out for cooperation; and Jayakar reported to Sapru that he found Gandhi 'very reasonable' and had 'never seen the Mahatma so anxious that we should intercede'. In view of this and the general consternation in Bombay's non-Congress circles at Gandhi's decision Jayakar asked Sapru whether they should join a mediatory deputation with Sethna, other Liberals and the Chamber of Commerce to see Gandhi and Willingdon. Gandhi had in fact cancelled his departure for Ahmedabad after discussion with Chamber of Commerce representatives, presumably in anticipation of a mediatory move. Sapru replied that neither of them should intervene because the Viceroy had London's support and because they could not guarantee that Gandhi would heed their advice. He was clearly irritated that Gandhi had not, as he had promised in London, consulted him on his return before seeing the Working Committee, but had rushed headlong into this confrontation contrary to Sapru's advice to go slow and his promise to accompany the Mahatma in an interview with Willingdon. At the same time he judged that British Tories would resent their attempt, as would Congressmen; and the public would say that they were acting as government emissaries.[40] Prospects for mediation were swiftly shattered: within hours of his conversation with Jayakar Gandhi was arrested before daybreak on 4 January and removed to Yeravda.

These crucial days in Bombay indicated the Government of India's reassessment of Gandhi's potential value as an ally in solidifying Indian support for reform, when weighed against the repercussions of dealings with him on the services and public opinion. They also demonstrated the

[40] Daily report of Bombay Commissioner of Police, 2 January 1932, Home Poll., 1932, File No. 5/82; 1–3 January 1932, Gandhi's diary, *CWMG*, XLVIII, 492–3; Jayakar to Sapru, 3 January 1932, Sapru to Jayakar, 4 January 1932, Sapru to H. Polak, 15 January 1932 (P2), Sapru Papers, Series II; Sapru to Lord Sankey, 24 January 1932, Jayakar Papers, Correspondence File No. 456; Willingdon to Hoare, 10 January 1932, Mss. EUR.E.240 (5); Gandhi to P.S.V., telegram, 3 January 1932, *India in 1931–32*, p. 238.

nature of the Mahatma's leadership in the Working Committee. None of its members was prepared to embark on a continental civil disobedience campaign in his absence. Most of them were close friends whom he had picked for committee membership and they waited for his advice, not just until his return but until he had taken his own time to explore the situation. Yet officials and non-Congressmen close to Gandhi were convinced that he was pushed into civil disobedience by the arguments of Vallabhbhai and others and by the arrests of Jawaharlal and Abdul Ghaffar; though observers such as Jayakar and Sapru laid the blame also on Willingdon for imposing such conditions on an interview. Even Sir Stanley Reed, a journalist of long Indian experience who had presided over the evening meeting on the day Gandhi arrived, and was deeply distressed at the break between him and Willingdon, wished that the Viceroy had seen Gandhi, though he judged that at some point a breach was probably inevitable. He told Sapru,

> I too saw Gandhi when he arrived, and he said he would strain every nerve to cooperate. Hoare had shown him exceptional consideration, and...I think the little man was genuine. But he was surrounded from the moment of his arrival by men who were determined that he should not cooperate. He was obsessed by the Ordinances and at once assumed that Government was entirely wrong. Bose and the Patels, and the local crowd were bent on driving him into the wilderness.[41]

Gandhi denied that he was pushed by Working Committee members – publicly, and privately to Hoare, assuring him that he reached Bombay 'with every intention of cooperating...The initiative for every step was mine and it was a logical outcome of my creed of satyagraha. I cannot wish for more loyal colleagues. In matters of satyagraha they yield to my judgement as if an expert.'[42] However, there were strong pressures on him against continued cooperation, generated by the actions of the government and his colleagues, and by his inner perception of effective and moral political action. Had he agreed to Willingdon's conditions he would publicly have rejected key Congress leaders whose support was essential for his own position, and would have placed himself in a negotiating position vis-à-vis the government far worse than in mid-1931 when he had striven to establish Congress's status as that of people's representative. He believed the Viceroy's attitude indicated government withdrawal from its position not only at the Delhi pact but also at the Simla settlement, and the denial of the growing power of Congress in public life. Moreover, Willingdon's rebuff was just the sort of action which Gandhi would take as a grave personal affront and a sign that the Viceroy would play no part in his peculiar mode

---

[41] Reed to Sapru, 21 January 1932 (R3), Sapru to H. Polak, 15 January 1932 (P2), Sapru Papers, Series II; Sapru to Sir Evelyn Wrench, ed. of *The Spectator*, 24 January 1932, Jayakar to Ramsay MacDonald, 23 March 1932, Jayakar Papers, Correspondence File No. 456.

[42] Gandhi to Hoare, 15 January 1932, Mss. EUR.E.240 (16); talk with Welfare of India League deputation, 2 January 1932, *CWMG*, XLVIII, 480.

of political encounter and exchange. Clearly contrasting it with Irwin's sympathy for his political style and intentions, he cabled the former Viceroy on the eve of his arrest, regretting the failure of his attempt to cooperate with Willingdon, but declaring that he hoped to 'retain the spirit which you believed activated me during that sacred week in Delhi'.[43] At the same time there was within Gandhi a conviction strengthened by the unpleasant interchanges of ordinary politics that ultimately satyagraha was the only pure mode of political action because it was itself both ends and means. In this particular situation it seemed the way to convert the services who he thought stood in the way of British concessions; and long term it was of world-wide significance. Caught between the actions of crucial colleagues and an obdurate government, Gandhi ignored the indications that satyagraha might attract less sympathy than in 1930 and would not escape repression: reluctantly he launched a movement which had the supreme merit of publicizing his ideals. Calling on Americans to watch and help the campaign he proclaimed, 'This Indian struggle is more than national. It has international value and importance. I am convinced that if my countrymen and women retain up to the last the spirit of non-violence, they will have inaugurated a new era upon earth.'[44]

II   THE PATTERN OF CONFLICT

The British responded to Congress resumption of civil disobedience with the measures they had prepared to squash all manifestations of the campaign and neutralize its guiding organizations and individuals, in stark contrast to the 1930 policy of using just enough force to control the situation. The four Ordinances they had in readiness were promulgated on 4 January, and from that day the AICC and Working Committee and many local Congress bodies were banned, their premises and funds seized, and leading Congressmen were swiftly incarcerated. In January nearly 15,000 were convicted and in February nearly 18,000: most of these went to jail for varying periods, the peak number in prison at one time – 32,458 – being reached in April.[45]

The circumstances of the Congress decision and the speed of the government crackdown had marked repercussions on the organization and

[43] Gandhi to Irwin, telegram, 3 January 1932, Gandhi to J. F. Horrabin, telegram, 3 January 1932, *ibid*, pp. 487, 485–6.
Hoare thought that Willingdon did not understand Gandhi's personality, though he was not prepared to challenge the judgement of his viceregal colleague as the man on the spot: he guessed that Irwin would have seen Gandhi without any condition. Templewood, *Nine Troubled Years*, pp. 66–7.

[44] Message to America, 3 January 1932, interview to Associated Press of India, 3 January 1932, *CWMG*, XLVIII, 492, 488.

[45] For statistics of convictions during civil disobedience, 1932–33, see Table 8. Text of Emergency Powers Ordinance, Unlawful Instigation Ordinance, Prevention of Molestation and Boycotting Ordinance, *The Civil Disobedience Movement, 1930–34*, pp. 151–70.

planning possible for the renewed campaign. From the start it was recognized that provinces and districts would be out on their own far more than in 1930, and that individuals would have to take the initiative for themselves when external direction became impossible. Consequently there was no planned escalation of conflict as in 1930: the Working Committee merely suggested boycott of foreign cloth and all British goods, picketing of cloth and liquor shops, unlicensed manufacture and collection of salt, non-payment of taxes, the breach of all 'non-moral' laws and disobedience to unjust orders under the Ordinances. It was the same recipe as before: but no place was bound to participate unless its people were willing to be non-violent, nor were there to be 'hired volunteers', or social boycott intended to injure government's servants and allies since this was inconsistent with the spirit of the movement. Gandhi himself advised that if he was arrested the campaign should begin with a hartal and fast, and then each place should begin such civil disobedience as was locally possible. He said that the Working Committee resolution had been purposely open and flexible to cater for a situation when all leaders were removed to jail. 'The situation will develop so suddenly that it is not possible to be more definite than the resolution is. After experience of nearly 12 years satyagraha in a more or less acute form, individuals are expected to know what the change in circumstances will require.' This declaration was a measure of Gandhi's dilemma as an all-India leader. Advocate of carefully controlled satyagraha by qualified exponents adjusted to meet the precise needs of the particular situation, he was now forced to recognize that the imminent campaign would be beyond central control once it had begun. The problem he had failed to solve in 1920 or more than temporarily in 1930 confronted him yet again. Manoeuvred into a conflict for which neither he nor potential satyagrahis were prepared he masked the harsh political reality with the somewhat ingenuous assertion of the visionary that individuals now had sufficient training to proceed without direction. Subsequent AICC circulars to the localities were more forthright in their realism. They stressed the fluidity of the programme and the need for all organizations and individuals to be resourceful and evolve strategies suitable for the occasion: there were to be no orthodoxies in the matter of strategy, only the criteria of non-violence and efficacy.[46]

Despite the ban on the central Congress bodies considerable all-India organization remained. By a resolution of the Working Committee in Bombay Congress Presidents exercised the powers normally belonging to the Committee, and each President could nominate a successor as he was jailed. Under this provision Vallabhbhai nominated Rajendra Prasad who was followed by Ansari, Sardul Singh, A. K. Azad, Sarojini Naidu, G.

[46] Civil Disobedience resolution issued in AICC Bulletin No. 9, 3 January 1932, AICC Papers, 1932, File No. 12 Misc.: interview to *The Bombay Chronicle*, given by Gandhi on 3 January, published in 4 January edition, *CWMG*, XLVIII, 490–1; AICC Circular No. 16, 17 January 1932, AICC Papers, 1932, File No. P-22.

TABLE 8. *Convictions for civil disobedience, 1932–3*

	Madras			Bombay			Bengal			U.P.		
	Men	Women	Total	Men	Women	Total	Men	Women	Total	Men	Women	Total
January 1932	784	95	879	2,132	141	2,273	1,592	101	1,693	3,544	83	3,627
February	408	47	455	2,692	200	2,892	5,133	323	5,456	2,893	115	3,008
March	280	16	296	1,397	88	1,485	1,116	76	1,192	1,100	60	1,160
April	244	17	261	1,408	74	1,482	601	47	648	1,051	78	1,129
May	208	35	243	732	42	774	481	24	505	545	32	577
June	290	17	307	740	43	783	395	29	424	664	17	681
July	142	8	150	675	45	720	276	17	293	585	22	607
August	142	7	149	556	23	579	330	12	342	623	17	640
September	147	9	156	450	38	488	368	31	399	501	32	533
October	56	10	66	572	34	606	255	3	258	308	25	333
November	122	2	124	407	43	450	340	17	357	312	28	340
December	70	2	72	290	35	325	209	10	219	346	36	382
January 1933	74	6	80	336	47	383	279	26	305	331	41	372
February	103	3	106	264	18	282	303	24	327	802	49	851
March	54	10	64	252	29	281	191	21	212	281	15	296
April	75	7	82	259	39	298	146	15	161	117	6	123
Total: January 1932–April 1933	3,199	291	3,490	13,162	939	14,101	12,015	776	12,791	14,003	656	14,659
Total population (1931 Census)	46,740,107			21,930,601 (incl. Aden)			50,114,002			48,408,763		
Convicts as percentage of population	0.007			0.064			0.026			0.030		

TABLE 8 (cont.)

	Punjab			Bihar & Orissa			C.P.			Assam		
	Men	Women	Total	Men	Women	Total	Men	Women	Total	Men	Women	Total
January 1932	174	15	189	2,499	41	2,540	460	17	477	37	5	42
February	442	33	475	1,972	79	2,051	1,124	117	1241	286	36	322
March	376	45	421	901	17	918	660	90	750	350	30	380
April	87	7	94	813	28	841	395	40	435	161	5	166
May	128	—	128	658	46	704	327	21	348	124	9	133
June	146	12	158	563	23	586	233	10	243	74	—	74
July	50	—	50	1,238	33	1,271	173	1	174	21	—	21
August	35	—	35	951	9	966	104	—	104	29	2	31
September	62	8	70	770	14	784	59	—	59	11	1	12
October	22	—	22	437	—	437	34	—	34	16	—	16
November	22	—	22	515	1	516	18	1	19	17	—	17
December	32	1	33	364	3	367	33	—	33	8	—	8
January 1933	24	—	24	784	10	794	51	1	52	10	—	10
February	8	—	8	1,132	28	1,160	13	—	13	17	3	20
March	15	—	15	318	12	330	17	1	18	11	2	13
April	30	—	30	618	26	244	14	—	14	6	—	6
Total: January 1932–April 1933	1,653	121	1,774	14,533	370	14,903	3,715	299	4,014	1,178	93	1,271
Total population (1931 Census)		23,580,852			37,677,576			15,507,723			8,622,251	
Convicts as percentage of population		0.008			0.040			0.026			0.015	

TABLE 8 (cont.)

	N.-W.F.P.			Delhi			Coorg			Ajmer-Merwara			Total		
	Men	Women	Total	Men	Women	Total	Men	Women	Total	Men	Women	Total	Men	Women	Total
January 1932	2,760	1	2,761	100	26	126	127	3	130	64	2	66	14,273	530	14,803
February	1,557	—	1,557	257	4	261	65	—	65	35	—	35	16,864	954	17,818
March	160	—	160	105	1	106	5	—	5	36	—	36	6,486	423	6,909
April	98	—	98	66	2	68	4	—	4	28	—	28	4,956	298	5,254
May	227	—	227	155	8	163	—	—	—	15	1	16	3,600	218	3,818
June	170	—	170	72	2	74	—	—	—	28	3	31	3,375	156	3,531
July	185	—	185	86	6	92	—	—	—	32	—	32	3,463	132	3,595
August	133	—	133	55	2	57	3	—	3	15	1	16	2,973	73	3,046
September	266	—	266	11	6	17	12	—	12	4	—	4	2,652	139	2,791
October	110	—	110	29	4	33	5	—	5	10	—	10	1,861	76	1,937
November	41	—	41	3	—	3	9	3	12	4	—	4	1,806	92	1,898
December	82	—	82	16	—	16	18	3	21	2	—	2	1,461	90	1,551
January 1933	35	—	35	4	3	7	9	—	9	3	—	3	1,949	137	2,086
February	42	—	42	23	2	25	3	—	3	11	2	13	2,727	129	2,856
March	41	—	41	—	—	—	3	—	3	1	—	1	1,184	90	1,274
April	145	1	145	—	—	—	—	—	—	1	—	—	1,411	93	1,504
Total: January 1932–April 1933	6,052	1	6,053	982	66	1,048	260	9	269	289	9	298	71,041	3,630	74,671
Total population (1931 census)	2,425,076			636,246			163,327			560,292					
Convicts as percentage of population	0.250			0.165			0.165			0.053					

SOURCES: Home Poll., 1933, File No. 3/11; *India in 1931–32*, p. 54.

NOTE: In 1932 of the total convictions a little over ¼ were under the Ordinances; the rest were under the ordinary law. The peak figure of civil disobedience convicts actually in jail was 32,458 in April 1932. In December 1932 there were 14,919 and in March 1933 12,620.

Desphande, S. Kitchlew, Rajagopalachariar and back again to Prasad during 1932. These temporary Presidents did their best to guide the campaign, Mrs Naidu, for example, taking great pains to organize a National Week in April before a Congress session in Delhi. The AICC office which continued to function – in Jawaharlal's estimation 'with a fair measure of success' – was their main channel of communication with the provinces. The first AICC circular despatched in March announced that the AICC still functioned, was in touch with provincial headquarters by a special messenger service, and would help PCCs with programmes, propaganda literature, and in cases of special need with money. It went on to give precise suggestions for two broad programmes – boycott aimed at reducing government income (including railways, post and telegraphs, foreign goods which brought in customs revenue, and liquor, specially in provinces like Bihar where it formed a large part of revenue) and civil defiance (including processions, meetings, leaflets and song processions) to harass the government and generate an atmosphere of resistance. A subsequent stream of circulars, some printed and some typed and cyclostyled, made suggestions for the National Week programme and for various special 'days', reminded local groups of the monthly flag salutation ceremonies, emphasized the importance of keeping up the procession of jailgoers, gave guidance on the content and tone of local bulletins and in mid-June suggested a new tactic of raids on confiscated Congress buildings. Thereafter there was a gap in the bulletins mainly because the AICC office and its communications network were disorganized. They appeared again somewhat erratically from mid-October. Chiefly responsible for the circulars were the two acting AICC secretaries, J. P. Narayan and Lalji Mehra, who also toured the provinces and tried to gather provincial information about the campaign's progress.[47]

The AICC's preparation of circulars did not mean that there were active provincial organizations to receive them. As the government attacked formal Congress organizations most localities went over to informal and often secret 'War Councils' and successions of 'Dictators'. Evidence of these is understandably sketchy. The U.P. PCC, for example, continued secretly to send instructions to the districts, issue printed or cyclostyled bulletins and pay regular workers until Gandhi advised the suspension of the whole Congress organization in mid-1933. Local activity often originated in more erratic and individual endeavours, as in the case of a Benares Hindu University student who on vacation at home in Banda organized the cutting of telegraph wires. Bombay City was divided into seven wards, each with its local organizing 'Dictator', and by the end of March twenty emergency councils had been arrested. As the organization became more

[47] Secret report of Bombay Deputy Commissioner of Police, Special Branch, 17 August 1932, Home Poll., 1932, File No. 14/25; typed report on progress of civil disobedience, April 1932 – March 1933, AICC Papers, 1932, File No. 15 Misc.; AICC Circulars of 1932-3, are in AICC Papers, 1932, File Nos. P-22 & 12 Misc.; J. Nehru, *An Autobiography*, p. 336.

diffuse so the police found greater difficulty in suppressing it. In August 1932 they tried in vain to locate a radio transmitter which was broadcasting Congress propaganda in Hindi and English near Bombay. In February/March 1933 they raided various Congress propaganda centres in Bombay, seizing typewriters and duplicating machines, and arresting several Gujarati youths and a barrister, A. K. Amin, who they believed was the principal organizer. However, these swoops only stopped the appearance of the local Congress bulletin for short periods.[48] Often provinces were far less effective organizationally, failing, for example, to send in reports to the AICC. Narayan levelled pungent criticisms at those he did receive; they tended to be wordy, unsubstantiated generalizations, hopeless as evidence on which he could base reports and the acting President could guide PCCs.[49]

Civil disobedience was meant to be financially self-sufficient and independent of central funding, according to the Working Committee's Bombay resolution. The AICC did attempt to help needy provinces, and between January 1932 and March 1934 appears to have dispensed in the region of Rs. 126,150 to the provinces. Most of this was paid out before July 1933, the chief recipients being Bihar, Karnatak, U.P. and the Frontier, in that order. The money at the AICC's disposal came largely from donations.[50]

The Government of India, remembering its failure to lay hands on Congress funds in 1930, stressed to provincial governments the need to deprive the movement of cash; and in the first week suggested how they might obtain information about Congress funds and prevent contributions. Recommended tactics included not only seizure of money belonging to illegal associations but orders that suspected contributors should show weekly statements of all their disbursements to an official. Congress organizations naturally tried to hide their funds. News came into Delhi from many provincial administrations that just before the police searched banks, firms and individuals who were known to have been holding funds these were withdrawn and hidden. However, substantial amounts were forfeited (see Table 9). Congressmen complained bitterly that they were harassed even when they held no Congress funds and in such cases were jailed for other offences if they failed to pay up.[51]

---

[48] *ibid.* p. 337; U.P. FR1, May 1932, Home Poll., 1932, File No. 18/8; Bombay FRs 1 & 2, August 1932, *ibid*, File No. 18/11 Bombay FR2, February 1933, FRs 1 & 2, March 1933, Home Poll., 1933, File Nos. 18/2 & 18/4; AICC Bulletin No. 2, 15 April 1932, AICC Papers, 1932, File No. 12 Misc.

[49] AICC Bulletin No. 5, 15 October 1932, *ibid.*; J. P. Narayan to all PCC secretaries, 21 June 1932, AICC Papers, 1932, File No. P-22.

[50] Typed report on progress of civil disobedience, April 1932–March 1933, AICC Papers, 1932, File No. 15 Misc.: AICC statement of income & expenditure, January 1932–July 1933, revised AICC statement of income & expenditure, 1 January 1932–31 March 1934, AICC Papers, 1932, File No. F-3.

[51] Govt. of India to all local govts., 7 January 1932, *The Civil Disobedience Movement 1930–34*, pp. 67–8; Bombay and Bihar & Orissa FR1s, January 1932, Bombay, U.P., Delhi FR2s, January 1932, Home Poll., 1932, File No. 18/1; undated typed report from Surat, AICC Papers, 1932, File No. P-35, part II.

TABLE 9. *Seizure of Congress funds in Bombay Presidency, January–April 1932*

Month	Description	Amount
January	Tilak Swaraj Fund balance	Rs. 40,000
	Bombay PCC	Rs. 246
February	Congress balances in three Karachi banks	Rs. 1,489-10-4
		Rs. 449-12-2
		Rs. 114-1-7
	Bombay PCC	Rs. 215
	Ahmedabad (Gujarat PCC)	Rs. 3,797
	Surat (sent from Ahmedabad to private individual in Surat for Congress use in Bardoli and Surat)	Rs. 10,800
March	Swadeshi Sabha, Ahmedabad	Rs. 35,705-8-3
	Chiplun taluka CC, Ratnagiri	Rs. 340-5-4
April	Ahmedabad (fixed deposits in joint name of G. V. Mavlankar and Vallabhbhai Patel on behalf of Gujarat Sabha)	Rs. 17,199
		Rs. 16,819

SOURCE: Bombay, FRs, January–April 1932, Home Poll., 1932, File Nos. 18/1, 18/4, 18/5, 18/7.

Lack of money became an almost insuperable problem for most provinces during 1932–33. In July the Madras PCC told Narayan that although it had received the 'five hundred' he had sent they needed the same again if they were to carry on. Early in 1933 Konda Venkatappayya from Guntur said they must have Rs. 1,000 a month as the AICC had promised, because it was not possible to manage on local contributions as they had in 1932. Kerala's 23rd 'Dictator' simultaneously demanded Rs. 1,000, complaining that he had been pressing the AICC repeatedly through its messengers to regard Kerala's financial plight. Bihar continually petitioned the AICC for funds and protested vigorously when it heard in April 1933 a rumour that its monthly grant was to be cut. Its volunteers dried up as the money ran out in September 1932, a fate Bengal had suffered as early as January, and Punjab by July. In Assam too lack of cash was a major handicap to the movement's progress.[52] U.P.'s financial position appears to have been stronger. Between January 1932 and August 1933 the PCC spent *c.* Rs. 63,000 and some strong DCCs, like Allahabad, Agra, Cawnpore and Lucknow were spending separately on their own account. As these were districts with major urban centres it seems likely that their funds came from business sources: and in Bombay, despite the seizures early in the year, Congress activities were subsidized by local merchants, in May apparently

[52] Madras letter to J. P. Narayan, 12 July 1932, Home Poll., 1932, File No. 14/25; K. Venkatappayya to AICC, 5 March 1933, A. K. Warrier to AICC, 5 March 1933, Bihar PCC to AICC, 11 April 1933, AICC Papers, 1933, File No. 4 Misc.; Bihar PCC to AICC, 2 April 1932, AICC Papers, 1932, File No. 17 Misc.; Assam report on civil disobedience, October–December 1932, AICC Papers, 1932, File No. P-35, part 1; secret report on Congress activities (*re* Punjab), 17 July 1932, Home Poll., 1932, File No. 5/67; *Report on the Administration of Bengal 1931–32* (Calcutta, 1933), pp. xi–xv.

to the tune of Rs. 30,000 a month. Gandhi's close business colleague, G. D. Birla, on his own admission 'liberally financed' Gandhi's anti-Untouchability and *khadi* campaigns, and Willingdon held him responsible for much of the money behind civil disobedience, though Birla firmly denied this – as indeed he had to in the circumstances prevailing in 1932 if he wished to keep out of jail.[53]

The initial government thrust against civil disobedience made the natural difficulties of organizing and financing a mass movement infinitely greater, and largely as a result of this onslaught the pattern of the conflict was very different from 1930. There was a surprising uniformity of types of disobedience at least in the early months while the AICC bulletins went out regularly. Processions, flag-raising, boycott and picketing started again, encouraged by observance of spcial 'days', National Week and a series of local political conferences. Raids were organized to recapture buildings which the government had seized as part of the crack-down which was now manifest in mass arrests, confiscation of property and tough police action against demonstrators. The intensity of the campaign varied from area to area, and some localities modified the all-India suggestions to suit themselves. The emergency council of the Bombay PCC for example had its own plans for National Week in disregard of Sarojini Naidu's suggestions; and the raids went on throughout the country far longer than the AICC had intended. However, there was no expansion of support and deepening of the Congress appeal as there had been in 1930 when many provinces developed those tactics which served local drives and concerns. Instead of gathering momentum in the first months the 1932 movement never really took off, and fairly swiftly died away; nor did it ever strike significant rural roots. The waning of active support and participation from March onwards was reflected in the numbers of arrests, the local administrations' weekly telegraphic reports and their routine fortnightly reports.[54] Contemporaries of varying political hues agreed on the timing and rate of the decline. Willingdon's Home Department reported at the end of March on the basis of local reports that civil disobedience was 'now definitely on down grade' and had not developed anywhere into rural agitation. Simultaneously Jayakar commented that the Congress agitation was practically dead except in Bombay; and in retrospect Jawaharlal agreed that after the first four months 'there was a gradual decline with occasional bursts'. By the last week of May Willingdon was reporting to Hoare that civil disobedience was 'in a pleasant state of lull', and in the

[53] J. Nehru, *An Autobriography*, p. 338; Jayakar to Sapru, 3 February & 24 May 1932, Sapru Papers, Series II; Birla to Hoare, 14 March 1932, enclosed by Hoare in letter to Willingdon, 8 April 1932, Mss. EUR.E.240 (1); Willingdon to Hoare, 9 October 1932, Mss. EUR.E.240 (6).

[54] Statistics of convictions, Table 8; weekly telegraphic reports by local administrations, Home Poll., 1932, File No. 5/46, 1933, File No. 3/1; provincial FRs, 1932, Home Poll., 1932, File Nos. 18/1, 18/4, 18/5, : 18/7–15, 1933, Home Poll., 1933, File Nos. 18/1, 18/2, 18/4–14, 1934, Home Poll., 1934, File Nos. 18/1–12.

last quarter of the year he constantly referred to the campaign as moribund and on its last legs.[55]

The scale of the response to Gandhi's call in January 1932 and the type of participants in the campaign can be gauged in part from the statistics for convictions and reports by local governments at the end of 1932 on the 'character and class' of civil disobedience prisoners. In the period ending April 1933 nearly 75,000 people were convicted, of whom about 70,000 were jailed, though not all of these were in prison at any one time. The provinces with the highest number of convicts were Bihar and Orissa (14,903), U.P. (14,659), Bombay (14,101) and Bengal (12,791). Of the major provinces Assam and Punjab produced the fewest – under 2,000 each. However, in proportion of prisoners to the provincial population the honours went to the Frontier (.250%), Bombay (.064%), Bihar and Orissa (.040%) and U.P. (.030%).[56]

Few convicts were Muslims except on the Frontier, a pattern reminiscent of 1930. In Peshawar Central Jail of *c.* 1,500 civil disobedience prisoners all were Muslims except five Hindus and two Sikhs: in Haripur Central Jail 1,983 were Muslims and only 24 Hindus: and 297 of the former were mullahs. Of the other provinces with Muslim majorities Punjab admitted 89.6% Hindus and Sikhs and only 10.3% Muslims among its 'better class' civil disobedience prisoners, and 59% Hindus, 35% Sikhs and 6% other communities among its lowlier prisoners; while in Bengal of 2,957 civil disobedience prisoners in Hijli special jail only 33 were Muslims, the rest being Hindus, and in two Dum Dum jails virtually all the prisoners were Hindus. Other provinces with significant Muslim populations reported a similar Muslim abstention from the movement. Only 2% of prisoners in Assam were Muslims, 1% in Bihar, about 2% in U.P., and 9% in Delhi. In Bombay 95% of prisoners were Hindus.[57]

A sizeable bloc of women (3,630) were among the civil disobedience convicts – the Frontier being the understandable exception in this pattern. Female participation had been a novel feature of the 1930 movement, and the phenomenon was again noted by some provinces. Bengal listed 90 in

[55] V (Home Dept.) to S of S, telegram, 27 March 1932, Home Poll., 1932, File No. 5/46; Jayakar to H. Polak, 1 & 7 April 1932, Jayakar Papers, Correspondence File No. 407, part II; J. Nehru, *An Autobiography*, p. 336; Willingdon to Hoare, 23 May 1932, Mss. EUR.E.240 (5); Willingdon to Hoare, 12 September, 3 & 17 October, 6 November 1932, Mss. EUR.E.240 (6).
[56] See Table 8. There are no comparable figures for convictions collected by Congress, which however claimed that the convictions were much more numerous than government admitted. It claimed, for example, that by mid-March 1932 Bihar had produced 6,500 Bengal 9,000, U.P. 10,300; published report of I.N.C. 1931–2, pp. 17–18, AICC Papers, 1932, File No. 17 Misc.
[57] These and subsequent provincial breakdowns of civil disobedience prisoners are in Home Poll., 1932, File No. 23/66, which gathered provincial reports on the character and class of convicts: each province provided statistics for jails where most of the political convicts were housed. Further information on the jail population is available in the annual provincial administration reports and occasionally in provincial FRs.

a special female jail, all of them Hindus: some were of good family but the female satyagrahis from notorious Midnapore included some prostitutes and many village widows. Bombay's Commissioner of Police commented that in the Gujarati part of the city women were wielding great influence and were fanatical supports of Gandhi: Bombay Presidency produced the largest number of women convicts. U.P. also had a large number, and Meerut's Commissioner reported with a certain masculine smugness from his part of the province:

> A feature, which is very difficult to estimate but which is becoming more and more important, is the position taken up by women. All women are now becoming politicians. Only a few are ready to take part in picketing or processions but all the younger women, whether Hindu or Muhammadans, who have received any form of education, are full of 'nationalist' sympathy. Being possessed of less sober judgement they are more and more led away by what they see in the papers and they are ready to believe any statement which is circulated in the English or vernacular press.[58]

The age of convicts also attracted official note. The number of prisoners under 21 in Assam jails shot up in 1932 and a large number of Assam's civil disobedience prisoners were students or unemployed ex-students. Madras, Punjab and U.P. also reported that they had jailed a certain number of students. In Bengal's Hijli jail only 56% of inmates were over 21, and the government commented that its young and illiterate prisoners came mostly from the west of the Presidency and were the sons of small landholders who could find no work. Of the convicts neighbouring Bihar had imprisoned, 70% were aged between 13 and 22.

When asked to comment on the 'class' of their civil disobedience prisoners local administrations found categorization difficult. All agreed, however, that while a large proportion were 'hirelings', known criminals cashing in on the Congress ticket, or people glad of jail food, a sizeable group were educated men and women of genuine political beliefs. One indication of this was their higher rate of literacy than among convicts in ordinary years. In Assam, for example, only 38 of of 1031 civil disobedience prisoners were illiterate; in Bombay's Yeravda and Visapur jails 1,977 out of 3,084 were literate; in Patna Camp jail the literacy rate was 45%. In U.P. early in 1932 petty tenants and labourers formed the bulk of political prisoners – 1,397 out of 2,004: only 454 of the total were literate. At the end of the year Lucknow's two jails had an average literacy rate of 23% whereas in Fyzabad, where superior prisoners were housed, of 140 B class prisoners five were lawyers, ten were BAs, four MAs or MScs and forty-two were students. In Madras, however, 759 out of 904 civil disobedience prisoners were illiterate; and on the Frontier the majority were illiterate

---

[58] P. W. Marsh, Meerut Commissioner, to U.P. Govt., 5 May 1932, Home Poll., 1932, File No. 14/28; note by H. Haig, 25 March 1932, based on information from P. A. Kelly, Bombay Commissioner of Police, Home Poll., 1932, File No. 5/82.

agriculturalists, precipitated into jail by loyalty to Islam and the hardships of unemployment and low prices affecting even that remote corner of the subcontinent. Punjab estimated that well over 80% of its prisoners were illiterate and hired men. In Bombay City the official estimate was that 20% of political prisoners were known criminals, while another large group were criminals imported from other provinces: the government's assertion that Congress imported 'hooligans' from Madras and U.P. (the latter being particularly rough and turbulent) found some substantiation in Jayakar's estimates of Congress activities in the city.[59] However, it was officially conceded that Gujarati convicts in the city were 'of better type'.

Reporting in mid-1932 on the degree of support for the movement, the government made a continental assessment which the statistics for conviction substantiated. The overwhelming majority of the population were not implicated in the campaign, and Muslims as a community were right outside it. Rural areas were much less affected than towns; while those who supported it were a minority of the Hindu intelligentsia and middle class.[60] Active participation was only part of the government's problem, as it admitted: there was a far wider band of peripheral sympathizers from all strata of Hindu society. For this reason statistics for arrest are not by themselves a reliable measurement of the temper of the country. Moreover, as the government policy was harsher than in 1930 and led to the rounding up of large numbers, and as different provinces experienced different manifestations which exposed their exponents to jail in different degrees, statistics alone are an inadequate guide to provincial variations and to the contrast with the pattern of conflict in 1930.[61]

Bombay Presidency was, as in 1930, the storm centre of the campaign. Excepting the Frontier it was the only area which posed real problems for the government. Even there the administration was never under such severe pressure as in 1930, partly because there developed no deep-rooted rural movement. Once again the lamentable economic conditions produced in part by the world-wide depression were fertile soil for unrest. The economic landslide continued in full force throughout 1931–2, though the depression eased slightly in 1932–3. In 1931–2 Bombay's imports were down nearly 13% on the previous year, most commodities falling in quantity and value simultaneously; in 1932–3 there was an improvement of 9% in value. Exports fell nearly 41% in value in 1931–2, the most catastrophic decline being that of raw cotton which formed half of Bombay's total exports; in the following year exports fell again – by 26% in value. In both years the entrepot trade declined. Yet another indicator of the plight of Bombay's

[59] Jayakar to Sapru, 3 February & 24 May 1932, Sapru Papers, Series II.

[60] V to S of S, 16 June 1932, Home Poll., 1932, File No. 14/28.

[61] Bihar & Orissa reported to Delhi, 12 April 1933, that its arrests appeared more numerous than in other provinces because there was probably more picketing and disturbances by unemployed and hungry 'bazar riff-raff' than elsewhere; therefore the statistics were an indicator of economic conditions rather than political allegiance: Home Poll., 1933, File No. 3/11.

premier industry was the collection of income and super tax from the textile millowners. In 1931–2 only Rs. 13 lakhs were collected, compared with Rs. 15 lakhs the previous year, despite an increase of almost 50% in the rate: the Ahmedabad mills paid all but one lakh of this. 27 out of 41 of Bombay City's mills were working at a loss, while in the next year in the wake of competition from Japanese products 17 out of 32 of Bombay's mills showed a loss and some had closed temporarily because they could not dispose of their stocks in the adverse market conditions.[62]

The state of Bombay's economy was aggravated by the boycott campaign which as in 1930 reached significant proportions. Again a vicious circle developed – of depression generating support for Congress and its tactics, and those tactics contributing to the disruption of the city's economic life. Picketing was resumed, particularly against foreign-cloth shops but in lesser degree against chemists and druggists; and there were protracted hartals in the Mulji Jetha market, and the Stock, Bullion and Cotton Exchanges. The cotton trade was the hardest hit. The Mulji Jetha market observed hartal for the first three months of the year, but even when dealers began to trade there again in *swadeshi* cloth in April the threat of picketing dissuaded them from opening the foreign section, and many foreign-cloth dealers moved into Kalbadevi and adjacent areas. Not until October did the East India Cotton Association decide to remove the boycott. The market's proprietors offered to reduce rents by over half if dealers would return: over eighty did, but they were nervous of stocking goods there and dealt covertly for fear of picketing. British cotton firms were subject to severe pressure. Some were black-listed for boycott in a Congress leaflet, and the Japanese consul admitted that his compatriots feared to have dealings with British firms lest they should be boycotted, too. Bombay's European firms, unlike their Calcutta counterparts, were heavily dependent on Indian cooperation and were ambivalent about resorting to government help in these circumstances. Some of them began to negotiate with their Indian associates for terms of open trade: in October a group of them, against the Bombay government's advice, to gain a relaxation signed a statement that they shared the national sympathies of their Indian colleagues in the cotton trade, and agreed among other things not to trade on Mondays which were 'Gandhi Days'. Not all Indian businessmen were in favour of the Congress campaign, but prominent among the boycott's supporters were the Bombay Cotton Brokers, the Native Share and Stock Brokers, and the Bombay Shroffs' Association. The local government was seriously worried that such groups could disrupt whole markets, and that the East India Cotton Association appeared unable to control the cotton market. In September, therefore, it passed the Bombay Cotton Contracts Act to regulate dealings in the cotton market; by this act it could supersede the Association's Board of Directors to secure

[62] *1931–32 Bombay Administration Report*, pp. vi–vii, xviii, 86; *Bombay – 1932–33. A Review of the Administration of the Presidency* (Bombay, 1934), pp. vi–vii, 73–4.

free trading. However the power was not used because the boycott tailed off from the autumn.[63]

At the height of the movement Sykes noted that his Commissioner of Police believed that Congress had more power than government in the cotton market, and he himself admitted 'that up to the present they have achieved a considerable measure of success if success is to be measured by interference with normal trade and influence over a particularly susceptible section of the Bombay commercial community'.[64] The effects were reflected in India's piece-goods import figures, since Bombay was the major port touched by the boycott. In 1931–2 776 million yards were imported compared with 890 million in 1930–1, and their value was down from Rs. 20 crores to Rs. 14.7 crores.[65]

The support of many of the Presidency's businessmen for civil disobedience was crucial for its momentum, not just in declaring hartals and boycotting British firms and goods, but also in financing Congress activities. Their reasons for doing so varied from group to group, but they differed little from the rationale behind their support of the 1930 campaign. For Ahmedabad millowners the *swadeshi* doctrine spelt profits for their mills, though they did not hesitate simultaneously to invest in British machinery. Kasturbhai Lalbhai and Ambalal Sarabhai also had close personal ties with the Gujarati whom they had revered for years; and believed that he was a bulwark against revolutionary tendencies so long as he remained pilot of the Congress. Reverence for Gandhi and distrust of British intentions were potent drives behind much business support for Congress, confirming a natural reluctance to avoid social ostracism and boycott's pressure. Many who disapproved of the boycott methods were driven into the arms of Congress by fear that real Indian autonomy and particularly control over the country's economy was still far off; and that without this India would continue to be governed for the satisfaction of British interests.[66]

The Ordinances promulgated in January saved Bombay City from becoming enemy territory from the government's point of view, as it had

[63] For reports on the Bombay boycott campaign see monthly reports by Bombay Commissioner of Police and Collector of Customs, Home Poll., 1933, File No. 3/20; Bombay FRs, 1932, Home Poll., 1932, File No. 18/subsections; *1932–33 Bombay Administration Report*, p. ii; Willingdon to Hoare, 1 May 1932, Mss. EUR.E.240 (5); Sykes to Willingdon, 19 March & 13 May 1932, Sykes to Hoare, 6 March & 5 November 1932, Mss. EUR.F.150 (4).
   Several Bombay Congress Bulletins-Boycott Supplements for 1932, 4-page printed pamphlets, price ½ anna, are in AICC Papers, 1932, File No. 12 Misc.
[64] Sykes to Willingdon, 13 May 1932, Mss. EUR.F.150 (4).
[65] *India in 1931–32*, p. 137.
[66] Sykes to Hoare, 19 June 1932, Mss. EUR.F.150 (4); Govt. of Bombay to Govt. of India, 18 May 1932, and particularly 2 May 1932 report by Monteath, Bombay I.C.S. officer, on which Bombay's letter was partly based, Home Poll., 1932, File No. 14/28; Lalji Naranji to Jayakar, 27 January 1932, Jayakar Papers, Correspondence File No. 456.

been in 1930. Sykes reported that one could drive from one end of the city to the other without knowing that civil disobedience existed, though he realized that Congress had adapted its tactics to meet the constraints of the new situation and was concentrating on the disruption of trade. His Police Commissioner told Haig that the Gujarati part of the city was as hostile as ever. Not only was Congress able to show its power in the cloth market and in picketing, but it kept up publication of its bulletin despite police attempts to track it down and destroy its production network. Mass demonstrations had stopped by mid-March but though there was increasing public reluctance to fall foul of the Ordinances large crowds, generally hostile to government, came to watch individual demonstrations. The National Week in April attracted scant support, however, and from then on incidents of law-breaking were largely the work of hooligans and hired men. Observers were unanimous that it was the Gujarati sympathy for Gandhi and civil disobedience which, combined with businessmen's compounded fears, made the city 'the Keep of Gandhism' – in Sykes's words. It was Gujaratis who in the early phase provided much of the man and woman power and the finances of the campaign; their community whose web of business connections through the provision of capital and men which made it impossible for others to carry on business without their cooperation. Moreover Bombay was a vast rabbit warren of a city where propaganda could flourish unchecked, where large numbers of unemployed could be hired and outsiders brought in to agitate; where in fact the old-style paternalism of the raj was outdated as a mode of social and political control.[67]

The city's mill areas were barely affected by civil disobedience, and few Muslims became involved. Bloody strife rather than joint opposition to government characterized communal relations in mid-1932. Communal rioting erupted in the city on 14 May, a contributory factor being Congress pressure on Muslim traders, one of whom had been placed on the boycott list. Although troops and police contained the situation antagonism smouldered on, and there was a fresh outbreak late in June. By the end of July 217 people had been killed and 2,710 injured; of the fatal

[67] Note by H. Haig, Govt. of India Home Member, 25 March 1932, based on information from P. A. Kelly, Bombay Commissioner of Police, Home Poll., 1932, File No. 5/82; Bombay Commissioner of Police report to Govt. of India, 2 May 1932, *ibid.* File No. 14/28: Govt. of Bombay, Home Sec., to Govt. of India, Home Sec., 27 April 1932, forwarding note on National Week in Bombay, *ibid.* File No. 5/82; Jayakar to Sapru, 3 February, 7 April & 24 May 1932, Sapru Papers, Series II; Sykes to Hoare, 6 March 1932, Mss. EUR.F.150 (4); Sethna to Mrs Barns, 16 March 1932, Sethna Papers.

Copies of the Bombay Congress Bulletin are in AICC Papers, 1932, File No. 8 Misc. & Thakurdas Papers, File No. 101/1930. These were issued by the Bombay PCC Emergency Council and consisted of one or two foolscap typed and cyclostyled sheets, price 1 pice. They were headed 'Freedom Be Thou My Soul' and 'Sedition Be Mine Song', and contained comments on current events, messages from Congressmen, plans for future agitation. names of the current Emergency Council etc.

casualties 132 were Hindus and 84 Muslims, while the two communities suffered almost equal numbers of injured.[68]

Muslim hostility to civil disobedience was clear in Sind, and this largely ensured the area's quiescence. One young British official noted in January, 'The political situation so far as Sind is concerned is perfectly quiet and well in hand. In fact I feel that we are using a sledge hammer to kill flies, with these savage ordinances...the "movement" in Sind never really had much guts.'[69] A similar tranquility prevailed in the rest of the Presidency countryside almost without exception, even in those areas which had generated wide support for civil disobedience in 1930; and this was no reflection of an upswing in the economy as prices of agricultural produce continued to fall. In Gujarat there remained obvious sympathy for Congress tactics, particularly among the Patidars, and a continuing elevation of Gandhi to the status of hero and prophet. In the words of Maxwell, now acting as Bombay's Home Secretary.

> ...among Gujaratis, wherever they may be and however little apprecia-
> tion they may have of political questions, there is a strong feeling of
> personal loyalty to Mr. Gandhi which is not based on any reasoned
> support of his programme and could almost be described as a non-political
> factor if it did not so easily lend itself to exploitation for political purposes.

Civil disobedience in Gujarat in 1932 manifested itself in attempts to withhold land revenue, the village of Ras again being one of the most spectacular centres; and a rash of district conference in June, followed by *taluka* conferences in August and September. But the Ordinances took the life out of the new campaign from the start – by arrests and by forfeiture of the networks of ashrams and *chhavnis* which had been the core of the local organization in 1930. Moreover at the prompting of the Political Department the Baroda government secured its frontier with Gujarat to prevent the mass exodus which had occurred two years before and the assistance of Baroda Patidars to their caste fellows in Gujarat.[70] The neighbouring princely state of Mysore provided a refuge for the organizers of a no-tax campaign in Siddapur, Ankola and Kumta *talukas* of Kanara, the only rural area where the Bombay government admitted that it experienced real difficulty in 1932. The local Congress reckoned that over 1,000

[68] Bombay FRs, May–July 1932, Home Poll., 1932, File Nos. 18/8–10.

[69] Letter home, 27 January 1932, quoted in H. T. Lambrick, 'Prospects for a United India, after the Cessation of British Rule, as these appeared in Sind 1930–46', Phillips & Wainwright (ed.), *The Partition Of India*, p. 509; confidential memorandum by Sind Commissioner, 4 May 1932, Home Poll., 1932, File No. 14/28.

[70] R. M. Maxwell to Govt. of India, 18 May 1932, *ibid.*
For civil disobedience in Gujarat in 1932 see local officers' reports in *ibid.*; C. Clee, Officiating Bombay Home Sec. to Govt. of India, Home Sec., 29 August 1932, Mss. EUR.F.150 (4); files containing reports from Gujarat, AICC Papers, 1932, File Nos. P-12, P-35, part II.
For the cooperation of the Baroda government see file on States' cooperation in combatting civil disobedience, Home Poll., 1932, File No. 5/4; Bombay FR1, January 1932, *ibid.* File No. 18/1.

agriculturalists were withholding tax, but they were eventually coerced into submission by the imposition of additional police at the cost of the inhabitants of the affected *talukas*.[71] In the Presidency as a whole there was none of the turbulence which had marked 1930: salt satyagraha barely left the ground, forest satyagraha never reached major proportions, and revenue collections were satisfactory.

On the Frontier the situation remained disturbed through January, and in Peshawar district until April. There, as the type of prisoners indicated, the main participants were landless labourers who in normal times existed on the wages paid by Pathan landlords. The latter's profits were cut drastically by the depression, and many of their dependents now found themselves without work or means of support and became willing converts to the Red Shirt campaign. The lure of promised redistribution of land and wealth in the new era was reinforced by reverence for Abdul Ghaffar as a religious leader in conflict with an infidel government. Troop movements in all districts (excepting Hazara where they had not been needed) had controlled the situation by early April. However in April elections to the new legislative council provided a sitting target for Red Shirt opposition. Stones were thrown at lorries carrying voters, women with Korans on their heads persuaded people not to vote, one candidate was penned up in his house, and the climax came with huge demonstrations in various places when police and many voters were injured and the police opened fire. Not surprisingly only 25% of the electorate voted. Partly as a result of this behaviour there was a considerable backlash of Hindu opinion against the Red Shirts, deepening the rifts and suspicion which had plagued the local Congress in 1931. Red Shirt activity decreased thereafter, and even in Peshawar district it was reduced to sporadic picketing and secret meetings – dislocated largely by the arrest of the main organizers who were still at large. During the following year the return to normal conditions continued as government still exercised tight controls, particularly the imposition of collective fines on acknowledged Red Shirt villages; but partly, too, as a result of an upswing in the rural economy produced by a good harvest and rise in the price of food grains.[72]

In three other provinces, U.P., Bihar and Orissa and Bengal, large numbers were convicted during 1932. In each the numbers were evidence of the new government policy in the early stages of the movement rather than wider support for the campaign than in 1930. Local evidence showed that the drives behind civil disobedience were less intense than in 1930, and

[71] File on civil disobedience in Karnatak, AICC Papers, 1932, File No. P-13; *1932–33 Bombay Administration Report*, p. 20; *Bombay – 1933–34. A Review of the Administration of the Presidency* (Bombay, 1935), p. x.

[72] N.-W.F.P. report to Govt. of India, 26 May 1932, Home Poll., 1932, File No. 14/28; note on the Frontier by G. Kripalani, 13 July 1932, AICC Papers, 1932, File No. P-16; *1932–33. Administration Report of the North West Frontier Province* (Peshawar, 1934), pp. i–v; *1933–34. Administration Report of the North West Frontier Province* (Peshawar, 1935), pp. i–ii.

were swiftly repressed by the Ordinance powers. In U.P., whence came the severest pressure on Gandhi to re-start civil disobedience, there had been considerable doubt even among Congressmen at the wisdom of Jawaharlal's enthusiasm for another local campaign, and scepticism about the village level drive behind it. As 1932 progressed it became clear that the no-tax campaign was a damp squib compared with the outburst of late 1930 and early 1931. It was strongest in Allahabad district, but even there it was petering out in February; and by early March 70 % of the district's revenue was in. Arrest of the organizers was certainly a factor in this; but a slight rise in food grain prices lifted the rural depression somewhat in 1932, and the remissions granted as a result of the Rent and Revenue Commission's deliberations helped to blunt rural enthusiasm. The Commission met again in July and rent and revenue remissions were continued for the next agricultural year, though the former were at a lower level. Consequently in U.P. the 1932 civil disobedience was, unlike its predecessor, a largely urban phenomenon in which Allahabad and Cawnpore figured particularly prominently. There was some picketing, a little illicit salt manufacture, illegal processions, raids on seized buildings, distribution of leaflets, fires in letter boxes and some cutting of telegraph wires. Attempts to hold district conferences in June showed the ingenuity of the organizers still at large more than popular support for them: at Cawnpore a 'conference' was held on a boat in the Ganges, and in Muzaffarnagar a conference president disguised himelf in a *burqa*! Support for these feats of imagination was poor, and in July local leaders meeting in Benares and Allahabad acknowledged the position and decided to concentrate on fund raising and training volunteers in the hope of a later revival rather than waste energy on immediate developments.[73]

In neighbouring Bihar prices continued to fall, but there was less landlord pressure than in U.P. to precipitate rural conflict. There was real distress however in Tirhut division in August, but this did not coincide with the outbreak of rural turbulence in north Bihar which occurred from late January until March. This took the form of massed attacks on police and police stations, and attempts to raise the Congress flag on public buildings. The administration retaliated with police firing and the imposition of seven forces of additional police in Muzaffarpur, Champaran and Monghyr. Outside this area there was little public sympathy for civil disobedience. Once the leaders were incarcerated early in January the movement fell

[73] *1931-32 U.P. Administration Report.* pp. iv, xvi-xx, U.P. FR2, June 1932, Home Poll., 1932, File No. 18/9; U.P. Chief Sec. to Govt. of India, Home Dept., 16 May 1932, *ibid.* File No. 14/28; weekly telegraphic reports from U.P., 1932, *ibid.* File No. 5/46; file on U.P. L/P&J/7/293; J. Nehru, *An Autobiography*, p. 330.

An example of leaflets being circulated was an appeal to ' *Police ke Bhaiyo* ' (police brethren) issued by the PCC President; U.P. FR1, April 1932, Home Poll., 1932, File No. 18/7.

The upswing in figures for convictions in February 1933 was due to celebrations of Independence Day and some revival in no-rent propaganda and picketing.

flat, provincial planning and organization became impossible, and those who produced the various manifestations of resistance – picketing, processions, flag raising and the like – were mostly juveniles and hired participants, while funds lasted. But they received little of the popular acclaim which had greeted convicts in 1930, and even older students kept aloof. That there was little heart in the movement was clear when in Patna the total attendance at a celebration of Gandhi Day on 4 January 1933 was two leaders, two volunteers, two women and one baby. The excise department was still in trouble however. Picketers were disposed of under the Ordinances but anti-excise propaganda continued through printed and cyclostyled pamphlets, and this, combined with people's low purchasing power, led to a further decrease in excise revenue. In 1932 it was down by over Rs. 6 lakhs on 1931 and in 1930–1, 1931–2, and 1932–3 it dropped steadily from Rs. 142 lakhs to Rs. 122 lakhs and Rs. 120 lakhs.[74]

Although Bengali conviction figures were near Bihar's they represented a far lower percentage of the population. Here, too, the swift arrest of the Congress leadership paralyzed any provincially organized campaign and it was left to individuals and local groups to respond to Gandhi's call in the way which suited them best, or to turn a deaf ear. Although Bengal had been a significant factor in Gandhi's decision to revive civil disobedience there was little widespread militancy in the Presidency. The 1931 Ordinances were reaction not to mass unrest but to terrorism, the symptom of the frustrations of a minority, the younger and often unemployed *bhadralok*. Calcutta itself provided the largest number of convicts early in 1932. Here there was a fairly effective boycott campaign and the piece-goods market only reopened properly in March. The PCC issued an illegal paper, *The Challenge*, but its appearance, illegal processions and letter box fires were no real challenge to the administration, and the capital grew increasingly quiet after the first months of the year. In the rural areas of east Bengal support for civil disobedience was either non-existent or waned swiftly, and by the first week in April the government reported it as 'nearly dead'. In Tipperah and Mymensingh where anti-rent agitations developed among jute cultivators, hard hit by the depression in jute prices, these were no part of civil disobedience, and in an area where Hindus were landlords and money lenders only ranged the rural activists, Muslims and low caste Hindu tenants, against the supporters of Congress. In Bengal's western districts civil disobedience struck rural roots only where its tactics served an existing local grievance, particularly in Arambagh (Hooghly district) where resettlement had begun late in 1931 and a vigorous boycott of the operations ensued; and in Midnapore, that old Congress stronghold. In the latter

[74] *1931–32 Bihar & Orissa Administration Report*, pp. xvii–xviii, xxi, 9–16, 20–2, 89–97; *Bihar and Orissa in 1932–33* (Patna, 1934), pp. ii–iii, 18, 63, 71–6; Officiating Chief Sec., Bihar & Orissa, to Govt. of India, Home Dept., 12 May 1932, Home Poll., 1932, File No. 14/28. The high figures for convictions in February 1933 appear to have been due to Independence Day celebrations.

agitation against the chaukidari tax was renewed, salt laws were broken and extra police were imposed to deal with disorderly mass demonstrations. However the fines for the upkeep of the police proved as difficult to collect as unpopular taxes, and the whole district continued to be a centre of Congress influence well into 1933 when all other districts were quiet. The momentum and organization were in both districts of local origin, and owed little either to Gandhian inspiration or Bengal PCC direction.[75]

C. P. Assam, Punjab and Madras had few such local groups with particular incentives to heed the Congress call, and their contribution to civil disobedience was marginal. In C.P. the campaign was confined to a few urban areas and there was no parallel to the enthusiastic wave of forest satyagrahis in 1930. Since then the local administration had made a detailed enquiry into grievances over forest regulations and an attempt to revive forest satyagraha in Betul in March collapsed swiftly for lack of support. By the end of the last week in April all the local government could find to report was one burning rag in a pillar box.[76] The Assam government reported that there was no mass response to civil disobedience as there had been in 1920–1, or to a lesser extent in 1930. Its manifestations in the early months of 1932, picketing, speeches, processions and the enrolment of volunteers, were limited to a few centres, particularly Sylhet, and as a local Congress report bemoaned in April, the educated were largely indifferent to the renewed campaign.[77] Muslim opposition to civil disobedience in Assam was parallelled in Punjab, depriving it of any popular thrust. Moreover in Punjab the Sikh community as a whole gave the movement no support despite overtures from Congressmen such as Dr Kitchlew. Pro-Congress Sikhs tried in vain to persuade the Shiromani Akali Dal as a body to support Congress. There was some picketing and disruption of the cloth trade, but by July Punjabi Congressmen still at large admitted that there was no prospect of a revivified campaign, and blamed Jawaharlal and Abdul Ghaffar Khan for precipitating a fight for which the country was unready. Among the reasons they listed for their local stagnation were shortage of funds because of public apathy, people's reluctance to go to jail for long periods, communal tension, dislocation of their organization

[75] *1931–32 Bengal Administration Report*, pp. xi–xv, xxv–xxvi; Bengal's weekly telegraphic reports on civil disobedience, 1932, Home Poll., 1932, File No. 5/46; reports on civil disobedience in Bengal, 1932, AICC Papers, 1932, File No. 4 Misc.
Evidence of the distribution of support for civil disobedience is in the regional variation of numbers of arrests: according to Congress sources, between April & June 1932 few were arrested in eastern districts, Calcutta's figure was 1,258 of a total of 4,499, Hooghly produced 280 & Midnapore 510: *The Challenge*, 25 July 1932, *ibid.*
[76] C.P.'s weekly telegraphic reports on civil disobedience, 1932, Home Poll., 1932, File No. 5/46; *The Central Provinces and Berar, 1931–32. A Review of the Administration of the Province. Volume I* (Nagpur, 1933), pp. 1–2, 14.
[77] Letters from Commissioners of Surma & Assam Valleys to Chief Sec., Govt. of Assam, 3 May 1932, Home Poll., 1932, File No. 14/28; Assam's weekly telegraphic reports on civil disobedience, 1932, *ibid.* File No. 5/46; reports on civil disobedience in Assam, 1932, File Nos. P-3, P-35, part 1.

by government action, lack of leaders, and public preoccupation with economic problems which spilled over into criticism of Congress for helping to cause unemployment by its disruptive tactics.[78] A repercussion of the communal tension in the province was growing Hindu suspicion of Congress and fear that Gandhi and the Working Committee could not be trusted to protect them against Muslim domination in the forthcoming constitutional changes.

In Madras Presidency swift repressive action under the Ordinances dislocated civil disobedience. The local government paid particular attention to the Telugu delta districts where an anti-land revenue campaign was already under way, and by mid-1932 its manifestations had subsided. In the rest of the Presidency there were few such issues which could serve as recruiting bases for widespread rural satyagraha. Moreover the activity which had proved most popular during the 1931 settlement, picketing, now incurred jail sentences. Picketing remained the most significant feature of the campaign, particularly in the Tamil areas, its object being not only to secure the boycott of foreign cloth and liquor but to collect large crowds and precipitate conflict with the police as a form of political advertisement. It was an almost entirely urban phenomenon, the main centres being Madras itself, Virudunagar in Ramnad district and Madura. Malabar too presented problems for the local administration through the year. As late as March 1933 it sprouted a well-organized attempt to establish a Congress postal service. But as with the Presidency's other manifestations, this too was suppressed with the embracing powers at the government's disposal.[79]

In such circumstances it was extremely difficult for Congressmen to embark on any all-India activity or policy discussion. When those leaders who were out of jail did manage to meet their encounters proved how frustrating the conflict was becoming both for them and the rank and file now that government had armed itself so massively. As jail became the almost inevitable result of participating in civil disobedience it ceased to be an attractive pastime except to those who were deeply committed ideologically to Gandhi and the attainment of independence by this means, or were glad of the shelter and food jail provided. To provincial leaders it meant not only certain jail but a campaign which did nothing to cement a local following or forward their long-term constitutional ambitions. Civil

[78] Secret report on Congress activities, 17 July 1932, Home Poll., 1932, File No. 5/67; Punjab's weekly telegraphic reports on civil disobedience, 1932, Home Poll., 1932, File No. 5/46; Punjab FR2, January & February 1932, Home Poll., 1932, File Nos. 18/1 & 4.

[79] *1931–32 Madras Administration Report*, pp. xi–xiv; V to S of S, telegram, 28 February 1932, Mss. EUR.E.240 (11); Govt. of Madras, Acting Chief Sec., to Govt. of India, Home Sec., 12 May 1932, Home Poll., 1932, File No. 14/28; Madras FR1, March 1933, Home Poll., 1933, File No. 18/4; Madras weekly telegraphic reports on civil disobedience, 1932, Home Poll., 1932, File No. 5/46; Congress reports on civil disobedience in Tamil Nad & Andhra, 1932, AICC Papers, 1932, File Nos. P-2, P-19, P-35, part 1; *Police Raj under Emergency Ordinance* (B.M., PIB 9/31), which is a summary of civil disobedience in Tamil Nad, 4 January – 30 June 1932.

disobedience had consequently become in 1932 a force making for disintegration in Indian politics rather than integration as it had been in 1930. But the barriers to discussion meant that Congressmen would find it extremely difficult to inaugurate any continental change of programme despite their frustration.

In April an attempted Congress session in Delhi demonstrated the disarray in the Congress ranks. It was the brain child of Sarojini Naidu, then Acting President, and Pandit Malaviya, who agreed to preside: it was intended to demonstrate the continuing vitality of Congress. Apart from Malaviya's speech there were to be three resolutions, reaffirming the Congress goal of complete independence, endorsing the Working Committee's civil disobedience resolution and affirming that Gandhi was the sole representative of Congress. From several provinces came the response that the suggestion was madness: government would clamp down on it, provincial delegates would be reluctant to face certain incarceration particularly in a strange region, and the resulting fiasco would harm Congress prestige. Nonetheless Malaviya and Mrs Naidu went ahead with the plan. In the event the session was formally prohibited. Local governments picked off many of the delegates who planned to attend (including Mrs Naidu) and the occasion degenerated into a debacle when within five minutes of the start of the proceedings the police arrested the 200 odd who had gathered.[80]

By July Malaviya and Kitchlew who were attempting to coordinate Congress activities were receiving reports from the provinces of the dislocation of the campaign – a melancholy tale of incarceration of leaders, lack of new participants and shortage of funds. Madras noted that enthusiasm had collapsed far more swiftly than in 1930, and from U.P. came news that the present movement there was disintegrating. There was some talk of a new programme in conjunction with Sapru and Liberal politicians, but eventually Malaviya and Kitchlew decided not to attempt a change of programme as this might kill the movement. When they discussed the matter with members of the Working Committee who were free in early August at Benares their advice was accepted and the meeting issued a holding statement stressing the boycott campaign. Those present clearly hoped that the Communal Award the British Government had just made might generate more support for their failing movement. Sapru and Jayakar discussed the situation by letter in August. Both agreed that having burnt their fingers in two previous peace attempts they were not going to embark on another. They considered that despite the frustrations in Congress circles at the impasse into which conflict had landed them it was highly

---

[80] S. Naidu to PCCs, 29 March 1932, AICC Papers, 1932, File No. P-22; papers relating to Delhi Congress including letters of protest, *ibid.* File No. 17 Misc.; Delhi FR1, April 1932, Provincial FR2s, April 1932, Home Poll., 1932, File No. 18/7; *India in 1931–32*, pp. 44–5; Jayakar to H. Polak, 9 May 1932, Jayakar Papers, Correspondence File No. 407, part II.

improbable that any change of policy would occur since the main leaders were in jail and any discontinuation of the campaign would result in loss of prestige.[81]

The Government of India showed no sign of frustration at being in renewed conflict with Congress. Indeed Willingdon and some of his colleagues exuded a positive relief that a fight was on at last after the ambiguities and strains of having to observe Irwin's settlement. Symptomatic of this attitude was the renewal of the Ordinance powers virtually *in toto* by a consolidating Emergency Powers Ordinance promulgated on 30 June just before the existing Ordinances expired. Within two weeks of the initial Ordinances Sykes had pressed Willingdon unsuccessfully for a public declaration that their powers would not be withdrawn until illegal activities had ceased. His intention was to squash any hopes among Congressmen that there might be an early settlement and jail delivery. He returned to the question in March and April, arguing that a lapse in the Ordinances would strengthen Congress and do nothing to rally moderate opinion. In the event his fears proved unjustified. Delhi called for the views of local governments in April and on their evidence the powers were not allowed to lapse, despite the anxieties of Ramsay MacDonald about the final political outcome of Ordinance rule.[82]

MacDonald had asked outright:

> Will a point come when Mr. Gandhi will be allowed to enter into political conversations for the purpose of reaching an agreement; or must we go on keeping him in prison, whilst a policy of smashing Congress is being pursued by Ordinance methods? If the former, are opportunities now being watched for, or has the time not come?

On this point Willingdon and his colleagues were adamant. From the time Gandhi was incarcerated they maintained that they had no need of his cooperation and that any suggestion of negotiations with him or permission to let him engage in discussions with his colleagues and sympathizers would be damaging to the government's present policy and boost the prestige of Congress. Consistently they refused requests for permission to interview Gandhi from Thakurdas, for example, and a large number of sympathizers

[81] Jayakar to Sapru, 13 August 1932, Sapru to Jayakar, 18 August 1932, Sapru Papers, Series II: secret reports on Congress activities, 16 & 17 July 1932, Home Poll., 1932, File No. 5/67; report on progress of civil disobedience, April 1932 – March 1933, AICC Papers, 1932, File No. 15. Misc.; Delhi FR1, August 1932, Home Poll., 1932, File No. 18/11.

[82] MacDonald was in an awkward political position, inundated with left-wing letters and constantly attacked by such papers as *The Daily Herald, The Nation,* and *The Manchester Guardian*; this lay behind his worried query to Willingdon, 31 March 1932, enclosed in Miéville (P.S.V.) to Haig, 10 April 1932, IOL, Haig Papers, Mss. EUR.F.115 (1); Hoare to Willingdon, 22 April 1932, Mss. EUR.E.240 (2).

Sykes's pressure on Willingdon in telegrams, 18 January & 26 April 1932, letters, 19 March & 19 April 1932, Mss. EUR.F.150 (4).

Govt. of India to all local govts., 20 April 1932, *ibid.*; text of June Special Powers Ordinance, *The Civil Disobedience Movement 1930–34,* pp. 171–87.

and pressmen.[83] Hoare had announced in the Commons on 29 April that Gandhi could contact the government without intermediaries, but in June he raised the question of allowing Gandhi a private talk with someone like Rangaswami Aiyengar, editor of *The Hindu*, not with a view to negotiation but in order to let Gandhi know that if he did contact the government he would not be snubbed or confronted with humiliating conditions. He was moved to reopen the question by pressure from the Archbishop of York, who believing that Gandhi was out for peace, wished the way to be made as easy as possible for him. Willingdon replied sharply that he did not believe Gandhi desired peace on terms acceptable to the government; and that any such interview would be interpreted as the start of negotiations and would shake the government's position which depended on the confidence of its officials and supporters that it would maintain its present policy. Bluntly he wired to Hoare that government had no need of Gandhi and would be glad to see his political influence eroded.

> I sometimes wonder whether there is not a tendency in England to attach too much importance to Gandhi, and to suppose that India can have no peace until we have reached an agreement with him. In the past, his influence has varied greatly with the treatment that he has received from the Government. I think that it is right to say it was at a very low ebb when he was released from jail just after the non-co-operation movement. It was at its height after the Delhi pact. Six months hence, if we continue our present policy, it will, I think, be seriously diminished.[84]

Hoare accepted Willingdon's reasoning and dropped the idea of a visit by Aiyengar. He wondered instead whether Bombay government officials could visit Gandhi regularly, instead, and was told that the District Magistrate, the Prison Superintendant and the Inspector-General of Prisons did.

Although Willingdon maintained that his government had no need of Gandhi, and despite the fact that the Mahatma's new campaign had been mortally wounded by repression, the raj's position was still precarious. It desperately needed a swift reform package to ensure the collaboration of its tentative supporters in building new foundations of imperial stability. This was implicit in the Viceroy's speech to the Legislature on 25 January when he sweetened his justification of the disagreeable medicine of repression with the promise that the programme of constitutional discussion and advance outlined by MacDonald at the end of the second Round Table Conference would continue. Haig, who had succeeded Crerar as Government of India Home Member in March, underlined the urgency of reform

[83] V to S of S, telegram, 19 January 1932, Mss. EUR.E.240 (11); Willingdon to Hoare, 22 February 1932, Mss. EUR.E.240 (5).

[84] V to S of S, telegram, 25 June 1932, Mss. EUR.E.240 (11). For the rest of this exchange see S of S to V, telegrams, 18 & 23 June 1932, V to S of S, telegrams, 21 June & July 1932, *ibid.*; Hoare to Willingdon, 24 June 1932, Mss. EUR.E.240 (2), V to Governor of Bombay, telegram, 29 June 1932, Governor's telegraphic reply, 30 June 1932, Mss. EUR.F.150 (4). *The Hindu*, through basically pro-Congress, was ambivalent on the current civil disobedience programme.

when he was confronted with MacDonald's query about the wisdom of rule by Ordinance. He argued that they were not trying to rule by Ordinance and crush a spirit of Nationalism; and though it was vital to defeat civil disobedience it was equally vital that constitutional reforms should come as swiftly as possible, because only this could bring contentment to political India.[85] In fact Willingdon had urged Hoare to consider the possibility of a British Indian Federation if the All-Indian Federal scheme was wrecked, as seemed likely, by princely opposition. When Hoare replied that this was impossible in the existing state of British opinion and party politics Willingdon went so far as to warn that if the security of princely conservatism in an All-India Federation was seen to be the precondition of advance all British Indians would become Congressmen and the government would have no supporters: 'if you lay this down as a basic proposition...then I look forward to the future with the gravest possible anxiety.'[86]

Although Willingdon recognized that it was urgent to press on with reform once he had closed the door to cooperation with Congress he found his path beset with obstacles from a number of sources. He spent much of the early part of 1932 having what he called a terrible time with the Princes, who were divided among themselves yet determined to protect their autonomy in any new dispensation.[87] Then from London came renewed pressure in April/May for a two-phased reform, provincial autonomy preceding an all-India Federation with responsibility at the centre. For Hoare this plan afforded a means of soothing Tory opinion in Parliament which had been hardening in reaction to the new Congress campaign. This was the idea which had created such a furore during the second London conference, and again the Hindu Liberal politicians opposed it bitterly. Sastri told the Prime Minister bluntly that such a scheme, attractive no doubt to Muslims and some highly ranked civilians, would never satisfy Congress. 'The followers of the Congress, who cannot be kept out of action indefinitely, will be strong enough to obstruct effectively the working of provincial autonomy; and if the Government of His Majesty is to be carried on it will have to be through the nearly exclusive agency of those minor communities whose claims are fully conceded.' He also pointed out that the delay in implementing the reforms was giving every interest and community, including the Princes, time to raise their demands.[88] Hoare

---

[85] H. Haig to E. Miéville, 13 April 1932, Mss. EUR.F.115 (1); *India in 1931–32*, pp. 46–7.

[86] Willingdon to Hoare, 8 February 1932, Mss. EUR.E.240 (5); also Willingdon to Hoare, 17 January & 6 March 1932, *ibid.*
Hoare judged that if an All-India Federation proved impossible they would be 'back on the pre-Round Table Conference status quo and 80 per cent. of the House of Commons will go back to unadulterated Simon Report'. Hoare to Willingdon, 3 March 1932, Mss EUR.E.240 (1).

[87] Willingdon to Hoare, 27 March & 4 April 1932, Mss. EUR.E.240 (5); Moore, *Crisis of Indian Unity*, pp. 270–84.

[88] V.S.S. Sastri to Ramsay MacDonald, 15 April 1932, Jagadisan, *Letters of Srinivasa Sastri*, pp. 224–7; Sastri to V. Rao, 10 April 1932, S No. 573, Sastri Papers; Hoare to Willingdon, 27 May 1932, Mss. EUR.E.240 (5).

dropped the scheme in view of Delhi's difficulties with its potential non-Congress Hindu allies. In June, however, with Cabinet support he made another proposal which threatened to rupture that alliance. Looking to his own Parliamentary position and the state of Tory opinion he suggested abandoning the third Round Table Conference, with all the expense involved and the opportunity it gave Indians to alienate their compatriots and British opinion by making set speeches rather than engaging in genuine negotiation. Instead Indian opinion would be heard through the Consultative Committee set up after the second conference which was already at work, and through Indian experts brought to London to discuss details. News of this rapidly reached the non-Congress Hindu politicians who had staked their prestige and expended months of their time on earlier conferences. A howl of wrath went up that this was the end of constitution-making by agreement, whereby Indians enjoyed equality with their rulers in the process. Jayakar and Sapru resigned from the Consultative Committee in protest; with others including Sethna, Chintamini and Sastri they issued a public denunciation of the new procedure. Eventually Hoare caved in, as he had on the two-phase plan. London agreed that there should be a small conference held in private with an agenda fixed by the government. Reluctantly Sapru and other Liberals agreed to the proposal, and Jayakar and his associates among the Hindu communalists also accepted the idea.[89]

Indian pressure on the Delhi government over constitution-making procedures was symptomatic of a growing suspicion and frustration generated by the conflict between Congress and the raj in a broad spectrum of politically conscious Hindus. It was most acute and articulate among the politicians who were loosely aligned with or sympathetic towards Congress. Their position as Nationalists yet non-Congressmen was made extremely difficult by the renewal of civil disobedience, and even more so by the savagery of the government's response. Looking ahead they could see no prospect of a generous reform which would elicit widespread Indian cooperation: the future seemed to hold only personal bitterness and embarrassment, and limited constitutional advance, whether through Simon-type proposals or an All-India Federation, under which the Princes and the Muslims would have predominant influence.

Malaviya, on the fringes of Congress and reluctant, as in London, to stand out against Gandhi was one of the first to give vent to this feeling. In January he sent Willingdon a virulent denunciation of his refusal to see Gandhi – 'the greatest Indian living....adored by countless millions in India and widely respected in all parts of the world', who would probably under

---

[89] Moore, *op. cit.* pp. 255–61; Willingdon to Hoare, 10 July 1932, Mss. EUR.E.240 (5).
Sapru's papers are full of evidence on the reasons for his resignation from the Consultative Committee: a good example of his disillusion with the government's handling of the political situation was his letter to H. Laski, 16 July 1932, with which he sent a copy of his resignation; (L 39) Sapru Papers, Series II.

the new constitution 'take over charge of the country's affairs' from the
Viceroy – and the subsequent repression of civil disobedience. He pleaded
for the withdrawal of the Ordinances, release of Gandhi and other satyagrahis; and negotiation with Gandhi first on the points at issue in particular
provinces which had led up to civil disobedience and then on the constitutional question to enable India and Britain to reach what he called a
mutually beneficial friendship between equals. When the government
failed to budge he publicly aligned himself with Congress by engineering
the emergency session in Delhi. In the same month he published a statement
designed to show the 'brutality, the meanness and the revolting nature of
the acts of repression which Government agencies and officials are inflicting
upon the men and women of my country'. He concluded that the last three
months had shown that Congress alone could speak for India and that no
reform would succeed unless Congress accepted it.[90] M. R. Jayakar was
equally dismayed at the renewal and results of conflict; and like Malaviya
strongly criticized Willingdon for refusing to see Gandhi and for rejecting
subsequent attempts he and Sapru made to draw Gandhi and other Congressmen into discussion. He was convinced that government had no desire
for peace; but unlike Malaviya he also blamed Congress for being intransigent and foolish. Considering how to reply to Lalji Naranji, who accused
him of being a government tool, he spelt out his belief that satyagraha could
never bring the alteration in government's economic and political policies
which they both desired.

> I honestly believe that the Congress policy is a hybrid mixture of
> philosophy and unpractical politics. It is neither plain revolution which
> I can understand, nor plain constructive work. It is a curious admixture
> of both, and in my frank opinion, is a disastrous blunder. It has
> emasculated the nation, brought rogues into prominence, and in spite
> of Mahatma Gandhi's honest wishes, the guidance of the movement is
> in the hands of charlatans if not rogues.[91]

It was Sapru who as 1932 wore on with its procession of prisoners, its
tally of confiscations, *lathi* charges and clashes between satyagrahis and the
police, voiced most eloquently the exasperation felt by men in his position
at the impasse into which Indian politics had drifted as the result of
the conflict between an equally stubborn Congress and Government. To
colleagues, to officials in India and Britain, and to representatives of
unofficial opinion in Britain he castigated the Ordinances and the manner
of their administration and argued that the extraordinary bitterness they
were creating among ordinary people was driving more and more educated

[90] *Pandit M. M. Malaviya's Statement on Repression in India up to April 20, 1932*
(Benares, April 1932), B. M. PIB. 1.35. No. 9; M. M. Malaviya to Willingdon, 29
January 1932, J. Nehru Papers, part I, vol. XXXXV.

[91] Jayakar to L. Naranji, undated draft reply to letter of 27 January 1932, Jayakar
Papers, Correspondence File No. 456; Jayakar to H. Polak, 18 April 1932, *ibid.*
Correspondence File No. 407, part II.

Hindus into sympathy with Congress. His personal frustration increased as the government rebuffed his suggestions of a more accommodating policy and as he saw the prospects receding of an All-India Federation on which he had staked so much of his recent political career. Moreover long term there would have to be some settlement with Congress, he reasoned, and if that was delayed Congress with its consequent accession of support would be in a commanding position, able to wreck proposals unacceptable to them. He was convinced that even at this juncture there were 'reasonable' Congressmen who would accept real responsibility in the provinces, and at the centre subject to safeguards during a transition period: it was to pave the way for cooperation between such men and the government that he and other moderates had been engaging in constitutional discussions. The government's rejection of the conference procedure appeared a death blow to this hope, thus compounding his despair at the political impasse.[92]

Sapru told the Lord Chancellor in April that because of the continuing conflict 'feeling is tense and the general temper of the people is sullen', an assessment echoed within days by Srinivasa Sastri to the Prime Minister, in a letter graphically depicting the activities of the police under Ordinance rule.[93] The Government of India took such allegations seriously and asked all local administrations to produce assessments of public feeling towards civil disobedience and the preventive measures against it. Their replies understandably played down hostility to government action, but they nonetheless showed that the frustration voiced by moderate politicians was very widespread among educated Hindus. The vast majority of this group had nothing to do with civil disobedience, yet they were increasingly sceptical of the government's intentions over constitutional reform, a scepticism compounded by dislike of the way officials were suppressing civil disobedience, by conviction that Congress generally represented their interests, and by admiration for Gandhi.[94]

Businessmen shared much of this ambivalence towards Gandhi and the Congress campaign. Their reaction also depended on the particular

[92] Sapru to Sir B. L. Mitter, Govt. of India Law Member, 18 January 1932, Sapru to Jayakar, 18 April 1932, Jayakar Papers, Correspondence File No. 407, part II; Sapru to Lord Sankey, 10 April 1932, *ibid.* Correspondence File No. 456; Sapru to H. Polak, 24 January, 1 May & 12 June 1932, Sapru to Sir Evelyn Wrench, ed. of *The Spectator*, 21 May 1932, Sapru to Graham Pole, 12 June 1932, Sapru to H. Laski, 16 July 1932 (L 39) Sapru Papers, Series II.

[93] Sapru to Lord Sankey, 10 April 1932, Jayakar Papers, Correspondence File No. 456; Sastri to Ramsay MacDonald, 15 April 1932, Jagadisan, *op. cit.* pp. 226–7. Sastri repeated his complaints of police brutality to MacDonald, 6 May 1932, *ibid.* pp. 228–30. He based them partly on evidence from Mangalore, where 17 citizens including 2 MLCs had written on 24 April 1932 to the District Magistrate to protest against police beatings of picketers and to request a public enquiry: a copy of this is in Sastri's papers.

[94] Govt. of India to all local govts., 20 April 1932, and govt. replies including many local officers' reports, Home Poll., 1932, File No. 14/28. See also P. Spear's study of educated Indian opinion, 'A Third Force in India 1920–47: A Study in Political Analysis', Phillips & Wainwright (ed.), *The Partition of India*, pp. 500–1.

interests they had at stake and the part of the country in which they did business. Most, from the humblest shopkeeper to the richest millowning magnate, realized that disorder was bad for production and trade. But at the same time many believed that Congress alone could wrest control of Indian finances from a reluctant raj, or hoped that Gandhi would restrain his more radical colleagues. Others feared to stick their necks out and court picketing when valuable stocks were at risk, or preferred a show-down to the suspense of the preceding years. Consequently many big businessmen and small traders supported Congress or at least refrained from open criticism of its tactics. FICCI (the Federation of Indian Chambers of Commerce and Industry) resolved in March not to participate in the Consultative Committee in view of governmental repression and its experiences at the Round Table Conference, unless the government would discuss questions of financial policy with representatives of nationalist opinion and agreed to refer detailed financial questions to a body of British and Indian experts.[95] Despite this resolution some of its members were unhappy at the prospect of continued conflict with the government. Willingdon tried hard to secure the cooperation of Thakurdas and Birla in his Consultative Committee before FICCI met, and was sure that they really wished to participate in discussions of the future constitution. His attempts at bridge-building to enable them to do this failed; but Birla indicated to Hoare that even though the Committee was not an acceptable forum of discussion Thakurdas could go to the Imperial economic conference in Ottawa without objections from FICCI. He also pleaded for a constitution acceptable to nationalist opinion outside Congress, and argued that Gandhi would certainly give it his blessing. Later to Sapru he repeated his argument that it was essential to get Gandhi back into 'direct or indirect cooperation', insisting that without this no constitution stood a chance of success.[96] Thakurdas did go to Ottawa in the middle of the year; and later his public hostility to boycott activities in Bombay earned him a scathing rebuke in the local Congress bulletin. By the beginning of October Birla had given the Governor of Bengal the impression that he regarded civil disobedience as a lost cause and would be glad to see it abandoned, though this would need Gandhi's fiat. Even so prominent a business supporter of the campaign as Bombay's Lalji Naranji was by mid-1932 less sure of the

[95] FICCI's resolution, 28 March 1932, enclosed in Birla to Sapru, 19 July 1932 (B 241), Sapru Papers, Series II.

For evidence of the wide range of businessmen's attitudes to civil disobedience see N. N. Sircar to Sapru, 1 & 12 January 1932 (S 77 & 79), *ibid.*; L. Naranji to Jayakar, 27 January 1932, Jayakar Papers, Correspondence File No. 456; Monteath to Govt. of Bombay, 2 May 1932, Chief Sec., Bengal Govt., to Govt. of India, Home Sec., 16 May 1932, Home Poll., 1932, File No. 14/28.

[96] Birla to Sapru, 2 August 1932 (B 243), Sapru Papers, Series II. For the earlier exchanges between Birla & Thakurdas, Hoare & Willingdon see Willingdon to Hoare, 15, 22 & 29 February, 14 & 21 March 1932, Mss. EUR.E.240 (5); Hoare to Willingdon, 1 & 8 April 1932, in the latter enclosing letters from Birla to Hoare, 14 & 28 March 1932, Mss. EUR.E.240 (1).

wisdom of his stand, as Bombay's business conditions sank lower into the doldrums in contrast to Ahmedabad, and as officials put increasing pressure on him for his support of Congress.[97]

Even from abroad came news that Gandhi's most loyal supporters such as C. F. Andrews, the Swiss, Edmond Privat, and Verrier Elwin, were appalled at the impasse into which civil disobedience had led their friend and his country. The latter confessed 'to considerable depression of spirit' as opinion in Britain appeared to be hardening: satyagraha seemed to have changed no hearts except those of 'a motley crew of food-reformers, theosophists and new-thought devotees'. Consequently he believed that Congress could only lose by continuing civil disobedience.[98]

III GANDHI'S 'POLITICS'

Gandhi's initial reaction to the conflict with the raj was not frustration. For him Yeravda allowed recuperation after the strains of 1931 which had brought him to the verge of physical breakdown; and on his own admission it meant a respite from apparently insoluble political problems, particularly the communal question and the Red Shirts' activities.[99]

With Mahadev Desai and Vallabhbhai Patel as companions he settled easily back into jail life. He was up before 4.0 a.m. each day, and spent his time praying, reading, writing, walking and spinning. To catch up on lost sleep he took two naps during the day, and was in bed by 9.0 p.m., sleeping in the open. He lived on toast, fruit, vegetables, nuts, honey and soda, supplemented for a time with milk. On this regime he kept in good health despite a painful elbow from spinning; and except when he was fasting he kept at a fairly constant weight of seven and a half stone. He was allowed a selection of papers – *The Times of India*, *The Bombay Chronicle*, *The Leader* from Allahabad, *The Tribune* from Lahore and *The Hindu* from Madras, *The Indian Social Reformer*, *The Modern Review*, and his own two, *Young India* and *Navajivan*. He took some books with him to jail and others were sent to him: he studied not only religious writings (his usual literary diet in prison), but political economy, Urdu and astronomy, and, interestingly, read two books written by Hoare and Ramsay MacDonald. For a time news of the outside world reached him through visitors as well as the press, though he was only allowed to see relatives and 'non-political' ashramites and friends. In June however he gave up even this favoured condition of imprisonment after an altercation with the local government which banned Mirabehn from seeing him on her release from jail on the grounds that

[97] Bombay Congress Bulletin, 29 September 1932, Thakurdas Papers, File No. 101/1930; V to S of S, telegram, 4 October 1932, Mss. EUR.E.240 (11); 12 & 13 June 1932, Diary of B. S. Moonje.

[98] V. Elwin to Jayakar, 27 July 1932, Sapru Papers, Series II.

[99] 17 March 1932, *The Diary of Mahadev Desai, Volume I* (Ahmedabad, 1953), p. 17; Gandhi to H. G. Alexander, 25 March 1932, *CWMG*, XLIX, 236.

she had participated in civil disobedience. He also wrote irritably to the government about delays in his correspondence because of censorship procedures. This problem was ironed out and he engaged in a massive correspondence which took up much of his time and to which he attached great importance. Through it he kept in touch with a wide range of friends and enquirers, particularly the ashramites, confining himself to discussion of moral and religious questions and advice on health. He also completed his discourses on the *Gita* for the ashram prayer meetings which he had begun in Yeravda in 1930, and wrote a history of the ashram. Meanwhile under the Mahatma's eagle eye his two companions were also making good use of their sentences. Mahadev, when he was not doing secretarial work for Gandhi and Vallabhbhai or cooking bread, learnt French and Urdu, while Vallabhbhai took up Sanskrit. Both did time with the spinning wheel.[100]

Although Gandhi had perforce to occupy himself with what the government accepted as non-political matters the political situation was always in his mind. With his two co-prisoners he discussed the campaign's progress, and their proper attitude to the forthcoming constitution. In the early phase of the conflict he saw no reason to change his political stance or to contemplate a settlement, and he trusted those outside to do what they considered best.[101] He discussed politics with the jail authorities and visiting government officials, and despite his prisoner's status kept in touch by correspondence with high officials of the raj. Within days of his imprisonment he wrote to Hoare giving his version of the renewal of conflict: he denied the allegation that he had been forced into civil disobedience by his colleagues and laid the blame wholly on Willingdon for imposing impossible conditions on an interview. Continuing the exchange he reminded Hoare again of his desire to cooperate on his return and rebuked him for making a hurtful reference to Congress in a recent broadcast. He reiterated this theme of cooperation in letters to Sykes, condemning 'excesses' committed under the Ordinances, and to Emerson, deploring Bombay's published intention to sell the lands of farmers in Ras and other villages who withheld their revenue. In both he underlined the need for either side in the conflict to prevent legacies of bitterness – an indication that the necessity of a settlement was in his mind though he felt the present time was not ripe for it.[102]

[100] For Gandhi's jail routine, reading, correspondence etc., see *CWMG*, XLIX–LII, *Desai's Diary – I*; letters on the *Gita* written in 1932, *CWMG*, XLIX, 138–49; history of the Sabarmati ashram, *CWMG*, L, 188–236; government correspondence on Gandhi's jail conditions, *HFM*, III, IV.

[101] 27 & 28 March, 24 & 28 June 1932, *Desai's Diary – I*, pp. 34, 37, 193–5, 198–9; Gandhi to A. Harrison, 15 June 1932, Gandhi Papers; Gandhi to M. A. Khan, 14 July 1932, *CWMG*, XL, 239–40.

[102] Gandhi to Hoare, 15 January & 28 February 1932, Hoare to Gandhi, 8 February & 24 March 1932, Mss. EUR.E.240 (16); Gandhi to Sykes, 23 January 1932, Gandhi to H. W. Emerson, 28 March 1932, Gandhi Papers.

However Gandhi's main point of contact with the upper echelons of the raj and his major endeavour to continue while a prisoner to influence Indian public life was his fast over the Communal Award. At the Round Table Conference he had spoken of resisting with his life the grant of a separate electorate to Untouchables. On 11 March he wrote to remind Hoare of that fact since he gathered that an announcement of an award was imminent. He argued that he wanted Untouchables to be fully represented, possibly by giving them immediate, total adult suffrage, but that the mechanism of a separate electorate would only 'vivisect' Hinduism and would do nothing to lessen the Untouchables' social degradation. He maintained that for him it was a moral and religious question, and he proposed to fast to death even if released, if the government granted a separate Untouchable electorate, though he realized the inferences which might be drawn from such a step and its possible repercussions.

> I am painfully conscious of the fact that such a step whilst I am a prisoner may cause grave embarrassment to His Majesty's Government and that it will be regarded by many as highly improper on the part of one holding my position to introduce into the political field methods which they would describe as hysterical, if not much worse. All I can urge in defence is that for me the contemplated step is not a method, it is part of my being. It is a call of conscience which I dare not disobey, even though it may cost whatever reputation for sanity I may possess.

It was a carefully designed letter deliberately playing down the fact that separate electorates for Untouchables on top of those for Muslims would destroy the single body politic for which Gandhi and Congressmen had striven, though Gandhi's intention in so doing had often differed from that of his colleagues. As he explained to Mahadev, 'If we tried to make this clearer, we would have to describe the Muslims' share in this sordid business. And that would increase Hindu–Muslim tension.' Neither Mahadev nor Vallabhbhai understood or wholly approved of the letter, Vallabhbhai in particular judging that it would harm Gandhi's reputation and lead to a series of ill-conceived imitative fasts.[103]

For the government the announcement of an award was an increasingly urgent political necessity. Not only did the communal impasse hold up vital decisions on the Federation: there were also clear signs that Muslim politicians might withdraw completely from constitutional discussions if their demands were not met – just at the time when the government was busy quelling civil disobedience and trying to mollify non-Congress Hindu

[103] Gandhi to Hoare, 11 March 1932, Mss. EUR.E.240 (16); 10 March 1932, *Desai's Diary – I*, pp. 4–5.
Hoare replied briefly that he realized the strength of Gandhi's feeling and that the government would take its decision on the merits of the case as it saw them after considering the report of Lothian's Committee and the views that Gandhi among others had expressed. Gandhi accepted this assurance. Hoare to Gandhi, 13 April 1932, Mss. EUR.E.240 (16); Gandhi to Hoare, 2 May 1932, *CWMG* XLIX, 391–2.

politicians. Assured that an award would be made, the Muslim Conference resolved late in March to delay its planned non-cooperation in the Round Table Conference and its sub-committees; but fear of losing Muslim support continued to dominate at least Willingdon's thinking as the award was hammered out. The award was made on 4 August and Muslims, Sikhs and other minorities received separate electorates. The Depressed Classes received not only a separate constituency in areas where they were numerous but a vote in the ordinary general constituencies.[104]

Indian reactions to the Communal Award were swift. Only moderate Hindu politicians accepted it with equanimity. Kelkar and Jayakar on the communalist wing thought it disappointing and divisive but felt that outright opposition to it would be of little use. With many of their associates they adopted a wait-and-see attitude, though the Mahasabha denounced it, and ultimately decided to boycott it and the third conference. Jayakar and Moonje declined to follow this line. In Punjab and Bengal, however, Hindus and Sikhs were virulent in their condemnation since in both provinces Muslims were assured of a majority in practice although they were not given statutory majorities. Muslims generally welcomed the Award although the Muslim Conference pronounced it disappointing since it fell short of their standing demand and particularly their claim for statutory majorities in Bengal and Punjab. Even Ambedkar complained to Hoare: he believed that Untouchables' representation was still inadequate and was worried about the Awards' proposal that their special constituencies should last only for a limited time.[105] No particular notice was taken of the provision for Untouchables except by Ambedkar, for Gandhi had kept his intention a confidence between himself, the government and his two jail companions. The Mahatma slept on the news of the Award and discussed his response with Vallabhbhai and Mahadev. Although he realized that people would say it was a stunt to obtain freedom and that among their colleagues Jawaharlal would certainly be critical, he nevertheless wrote to the Prime Minister announcing that he would begin to fast on 20 September unless the decision as applied to the Untouchables was revoked and they

---

[104] Muslim Conference Working Committee Resolution, 5 March 1932, Muslim Conference Resolution, 22 March 1932, Aziz, *op. cit.* pp. 84, 101–2; Hoare to Willingdon, 14 July 1932; Mss. EUR.E.240 (2); *East India (Constitutional Reforms.) Communal Decision,* Pp. 1931–2, XVIII, Cmd. 4147.

[105] Provincial FR2s, August 1932, Home Poll., 1932, File No. 18/11; N. C. Kelkar to Jayakar, 17 August 1932, Jayakar to Kelkar, 21 August 1932, reporting a small meeting of Hindus at his house, press statement on Award by Jayakar, 21 August 1932, Jayakar Papers, Correspondence File No. 445; Muslim Conference Executive Board Resolutions, 21 August 1932, Aziz, *All India Muslim Conference 1928–1935,* pp. 111–12; B. R. Ambedkar to Hoare, 21 August 1932, Mss. EUR.E.240 (16).

In the Punjab Muslims received 49% of seats (86 cf. 30 in the old legislative council), Hindus 27.4% (43 cf. 29), and Sikhs 18.9% (32 cf. 12). In Bengal Muslims received 48.6% and this gave them 119 seats compared with 39 in the old legislative council, whereas Hindus were awarded 80 general seats compared with their previous 46 seats: Muslims gains were therefore particularly dramatic here.

were included in the general electorates under a common franchise. Mac-Donald tried to dissuade him with the argument that the Untouchables would remain part of the Hindu community under the proposed mechanism, but he was firm that there could be no change in the proposal unless the communities themselves agreed. The Inspector-General of Prisons also saw Gandhi twice to ensure that he understood the implications of the Award and the possibility of a revision by agreement before it became law. Gandhi however remained as firm as MacDonald in acknowledging his letter. He added that he objected to the Award's other provisions though he did not feel obliged to fast against them. Despite Vallabhbhai's suggestion that he should state his total objection to the Award in the first letter to MacDonald he had deliberately refrained lest people should say he was seizing on the Untouchable provision as a means of securing the overthrow of the whole package.[106]

Not even Gandhi's closest colleagues understood the Mahatma's compulsion into this dramatic gesture. Officials unanimously interpreted it as a devious political manoeuvre – though they disagreed on its purpose. The Government of India told local governments that the fast was intended to change government policy not to obtain release, while the Bombay government asserted that Gandhi's primary intention was not to secure an alteration of the Award but to infuse life into civil disobedience, a view Willingdon held privately. 'There is no doubt from the general atmosphere all round that the civil disobedience movement is at a very low ebb; Gandhi is I think well aware of this, and this is I fear his least desperate effort to regain his prestige and authority.'[107] Gandhi consistently maintained in private discussion with Vallabhbhai and Mahadev, in personal letters and in press statements, that it was not a political move. He argued that for him the issue was religious: Untouchability was a blot on the face of Hinduism and the work of its eradication would only be stifled by separate electorates. Moreover his fast was intended not as a manoeuvre to force the British to change their position but a means of throwing his whole weight against the evil of Untouchability and stinging the conscience of caste Hindus into right action. The technique of fasting was hallowed by Christianity and Islam as well as Hinduism, within which the fast was a well-known method of purification and penance.[108]

[106] Gandhi to MacDonald, 18 August & 9 September 1932, MacDonald to Gandhi, 8 September 1932, Mss. EUR.E.240 (16); Govt. of Bombay to V, telegram, 10 September 1932, Home Poll., 1932, File No. 31/113; 18 August 1932, *Desai's Diary – I*, pp. 292–4.

[107] Willingdon to Hoare, 4 September 1932, Mss. EUR.E.240 (5); Bombay Govt. to Govt. of India, telegram, 14 September 1932, Govt. of India to all local govts., telegram, 11 September 1932, Home Poll., 1932, File No. 31/113.

[108] Discussions in jail, 20, 21, & 22 August 1932, *Desai's Diary – I*, pp. 296–304; statements to press, 16, 20 & 23 September 1932, *CWMG*, LI, 62–5, 116–20, 132–3; Gandhi to B. Bijoria, 10 October 1932, *ibid.* p. 226.

Gandhi insisted in the face of criticism that the fast was not intended to coerce

Although in justifying his fast Gandhi tried to separate out Untouchables'
representation as a purely religious issue, he himself had always insisted
that politics and religion were inseparable: and there seems no doubt that
this was an attempt, both 'political' and 'religious', to influence public life
in a novel way since jail prevented other activities, and as his supreme
remedy for all ills, satyagraha, seemed to be having little effect when
applied on a continental scale. By mid-1932 he was himself increasingly
frustrated at the impasse into which conflict had led him, and in two
particular respects by the failure of civil disobedience. It had manifestly
failed to create that unity for which, as the foundation of swaraj, he had
striven by this means since early 1930; and he turned to fasting on the
Untouchables' representation as another approach to the ultimate goal. As
he wrote to a correspondent in January 1933:

> Why do you believe that swaraj is something apart from the eradication
> of untouchability? Swaraj is not like a straight rod. It is rather like a
> banyan tree. The latter has innumerable branches each of which is as
> important for the tree as the original trunk. Feeding any of them means
> feeding the tree. Nobody can lay down a rule as to which of the
> branches should be fed when. Circumstances determine that.

That the unity of Indians in this wider context was in his mind at the time
of the Poona fast was evident from his assurance to Syed Mahmud that
'the whole time the fast was on, I was thinking too of the Hindu Muslim
question', and his statement after the fast that he hoped that the ensuing
settlement heralded a recognition of Indians' fundamental unity and a
settlement of the Hindu–Muslim–Sikh question.[109] Civil disobedience had
also failed to move the British or to open the way to discussion: and
for Gandhi satyagraha campaigns were always intended as preliminaries
to talks. In fact Jawaharlal in jail had been worried even in May that
Gandhi might discuss conditions of a settlement with Hoare. Now an
element in Gandhi's thinking was almost certainly the hope that he might
renew contact with the government. Although by saying that release
would not prevent his fast he was not trying to force the government to
release him, he admitted to Vallabhbhai that he expected to be set free
and enabled to start a new phase of public work.[110] Whatever the
precise blend of intentions and considerations behind his decision to fast,
by the time it began he had generated within himself a sense of tremen-
dous spiritual exaltation and excitement. He wrote of it in a series of
letters to friends, disciples and relatives as his supreme *dharma*, a

anyone but to arouse consciences, though he admitted that some might unfortunately
feel coerced; Gandhi to S. M. Mate, 2 October 1932, *ibid.* p. 167.
[109] Gandhi to Parmananda K. Kapadia, 8 January 1933, *CWMG*, LII, 399; Gandhi
to Syed Mahmud, 9 October 1932, Gandhi Papers; statement to press, 26 September
1932, *CWMG*, LI, 144–5.
[110] Discussion with Vallabhbhai, 6 September 1932, *ibid.* p. 457; 31 May 1932, J.
Nehru's Diary, *SWJN*, 5, pp. 385–6.

call from the 'inner voice', a rare privilege and the crown of his career.[111]

However, the repercussions of Gandhi's fast depended partly on the British responses, and the facilities they afforded him for publicity. At the outset London, Delhi and Bombay agreed to follow the plan laid down in 1930 should Gandhi hunger-strike in jail – as it was clearly impolitic either to force feed him or to let him die in jail they would release him when he became dangerously weak and rearrest him later if he broke the law. When Gandhi's fast was imminent Willingdon's Council decided that it would be impossible to change the Award as a result of the threat and that Gandhi should be released unconditionally at the beginning of the fast to avoid the build-up of anti-government feeling, rather than wait for him to become dangerously weak. Sykes's government was apprehensive that this would give him a chance to renew agitation particularly in Bombay City (where it thought two weeks of Gandhian agitation would mean the loss of ground government had taken six months to gain). Hoare, too, was perturbed by the prospect of reactivated civil disobedience resulting from Gandhi's release; his fear in London was that such a development in India might add to the disquiet of Tories already anxious at the prospect of a third Round Table Conference, and might give a handle to Winston Churchill and his press backer, Rothermere, who were planning a campaign against the government's Indian policy and would gladly work on any suspicion of weakness. Moreover the king was personally interested in the question and anxious that his Indian empire should not be plunged into further confusion. Eventually it was decided to move Gandhi to his Sabarmati ashram on his release and restrain him there under the Special Powers Ordinance in order to prevent him visiting Bombay City; though Delhi and Bombay could not agree on the policy to adopt if he then broke the restraining order. The issue never arose in practice because Gandhi, on hearing of Haig's announcement on 15 September that he was to be detained in a private residence and that further restrictions would depend on whether he used his liberty to promote civil disobedience, replied to Willingdon that he wished to stay in Yeravda. He expressed pain at the news and said that a move would cause public expense and worry to himself and he could not accept any conditions restricting his movements after release. After a Council meeting Haig told the Legislative Assembly on 20 September that the government would leave Gandhi in jail as he wished but would let him see and correspond with anybody he desired in order to discuss the problem of the Depressed Classes; and Gandhi was informed of this decision.[112]

---

[111] Gandhi to M. M. Bhatt, D. Gandhi, Kasturba Gandhi, N. Gandhi, all on 13 September, 1932, *CWMG*, LI, 50–3; Gandhi to Mirabehn, 15 September 1932, Gandhi Papers.

[112] For the discussions between Delhi, London and Bombay on treatment of Gandhi see Home Poll., 1932, File No. 31/113; Mss. EUR.E.240 (2) (6) (11); Mss. EUR.F.150 (4). Text of Haig's statements to Assembly on 15 & 20 September 1932,

Gandhi's correspondence with the government on the fast was published on 12 September; reaction among India's public figures was swift and strong, because they realized it was no idle threat and that the Mahatma's death would have unpredictable repercussions. Most of them felt considerable reservations, if not revulsion, at the Mahatma's enterprise. Ambedkar condemned it as a political stunt, a view echoed privately by Sethna who thought it was intended to revive civil disobedience. Jawaharlal, on hearing the news in jail, was annoyed at Gandhi's 'religious and sentimental approach to a political question' and his emphasis on what to Jawaharlal was a side issue compared with the central one of freedom. As his anger blended with personal devastation at the prospect of Gandhi's death he experienced a brief period of total emotional confusion, but surfaced with the thought that 'Bapu had a curious knack of doing the right thing at the psychological moment and it might be that his action...might lead to great results – not only in the narrow field in which it was confined, but in the wider aspects of our national struggle.' Srinivasa Sastri, appalled at this apparent flight from reasoned persuasion, thought it 'moral coercion and the result achieved *whitemail*'; though in public he merely expressed hope for the survival of one whose life was 'of supreme consequence to our kind'.[113]

Messages poured into Yeravda expressing concern, and many of Gandhi's colleagues and sympathizers tried to get him to call off the fast, including C. F. Andrews, Birla and Sapru. Hindu leaders who were at liberty swung into action to avert the Mahatma's self-martyrdom, and Malaviya convened a conference in Bombay. Their intentions in so doing were diverse. The desire to save the life of a friend and revered leader and avoid the consequences of his death was of course paramount; but there was also a keen sense that the crisis had implications for the conflict between Congress and the raj. Birla pressed Sapru to work for Gandhi's release in the hope that Gandhi's influence could bring about a pact with the Untouchables and so avert his death; but he also felt that Gandhi's release might bring other important results, and encouraged Sapru to go to Bombay not only to help settle the immediate question but to get Gandhi involved in renewed constitutional discussions. He hinted at the same idea to Thakurdas, encouraging him 'to do our bit to save the life of the old man'.

I personally feel that if we can succeed in settling up this representative question, many other important decisions may be arrived at once

Home Poll., 1932, File No. 31/113 & Mss. EUR.F.115 (1). Gandhi to P.S.V., telegram, 16 September 1932, Gandhi Papers. The three governments still had not decided whether to let Gandhi die in jail if no agreement was reached as a result of discussions on the Untouchables; though Bombay & London both thought that in the final stages he should be removed to a private house, and Bombay was in fact preparing to do this when agreement was reached.

[113] Sethna to Lindsay, 16 September 1932, Sethna Papers; 22 September 1932, J. Nehru's Diary, *SWJN*, 5, pp. 407–8; speech by Sastri, 22 September 1932, Sastri to P. K. Rao, 10 October 1932, Jagadisan, *op. cit.* pp. 235, 237–9.

Gandhiji is out, and therefore we ought to take full advantage of the situation...The R.T.C. will now dwindle into insignificance. Once Gandhiji is out I anticipate a great change.[114]

Sapru, horrified that the government had let the question slide since March and that even now it appeared reluctant to liberate Gandhi swiftly and unconditionally, had already been in contact with both Gandhi and Willingdon when he received Birla's request. His intention was not so much to use the situation to seek a way out of the frustrations generated by the conflict between Congress and raj, but to prevent further embitterment of Hindus which would make a reconciliation with government even more remote. He had not wanted to attend Malaviya's conference, fearing that he would be a fish out of water in a communal matter: but he decided to go after he received a wire from Gandhi indicating a hope that he would help solve the problem, and after a visitation from Devadas Gandhi who urged him to go.[115]

At the Bombay gathering Sapru joined Malaviya, Moonje, Aney, Jayakar, Sir Chunilal Mehta, Rajagopalachariar and Rajendra Prasad among others. Present too were Ambedkar and his opponent, M. C. Rajah, who also claimed to represent Untouchables but favoured joint electorates with the Hindus. Before they assembled for the first time on 19 September Gandhi had indicated to a small deputation, including Mehta, Birla and Thakurdas, that he would consider a compromise with reservation of seats for Untouchables (though he disliked even that degree of separation), provided that separate electorates were done away. At the 19 September meeting of Malaviya's conference there was much emotional insistence that Gandhi must be saved, and that Untouchability must go. However Ambedkar, reacting to the extreme pressure of the situation, stridently refused to discuss the constitutional question until he knew precisely what Gandhi had in mind. The next day Mehta told the conference on behalf of the deputation which had been to Yeravda that he thought Gandhi would agree to reservation of seats, and Ambedkar was pressed to accept this. Understandably he complained that he was being made to look the villain of the piece, and said that although he was willing to compromise they still had no concrete proposals from Gandhi. He felt that Gandhi was pointing a gun at their heads and that he should postpone his fast and give them two weeks to negotiate. Informal bargaining then began; and by the evening Sapru and Jayakar had produced a draft settlement to which Ambedkar tentatively agreed. Essentially it was a system of primary and secondary

[114] G. D. Birla to Thakurdas, 14 September 1932, Thakurdas Papers, File No. 129/1932; Birla to Sapru, telegrams, 13, 14 September (B 246 & 247), letter, 15 September 1932 (B 249), Sapru Papers, Series II. Birla also put pressure on Moonje to attend the Bombay Conference; 16 September 1932, Diary of B. S. Moonje.

[115] Sapru to Birla, telegram, 15 September 1932 (B 248), to B. Rama Rao, 14 & 17 September 1932 (R 112 & 114), to H. Polak, 17 September 1932, Sapru Papers, Series II; Sapru to Jayakar, 13 September 1932, Jayakar Papers, Correspondence File No. 421; Gandhi to Sapru, telegram, 16 September 1932, *CWMG*, LI, 60.

electorates for a certain number of seats, by which Untouchables voting alone in the primary election would choose between the candidates thus chosen. Sapru and Jayakar, Birla, Devadas, Rajagopalachariar and Prasad then went by the night train to Poona to put this to Gandhi, who had begun his fast that day as planned.

Gandhi's reaction was favourable, but he refused to agree until he had seen the plan in writing and talked to Ambedkar and Rajah. There followed three days of detailed discussions on the primary/secondary formula, on the number of reserved seats for Depressed Classes, and on the length of time primary electorates and reservation of seats should last. Gandhi proved amenable. In Sapru's words,

He gave practically no trouble to us when we saw him in Poona. He readily accepted my formula about Primary Election though it was not so easy to get it accepted by some of the Congressmen and the Hindu Sabha men. On the other questions too he was extremely reasonable. The real fight was between Ambedkar and others.

Gandhi, subsisting on water, salt and soda, was growing markedly weaker; by 24 September his condition had so deteriorated that the government medical authorities believed he would collapse mentally and physically within two days. By this time all the issues had been settled except the date of a referendum among Untouchables to decide on the termination or continuation of the reserved seats. Gandhi wanted it to be after five years, Ambedkar stuck out for ten years. When no agreement appeared possible Ambedkar reached a compromise with the caste Hindu negotiators outside Yeravda, by which they agreed to leave the question open to future settlement by mutual agreement. Gandhi acquiesced and the 'Poona Pact' was drawn up to embody the agreed package: it was signed by Ambedkar, Rajah, Malaviya, Jayakar, Sapru, Mehta, Birla, Thakurdas, Rajagopala-chariar and Rajendra Prasad among others.

The terms of the Pact showed that Ambedkar, although pushed into a tight corner by the Mahatma's imminent death, Hindu pressure and divisions among the Untouchables symbolized by Rajah's presence, had driven a hard bargain. He had given up the demand for separate electorates and agreed to the compromise system of primary and secondary elections, but in return had secured the reservation of 148 seats in the provincial legislatures for the Depressed Classes, compared with 71 (excluding a possible 10 for Bengal) awarded by the British under the separate electorates' system, and the guarantee of 18% of general seats for British India in the federal assembly. Moreover it was laid down that a sum should be earmarked from every provincial budget for the education of Untouchables. Most of the signatories then returned to Bombay, where a formal session of Malaviya's conference ratified the Pact and passed a resolution drafted by Gandhi, that henceforth no Hindu should be regarded as Untouchable because of his birth and that those who had been so regarded would now have equal rights with other Hindus to use public wells, roads, schools and other public institutions. When Gandhi heard on the 26th that the Cabinet had accepted the Pact's provisions in place of the corresponding parts of the Communal Award he broke his fast – ceremoniously in front of 200 people after prayers led by Rabindranath Tagore.[116]

Gandhi's conscience was salved by the Pact, and though Moonje at least considered it a climb-down on his part, he assessed it as 'a generous gesture on all sides'. He saw it however only as the beginning of a vast social transformation, the complete removal of the Untouchables' social and religious disabilities, and he warned caste Hindus in a press statement the very day he ended the fast that he would resume it 'if this reform is not relentlessly pursued and achieved within a measurable period'. He also appealed to the Untouchables, Harijans or 'Children of God' as he now began to call them, to play a part in this reform by observing laws of cleanliness and abstaining from intoxicants. A radical he might be in opposing Untouchability, but his remedies were firmly embedded in Hindu standards and did not seek to overthrow them.[117]

Immediate Hindu reaction to the Pact was relief that Gandhi's life was saved. Even the sceptical Jawaharlal, who still feared that others might imitate Gandhi's method and that the central issue of freedom might be obscured by Gandhi's gesture, marvelled at the almost hysterical public response to the fast. Temples and wells were thrown open to Untouchables, caste Hindus publicly embraced Untouchables, and inter-caste dinners were held. These manifestations were focussed by an Untouchability Abolition Week from 27 September; and at a public meeting in Bombay on the

[116] Bombay Govt. to Govt. of India, telegram, Home Poll., 1932, File No. 31/113. This wire forwarded a letter from Malaviya enclosing the text of the pact. The provincial allocation of special seats as compared with those granted under the Communal Award was:

Province	Award:	Pact:
Madras	18	30
Bombay & Sind	10	15
Punjab	0	8
Bihar & Orissa	7	18
C.P.	10	20
Assam	4	7
Bengal	not decided *c.* 10	30
U.P.	12	20

The British government's agreement to the Poona Pact's provisions in place of the appropriate sections of the Award was wired to V by S of S, 25 & 26 September 1932, Mss. EUR.F.115 (1).

This account of the fast and negotiations in Poona and Bombay is based on Sapru to Ramaswami Aiyar, 28 September 1932 (A 81), Sapru Papers, Series II; 19, 20, 21 September 1932, Diary of B. S. Moonje; discussion between Gandhi and Ambedkar, and statement of Gandhi, 22 September 1932, *CWMG*, LI, 458–61; Tendulkar, *Mahatma*, vol. 3, pp. 166–76.

[117] Press statement, 26 September 1932, note to P. N. Rajbhoj, 28 September 1932, *CWMG*, LI, 143–5, 149.

Moonje wrote in his diary, 25 September 1931, 'Those who had kept their reason in tact could see that Mahatmaji has climbed down and accepted Separate Electorates to save his life though they w[oul]d not like to say so openly.'

30th an All-India Anti-Untouchability League was formed, with Birla as President and A. V. Thakkar as Secretary.[118] However, this enthusiasm very soon waned and undercurrents of reaction came to the surface. Untouchables were often apathetic if not openly suspicious of the motives behind caste Hindus' sudden generosity; while among orthodox Hindus opposition to the long-term social implications of Gandhi's stand became overt. In Bihar some temples were thoroughly washed out after Untouchables had entered, the operation taking three days in one case; while in C.P. the very orthodox Marwari community of Drug reacted to attempts to throw open wells and temples by breaking the seals on their stocks of foreign cloth and beginning that trade again.[119]

Moreover the political implications of the Poona Pact soon dawned on caste Hindus, though their natural champion, the Mahasabha, had ratified it. As the C.P. government reported in late September, 'Only the glamour of Mr Gandhi's name has hitherto been able to camouflage the plain fact that the essence of separate electorates has been retained and much searching of heart has begun among politicians who find that ten seats in the local legislature have been bartered for the dubious advantage of a joint election of candidates already separately selected by the depressed classes.' But a hard look at the figures produced far stronger reaction in Punjab and Bengal, the two provinces where Hindus were a minority struggling for seats, neither of which had been represented at Yeravda. Punjabi Hindus now found themselves told by the Poona negotiators to give up eight of their precious seats, whereas the Communal Award had made no special allocation for Untouchables in their province. Within days they were asking for exemption from the Pact.[120] Bengali Hindus, their representation in the provincial legislature already savagely cut by the Award, found that Gandhi and his associates had given away thirty of their seats. As Sir N. N. Sircar put it to Sapru in a letter bitterly critical of Gandhi and the Pact, 'The Bengal Hindus who had been almost finished by the Communal Award have been given the finishing touch by the Poona Pact.' In the new year they began to campaign for reconsideration of the Pact as it affected them. On hearing this Gandhi gave private reassurances to Untouchables

[118] Provincial FR2s, September 1932, Home Poll., 1932, File No. 18/12; booklet published November 1932 on origins, aims & objects of The All-India Anti-Untouchability League, Thakurdas Papers, File No. 121/1932. For J. Nehru's views see his diary, 22 September 1932, *SWJN*, 5, p. 408; J. Nehru to Gandhi, telegram, 25 September 1932, J. Nehru Papers, part I, vol. XXIII.

[119] Madras, Bihar & Orissa, C.P. & Berar FR1, October 1932, Home Poll., 1932, File No. 18/13; Bihar & Orissa FR1, November 1932, *ibid.* File No. 18/14.

[120] S of S to V, telegram, 28 September 1932, forwarding wire from Gokal Chand to the Prime Minister asking that Punjab should be exempted from the Pact, Mss. EUR.E.240 (11); Jayakar to Raja Narendra Nath, 1 October 1932, replying to his complaint about the Pact's effect on Punjabi Hindus, Jayakar Papers, Correspondence File No. 421.

For reaction in C.P. see C.P. & Berar FR2, September 1932, Home Poll., 1932, File No. 18/12.

that the Pact would not be changed without the unanimous consent of all concerned, and to caste Hindus he said he felt that Harijans could not be given too many seats. Caught unawares by an opposition which threatened to alienate Untouchables and destroy his work for unity, but if unplacated to deprive Congress of Hindu support in Bengal, he maintained a studied public silence on the question and urged Birla to do likewise.[121]

Gandhi envisaged his fast and the Pact as inaugurating a new era in India's public life, one of social reform and a new approach to Indian realization of a fundamental nationhood uniting not only castes but communities. He also saw it as a new beginning for himself, and intended to embark on a new public role even though he had not been released. Before the fast ended he told the jail authorities that he expected to have continued facilities to pursue Untouchability work, and it was soon evident that he contemplated seeking a new relationship with the government. Jayakar and Sapru had talked privately with him after the Pact was concluded, urging him to seize the opportunity to call off civil disobedience, if only because the anti-Untouchability campaign could not flourish during conflict with the raj. He did not immediately dismiss their suggestion, and within days, when he was on the road to recovery,[122] he took them up on their promise to be available if he wished to see them.

On 28 September Jayakar received a summons from Gandhi through Malaviya. Immediately he left for Poona; he was not optimistic about a settlement, however, because he thought Gandhi would probably insist on terms similar to those of February 1931 while the present Government of India, secure in the knowledge that it had quelled the outward signs of civil disobedience, would doubtless demand a higher price than had Irwin. Jayakar had a preliminary talk with Malaviya and gathered not only that Gandhi was in a receptive mood but that H. N. Kunzru had persuaded Rajendra Prasad and Rajagopalachariar that it would be reasonable to end the conflict on an honourable basis. Kunzru was with Jayakar and Malaviya when they talked with Gandhi for over two hours on 29 September, and proved a great asset in arguing for peace, though Malaviya seemed more belligerent than Gandhi at this juncture. By the end of the discussion the

[121] Gandhi to Birla, 21 January 1933, to A. D. Ray, 19 January 1933, to R. Chatterjee, 20 January & 11 February 1933, *CWMG*, LIII, 110, 92, 99, 272–4.
For Bengali opposition to the Pact see Sir N. N. Sircar to Sapru, 17 February 1933 (S 83), Sapru Papers, Series II; Willingdon to Hoare, 15 January 1933, reporting deputation from Bengali Hindus on 14 January, Mss. EUR.E.240 (6); group of Bengali Hindus to Jayakar, 27 January 1933, Secs. of British Indian Association to Jayakar, 23 February 1933, Jayakar Papers, Correspondence File No. 421.

[122] By 28 September Gandhi was regaining strength and sleeping well; by 1 October he could walk again; and by the end of the month was virtually back to normal health. He admitted that the fast had caused him considerable suffering, but he clearly also experienced a kind of spiritual exaltation and illumination at the same time. Gandhi to N. Gandhi, 2 October 1932, to H. G. Alexander & E. Menon, both 4 October 1932, *CWMG*, LI, 174–5, 186, 187.

Mahatma had agreed to participate in a settlement provided that peace
could be established between Congress and the raj as equals. Jayakar looked
forward to evolving a formula for peace in a further meeting that afternoon. In the interval he discussed the matter with Kunzru, Thakkar, Kelkar
and Rangaswami Aiyengar, who all agreed with him, and the latter
managed to talk Malaviya round. The scene seemed set for progress: but
when they reached Yeravda jail they were told that interviews were now
forbidden. Delhi and Bombay had been in consultation for two days on
the best time to end the special facilities granted during the fast, and
Delhi decided to end them forthwith as Gandhi was receiving so much
publicity. For Sapru, who had been more optimistic than Jayakar about
manoeuvring a settlement in the wake of the Pact, this action by Willingdon's government only deepened his frustration at the impasse into
which the continuing conflict had led Indian politics. On this occasion he
laid the blame squarely on Willingdon, and lamented to the sympathetic
Polak in England Delhi's failure to use an occasion when he judged Gandhi
would have agreed to call off civil disobedience to enable his followers to
pursue the anti-Untouchability campaign.

> How long is Parliament to be kept under the delusion that the dual policy
> has succeeded in India? . . . I cannot congratulate the Government which
> shows such a peevish and petulant attitude and it is not creditable to
> its pretensions to statesmanship. Even Germany could not be compelled
> to admit its war guilt. Why then deny the ordinary human weakness to
> the Congress? It is silly for the Government to claim triumph or to be
> afraid of defeat. They could have carried a vast majority of people who
> want peace with them if they had not betrayed a spirit of this kind.[123]

Sapru had gauged the temper of Willingdon and his government rightly.
Delhi was determined to resist any attempt to soften its policy towards
Gandhi as civil disobedience leader and to open up the political situation
in the way Birla, Sapru and Jayakar had hoped. In its view the more
frustration the conflict generated the more potential collaborators in the
new constitution would part company with the Mahatma and current
Congress policy; and the only terms on which it would release Gandhi or
talk with him were if he did the job himself and called off civil disobedience.
Willingdon had told Hoare this the day Gandhi broke his fast; but before
the letter reached London the Secretary of State had wired to ask him to
consider releasing Gandhi. There was strong representation in Britain that
the government ought to take this chance of re-establishing contact with
Congress and ending the conflict; and he, MacDonald and other members
of the Cabinet thought it might be an opportune moment since the rationale

---

[123] Sapru to H. Polak, 9 October 1932, Sapru Papers, Series II.
For Jayakar's abortive attempt see Sapru to Ramaswami Aiyar, 28 September 1932
(A 81), Jayakar to Sapru, 28 & 30 September 1932, Sapru to Polak, 30 September
1932, Sapru Papers, Series II; telegrams between Govts., of India & Bombay, 27–29
September 1932, Home Poll., 1932, File No. 31/113.

could be implementation of the Pact, no negotiation would be involved and government would avoid having to negotiate unwillingly at a later date. Willingdon and all his colleagues except Mitter strongly opposed this suggestion. They believed that the Mahatma's release, even for a social campaign, would be hailed by Congress as a victory, and would undermine government's supporters, including the Muslims and the services: moreover it would be taken as a sign that government was prepared to negotiate and would generate demands for the release of more prisoners. In Delhi's view they must either stand firm on Gandhi or give away the whole position. When the governors backed Willingdon unanimously Hoare agreed not to press for Gandhi's release though he urged that they should give Gandhi reasonable facilities for carrying out the Pact and for talking to men like Rabindranath Tagore who might try to persuade him to give up civil disobedience. Hoare felt from his own contact with Gandhi that he would never abandon civil disobedience completely and therefore wished to keep the situation fluid, making it as easy as possible for the Mahatma to make a graceful surrender and saving the government from the position of having to keep him permanently in prison. Willingdon was also subjected to a barrage of Indian requests for Gandhi's release. But he and his Home Member, Haig, held to their position: there could be no negotiation with Gandhi and no release unless he called off civil disobedience, though Willingdon did agree with Hoare that some people should be permitted to visit Gandhi to encourage him to this end.[124] However even this small loophole was closed by the end of October. In consultation with a worried Bombay government Delhi decided to refuse all interviews at which civil disobedience was likely to be discussed, for fear of giving the impression that government would negotiate – despite strong pressure from Hoare and the Cabinet against this more rigid stand.[125]

Willingdon and his Home Department had calculated, in view of the current state of civil disobedience and the assured participation of a fair range of politicians in constitutional discussions, that government would gain nothing by contact with Gandhi; whereas the Irwin regime facing different pressures had judged that it was worth giving Gandhi a chance to exercise a continental leadership role. The present government believed that Gandhi could perform no useful function for it except that of ending

[124] Willingdon to Hoare, 26 September, 3 & 9 October 1932, Mss. EUR.E.240 (6); S of S to V, telegrams, 29, 30 September, 2 & 5 October 1932, V to S of S, telegrams, 1, 4, 5 October 1932, Mss. EUR.E.240 (11); Hoare to Willingdon, 30 September, 5 October 1932, Mss. EUR.E.240 (2); Governor of Bombay to V & S of S, telegram, 2 October 1932, Mss. EUR.F.150 (4); file of wires asking for Gandhi's release, e.g. President of Madras Liberal League to Viceroy, 6 October 1932, Home Poll., 1932, File No. 31/106.

[125] For the hardening of policy on selected 'political' interviews which followed a meeting between Willingdon, Sykes and Bombay's Home Member on 16 October see communications between Hoare and Willingdon, 14 October–8 November 1932, Mss. EUR.E.240 (2) (6) (11); also Sykes to Willingdon, 11 October 1932, Mss. EUR.F.150 (4).

civil disobedience, and by the later part of 1932 it had doubts whether he could even do that if he wished to. Willingdon, Haig and the Governors of Bombay and U.P. all stated that the issue was not now in Gandhi's hands, and though some Congressmen were willing to cooperate Vallabhbhai, Jawaharlal and Abdul Ghaffar Khan would probably sabotage any attempt by Gandhi to abandon the movement.[126]

Delhi's position was plain and unchanged when at the end of December Hoare returned to the question on which he disagreed with Willingdon's government – whether to allow Gandhi selected 'political' interviews. He pressed the suggestion that Sapru and Jayakar should be allowed to see Gandhi to explain the results of the third Round Table Conference. Backed by his Home Department and almost all his governors, Willingdon resisted. They argued that such an interview would be counterproductive, in that it would destroy the position the government had constructed during 1932 and dishearten those who were currently cooperating with government: while in return there was no guarantee that Gandhi either would or could call off a movement which now had little force, though there would certainly be a repetition of the extended mediation and escalating demands which had occurred in 1930 and 1931. Haig, moreover, going behind Hoare's proposal to the question implicit in it of releasing Gandhi after the third conference as he had been released after the first, bluntly minuted that in 1933 unlike 1931 'it is in no way necessary to secure the co-operation of the Congress in order that the new constitution may be properly launched, and in fact if Government reach an agreement with the Congress, I think conditions would be set up which might in certain Provinces wreck the constitution at the outset'. If this was the case Gandhi's release could serve no useful purpose and would only generate a demand for a general amnesty. There was to be no using Gandhi, thereby re-establishing him in a position of political leverage.[127] Hoare demurred that Haig's note implied keeping Gandhi in jail until the new constitution came into operation, an idea he found unpalatable and impolitic in both Indian and British contexts. To this Willingdon replied that they would let him out as soon as possible, but only in the unlikely event of his calling off civil disobedience or when there was no chance of the movement's revival.[128]

Despite his fast and the Poona Pact Gandhi was therefore completely

[126] Note by H. Haig, 3 October 1932, Home Poll., 1932, File No. 31/95; Sykes to Willingdon, 11 October 1932, Mss. EUR.F.150 (4); U.P. Governor to V, telegram, 31 December 1932, Home Poll., 1932, File No. 31/97; Willingdon to Hoare, 29 January 1933, Mss. EUR.E.240 (6).

[127] For the December–January exchanges on allowing Jayakar & Sapru to see Gandhi, which began with Hoare's wire to Willingdon, 24 December 1932, see Home Poll., 1932, File No. 31/97; Mss. EUR.E.240 (3) (6) (11). Particularly important were note by H. Haig, 28 December 1932 (Home Poll. File) and V to S of S, telegram, 7 January 1933 (both sources). In the event Jayakar & Sapru did not ask to see Gandhi.

[128] Hoare to Willingdon, 12 & 26 January 1933, Mss. EUR.E.240 (3); Willingdon to Hoare, 29 January 1933, Mss. EUR.E.240 (6).

boxed in by the government. Deprived at the end of September of special facilities to pursue his anti-Untouchability campaign or the chance to extend peace feelers to the raj he responded to the frustration of the situation by throwing himself into the Harijan campaign in an attempt to break out of the impasse created by the political conflict for him personally as for Congress. He sought both a new role as the Untouchables' champion, and in the reform programme a way to build the foundations of swaraj which would not incur the penalties of repression as did civil disobedience.

The first round in the new move was a battle for concessions in his jail conditions which would permit him to perform such anti-Untouchablity work. On 29 September, the day the special concessions granted during the fast were withdrawn, Gandhi demanded the right to see anybody he thought necessary for the implementation of the Poona Pact, and on 18 October when he had received no reply he repeated the demand. Bombay informed him that he would be permitted a reasonable number of interviews with officially approved visitors on the Untouchability question and unrestricted correspondence on the topic provided that it was not published. To this the Mahatma replied on 24 October by threatening to put himself on the diet of Class C prisoners unless there was an end to all restrictions on visitors and publication of correspondence. In leisurely fashion the local government informed Delhi of the crisis which was brewing, noting that Gandhi would probably become ill rapidly on such food. Delhi was horrified that it had not been told of the Mahatma's earlier protests and that the news arrived only the day before Gandhi was to begin his 'fast'. Immediately Willingdon's Council recommended that he should have complete freedom for visitors and correspondence on the Untouchability question, a position to which Hoare readily agreed. Gandhi accepted the concession with thanks, and promised not to abuse the government's trust by using the concession to discuss civil disobedience. Although the Bombay government complained bitterly that this was surrender to threats Willingdon's government was clear that it could not expose itself to universal condemnation in India and Britain for preventing Gandhi from 'dealing solely with a question of moral and religious reform'. It also had more devious intentions in permitting Gandhi this freedom. It hoped that his immersion in this work would reduce his popularity among caste Hindus (a spin-off stressed by Fazl-i-Husain), would divert public attention from civil disobedience, and provide the Mahatma with a face-saving exit from the political conflict.[129]

That Gandhi's battle for concessions was part of a wider bid to re-establish a public role for himself and continue building the foundations of swaraj was rapidly confirmed. Within days he was asking why he had been refused contact with Shaukat Ali, Ansari, and A. K. Azad on the question

---

[129] Exchanges between Gandhi and the Govts. of Bombay & India, between Delhi, Bombay & London on this episode are in Home Poll., 1932, File No. 31/95, Mss. EUR.F.150 (4), Mss. EUR.E.240 (2) (6), Gandhi Papers.

of Hindu–Muslim unity, and whether such contact would be allowed in future if it did not concern civil disobedience. Willingdon was irate that 'the little devil', as he described Gandhi to Hoare, had proved unwilling to confine himself to anti-Untouchability work. All the Mahatma received was a curt reply that a prisoner could not expect to participate in public life or discuss political questions. Gandhi himself maintained in a press interview shortly afterwards that he could not abandon his political objective and say he intended to devote himself entirely to Harijan work.[130] His life, he argued, was a whole, dedicated to the vindication of truth and non-violence. This total view of his role was clearly a significant source of inner strength and adaptability, enabling him to pursue his goals by different paths according to the constraints of his current situation. Seeing ordinary political activity as only one path he was able to a greater extent than most politicians to circumvent the frustrations of the present political impasse by following other paths as these opened. To him social reform and communal unity were essential elements in the re-creation of Indian life, providing scope for constructive action despite the collapse of civil disobedience and the government's refusal to talk.

The Harijan campaign Gandhi conducted from Yeravda left him little time to brood on his exclusion from ordinary political contacts. It even occupied his dreams. Early in December Chhaganlal Joshi was transferred from a Hyderabad prison to help with the volume of work, and Gandhi, having already stopped spinning because of sore elbows, now gave up all reading to devote his time to correspondence and interviews. He regularly wrote twenty or more letters a day and received a growing flood of visitors who had to be accommodated in a special yard. In the first five days of December alone he saw 13, 22, 25, 42 and 37 people! He also issued a series of statements on aspects of Untouchability and the campaign to eradicate it. By the end of the year his main preoccupation was opening Guruvayur temple in Kerala to Untouchables, an issue on which he declared that he would fast from the beginning of January. Sympathizers and opponents alike disliked the coercive effects of the fasting tactic to which the Mahatma seemed increasingly to be resorting. Ambedkar complained that it was far more important to end Untouchables' other disabilities, but Gandhi argued that temple-entry was the crucial symbol of caste Hindus' willingness to eradicate Untouchability. To C. F. Andrews he confided that his explanations of the projected fast could never express the depth of his feeling on the matter: 'for me personally it transcends reason, because I feel it to be a clear call from God.' However, he postponed the fast indefinitely when

[130] Gandhi to Govt. of India, Home Sec., 7 November 1932, Govt. of India, Home Dept., to Govt. of Bombay, Home Dept., 16 November 1932, asking them to relay their reply to Gandhi, Home Poll., 1932, File No. 31/95; Willingdon to Hoare, 13 November 1932, Mss. EUR.E.240 (6).

The occasion for this request was a Unity Conference in Allahabad in mid-November engineered by Malaviya: it produced no permanent agreement. Gandhi's press interview, 21 November 1932, *CWMG*, LII, 37.

it was established that enabling legislation was necessary.[131] Thereafter he tried the tactic of cooperation with government to ensure the passage of the necessary laws through the central and Madras legislatures. He sought advice from Jayakar on legal points, urged the government to expedite the bills, and appealed to MLAs to listen to Rajagopalachariar as his representative when he solicited their cooperation in the matter. When taunted with inconsistency as a non-cooperator working with government and through the legislatures he argued that he could not answer because of the bar on political discussion. But he commented on the irony of his situation to Jayakar who told Sapru, 'we both laughed, and I could not help feeling a little pang that the strength of last year with which he began the civil disobedience movement had completely been replaced by a pathetic impulse seeking refuge in legislative reform to secure national unity'.[132]

Gandhi's extraordinary position at the close of 1932, as a prisoner who held daily levees, as a self-confessed rebel who cooperated with government on legislation, reflected the dilemma into which the continuing political conflict with the raj had thrust him. As Jayakar realized the Harijan campaign was no withdrawal from the political world: it was another route to the goal of national unity which had been his constant theme since the start of civil disobedience in 1930. Although it provided for Gandhi an alternative to the tactic of civil disobedience which had manifestly failed to forge that unity, he had still found no way of engaging in political discussion with the government, and whenever possible he hinted that he was open to suggestions of peace. He made this plain to the Liberal, Chintamini, early in October. Moreover though he maintained that he could not guarantee calling off civil disobedience as the government demanded he said that if he was released unconditionally he would consider the situation and might advise people to give up the campaign.[133]

[131] For evidence of Gandhi's Untouchability work see his letters, statements & diaries, *CWMG*, LI–LIII; Govt. of Bombay, Home Dept., to Govt. of India, Home Dept., 7 & 15 December 1932, Home Poll., 1932, File No. 31/95; Pyarelal to A. Harrison, 12 December 1932, sent by Miss Harrison to Sapru, 22 December 1932 (H 171), Sapru Papers, Series II.

Gandhi's reasoning on the Guruvayur issue; press interview, 7 November 1932, *CWMG*, LI, 376–8, letter to C. F. Andrews, 20 December 1932, *CWMG*, LII, 244–5; announcement of postponement of fast, 29 December 1932, *ibid.* p. 303.

[132] Jayakar to Sapru, 6 February 1933, Sapru Papers, Series II; Gandhi on his cooperation in the legislative process, *Harijan*, 11 February 1933, *CWMG*, LIII, 267; Gandhi's appeal to MLAs, *Harijan*, 18 February 1933, *ibid.* pp. 328–9; file on government attitude to temple entry bills, including Gandhi's correspondence of 1 & 19 February 1933, on the matter, Home Poll., 1933, File No. 50/II.

[133] Gandhi to C. Y. Chintamini, 8 October 1932, *CWMG*, LI, 205; Gandhi to C. F. Andrews, 9 December 1932, Gandhi Papers; discussion between Gandhi & visitors, 18 December 1932, *CWMG*, LII, 438–40.

Pyarelal told Agatha Harrison, 12 December 1932, that though Gandhi would not call off civil disobedience as was being widely suggested, 'One thing is certain...that if he is released now all his energies are sure to be absorbed by his Anti-Untouchability work.' Enclosed in A. Harrison to Sapru, 22 December 1932 (H171), Sapru Papers, Series II.

Gandhi's politics as a prisoner trying to escape the frustration of a fruitless political confrontation only increased the dilemmas of other Congressmen. Many were aggrieved, feeling that Gandhi's emphasis on a social issue was diverting attention from civil disobedience. Others felt that the Mahatma had let them down by his stand and was indifferent to the fate of compatriots who had ended in prison for supporting his campaign. Yet others were confused as to whether they should now confine themselves to Harijan work. Jamnadas Dwarkadas, on parole to enable him to have an operation, told Gandhi something of this confusion when he saw him in Yeravda on 26 December.[134]

In response to this news from outside Gandhi issued a statement with government permission that Congressmen at large must make their own choice between civil disobedience and Harijan work, and that he could not decide for them. Though Gandhi's later comments indicated that he meant Congressmen to stick to civil disobedience unless they felt a particular call to the anti-Untouchability campaign his statement was interpreted in a multitude of ways. *The Bombay Chronicle* took it at its face value as 'a restoration of the individual's freedom of thought and action'. The Bombay Congress bulletin saw it as a renewed call to civil disobedience; while another Bombay paper, the Gujarati *Hindustan ane Prajamitra*, interpreted it as a sign that Rajagopalachariar, Satyamurti, Sherwani and other Congressmen at liberty should call off civil disobedience and save Gandhi the unpleasant task – an interpretation the Home Department in Delhi tended to share. The practical effect however was to increase Congressmen's confusion and doubt as to the value to them of Gandhi's leadership in the conflict in which they were trapped. It also confirmed the Government of India's belief that Gandhi could not effect fundamental policy changes in Congress and its judgement that therefore contact with him and the chance to let him play an all-India role as in February 1931 would serve no useful purpose.[135]

The contrast between government policy in the wake of the first and third Round Table Conferences was stark. Now as it prepared its White Paper embodying proposals for reform to be considered by a Joint Select Committee Whitehall exerted no pressure for a general amnesty for prisoners.

[134] R. M. Maxwell to M. G. Hallett, 12 January 1933, Home Poll., 1933, File No. 44/35.
Other evidence of Congressmen's disarray and discontent, R. Prasad, *Autobiography*, pp. 354–5, J. Nehru, *An Autobiography*, p. 338; Bose, *The Indian Struggle 1920–1942*, p. 249, S. Reed, *The India I Knew 1897–1947* (London, 1952), p. 204.
[135] Willingdon to Hoare, 29 January 1933, Mss. EUR.E.240 (6).
Text of Gandhi's statement, 7 January 1933, in Bombay Govt. to Govt. of India, telegram, 11 January 1933, comment by H. Haig on its significance, Home Dept., to P.S.V., telegram, 11 January 1933, Home Poll., 1933, File No. 50/15; reports by R. M. Maxwell to M. G. Hallett on interpretations of statement, 23 & 30 January 1933, Home Poll., 1933, File No. 44/35.
Gandhi's comment, 31 January 1933, on his attitude to the decision between civil disobedience and Harijan work, in discussion with Vallabhbhai & Rajagopalachariar, *CWMG*, LIII, 495.

Cartoon by David Low (*Evening Standard*, 20 March 1933), by
arrangement with the Trustees and the London *Evening Standard*.

The National Government was pressed at home from the right by a pungent attack led by Churchill on its long-term India policy, and harried from the left with criticisms of stonewalling with Congress. It faced a Delhi administration determined to extract implicit if not explicit surrender from Congress. Consequently Hoare merely suggested that a quiet quickening of the pace at which civil disobedience prisoners were released would ease his position in London. To this Delhi agreed, insisting to its local governments that this marked no change of policy towards civil disobedience, but was merely a device to detach those with more moderate inclinations from the movement.[136]

Since the government made no move to end the conflict with Congress except by slow suffocation the political situation in the new year increased the despondency of many non-Congress Hindus who had participated in the Round Table Conference. Few of them were prepared to organize a direct challenge to Gandhi and preferred both to press Congressmen at large to take courage and modify their policy, and to exhort the government to put the Mahatma in a position from which he could end the conflict. Moonje, anxious that power under the new constitution should not fall by Congress's default into 'undesirable hands' publicly urged that Congress should enter the new legislatures, though this suggestion that council entry should operate in uneasy tandem with continued civil disobedience showed an understanding of the extreme difficulty for Congressmen, who had committed themselves to defiance in January 1932, of repudiating their policy in favour of collaboration. When he floated the idea of a new party to contest elections Jayakar even more forcibly put the view that an overt challenge to Gandhi and Congress would be impolitic. 'As for your suggestion', he replied,

> I am not sure whether it is not premature. Besides, the old Responsive Co-operation Party has been scattered to the winds, and I do not know whether you think it easy to reassemble the disintegrated forces. We broke up miserably on the first prospect of opposition to a popular movement set up by Gandhi's march from [sic] Dandi three years ago, and if as you say a new Party has to be formed, it must be proof against any repetition of similar misadventures.[137]

Sapru tried to induce movement in the political deadlock by private encouragement to Congressmen to be realistic and work the new constitution rather than let it fall into conservative hands; and, in the interview he and Jayakar had with Willingdon on their return from London, by urging the Viceroy to release Gandhi.[138]

[136] Hoare to Willingdon, 10 & 17 February 1933, Mss. EUR.E.240 (3); S of S to V, telegram, 20 February 1933, Mss. EUR.E.240 (12); Govt. of India to all local govts., 25 February 1933, Mss. EUR.F.150 (5).

[137] 13 March 1933, Diary of B. S. Moonje; Jayakar to B. S. Moonje, 1 February 1933, Jayakar Papers, Correspondence File No. 236.

[138] Sapru to Rangaswami Aiyengar, 2 February 1933, Sapru to Miss C. K. Cumming, 5 February 1933, Sapru Papers, Series II.
Demands for release of Gandhi and political prisoners were made at moderate

Meanwhile among Congressmen at liberty there was increasing disquiet at the situation into which civil disobedience and Gandhi's Harijan campaign, compounded by his January statement, had led them. A new programme seemed increasingly urgent when the White Paper containing the British government's reform proposals was published on 18 March 1933. Based on the deliberations of the three Round Table Conferences, the plan had two main elements: a federation of British India and the Princely states when sufficient of the latter agreed to cooperate, and immediate grant of autonomy to the provinces of British India which were for the first time to be freed from control by Delhi or London within certain safeguards. The appearance of the White Paper showed Congressmen that unparalleled power would now be on offer in the provinces to politicians who trod the path of electoral and conciliar politics. It also indicated that it might be possible to put pressure on government to liberalize the reforms further by joining with non-Congress politicians who chafed at their limited nature, particularly in relation to the federal centre. Sapru, for example, made quite clear what men of his persuasion felt about the reform proposals Hoare felt able to put to a Tory-dominated Parliament.

> The ultimate power is to remain with Parliament for ever, the Secretary of State must continue to control the Governor-General and the Governor-General in his turn must continue to control the legislature. We can not employ our own agents. Our agents must be found for us by the Secretary of State. When we may hope to get control over Defence, or when or how the safeguards will disappear, none of us can foresee. This is the line of criticism common to all the parties. The White Paper has no friends and such of us as have spent three years of our time over the R.T.C. feel the contrast between the spirit of the first Conference and that which presents itself today. I should, however, still stand by the idea of Federation and temporary safeguards and reservations in the spirit of 1930 but the offer of the Government is very different from that.

His private criticisms were echoed when the Liberal Federation met in Calcutta on 17 April.[139]

Rangaswami Aiyengar, trying to act as a bridge over which Congressmen could begin to walk towards a new programme in line with some of their non-Congress compatriots, discussed the impasse with prominent Congressmen including Rajagopalachariar just after Gandhi had issued his January statement, and urged that they should exploit its possibilities. He believed that if Sapru and other moderates extracted Gandhi's release from the government Congressmen might be induced to stop civil disobedience and consider cooperation in the Joint Select Committee's proceedings and

meetings for example in Bombay on 9 February where Sir Chimanlal Setalvad presided, and in Madras on 16 February where V. S. S. Sastri presided: Bombay FR1, Madras FR2, February 1933, Home Poll., 1933, File No. 18/2.

[139] Sapru to Graham Pole, 2 April 1933 (P 140), Sapru Papers, Series II; *India in 1932–33* (Delhi, 1934), pp. 14–15; text of White Paper, *Proposals for Indian Constitutional Reform*, P.P., 1932–3, xx, Cmd. 4268.

in the new legislatures. From various provinces news filtered to the government of private Congress gatherings expressing frustration at the continued conflict and a wish to call off civil disobedience. Aney, the current acting Congress President, appeared to favour such a change, and the Berar Congress President, Waman Rao Joshi, came out in support of it. Among other ex-civil resisters some like Jamnadas Dwarkadas and the fiery Gujarati student leader, Rohit Mehta, felt so strongly that they wrote urging Gandhi to call off civil disobedience. Moreover the Nationalist Muslims, such uneasy civil resisters from the start in 1930, were among those who argued for a change of policy; and as Congress could not ultimately risk their alienation the likelihood of a reversion to cooperation in the near future was clear.[140] However Aney was not willing to stick his neck out and use his temporary position to steer Congress into cooperation. When the government announced that it would not allow the Congress session which Malaviya had suggested in the press Aney went ahead with his plans for a session in Calcutta late in March although it was bound to precipitate conflict with the administration. Obviously the government's declared ban made it very difficult for him to draw back without losing face; but in Aney's thinking there also seems to have been both a reluctance to stand out publicly against the policy Gandhi had inaugurated and a wish that it should be proved a failure so that Gandhi could not revive it. Consequently circulars went out to PCCs urging them to despatch delegates to Calcutta on 24 March, giving them a week for the journey during which they should engage in propaganda. The aim was to demonstrate Congress strength by publicity and arrests; and moreover one of the proposed resolutions would endorse the Working Committee's 1932 decision to renew civil disobedience.[141]

Even while preparations were under way for deliberate confrontation with government Congressmen were urging Sapru and Jayakar, their well-tried mediators, to effect some compromise with the raj. Aney, accompanied by Kelkar, pressed Jayakar in Poona. While in Delhi and then at home in Allahabad Sapru had long talks with the Nationalist Muslims, Ansari, Khaliquzzaman and Asaf Ali, and was actually sounded out by them about joining and leading a coalition party. He realized their peculiar predicament as non-communalist Muslims. Although they could not accept

[140] Rangaswami Aiyengar to Sapru, 16 January 1933, Sapru Papers, Series II; Delhi and C.P. & Berar FR2s, January 1933, Home Poll., 1933, File No. 18/1; Bombay, C.P. & Berar FR1s, March 1933, *ibid*, File No. 18/4; R. M. Maxwell to M. G. Hallett, 23 February & 15 March 1933, *ibid*. File No. 44/35; 5 March 1933, Diary of B. S. Moonje.

[141] For Aney's attitude see 3, 5, 26 March 1933, Diary of B. S. Moonje. An element in Aney's attitude to Gandhi's current 'political' stand was his anger at the Mahatma's willingness for legislation dealing with Hindu practices: his bitterness on this score was shared by Malaviya. For the preliminaries to the Congress session see Govt. of India to local govts., 8, 25 February, 17 March 1933, the latter enclosing two Congress circulars of 6 March 1933, *The Civil Disobedience Movement 1930-34*, pp. 78-80, 82-6.

wholeheartedly the sort of constitution the British were proposing, they dared not leave the Muslim seats in the new legislatures of autonomous provinces to 'reactionary' Muslims: however they were hesitant to come out into the open against civil disobedience for fear of losing prestige and splitting the Congress on which their political careers depended. Sapru's response was to urge them as a start to give up the Calcutta session; and he organized a meeting in Benares at which he hoped to reiterate his plea and suggest that they think out a new policy. The meeting took place in Malaviya's house in Benares on 28 March. Although Ansari's professional commitments kept him away, Khaliquzzaman, Azad and Asaf Ali attended, with Aney, Rajagopalachariar and a few others. At this gathering their frustrations at the current deadlock were clear: so too were their hesitations and divisions at the prospect of modifying the policy of conflict. Sapru explained to them the working and outcome of the third Round Table Conference and urged them to enter the new legislatures to prevent reactionaries from doing so. He judged that a growing number of them favoured council entry as a means of demonstrating Congress influence and forcing the government to consider their wishes, though they expressed no collective opinion. However he got no change when he argued for the abandonment of the Calcutta session three days hence. 'They seemed to feel that things had gone too far and that to abandon the session would on the one hand alienate their own following and on the other be treated by Government as a confession of defeat.' He was greeted with silence when he suggested that they should engineer some means of indicating a wish for peace even though they could not formally call off civil disobedience while the Working Committee was out of action. However he believed they realized that civil disobedience had lost momentum, an impression confirmed by their apparent willingness to cooperate with Liberals in an all-India day of protest against the White Paper.[142]

Despite the obvious hesitations of these Congress leaders about the wisdom of their policy they pushed ahead with the Calcutta confrontation. Government likewise swung into action. Considerable numbers of intending delegates were arrested en route to Bengal, and extensive raids in Calcutta on the night of 30 March led to the arrest of about 500 who had slipped through the net. Aney, Malaviya and Mrs Motilal Nehru were detained as they arrived, and the 'session' ended up as meeting on Chowringhee attended by about 800 on 1 April, at which Mrs Sen Gupta began to read out the proposed resolutions. With about 240 others she was immediately arrested and the rest of the crowd dispersed. Calcutta people had taken little notice of this all-India gathering on their territory, partly

[142] Jayakar to Sapru, 13 March 1933, Sapru to Jayakar, 23 & 24 March 1933, Sapru to Ansari, telegram, suggesting Benares meeting, 23 March 1933, Sapru to Rangaswami Aiyengar, V. S. S. Sastri & K. N. Haksar, describing Benares meeting, 28 March 1933, Sapru to Graham Pole, 2 April 1933 (P 140), Sapru Papers, Series II.

because elections to the Calcutta Corporation occurred on 29 March; since control of an annual income of Rs. 24,178,000, quite apart from other perks, was at stake the rival Congress factions preferred to concentrate on that! Consequently of the delegates arrested between 28 March and 1 April in Calcutta, only thirty-two belonged to the city. U.P. provided the largest batch (440) followed by the rest of Bengal and Assam (204), Bihar and Orissa (154), Punjab (46), Madras (26), Bombay (10), Gujarat and C.P. (8 each) with one from the Frontier and one from Bhopal. That the session was a desperate gesture and no way out of the political deadlock was recognized. *The Hindu* subsequently called on Congress to give up civil disobedience, publicly urging what its editor, Aiyengar, had been trying to manoeuvre privately. Sapru lamented on the 'sort of spiritual affinity' and equal fear of Congress and the government of losing prestige which impelled both into fruitless conflict. He remained, however, convinced that though Congressmen would neither disown civil disobedience nor approve of the White Paper 'a considerable section of them...are biding their time and are determined to capture the legislative machinery everywhere'.[143]

Gandhi, still in Yeravda, was insulated somewhat from the growing tension in Congress circles and the pressure for a new programme. Yet as a prisoner there was little he could to to help his colleagues outside. All that would have been permitted was a repudiation of civil disobedience – which would have alienated those in jail and would not have provided those at liberty with the face-saving formula they so badly needed. Consequently he remained immersed in his Harijan work, fighting increasing orthodox hostility and finding a new outlet from February 1933 in writing for a new paper, *Harijan*, which though edited by R. V. Shastri under the auspices of the Servants of Untouchables Society was effectively his mouthpiece. His determination to influence public life even though a prisoner, and his frustration at the means available to him, were dramatically proven when on 30 April he announced that he would fast from 8 to 29 May in response to an inner call on the Harijan issue. He explained that the fast was not directed at any group or person but was a personal act of self-purification as the road to inward power to fight an evil which he now realized was of such proportions that it could not be fought by money, organization and political power alone. His private explanations followed the same course. Telling Jawaharlal, who he knew would probably not understand, he wrote, 'The Harijan movement is too big for mere intellectual effort. There is nothing so bad in all the world. And yet I cannot leave religion and therefore Hinduism, my life would be a burden to me, if Hinduism failed me...But then I cannot tolerate it with untouchability ...Fortunately Hinduism contains a sovereign remedy for the evil. I have

[143] Bengal FR2, March 1933, Home Poll., 1933, File No. 18/4; *Report on the Administration of Bengal 1932–33* (Calcutta, 1934), pp. x–xi, 58; Madras FR1, April 1933, Home Poll., 1933, File No. 18/5; Sapru to Jayakar, 3 April 1933, to B. Rama Rao, 9 April 1933, Sapru Papers, Series II.

applied the remedy.' Public and private evidence together indicate that Gandhi's battles for Untouchables since the Poona Pact had convinced him that the problem was far greater than he had originally thought. Moreover disquieting news of moral lapses in his ashram in his absence made him feel that in it he had no fit instrument to carry on this battle for reform. Consequently he embarked on a dramatic gesture of self-purification which was possible to a prisoner. The technique and the idea that purity generated power were deeply engrained in Hindu tradition; and his action was consistent with his own pronouncements over the years that public and private life could not be run on different standards and that he who wished to influence public life must first refine his own life and that of his helpers.[144]

Such reasoning and activity was appropriate to a Mahatma and a prisoner: but it did little to solve the problems of men looking for political leadership, who saw their former general confusing and diverting his followers and endangering his life. The press expressed bewilderment and some overt hostility, and a flood of letters and telegrams from appalled associates poured into Yeravda. Jawaharlal, Malaviya, Syed Mahmud, Ansari, A. K. Azad, Sri Prakasa and K. Natarjan among others protested vigorously; while Rajagopalachariar went to Yeravda and failed despite four hours' exhausting discussion to persuade Gandhi to call off the fast.[145] The Bombay government had warned Delhi that Gandhi would probably not survive a three-week fast, and the Government of India decided that the political repercussions of Gandhi's death in jail outweighed the risk of his presence at large giving new impetus to civil disobedience. Moreover as Delhi and London both realized, there were great advantages in terms of politics and public opinion in India and Britain to release him on humanitarian grounds and so forestall any suggestion that government was changing its policy or 'negotiating': and they emphasized that this should be the official publicity line. Consequently when Gandhi began to fast on

[144] Announcement of fast in press statement, 30 April 1933, published in *Harijan*, 6 May 1933, Microfilm, John Rylands University Library of Manchester; Bombay Govt. to Govt. of India, telegram, 1 May 1933, enclosing wire from Gandhi to Govt. of India announcing fast, Mss. EUR.F.150 (5); Gandhi to J. Nehru, 2 May 1933, J. Nehru Papers, part 1, vol. XXIII; Gandhi to Manibehn Patel, 6 May 1933, M. K. Gandhi, *Letters to Manibahen Patel* (Ahmedabad, 1963), pp. 65–6.

For Gandhi's concern about the ashram see a guarded allusion in his 30 April announcement and a definite assertion in letter to prisoners from ashram in Visapur jail, 6 May 1933, Balvantsinha, *Under the Shelter of Bapu* (Ahmedabad, 1962), pp. 25–6: further evidence on state of ashram, report by Ahmedabad District Magistrate, 27 July 1933, Home Poll., 1933, File No. 3/17.

[145] In Gandhi Museum, Delhi, the files of correspondence to Gandhi for May, May–June 1933 are full of such protests, of which these are only a selection. See also 8 May 1933, J. Nehru's Diary, *SWJN*, 5, pp. 474–5; reports on press reaction, provincial FRIs, May 1933, Home Poll., 1933, File No. 18/6; statement by Rajagopalachariar, 5 May 1933, *Harijan*, 6 May 1933.

8 May he was released in the evening and taken to the home of Lady Vithaldas Thakersey in Poona.[146]

The Viceroy was not sure what prompted Gandhi to undertake this fast, but he suspected that it was the attempt of a vain man to regain the limelight. 'He may of course be really sincere in wanting to confine himself during the later years of his life to helping on the untouchables. We shall see.'[147] The day Willingdon wrote that phrase he was made aware that the Mahatma intended to use his liberty to influence the political situation directly. In a statement on his release Gandhi said he would study the civil disobedience movement though at present his views on civil disobedience were unchanged; but he advised Aney as Congress President to suspend the movement for up to six weeks since satyagrahis would in any case 'be in a state of terrible suspense' during his fast. He then appealed to the government to use this suspension and release all civil resisters: only then was there a chance that the movement would be called off, and technically it could not be called off while the members of the Working Committee as it existed in December 1931 were in jail. However he made it clear that he would like to enter into discussions with the authorities once more and 'take up the thread at the point where I was interrupted on my return from England'. The next day Aney seized the opportunity to do what he had not dared to do on his own authority and declared the campaign suspended for six weeks.[148] Bombay and Delhi were at one in thinking that Aney and Gandhi must have decided this policy together when the President visited Yeravda on 6 May, though the interview was meant to be 'non-political'. Moreover Willingdon and Sykes agreed that Gandhi had made this gesture in an attempt to hold together the disintegrating Congress ranks, re-establish

---

[146] Govt. of India to Govt. of Bombay, telegram, 5 May 1933, Mss. EUR.F.150 (5); S of S to V, telegram, 7 May 1933, Mss. EUR.E.240 (12).
Because of the need for speed Delhi and London had decided on the policy with only a preliminary consultation with Bombay. This provoked an official protest from Sykes and his Home Department because Bombay had wanted to release Gandhi later in the fast when he was unlikely to be able to leave Poona. Sykes even argued that Delhi's decision meant abandoning the agreed policy and risking a return to the conditions of 1930 'simply because a man says that he is being spoken to by an inner voice'. Willingdon denied that Gandhi's release indicated a policy change, and reminded Sykes that he too had agreed that Gandhi must be released at some time during the fast. Gandhi was released on the first day of the fast to prevent agitation since later release would look like capitulation to agitation. Sykes to Willingdon, 6 May 1933, Willingdon's reply, 15 May 1933, R. M. Maxwell to M. G. Hallett, 6 May 1933, Hallett's reply, 17 May 1933, Mss. EUR.F.150 (5).

[147] Willingdon to Sykes, 7 May 1933, *ibid.*; Willingdon to Hoare, 8 May 1933, Mss. EUR.E.240 (6).

[148] Gandhi's 8 May 1933 statement, Home Poll., 1933, File No. 4/11; part of M. S. Aney's 9 May 1933 statement, quoted in R. M. Maxwell to M. G. Hallett, 12 May 1933, Home Poll., 1933, File No. 44/35.
Rangaswami Aiyengar talked to Gandhi on 9 May and assured the P.S.V. that Gandhi wished to get back to his position on his return from London in order to resume constitutional discussions; Willingdon to Hoare, 15 May 1933, Mss. EUR.E.240 (6).

his authority, and in relation to the raj to get back to a position similar to that of 1931 in which as Congress spokesmen he had participated in constitutional discussions and negotiated on equal terms with the government. In order to scotch any such developments or suspicion of a change in policy the government issued a communiqué on 9 May that its policy remained unchanged: there could be no cooperation until civil disobedience was definitely abandoned not merely withdrawn for a space, and there was 'no intention of negotiating with the Congress for a withdrawal of the civil disobedience movement or of releasing the leaders of that movement with a view to arriving at any settlement with them in regard to these unlawful activities'.[149]

So government foiled Gandhi's attempt to end the deadlock between Congress and the raj. Immediately the different groups in the political scene began to prepare for another Gandhian initiative at the end of the temporary suspension of civil disobedience – if he survived. The Mahatma, used to a spare and disciplined diet and to frequent lesser privations, lived on; though he was too weak for a month afterwards to take any political initiative. It was clear however that he would ultimately have to find a public role and a policy which not only satisfied his particular ambition to reform Indian public life but, if he wished to retain a continental leadership position in politics, also provided Congress with a credible stance towards the government.

In anticipation of this development the government immediately began to manoeuvre to prevent the renewal of Gandhi's leadership in politics. Willingdon, prodded by Hoare that their policy of releasing lesser civil disobedience prisoners seemed to be proceeding hesitantly in certain provinces, reminded local governments and the two prime offenders, Bombay and the Frontier, in particular. The Viceroy's intention in so doing was not merely to pacify the Secretary of State, who had his own problems of left-wing pressure on the National Government and the presence in London of Indians giving evidence to the Joint Select Committee on the White Paper. Indian witnesses included Sapru, Rangaswami Aiengar and spokesmen of the Mahasabha, and were proof of the frustration of Hindu politicians on the Congress peripheries at the continuing conflict between Congress and the raj. Willingdon now also wished to deny Gandhi any new leverage and limelight. He argued in a private exhortation to Sykes that Gandhi was likely to request an interview on his recovery and ask for the release of civil disobedience prisoners. If the actual numbers in jail were small 'Gandhi would get very little kudos if he came to see me and asked for their release...would it be possible for you to hasten up your jail delivery of these people in order that we may achieve this result? I am sure you will

---

[149] V to S of S, telegram giving text of 9 May 1933 communiqué, 9 May 1933, V to S of S, telegram, 10 May 1933, Home Poll., 1933, File No. 44/57 & K.-W.; Willingdon to Hoare, 15 May 1933, Mss. EUR.E.240 (6); Sykes to Willingdon, 13 May 1933, Mss. EUR.F.150 (5).

agree that it would be a great thing not to allow Gandhi to claim any credit and restore his prestige.' Sykes's government dug in its heels, fearing that releases would in fact decrease pressure within Congress for 'capitulation'.[150] Nevertheless Bombay agreed with Delhi on the need to prevent any build-up of Gandhi's political influence, and this lay behind their agreement by early June that no member of either government would grant Gandhi an interview unless civil disobedience was abandoned. Willingdon analysed the position as he saw it to Hoare on 1 July. Congress was divided on policy and many elements in it were disillusioned with Gandhi's leadership, but the Mahatma was the only one who given favourable ground could pull them all together: in the past his influence in Congress had depended largely on his influence with the government, and the government's readiness to treat with him. Willingdon was determined to prevent a recurrence of this syndrome. A further element in his calculation was the probability that Gandhi would not be able to ensure that Jawaharlal, Vallabhbhai or Abdul Ghaffar Khan observed the peace: his value to government was therefore minimal, compounding the disadvantages of boosting his leadership position. Willingdon's Council confirmed this policy on 3 July and stuck to it despite pressure from Hoare to grant an interview to Gandhi if he merely requested one and showed no wish to 'negotiate', even if civil disobedience had not been revoked. The Secretary of State and the Cabinet were worried that a blatant rebuff would alienate British Liberal and Labour politicians and Indian witnesses in London, but to the men under different pressures in India the benefit of depriving Gandhi of a negotiatory role far outweighed the dangers Hoare outlined.[151]

Meanwhile among Congressmen there was extreme uncertainty – 'demoralisation' in Jawaharlal's words – as they waited for Gandhi to recover. Most of them were looking for a lead from him, and civil disobedience was suspended yet again in mid-June until the end of July to enable the Mahatma to take the initiative. There was clearly a chance for him to take control of the situation, for as Jawaharlal commented from jail, 'All India, or most of it, stares reverently at the Mahatma and expects him to perform miracle after miracle and put an end to untouchability and get Swaraj and so on – and does nothing itself!'[152] It was not only Gandhi's

[150] Willingdon to Sykes, 27 June 1933, Sykes's reply, 3 July 1933, Mss. EUR.F.150 (5). Haig, after a conference with the Govt. of Bombay, thought Delhi should press Bombay no further on this issue; note by H. E. Haig, 10 July 1933, Home Poll., 1933, File No. 44/57 & K.-W.

See also Hoare to Willingdon, 26 May 1933, Willingdon's reply, 5 June 1933, Mss. EUR.E.240 (6); Govt. of India to all local govts., 26 June 1933, Mss. EUR.F.150 (5).

[151] M. G. Hallett to R. M. Maxwell, 27 May 1933, Maxwell's reply, 5 June 1933, note by Hallett on 3 July Council meeting, 4 July 1933, Home Poll., 1933, File No. 44/57 & K.-W.; Willingdon to Hoare, 26 June 1933, Mss. EUR.E.240 (6); V to S of S, telegrams 1, 8, 13 July 1933, S of S to V, telegrams, 6, 11, 12 July 1933, Mss. EUR.E.240 (12).

[152] 4 & 23 June 1933, J. Nehru's Diary, *SWJN*, 5, pp. 478, 485; note by M. G. Hallett, 14 June 1933, Home Poll., 1933, File No. 44/57 & K.-W.

position as civil disobedience expert which produced this stance. Once again Congressmen were deeply divided and looked to the Mahatma to compose their differences with a face-saving yet politically productive compromise. Throughout June small groups of Congressmen assembled to discuss their future policy. In almost every province there was dissension. Some argued that civil disobedience was dead and should be buried forthwith, while others pressed for its revival, eager for continued conflict on ideological grounds or out of need for the financial support of an agitational pro-gramme. Despite pressure for renewed conflict from Delhi, U.P. and Bombay in particular, those in favour of abandoning civil disobedience appeared to be growing in conviction and numbers. Most notable among them were Nationalist Muslims who had earlier contacted Sapru – Ansari, Sherwani, Khaliquzzaman and Asaf Ali. The latter went so far as to write an open letter to Gandhi arguing that Congress should turn from civil disobedience to the ballot box, an admission of the failure of civil disobe-dience so public that it distressed even Ansari. B. C. Roy also thought it premature to discuss council entry publicly, but he too hoped privately to discuss the possibility with Ansari, Asaf Ali and Khaliquzzaman. A further sign that Congressmen were reluctant to cut themselves off from positions of power within the constitution, whatever continental or provincial leaders might enjoin, was their increasing participation in elections to local boards though of necessity they campaigned under names other than Congress.[153]

Jail walls no longer insulated Gandhi from these conflicting pressures; and he was soon aware that the choice he would have to make would be as difficult as his earlier decisions to start or stop civil disobedience. Polak, writing from England, told him bluntly that 'the mere thought of civil disobedience, let alone its active prosecution' had arrayed all reactionary forces there against constitutional advance, and that judging from the evidence he had seen while visiting India two months earlier many Con-gressmen were anxious for a formal end to the campaign. He urged him not to play with words like suspension but to end the movement which had become a divisive force. At the time Asaf Ali penned his open letter, Gandhi deliberately took soundings from the Nationalist Muslims who were closest to him, and received a long statement from Ansari urging him to abandon civil disobedience and tour India with a triple programme of *khadi*, Harijan uplift and communal unity. His argument was that civil disobedience had not failed, since it had changed people's mentality dramatically, but that it was now at a standstill and people should be given a breathing space before they resumed it. During that space they should back Gandhi's triple

153 For local discussions on future policy and dissensions see provincial FRs, June 1933, Home Poll., 1933, File No. 18/7 (Asaf Ali's letter of 24 June is reported in Delhi FR2); 23 June 1933, J. Nehru's Diary, *SWJN*, 5, p. 485; B. C. Roy to M. A. Ansari, 18 June [1933], Ansari Papers.

For Congress participation in local board elections see e.g. *1932–33 Bihar & Orissa Administration Report*, pp. vi–vii; C.P. & Berar, FR1, July 1933, Home Poll., 1933, File No. 18/8.

programme with a campaign against the White Paper in company with non-Congressmen who also opposed it, and should consider entering the new legislatures. Clearly he was again hoping to forge links with Sapru and his kind in constitutional politics, and was tactfully trying to persuade Gandhi to give up satyagraha and to propel him into a role where his talents could be used without precipitating conflict with the raj.[154]

Gandhi meanwhile told C. F. Andrews that the political situation could hardly have been worse: Ordinances had silenced people and the civil service showed no intention of relinquishing power. But he said he would take no precipitate action and would try to secure an honourable peace. At least two factors made it highly unlikely that he would be able to reach a settlement which he considered honourable. He was determined not to sacrifice Abdul Ghaffar Khan, partly because he believed him to be genuinely non-violent, and partly because his support provided an argument against allegations that Congress was a Hindu organization: Abdul Ghaffar's release was as essential to a settlement as had been that of his allies imprisoned for their participation in the Congress-sponsored Khilafat campaign in 1921, notably the Ali brothers. Moreover, as he hinted to Andrews and spelt out in his reply to Asaf Ali, he could never give up satyagraha completely.

> Non-violence for me is not a mere experiment. It is part of my life and the whole of the creed of Satyagraha, Non-cooperation, Civil Disobedience, and the like, are necessary deductions from the fundamental proposition that Non-violence is the law of life for human beings. For me it is both a means and an end and I am more than ever convinced that in the complex situation that faces India, there is no other way of gaining real freedom.[155]

Nevertheless by mid-June he had decided to ask Willingdon for an interview when he was well enough. In this he was supported by Srinivasa Sastri, Rajagopalachariar and Mahadev Desai, but most other Congressmen close to him opposed the idea. Aney though it would invite a rebuff, and in any case if civil disobedience was to be withdrawn, as he thought most Congressmen wished, there was no need to seek an interview. Because of such differences a private conference of about 150 Congressmen was called at Poona for 12 July to enable Gandhi to take soundings before suggesting an appropriate policy in the light of the current situation and the diverse opinions within their ranks.[156]

[154] H. Polak to Gandhi, 1 June 1933, S.N. No. 21420, Gandhi Papers; Gandhi to S. Mahmud, 26 June 1933, S. Mahmud Papers, File No. 50; M. A. Ansari to M. Desai, 5 July 1933, enclosing statement signed by him that day to be shown to Gandhi, S.N. No. 21514, Gandhi Papers.

[155] Gandhi to C. F. Andrews, 15 June 1933, M. Desai to C. F. Andrews, 15 June 1933, S.N. No. 19098, Gandhi to Asaf Ali, 26 June 1933, S.N. No. 19108, Gandhi Papers.

[156] Gandhi to A. Harrison, telegram, c. 15 June 1933, Gandhi Papers; V. S. S. Sastri to Hoare, 22 June 1933, Jagadisan, *Letters of Srinivasa Sastri*, p. 255; M. Desai

When the delegates met it was clear that none contemplated the renewal of civil disobedience: the question at issue was whether they should end it unilaterally without contacting government or make its abandonment conditional on concessions. On the first day most speakers urged that Congress should withdraw the campaign unconditionally, one of the most committed exponents of this view being Satyamurti. The next day those in favour of bargaining for the end of civil disobedience held the field, prominent among them J. B. Kripalani. Gandhi held his fire until the following day, 14 July, though he had in earlier, private discussions made it plain that he would never renounce civil disobedience for all time, and had floated the idea of civil disobedience by individuals under the Congress banner or going on alone with satyagraha if Congress withdrew it. On the 14th Gandhi made a powerful eighty-minute speech in which (clearly remembering his letters from Ansari and Polak) he said that those who called for the end of the campaign were really asking for suspension for an indefinite period to give them breathing space to prepare for another campaign. This was dishonest: they had either to withdraw it completely or not at all, and complete withdrawal could not be unilateral but must follow negotiations with government. An hour's interval followed, during which there was brisk canvassing of opinion, and when the meeting resumed Malaviya publicly threw his weight behind Gandhi. The voting then took place and resolutions in favour of unconditional withdrawal and 'individual' civil disobedience were thrown out, while one authorizing Gandhi to seek an interview with Willingdon was passed unanimously.[157]

The vote was a triumph for the Mahatma as it went against the real sense of the meeting. Several elements in the dynamics of the gathering accounted for this. In the first place many of those most deeply committed to continuing the conflict were not present. Jawaharlal's savage note in his jail diary indicated how he would probably have argued had he been present. 'It is amazing how flabby-minded our people have got. They meet in Poona at a critical moment after nearly 2 years and they do not even trouble to discuss, much less lay down, the objective before us. Only talks of peace with a govt. that has insulted us in every way.' Since many of those present in Poona were seeing Gandhi for the first time after a year and a half in jail and two major fasts the circumstances were likely to be heavily charged emotionally, conducive to accepting his advice rather than overtly

---

to C. F. Andrews, 20 July 1933, S.N. No. 21529, Gandhi Papers, Gandhi's press conference, 18 July 1933, *The Bombay Chronicle*, 19 July 1933, Home Poll., 1933, File No. 4/11.

[157] M. Desai to C. F. Andrews, 20 July 1933, S.N. No. 21529, S. Satyamurti to Gandhi, 13 July 1933, S.N. No. 21524, Gandhi Papers; 12 & 13 July 1933, Diary of V. S. S. Sastri; J. B. Kripalani to J. Nehru, 11 July 1936, J. Nehru, *A Bunch of Old Letters*, p. 200; V to S of S, telegram, 15 July 1933, Home Poll., 1933, File No. 3/17; Bombay FR1, July 1933, Home Poll., 1933, File No. 18/8; Govt. of Bombay to Govt of India, 11 August 1933, Mss. EUR.F.150 (5).

rejecting his leadership or consigning him to the role of independent satyagrahi as he had suggested. Furthermore, as Gandhi put the issue, withdrawal of civil disobedience without securing conditions was made to appear abject surrender; while the prospect of Gandhi negotiating with Willingdon conjured up visions of a return to the prestigious days of February 1931 when Irwin had welcomed Gandhi as an equal to discuss the end of their first campaign. Added to these factors was the natural desire in such a gathering to reach a consensus rather than increase Congress weakness and lessen its prestige by a display of disunity which was bound to become public.[158]

Gandhi took great care over the wire asking Willingdon for an interview, casting out of the first draft reference to Congress and government reaching a settlement, as he rightly thought that this would provoke an immediately hostile reaction. Eventually the wire merely requested an interview 'with a view to exploring possibilities of peace'. The Viceroy's Council went into session when it received the request on 15 August, and decided unanimously that it should be refused. Willingdon referred the matter to Hoare. Realizing from recent telegraphic consultation that Hoare might press again that he should see Gandhi as he had imposed no conditions in his request, Willingdon took care to put a gloss on Gandhi's wire which the wording would not bear. He insisted that in the light of the Poona discussions this was clearly a request to negotiate under the threat of civil disobedience, and must therefore be refused. Hoare agreed, and on 16 July the reply went back that an interview would serve no purpose as Congress had not withdrawn civil disobedience and the government had no intention of bargaining with Congress as a condition of its cooperation. A small inner group of Congressmen considered this refusal, among them Rajagopalachariar, Aney, A. K. Azad, Bhulabhai Desai and K. Venkatappayya. Most of them opposed sending any reply, but Gandhi and Rajagopalachariar insisted on making a further attempt, and consequently Gandhi sent off a wire repeating his request, saying that he was a man of peace and could show the Viceroy that the sense of the Poona meeting was in favour of an honourable peace. The small gathering of Congressmen thought Willingdon would refuse even this advance, and laid tentative plans for the future in that event. Since mass civil disobedience was clearly impossible in some areas they virtually decided on individual civil disobedience whereby satyagrahis could be shuttled round the country to give

[158] 18 July 1933, J. Nehru's Diary, *SWJN*, 5, p. 489.

N. C. Kelkar gave a scathing comment to the press on 17 July about the Poona meeting quoted in Govt. of Bombay to Govt. of India, 11 August 1933, Mss. EUR.F.150 (5). 'It is quite clear that even the Congress workers were against continuing the civil disobedience movement and yet they defeated the first resolution about unconditional and immediate discontinuance out of loyalty to Mr. Gandhi. Lip sealing has been the bane of public life under Mr. Gandhi's regime. It may be glorious from Mr. Gandhi's point of view, but it is disastrous indeed from the point of view of the country.'

a good display even in provinces which could produce few home-grown resisters. This was a plan of Gandhi's own concoction of which he was, according to Sastri, very proud; though it was diametrically opposed to a vote taken at the Poona conference. Again divisions among Congressmen, leading to the postponement of a definite policy decision until after the interview with Willingdon on which they had been able to agree, placed Gandhi in the position of being able to advise on policy unfettered by a Congress gathering. Predictably the second telegram to Willingdon elicited only the same refusal.[159]

After their confabulations on messages to Willingdon the Congress leaders left Poona for their home provinces, and Gandhi went to Ahme-dabad to visit his ashram, though he did not stay there because of his vow on setting out for Dandi in 1930 that he would not return until he had won swaraj. The results of their Poona plans were made public on 22 July when Aney published a statement drafted at Poona. It suggested that in the light of the Poona discussions and Gandhi's advice civil disobedience should not be unconditionally withdrawn but should now take the form of individual civil disobedience. Aney also recommended that all secret activities should cease and that therefore Congress organizations, being illegal, should also cease to operate for the time being (with the exception that all-India and provincial 'dictators' should continue). Gandhi followed this up with a statement on 26 July in which he claimed responsibility for Aney's sugges-tions, disagreeing with him only on the continued existence of 'dictators', which he opposed. Satyagraha must go on as the only route to indepen-dence, Gandhi argued; but as 'the prolonged torture of the ordinance rule' made the end of mass civil disobedience a practical necessity it was now the task of individuals to infect the nation with a spirit which could not be crushed by repression. While only a few thousand Congressmen would become individual civil resisters the others should concentrate on con-structive activities which would also help to build up the nation – *khadi*, Harijan service, communal unity, and the development of village industries and agriculture. He suggested that it was premature to discuss working the reformed constitution until they knew its form, but refused to give any guidance on entering the existing legislatures, merely commenting, 'My head reels at the very thought of entering Councils for the sake of winning independence.'[160]

Reaction among Congressmen throughout the country to these state-

[159] Gandhi to P.S.V., telegrams, 15 & 16 July 1933, P.S.V. to Gandhi, telegrams, 16 & 17 July 1933, Home Poll., 1933, File No. 3/17 (also all are S.N. No. 21526, Gandhi Papers); V to S of S, 2 telegrams, 15 July 1933, S of S to V, telegram, 16 July 1933, Mss. EUR.E.240 (12); Willingdon to Sykes, 16 July 1933, Mss. EUR.F.150 (5); M. Desai to C. F. Andrews, 20 July 1933, S.N. No. 21529, Gandhi Papers; 17 July 1933, Diary of V. S. S. Sastri; secret report, 15 July 1933, received by D. I. B., Home Poll., 1933, File No. 3/17.

[160] M. S. Aney's statement, 22 July 1933, Home Poll., 1933, File No. 3/17; Gandhi's statement, 26 July 1933, Home Poll., 1933, File No. 4/11.

ments was one of incomprehension and growing disillusion with Gandhi's renewed attempt at political leadership. Instead of an attractive, face-saving policy to extricate them from the political impasse, they had been landed with a policy dead against the wishes of those who had gathered at Poona. For those who hankered after cooperation and exploitation of the constitutional structures it offered no base for an organized onslaught on the legislatures, only a muted confrontation with the raj which would still obstruct any change in official policy. For those who hoped for conflict it provided a feeble substitute for mass civil disobedience. Moreover the very organization which was a major attraction of Congress to local politicians was put in jeopardy. And all this came at a time when many Congressmen were deeply ambivalent about Gandhi's Harijan campaign. Feeling was particularly strong in the south, but the frustration and despair was echoed in the press and small Congress gatherings throughout the country. Few were prepared to break out openly and try to follow a new programme or found new organizations. U.P.'s leading Congressmen meeting in Allahabad on 30 July, for example, agreed reluctantly to obey Aney's instructions but registered a protest against the new policy. As Sapru put it, 'there is utter chaos and confusion in public life' and among Congressmen the 'present feeling is of despair & disappointment'.[161]

Gandhi's position as an all-India political guide after Willingdon had rejected his Poona advance was one of acute difficulty. His immediate colleagues and the local groups for whom they spoke were divided, and any decision clearly for or against the civil disobedience movement would have provoked opposition. Moreover mass civil disobedience was dead, and this had somehow to be recognized formally by Congress without abjectly surrendering its stand of the past three and a half years. Individual civil disobedience was his answer to these dilemmas. It also satisfied his personal commitment to satyagraha as an indispensable element in his philosophy of life and was consistent with his earlier teaching that only reform of his compatriots' attitudes could be the basis of swaraj. By dissociating the Congress organization from civil disobedience he may have hoped that there was a slim chance that government would agree to talk to Congressmen, and he concluded his statement with the assertion that Congress replace forced cooperation. Some of his close colleagues evidently thought that the temporary non-functioning of the Congress organization was an astute move to keep the organizational structure out of the hands of 'undesirables' which had been difficult when secrecy was at a premium during 1932–3, or prevent its takeover by those determined on council entry. Similarly the end of secret methods was not only a reflection of his

---

[161] T. B. Sapru to S. Sinha & to Jayakar who were both in London, 13 August 1933, Sapru Papers, Series II.

For evidence of the chaos in Congress circles see Willingdon to Hoare, 22 July 1933, Mss. EUR.E.240 (6); Bombay Govt. to Govt. of India, 11 August 1933, Mss. EUR.F.150 (5); Provincial FR2s, July 1933, Home Poll., 1933, File No. 18/8; U.P. FR1, August 1933, *ibid.* File No. 18/9.

satyagrahi's commitment to openness but a means of rooting out of Congress people and methods which had brought Congress into disrepute by violence and were outside the control of the Working Committee.[162]

Although Gandhi's decision made considerable sense in the context of the appalling constraints imposed on him by Congressmen and the Government of India he was by this time deeply frustrated at being in conflict with the raj and unable to force on the obdurate Viceroy an 'honourable' settlement. No other satyagraha he had master-minded had led to a total deadlock, and having suggested a compromise policy which recognized the situation and permitted Congressmen personal choice of activity he cast around for a personal campaign by which to influence his compatriots and force the government into some new move.

His first personal step was to announce to the Bombay government that he was disbanding the Sabarmati ashram on 31 July. He offered the land, buildings and crops to the government as he felt he could not hand these over, like moveable property, to friends and be party to their paying revenue. This proposal was greeted with incredulous incomprehension by the public. The reasons he gave were that government repression made it impossible for the ashram to carry on constructive work without dissociating itself from civil disobedience and thereby denying its creed; and that as government policy indicated that the struggle would be prolonged much greater sacrifices would be required of the people and he as author of civil disobedience must sacrifice what was dearest to him. Moonje interpreted this, taken with the disbanding of the Congress organization, to be a sign that Gandhi was trying to get back into a relationship with the government not similar to that of 1931 but to that which he had enjoyed before his 1920 confrontation with the raj. The Ahmedabad District Magistrate noted that 'all has not been well at the Ashram for a considerable time. Little practical work was being done, the moral standard was low and the conduct of affairs and of religious worship was utterly artificial. Doubtless these facts were in large measure responsible for Mr. Gandhi's decision.' In the light of Gandhi's concern over the ashram before his May fast it seems likely that at the heart of his decision was the realization that Sabarmati was no longer the fit instrument for his work which he had tried to build up in 1929–30, and that its disbanding would allow him to start again with a body of disciplined adherents at Wardha in central India. The dramatic symbol of renouncing the institution which had been his show-piece since his return from Africa was but the prelude to another move which, like his salt campaign and Dandi march, was a symbolic demonstration of his message. Just as early in 1930 he and picked companions had been the visual

[162] On the reasons for the temporary suspension of Congress organization, Jayakar to Sapru, 31 August 1933, Sapru Papers, Series II, J. Nehru to Gandhi, 13 September 1933, *SWJN*, 5, pp. 528–9. For evidence that Rajagopalachariar & Rajendra Prasad had earlier been anxious about the repercussions of secrecy on Congress see progress report on civil disobedience, April 1932 – March 1933, AICC Papers, 1932, File No. 15 Misc.

embodiment of civil disobedience when mass resistance seemed fraught with danger, now he reverted to the idea when mass resistance was impossible. Srinivasa Sastri, reading of the closure of Sabarmati in the paper, noted, 'Ominous! I should think he was planning a big stunt from the 1st August...Don Quixote II.' On 30 July Gandhi informed the Bombay government that he and thirty-two companions, half of them women, intended to march from the ashram in the direction of Ras, the Kaira village most deeply committed to civil disobedience: they would go without money, dependent on the good will of villagers, and would preach their gospel of individual civil disobedience, *khadi*, teetotalism and the end of Untouchability. Fearlessness and sacrifice were the qualities he hoped this new tactic would display – qualities he had long held essential prerequisites of swaraj.[163]

Even before Gandhi disclosed his plan to march to Ras the local government had wished to arrest him. The Government of India Home Department at first stressed that it would be politic from an all-India viewpoint to allow the escalation of criticism of Gandhi's leadership and programme which was now a feature of public comment, and to jail him only when he made an overt act of disobedience. Willingdon, on tour from Delhi, talked to Sykes and his advisers on 29 July and decided to support their line, since they viewed with misgiving the prospect of Gandhi and the ashramites wandering homelessly in Gujarat, and were anxious to avoid any repetition of the 1930 march when Gandhi was loose in Gujarat, generating wide support. Delhi agreed and gained Hoare's consent on 30 July; and on 1 August Gandhi and his 32 followers were arrested in Ahmedabad. Gandhi and Mahadev Desai were transferred to Teravda and released on the 4th under an order restraining them within Poona. When they announced they would disobey the order they were rearrested, tried and jailed for a year under the ordinary law rather than the State Regulation which had previously been invoked in Gandhi's case.[164] Despite the hopes of Congressmen at Poona the Mahatma had proved unable to

---

[163] Gandhi to Govt. of Bombay, 26 July 1933, S.N. No. 21535, telegram, 30 July 1933, Gandhi Papers. (Gandhi received a bare acknowledgement of his renunciation of the ashram, Maxwell to Gandhi, 28 July 1933, S.N. No. 21538, Gandhi Papers.) Press statement by Gandhi on his programme, 31 July 1933, Home Poll., 1933, File No. 4/11.

For comments on Gandhi's decision see report of Ahmedabad District Magistrate, 27 July 1933, Home Poll., 1933, File No. 3/17; Moonje to Jayakar, 24 March 1934, Jayakar Papers, Correspondence File No. 408; V. S. S. Sastri to Mrs S. Das, 26 July 1933, NMML, V. S. S. Sastri Papers (3rd instalment); V. S. S. Sastri to Vaman Rao, 7 August 1933, S No. 605, Sastri Papers.

[164] Govt. of India, Home Dept., to P.S.V., Viceroy's Camp, telegram, 28 July 1933; P.S.V.'s reply, telegram, 29 July 1933; Bombay Govt. to Govt. of India, telegram, 29 July 1933; Govt of India to S of S, telegram, 30 July 1933; S of S to Govt. of India, telegram, 30 July 1933; Home Poll., File No. 3/17: Govt. of Bombay to Govt. of India, 5 August 1933, Home Poll., 1933, File No. 3/1. Gandhi informed the Bombay Home Sec. in letter, 3 August 1933, that if he was released under restriction orders he would not obey them; Gandhi Papers.

break the deadlock with the government. He was back in Prison, leaving Congress saddled with a policy which its adherents neither desired nor understood, which acknowledged the disintegration of mass civil disobedience but provided no effective alternative either for renewing pressure on the raj or for enabling Congressmen to affect and exploit the imminent constitutional changes.

CHAPTER 7

The resolution of the leadership dilemma

Gandhi's re-incarceration in August 1933 brought to a head the dilemma of all-India political leadership which had developed during 1933. Gandhi's dilemma was that despite his recognition since 1929 as Congress's main continental leader the part he could now actually play in public life was intolerably restricted – by the government which jailed him and refused to negotiate even when he had scaled down civil disobedience, and by Congressmen who were disorganized by government action and his own advice, and lacked his apocalyptic commitment to satyagraha. Even if the raj had left him free Congress would not have been a suitable instrument for the creation of *purna swaraj* on his terms and in his way. For their part Congressmen faced the dilemma of needing a leader who could unite them and provide a programme suited to the changed political situation of an inadequate White Paper, a divisive Communal Award, yet the certainty of constitutional reform with increased power on offer in autonomous provinces. To Gandhi they looked to perform these functions, but he failed them because he adamantly refused to give up the principle of civil disobedience. Yet any other policy so far suggested was divisive and savoured of humiliating surrender to the government. Nor was any one willing to take the risk of challenging Gandhi for continental leadership: and no other individual had the resources of the Mahatma for such a position.

I GANDHI IN SEARCH OF A ROLE

Back in Yeravda Gandhi's options in searching for a means to continue moulding Indian public life were virtually restricted to Harijan work, and he immediately asked the government for the same facilities which he had enjoyed during his previous sentence. But he had been interned in August under the ordinary law rather than State Regulation partly because the government would thereby not be obliged to grant him special facilities for exercising this public role.[1] Delhi and Bombay adhered to their pre-arranged refusal to grant him any special facilities, a stand Willingdon

[1] Gandhi to Major Adwani, 1 August 1933, Gandhi to Bombay Home Sec., 4 August 1933, Gandhi Papers.
  On advantages of jailing Gandhi under the ordinary law, M. G. Hallett to R. M. Maxwell, 27 May 1933, Maxwell to Hallett, 5 June 1933, Home Poll., 1933, File No. 44/57 & K.-W.; note by H. Haig, 2 December 1933, *ibid.* File No. 4/20.

justified to Hoare on the grounds that compared with 1932 the reform movement was now well established and Gandhi was clearly not going to give up politics as had seemed possible then. However Hoare pushed for certain restricted facilities of correspondence, visitors and newspapers, because British public opinion approved of the Harijan movement and he wished to avoid any allegations that they were martyring Gandhi for this cause. This Delhi and Bombay accepted though both would have preferred to give Gandhi either all or none of the concessions he had previously received, and felt such a half-way position as Hoare suggested would be difficult to hold. Gandhi had meanwhile announced that he intended to fast if Harijan facilities were not given to him; and on 16 August when he was told the concessions government was prepared to give he began after some hesitation to fast.[2]

On this occasion Gandhi rapidly became very ill, and appeared to lose the will to live – a sign of the constraints he had experienced in the previous months and possibly of despair that he would again resume a personally fulfilling public role. He was removed to hospital on 20 August, where he said various goodbyes and gave away his scant personal belongings; but on 23 August when the medical authorities considered he had reached the danger zone he was released unconditionally. London, Delhi and Bombay were in agreement on this: they had no wish for him to die in jail even if release meant the trouble of rearresting him later if he broke the law. Gandhi stated briefly on his discharge that it was unexpected and he had no idea how he would use his life out of prison, though Harijan work would be supremely important to him. Two days later he did say, 'I shall seek peace much more eagerly than imprisonment and a possible repetition of the fast. I shall, therefore, again use this unexpected freedom from imprisonment for the sake of exploring avenues of peace.'[3]

Therefore Gandhi began to search for a role which would fulfil his personal aspirations and enable him to influence his compatriots and the government. It was no easy task now that the extraordinary position of a prisoner holding court as a social reformer was impossible, and personal civil disobedience would only have led to a humiliating and ludicrous 'cat and mouse' pattern of periodic rearrests. There was also increasing evidence that public opinion was perplexed by Gandhi's activities while some people were positively hostile, condemning him for fasting merely to gain

[2] Policy discussions between London, Delhi & Bombay, Home Poll., 1933, File No. 3/17; Willingdon to Sykes, 8 August 1933, Mss. EUR.F.150 (5); Hoare to Willingdon, 11 August 1933, Mss. EUR.E.240 (3).
Gandhi on his decision to fast to Bombay Home Sec., 14 August 1933, to Colonel Martin, 16 August 1933, Gandhi Papers.
[3] Statement by Gandhi, 23 August 1933, *Harijan* 26 August 1933; press interview, 25 August 1933, *The Hindustan Times*, 26 August 1933, Home Poll., 1933, File No. 4/11.
On Gandhi's state of health and mind, C. F. Andrews to J. Nehru, 4 September 1933, J. Nehru Papers, part 1, vol. III; J. Nehru, *An Autobiography*, p. 398.

release and keep in the public eye. Sapru was not alone in his anxieties when he told Rangaswami Aiyengar,

> Much as I admire Gandhi Ji personally I can not follow the working of his mind or the method he is pursuing. This 'fast business' is losing all its charm and effect. Apart from the fact that it is a very ancient or medieval form of spiritual purification reminding one of the philosophy of the mortification of the flesh for spiritual regeneration – which after all is a matter of individual faith – it seems to me that it exposes Gandhi Ji to many uncharitable criticisms even in friendly quarters. I may be a misguided person but it is my belief that modern political battles cannot be fought with ancient spiritual weapons.[4]

Gandhi's first tentative moves on his release were attempts to contact the administration. Aiyengar discussed with Sastri the possibilities of a settlement between Gandhi and the government, and sounded Sapru, who refused to have anything to do with another attempt at mediation. The message got through to the government from Thakurdas, though he had not been directly in touch with Gandhi, that his aim had throughout 1932–3 been a comparatively restricted one: not to extract an acceptable constitution but to revert to the status quo of a talking relationship between government and Congress which in Gandhi's eyes Willingdon had shattered in December 1931. Thakurdas pressed Hoare to explore some avenue of peaceful contact with Congress even if Willingdon would not see Gandhi.[5] It was C. F. Andrews who interpreted Gandhi's mind to officialdom most clearly when he saw Bombay's Home Secretary on 2 September. Gandhi was apparently searching for a way of making peace with the government and cooperating 'in neutral matters', but was determined not to humiliate himself or Congress in the process of coming to terms. During the following months Gandhi reverted to this theme that the government was intent on humiliating its opponents and him in particular – a belief which militated against any surrender of the principle of civil disobedience on his part. Moreover, as Andrews explained, though Gandhi had abandoned the idea of mass civil disobedience he could not abandon the principle because he saw it as the ultimate reply to any form of coercion and a means of converting the opponent. 'He even expects it to be a means of effecting reconciliation with authorities as alleged to have been the case in South Africa to which Gandhi frequently refers in his conversation.' Though the Mahatma hankered after his days of personal friendship with Smuts, Willingdon and his Home Secretary had no intention of allowing such personal contact, and Gandhi's feelers came to nought.[6]

[4] Sapru to Rangaswami Aiyengar, 31 August 1933 (A 60), Sapru Papers, Series II. For exceedingly hostile press reaction to Gandhi's fast see Bombay FR2, August 1933, Home Poll., File No. 18/9.

[5] Thakurdas to Hoare, 4 September 1933, Thakurdas Papers, File No. 132/1932; Aiyengar to Sapru, 26 August 1933, Sapru's reply, 31 August 1933 (A 60), Sapru Papers, Series II.

[6] Bombay Govt. to Govt. of India, telegram, 4 September 1933, reporting Home Sec.'s interview with Andrews on 2 September, Home Poll., 1933, File No. 3/17.

As Gandhi rethought his position in the light of the government's attitude he was subjected to pressure from men whose judgement he valued though it was often critical. One of these was Srinivasa Sastri. He was 'at heart out of sympathy with G. His fasts irr[i]tate me. His frequent invocation of his inner voice make[s] me impatient. His fetish civil disobedience and apotheosis of the jail, not without justification and merits within certain limits, have transcended reason and begun to do harm.'[7] Four days after Gandhi's release he wrote him a forthright letter saying that outside Congress and inside it to an increasing extent people felt that mass and individual civil disobedience must be given up to permit a new policy for the country's future, including not only the Congress constructive campaign but attempts at construction through legislation, finance and administration. As it was highly unlikely that Gandhi would adjust to such a programme or that anyone would challenge Gandhi for dominance, he pleaded with him to set Congress free from his leadership to try other methods, even if as an individual he persevered with civil disobedience. Gandhi agreed that he was not the man for 'constitution building' at present, and would gladly retire from Congress and devote himself outside it to civil disobedience and his Harijan campaign, as he had mooted privately during the Poona conference. But he did not see how he could do this, nor did he believe that Congressmen in general would agree to working reforms even on the lines of a modified White Paper though he realized that many of them were weary of continued conflict. Sastri replied with a further appeal to Gandhi to slacken his dictatorial grip on Congress policy, hammering home the argument that civil disobedience and constitutional activity could not coexist, and whatever the White Paper's faults it was vital for nationalists to combine forces and make themselves felt in every part of public life as it was clear that the Tories were firmly entrenched in Britain, and the minorities were eager to seize power under the reforms. Gandhi, unperturbed by Sastri's outspokenness, reminded him that as he had proved in the days of the Swarajists he was willing to make way for others, but now a repetition of his 'surrender' to Motilal and Das was 'not such a simple performance'. There was much truth in his assertion, because

For Gandhi's repetition of the theme that he and Congress were being deliberately humiliated see note by H. W. Emerson, 26 October 1933, on interview with Andrews that day, Home Poll., 1933, File No. 169; Gandhi to A. Harrison, 24 November 1933, Gandhi Papers.

Emerson noted on 15 November 1933 that Gandhi could still not be permitted interviews with officials, even on Harijan work, as C. F. Andrews had just requested. The policy remained as it had been since the end of 1931 – Gandhi had either to be friend or foe, he could not have the advantages both of attacking government and maintaining contact with it because 'thereby he secures a strong position for himself with his followers as an opponent of Government and at the same time creates considerable depression in the ranks of Government supporter[s] who feel that Government are afraid to treat him as, what he proclaims himself, an enemy'. Home Poll., 1933, File No. 169.

[7] V. S. S. Sastri to B. D. Chaturvedi, 24 November 1933, Sastri Papers (3rd instalment).

there was no established group with respected leaders committed to following a Swarajist line in 1933, only a medley of confused and conflicting aspirations to end the current impasse. He claimed, however, 'I do not want power. I look upon it as a privileged service. The moment I feel that I can get out of it to the benefit of the Congress, I will not fail. However, you may depend upon me that I shall strain every nerve to adopt your advice.'[8]

Gandhi was clearly confused about his future, thinking of his diverse experience in Africa and in India in the 1920s, and unsure what Congressmen really wanted. He told Sastri that much depended on the views of Jawaharlal, who had just been released from jail and was coming to see him on 9 September. Sastri and Nehru were poles apart politically – one the heir to Gokhale's liberalism and constitutional cooperation with the raj, the other deeply committed to the reconstruction of Indian society on more egalitarian lines and conflict with imperialism. Yet they shared a deep irritation with Gandhi's political style and programme. Jawaharlal confided to his jail diary his despair of Gandhi's emphasis on purity and sacrifice, his constant references to the Almighty and his apparent absorption in the next step rather than concern for the ultimate goal of their struggle. Though he admitted his strong emotional attachment to the Mahatma, he felt they were drifting apart politically, and after the Poona conference he wondered whether they could ever again cooperate in politics.[9]

When Jawaharlal and Gandhi met in September it was the first time for two years, the last occasion being Gandhi's departure for London. It must have been a moving occasion for both, and an unlikely time for a rift to develop between them. They conversed on a wide variety of topics which had agitated the younger man in jail; but their main preoccupation was Gandhi's immediate future. Three options were open, all undesirable politically. One was individual civil disobedience by Gandhi, his inevitable arrest, followed by a repetition of the Harijan facilities episode: as Gandhi refused to submit to this humiliating syndrome and intended to fast to death in such an event that course was eliminated. He could, as he told Jawaharlal, retire from Congress, but this would mean that Congress would either revert to constitutional collaboration and abandon its struggle, or would fight on, further weakened without Gandhi's presence. Moreover as Congress bodies were illegal there was no way a group could formally take over Congress or meet to produce a new policy. Consequently they arrived at a third course, the only practicable one, though they knew it would undermine what remained of civil disobedience. Gandhi would not court jail for the ten and a half months left of his August sentence and would devote himself to Harijan work, meeting Congressmen to advise them when necessary. This Gandhi announced in a press statement on 14 September, and simultaneously Jawaharlal issued one which said that they were exchanging letters which would subsequently be published, describing the issues they had discussed. He admitted that his attitude to their political campaign differed from Gandhi's; nevertheless the methods Gandhi had taught them were fundamentally right for India and 'for these methods his leadership is essential'.[10]

Their exchange of letters, a tactical mechanism for suggesting their continued cooperation despite differences of opinion, filled out the problems to which Jawaharlal had alluded in his statement. His basic concern was independence as a prelude to a radical restructuring of Indian society and a more egalitarian distribution of wealth, as part of a world struggle 'between the forces of progress and betterment of the masses and the forces of reaction and vested interests'. He showed too his anxiety lest the statements by Gandhi and Aney on the Congress organization should be taken as the dissolution of the organization rather than a recognition that there could be no regular organization under the existing ban; and underlined that Congressmen could still continue to cooperate in pursuit of the campaign. Moreover he stressed that the struggle should go on, and individual civil disobedience did not preclude corporate civil disobedience when any group felt itself strong enough to offer it. Gandhi's reply indicated that they disagreed on details such as the banning of secret Congress activities: but their major difference was that Gandhi, though agreeing with much that Jawaharlal had said about the goal of an egalitarian society, was far more interested in the means to that goal. For him the former implied the latter, as he had consistently maintained in his apologies for satyagraha.

> The clearest possible definition of the goal and its appreciation would fail to take us there if we do not know and utilize the means of achieving it. I have, therefore, concerned myself principally with the conservation of the means and their progressive use. I know that if we can take care of them, attainment of the goal is assured. I feel too that our progress towards the goal will be in exact proportion to the purity of our means. If we can give an ocular demonstration of our uttermost truthfulness and non-violence, I am convinced that our statement of the national goal cannot long offend the interests which your letter would appear to attack. We know that the princes, the zamindars, and those, who depend for their existence upon the exploitation of the masses, would cease to fear and distrust us, if we could but ensure the innocence of our methods. We do not seek to coerce any. We seek to convert them. This method may appear to be long, perhaps too long, but I am convinced that it is the shortest.

Gandhi was utterly convinced that truth and non-violence, even pursued by an individual civil resister, would ultimately triumph. Moreover he chided Jawaharlal for not mentioning Congress's constructive activities

[10] J. Nehru, *An Autobiography*, pp. 403–4; Gandhi's statement, 14 September 1933, Home Poll., 1933, File No. 3/17; J. Nehru's statement, 14 September 1933, *SWJN*, 5, pp. 531–2.

such as communal unity, anti-Untouchability and *khadi*, since these were important building blocks of swaraj and provided work for the vast majority of Congressmen who never went to jail.[11]

Their exchange demonstrated that two men with deep differences of approach to politics who did not wish to part company for political as well as personal reasons had reached a mutually beneficial accommodation. Gandhi solved his personal problem of finding a public role. This arrangement gave him a task to do without actively prosecuting civil disobedience; but though avoiding jail himself he would have in what remained of Congress an energetic protagonist of the struggle to which he was committed though for very different reasons from those which fired Jawaharlal. Moreover Jawaharlal's continued cooperation with him would probably restrain and keep within the Congress allegiance those who shared his ideals. The Bombay government rightly judged that so long as the two stood together 'it seems unlikely that they will either call off the civil disobedience movement unequivocally and unconditionally or that they will find their programme and themselves displaced'. Gandhi's recognition of Jawaharlal's strategic importance to him in the continuation of satyagraha by Congress was clear when he told him in January, 'So far as I am concerned, you do not disturb me at all. I should be myself in a wilderness without you in the Congress.'[12] For Jawaharlal the agreement of September was also a good proposition. He publicly affirmed his loyalty to one from whom he had contemplated parting company politically but thereby gained a guarded sanction for his ideas and implicit liberty to propagate them. By underwriting Gandhi's leadership he might secure pay-offs which were important for his own plans – unity in the only organization which was available under the major acknowledged leader, and assurance of an ally committed to the continuation of civil disobedience and to work among the rural population, both of which were as vital to him as to Gandhi though their significance for each man differed.[13]

From mid-September Gandhi had marked out his role for the coming months – as perambulating champion of the anti-Untouchability campaign

[11] J. Nehru to Gandhi, 13 September 1933, Gandhi's reply, 14 September 1933, Home Poll., 1933, File No. 4/11.

[12] Bombay Govt. to Govt. of India, telegram, 20 October 1933, Mss. EUR.F.150 (5); Gandhi to J. Nehru, 21 January 1934, J. Nehru Papers, part I, vol. XXIV.

Jayakar placed less emphasis on the strategic position of Jawaharlal in Gandhi's thinking, and commented to Sapru, 25 February 1934, 'I have come to realize the unpleasant truth that the Mahatma always yields to a dominant opponent, and what Jawaharlal thinks to-day the Mahatma will think tomorrow.' Jayakar Papers, Correspondence File No. 408.

[13] For Jawaharlal's emphasis on unity, continued conflict, rural work and carrying Congress as far as possible towards his goal, which he clearly hoped would be forwarded by cooperation with Gandhi, see letter to Subhas Bose, 4 February 1939, J. Nehru, *A Bunch of Old Letters*, p. 318; press interview, 24 September 1933, *The Tribune*, 27 September 1933, *SWJN*, 5, p. 544; J. Nehru to C. Mascarenhas, 10 November 1933, to Asaf Ali, 12 October 1933, *SWJN*, 6, pp. 17–18, 42–4.

and occasional political adviser to Congressmen. Willingdon was convinced that Gandhi's projected tour of India for Harijan uplift was basically a propaganda exercise in preparation for renewed civil disobedience. Jawaharlal clearly did not see it as such, and confessed to being 'not at all enamoured of Harijan work'. Its main merit in his eyes was to force orthodox Hindus into hostility and so 'bring real issues before the public. It is a good thing that the orthodox section of the Hindus is showing its true colours and behaving politically as a most reactionary group.' Gandhi himself felt that covert civil disobedience or Congress propaganda through the Harijan campaign would harm both Congress and the Harijan cause. 'Cases of this type have come under my notice,' he told Jawaharlal. 'I have expressed strong disapproval of any such work.'[14] Yet such a continental tour had significant political implications even if it was not designed as a cloak for the satyagraha message. Gandhi intended it to cement that national unity which he saw as indispensable to swaraj. Furthermore the continental publicity for Congress's major leader among the real masses and the collection of funds for the Harijan cause would have considerable political spin-off when Congress reverted to working within the constitutional framework and soliciting votes.

Gandhi was not fully recovered from his collapse in jail until early November, and meantime he rested at Wardha in C.P. which replaced Sabarmati as his base of operations. He started out on his mammoth Harijan tour on 7 November, beginning with C.P., going on to Delhi and then the south at the end of the year. By February he was touring the Karnatak, but then his plans were disrupted by events in Bihar. His message was simple – an end to the practices which made up the burden of Untouchability, temple entry for Harijans (except in orthodox centres such as Madura where he avoided the subject), and an appeal for funds for the cause. Wherever he went there were certain constant features of his reception. He attracted vast crowds, 20–25,000 at his main meeting in Nagpur for example, one of the largest ever seen in the city. Most of these were drawn by curiosity and veneration for Gandhi personally rather than by commitment to the Harijan cause. This was clearest in the south where Untouchability was firmly entrenched and Gandhi's political support was limited. One of the least flattering assessments of Gandhi's reception came from the Madras Government's Chief Secretary.

[14] Willingdon to Hoare, 24 September 1933, Mss. EUR.E.240 (6); J. Nehru to Asaf Ali, 12 October 1933, *SWJN*, 6, p. 43; Gandhi to J. Nehru, 13 November 1933, J. Nehru Papers, part I, vol. XXIII.
Gandhi did not attend the funeral of Vithalbhai Patel in Bombay in November largely because of his immersion in the Harijan campaign and his wish to avoid an occasion of conflict with the government if unacceptable conditions were imposed on his attendance. He told Manibehn Patel, 14 November 1933, 'I could not make the trip to Bombay because at present my place can only be in prison or among Harijans. I am out of prison only for the Harijan cause; this is my feeling at heart and not a show put up either for Government or for our own people.' *Letters to Manibahen Patel*, p. 69.

For the general public Gandhi is still a subject of curiosity, if not of veneration, but curiosity was more in evidence during his tour than veneration. Crowds came to gape at Gandhi and went away without bothering to listen to a word he had to say.

Yet he added that Gandhi was 'not yet a spent force and his personal magnetism is still a political factor with which it is necessary to reckon'.[15]

During these tours he collected considerable sums – Rs. 8,000 in Nagpur district, Rs. 6,000 in Raipur district, Rs. 12,000 in Delhi, Rs. 270,000 in south India, Rs. 30,000 in Karnatak. But in many places these collections did not come up to his expectations or those of his local associates, and he did not hesitate to say so publicly. Wherever he went there was evidence that the Depressed Classes were sceptical of the benefits to them of the campaign, and those who followed Ambedkar were openly hostile. Among the orthodox there was mounting hostility to his campaign, though its overt manifestations were small, amounting to a few boycotts of his meetings and black flag processions, However, even C.P. Marwaris who had been significant supporters of his and contributed to his triumph at the Nagpur Congress of 1920, were ambivalent about his reform venture; and in Nagpur many stipulated that their contributions should not go to the local Mahars who formed the bulk of the industrial labour force. In parts of the south the wider social implications of abolishing Untouchability also reinforced purely orthodox opposition, and in the northern Telugu coastal districts peasant farmers of higher caste objected to any movement which might make their Untouchable labourers more independent. In C.P. the long-standing split between the Hindi and Marathi speaking sections of Congress vitiated his visit; and some of the former dissociated themselves from it, attacking Gandhi for diverting Congress from its true political activities and describing his career as a series of blunders. In the long term the tours were probably of doubtful value either to Gandhi's political reputation or the uprooting of Untouchability, despite the spectacular nature of what Willingdon called Gandhi's 'processional career.'[16]

Gandhi's plans were disrupted by the aftermath of the earthquake which

[15] Madras Chief Sec. to M. G. Hallett, 14 March 1934, Home Poll., 1934, File No. 50/1.

[16] File of reports on Gandhi's C.P. tour, Home Poll., 1933, File No. 3/23: report by Delhi Chief Commissioner to Govt. of India, 18 December 1933, on Gandhi's Delhi visit, *ibid.*: on Gandhi's Madras tour, Madras FR2, December 1933, Home Poll., 1933, File No. 18/14, Madras FRs, January 1934, FR2, February 1934, Home Poll., 1934, File Nos. 18/1 & 2; file of reports on Madras tour, Home Poll., 1934, File No. 50/1: on Karnatak tour, Bombay FR1, March 1934, Home Poll., 1934, File No. 18/3; Home Poll., 1934, File No. 50/1: Willingdon to Hoare, 1 January 1934, Mss. EUR.E.240 (7). Accounts of Gandhi's tours are given in *Harijan*.

Jayakar refused to have anything to do with Gandhi's Harijan tours because he believed that donations would not be used 'for non-sectarian or non-political causes', and that some would be used to finance whatever political stunt Gandhi might start in August 1934; he had heard that 'part of his collections have found their way into the hands of the Charkha Sangh'. Jayakar to Sapru, 1 July 1934, Sapru Papers, Series II.

hit Bihar with shattering ferocity on 15 January. It was one of the world's largest recorded earthquakes and devastated a large part of north Bihar. In an area of 6,000 square miles virtually every masonry building was damaged or destroyed, and twelve towns were almost entirely demolished. Some of its most terrifying features were the huge fissures which opened in the ground, spewing forth water and fine sand which wrecked agriculture and communications for weeks: over 900 miles of railway track for example were destroyed. Over 7,000 people were killed – a figure which would have been far larger had the earthquake not occurred in the early afternoon when most villagers were outside, and had it not lasted so long that many people in towns managed to get out of buildings before they collapsed. Gandhi's response to this natural catastrophe reflected both his whole attitude to life and morality and his immediate preoccupation. In *Harijan* he commented that such calamities were divine chastisement for sin; though he could not know whether Untouchability was the sin which had called forth this disaster he felt that it merited such a punishment. Rabindranath Tagore voiced the incredulous and hostile response of many Indians, including Jawaharlal Nehru, to this statement when he denounced it as flying in the face of reason.[17]

Bihar Congressmen, headed by Rajendra Prasad, plunged into relief work in cooperation with other private relief organizations and the government. Of all the private funds established to help victims and provide for reconstruction the largest was that of the Bihar Central Relief Committee launched by Prasad. By mid-November it had collected Rs. 2,839,565 in cash and Rs. 330,587 in kind. Early in March Prasad appealed to Gandhi to visit Bihar, largely it would seem so that he could help organize the administration of the growing fund. Gandhi went at once, and on 18 March presided at a meeting of about 200 people from all over India to consider the Committee's problems. As a result a fresh executive committee was appointed with Prasad as its president. Gandhi and Malaviya together pushed through a resolution despite opposition from such men as C.P.'s Dr Khare and Gurdit Singh, by which the Committee tendered 'its respectful cooperation to the Government in the prosecution of the common object of relieving the unparalleled distress that has overtaken Bihar'. Gandhi subsequently issued nine principles of relief work which, besides publicizing his constant themes of abolishing distinctions between high and low in Indian society, efficient accounting of public money and village hygiene, also stressed that there should be no overlapping or rivalry between different relief organizations.[18] Here was an occasion which admirably suited his

[17] *Harijan*, 2 February 1934, contained Gandhi's original statement. Tagore's response and Gandhi's comments were published in *Harijan*, 16 February 1934. For Nehru's shock at Gandhi's statement see J. Nehru, *An Autobiography*, p. 490.

[18] Bihar Chief Sec. to M. G. Hallett, 27 March 1934, Home Poll., 1934, File No. 50/1; Bihar & Orissa FR2, March 1934, *ibid.* File no. 18/3; Willingdon to Hoare, 13 March 1934, Mss. EUR.E.240 (7); *India in 1933–34* (Delhi, 1935), pp. 67–8.

Moonje grumbled to Jayakar, 24 March 1934, about Gandhi's swing from denounc-

concern since leaving Yeravda to bring Congressmen and government into cooperation on uncontroversial matters and to engage in constructive work those who would not offer individual civil disobedience.

Although Gandhi's advice to cooperate with government in relief work was in line with the natural wishes of Bihari Congressmen, the rumblings of opposition at the March meeting and the reactions to his call to repentance in the wake of national chastisement indicated that his priorities and preoccupations were not those of most Congressmen. He had been made increasingly aware of this fact as in the interstices of his Harijan campaign he performed the other part of the role he had marked out for himself in Poona and advised Congressmen on political matters. By the time he reached Bihar the pressing political problem was still unsolved, and for many Congressmen their leadership dilemma remained.

II CONGRESS IN SEARCH OF A PROGRAMME

The programme of individual civil disobedience which Gandhi had foisted on Congressmen attracted little support. There was an upswing in the number of convictions for civil disobedience in August and September compared with July in all provinces, but the numbers tailed away in October, a decline aided by the beginning of the Durga Puja holiday at the end of September (see Table 10). Bihar and Orissa produced the most convictions during this temporary revival. There disobedience took the form of picketing liquor shops, waving flags in court, shouting slogans, distributing leaflets and taking out illegal processions. 'Dictators' organized this though Gandhi had publicly disagreed with Aney in advising that even this rudimentary form of organization should be abandoned. Despite this upsurge Congressmen continued to contest the local board elections then in progress. Elsewhere individual civil disobedience mainly took the form of picketing. In Bombay City hand-written Congress bulletins were produced and seven Congressmen tried to manufacture salt and organize a flag salutation ceremony; while in Ahmedabad two men tried to retake possession of a Congress house. In Wardha and Akola districts of C.P. there was an outbreak of forest satyagraha for which Aney was arrested. Only Midnapore continued to show interest in the campaign right through the year, and it was indicative of the decline of the Congress appeal among the Bengali *bhadralok*, those early leaders of political agitation and exponents of passive resistance, that virtually none of Bengal's convicts came from Calcutta after October.[19] Throughout the subcontinent individual civil disobedience was an unattractive programme except for those who

ing the government to advising 'respectful cooperation', and claimed that his Responsivist group had been consistent: Jayakar Papers, Correspondence File No. 408.

[19] Provincial FRs, August–December 1933, Home Poll., 1933, File Nos. 18/9, 10, 12, 13, 14; weekly telegraphic reports on civil disobedience from local govts. for 1933, Home Poll., 1933, File No. 3/1.

TABLE 10. *Convictions for individual civil disobedience, July–October 1933*

Province	July 1st half	July 2nd half	August 1st half	August 2nd half	September 1st half	September 2nd half	October 1st half
Madras	1	0	32	14	7	10	13
Bombay	10	29	102	82	61	29	34
Bengal	19	33	28	Not given	63	31	31*
U.P.	3	3	21	132	109	32	6
Punjab	18	0	60	53	37	40	17
Bihar & Orissa	1	2	111	263	165	160	15
C.P.	3†	0	7	c. 34	c. 10	0	6
Assam	0	0	1	0	3	0	0
N.-W.F.P.	20	0	3	48	26	33	5
Delhi	0	0	6	0	1	0	0

SOURCE: Provincial fortnightly reports, July–October 1932; Home Poll., 1933, File Nos. 18/8–10, 18/12.

* Arrests only.   † Prosecutions.

shared Gandhi's belief in the revolutionary qualities of satyagraha, or like Jawaharlal were determined to keep at least a symbolic conflict going. Even in Bihar where individual satyagraha was most successful in numerical terms, Congress leaders gathered at Patna on 14 September decided that it had failed and that they must try again to enlist volunteers and establish secret ashrams. Their lack of enthusiasm was apparent when one of them refused to act as provincial 'dictator', quoting Gandhi's decision not to court arrest as an example. This drew from a Bhagalpur man the retort that since Patna men were so timid he would organize work in his district on his own account.[20]

The confusions felt by Congressmen as Gandhi's programme petered out and he excluded himself from overt political activity were evident in the discussions and realignments which occurred in the provinces. In U.P. about ninety Congressmen met in Lucknow on 20 September to discuss Aney's statement, the question of council entry and the idea of holding an AICC meeting. There was a sharp difference of opinion between Jawaharlal, backed by G. B. Pant, P. T. Tandon and R. A. Kidwai, who wanted to begin a movement among peasants and labourers based on economic improvement, and more moderate men who supported Aney's programme and argued for re-entry into the legislatures. Almost their only point of agreement was that individual civil disobedience was an inadequate programme, and ultimately all they decided was not to disband existing Congress committees, and to entrust to a committee selected by Jawaharlal

[20] Bihar & Orissa FR2, September 1933, Home Poll., 1933, File No. 18/10.

the preparation of another plan of campaign.[21] Although a majority of U.P. Congressmen opposed Nehru's commitment to continued conflict, rural propaganda and ultimate social reconstruction, his dominance as thinker and organizer was clear when a further meeting of about eighty local Congressmen took place between 10 and 12 October in Allahabad. The whole political situation was reviewed, and Jawaharlal delivered a series of lectures on such topics as 'economic problems' and 'socialism'. Simultaneously there appeared in the press a series of articles by him later reprinted as a pamphlet, *Whither India?*, in which he expounded the views he had put to Gandhi in September. The resolutions passed at the Allahabad gathering bore his stamp. The struggle for independence accompanied by social and economic freedom for the exploited masses was to continue, with civil disobedience as its main weapon. In the short term Congressmen were to continue the individual resistance programme as a gesture, but they were not to go out of their way to court arrest and were to concentrate on rural education and organization.[22]

In other provinces where Jawaharlal's influence was felt less, the search for a new programme veered more towards abandoning civil disobedience, and those who went as far as advocating council entry were not so easily silenced. In Bombay at an All-Maharashtra Political Conference on 28/29 October the Democratic Swaraj Party was formally inaugurated, its creed identical to that of Congress but its membership open to non-Congressmen. Its programme was the capture and acceptance of all places of power in the state structure from village *panchayat* to legislature, backed by an economic programme to help peasants and industrial workers, and the abandonment of civil disobedience. It was the brainchild of Jamnadas Mehta who even in 1930 had spoken for the group of Congress MLCs in Bombay who opposed Gandhi's civil disobedience plan. At a preparatory meeting he castigated the Mahatma as 'a great reactionary force in a democratic party...unfit to be a political leader', whose greatest blunder had been to advise boycott of the legislatures. Mehta's main ally in this venture was N. C. Kelkar, that old stalwart of Tilak's Maharashtrian group which had reluctantly bowed to the Mahatma's all-India forces on their leader's death, but had fought back through the Swaraj Party and Responsive Cooperation group in the 1920s and continued to lambast Gandhi's leadership in the papers Tilak had founded. This new party was not only the latest manifestation of long-standing rivalries within and on the

[21] U.P. FR2, September 1933, *ibid.*; Sapru to Polak, 25 September 1933, Sapru to Rangaswami Aiyengar, 26 September 1933, Sapru Papers, Series II.

[22] U.P. FRs, October 1933, Home Poll., 1933, File No. 18/12; note on 10–12 October meeting by V. N. Pathak, Home Poll., 1933, File No. 4/19; J. Nehru, *An Autobiography*, p. 474.

Whither India?, *SWJN*, 6, pp. 1–16. Jawaharlal did not rule out later participation in councils as a front on the anti-government fight, but thought the idea irrelevant at the present stage; J. Nehru to V. V. Giri, 30 September 1933, J. Nehru Papers, part I, vol. XXVIII.

peripheries of Congress in western India, and a means of forestalling old rivals in the exploitation of the new constitution. It also reflected increasing anxiety on the part of men like Kelkar who shared the Hindu Mahasabha's determination to capture legislative seats and prevent Muslims from dominating the new constitutional structures in alliance with the bureaucracy. It was no coincidence that barely a fortnight earlier the Mahasabha had resolved at its annual session that the Hindu community could 'no longer afford to ignore the various means open, in and out of the constitution, to promote and protect its interests'. The Mehta–Kelkar move did not go unchallenged locally; and a manifesto condemning it was issued by thirty-nine Maharashtra Congressmen including D. D. Sathaye and G. A. Deshpande.[23]

Simultaneously Satyamurti, who had argued at Poona against continuing civil disobedience, started a Congress Swaraj Party in Madras, with a programme of contesting elections to local bodies and the legislatures. Thereafter he began to tout for support for an All-India Congress Swaraj Party on similar lines. Like the Maharashtrian party this too was largely the work of a pre-existing faction within the local Congress. Its representative character was immediately challenged by other Congressmen, and it attracted very little support.[24]

The replies Satyamurti received indicated some of the difficulties Congressmen felt in searching for a new programme, however much they disliked the present stagnation. Govindanand from Sind, for example, agreed that a revolt from Gandhi's leadership of Congress was long overdue. But he argued that Satyamurti had set about it in the wrong way: by founding a new party he had cut himself off from Congress and in practice set up as a splinter group, and by making council entry its main rallying cry was raising a highly divisive issue. Govindanand was also ambivalent towards Gandhi. Although he condemned his leadership he realized that there was a solid bloc in the AICC apart from Gandhi's hand-picked men in the Working Committee who would not easily revolt against the Mahatma. Consequently no effective reversal of policy was possible until these key decision-makers were convinced of the folly of Gandhi's programme. Give Gandhi a long rope to hang himself was his advice. The Nationalist Muslim editor of *The Bombay Chronicle*, S. A. Brelvi, likewise condemned the council entry policy as divisive and urged Satya-

[23] Bombay FR2, September 1933, FRs, October 1933, Home Poll., 1933, File Nos. 18/10 & 12; *The Times of India*, 10 October 1933, *Free Press Journal*, 17 October 1933, Jayakar Papers, Correspondence File No. 236; Sapru to Jayakar (in U.K.), 5 November 1933, Sapru Papers, Series II. On the Mahasabha session in Ajmer, 14–16 October 1933, *India in 1932–33*, p. 46.

[24] Madras FR1, October 1933, Home Poll., 1933, File No. 18/12; S. Satyamurti's circular, 7 November 1933, was sent among others to S. A. Brelvi, Swami Govindanand & B. C. Roy: it is in Brelvi Papers, file of correspondence with Satyamurti, in NMML, B. C. Roy Papers, File Nov. 1933 – May 1934, All India Swarajists' Conference, and in Home Poll., 1933, File No. 4/19.

murti even more strongly, though for a different reason, to recognise the key position of Gandhi in any successful change of programme.

> The most urgent task before Congressmen is to restore the re-functioning of the Congress organisation and the restoration of political life by the calling off of the individual civil disobedience. It is to the accomplishment of this task – which we must and can fulfil without undermining the influence of Mahatma Gandhi who is the greatest national asset that we possess and that we can utilise in the near future – that we must devote our present efforts and I fear the talk of Council entry will merely hamper the performance of this task.[25]

In the minds of most Congressmen who cast around for an escape from their predicament there was this two-fold consideration. They needed to retain the benefits of Gandhi's continental reputation, and the organizational network which only a united, revived Congress could guarantee; for without these there would be little hope of influencing the government or eventually of winning votes. Although entry into the legislatures was their ultimate aim many felt it premature to press it as immediate policy because with its history of division in the 1920s and opportunities for future strife it threatened their precarious unity and would immediately alienate the Mahatma whose sights were set on satyagraha. Since the new councils were unlikely to come into existence that year there was all to be gained from delaying a decision so fraught with difficulty. Jayakar gauged their temper rightly when he discounted any hope of an alliance between pro-council Congressmen with politicians like Sapru and Srinivasa Sastri. 'They will try to keep the badge burnished that they are Congressmen; that is their best strength at Polls and they are not going to give it up for the doubtful benefits of common action.'[26] The determination to extract the Mahatma's sanction and retain the resources of the Congress name and organization lay behind the two formidable attempts by K. F. Nariman and then by Drs Ansari and Roy to secure a new programme which followed the splinter activities of Mehta and Satyamurti.

Nariman's tactic was to attempt to secure an AICC meeting as the prelude to a new Congress programme, though he kept off the thorny question of the legislatures. The idea of an AICC meeting was abroad early in September but Jawaharlal and Gandhi, committed as they were to continued civil disobedience, both declined to take the initiative in calling one. Jawaharlal, insisting on acting as Congress General Secretary despite the supposed suspension of the organization, maintained publicly that he would willingly summon a meeting if its members requested one though

[25] S. A. Brelvi to S. Satyamurti, 12 November 1933, Swami Govindanand to S. Satyamurti, 17 November 1933, Home Poll., 1933, File No. 4/19.

[26] Jayakar to Sapru, 13 October 1933, Sapru Papers, Series II. See also Sapru to Jayakar, 11 January 1934, Jayakar Papers, Correspondence File No. 408; Haig's note on Nariman's insistence on staying within Congress rather than taking the Mehta line in manoeuvring for a new programme, 9 March 1934, Home Poll, 1934, File No. 4/4.

he judged that there was no widespread dissatisfaction with the existing programme. Gandhi took the same line in a letter to Malaviya, having already told Jawaharlal,

> I adhere to the opinion that it will be no good to have the A.I.C.C. meeting. But that does not mean that it will deeply hurt me if such a meeting was held. On the contrary if a sufficient number desire it, it is their duty to send a requisition for the meeting. What I feel is that we may not take the initiative.[27]

Their joint stand made it tactically difficult for anyone else to secure a meeting. It would need considerable lobbying among AICC members unless a Working Committee member was prepared to take the onus on himself; and such lobbying implied both a public declaration of dissatisfaction with Gandhi's programme and presentation of an alternative. These internal difficulties were superimposed on the continuing government ban on the AICC.

Nariman, a Working Committee member, seized the nettle soon after he was released. At the end of October he visited Gandhi at Wardha, telling him frankly that he intended to campaign for a new programme. He argued that the present impasse was leading to disintegration and demoralization within Congress and inviting the emergence of hostile cliques outside its ranks. (He was clearly disturbed by the Mehta–Kelkar move and anxious lest they should walk away with seats in the Bombay legislature if Congress refused to abandon its conflict with the raj.) He also urged that Congress's guideline should be political expediency, not a spiritual belief. His aim was to restore the authority of Congress and summon the AICC to consider the situation in a rational light. Gandhi referred him to Jawaharlal, reiterating his conviction that most Congressmen did not want to abandon civil disobedience. However he did say that he would not resist any programme an AICC might wish, though he could not approve the suspension of civil disobedience.[28]

On 2 November Nariman publicly asserted that differences among Congressmen were being swept under the carpet, and made a clear though veiled criticism of the tendency to defer to Gandhi rather than consider opinion within Congress. Jawaharlal shot off an acid telegram deploring

[27] Gandhi to J. Nehru, 28 September 1933, to M. M. Malaviya, 15 October 1933, J. Nehru Papers, part I, vol. XXIII: press interviews to J. Nehru, 17 September 1933, *The Bombay Chronicle*, 18 September 1933; 24 September 1933, *The Tribune*, 27 September 1933, *SWJN*, 5, pp. 535, 544.

[28] Nariman's account of interview in circular to various politicians, 11 November 1933, Home Poll., 1933, File No. 4/19, to M. A. Ansari, 11 December 1933, Ansari Papers; Gandhi to J. Nehru, 1 November 1933, J. Nehru Papers, part I, vol. XXIII. In taking this line Gandhi was repeating what he had said in September to Rangaswami Aiyengar that he would welcome a group within Congress anxious for constitutional activity, though Congressmen committed to civil disobedience should have the same liberty to function within Congress: Aiyengar to Sapru, 23 September 1933 (A 61), Sapru Papers, Series II.

such criticism of his Working Committee colleagues, which brought Nariman hot foot to Allahabad in company with Brelvi. Nehru deplored such public infighting; but Nariman insisted that it was his right to air his opinion and try to secure support, particularly as so many people were reluctant to disagree openly with Gandhi whatever their private misgivings. His complaints were similar to those he had made of Gandhi's 'autocracy' at the time of the pact with Irwin. Nehru suggested that the members of the Working Committee who were not in jail should meet to discuss the position, and if necessary an AICC meeting should be called; to this Nariman agreed. Nehru's attempts to arrange an informal Working Committee meeting fell through because most of the members could not manage the only date Gandhi could offer in the midst of his Harijan tour, and he suggested that Nariman should go ahead with a requisition for an AICC. The irritated Nariman retorted,

> This is an apt illustration to show how important political work is being subordinated and side-tracked to non-political comparatively unimportant activities. If the same attitude continues and pre-arranged Harijan programme is to have precedence over matters of supreme All India National interest A.I.C.C. may have to wait till the end of this Harijan campaign.[29]

Meanwhile Nariman had been soliciting support with a circular to prominent Congressmen, describing his interview with Gandhi and stressing that they must find a formula for a new programme which would unite rather than divide the AICC, a meeting of which he deemed essential if they were to get to grips with the realities of their situation. He enclosed a draft programme for consideration. This included the reiteration of Congress's faith in non-violent civil resistance as the best means of attaining their goal, but the revocation of the Working Committee resolution inaugurating civil disobedience in 1932 as a matter of political expediency in the present situation. Individuals would still have the right to offer civil disobedience on their own responsibility, but the official Congress policy would be constructive activities and an economic programme to be settled later. It was a brave attempt to soothe Gandhians, convince men of Nehru's outlook that a radical economic programme might be forthcoming if they cooperated in the initiative, and to pave the way for change without raising the bogey of council entry. As he said in a postscript to B. C. Roy and A. K. Azad, 'I think Council Entry Question should for the time being give way to the main issue of restoring the organization; if schism now it may prejudice the main issue.' He stressed to his correspondents the necessity of sticking to their principles once they had made a careful decision, and not as in July at Poona shifting their position for personal or sentimental reasons. Late in November he expounded his views more fully in a book,

---

[29] Nariman to J. Nehru, 15 November 1933, Home Poll., 1933, File No. 4/19. See also Weekly Report of D.I.B., 16 November 1933, Nariman to Nehru, 12 November 1933, *ibid.*; J. Nehru to Gandhi & to Nariman, 8 November 1933, *SWJN*, 6, pp. 59–62.

whose title, *Whither Congress?*, was an implicit retort to Jawaharlal's condemnation of public disagreement since he had just published *Whither India?* Nariman's circular elicited a number of unfavourable replies, and some which hedged their bets. Among those in favour were Asaf Ali, Sherwani, Satyamurti, the Ahmedabad Youth League and the Andhra PCC.[30]

Although Jawaharlal decried Nariman's efforts and insisted that most Congressmen did not wish for a change of programme, he was told bluntly that Roy and Azad were anxious to have the meeting with Gandhi which had earlier fallen through. 'They say', reported Syed Mahmud, 'that the provinces will separate themselves and revolt if this state of affairs is continued.' Jawaharlal replied that he had fixed a meeting with Gandhi in Jubbulpore in early December; and in the intervening period he circularized all AICC members asking if they wanted a meeting. Despite his reluctance to take the initiative he now evidently felt that they must clear the air though he had not received a formal requisition for a meeting. The replies showed that opinion was very divided. A large proportion of those in favour came from Bombay, while among those against there was evidence of despair at the present programme yet fear of further controversy if differences were aired at an AICC. Congressmen's hesitations were symbolized by Sherwani who voted for an AICC and reversed his decision on the advice of friends![31]

While these reactions were coming in Gandhi squeezed a meeting with Nehru, Nariman, Ansari, Mahmud, Azad and Jamnalal Bajaj into his schedule. No decision was reached on a change of programme and the subject was postponed for further discussion in Delhi as opinion among them was nicely balanced. Nariman, Ansari and Azad argued that civil disobedience should be called off. Mahmud was undecided, and as Gandhi threw his weight against a change an impasse resulted. However they decided that if an AICC meeting was banned they would not defy the order and precipitate a confrontation with the raj.[32] The government effectively closed this phase of Congress agonizings over the future. At the end of October it had decided not to permit an AICC meeting before Congress had abandoned civil disobedience on the grounds that it would be a policy change unsettling to its supporters. This decision was announced in the

[30] Nariman's circular to various politicians 11 November 1933, and draft programme, Home Poll., 1933, File No. 4/19; p.s. to B. C. Roy in copy of circular in Roy Papers, File Nov. 1933 – May 1934, All India Swarajists' Conference; note by Sir Horace Williamson, D.I.B., 16 February 1934, Home Poll., 1934, File No. 4/4. Bombay FR2, November 1933, Home Poll., 1933, File No. 18/13. Description of Nariman's *Whither Congress?* in Bose, *The Indian Struggle 1920–1942*, pp. 264–5.

[31] S. Mahmud to J. Nehru, 20 November 1933, Datta & Cleghorn (ed.), *A Nationalist Muslim and Indian Politics*, p. 131; J. Nehru to S. Mahmud, 23 November 1933, S. Mahmud Papers, File No. 121 (x); J. Nehru to AICC members, 24 November 1933, *SWJN*, 6, pp. 75–6; file of answers of J. Nehru's circular (dated here as 25 November), AICC Papers, 1933, File No. 10.

[32] C. P. Home Sec. to M. G. Hallett, 12 December 1933, Home Poll., 1933, File No. 3/23; K. F. Nariman to Ansari, 11 December 1933, Ansari Papers.

Legislative Assembly on 11 December.[33] Consequently when Gandhi, Nehru and other Congressmen met in Delhi they dropped the idea of an AICC, though significantly Gandhi said that if any Congressmen thought council entry would benefit the country he should follow his convictions rather than remain idle. Nariman, his tactic thwarted, now began to press for a referendum of all members of Congress organizations on the question whether the Working Committee resolution restarting civil disobedience in 1932 should be revoked, modified or retained. It was the only way he could see to marshal the views of those who shared his opposition to the current programme.[34]

Within days of the collapse of Nariman's enterprise M. A. Ansari and B. C. Roy tried to manoeuvre a change of programme by another means. Both had powerful reasons for wanting a revival of the Congress organization and the end of civil disobedience as the only official Congress programme. The one was a leading Nationalist Muslim, opposed to civil disobedience even in 1930, eager for its suspension at the Poona conference though he could not be present to argue the case, who realized the danger that Muslim seats in the new legislatures would all go to communalists unless Congress could rehabilitate itself in his co-religionists' eyes. Moreover a recent visit to Britain had convinced him that while the Tories were well entrenched in Parliament no good could come of continued conflict with the raj and they must exploit what was on offer. The other was a prominent Calcutta politician, keenly aware that growing hostility within his province to Bengal's 'betrayal' by the all-India Congress over the Communal Award was eroding Congress support, and that it must take action to restore its credibility and provide an efficient machine for caste Hindus bent on fighting for the maximum influence in the legislature. Even the Mahatma's Harijan campaign had failed to attract the lower castes whose cooperation was essential if Bengali Hindus were to put up any challenge to the Muslim majority.[35] The two men had been in touch in June, airing the possibilities of legislative work in the new dispensation. Then they had thought public discussion of this premature, and now they did not explicitly state what was their basic reason for wishing to get the Congress back into working trim. Ansari had chided Nariman for the brashness of his attempt to engineer a policy change in Congress, and the two walked warily.

Late in December they met in Bombay to discuss the situation, consulting,

[33] Note by M. G. Hallett, 17 February 1934, Home Poll., 1934, File No. 4/4. Bombay Govt. to Govt. of India, telegram, 20 October 1933, Mss. EUR.F.150 (5).

[34] Delhi Chief Commissioner to Govt. of India, Home Sec., 18 December 1933, Home Poll., 1933, File No. 3/23; Nariman to Ansari, urging a referendum, 12 December 1933, Ansari Papers; report of Nariman's press statement, 20 December 1933, arguing for a referendum, Bombay FR2, December 1933, Home Poll., 1933, File No. 18/14.

[35] For increasing Bengali opposition to Gandhi and the All-India Congress see Bengal FR1, August & December 1933, Home Poll., File No. 18/9 & 14; J. Gallagher, 'Congress in Decline: Bengal 1930–39', Gallagher, Johnson & Seal (ed.), *Locality, Province and Nation*, pp. 269–325.

too, with Rangaswami Aiyengar and K. M. Munshi who had both been arguing privately to Gandhi the need to permit a council entry group within Congress. The four men concocted a letter which was seen and slightly modified by Gandhi, Sarojini Naidu and A. K. Azad. As sent to about forty prominent Congressmen early in January it was an invitation to meet to draw up a scheme to 'implement the constructive programme outlined in the Poona Conference and later amplified in his statement by Mahatma Gandhi'. Tactfully there was no whisper of council entry, and the letter concluded with the assurance that any decision of the meeting would be 'duly placed before Mahatmaji for his consideration before any action is taken on it'. It did however ask recipients to sound out their provinces on the practicability of continuing civil disobedience and the attitude of people to its withdrawal.[36] Aiyengar died early in February and the burden of the venture fell more heavily on Roy and Ansari, though Roy was confined to bed for ten weeks after a car accident late in December. The Bihar earthquake distracted people's attention from political gatherings, but gradually replies began to come in. Sind's representative agreed with the idea, and Satyapal from Punjab answered the query about provincial support for civil disobedience with the assertion that it was completely dead. Satyamurti reported that Madras favoured the end of conflict but was divided whether civil disobedience should be formally withdrawn. Ansari also conferred with Sherwani from U.P., Asaf Ali from Delhi, and Sidhwa from Sind, and the meeting was arranged for mid-March in Delhi. Ansari's hope, as he told Brelvi, was that the Swaraj Party would be revived 'and a programme of constructive work, not for the time being, either excluding or stressing the matter of council-entry should be formulated'.[37] Memories of the aftermath of Non-cooperation were still green; and he had no intention of precipitating a conflict reminiscent of that between Gandhi and the Swarajist leaders in 1924.

Evidence was accumulating in the provinces that Congressmen were determined not to remain isolated from the sources of power available at various levels in the constitutional structure, either now or in the future. A local Swaraj Party was formed in Andhra, stressing participation in the legislatures and all self-government insitutions, and held itself in readiness to affiliate with an all-India Swaraj Party when one was formed. Moreover in Delhi Congressmen set up a board of about thirty to organize their contests in the municipal elections: when Jawaharlal's ire led to its disbanding the aspirant Congress councillors merely operated under a new name,

[36] Ansari & Roy to prominent Congressmen, 10 January 1934, K. M. Munshi, *Indian Constitutional Documents. Volume I. Pilgrimage to Freedom (1902–1950)* (Bombay, 1957), pp. 358–9.
 For the background to this letter see Gandhi to Munshi, 8 January 1934, Ansari to Munshi, 20 January 1934, *ibid.* pp. 357–9, also Munshi's narrative, *ibid.* pp. 33–4; note by Sir Horace Williamson, D.I.B., 16 February 1934, Home Poll., 1934, File No. 4/4.
[37] *idem*; Ansari to Brelvi, 1 February 1934, Brelvi Papers, File of correspondence with Ansari; Roy to Munshi, 26 February 1934, Munshi, *op cit.* p. 362.

the People's Municipal Party.[38] Despite the death of civil disobedience and the gradual reversion of Congressmen to constitutional politics in intention and practice, observers outside Congress saw Gandhi still as a force to be reckoned with in politics. Sapru echoed Hallett's argument that just because of Congressmen's uneasiness at their leadership and the Mahatma's immersion in Harijan uplift 'it would be rash to underestimate him at the present stage. He may be merely marking time till his year of self-imposed abstinence from politics has expired, and if at this stage any change of policy by Government enabled Congress to re-organise itself, he would be in a strong position to cause further trouble after that year has expired.'[39] Gandhi's continued influence was powerfully demonstrated in the fate of the meeting Ansari and Roy had proposed.

On 12 March Ansari advised Roy by telegram to call off the meeting, after he had had long discussions with Congress people in Bombay, including Mrs Naidu. The latter had just seen Gandhi and reported that though he favoured the formation of a Congress group to do constructive work he did not approve of Congress officially endorsing any new policy or calling off civil disobedience. In these circumstances it looked as if nothing could come of the planned meeting since Congressmen not offering civil disobedience were already permitted by Aney's July statement to engage in constructive activity; and the object of the exercise was to get an official reorientation of policy blessed by Gandhi. Sarojini thought that Gandhi was slightly more amenable to the idea of a change than he had been in December at Jubbulpore, and his attitude was clear in a letter he wrote to Aney on 7 March.

> In my opinion it is desirable that those who do not have faith in C.R. or have lost the spirit for it should organise as congress men such constructive activities as may command [sic] themselves to them and prosecute them vigorously. In these I include even the council entry programme for those who believe in it. Only they may not follow them as the official congress programme. The present paralysis is demoralising and difficult for one to understand.

Moreover on 12 March *The Times of India* reported the forthcoming meeting as a revolt against Gandhi. This was exactly the impression Ansari wished to avoid, and he abandoned the project rather than risk dividing Congressmen still further and lose for those who wished to modify the programme the resources of Gandhi's authority and the Congress machine[40]

K. M. Munshi's comments when he told Moonje of this volte-face under-

[38] Delhi FRs, February 1934, Madras FR1, March 1934, Home Poll., 1934, File Nos. 18/2 & 3.

[39] Note by M. G. Hallett, 17 February 1934, Home Poll., 1934, File No. 4/4; Sapru to A. Inglis of *The Times*, 4 February 1934, Sapru Papers, Series II.

[40] Gandhi to M. S. Aney, 7 March 1934, enclosed in Aney to B. C. Roy, 28 March 1934, Roy Papers, File Nov. 1933 – May 1934, All India Swarajists' Conference; Ansari to Roy, telegram, 12 March 1934, Nariman to Roy, 13 March 1934, *ibid.*: Bombay FR1, March 1934, Home Poll., 1934, File No. 18/3.

lined the reluctance of many to challenge the Mahatma and the dynamics within any group of Congressmen which militated against such a course.

> ...we have all seen the futility and impracticability of the C. D. movement and we want to revive our old Constitutional methods of Congress politics. We have seen the harm done by the Council Boycott and we all want to go in for Council entry but the point is that no one has the courage to stand up against Mahatmaji for fear of loosing [sic] his leadership and popularity. Individually we all hold these views but when we meet to consider these points collectively, Mahatma is on the brain of all of us. Then everyone vies with each other to justify the position of the Mahatma. Besides there is a section who are the unthinking followers of the Mahatma. They still believe that the Mahatma will find a way out as soon as his period of abstaining from politics is over.

When Moonje suggested that the crying need was for an all-parties conference and a common programme, Munshi replied, 'That's the rub. There is no one strong enough in the Congress to bell the cat.'[41]

Roy however decided to confront Gandhi in person now he had come to Bihar; and, still in splints, he left Calcutta to catch him in Patna on 17 March. Roy's appeal was doubtless made easier by the fact that there was now no Jawaharlal, back in jail since mid-February, to produce counter-arguments and assure Gandhi that Congressmen wished for no change of programme. Roy argued for the withdrawal of civil disobedience, using the metaphor of the general who halts or even retires to regroup his forces and resharpen his weapons, and of the surgeon who needs a sharp knife to remove a growth as a blunt instrument would merely exacerbate the trouble. Civil disobedience, he urged, was no longer a sharp scalpel for Gandhi to use on India's body politic. Gandhi was evidently impressed by Roy's arguments because the next day he wrote a letter to Ansari on the evidence of which Ansari decided that it was worth calling the ill-fated meeting after all. Its key passage was a clear indication that Gandhi would not stand in the way of a council entry party or of the withdrawal of the Poona resolution – marked changes from his response earlier in the month to Sarojini Naidu and Aney.

> My emphatic opinion is that this paralysis of the intelligent[s]ia must be removed. However much therefore I may differ on the Council-Entry programme. [sic] I should welcome a party of Congressmen prosecuting the programme rather than they should be sullen discontented and yet utterly inactive. I still retain the view that the congress cannot without committing suicide give up the Poona resolution authorising restricted individual civil disobedience. But there too if the majority of congressmen do not feel like it, I would warmly welcome a meeting of the All India Congress Committee at which it should express its opinion and withdraw the Poona resolution and suspend or discontinue civil resistance.[42]

[41] 12 March 1934, Diary of B. S. Moonje.
[42] Gandhi to Ansari, 18 March 1934, Home Poll., 1934, File No. 3/6; Roy to Satyamurti, 15 March 1934, Ansari to Roy, telegram, 22 March 1934, Roy Papers,

Although the way was now clear for the meeting Ansari and Roy proposed, the letters which came to them in anticipation of it showed that they would have great difficulty in reconciling the views even of those who wanted a change of programme. Brelvi, who could not attend, argued to Ansari that it was vital to end civil disobedience and get Congress forces reorganized for a constructive programme: resistance and construction could not be Congress policies in tandem, as Sastri had also argued in August. However Brelvi still maintained that talk of council entry was inopportune. Aney echoed his stress on refurbishing the Congress organization and the impossibility of holding civil disobedience and constructive work as simultaneous policies, but he advocated acceptance of the principle of council entry as a means of fighting the bureaucracy, though a definite decision on the practical question of entering the legislatures should be delayed. From Punjab Duni Chand pressed for an end to civil disobedience and Congress participation in the next Assembly elections on the grounds of fighting the White Paper; while Satyapal urged the necessity of getting Gandhi to change his attitude on civil disobedience because without that many people would oppose the formal end of the movement although they had no intention of carrying it on in practice.[43]

In this delicate situation the meeting took place on 31 March/1 April at Ansari's Delhi home. The doors were barred to outsiders, doubtless as a precaution against press reports of the nature which had nearly wrecked the enterprise before. Among the twenty-six present were Roy and Ansari, Satyamurti, Malaviya, Khaliquzzaman, Mohanlal Saxena, Asaf Ali, Munshi, Nariman and Bhulabhai Desai. Delhi produced six men, Bombay five, Bengal and Punjab four each, U.P. three, Madras two, and Andhra and Sind one each. They were joined by others on the second day. At the start of proceedings Ansari read out various letters including those from Gandhi, Brelvi and Aney. Then those present reported on the state of civil disobedience in their provinces and local feeling about its withdrawal. It was soon clear that civil disobedience was dead, but that there was disagreement whether formally to end it. The most influential there, Ansari, Roy, Malaviya and Bhulabhai Desai, all disliked the movement but thought the barriers to its formal withdrawal were formidable, largely because it was important to carry Gandhi with them in any new venture. Ansari's advice was to leave the question alone and concentrate on contesting the next Assembly elections, a course Malaviya also urged.

The idea of contesting Assembly seats under the existing constitution was a novel element in the discussions. Roy, in pressing for the reconvening

File Nov. 1933 – May 1934, All India Swarajists' Conference; K. P. Thomas, *Dr. B. C. Roy* (Calcutta, 1955), pp. 181–2. Government of India officials could not decide whether Gandhi meant this or not; note by Sir Horace Williamson, D.I.B., 27 March, note by M. G. Hallett, 28 March, Home Poll., 1934, File No. 3/6.

[43] Brelvi to Ansari, 26 March 1934, Aney to Roy, 28 March 1934, Duni Chand to Roy, 31 March 1934, Satyapal to Roy, 27 March 1934, Roy Papers, File Nov. 1933 – May 1934, All India Swarajists' Conference.

of the meeting, had only envisaged forming a party to do constructive work as a generator of public support in preparation for council entry, while deliberately avoiding the question of entering the new legislatures at this stage for fear of losing popularity. Two days before the Delhi gathering, Ansari had gathered from a journalist that the government intended to hold Assembly elections in the autumn, and he seized on this as a handle for a new programme which would enable a challenge to the government but would side-step the thorny questions of withdrawing civil disobedience and making an immediate decision on the new legislatures. He put his argument to Brelvi, who had resisted any discussion of council entry.

> I admit that the scheme has many draw backs and is far from perfect, but I want to see what other scheme could have been devised which would be dynamic, would catch the imagination of the people, would offer a challenge to the government and would at the same time be fighting the government on constitutional lines and thus circumventing any interference from them such as application of ordinance laws. You would also see that, as it confines itself to the election of the Assembly, it would be possible for the Swaraja Party to send the most outstanding men to the elections and thus ensure not only their return but the raising of the morale of the opposition in the Assembly and all Congressmen in the country. It has an additional advantage of immediately setting up the machinery of the Swaraja Party in motion and working it in every Province and have your constituencies ready should it be decided later on by the Swaraja Party to contest elections after the new reforms have come in.[44]

Only Nariman argued against the idea because he thought they would win insufficient seats to make an effective demonstration. The upshot of the meeting was a unanimous decision to revive the Swaraj Party – the very name being a claim to continuity and respectability in terms of Congress history. Its constructive programme was to include contesting and taking up Assembly seats on the issues of ending repressive laws and rejecting the White Paper in favour of a National Demand on the lines of that placed before the Round Table Conference by Gandhi. It was also agreed that Ansari, Roy and Bhulabhai Desai should go to Patna and put the idea to Gandhi, as this had been promised in the original invitation. They went at once to see whether at last the Mahatma could help lead them out of their impasse.

[44] Ansari to Brelvi, 10 April 1934, Brelvi Papers, File of correspondence with Ansari.

For the Delhi meeting see Munshi to Gandhi, 2 April 1934, Munshi, *op. cit.* pp. 365–6; notes by G. V. Subba Rao (who was present) on the meeting, Roy Papers, File Nov. 1933 – May 1934, All India Swarajists' Conference; note by source for Intelligence Bureau, 23 March 1934, *The Statesman*, 1 & 2 April 1934, Home Poll., 1934, File No. 3/6.

III THE LEADERSHIP DILEMMA RESOLVED

When the three Delhi emissaries reached Patna on 4 April they found to their surprise that Gandhi had independently begun to resolve his own dilemma as an all-India leader of civil disobedience. He confronted them with a statement which he had drafted on 2 April but which had been in his mind and a topic of discussion with companions such as Rajendra Prasad several days earlier as he toured the areas hit by the earthquake. Its essence was that Congress should suspend civil disobedience. He had been about to issue it to the press when a wire arrived from Delhi telling him that the emissaries were en route; whereupon he held it back until they arrived and released it in its final form on 7 April after long discussions with them. The argument he used in it echoed the analogies Roy had employed in their mid-March conversation. Satyagraha was a weapon and a surgical instrument, to be used at its sharpest by properly qualified practitioners: he now felt as an expert in satyagraha that Congress must leave it to him alone as a weapon in the struggle for swaraj as distinguished from the remedy for specific grievances.[45]

The timing of Gandhi's decision shows that it was not the result of pressure from the Delhi meeting. Nor was it in Gandhi's mysterious mind a face-saving admission of defeat. Although his advised withdrawal of the Poona programme looked like a pragmatist's end to a frustrating conflict it was also a visionary's means of refining a revolutionary implement. He insisted publicly and privately that this was a 'spiritual' decision. An earlier draft of the statement had made clearer that Gandhi saw himself as reburnishing his weapon for renewed conflict; and he later spoke of saving the weapon for India's future use. He told Vallabhbhai who was still in jail, 'I have no doubt about it myself. There is now no danger of lowering the standards of Satyagraha.'[46]

Gandhi's internal turmoil prompting this decision was largely generated by his recent experiences in Bihar. His statement indicated that conversation with close associates just out of jail convinced him that he had been blind in thinking that they shared his apocalyptic commitment to satyagraha. If this was so, the April decision was a logical continuation of the advice he had given at Poona; true satyagraha would ultimately infect the

---

[45] The full statement is in Tendulkar, *Mahatma*, vol. 3, pp. 259–61. For the timing of it see Bihar & Orissa FR1, April 1934, Home Poll., 1934, File No. 18/4; Prasad, *Autobiography*, pp. 378–9; statement by Gandhi, *The Hindu*, 8 April 1934 (courtesy of collectors of material of *CWMG*).

[46] Gandhi to Vallabhbhai, 13 April 1934, *Letters to Sardar Vallabhbhai Patel*, p. 54. For further evidence that Gandhi intended the decision to be the prelude to the vindication of satyagraha see Gandhi to Vallabhbhai Patel, 3 May 1934, *ibid.* p. 59; note by M. G. Hallett, 20 May 1934, Home Poll., 1934, File No. 4/4; G. Deshpande to S. A. Brelvi, 10 April 1934, Brelvi Papers, file of correspondence with Deshpande; G. V. Subba Rao to Ansari, 20 April 1934, Roy Papers, File Nov. 1933–May 1934, All India Swarajists' Conference; Gandhi to Balvantsinha, 6 May 1934, Balvantsinha, *Under the Shelter of Bapu*, pp. 29–30.

masses and purify public life even if practised by a few, and now that even the few seemed to fail by Gandhi's standards as true satyagrahis the experiment with truth fell to him alone. Moreover, less esoterically, as Rajendra Prasad recalled, 'In my own province, apart from the slackness in satyagraha, the atmosphere had completely changed as a result of the earthquake. No one was offering or intended to offer satyagraha. Political workers when released from jail devoted themselves entirely to relief work.' This tendency had worried Jawaharlal before he was reimprisoned, but Gandhi was deeply moved by the opportunities for engaging men in constructive work in cooperation with the government which Bihar's predicament presented. His statement came only days after he had spoken of 'respectful cooperation' in relief action.[47]

For Gandhi this decision and his response to the proposition brought from Delhi were independent, and the former was to him much the more important.[48] However it cleared the way for him to give wholehearted support to the revival of the Swaraj Party. He did not mention this in his statement but dealt with it in a letter to Ansari on 5 April, published the next day, in which he welcomed the decision to revive the party and contest Assembly seats.

> My views on the utility of Legislatures in the present state are well known. They remain on the whole what they were in 1920, but I feel that it is not only right, but that it is the duty of every Congressman who for some reason or another, does not want to, or cannot take part in civil resistance, and who has faith in entry into the Legislatures, to seek entry and form combinations in order to promote the programme, which he or they believe to be in the interest of the country.

He placed himself at the party's disposal and actually drafted a statement of its aims and programme.[49] For months he had said that Congressmen who hankered after the legislatures should organize to enter them rather than remain inactive and disgruntled. He pressed this home to the puzzled Vallabhbhai:

> I feel that it is our duty to give a free rein to the parliamentarians. It is only fair that those who daily attend the councils in spirit should be permitted to enter them in fact; then alone can they realize the advantages and disadvantages of such action. Don't you think it is better for someone who is always dreaming of *jalebi* to eat it and find out its actual taste for himself?[50]

[47] Prasad, *Autobiography*, p. 378; J. Nehru, *An Autobiography*, p. 491. It may be, too, that Gandhi saw this as a way of convincing Willingdon of his desire for peace: he had on 15 March written to him refuting the opinion he gathered Willingdon held of him – that he was insincere in saying he was England's friend: Gandhi Papers.

[48] Gandhi to J. Nehru, 14 April 1934, J. Nehru Papers, part I, vol. XXIV.

[49] Gandhi to Ansari (obviously 5 April 1934), *The Statesman*, 6 April 1934, C. P. Shukla (acting as Gandhi's secretary) to correspondent in Delhi, 6 April 1934, Home Poll., 1934, File No. 3/6.

[50] Gandhi to Vallabhbhai Patel, 18 April 1934, *Letters to Sardar Vallabhbhai Patel*, p. 56.

The difference now was that his advice to suspend civil disobedience enabled such men to pick the fruits of conciliar work in the Congress's name.

Reaction to Gandhi's two decisions was mixed. Ansari and those who had met in Delhi were well satisfied with Gandhi's public acceptance of their proposal and with the liberation his statement gave them from their ambiguous position on civil disobedience. Most Congressmen were relieved at the suspension of satyagraha, though many disliked the reasons Gandhi had given for it. To the imprisoned Jawaharlal the statement seemed an insult to the nation, and combined with Gandhi's apparent desertion of the struggle while his colleagues were still in jail, shattered him. He read it over and over, and concluded that it marked the end of his allegiance to the Mahatma, the close of an epoch in his personal life and in the political struggle. Vallabhbhai too was at a loss, though his reaction was not the emotional desolation which Jawaharlal experienced. Moonje, always critical of Gandhi, took it as an admission of defeat, and bemoaned the probability that Hindus, steeped in the tradition of venerating gurus, would once again follow the Mahatma despite his change of tune.[51]

Gandhi's advice to end civil disobedience solved Congressmen's immediate leadership dilemma; but there remained for Gandhi and for them the question of his future. He had unequalled resources of prestige, popular devotion and skill which might be deployed in a new leadership role even though his expertise in satyagraha no longer qualified him to guide Congressmen. For his part, Gandhi felt unsure of his course and isolated from those who had been among his closest associates.[52]

In the following weeks splits appeared among Congressmen over the relationship of the Congress and the party envisaged at Delhi. It was crucial to the multifarious groups which composed the all-India Congress because local factions, ideological camps, opponents of and adherents to the Communal Award all wanted to control the proposed electioneering machine and to prevent their opponents from so doing. The problem became acute when the government announced on 16 April that it would not prohibit an AICC meeting called to ratify Gandhi's decision; and when on 1 May it declared that elections for a new Assembly would be held in the autumn.[53] In the ensuing confusion within Congress ranks it looked

[51] Ansari to Brelvi, 10 April 1934, Brelvi Papers, file of correspondence with Ansari; Prasad, *Autobiography*, p. 379; 13 April 1934, J. Nehru's Diary, draft note on Congress programme written probably early August 1934, *SWJN*, 6, pp. 247–8, 272–3; J. Nehru, *An Autobiography*, pp. 504–7; Gandhi to Vallabhbhai Patel, 23 April & 3 May 1934, *Letters to Sardar Vallabhbhai Patel*, pp. 57–9; 6 April 1934, Diary of B. S. Moonje.

[52] Gandhi to Munshi, 16 April 1934, Munshi, *op cit.* pp. 372–3.

[53] For the manoeuvrings of various groups to control the electoral machinery see Khaliquzzaman to B. C. Roy, 19 April 1934, Roy Papers, File Nov. 1933 – May 1934, All India Swarajists' Conference; M. Saxena to Gandhi, 20 April 1934, Home Poll., 1934, File No. 4/7; Rajagopalachariar to Gandhi, 21 April 1934, Home Poll., 1934, File No. 4/4. Government policy discussions leading to permission for AICC, *idem;*

as if Gandhi would re-establish his ascendancy by his manipulatory skill. At a Swaraj Party Conference in Ranchi on 2/3 May, and then at an AICC meeting in Patna on 17/18 May, the Mahatma excelled as broker and political manager. He arranged a package of judicious compromises to balance the conflicting forces and hold Congressmen together. The Swarajists received the Congress imprimatur for their policy, but the organization of the programme was to be controlled by a Congress Parliamentary Board rather than an autonomous party. No opinion was delivered on the Communal Award, thereby alienating neither the Bengalis and Communalists who opposed it, nor the Nationalist Muslims whose standing in their own community depended on its acceptance. Those who were aligning behind a socialist ideology were placated by the promise of a Congress session in October, though their opposition to entering the legislatures had been defeated. Subsequently the Government of India Home Secretary was not alone when he judged that these gatherings had re-established the Mahatma as Congress's premier leader.[54]

Despite this personal triumph Gandhi was soon confiding to close friends that he was thinking of leaving the Congress. In mid-August he told Vallabhbhai that he had no option but to quit; because he was convinced that most Congressmen did not share his preoccupation with the issues of truth and untruth, violence and non-violence, and *swadeshi*, and their lip service to his ideals was rank hypocrisy. Since he could never agree to the relaxation of Congress standards on such matters the only way for it to maintain an honest position was to disregard and so virtually expel him: he preferred, therefore, to retire.[55] Gandhi's despair at exerting influence within Congress according to his lights was generated by his experience of the disunity and fevered place-seeking which erupted when the government announced the withdrawal of its ban on Congress organizations on 6 June.[56] The bitterest source of division was the Communal Award. Gandhi attempted in meetings of the Working Committee and the Parliamentary Board to

for the controversy between Delhi and London on the wisdom of holding Assembly elections in the autumn, see Mss. EUR.E.240 (4) (12). London eventually gave way though Hoare and the Cabinet feared that Indian electioneering against the White Paper would give further ammunition to the die-hard Tory attack on the reform proposals.

[54] Note by M. G. Hallett, Govt. of India Home Sec., 20 May 1934, Home Poll., 1934, File No. 4/4; Jayakar to Sapru, reporting Mrs Naidu's assessment, 29 May 1934, Sapru Papers, Series II. On the Ranchi and Patna meetings see Bihar & Orissa Home Sec. to Govt. of India Home Sec., 4 May 1934, Govt. of Bihar to Govt. of India, telegrams, 2 & 3 May 1934, Home Poll., 1934, File No. 4/7; *India in 1933–34*, pp. 15–16; *Report on the Administration of Bengal 1933–34* (Calcutta, 1935), p. viii.

[55] Gandhi to Vallabhbhai Patel, 19 August 1934, *Letters to Sardar Vallabhbhai Patel*, p. 71; Gandhi to Agatha Harrison, 7 & 22 August 1934, Gandhi Papers. Polak wrote to Sapru (7 September 1934, Sapru Papers, Series II), 'I have known for some time that he was contemplating the possibility of...withdrawal owing to his disgust and dissatisfaction with dissensions and corruption that he found within the organization.'

[56] Home Poll., 1934, File No. 4/4.

stave off disaffection by the Nationalist Muslims or the Communalists by urging that Congress should neither accept nor reject the Award; he failed and in August the Communal wing, under Malaviya and Aney, broke away and formed a Nationalist Party to fight the elections on this issue. Divisions were further compounded by the emergence of a small but vocal group of younger Congressmen, calling themselves Socialists, who were disgruntled at the impasse into which civil disobedience had led them, and the apparently defeatist exit Congress had chosen with Gandhi's blessing. These major disputes, added to long-standing personal and factional rivalries, precipitated fratricidal strife when Congressmen began to revive their organizations and to hold elections to Congress bodies and offices. Virtually no province escaped infighting, which in places degenerated into physical violence. In Sapru's words, 'Almost everywhere the Congress is disgustingly carrying on a domestic war among its own ranks.'[57]

Jayakar, apparently unaware of Gandhi's hardening intenton to quit this scene of disarray, hazarded a guess that this might be the Mahatma's most politic course. 'You ask me what I think Gandhi means to do' he replied to Srinivasa Sastri.

> I wonder if he himself knows that. Perhaps he is waiting to get a call, but I strongly suspect he will have some stunt only remotely connected with politics. The present situation of the Congress is such that the Mahatma, with his usual astuteness, will prefer to hover on the verge of political questions rather than plunge at the centre. That is his only chance of surviving the present disintegration of the Congress.[58]

Gandhi first broached the subject publicly at a meeting of the Working Committee and the Parliamentary Board in early September; he there postponed a final decision at the urging of those present. But on 17 September he published a long statement on his intended step, explaining that he felt there were fundamental differences between himself and the majority of Congressmen on issues which were at the heart of his philosophy of life. He included *khadi* and the spinning-wheel, Untouchability and non-violence, and the very nature of *purna swaraj*: while of the Socialists he said, 'I may not interfere with the free expression of those ideas, however distasteful some of them may be to me. If they gain ascendancy in the Congress... I cannot remain in the Congress.' He insisted that his life was dedicated to the satyagraha experiment, and for this he needed complete freedom; and if he could not have Congressmen's full-hearted acquiescence he would conduct the experiment alone. To test Congress opinion he suggested several amendments to its constitution, including a spinning qualification for membership.[59]

[57] Sapru to Polak, 13 August 1934, Sapru Papers, Series II.

[58] Jayakar to V. S. S. Sastri, 16 August 1934, Jayakar Papers, Correspondence File No. 408.

[59] Gandhi's 17 September statement, *Mahratta*, 23 September 1934, NAI, N. K. Bose Papers, Press Clipping Books, 1930–46. Gandhi expounded his argument more

This statement appeared a similar move to his ultimatum to the AICC in 1924 when he redefined his role in relation to Congress in the aftermath of Non-cooperaton: but it was soon clear that it was a declaration of faith rather than a serious bid for leadership on his own terms. Before Congress had time to accept or reject his ideas he told Mirabehn, 'My mind is certainly set on going out of the Congress. I feel quite sure that it will do good to the Congress and to me. I shall better influence the Congress by being outside. I shall cease to be the weight that I am just now, and yet I shall be passing my views on to the Congress whenever occasion demands it.'[60] Within a year he had come to the decision with Srinivasa Sastri had urged on him when he left Yeravda. In his eyes the situation had changed. Now there was a working Congress organization to make decisions: but, more important, he was convinced that most Congressmen had no time for civil disobedience while their conflicts proved to him that their priorities differed radically from his. Now he knew that if he continued as a central figure in the Congress organization he would be subjected to conflicting pressures from its component groups and would have no well-tempered implement at his disposal: position in Congress would be as much a prison as Yeravda had been. He therefore determined to find a means of influencing public life unfettered, since this was for him far more important than the conventional appearance of political power.

When Congress met in Bombay Gandhi achieved precisely the position of detached influence he desired. On its final day the session unanimously accepted his retirement 'reluctantly', but recorded 'its deep sense of gratitude for the unique services rendered by him to the Nation' and noted 'with satisfaction his assurance that his advice and guidance will be available to the Congress whenever necessary'. For Gandhi influence at the heart of the Congress organization from outside could scarcely have been made easier: the President was his Bihari stalwart, Rajendra Prasad, and an amendment to the constitution just passed gave the President power to appoint the Working Committee from among the AICC. As important to Gandhi was the resolution establishing an All-India Village Industries Association under his guidance, which though part of Congress was to be an autonomous body, controlling its own organization and funds, designed to work for the revival of village industries and the moral and physical advancement of villages. In 1925 he had secured the All-India Spinners' Association as his own organization, and *khadi* as his particular zone of work: now he had another organization which would permit him to work in rural India, pursuing his vision of swaraj and building up his own area of influence, unhampered by Congress politicking.[61]

concisely to Valabhbhai in an undated September 1934 letter, Tendulkar, *Mahatma*, vol. 3, pp. 317–19.
   [60] Gandhi to Mirabehn (in London), 12 October 1934, Gandhi Papers.
   [61] On the Bombay Congress, *Report of the 48th Annual Session of the Indian National Congress*, IOL, Microfilm Pos. 2274; Govt. of India, Home Sec., to all local govts.,

There was considerable bewilderment at Gandhi's new position, but many were convinced that it marked no retirement either from Congress or from politics. Sapru noted, 'I do not attach much importance to the so called retirement of Mahatma Gandhi. In my opinion he will still continue to dominate the Congress.' Willingdon and his Home Department were convinced that Gandhi's intention was to organize an efficient Congress to harry the government in the legislatures while himself setting up as a rural propagandist to instil Congress's name and ideals into the minds of villagers as a prelude to renewed civil disobedience.[62] Gandhi himself saw no prospect of renewed civil disobedience by himself for years. His intention, as he admitted, was 'to disarm all suspicion about the character of civil disobedience' and to spread the constructive programme. Yet he believed that programme to be the way to self-reliance among ordinary people, a change of attitude which would ultimately erode the acquiescence on which the raj was founded and produce *purna swaraj*, while it would train them for a final conflict with the British if that proved necessary.[63]

So the all-India leadership dilemma posed brutally to Gandhi and Congress in August 1933 was by slow and painful stages resolved. By October 1934 Congress was once more a legal organization on the road to constitutional politics, free of a movement which had stifled it and reduced its members to political impotence. Yet in the process of disentangling itself from the Mahatma's leadership as civil disobedience 'expert' it had retained an option on his services and had made no humiliating surrender to government by overt disavowal of him or his campaign. For his part Gandhi was still committed to satyagraha. He retained the driving conviction that he alone had the message of political, social and moral renewal for his country; and at Bombay had secured his liberation from the constricting demands of his colleagues and the restraining hand of government in order to spread that message and influence public life without the trappings of formal political position. Yet he had not retired from politics, nor ever would; because he believed passionately not only that the transformation of individuals and society were inseparable and that morality must be displayed and vindicated in public affairs, but that while the British ruled Indians as a subject people the outcome of that moral reformation, the state of *purna swaraj*, could never be attained.

---

23 November 1934, Home Poll., 1934, File No. 3/16 & K.-W.; Bombay FR2, October 1934, *ibid.* File No. 18/10.

[62] Sapru to A. Inglis of *The Times*, 7 November 1934 (1 18), Sapru Papers, Series II; Willingdon to Hoare, 11 & 19 November 1934, Mss. EUR.E.240 (8); Govt. of India, Home Sec., to all local govts., 23 November 1934, Home Poll., 1934, File No. 3/16 & K.-W.

[63] Gandhi to A. Harrison, 31 October/2 November 1934, Gandhi Papers; M. Desai to J. Nehru, 6 September 1935, J. Nehru Papers, part 1, vol. XVII.

Conclusion

India's political development in the first half of the twentieth century was the product of novel forms of political encounter in which the participants experimented and learnt from experience in situations for which there were often few precedents. Ideologies were in the process of creation; patterns and standards of behaviour were not clearly defined; nor were institutions deeply entrenched as in longer-established political systems. The British encountered their Indian subjects at the different levels of the administrative structure; but increasingly political interaction occurred in the western-style constitutional edifices the British erected as a means of buttressing their raj in changing social and economic conditions. In turn these new structures produced political change, eliciting from Indians appropriate styles of activity and prompting new alliances. For the first time British imperialists had to face political ambition among non-white subjects which used the rhetoric and many of the techniques of a nationalist movement, and to grapple with the problems of devolving power as a conciliatory procedure in a plural society where white settlers were not among the claimants. The British–Indian political encounter spanned a wide spectrum of collaboration and conflict, as different groups and individuals among the rulers and the ruled moved from cooperation to confrontation according to the issue at stake and the arena of interaction. Increasingly they were watched and influenced by opinion outside the subcontinent, particularly that of British M.P.s and their electorate and Americans with international interests. Interwoven with the relations between Indians and their rulers were the changing political encounters among Indians, as existing values, institutions and relationships was modified by the experience of economic and social change, new ideas and new forms of government, once the different areas of the subcontinent were forced into contact with each other and a wider world community under the aegis of the raj. Such changes dislocated established relationships between different regions, communities and social groups, and altered the importance of different arenas and styles of politics. On the linkages formed between Indians in these processes of change were built their relationships with their rulers, while the latter in turn impinged upon the former.

In the 1920s and 1930s, despite and in a sense because of the growing experience of reformed political institutions in Delhi, the provincial capitals and the localities, India did not have a single well-defined political system in which Indians encountered their compatriots and their rulers, but a cluster of intermeshing systems in each of which ideals, strategies and alliances were being created. In this complicated environment of political interaction Gandhi played a crucial role for over a quarter of a century. He was for much of the period the figurehead of the Indian National Congress; and at particular times led agitations which constituted a serious challenge to the raj's moral authority and its power to control its subjects.[1] He evoked popular adulation of a kind and to an extent never before enjoyed by an Indian politician; and he attracted the respect of numerous idealists outside India. Gandhi's role and standing in Indian politics were extraordinary phenomena when seen against the barriers to continental political leadership created by regional and social divisions and the limited development of mass media. Accumulating evidence about the extent of regional diversity and the continuity of existing political interests and allegiances has turned the focus of many historical studies of Indian politics to the local arena, in the hope of unearthing in region, town and district the drives and connections which were the basic building blocks of politics. This trend is in marked contrast to the Nationalist slogans and arguments of many politicians at the time, and to later generalizations which have portrayed the British–Indian encounter alone as the main strand in Indian political development, explicable in terms of a nation's frustration at imperial rule and imperialists' resistance to nationalists' claims. Nonetheless continental political leaders existed, supreme among them Mahatma Gandhi. They led campaigns, established parties, evoked support, arranged alliances. Without reverting to older, more simplistic accounts, analysis of Indian politics must give weight to the function and influence of the all-India leader while acknowledging the powerful impulses generated in the localities.

Gandhi's political career between 1928 and 1934 has been chosen for study not only because of its intrinsic importance. This particular phase saw his rapid accumulation of continental influence followed by its even swifter erosion. Analysis of these two processes should therefore illuminate the nature of continental leadership, its strengths and weaknesses. The framework of the argument is that an all-India leadership role depended on an

[1] The extent to which either Non-cooperation or Civil Disobedience seriously challenged the raj was limited in time and geographical location. But Haig as Home Member underlined the weakness of the British position even when the Ordinance crackdown seemed to be highly effective. 'We are being watched very narrowly in India. It is a mistake to regard our power as overwhelming and our resources as limitless. At the moment, we are in a strong position, because the Army and the Police and large sections of the population, including probably the majority of the Muslims, believe that we shall persist in our struggle with civil disobedience. But it would take little to shake that confidence, and the results of its being shaken might be very formidable.' Haig to Miéville, P.S.V., 13 April 1932, Mss. EUR.F.115 (1).

For an investigation of some of the weaknesses of the British raj see J. M. Brown, 'Imperial Façade: some constraints upon and contradictions in the British position in India, 1919–35', *Transactions of the Royal Historical Society* 5th series, vol. 26 (1976), pp. 35–52.

individual's impulsion, the needs and aspirations of others, and their mutual satisfaction in a particular political context. As any of these three aspects of the situation changed so could the creation or disintegration of a leadership position occur.

At the level of conscious aspiration Gandhi was compelled into politics by a consuming vision of the nature of man and the type of society and government which permitted men to realize their true nature. He believed that in satyagraha he possessed the perfect mode of political action because he saw it as means and end, by its action producing the sort of people whose personal transformation was the foundation of the Indian society which had been his ideal since he wrote *Hind Swaraj* in 1909. At an unconscious level Gandhi's childhood and adolescent experiences also contributed to his political drive: and there are indications that he found in political action, particularly in opposition to the British, a way of resolving inner tension and working out buried guilt and anger.[2] Here was an explosive political mixture: a man careless of the conventional trappings of power, with the iron will of a fanatic, who entered politics with a messianic zeal for the purification of individuals and their relations with each other, one who was willing to bend on many matters but refused to compromise on what he considered essentials though others considered them mere fads, one who would only participate in organized politics if he was undisputed leader. He claimed to be guided by an 'inner voice'; and his willingness to suffer privation and the prospect of death in the pursuit of what he perceived as Truth suggests that he was utterly convinced of the reality of his inner guidance and was neither charlatan nor humbug, covering the tracks of self-seeking ambition with the cloak of religion.

Gandhi's vision of the span of public work essential to his pursuit of swaraj was a significant aspect of his perception of his public role. His interest in health, diet, hygiene, clothing, social customs and religious practice was as strong as his concern for politics. Such activities contributed to Gandhi's continental and international reputation, generating respect for him among segments of Indian society which it was difficult to touch with a more conventional political appeal. They also gave him a flexibility which few other political leaders possessed. If he felt at a particular juncture that he could not act as a political leader without compromising his ideals, he could devote himself to these matters temporarily without a sense of defeat, secure in the belief that they were as important steps on the road to the final goal as promoting resistance to the raj through civil disobedience. The absence of any internal constraint of aspiration to a political career through office in Congress or the governmental structures gave the Mahatma a flexibility which paradoxically was vital in enabling his continued political importance in a period of rapid change.

[2] There is a stimulating discussion of what drove Gandhi at an unconscious level into political opposition in E. V. Wolfenstein, *The Revolutionary Personality. Lenin, Trotsky, Gandhi* (Princeton, 1967).

However Gandhi's personal aspirations and expertise only led him to continental leadership when others were willing to accord him that position. Most obvious among these were men who followed or allied with him. They included many different individuals and groups, in whose response to Gandhi the blend of admiration, shared interests and other calculations differed markedly, as did the permanence and importance of their support for him.

The most dramatic manifestations of public response to Gandhi were the crowds who flocked to see him and hailed him as a Mahatma. But theirs was not truly political support. Curiosity and veneration were rarely emotions which impelled men into following his exhortations, whether to wear *khadi*, to abandon the observation of Untouchability or to join the ranks of the satyagrahis. Nonetheless Gandhi's public image across the land among vast multitudes was a factor which impinged on the attitudes towards Gandhi of men who were active in politics. The British acknowledged this in their agonized discussions on the time and place to jail him, and the need to avoid his death in prison. Responsivists became reluctant satyagrahis, and moderates refrained from public criticism, in deference to the Mahatma's unprecedented repute among their compatriots.

Among those who were active followers of Gandhi in his political enterprises the most committed were the members of his ashram and other devotees. Moved by a blend of religious and emotional loyalty to a guru who tended their souls and showed a motherly concern for their personal lives, the nature of their relationship with him was indicated by their use of the name Bapu for him, and the images of protective authority they used of their connections with him, as for example, Balvantsinha's *Under the Shelter of Bapu*. Such followers were important in Gandhi's political career as dedicated satyagrahis who could spearhead a campaign or bear the brunt of one when wider participation was unlikely or impolitic. They were rarely leaders in their own right who could guarantee widespread support for Gandhi, nor were they numerous enough to influence voting patterns in Congress gatherings. Their inner need which Gandhi's authority and care satisfied, was present, too, in his relationship with many who were far more important generators or guarantors of political support. Many hard-headed political or business careerists were bound to him by subtle emotional ties. Jawaharlal Nehru was one example. G. D. Birla also succumbed to the Mahatma's attraction, telling him in a quite extraordinary affirmation, even allowing for an element of flattery:

> We are so much dazzled with your superhuman personality that we have almost lost self-confidence in ourselves. The result is that whenever I feel doubtful about your actions I console myself with an explanation that the fault may be with my own capacity to understand the implications of your decision.[3]

[3] Birla to Gandhi, 21 December 1932, Birla, *In the Shadow of the Mahatma*, p. 75. (Here again the title is significant.)

Gandhi increasingly assumed a paternal role in the Nehru family after Motilal's

Although Gandhi deprecated slavish adulation he strengthened personal ties with hundreds of associates by his concern for their lives, and many found in him not only personal care and guidance but security in a time of rapid change, the reassurance of contact with one who judiciously blended many of the older standards of Hindu society with more modern ideals of equality and efficiency.[4]

Far more important than emotional bonds were the judgements Gandhi's crucial supporters made of the functions he could perform for them as a continental leader. At local level widespread participation in Gandhi's campaigns depended on the extent to which his tactics suited local interests and proved a means of forwarding the aspirations and ambitions of local men. Gandhi could rarely attract support directly. He needed the support of key intermediaries who brought their clients, associates and followers into his political campaigns; and potential local intermediaries reacted to him with deliberate calculations of the pros and cons of following advice which emanated from all-India sources and might be inconvenient in their local situations. They were out to cement their local support, and to forward their particular interests: his name and tactics might be an asset in their local politics, but they were not readily amenable to all-India direction if support for him jeopardized those interests.

However, Congress as an all-India body was not apart from local politicians, though between AICC meetings and annual sessions it sometimes appeared to be the preserve of a handful of leaders. These potential intermediaries or sub-contractors were the men who manned not only the local Congress bodies but the AICC, and attended the annual meetings of the whole organization. They operated uneasily in the two worlds of local and all-India politics, balancing the needs and opportunities of the former against the benefits of cross-regional alliance and joint action with men from other localities, and the resources which the Congress name and organization could give them. Their dilemmas of priority reflected the intermeshing of India's diverse political systems, and the fact that the regions were no longer able to operate in isolation, such was the nature of the raj and the problems confronting men ambitious for various kinds of power. Gandhi needed the votes of these men in the decision-making bodies of the Congress if his programmes were to be accepted as nation-wide policy and he was to be acknowledged as a continental leader. Paradoxically they were sometimes impelled into supporting his claims and policies because these made sense in continental terms though they were difficult to justify or implement in their local situation.

death. For example, during his Poona fast he wired to Jawaharlal telling him that he had seen members of the family including Indira, who looked well and happy; 24 September 1932, *CWMG*, LI, 134. This caused Jawaharlal to write to his sister, 'Nan', on 4 October 1932, 'How extraordinarily considerate he is and how he thinks of others. In spite of his fast it was he who issued directions as to where Mother and Kamala were to stay in Poona.' V. Pandit Papers.

[4] For a discussion of this see L. I. & S. H. Rudolph, *The Modernity of Tradition. Political Development in India* (Chicago & London, 1967), pp. 157–249.

It was in the all-India gatherings that Gandhi achieved his greatest prominence and influence because as all-India leader he performed a multiplicity of service roles in the particular context of 1928–31. He proved pre-eminent among Congressmen as an arranger of compromises because of his skill with words, his aloofness from factional strife and his ability to set a goal which could provide a focus of unity and a propaganda weapon. It was to achieve a vital unity that some of them deliberately called him back to Congress in 1928, and because of his success in satisfying this need that he was able to assert a new authority at the Calcutta session with the acquiescence of the majority.

Thereafter, as the civil disobedience 'expert', Gandhi was of extraordinary value to Congressmen in circumstances where a campaign of opposition to parts of the imperial structure seemed the best tactic to exert pressure on the raj and to mask their own divisions. Satyagraha solved many of the dilemmas conflict posed in their relations with their rulers and their compatriots. It was a mode of direct action which permitted them temporarily to leave the paths of cooperation while avoiding the pitfalls of violent resistance, which they were ill equipped to organize, and would not only have threatened many of their vested interests but also alienated many Indians and foreign observers whose sympathy was important if they were to put pressure on the British. Civil disobedience provided an umbrella for a host of individual and corporate protest movements, as it coincided fortuitously with the onset of the depression. It helped them to cement local followings, to elicit support from businessmen, and to exert pressure on more moderate Hindu politicians who felt themselves isolated and their constitutional endeavours threatened by the evidence of widespread support for the movement. It also attracted considerable foreign sympathy. Gandhian civil disobedience thereby exerted significant pressure on the raj. Although it only threatened the administration in a few distinct areas, it embarrassed a government which hesitated to crack down on a non-violent movement, and was anxious to retain the cooperation of moderate politicians at least in creating the new constitutional structures which it hoped would be the buttress of a new imperial order. Consequently the British did a deal with Gandhi. They resurrected their old technique of alliance with a notable who could bring his followers with him, and in so doing reinforced his continental standing. Gandhi's satyagraha doctrine and previous experience enabled Congress to take advantage of the British move and revert gracefully through a negotiated settlement to guarded cooperation with the raj when this seemed more productive than conflict. Added to the advantages of placing Gandhi in a leadership position as civil disobedience 'expert' were his skill in fund-raising and his energy as an organizer, qualities which convinced Vallabhbhai Patel, for example, that the Mahatma was a man who meant business and was worth following.[5]

[5] F. Moraes, *Witness to an Era. India 1920 to the present day* (London, 1973), p. 52.

Gandhi reached the peak of his influence early in 1931. His dominance was however only in the realm of all-India politics, because only in that context were his skills valued. Even in that arena the pressures to which he was subjected by those who looked to him for leadership, and his failures in asserting authority, most markedly among Muslims, showed the weakness inherent in a position which hinged on the ability to perform a lubricant function in the processes of political action rather than the capacity to forward the clear interests of a cohesive group. The nature of his leadership was even clearer in 1933–4, when his position of ascendancy was rapidly eroded. The civil disobedience campaign inaugurated in 1932 elicited far less popular support than the 1930 campaign, and was soon stifled by the government. Consequently it strengthened neither Congressmen's cross-regional alliances nor their links with those who should have been the rank and file. It failed to exert pressure on the Communalist Hindus and eventually provoked the Mahasabha's open deviation. It had far less influence than the 1930 campaign on moderate politicians who continued, though with considerable gloom, to cooperate in British reform plans. Ultimately it even alienated those Bombay businessmen who had financed it in the hope that it would assist them in gaining control over economic policy.[6] The cumulative result was the campaign's failure to put pressure on the British and bring Congress into negotiation on the forthcoming constitution. Now Gandhi's tactic was a force isolating and dividing Congressmen instead of uniting them and integrating their different levels of political activity. Moreover Gandhi's skills and potential as an ally were judged of little use by the British. They had recalculated his value to them before civil disobedience began again, in the light of Indian attitudes, the state of the services, and British party politics, and the repercussions of these on their proposed reforms. The government's consequent decision to suppress his campaign and refuse to treat with him steadily diminished his value to his compatriots and undermined his all-India standing.

In 1934 Gandhi recognized that in the changing circumstances he could no longer act as continental leader in the role of civil disobedience 'expert'. Such were his personal aspirations and priorities that he preferred to solve the dilemma his presence and insistence on satyagraha created for his Congress colleagues by liberating them from a technique which for them was a mere tactic and so preserve it and his own integrity, and 'retire' rather than retain an all-India leadership position by performing the functions they now desired of him. However, these decisions did not mean the end of Gandhi as an all-India political leader. Congressmen would not lightly ignore him; and civil disobedience remained an important tactic for use when confrontation with the raj offered more benefits than cooperation, or when no other programme could secure among them an essential unity.

[6] D. G. Dalvi to Sapru, 17 November 1934 (D 17), Sapru Papers, Series II; Sapru to V. Subbarayan, 29 October 1933, Sapru Papers, Series II.

Nor had Gandhi himself lost interest in politics: he had merely redirected his energies to preserve himself and his technique from compromise. Ironically, by 'retiring' Gandhi did for himself what the British had done for him in 1922. He took time to review the changing situation where the politics of elections, conciliar activity and even acceptance of office would probably become Congressmen's primary concerns. In this political context men like Vallabhbhai Patel who could weld the disparate elements in the Congress movement into a coherent and disciplined party would be of supreme importance. It was a leadership function Gandhi was ill fitted to perform either by inclination or by expertise. What his role might be in the new context was unclear late in 1934; but by abandoning a role which had proved redundant for his contemporaries he freed himself to adopt another on which a new position of continental leadership could be based, if a situation developed where his personal inclinations and expertise dovetailed with the needs of contemporaries, and offered him a sphere and mode of political action which could forward both their aims and his vision of swaraj.

Nonetheless, Gandhi's civil disobedience campaigns between 1930 and 1934 were of lasting importance in the development of Indian politics. Although civil disobedience neither led to *purna swaraj* nor very significantly influenced the process of constitutional reform, it proved a powerful bonding agent among Indians within and across regions under the Congress banner. It gave many activists a new sense of unity born of shared illegal activities and sojourns in jail. Participation in it became one qualification for political place and a source of prestige in the years which followed. Moreover the campaigns were recruiting grounds for Congress, involving younger people and numbers of women in Congress organizations and activities for the first time and educating them for future positions in the Congress and state structures. The experience of running a continental campaign and Gandhi's emphasis on efficiency were also significant factors in Congress's success in turning itself into an all-India party geared to attract the votes of an enlarged electorate. The Congress name and organization, sketchy though the latter was, had been an important resource in politics in the 1920s. This importance was magnified as Congress emerged from civil disobedience into constitutional competition for power. Few Hindus would now lightly isolate themselves from it, and the influence of those who controlled its central organs was increased because they offered rewards and wielded sanctions which the Mahatma had never had at his command.

In less material ways civil disobedience also equipped Congress for a new political dispensation. It had been a remarkable publicity operation, demonstrating political ideas and actions throughout the land and generating political awareness even in remote villages. It convinced many Indians, and to a lesser extent their rulers, that Congress was a significant factor in political life which could not be ignored. Although its claims to be the people's intermediary with government had not received formal recognition, once Congress returned to constitutional politics most Hindus with political ambitions regarded it as the natural channel through which to pursue them, while the majority of the community who had no aspirations to political activism were sympathetic to its aims and claims. Gandhi's political activities had provided Congress with a pedigree: they had also to some extent modified the manner in which Hindus at least perceived themselves. His ultimate aim was to create among all Indians a totally new cognitive structure, to achieve a conversion of heart and mind, whose outward manifestations would include *swadeshi*, communal unity and an end to Untouchability, as aspects of a common awareness of national identity. He failed to forge that inter-communal unity which he had envisaged when he launched civil disobedience in 1930; but his reiterated ideals, his use of traditional styles and symbols, and the dynamics of his campaigns had done much to create among Hindus a new sense of identity and nationality of which Congress was now the focus and champion.

As an all-India political leader Gandhi had for a short time satisfied the immediate political needs of many of his contemporaries. He had also helped to equip them with the means and material to turn Congress into a party which could organize the relationship of different groups within and across regions, compromise their differences, set their goals and direct their activities on a permanent basis in order to exploit the opportunities offered in the changed political environment. He thereby contributed to an organization which was in a sense to replace him and perform in the new circumstances the unifying and integrating functions he had performed in attempting to hold together an all-India campaign of civil disobedience. This was soon clear, in the 1934 Assembly elections, when the poll was higher than in any previous Assembly election and Congress successes outstanding. No other group came near it in organization, resources and appeal. As Sapru commented, 'In the first place the Congress has got a powerful organization. It has got energy and has got money and manpower and it does appeal to the imagination of the people firstly because it professes to represent the forces of freedom and secondly because it has gone through some suffering.'[7] But the legacy of civil disobedience was political capital on which Congress was to live for at least three more decades. Gandhi, as architect of civil disobedience, despite the weaknesses inherent in his position and his withdrawal from Congress, had performed a vital function in the evolution of the political relationships of Indians with each other and their rulers. His career demonstrated the significance of all-India leaders and their politics, in conjunction with those of local leaders, in the processes of political change. Theirs was the work

[7] Sapru to A. Inglis of *The Times*, 7 November 1934 (I 18), Sapru Papers, Series II. Also Willingdon to Hoare, 19 November & 22 December 1934, Mss. EUR.E.240 (8); provincial FRs, November 1934, Home Poll., 1934, File No. 18/11.
For the % poll compared with previous Assembly elections see Appendix II.

of conciliation, compromise, instruction and inspiration which gave substance to the rhetoric of Nationalism, and helped to create out of the particularities of local politics the heroes and myths of an independence movement and an independent nation.

Percentage poll in elections to provincial Legislative Councils, 1923–30

Province	Type of constituency	Percentage poll		
		1923	1926	1930
Madras	Non-Muslim Urban	60.5	69.69	47.4
	Non-Muslim Rural	34.0	46.59	42.2
	Muslim Urban	59.5	50.78	35.5
	Muslim Rural	52.8	56.52	53.5
	Indian Christians	59.3	69.35	66.0
	European	—	—	—
	Anglo-Indian	—	68.30	58.0
	Landholders	73.1	94.83	90.0
	University	55.8	—	46.0
	Planters	—	—	—
	European Commerce	—	—	—
	Indian Commerce	—	97.8	—
	Total	36.3	48.29	43.1
Bombay	Non-Muslim Urban	37.5	35.59	8.0
	Non-Muslim Rural	30.40	42.92	13.5
	Muslim Urban	39.7	36.50	12.0
	Muslim Rural	52.1	38.32	46.8
	European	—	—	—
	Landholders	38.5	63.51	47.2
	University	60.5	65.73	22.3
	European Commerce	—	—	—
	Indian Commerce	68.6	60.94	—
	Total	40.55	48.2	16.5
Bengal	Non-Muslim Urban	50.1	48.36	25.0
(Election held	Non-Muslim Rural	42.8	39.45	33.9
in 1929, not	Muslim Urban	49.6	41.07	38.8
1930, because	Muslim Rural	32.4	37.03	20.2
of local	Landholders	82.9	72.01	76.7
circumstances)	Universities	76.8	77.78	79.8
	European General	—	—	6.0
	European Commerce	91.2	—	—
	Anglo-Indian	—	35.8	—
	Indian Commerce	77.1	94.7	87.7
	Total	39.0	39.25	26.1

Province	Type of constituency	Percentage poll		
		1923	1926	1930
United Provinces	Non-Muslim Urban	46.7	45.59	6.0
	Non-Muslim Rural	40.2	49.3	21.8
	Muslim Urban	49.1	42.04	53.8
	Muslim Rural	54.8	64.5	57.1
	European	—	14.2	—
	Landholders	42.6	57.0*	42.8†
	Commerce European	—	—⎱ Chbrs of Commerce	
	Commerce Indian	94.0	—⎰	—
	Total	33.0	50.2	24.6
Punjab	Non-Muslim Urban	59.0	52.0	19.0
	Non-Muslim Rural	49.0	53.0	41.0
	Muslim Urban	61.0	59.0	47.0
	Muslim Rural	52.0	54.0	50.0
	Sikhs	38.0	45.0‡	15.0‡
	Landholders	78.0	—	84.0
	University	84.0	80.37	—
	Commerce	79.0	—	—
	Industry	—	86.63	—
	Total	49.3	51.42	38.5
Bihar and Orissa	Non-Muslim Urban	46.7	49.4	29.7
	Non-Muslim Rural	52.8	62.5	25.3
	Muslim Urban	52.9	61.2	48.2
	Muslim Rural	60.6	64.5	59.8
	European	—	—	—
	Landholders	81.7	85.5	81.1
	University	76.7	85.5	66.3
	Planters European	—	—	—
	Mining Indian	—	—	—
	Mining European	—	—	—
	Total	52.2	60.54	33.2
Central Provinces and Berar	Non-Muslim Urban	56.6	58.18	21.2
	Non-Muslim Rural	57.4	58.88	36.0
	Muslim Urban	65.6	—	64.8
	Muslim Rural	56.8	67.12	53.2
	Landholders	61.6	70.05	20.1
	Mining	83.3	68.0	—
	Commerce & Industry	71.7	72.9	—
	University	93.0	91.36	54.5
	Total	57.7	61.9	33.3
Assam (Election held in 1929 not 1930, because of local circumstances)	Non-Muslim Urban	52.2	53.3	60.9
	Non-Muslim Rural	38.2	38.83	26.4
	Muslim Rural	49.9	53.59	34.7
	Planters	—	—	—
	Commerce European	—	92.1	62.0
	Total	42.1	44.17	28.3

* Agra Landholders 58.0, Talukdars 53.3.

† Agra Landholders nil, Talukdars, 42.8.

‡ Rural, no urban contest, 1926 or 1930.

NOTE: Blank denotes uncontested election.

SOURCE: *Return Showing the Results of Elections in India 1925 and 1926*. Cmd. 2923, 1927.

Return Showing the Results of Elections in India 1929 and 1930. Cmd. 3922, 1931.

Percentage poll in elections to Legislative Assembly, 1923–34

Province	Type of constituency	Percentage poll			
		1923	1926	1930	1934
Madras	Non-Muslim	42.8	41.33	30.4	58.4
	Muslim	52.6	61.0	56.0	62.7
	European	—	—	—	—
	Landholders	41.0	82.0	73.0	88.07
	Indian Commerce	—	—	—	89.04
Bombay	Non-Muslim	39.3	48.94	10.0	60.38
	Muslim	33.8	39.51	58.4	55.52
	European	—	—	—	—
	Landholders	51.2	—	—	76.98
	Indian Commerce	94.9	—	—	83.09
Bengal	Non-Muslim	39.4	39.0	—	26.7
	Muslim	39.4	46.48	40.3	34.1
	European	—	—	—	—
	Landholders	24.4	76.1	—	60.4
	Indian Commerce	—	—	87.0	94.6
U.P.	Non-Muslim	43.1	51.4*	14.2*	56.76*
	Muslim	51.1	{64.3* {26.9†	{43.7* {—†	{70.00* {57.00†
	European	—	—	—	—
	Landholders	29.2	—	—	—
Punjab	Non-Muslim	61.0	62.0	41.0	64.0
	Muslim	64.0	64.0	62.0	75.9
	Landholders	84.0	87.0	—	—
	Sikhs	53.0	52.0	50.0	60.6
Bihar & Orissa	Non-Muslims	42.1	52.3	8.7	64.1
	Muslims	55.2	59.04	53.9	73.3
	Landholders	67.4	—	62.7	85.7
C.P. & Berar	Non-Muslims	44.1	76.65	—	58.2
	Muslims	—	—	41.0	62.9
	Landholders	—	37.8	—	—
Assam	Non-Muslims	—	56.40	—	45.8
	Muslims	44.0	52.43	—	—
	Europeans	—	—	—	—
Delhi	(General)	30.0	65.0	22.8	38.62
Burma	Non-European	23.3	13.77	17.7	29.99
	European	—	—	(No figure)	—
Ajmer–Merwara	(General)	74.5	66.42	35.9	76.6
North–West Frontier	—	‡	‡	‡	73.0
	Total:	41.9	48.07	26.1	53.54

NOTE: Blank denotes uncontested election. * Rural constituencies only contested.
† Urban constituencies only contested. ‡ 1934 was the first election in N.-W.F.P.
SOURCE: *Return showing the Results of Elections in India 1925 and 1926.* Cmd. 2923, 1927. *Return Showing the Results of Elections in India 1929 and 1930.* Cmd. 3922, 1931. *Return Showing the Results of the General Election to the Legislative Assembly in India 1934.* Cmd. 4939, 1935.

APPENDIX III

Index of retail prices of 17 food articles in Bombay Presidency, 1929–34

Articles	N. Division					C. Division					S. Division				
	1929–30	1930–1	1931–2	1932–3	1933–4	1929–30	1930–1	1931–2	1932–3	1933–4	1929–30	1930–1	1931–2	1932–3	1933–4
Rice	89	80	65	60	54	91	80	62	59	55	88	77	56	53	45
Wheat	91	74	56	55	55	86	68	51	53	50	79	67	48	50	48
Jowari	88	67	44	54	53	97	66	42	51	49	94	73	47	53	56
Bajri	98	73	47	54	56	99	73	45	52	56	95	72	46	44	47
Gram	102	94	64	54	53	114	87	58	50	52	119	97	67	59	58
Turdal	93	86	66	62	57	103	87	70	56	53	102	91	73	72	58
Sugar (refined)	76	74	81	87	85	79	75	81	86	84	79	75	79	85	81
Sugar (raw)	91	79	68	56	55	112	86	68	61	51	100	80	65	62	50
Tea	99	91	79	72	61	94	89	75	69	65	92	88	84	79	71
Salt	100	102	103	107	111	95	94	94	117	112	105	99	105	111	132
Beef	100	96	89	87	91	100	100	91	86	86	75	80	80	80	80
Mutton	101	98	88	83	77	85	87	88	82	77	91	89	87	84	80
Milk	90	85	80	75	68	98	92	86	77	70	99	94	88	85	81
Ghee	95	85	92	82	60	96	88	79	70	62	96	89	80	74	63
Potatoes	84	72	77	64	65	78	72	73	57	58	88	81	80	71	62
Onions	74	61	71	59	55	56	56	54	41	42	71	62	60	58	57
Coconut Oil	93	75	65	66	59	92	85	68	66	55	89	78	68	70	56

| | Sind | | | | | Bombay City | | | | |
Articles	1929–30	1930–1	1931–2	1932–3	1933–4	1929–30	1930–1	1931–2	1932–3	1933–4
Rice	90	63	54	53	47	120	93	75	76	57
Wheat	91	57	42	54	50	109	74	50	57	62
Jowari	97	69	49	52	50	102	83	60	68	56
Bajri	93	61	45	47	48	103	79	60	62	56
Gram	125	73	49	47	47	117	85	78	71	58
Turdal	104	87	71	67	59	103	88	72	70	57
Sugar (refined)	81	77	84	90	89	87	79	83	86	80
Sugar (raw)	86	80	64	49	49	96	80	74	67	53
Tea	102	102	101	86	80	98	98	98	86	76
Salt	98	94	101	104	105	96	78	80	84	101
Beef	99	98	92	88	78	89	82	82	81	71
Mutton	93	91	81	79	69	79	78	75	73	73
Milk	99	84	69	66	56	100	95	81	81	77
Ghee	97	79	68	68	56	96	96	92	89	78
Potatoes	98	74	71	55	56	92	91	76	77	69
Onions	129	81	87	56	86	61	61	58	49	34
Coconut Oil	97	81	63	67	56	98	92	69	65	62

100 = average price in 1926–7

SOURCE: 1930–31 *Bombay Administration Report*, p. 72; 1931–32 *Bombay Administration Report*, p. 66; 1932–33 *Bombay Administration Report*, p. 52; 1933–34 *Bombay Administration Report*, p. 52.

Glossary

Note: in the text Indian words are not italicized if they occur often or if they have entered the English language as indicated in *The Shorter Oxford English Dictionary.*

ashram   Hindu religious community (hence *ashramite*, member of an *ashram*)

Bande Mataram   title of poem by Bankimchandra Chatterjee (*Mother I bow to thee*) which became a nationalist slogan
Bapu   'Father': pet name for Gandhi
bhadralok   'Respectable folk' in Bengal: used of the three highest Bengali castes
burqa   Muslim woman's veiling garment

chaukidar   watchman (adj. *chaukidari*)
chhavni   roof, encampment
crore   10,000,000

dharma   in Hindu thought one's religious duty, one's allotted role in life
durbar   public audience

Fasli   revenue year

gurdwara   Sikh place of worship
guru   spiritual teacher

Harijans   'Children of God': Gandhi's name for Untouchables
hartal   strike, traditionally used to indicate mourning or protest
hat   market

jalebi   Indian sweet

karma yogi   in Hindu tradition one who seeks spiritual realization through action
khadi   hand-spun cloth
kharif   autumn harvest
Khudai Khitmatgars   'Servants of God': Red Shirts on the North-West Frontier
kisan   peasant

lakh   100,000
lathi   cane used by police

mahal   part of a *taluka* (q.v.)
Mahatma   'Great Soul': Hindu title of great respect

Mahatma-Gandhi-ki-jai   Victory to Mahatma Gandhi

maulana   title applied to Muslim learned man

maund   measurement of weight which varied from place to place: standard maund = just over 82 lbs.

mohulla   division or quarter of a town

moksha   in Hindu thought salvation, spiritual realization

mullah   Muslim theologian, often at village level

panchayat   court of arbitration, from *panch*, five: caste governing council

pandal   shady covering: tent

Pandit   Man learned in Sanskrit: honorific title to learned Hindu

patel   village head man

peon   messenger

prabhat feris   dawn song processions

rabi   spring harvest

satyagraha   'Truth Force', 'Soul Force': Gandhi's name for non-violent resistance (hence *satyagrahi*, one who practises *satyagraha*)

siapa   mock mourning

swadeshi   produced in one's own country

swaraj   self rule, Home Rule (*purna swaraj*: complete independence)

tahsil   revenue division of a district

talati   subordinate revenue officer

taluka   revenue division of a district

thana   police station

ulema   pl. of *alim*: learned Muslim, priest

varnashramadharma   ideal four-fold division of Hindu society

wallah   Hindi adjectival affix denoting someone who does, owns or purveys something

zamindar   landholder who pays revenue directly to government

zulum   oppression

Sources and Bibliography

Note: only sources and works cited are listed here.

UNPUBLISHED SOURCES

(i) *Private Papers*

India Office Library, London
Papers of Sir George Cunningham, Mss. EUR.D.670
Papers of Sir Harry Haig, Mss. EUR.F.115
Papers of the Earl of Halifax (then Lord Irwin), Mss. EUR.C.152
Papers of Lord Reading, Mss. EUR.E.238
Papers of Sir Frederick Sykes, Mss. EUR.F.150
Papers of Lord Templewood (then Sir Samuel Hoare), Mss. EUR.E.240
  Note: there are no papers of Lord Willingdon relating to the period of
    his Viceroyalty: his letters as Viceroy have to be consulted in the papers
    of his major correspondents such as Sykes and Hoare.
Papers of Sir T. B. Sapru (available in the India Office Library, but con-
    sulted in xerox form in the Research School of Pacific Studies,
    Australian National University, Canberra).

Gandhi Memorial Museum, New Delhi
Gandhi Papers

Nehru Memorial Museum and Library, New Delhi
M. A. Ansari Papers (microfilm)
S. A. Brelvi Papers
N. S. Hardikar Papers
Diary of B. S. Moonje (microfilm)
J. Nehru Papers
M. Nehru Papers
V. Pandit Papers
B. C. Roy Papers
V. S. S. Sastri Papers (recently transferred from Madras in instalments:
    instalment no. is given in footnotes to distinguish them from Sastri
    Papers in NAI): these include Sastri's Diaries, 1929–34
S. Satyamurti Papers
Sir Phiroze Sethna Papers
Sir Purshotamdas Thakurdas Papers

AICC Papers

National Archives of India, New Delhi
N. K. Bose Papers
M. R. Jayakar Papers
V. S. S. Sastri Papers

(ii) *Government Records*

India Office Library, London
Files of Public & Judicial Department (L/P & J)
Files of Private Office (L/PO)

National Archives of India, New Delhi
Files of Home Political Department

PUBLISHED SOURCES

(i) *Newspapers*

Young India (1919–31)⎫ John Rylands University Library of
Harijan (1933–5)   ⎭ Manchester (microfilm)
The Manchester Guardian (1931) Central Reference Library, Manchester

(ii) *Material in Proscribed Book Collection,*
the British Library, London

PIB 29/3 *The Black Regime at Dharasana* [*A brief Survey of the 'Dharasana Raid'*] (1930, Ahmedabad, Sec. of Gujarat PCC).
PIB 9/32 *Law and Order in Midnapur. 1930. As Contained in the Reports of the Non-Official Enquiry Committee.* Published by D. C. Lodh, Calcutta.
PIB 9/31 *Police Raj Under Emergency Ordinance* (Survey of civil disobedience in Tamil Nad, 4 January 1932 – 30 June 1932).
PIB.1.35. No. 9. *Pandit M. M. Malaviya's Statement on Repression in India up to April 20, 1932* (April 1932, Benares).

(iii) *Parliamentary Papers*

Return Showing the Results of Elections in India 1925 and 1926. P.P. 1927, XVIII, Cmd. 2929.
Return Showing the Results of Elections in India 1929 and 1930. P.P. 1930–1, XXIV, Cmd. 3922.
Return Showing the Results of the General Election to The Legislative Assembly in India 1934. P.P. 1934–5, XVI, Cmd. 4939.
Report of the Indian Statutory Commission Volume I – Survey. P.P. 1929–30, XI, Cmd. 3568.
Statement Issued on 5th September by Sir Tej Bahadur Sapru and Mr M. R. Jayakar, of the Course of their Conversations with the Congress Leaders, July–September 1930. P.P. 1930–1, XXIV, Cmd. 3728.
Indian Round Table Conference, 12th November, 1930 – 19th January, 1931. P.P. 1930–1, XII, Cmd. 3772.
Indian Round Table Conference (Second Session) 7th September, 1931 – 1st December, 1931. Proceedings. P.P. 1931–2, VII, Cmd. 3997.
Indian Round Table Conference 7th September – 1st December 1931. P.P. 1931–2, XVIII, Cmd. 3972.
East India (Constitutional Reforms.) Communal Decision. P.P. 1931–2, XVIII, Cmd. 4147.
Proposals for Indian Constitutional Reform. P.P. 1932–3, XX, Cmd. 4268.
The Parliamentary Debates. 5th Series, Volume LXXV, House of Lords, 1929–30.
The Parliamentary Debates. 5th Series, Volume 231, House of Commons, 1929–30.
The Parliamentary Debates. 5th Series, Volume 249, House of Commons, 1930–31.

(iv) *Government Publications*

Report on the Administration of Assam for the year 1929–30. Shillong, 1931.
Report on the Administration of Assam for the year 1930–31. Shillong, 1932.
Report of the Administration of Bengal 1929–30. Calcutta, 1931.
Report on the Administration of Bengal 1930–31. Calcutta, 1932.
Report on the Administration of Bengal 1931–32. Calcutta, 1933.
Report on the Administration of Bengal 1932–33. Calcutta, 1934.
Report on the Administration of Bengal 1933–34. Calcutta, 1935.
Bihar and Orissa in 1929–30. Patna, 1931.
Bihar and Orissa in 1930–31. Patna, 1932.
Bihar and Orissa in 1931–32. Patna, 1933.
Bihar and Orissa in 1932–33. Patna, 1934.
Bombay – 1928–29. A Review of the Administration of the Presidency. Bombay, 1930.
Bombay – 1929–30. A Review of the Administration of the Presidency. Bombay, 1931.
Bombay – 1930–31. A Review of the Administration of the Presidency. Bombay, 1932.
Bombay – 1931–32. A Review of the Administration of the Presidency. Bombay, 1933.
Bombay – 1932–33. A Review of the Administration of the Presidency. Bombay, 1934.
Bombay – 1933–34. A Review of the Administration of the Presidency. Bombay, 1935.
The Central Provinces and Berar 1929–30. A Review of the Administration of the Province. Nagpur, 1931.
The Central Provinces and Berar 1930–31. A Review of the Administration of the Province. Nagpur, 1932.
The Central Provinces and Berar 1931–32. A Review of the Administration of the Province. 2 vols. Nagpur, 1933.
Report on the Administration of the Delhi Province for 1930–31. Calcutta, 1932.
Report on the Administration of the Madras Presidency for the year 1929–30. Madras, 1931.
Report on the Administration of the Madras Presidency for the year 1930–31. Madras, 1932.
Report on the Administration of the Madras Presidency for the year 1931–32. Madras, 1933.
1929–30. Administration Report of the North West Frontier Province. Peshawar, 1931.
1930–31. Administration Report of the North West Frontier Province. Peshawar, 1933.
1931–32. Administration Report of the North West Frontier Province. Peshawar, 1934.
1932–33. Administration Report of the North West Frontier Province. Peshawar, 1934.
1933–34. Administration Report of the North West Frontier Province. Peshawar, 1935.
Punjab Administration Report, 1930–31. Lahore, 1932.
Report on the Administration of the United Provinces of Agra and Oudh. 1929–30. Lucknow, 1931.

Report on the Administration of the United Provinces of Agra and Oudh.1930–31.
   Lucknow, 1932.
Report on the Administration of the United Provinces of Agra and Oudh. 1931–32.
   Lucknow, 1933.
Report on the Administration of the Salt Department of the Bombay Presidency
   (excluding Sind and Aden). For the year 1929–30. Calcutta, 1930.
Report on the Administration of the Salt Department of the Bombay Presidency
   (excluding Sind and Aden). For the year 1930–31. Calcutta, 1931.
Census of India, 1931. Vol. I. – India. Part 1 – Report. Delhi, 1933.
Progress of Education in India 1927–32. Tenth Quinquennial Review. Vol. I.
   Delhi, n.d.
Statistical Abstract for British India from 1924–25 to 1933–34. Delhi, 1936.
India in 1928–29. Calcutta, 1930.
India in 1929–30. Calcutta, 1931.
India in 1930–31. Calcutta, 1932.
India in 1931–32. Calcutta, 1933.
India in 1932–33. Delhi, 1934.
India in 1933–34. Delhi, 1935.
The Civil Disobedience Movement 1930–34. New Delhi, 1936.
Hale, H. W. *Political Trouble in India 1917–1937.* reprint, Allahabad, 1974.

(v) *Congress Reports* (on microfilm in IOL)

Report of the Forty-Third Session of the Indian National Congress held
   in Calcutta in December 1928.
Report of the 44th Annual Session.
Report of the 45th Annual Session.
Report of the 48th Annual Session of the Indian National Congress.

(vi) *Collections of Source Material*
(Autobiographical works are listed under secondary works)

Aziz, K. K. (ed.). *The All India Muslim Conference 1928–1935. A Documentary*
   Record. Karachi, 1972.
Bose, S. K. (ed.). *Subhas Chandra Bose. Correspondence 1924–1932.* Calcutta,
   1967.
Datta, V. N. & Cleghorn, B. E. (ed.). *A Nationalist Muslim and Indian*
   Politics. Delhi, 1974.
The Diary of Mahadev Desai, Volume 1. Ahmedabad, 1953.
The Collected Works of Mahatma Gandhi. In process of publication, New
   Delhi. (Up to vol. LIII at time of writing.)
Gandhi, M. K. *Bapu's Letters to Mira [1924–1948].* Reprint of 1949 edition,
   Ahmedabad, 1959.
   The Removal of Untouchability. Reprint of 1954 edition, Ahmedabad, 1959.
   Letters to Sardar Vallabhbhai Patel. Ahmedabad, 1957.
   Varnashramadharma. Ahmedabad, 1962.
   Letters to Manibahen Patel. Ahmedabad, 1963.
   The Hindu–Muslim Unity. Bombay, 1965.
Jagadisan, T. N. (ed.). *Letters of the Right Honourable V. S. Srinivasa Sastri.*
   2nd edition, Bombay, 1963.
Mansergh, N. & Lumby, E. W. R. (ed.). *Constitutional Relations between*
   Britain and India. The Transfer of Power 1942–7. Volume IV. London,
   1973.

Munshi, K. M. *Indian Constitutional Documents. Volume 1. Pilgrimage To Freedom (1902–1950).* Bombay, 1967.
Selected Works of Jawaharlal Nehru. In process of publication, New Delhi. (Up to vol. 6 at time of writing.)
Nehru, J. *A Bunch of Old Letters.* 2nd edition, Bombay, 1960.
Philips, C. H. (ed.). *The Evolution of India and Pakistan 1858 to 1947. Select Documents.* London, 1962.
Source Material for a History of the Freedom Movement in India Vol. III Mahatma Gandhi Part II: 1922–1929. Bombay, 1968.
Source Material for a History of the Freedom Movement in India Vol. III Mahatma Gandhi Part III: 1929–1931. Bombay, 1969.
Source Material for a History of the Freedom Movement in India. Mahatma Gandhi Vol. III, Part IV 1931–32. Bombay, 1973.

SECONDARY WORKS: PUBLISHED AND UNPUBLISHED

Baker, C. J. *The Politics of South India 1920–1937.* Cambridge, 1976.
Baker, D. E. U. 'The Break-Down of Nationalist Unity and the Formation of the Swaraj Parties, India, 1922 to 1924.' *University Studies in History,* vol. v, no. 4, 1970.
Balvantsinha. *Under the Shelter of Bapu.* Ahmedabad, 1962.
Barrier, N. Gerald. *Banned. Controversial Literature and Political Control in British India 1907–1947.* Missouri, 1974.
Bayly, C. A. *The Local Roots of Indian Politics. Allahabad 1880–1920.* Oxford, 1975.
Birla, G. D. *In the Shadow of the Mahatma. A Personal Memoir.* Bombay, 1968.
Bose, S. C. *The Indian Struggle 1920–1942.* 2nd edition, New York, 1964.
Brecher, M. *Nehru A Political Biography.* London, 1959.
Brown, J. M. *Gandhi's Rise to Power. Indian Politics 1915–1922.* Cambridge, 1972.
  'Imperial Façade: some constraints upon and contradictions in the British position in India, 1919–35.' *Transactions of the Royal Historical Society* 5th series, vol. 26, 1976.
Coatman, J. *Years of Destiny. India 1926–1932.* London, 1932.
Coupland, R. *The Indian Problem 1833–1935.* London, 1942.
Desai, M. *The Story of Bardoli.* Reprint of 1929 edition, Ahmedabad, 1957.
Gallagher, J., Johnson, G. & Seal, A. (ed.). *Locality, Province and Nation. Essays on Indian Politics 1870 to 1940.* Cambridge, 1973.
Gandhi, M. K. *Satyagraha in South Africa.* Revised 2nd edition, Ahmedabad, 1961.
Gopal, S. *The Viceroyalty of Lord Irwin 1926–1931.* Oxford, 1957.
Gordon, R. A. 'Aspects in the history of the Indian National Congress, with special reference to the Swarajya Party, 1919–1927.' Unpublished D.Phil. thesis, 1970, Oxford.
  'The Hindu Mahasabha and the Indian National Congress, 1915 to 1926.' *Modern Asian Studies,* vol. 9, no. 2, 1975.
Gould, H. A. 'The Emergence of Modern Indian Politics: Political Development in Faizabad.' *The Journal of Commonwealth & Comparative Politics,* vol. XII, no. 1, 1974.
Halifax. *Fulness of Days.* London, 1957.
Hardy, P. *The Muslims of British India.* Cambridge, 1972.

Heeger, G. A. 'The Growth of the Congress Movement in Punjab, 1920–1940.' *The Journal of Asian Studies*, vol. XXXII, no. 1, 1972.

Huttenback, R. A. *Gandhi in South Africa British Imperialism and the Indian Question, 1860–1914*, Ithaca and London, 1971.

Iyer, Raghavan N. *The Moral and Political Thought of Mahatma Gandhi*. New York, 1973.

Kothari, R. (ed.). *Caste in Indian Politics*. New Delhi, 1970.

Low, D. A. (ed.). *Congress and the Raj*. (forthcoming).

Mahar, J. M. (ed.). *The Untouchables in Contemporary India*. Arizona, 1972.

Mason, P. (ed.). *India and Ceylon: Unity and Diversity*. London, 1967.

Moon, P. *Gandhi and Modern India*. London, 1968.

Moore, R. J. *The Crisis of Indian Unity 1917–1940*. Oxford, 1974.

Moraes, F. *Witness to an Era. India 1920 to the present day*. London, 1973.

Nanda, B. R. *Mahatma Gandhi. A Biography*. Boston, 1958.

The Nehrus. Motilal and Jawaharlal. London, 1962.

Gokhale, Gandhi and the Nehrus. Studies in Indian Nationalism. London, 1974.

Neale, W. *Economic Change in Rural India. Land Tenure and Reform in Uttar Pradesh, 1800–1955*. Reissue of 1962 edition, London, 1973.

Nehru, J. *An Autobiography*, London, 1936.

Pandey, G. N. 'The Indian National Congress and Political Mobilisation in the United Provinces 1926–1934.' Unpublished D.Phil. thesis, 1974, Oxford.

'Mobilization in a Mass Movement: Congress "Propaganda" in the United Provinces (India), 1930–34.' *Modern Asian Studies*, vol. 9, part 2, 1975.

Park, R. L. & Tinker, I. (ed.). *Leadership and Political Institutions in India*. Princeton, 1959.

Peele, G. 'A Note on the Irwin Declaration.' *The Journal of Imperial and Commonwealth History*, vol. 1, no. 3, 1973.

Philips, C. H. & Wainwright, M. D. (ed.). *The Partition of India. Policies and Perspectives 1935–1947*. London, 1970.

Prasad, R. *Mahatma Gandhi and Bihar. Some Reminiscences*. Bombay, 1949.

Autobiography. Bombay, 1957.

Reed, S. *The India I Knew 1897–1947*. London, 1952.

Rudolph, L. I. & S. H. *The Modernity of Tradition. Political Development in India*. Chicago and London, 1967.

Ryburn, M. 'Mahatma Gandhi 1922–28.' Unpublished M.A. thesis, 1974. Canterbury University, N.Z.

Sharp, G. *Gandhi Wields the Weapon of Moral Power*. Ahmedabad, 1960.

Sitaramayya, B. P. *History of The Indian National Congress Volume I (1885–1935)*. Reprint of 1935 edition, New Delhi, 1969.

Sykes, F. *From Many Angles. An Autobiography*. London, 1942.

Templewood. *Nine Troubled Years*. London, 1954.

Tendulkar, D. G. *Mahatma*. Vols. 2 & 3. Revised edition. Delhi, 1961.

Thomas, K. P. *Dr. B. C. Roy*. Calcutta, 1955.

Wang, Gungwu (ed.). *Self and Biography: Essays on the Individual and Society in Asia*. Australian Academy of the Humanities, 1975.

Wolfenstein, E. V. *The Revolutionary Personality. Lenin, Trotsky, Gandhi*. Princeton, 1967.

Index